Jack Goody's new book takes as its theme the symbolic and transactional uses of flowers. He begins his study by asking why there are so few uses of flowers in Africa, either domesticated or wild, either in reality or in representation, and goes on to initiate a world-wide enquiry into the place of flowers in secular life and religious ritual from ancient Egypt to modern times. He links the use of flowers to the rise of advanced systems of agriculture, the growth of social stratification and the spread of luxury goods, looking at the history of aesthetic horticulture in Europe and Asia. Other themes that emerge are the role of written texts in building up a culture of flowers; the importance of trade and communications in disseminating and transforming attitudes to flowers; the rejection on puritanical grounds of flowers and their artistic representation; and the multiplicity of meanings that flowers possess.

A particular feature of the book is its analysis of the role of flowers in the Far East and of the aesthetic and political implications of flowers in China during the cultural revolution. The conclusion returns to earlier themes of long-term developments in cultural history, treating uses of flowers in the context of theology and ideology as well as of processes of production and systems of 'class'.

Written from a broad temporal and geographical perspective, this wide-ranging book will appeal not only to anthropologists and social historians, but also to anyone interested in flowers and their symbolic function across the centuries.

The culture of flowers

THE CULTURE
OF FLOWERS

JACK GOODY

Formerly Professor of Social Anthropology
University of Cambridge and Fellow of St John's College

CAMBRIDGE
UNIVERSITY PRESS

Published by the Press Syndicate of the University of Cambridge
The Pitt Building, Trumpington Street, Cambridge CB2 1RP
40 West 20th Street, New York, NY 10011–4211, USA
10 Stamford Road, Oakleigh, Melbourne 3166, Australia

First published 1993
Reprinted 1993

Printed in Great Britain by Woolnough Bookbinding Ltd, Irthlingborough, Northants

A catalogue record for this book is available from the British Library

Library of Congress cataloguing in publication data

Goody, Jack.
The culture of flowers / Jack Goody.
  p. cm.
Includes bibliographical references.
ISBN 0 521 41441 5. – ISBN 0 521 42484 4 (pbk)
1. Ethnobotany. 2. Ethnobotany–Africa. 3. Flowers–History.
4. Flowers–Social aspects. 5. Symbolism of flowers. I. Title.
GN476.73.G66 1992 92–3740
302.2'22–dc20 CIP

ISBN 0 521 41441 5 hardback
ISBN 0 521 42484 4 paperback

Contents

Illustrations

x   *List of illustrations*

TABLES

Preface

> I sing of Brooks, of Blossomes, Birds, and Bowers:
> Of April, May, of June, and July-Flowers.
> I sing of May-poles, Hock-carts, Wassails, Wakes,
> Of Bride-grooms, Brides, and of their Bridall-cakes.
> I write of Youth, of Love and have Accesse
> By these, to sing of cleanly-Wantonnesse.
> I sing of Dewes, of Raines, and piece by piece
> Of Balme, of Oyle, of Spice, and Amber-Greece.
> I sing of Times trans-shifting; and I write
> How Roses first came Red, and Lillies White.
> I write of Groves, of Twilights, and I sing
> The Court of Mab, and of the Fairie-King.
> I write of Hell; I sing (and ever shall)
> Of Heaven, and hope to have it after all.
> (R. Herrick, *Hesperides*, lines 1–14)

most people actually laugh at me for carrying on research in these matters, and I am accused of busying myself with trifles. It is, however, a great comfort to me in my vast toil to know that Nature too, not I alone, incurs this contempt. (Pliny, *Natural History*, XXII.vii.15)

I describe this endeavour as a personal ethnography for two reasons. Firstly, I want to indicate that while much of the material I use is derived from the books that others have written – travellers, poets, scholars of all kinds – I have conducted my enquiry along two other lines. My original question arose partly out of my own observations in Africa, which were intensive in kind and scholarly in intent. But they were crystallised by spending time in other cultures where I knew almost nothing of the language and little of the culture, for I decided to extend these observations to India, Japan, China and elsewhere. On Africa I needed more information than I had myself gathered and since I could find little in books, I asked the help of a number of other ethnographers. Most importantly there was contemporary Europe. One reason that I have had to make this such a personal account and to rely on the experience of my friends and myself is that so little of a systematic nature has been written on the subject. Of course there are countless books on botany, on flowers, on gardens. But there is remarkably little of an 'ethnographic' kind, examining the uses, practical and 'symbolic', made of flowers in particular societies, let alone anything that compares such uses across the board and begins to ask questions about the internal and external facets of that distribution. I intended this book to be an 'ethnography' in the sense of recording contemporary usages but the questions that arose demanded a historical treatment as well as an observational one, so I have had to cut down on that side. The nature of the enquiry led me to search through a variety of sources, one of the most useful being the surveys put out by governments and trade associations, whose very existence points to the great importance of flowers in the national and international economies of today.

During my enquiry, I became interested in the 'Language of Flowers' as it developed in Europe in the nineteenth century, mainly because of the question of the relationship between 'specialist' and 'everyday' usage, which parallels an earlier interest in cooking terms. My hypothesis was that this language represented not an underlying semiotic of current practice that had hitherto remained hidden, but an 'expert' system, constructed in particular circumstances but much influenced by developments in literacy and among literateurs. I had been working for some time in the Bibliothèque Nationale in Paris on the history of this recent tradition when I came across the work of Beverley Seaton (and later that of Philip Knight) which had gone further than mine in some respects and helped me fill in a number of gaps. I was later able to look at some of the American material in the Sterling Library at Yale University, in the Library of Congress and elsewhere, but the ephemeral nature of these publications has meant that they are often hard to track down.

Although I am dealing with the culture of 'flowers', that is not the exclusive focus since I touch upon the notions of foliage as well. In bouquets and chaplets and for decorative use, as with the holly and the ivy, it is not possible to keep them altogether apart. In any case, other societies may not draw the same boundaries between these categories as we do, although in fact I myself have not found that to be so in any significant degree.

More importantly, I was drawn into the use of flowers in worship and in representation, which led me to think about why flowers were sometimes rejected even in circumstances where they might have been present (and were so at other periods). That raised the question of the contradictions in 'cultures of luxury' which preceded cultures of mass consumption, and the varied reactions of puritans, of revolutionaries and many others not only to luxuries but to representations of all sorts, giving rise to forms of iconoclasm and rejection. That was the direction the enquiry took and it led me to depend heavily on libraries, friends and the work of others in addition to my own ethnographic observations.

It was when I was leaving the Department of Social Anthropology after many years that I decided to give a farewell seminar on 'The culture of flowers', the origin of my interest in which is explained in Chapter 1. The busy fingers of Asha Sarabhai and Deborah Swallow fashioned a garland during my talk and it was largely their Indian connections that led me to widen my study and to spend time in Ahmadabad, enquiring among other things into flower usage, flower markets and gardeners. The invitation to spend a few months at the National Museum of Ethnography in Osaka helped me acquire some knowledge of flowers in Japan. Later on I visited South China with the same idea in mind.

The subject of flowers has provided a never-ending topic of conversation among friends, acquaintances and those I met more casually. I cannot give a comprehensive review of my 'informants', as anthropologists so unkindly call their friends and acquaintances (the word always reminds me of the infamous role of 'informers' in Irish history). But I am particularly grateful to Martine Segalen of the Centre d'Ethnologie française, especially for taking the risk of having me address a French audience on a French theme on the occasion of her succession to the headship of that group. Jean La Fontaine (of the London School of Economics) and Cesare Poppi (of the University of East Anglia) overwhelmed me with information about the British middle class and about Italian customs in the Plough at Coton, Julian Pitt-Rivers (of the Ecole des Hautes Etudes) was helpful about England, France, Spain and Mexico in more decorous surroundings. Sheila Murnaghan took an interest in the project and accompanied me to the Catholic cemetery of St Lawrence in New Haven on All Saints' Day as well as sending me photographs of other graveyards in New England and the Caribbean. I had the benefit of expert advice in Bogota thanks to a visit to the University of the Andes. Sandy Robertson escorted us around the cemeteries of Santa Barbara on Christmas Day 1988, and Ellen Paden did likewise in Los Angeles on All Saints' Day, with Christiane Klapisch helping out at Glendale for St Valentine's and Pam Blackwell at Eastertime in Santa Monica. Olga Linares guided us around a Panamanian cemetery, Barbara Sahlins gave me a tour of Chicago burial places, Birgit Müller drove me around the Friedhöfe of East and West Berlin, Manuela Carneiro da Cunha took me to the flower market in São Paulo, Patricia MacGrath showed me gardens and catalogues in Washington, and Arthur Wolf assisted on my visits in California and helped me see something of Taiwan. Kim Kwang-ok (of the University of Seoul) took me to Confucian lineage rites, having arranged for a visit to Korea through the International Cultural Society. Shigehu Tanabe (of Minpaku) was a superb host for three months in Japan and Lucia Szeto Yiu in Hong Kong. Through her connection with 'Chrysanthemum Town' in the Pearl River delta, Helen Fung-Har Siu (of Yale) was a great support in matters Chinese; she most generously took me to visit her field site as well as introducing me to the culture of flowers in Hong

Kong and Guangdong where we were accompanied and assisted by Ye Xian'en, Professor of History at the Guangdong Academy for Social Sciences, Guangzhou, and Liu Xhiwei, Lecturer in History at the Zongshan University, Guangzhou. The account of the contemporary situation in China owes much to her and by rights her name should appear as co-author. David McMullen and Joe MacDermott helped with literary aspects of the medieval history of flowers in China and Deborah Swallow (of the Victoria and Albert Museum, London) with Indian references. David Allen (of the SSRC) put me in touch with survey material as well as assisting with bibliographic references. At Cambridge Stephen Hugh-Jones, Gilbert Lewis and Stephen Levinson tried to restrain my old world biases. I remember too discussions with Ray Abrahams, Fred Adler, Jeanne Augustins, Pascale Baboulet, John Baines, Chris Bayly, John Aubrey, Maria Pia di Bella, George Bush, Brendan Bradshaw, David Brockenshaw, Peter Brooks, Elizabeth Colson, Elizabeth Copet-Rougier, Marie-Paul Ferry, Anthony Forge, Takeo Funabiki, Ariane Gastambide, Michelle Gilbert, Heather Glen, Aaron Gurevich, Colette de la Cour Grandmaison, Françoise Héritier-Augé, Alicia Holy, Christine Hugh-Jones, Sara d'Incal, Joseph Kandert, Junzo Kawada, John Kerrigan, Pratina Khilnani, Hilda Kuper, Stephen Lansing, Peggy McCracken, Malcolm McLeod, John Middleton, Birgit Müller, Rheinhold Müller, Gyoko Murakami, Sue Naquin, Colette Piault, Zdenka Polednová, Elaine Scarry, Regina Schulte, Michaela Settis, Monika Zweite-Steinhausen, Amrit Srinivasan, Lucia Szeto, Francine Thérondel, Douglas Tsui, Dan Sperber, and Ruth Watt. Offprints or correspondence have come from Griet Kershaw, Beverley Seaton, and Roy Vickery. Ellie Apter found me a book. Esther Goody has endured many a graveyard and Mary Goody has been helpful in producing photographs of flower shops and markets in London, John Sawyer of cemeteries of Cambridge at All Saints', Claudio Poppi of those around Bologna at the same period, Mike and Sonia Cole of San Diego, Bogumil Jewsiewicki of Quebec, Pam Blackwell of Los Angeles and Helen Siu of New Haven; as always, I am indebted to Asha and Suhrid Sarabhai in Ahmadabad where flowers were always unforgettable. I thank too Lokamitra for his instruction in Buddhism, and my daughter-in-law, Ranjana, in Pune for her more earthy examples of flower use.

The bibliographical work I did in the Bibliothèque Nationale and the Maison des Sciences de l'Homme in Paris, the Sterling Library at Yale, the Green Library at Stanford, very briefly at the Widener Library in Harvard, the Smithsonian Libraries (and the Library of Congress), the Newberry Library at Chicago, the Wissenschafts Kolleg zu Berlin and extensively in the Library of the Getty Center for the History of Art and Humanities (drawing on that of the University of California, Los Angeles), and the University Library at Cambridge. Some libraries were not so helpful and it has always seemed to me that they deserve mention in order to encourage their staff and management to more user-friendly behaviour. But I have been persuaded not to name names on this occasion.

I am grateful to Josselyne Chamarat of the Centre d'Ethnologie française for giving me access to her references on flowers in France as well as indirectly to A. de Carle Smith who deposited a collection of twenty-six manuscript volumes in the Norwich Museum under the title of 'Flowers in painting' (and to Jane Thistlewaite who drew my attention to it).

For general advice I am, as always, grateful to Patricia Williams and, at Cambridge University Press, to Richard Fisher. The following have read various versions of chapters of the book: 1, Anthony Forge, Stephen Hugh-Jones, Christine Hugh-Jones, Gilbert Lewis, Cesare Poppi; 2, Dick Whittaker (and 3), Salvatore Settis, Graeme Clark (and 3); 3, Aaron Gurevich; 4, Ziba Mir-Hoseini; 5 and 7, Richard Beadle; 6 and 7, Peter Burke; 10, Martine Segalen, Pascale Baboulet; 11, Asha Sarabhai, Chris Bayly, André Béteille, Lokamitra; 12 and 13, Helen Siu, Joe McDermott, David McMullen, Francesca Bray. Keith Hart braved the lot.

For wordprocessing in Cambridge I am indebted to Antonia Lovelace, Dafna Capobianco, Janet Reynolds, Andrew Serjent, Jaya Pankhurst, Sue Kemsley, Hamish Park and Samata; for much help in Santa Monica to Bill Young, Neil Hathaway, Brigitte Buethner and especially to Julie Deichmann. For checking the romanisation of the Chinese I have to thank Oliver Moore. For correcting the proofs I am indebted to Ruth Daniel and for much checking to Sue Kemsley.

As earlier with cooking, my practical skills with flowers are minimal. The limited empirical knowledge I acquired, in the house rather than from books or even from observation, came from my mother, Lilian Rankine Goody, above all from my wife, Esther Newcomb Goody, and from my daughter, Rachel Mead Goody.

The acknowledgements point to the fact that, like most such works, this is in many ways predatory, relying on knowledge that is more secure in the hands of women than of men. But I began such an enquiry not simply for purposes of self-aggrandisement, to exalt the male ego, but in order to make sense of my experiences as an 'observer of man' (to use the title of a French society of anthropologists founded in the Napoleonic era), as well as to try to contribute towards the understanding of the differences and similarities between North and South on the one hand, and West and East on the other. Above all I have enjoyed the undertaking which has taken me to interesting places and to friendly people, often somewhat outside the usual range of scholarly contacts. For one great advantage of the topic is that almost anywhere, outside Africa, people are only too willing to talk about flowers, however great or small their knowledge. It has not been a case of 'with a little help from my friends', but of a great deal.

Acknowledgements

The publishers wish to acknowledge the following institutions as sources for the illustrations. Every effort has been made to obtain permission to reproduce the illustrations, and the Press acknowledges with gratitude those institutions that have given formal permission.

British Museum; British Library; Topkapy Seray Museum; Musei Civici di Verona; Museum of Archaeology and Anthropology, University of Cambridge; Oxford University Press; Österreichische Nationalbibliothek, Vienna; Museo Nacional del Prado, Madrid; M. H. de Jong Museum, San Francisco; Staatliche Kunstsammlungen, Dresden; Musée National des Arts et Traditions Populaires, Paris; Bibliothèque Nationale, Paris; Victoria and Albert Museum; Thyssen-Bornenisza Collection, Lugano; Cambridge University Library; Metropolitan Museum of Art, New York; St John's College, Cambridge, Simon Jervis, Fitzwilliam Museum, Cambridge.

Every effort has been made to reach copyright holders: the publishers would be pleased to hear from anyone whose rights they have unwittingly infringed.

A note on terminology

In ordinary life and in academic talk the word 'culture' is used in a variety of ways, mostly unsatisfactorily. I have employed the term as a signpost to an arena of human performance, very much part of the social and in no sense opposed in the way that some try to mark out a cultural from a social history, anthropology or sociology. I speak of 'utilitarian' and 'aesthetic' horticulture in a similar way; growing flowers I treat as aesthetic even though they have some uses as medicine, for perfume, as food but above all as offerings to or for the gods. I do not defend these usages; I simply know nothing else apart from neologisms that would convey my meaning. 'Representations' in principle cover the range of senses, but especially words (imagery) and sight (images); 'icon' I try to reserve for images that are weighted or marked in some way, generally by religion.

1 · No flowers in Africa?

Is the culture of flowers universal? Is it part of an interest in the natural world that in some form is found in all human societies? I may have implicitly assumed, like many others, that the attraction of flowers was present throughout the world, operating at an almost biological level. Their colour, perfume, sweetness and shapes, which played so prominent a role in plant reproduction, seemed to attract humans as well as animals, rather like the bright feathers of the blue jay and the golden pheasant, or the rich scales of the carp or tropical fish. There seemed something in common in mankind's use of flowers and feathers as well as with his propensity to collect and create coloured objects; in this feathers have one advantage – they endure in a way that only artificial flowers can do. A cultural anthropologist might make different but none the less universalistic assumptions, perhaps following the idea of Blondel in his study of garlands published a century ago in which he associated flowers with femininity and declared, 'Every people has gained pleasure in weaving flowers into garlands and crowns and in gathering them in bouquets.'[1] In his account of their influence on French poetry, Philip Knight writes of this continuous intertextual 'culte des fleurs' which was elaborated into 'a new flower rhetoric' in the nineteenth century.[2] In this view every people would have different usages, that is culture. Nevertheless the culture of flowers itself would be universal.

On the other hand, some accounts dwelt on the growth of interest in flowers as an aspect of the rise of the West and the expansion of Europe, recounting the successful introduction of foreign species, the popularisation of the garden, developments in plant breeding and the proliferation of new varieties.[3]

A similar duality accompanies the cultural history of man's attitudes to nature itself. Some writers treat such a concern as accompanying the growth of urban society; the nature we are destroying is a matter for contemplation and inspiration in the Romantic manner. Others would put the emergence of modern attitudes earlier in the Renaissance. On the other hand, another group argue that, while their interest took less explicit forms, man the hunter and

[1] Blondel 1876:6.   [2] Knight 1986:3.   [3] E.g. R. Gorer, *The Growth of Gardens*, London, 1978.

woman the gatherer were both concerned with the conservation of resources and with a mystical communion with the world about them that presaged many later attitudes towards the environment.

There is a problem here of periodisation, a problem of continuity and discontinuity and above all a problem of definition of what is at stake. The last is the most intractable. One author of a book on Chinese miniature gardens writes that generalities like the 'love of looking at nature' are 'common to too many civilizations to be characteristic in itself'.[4] Vague usages make any assessment of continuity or discontinuity difficult to support. At a general level much has continued; on a more particular one differences exist and some of these can be treated historically. By concentrating on flowers, which are part of nature and of society's views about nature, one has a better chance of approaching problems that are less easily approached at the general level. For flowers are also part of culture: firstly, because they have been brought under cultivation by mankind and, secondly, because they are used throughout social life, for decoration, for medicine, in cooking and for their scents, but above all in establishing, maintaining and even ending relationships, with the dead as with the living, with divinities as well as humans.

Clearly there have been important changes over time, influenced by the growth of botany, the uses of written knowledge and literature, the nature of leisure, the arts of reproduction, by modes of production and by more immediate concerns. But there have also been continuities which derive from the human condition itself, generalised but by no means always general. It is important to try to disentangle these different aspects. An enquiry of this kind helps to make more concrete the problem of attitudes to nature by linking them to wider social transformations. For in taking the subject of flowers, we are already dealing with the domesticated as well as the wild, with image or representation as well as 'reality' or what is represented, in other words, with objects and their uses that are influenced by wider sets of practices and beliefs.

The evidence for particular changes and differences of attitude has to be assessed in a wide historical and geographical context, especially if there is the slightest implication that we are dealing with one aspect of the so-called 'Uniqueness of the West'. In other words, the edge of my argument has to do with the comparison of systems of knowledge and practice in the East and West, especially at the time of the Renaissance, and in their relative positioning regarding the growth of the modern world. When I began to reconsider the problem, it seemed important to be wary of inappropriate assumptions of a universalistic kind. On the other hand, many had fallen in another trap, which is common among European scholars, that of concentrating on the modern achievements of that continent, especially those of England, and taking them out of the wider context of Eurasian developments,

---

[4] Stein 1990:49.

either because of 'practical' ethnocentricism or 'theoretical' notions of the process of modernisation. By so doing they tend to overlook the implications of Europe's earlier backwardness and the enormous contribution made by the East and the Near East to the culture of flowers, our own and the world's. My own approach attempts to 'rationalise' and at the same time to lessen the gap between the West and the East, and even between the Eurasian North and the African South, by pointing to factors behind the similarities and the differences. In some respects the argument, overwhelmed as it may become in the welter of floral particularities, represents a paradigm for reconsidering this very problem of the uniqueness of the West that underlies so many approaches to the study of the growth of capitalism, of knowledge and of modern life as a whole. My justification for presenting a *tour du monde*, apart from the pleasure I have had in making it, is precisely to provide the context for historical transfers and for adequate comparison.

A FLOWER IS . . .

Before presenting the particular problem with which I began, let us turn to the question of what makes a flower. Each society has its variation on this theme, but in the languages I have known or am acquainted with there is some concept that can be reasonably seen as corresponding to the English term (unlike the wider concepts of 'nature' and 'culture'). However, it is with the observer's rather than purely the actor's frame of reference that I am first concerned, with the etic rather than the emic, so I turn to the *Encyclopaedia Britannica* which defines a flower as 'a term popularly used for the bloom or blossom of a plant, and so by analogy for the fairest, choicest or finest part or aspect of anything'.[5] It is characteristic of the highest group of the plant kingdom, the flowering plants or *Phanerogamia*, the name being given to the association of organs, more or less leaf-like in form, which are concerned with the production of the fruit or seed; of this order there are two subdivisions, the gymnosperms (the 'naked seeds') and the angiosperms (the 'covered seeds').

From the botanical standpoint, flowers represent a method of continuing the life of plants. Early vegetative life required direct access to water and reproduced by fertilisation through sperms. The end of the Age of Reptiles saw the appearance of angiosperms, the 'encased seeds' of the flowering plants emerging out of pollen-disseminating varieties. Instead of spores the angiosperms produced seeds that could be scattered by the birds and animals as well as by the wind, providing a surer method of dispersal. Reproduction depended on the flower attracting other species, by its colour, its odour, its sweetness and its shape, all of which developed during the Cretaceous period. Sexuality lies at the core of the flower's existence and played a prominent part

[5] *Encyclopaedia Britannica* (11th edn), vol. 10, p.553.

when it was taken up in human life. At the same time, the process gave the burgeoning population of animal life the energy it needed by producing concentrated food, the nectars and pollens to bring insects, the fruits to draw larger animals and the contents of the seeds themselves to nourish the growing plant. The bees flourished with the flowers. So it was the emergence of wild flowers, in the broadest sense, that paved the way for the dominance of terrestrial mammals and so for the emergence of man himself.

So much for the technical sense of flower, but this is not the common one. Let us explore its range of meaning in English (we will later consider its range in Eastern languages). To the West European of today, flower means primarily 'ornamental flower'. Say you are interested in the culture of flowers and people talk of roses, peonies and daffodils, or they speak of gardens. Even in rural areas in nineteenth-century England the flower garden was separated from the vegetable garden, which has of course its own flowerings, its own blossoms, but these are precursors to vegetables and fruit, to productive ends, to consumables, to food, rather than ends in themselves, as with garden flowers. The very word garden, as in 'an English garden', tends to conjure up the decorative rather than the productive aspects of cottage horticulture. Garden flowers are for display; the vegetable garden tends to be hidden behind a walled enclosure in country houses, allocated to the bottom of the lawn in suburban dwellings, pushed out to the allotment in council houses. The competitive displays of vegetables are of a different order; they tend to form part of working-class culture, of sales of produce for good causes and of harvest festivals in country churches. Flowers, on the other hand, are displayed in front (and back) gardens, inside houses, publicly in municipal gardens and country houses, competitively at upper-class events like the Chelsea Flower Show, formally opened by royalty.

It is not only the flowers in themselves that are prized but in their combination with others, both in the garden and in the house. The layout of the vegetable garden is largely 'functional', that of the flower garden 'aesthetic'. And while fruit may form the subject of display in the house, vegetables rarely do. Flower arranging, in specially created containers, is an art, posing one shape, one colour, one height against another, relating this pattern to the room, hall or church in which it stands.

The extreme of such a separation of food (or reproduction) from decor, of the 'functional' from the 'aesthetic', occurs in East Asia where many fruit trees such as the cherry were specialised for flowers *instead* of fruit.[6] In China and especially in Japan voyages were made, platforms built, picnics arranged, to 'view' these and other plants in all their glory at the right time of the year.

To prefer the flower to the fruit raises the kind of qualms many a European experiences on breaking off a branch of a fruit tree in blossom, the abortion of

---

[6] Grimal (1969:81) writes of sterile fruit trees in Rome but the scale was much different.

a birth. And this ambivalence between the delight in beauty and the critique of conspicuous waste will often emerge as an explicit or implicit feature of these highly developed cultures of flowers.

As a bud, a forerunner, the flower is 'the essence', one of its central meanings in English as in French (*la quintessence*); the 'flowers' or *les fleurs* of sulphur is the essence of that mineral, just as the flower of the ground wheat is its essence and hence its 'flour', giving rise to the English doublet, only possible in a written language, of 'flower' and 'flour'. Medieval French had *flour de farine* for fine-ground wheatmeal and *fleur de farine* is still possible, being derived from the Latin, *flos farina*, which carried the similar meaning of the 'best', the 'finest' specimen.

But both in Latin and in French the flower is not only the essence but at times the surface (*fleur d'eau*), like the bloom in English – *le velouté, le duvet du raisin, d'une pêche*. The logic lies in the flower being a reproductive organ, coloured and perfumed for that end, so that what is displayed is also the means of reproduction; the surface is at the same time the essence, or becomes so when it gives way to fruit and seeds which in the hands of Renaissance scholars such as Cesalpino came to be the basis of later botanical classification.[7]

It is perhaps the connection of the flower with generation that has given the name of 'flowers' to the menstrual activity of a woman, but the notion of the deflowering of a virgin, the breaking of her hymen through sexual penetration, has more to do with the plucking of a flower, the taking away of her 'essence' (as a virgin), leading to her 'blossoming forth' as a woman. Like a flower, she may of course blossom too much and become 'full-blown', 'over-blown', even 'blowzy' or 'blousy', a word possibly deriving from the verb, to blow, meaning to bloom, as in Shakespeare's line 'I know a bank where on the wild thyme blows' (*Midsummer Night's Dream*, II.i.249), giving the nouns 'blowing', a bloom, and 'blowen' and possibly 'blowze', a whore.[8]

English is once again able to draw upon both the Romance and Germanic contributions to the language, 'flower' from French and 'bloom' and 'blossom' from Teutonic roots. 'Blossom' was the word used in Old English before 'bloom' came from the Old Norse and 'flower' from the French. While there is a large area of overlap in their meanings, this reduplication allows for subtle discriminations as well. Unlike its companions, 'flower' may refer to the plant as a whole. 'Bloom' means a delicate flower, even the powder on the skin of a grape; it is a surface phenomenon. Blossoms, according to Dr Johnson, generally mean those flowers 'which are not much regarded in themselves, but as a token of some following product'.

---

[7] See Atran 1986:78.
[8] 'Sweet blouse, you are a beautious blossome sure', Shakespeare, *Titus Andronicus*, IV.ii.72. 'Blowen' occurs in Herrick's *Hesperides*. By association rather than derivation we get into 'blouse' from the French, but in modern English usually confined to woman's clothing, as well as into 'bloomers', so called after the American lady who created them.

thou prun'st a rotten tree,
That cannot so much as a blossom yield.
(Shakespeare, *As You Like It*, II.iii.64)

But while cherries blossom and daffodils bloom, the former word has also come to be largely specialised for large, heavy flowers associated with trees, whether they fruit or not, and with tall plants in flower. In each case it is the ornamental, aesthetic sense that predominates in current usage, not only in the town but in the country too.

ABUNDANCE IN BALI

Having outlined the general context of the enquiry, let me turn to the particular situation that brought this topic to my notice and raised the question about flowers in Africa. In Ubud, a Balinese town with a princely past and an artistic present situated in the hills of Bali some two hours drive from the International Airport, a festival was being celebrated at one of the many temples. There was nothing unusual in this. Temple festivals, with their formal dancing, their gamelan music, their *wayang kulit* shadow puppet shows based on the Mahābhārata and the Rāmāyaṇa running late into the night (Plate 1.1), seemed to follow one another in a continuous flow, in parallel to the seamless pattern of planting, growing and harvesting the rice, a process that knew no season, no set time of sowing or of gathering. For the extraordinary complex pattern of man-made channels leads irrigated water down from the mountains to the coast, sometimes along small wooden aqueducts passing above the road, and at others making spectacular sweeps as they wind down the valleys of the tropical landscape, bringing a variable but perpetual supply to countless small fields on the way in a remarkable feat of human organisation.[9]

I had gone to Bali on a brief visit to gain some idea of an island on which so many anthropologists had worked, Margaret Mead, Jane Belo, Clifford and Hildred Geertz, and many others, but particularly, for me, Gregory Bateson who, like his father and grandfather before him, had been a fellow of the same college at Cambridge in which I have always worked. Their studies did much to prepare me for what I saw.[10] As I walked towards the ruins of the house of Colin McPhee where Bateson and Mead had stayed, I came across a cockfight at the side of the road.[11] Facial expressions, body movements, had been caught

[9] In order to spread the available water, the members of one irrigation group plant at different times. Every terrace or group of terraces has rituals at planting and harvesting. The old rice took 210 days to grow, determining the length of the Balinese year on which the main temple rituals are based. But new varieties mature in 100 days so that the cycling is much faster.

[10] The works I refer to are those of Mead and Macgregor (1951), Bateson and Mead (1942), Belo (1953, 1960, 1970), C. Geertz (1966, 1980) and C. and H. Geertz (1975). I have not looked at work in Dutch, nor done little more than glance at the specialist studies of music (McPhee 1966), dance and drama (de Zoete and Spies 1939), and at the more recent research of Boon (1977), Hobart, Lansing and others.

[11] Colin McPhee, a musicologist, has written about his house in Bali (1946).

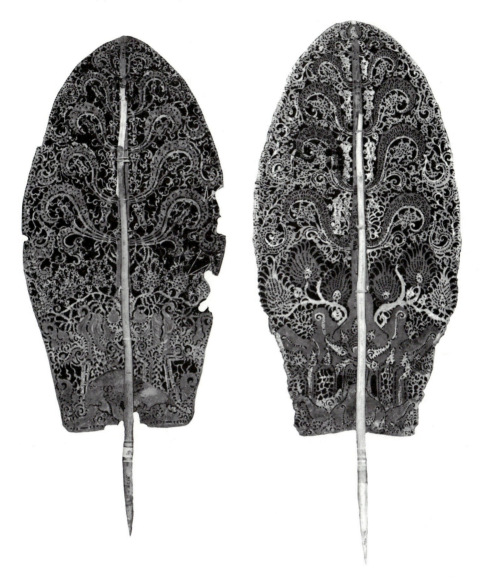

1.1 The Tree of Life, one of the shadow puppets of the *wayang kulit*, associated with the trees of the Garden of Eden. (Cambridge University Museum of Archaeology and Anthropology)

in the eye of the ethnologists' lens as well as in their words. The entire ambiance was indeed theatrical. But I soon found that my understanding lacked a significant dimension.

That was partly my fault. I should have looked more deeply at the scholarly sources, the written records, instead of relying so heavily on those whose interests and capabilities lay in the oral field. I should have recalled the remark of Belo that 'To write of Bali . . . is not like writing of a primitive society.'[12] I

[12] Belo 1949:1.

should have remembered too that important work by Geertz on *The Religion of Java* where within an Islamic frame many of the earlier features of the religious system were maintained. As a result of my neglect of these sources, I was surprised at the development of the graphic arts and the strength of their links with India, surprised too at the levels of linguistic complexity associated with the written as well as with the oral mode, that is, the reference back, in the present as well as the past, to Hindu and Buddhist sutras, the iconographic adaptations to 'another civilisation', surprised at the elaborateness of temple rituals, musically, dramatically, visually, surprised beyond anything by the 'luxury' of it all, as well as by the productivity and development of the agriculture, above all in comparison with the savannah areas of Africa in which I had lived, or even the wheatfields of East Anglia, which have long been my home.

Preparing for the festival, women spent hours creating many-coloured offerings of cooked ricecakes, fruits and flowers, all vegetable gifts which were arranged as a tall, elegant pyramid on a platter to be carried on their heads from house to temple (Colour plate 1.1). In the service itself the priest (a brahmin) made offerings, placing a flower behind his ear, according to Belo, as a sign of dedication to god.[13] When the offerings are set down, prayers are recited to the gods accompanied by incense and flowers, especially the marigold, which waft the words towards the divinities.[14] At the ceremony I attended in Ubud, the women, who filled the front of the temple, were first blessed by being asperged with the Holy Water (*tirta*) on the surface of which petals gently float; then they pulled off the petals of the flowers they held and cast them in the direction of the altar, three times in all, once for Brahma, once for Vishnu and once for Śiva.

This food offering is the *mbantĕn*, the equivalent of the *slametan* or 'communal feast', described for Java by Geertz,[15] which can be used to 'celebrate, ameliorate, or sanctify almost any occurrence'; there is always incense and special food, including dishes of rice variously coloured and moulded. A simple *slametan* to the shrine of *mBah Buda*, Grandfather Buddha, consisted of food, incense and flowers;[16] the caretaker takes the food, burns the incense and places the flowers on the head of Ganesh, the Hindu elephant god.[17] Then he gathers up some old flowers from the shrine, forms them into a packet and gives it to whoever brought the offering to take home so that it can be mixed with water and drunk by those who had participated. Both rice and flowers can be bought in the market for this purpose, and in his budget of a funeral, Geertz includes an average figure of 15

---

[13] It is not essential to have a brahmin *Pedanda* at such a ritual; most ceremonies are carried out by the temple priest who can be of any caste but then he has to officiate from the ground. Some of the offerings consist almost entirely of flowers, see Belo 1970: Plate XIX.

[14] Belo 1953:24–5.   [15] Geertz 1960:11ff.   [16] Geertz 1960:25.

[17] Gaṇeśa (Ganesh) was the elephant-headed son of Śiva and Parvati, the patron of learning, composer of the Mahābhārata, whose shrine is often placed at the entrance to temples so that it is the first to be worshipped.

rupiah for the cost of flowers, one-quarter that of the food provided; they enter market transactions as part of worship. In addition, flowers are placed on the graves of parents on the anniversary of their deaths.[18]

The complexity of such offerings, including the large rice 'pyramid', reaches greater heights in the ceremonies for births,[19] while at marriages flowers become yet more prominent. Before the actual wedding, the bride is seated in front of a ceremonial bedroom and her mother performs the ritual of the burying of the *kembang majang* – the 'blossoming flower(s)'. This large composite plant consists of a banana-tree-trunk as a stem and 'blossoms' of scalloped leaves from various trees, wrapped in green coconut branches, and represents the virginity of the bride and groom. Many others are used. For the traditional wedding the bride is dressed up as a princess, her black blouse trimmed with flowers; three necklaces of silver or of flowers hang down in front of her. The groom too is draped with blossoms, and in his belt is stuck a huge, flower-covered *kris*, a conscious symbolisation of the phallus.[20] His feet are washed in flower water by the bride as a sign of the respect she owes him. Flowers are widely used throughout the East for giving a fragrance to water which may then refresh the human body or the palate. They also decorate the hair of girl dancers, sometimes in combination with a metal crown or even metal flowers (Plate 1.2).[21] But apart from personal decoration, and apart from their role in ceremonies, they play a major part in Hindu, Buddhist and even in some Islamic art, as well as in the adornment of the home and temple where flower petals are strewn in bowls of water.[22] In these various ways, the use of flowers for 'dressing up the bride', for funerals as well as in temples and houses, the culture of flowers bears many resemblances to the contemporary West.

In Bali these offerings to men and gods are not a matter of collecting colourful wild flowers from the fields and forests, though many exist in the Asian tropics. Flowers are grown around the houses to be offered to the gods, not only on public occasions in the temple but also at private shrines in the house where they are used for worship rather than for decoration. The plants are grown in small plots largely devoted to particular specialist crops which include what we would call herbs and spices – the vanilla pod is conspicuous as a vine. They are grown to offer to the gods, like music, dance and drama at the temple festival, to attract them down to earth to bring help to mankind. Frangipani (*Plumifera acutifolia*) and jasmine are especially in demand for ritual offerings and small children collect the flowers for sale early in the morning. In the mountains there is also a commercial growth of marigolds, which are liked because of their strong colours, their toughness and their durability. Every morning they are brought down in truckloads to be sold, very much as in Indian markets.

---

[18] Geertz 1960:72.   [19] Geertz 1960:39ff.   [20] Geertz 1960:57.
[21] Ramseyer 1977:79, plate 82; 231, plate 373; 232, plate 375.   [22] Geertz 1960:42.

1.2 Girl dancer wearing headdress decorated with fresh flowers, Bali. (Ramseyer 1977:231)

The growing of flowers for such purposes is an important part of Indian culture which provides a significant element in Indonesian religion, ritual and iconography. Our friend Bikubhai Sharma in the Midlands town of Leicester, England, grows roses in his garden specifically for offering to the household shrine.[23] The same is true in rural areas in China, Japan and India itself, possibly even in parts of Europe.[24] Gardens for display and for sitting in, flowers for decoration inside or outside the house, are for the rich rather than the poor, but the poor need flowers for worship in Hindu rituals and most notably in Buddhism. Indeed the 'Indian' lotus found in China (*Nelumbo nucifera*) is sometimes known in the West as the 'Buddhist' lotus.[25]

ABSENCE IN AFRICA

In Indonesia I was struck by what I saw partly because of the rich unfamiliarity of the scene, although I had spent time in other parts of Asia, which like Europe too has its culture of flowers. But I was struck above all by the extreme contrast with West Africa. I had attended many ceremonies and had seen food, the raw and the cooked, offered at innumerable shrines – but never flowers. Nor did one see flowers grown around the house, let alone in the fields. This I encountered only once in a 'traditional' context, in the town of Damongo in Gonja, where I found a creeper with a blue flower growing in the compound of a well-travelled Muslim trader. Islam certainly has its culture of flowers, at least in Asia, the Mediterranean, and to some extent in East Africa. John Middleton observed that the Swahili of Lamu, in the coastal area of East Africa, grow red roses and jasmine.[26] However, their culture has been much influenced by Islam, by India and by Indonesia. Bouquets of petals of pink Bourbon roses are made up, sewn together with jasmine on a base of basil leaves.[27] These bouquets are worn by women in their hair and as corsages or are put under their pillows. All house gardens in Lamu grow herbs, including basil, while the rose and jasmine petals are obtained from specialist growers who raise them both in household plots and in the small farms outside the town that are mainly planted with coconut palms. Roses are also grown in northern Madagascar and in Réunion (Bourbon itself) where

---

[23] A photograph, taken by E. Goody, shows a flower in the temporary Randal Mata shrine, part of which will be incorporated in the household shrine or *mundir*.

[24] Of a much later period, the Renaissance, Tapié (1987:26) writes: '[Flowers] actualise the idea of sacrifice, they are living creatures offered to God.'

[25] There are two main types of 'lotus', the Indian or Buddhist lotus (*Nelumbo nucifera*, an edible plant), indigenous to China although it had reached Egypt from India at about the time of the Persian conquest (c.708 BC), and the Egyptian lotus (*Nymphaea sp.*), a type of waterlily.

[26] J. Middleton, personal communication.

[27] Bourbon roses are said to have been the result of a chance crossing of the *R. chinensis* with a Damask rose, 'Rose de Quatre Saisons', which French farmers on the island of Réunion used for hedging because of their thorns. The eighteenth-century importation of Chinese roses gave birth to the parent of the hybird musks (Coats 1970:178–9).

they have run wild. In that dominantly Islamic area lies the Francophile island of Mayotte, Comores, where modern cash crops include the ylang-ylang whose flowers yield an oil used as a stabiliser by the French perfume industry.[28] In Malagasy-speaking villages, cologne (*marashi*) is an important offering in the spirit cults; the Swahili word is translated as 'rosewater and scent in general' and in Islamic poetry sometimes refers to scholarship and to piety, a version of the 'odour of sanctity'. Odour has a central place in many rites and prayers are generally said over a dish of lighted incense. Fragrant smells (*haruf*) include not only cologne and lemons but some flowers as well as some spices. Despite the dried flowers women wear on their heads, it is claimed that flowers 'are selected for their fragrance, not for their color or form'.[29]

Rosewater (again, *marashi*), which is widely found throughout Arabia and India, is also used in Lamu both to attract spirits to take possession of a person and to spray on the bride on her wedding day when she is adorned with heavy cosmetics; 'it is extraordinary', comments the ethnographer, 'to see someone totally changed cosmetically as to become a kind of sexual doll in which her normal personality must be extinguished'.[30] The Asiatic influences are clear, not only in the cultigens themselves, the jasmine from India, the roses from China, but in the use of incense, perfume and other features of adornment, for aloewood and other materials are burnt to give pleasure to the spirits. Even some non-Islamic peoples of East Africa may have been affected, for Middleton also reports that when unmarried Lugbara girls go to dances they will put the exotics, frangipani or scarlet flamboyant flowers, in their hair; otherwise in the 1950s they were naked except for pubic leaves, beads and cicatrisations.

But in general the peoples of Africa did not grow domesticated flowers. Nor yet did they make use of wild ones to any significant extent in worship, in gift-giving or in the decoration of the body. That is understandable in the light of what I have said about worship, since one gives to the gods the best of what one gives to humans: the bread and the wine are the basis both of secular and of religious life, at least in the area where the religion was born. But what is perhaps more surprising is that flowers, neither domesticated nor wild, play so little part in the domain of design or the creative arts. I certainly have not reviewed the entire corpus of the graphic arts in Africa but I have come across little or nothing in my own experience.[31] African sculpture provides no examples; there are some decorations of a possibly floral type on Benin bronze plaques and there are similar 'abstract' designs on some of the Moorish or Egyptian brass ware that has entered into Africa south of the Sahara for nearly a thousand years. But these 'rosettes' of the Islamic tradition are explicitly

---

[28] These flowers are also grown in Zanzibar. The name is derived from the Tagalog for *Canangium odoratum* found in Malaysia and the Philippines.   [29] Lambek 1981:16, 119–120, 200.

[30] J. Middleton, personal communication.   [31] For a compendium of African design, see Williams 1971.

alternatives to the representations of flowers, a rejection rather than an image.[32]

What about the verbal arts? Is there any parallel to the myriad references to flowers and to the development of flower symbolism resembling that we find in Chinese poetry from the earliest times as well as in Indian, Arabic and European literature?[33] Again it would be impossible to scan the whole of African 'literature', even that small part of the oral tradition that has been written down. Let me take one central example. Over a number of years I have been recording, transcribing and editing one of the longest African recitations which belongs to the Bagre society of the LoDagaa of West Africa; of these recordings two versions have been published and I have prepared many others with my collaborator, S. W. D. K. Gandah.[34] In these long 'myths' little or no use is made of flowers, certainly as Europeans usually understand the term. There are some limited references to flowers as forerunners of crops, a theme to which I will return soon. Just as the absence of visual images of plants is in stark contrast to the still-life tradition of Dutch painting, so the paucity of verbal ones stands opposed to the 'Daffodils' of Wordsworth, to the work of Clare and in a totally different way of Baudelaire, to the imagery of Shakespeare conjured up in the speech of the mad Ophelia, let alone to the abundant references to flowers in Asian poetry.

When this contrast first struck me, I consulted other Africanists to see if their experience tallied with my own. My French colleagues were encouraging. Alfred Adler strongly agreed that such was the case among the Moundang people of Chad whom he studied. Elizabeth Copet-Rougier, who worked with the Nkaka in the Cameroons, had been particularly impressed by the lack of interest in flowers as well as by another, perhaps surprising, feature, the relative absence of wild flowers in the tropical forest itself. In northern Ghana, the flamboyant tree with its mass of bright red blossoms stands out in the sea of greenery,[35] but like many other savannah trees (such as the mango, teak and neem) it was apparently introduced by European colonialists.[36] Cesare Poppi wrote to me of the disappointment he felt on going to the Ghanaian Botanical Gardens at Aburi to walk in the rain forest and 'realized there were very few flowers – or none at all . . . Only a monotonous, maddening deep-green foreground, midground, background and horizon – butterflies were the only

[32] On the art history, see Bravmann (1974). We find some rosettes on the Muslim house decorations of the savannah zone and 'flowers' of a different design, including the fleur-de-lis, on Benin plaques, which were probably influenced by the Portuguese. Both are formal designs, adapted from outside, not flowers as such. Some daisy-type patterns appear on Yoruba indigo cloths from Ibadan (Willett 1971:122; Williams 1974:90; V. Ebin, personal communication).

[33] References to flowers pervade classical Javanese literature of the court, as they do their Indian models. See Zoetmulder 1974:196ff., for which reference I am grateful to Steven Lansing.

[34] Goody 1972; Goody and Gandah 1981.

[35] The flamboyant tree, peacock tree or royal poinciana (*Delonix regia*) is a native of Madagascar.

[36] Mango, *Mangifera indica*, a fruit tree native to East Asia; teak, *Tectona grandis*, a timber native to India, Burma and Thailand; the neem, or nim, is an East Indian tree.

"flowers" around.' In the savannah too flowers are few and far between, practically the only spectacular kind being some large white and purple lilies that last for a brief moment in the rainy season. Flowers do not endure; 'African decorations imply *dry* matter.' In the Cameroons, the only flower to be used today is the amaryllis which was imported by some 'colon' and whose leaves and bulbs serve as medicine.[37] As among many African peoples, it is the leaves, bark and roots of trees and plants that are important; the LoDagaa words for both medicine (*tĩĩ*) and shrine (*tiib*) are apparently related to that for tree (*tie*), and from the word for root comes one of the main terms for a herbalist or curer (*daanyigr*). Once again no use is made of flowers in the local recitations though, as always, there are plenty of animals.[38]

The absence of flowers in Africa is reinforced by the relative lack of attention paid to perfumes, or to smell in general, and possibly by the limited vocabulary for colours. I do not know of any indigenous use of odours, either in ritual, in myth, or yet for personal adornment. Certainly perfumes are now imported into African countries, often the stronger Indian varieties.[39] And they were much used in the areas under Islamic influence.[40]

As with perfume and the sense of smell, there is no question of Africans being unable to recognise colours, but their use of them is limited in range, if we think either mentally about colour terminology (which is basically a tripartite division between white, blue/black, and red/brown) or visually about the uses of colour in weaving or in painting and colouring.[41] In weaving the main dyes known in West Africa were indigo (blue/black) and red or rather brownish red; white was the absence of dye, being the colour of the

---

[37] The amaryllis is a genus of bulbous plants of South African origin.

[38] Occasional uses of flowers do occur in West Africa. In her recent fieldwork among the LoBirifor in northern Ghana, Esther Goody noted some young girls using wild flowers behind their ears (though straw is a more usual decorative feature placed in the lip drilled for display). Christine Kreamer saw the same among the Bimoba of the Togo–Ghana border; she also remarks that one *kente* cloth pattern in Asante is known as 'yam flower', though this is again prized for what it becomes rather than what it is.

[39] These points were brought out in a discussion with Elizabeth Copet-Rougier. Of course African societies take cognisance of 'bad' smells, sometimes employing smoke in curative rituals. Indian attar (or otto) of roses is produced by distillation, acquired through Islam; their heavy flavour comes from the admixture of shavings of sandalwood, which facilitates distillation (Rimmel 1865:9).

[40] I once went with a Muslim friend to visit the disused Rest House situated at the top of a hill near Jirapa, northern Ghana, when we were attacked by a swarm of African bees and fled in opposite directions. The bulk of the swarm followed my friend as he ran down the steep slope, largely because he had used some toilet water in a liberal fashion. The local inhabitants were doubtless pleased to see followers of religions of the book being treated in such a way, since the former colonial government had built the Rest House on a hill inhabited by the 'beings of the wild' (*kontome*). Much more widely, bees are seen as being protectors of local interests, as for example at Senyon in Gonja, the site of a noted shrine. At the end of the nineteenth century, bees successively attacked the Muslim cavalry of Samory and the Christian invaders from Britain, forcing them into humiliating situations. On these incidents see the account of Duncan-Johnstone. The aggressiveness of African bees has become well known as the result of their invasion of the Americas; they are to European bees as the wild to the domesticated.

[41] It is doubtful if too much significance can be read into this linguistic fact since Roman colour terms were also very restricted, despite the wide range of pigments in paintings, the cultivation of flowers and for dyes for cloth. Alternative ways are usually found for talking about a wider range of colours, possibly using names of objects such as orange or pink.

natural cotton or hair. As for colouring houses and pottery, the same limited vocabulary and shades covered virtually the whole range that we find.

I also had the opportunity of discussing the problem of flowers with a Japanese anthropologist, Junzo Kawada, who worked among the Mossi of Tenkodogo in Burkina Faso. He remarked that the local chief was totally surprised at any enquiry on this topic and Kawada concluded that his response and those of others represented a wider lack of interest in natural beauty as distinct from man-made things. There may be some truth in this suggestion, although three points should be borne in mind. In art European interest in such beauty was not 'indigenous' but largely an outcome of the Renaissance, although some claim it to be the rediscovery of the Middle Ages.[42] Secondly, the possible absence of interest in natural beauty for its own sake certainly did not mean an absence of interest in nature in Africa, for that was always of intense concern, both in its wild and in its domesticated state. But interest was not in flowers as such, which hardly impinge upon man and his works. Clearly that does not mean that there was no developed aesthetic but in the verbal as in the plastic arts interest centred on men and animals rather than on less animate nature.[43] Thirdly, and here I want to introduce a further theme to be developed later, it is possible that in his circumstances the chief of Tenkodogo saw attention to flowers as a moral failing, as well it might seem to others contemplating Africa's continuing encounter with hunger and famine. It was an attention of those who had not got their priorities right.

I have remarked that the general assertion about flowers in Africa needs tempering. I can best make the point by referring to the 'Myth of the Bagre', which is chanted in the course of the rites initiating newcomers into the association. These rites continue for several months during the dry season and the timing of the component phases turns around the ripening of various food plants that are at first forbidden to the neophytes until the appropriate ceremony has been performed when they are released from the prohibition. This laying down and lifting of a taboo on foods emphasises the significance of those products to the whole society as well as the importance of the elders, the Bagre itself and its associated gods and deities all of whom are able to control man's basic needs in this way, just as they claim (and then finally admit their impotence) to control life and death itself.

The first of the ceremonies is heralded by the ripening of the fruit surrounding the shea-nut, a more or less wild tree the nuts of which are used to make a basic fat (shea-butter) as well as soap, and the fruit of which has a date-

---

[42] Evans 1931:i, 40, referring essentially to the Gothic tradition.
[43] It is significant that in the ancient literature of Egypt (Joret 1897:249) and of Mesopotamia (Joret 1897:444) plants speak, whereas in African tales it is largely, if not only, animals. At a more 'serious' level, that of myth, we find only men and gods speaking; I am thinking here of the Bagre myth of the LoDagaa, and of the epics of the Saharan fringe, but the proposition seems to hold more widely.

like sweetness when fully ripe. The myth recounts how a fruit bat found a ripe shea-nut (*tãã̃n*) which he began to eat. His mate wanted to taste some but he refused to give any to her, saying that since she had refused him sex the night before, he was going to refuse to share the sweet fruit. At a later ceremony a similar tale is told about the male and female guinea-fowl who fight over a bean flower and drop it in their struggle. An elder thinks he sees a cowry shell, used as money, but when he goes there to pick it up he finds it is the flower (*puru*) of the white bean, which like the shea-fruit is at first forbidden to the neophytes:

One day
the elder
went to sleep
and put down his skin bag.
The elder was a fool
to go off to sleep.
An old guinea cock
and his mate
last night
fought together.
He wanted to sleep with her
and she refused him.
He got up
the next morning,
walked around
among the guinea corn leaves
and saw
a bean flower
which he picked.
And his mate
hurried along
and said to him,
'What is it?
Let's eat it.'
He replied,
'Why was it
that yesterday
I asked you
to lie with me
and you refused me?
And now look at today.'
The two guinea fowl
were struggling
and found themselves
in front of the elder.

He saw the white flower
and, taking a stick,
hurled it,
crying, 'Oh,
my bag
has a hole in it.
My shell money
has dropped out
and the guinea fowl
is eating it.'
He threw [his stick],
picked it up,
and as he did so,
he realized
it was a bean flower.
He exclaimed, 'Well,
this is just the way
our children
might have sinned.'[44]

So while the LoDagaa make little use of flowers, they do possess the concept. But the nature of this concept is highly significant. 'Flower' is probably part of the plant terminology of all or the large majority of languages.[45] I had originally thought that the LoDagaa word for flower (*puru*) was cognate with that for greeting (*puoru*) and that the phase *ben puru*, the bean flower, could also mean 'greeting' the bean; that is, the flower seemed to be seen as a bud, as a promise of the fruit to come. I am now less sure of the etymology but the idea behind it remains true for the LoDagaa; the 'flowering' of the maize corn heralds the harvest and signals the time for the Dance of the Hoe to take place in the market places of the district. In a technical sense, the same holds true in English and other European languages. It is significant in this regard that the goddess Flora, so long established in central Italy, at first looked after the flowering of cereals, of vines and of fruit trees. It was only later that she became goddess of flowers 'in the full meaning of the word'.[46] Her cult, initially concerned with bad harvests, was given official recognition and in 240 BC the Floralia or floral games were instituted in her honour, being celebrated annually from 173 BC. Historically the 'flower' seems first to have been the promise of fruit, not a thing itself.

[44] Goody 1972:128.
[45] By terminology I mean, following Joseph Needham (1986:117), the naming of parts; by nomenclature I mean the given names of the plants, which also represent a system of classification.
[46] Hild 1896:1189; the author provides detailed references for this sequence, although the evidence is necessarily thin. However the sexual and floral aspects of the ceremony are reported only later; Flavius Philostratus (c.170–c.245 AD) claimed that the Festival of Roses (Rosalia) celebrated at Rome included a race whose participants clasped a rose, signifying the passing of youthful beauty (*Ep.*, 55).

WHY?

A realisation of the differences in these notions and their accompanying usage gave rise to the first question. Why did flowers play so little a part in African life and so great a role in Asia and Europe? The question had similar roots to an earlier interest in differences in cooking and cuisine, and indeed in a wider set of features, between Africa and the major civilisations of Eurasia. African cooking displayed limited differentiation, and indeed elaboration, having little by way of a haute cuisine; the cultures were largely homogeneous from this point of view, even in states composed of a number of social strata. That was certainly not the case in Europe and Asia, where strata tended to eat, as they married, in a circle, with their own recipes, ingredients, methods, table manners and social rituals; each had its own place in the system of consumption as well as in that of production, in the culture as in society (if we may use that unsatisfactory opposition). These broad differences between the continents I saw as linked to the nature of social systems and specifically to the relations between 'classes'. In most of Africa members of groups intermarried frequently and hence did not establish their own distinct sub-cultures, nor greatly elaborate the culinary art. I argued that in societies based on hoe cultivation and lacking many of the major inventions of the Bronze Age, the main differences between individuals and groups did not centre upon either the ownership of the means of production nor yet the relations between those involved in the process. Equally the absence of writing, except in Muslim areas, meant that there was little differentiation resting on the mode of communication. Of course there were internal distinctions, especially with regard to slaves and chiefs, as well as those based on sex and generation. But by and large access to land under systems of shifting hoe cultivation was relatively open, since the amount of land used, the quantity of the produce and the density of the population were all limited. Not only the quantity but the type, for there were no cultivated species of blossoming fruit trees, though citrus has been brought down from the North, nor yet domesticated flowers, except in the areas influenced by Islam. Into other regions the system of cultivation put little effort either to invent or to adopt; attention was focused on more basic food crops under a largely shifting agriculture that had little time for the cultivation of flowers for their own sakes.

In the case of Africa ecological factors may also enter into the low level of interest in flowers and in perfumes (which are closely linked). Asia possessed a much wider range of flowering plants than Europe or Africa, and had more distinctive odours in consequence. Even a group of hunters and gatherers like those inhabiting the Andaman Islands in the Bay of Bengal displays a greater interest in wild flowers. Among these people, Radcliffe-Brown writes, girls acquire an additional name at puberty drawn from a tree or plant which is flowering at that time. A succession of these come into flower one after another throughout the year and people describe the different seasons by particular species in flower. All of those selected in this way have flowers from which honey is made. Each has a distinctive scent which gives the honey a special flavour.[47] Some of those distinctive odours are very strong; when a certain species of *Sterculia* comes into blossom 'it is almost impossible to get away from the smell'.[48] But weak or strong, they mark out the year. In fact, 'their calendar is a calendar of scents', with each flower period seen as possessing its own particular kind of generative force of which the scent is the manifest sign.[49] 'When a girl reaches puberty the natives think of her as having blossomed . . . under the influence of the same natural forces', so she is given her flower name which is no longer used after she gives birth.[50]

In many pre-industrial societies honey from flowers is the main source of sweetness, the equivalent for taste to perfume for the sense of smell.[51] Both are intimately associated with flowers. In the absence of domesticated cane, men and women make extraordinary efforts to obtain this luxury. Today sugar forms one of the main imports of many new nations in Africa and the Pacific just as it did in eighteenth- and nineteenth-century Europe.[52] It is little wonder that in the Andamans the source of the sweetness should so mark the yearly round. In any case, flowers are an outstanding feature both of the ecological and social landscape of continental Asia. Honey is also a major source of sweetness in Africa, though its bees are wilder. Nevertheless, even wild flowers are not as common as in other continents, which may have some bearing not only on the absence of domesticated flowers but the minimal use of any blossoms.[53]

---

[47] Radcliffe-Brown 1922:119.   [48] Radcliffe-Brown 1922:34.   [49] Radcliffe-Brown 1922:312.

[50] There is some archaeological evidence for the use of flowers by Neanderthal man in the Zagros mountains some 50,000 years ago. In a pollen examination, clusters of pollen were found of *Achillea* – type, *Senecio* – type, *Centaurea solstitialis* – type, Liliaceae (*Muscari* – type) and *Ephedra altissima* – type. The first four species contain herbaceous plants, the flowers of which have brilliant colours, blue for the *Muscari* and yellow for the *Senecio*. Leroi-Gourhan concludes that burials took place on a bed of ramose branches and flowers (1975).

[51] There were of course other sources of sweetness such as wild fruits, trees such as the maple, then as cultigens, dates and other dried fruit (raisins, prunes) as well as sugar cane which was apparently known in India as early as 3000 BC. When the Greek general Nearchus came across it in the fourth century BC he described it significantly as 'beeless honey'. By the eighth century AD sugar was being grown in Muslim Spain and even southern France. Venice became the centre for refining the product, followed by Antwerp. Its introduction to the new world led to much increased production, largely by slave labour, but it remained a luxury as late as 1736 when it was listed with precious stones among the wedding gifts of Maria Theresa, future Empress of Austria. For a more general account, see Mintz 1985.   [52] Goody 1982:168, 176; Mintz 1985.

[53] The behaviour of African bees may be related to the absence of domesticated flowers and their reliance on shorter-lasting and possibly rarer resources. European bees seem to be adapted to clusters of flowering plants whereas African bees forage more widely, in type and in distance. Domesticated bees largely depend upon domesticated flowers and are less unhappy about being moved around. However, whether these features are linked to greater aggressiveness is a moot point. (I am indebted to David Roubik of the Smithsonian Tropical Research Institute, though the suggestions concerning the sources of aggressiveness are not ones with which he would agree.) This absence of wild flowers is only relative; a recent volume on flowers in Black Africa includes photographs of 91 flowers, of which some 58 per cent were indigenous and 36 per cent exotic (Assi 1987). South Africa, with its Mediterranean climate, was an exception. In the early seventeenth century the Dutch sent back flowering plants from their colonies, which were gradually introduced to British gardens, especially after the advent to the throne of William III (Gorer 1978: chapter 4).

'Material' factors may also have something to do with the broad difference between Africa and Eurasia regarding the use of the flowers in the visual arts, for there are important differences in the nature of the media which relate partly to the presence or absence of writing. African art, as we usually understand the term, was largely sculptural, in wood, in clay, in bronze in parts of Nigeria, a little in stone. There was some pictorial design on cloth (appliqué and embroidered), some engraving on calabashes, some low relief. But of figurative painting there was little, except in caves and on rocks by hunters, gatherers and some pastoralists.[54] Sculpture deals with men and animals, as did rock art, not with plants and flowers. There were few of the architectural or decorative contexts in which we find flowers being used in the ancient world. Design was largely abstract, with representational painting or drawing little developed, using mud walls rather than rock surfaces. In other traditions the appearance of flowers is linked, strongly but not exclusively, to the use of the brush and pen on flat, portable media such as paper, hide, cotton and canvas, and to the motor skills associated with writing.

This said, I see one part of my question as covered by the broad argument about differences between Africa and Eurasia that I have applied not only to cooking but to other factors of more central significance. I refer specifically to *Technology, Tradition and the State in Africa* (1971), *Production and Reproduction* (1976), *The Oriental, the Ancient and the Primitive* (1990), and on a more general level to my work on the broad differences between societies with and without writing. Cultivated flowers are essentially products of advanced agriculture, of gardening, so we rarely find them under simple hoe agriculture, except where they have been borrowed or adapted from neighbours. That general aspect is related to the complexity of the system of 'class', of roles and of culture. However, there are two aspects to the opening question; the second has to do with why even *wild* flowers play so little part in African culture. The ecological argument is not in itself sufficient, for in many societies with shifting cultivation the situation is not dissimilar to that in Africa. Of the Barasana of the Amazon region of South America, who are certainly not without a rich floral environment, Stephen Hugh-Jones writes:

The Barasana are totally uninterested in *wild* flowers including beautiful and exotic orchids (which they call 'monkey's love potion') except insofar as they are indices of seasons, promises of future fruits, etc. They do occasionally use flowers (wild) as body decoration mostly either stuck in holes in their earlobes or worn over the ear like carpenters wear pencils. I have seen photos of other South American Indians, notably the people of the Choco in Colombia (Embera, Noanama, Waunan and even the Cuna) also wearing flowers stuck over their ears. Most South American lowland Indians have 'kitchen gardens' round their houses which are also used as experimental plots for trying out new cultigens, growing 'magical' plants, etc. Some magical plants are clearly selected on the basis of the fact that they have pleasant or

[54] See for example Leakey, 1983.

pungent *smells* and some of them produce smells from the flowers rather than the leaves – but here the emphasis is on the *smell*. Other magical plants have brightly coloured and patterned leaves, notably Calladium species which are widely used and cultivated. Calladiums are popular houseplants in the West. My impression, from the Barasana, is that with the Calladiums, 'magic' and aesthetics begin to merge – they plant them partly because they are (magically) useful but also because they *look* nice. So here we have a kind of incipient form of non-utilitarian gardening.

In these same kitchen gardens the Barasana also sometimes plant entirely useless flowers which they get as cuttings from the local missions. It is characteristic of both Protestant and especially the Catholic missions that they have flower beds tended by Nuns with Indian labour and that they have pots of flowers and pretty leaves (including Calladiums) growing around the place. I suspect that the reason the Barasana also plant such flowers in part has to do with an imitation of missionary practice. In their own reports of a kind of messianic cult that they had around the turn of the century, the Barasana also mention that the cult adepts arrived at meetings carrying bunches of tree-flowers and one of the cult songs also mentions these flowers. I don't yet know what is going on here but they say that they had altars like the Catholic church and I suspect that the flowers were again an imitation of Catholic practice (flowers on the altar). Finally, although this is not flowers in the strict sense, the Barasana garden layout is not strictly utilitarian – although manioc is planted in a kind of random blanket, coca bushes are planted in neat rows forming a kind of grid pattern over the garden. I have seen reports of other examples of careful 'symbolic' layouts of Amazonian gardens, notably from the Kreen Akore in Brazil. I think that's really all there is to say about flowers in this area – in short they are not very important in real life nor do they figure much in mythology, ritual, etc.[55]

The situation Hugh-Jones describes, including the adoption of flowers from the gardens of missions, differs little from the parts of Africa with which I am acquainted. The LoDagaa do not even make any general use of coloured leaves, nor do the Gonja to the south. But it is always possible that some individual might discover desirable properties in this or that leaf or flower, either medicinal or aesthetic, and so create a window for such behaviour in the society.

In the rain forest to the south, Asante culture is much richer from the artistic and material point of view and makes use of many colours, for example, in the *kente* cloths, first woven in the 1720s from silk and cotton materials imported from the coast which they unravelled and reconstituted,[56] just as they appear to have done with the glass of variegated beads.[57] But apart from the

---

[55] S. Hugh-Jones, personal communication.   [56] McLeod 1981:153.

[57] The Asante traded gold with the North and were much influenced by the designs on vessels which they received in return. These were largely Islamic, especially the brass bowls to which I have referred; the palm-tree motif (McLeod 1981:111) and many of the patterns on the stamped Adinkra cloth came from such sources. The foreign models they adapted included European ones, not only Venetian beads but the Richard II ewer and other metal jugs which had been traded across the Sahara and were incorporated into royal shrines (Goody 1971); their shapes may well have influenced subsequent brass ware in the kingdom. Despite these foreign influences and the greater richness of their culture, there were only the same three basic colour terms that we find further north.

occasional embroidery, in Gonja sometimes of animals, elsewhere mostly of abstract designs of Islamic origin, the locally woven cotton cloth was rarely decorated, except by the colour of the woven thread, never painted or printed in the way cotton and silk were in Asia. Indeed, the heady splashes of colour provided by Indian cloth, imported to West Africa by the Portuguese under the name of *pintados* long before the imitative manufacture of such cloth began in Europe, was surely one reason, together with its lightness, for its enormous popularity right down to today. But my general impression is that, even so, the preference is for designs of animals and men (including the faces of politicians) rather than of flowers, although these inevitably appear in any cloth of Indian inspiration.[58]

Lying on the outskirts of the village, an Asante cemetery is planted with bushes which have a characteristic green and yellow leaf that parallels the russet colours of the cloth used in funeral performances. Leaves, as distinct from flowers, have many uses in the region.[59] Among the 'tribal' peoples of West Africa, women regularly wore them as 'clothing' to cover their nakedness.[60] In the Kingdom of Asante, cloth, first of bark, then of cotton, was worn on ordinary occasions. But at funerals, in which the normal actions of men are so often reversed, the widow would wear what the anthropologist Rattray calls 'wreaths' of the *asuani* plant (*Cardiospermum grandiflora*), an Asante word meaning 'tears'. These vines were passed over the shoulders and crossed under the other arm.[61] Rattray also attended a second funeral for two senior women, long dead, in which those men and women who stood in distant relationship to the deceased (the *wirempefo*) made chaplets of the same creeper before rushing through the village and crying out in a wild and extravagant manner.[62] But despite the surrounding tropical forest and the extent of man's dependence on it for medicines and for gods, often enough related, the floral component in culture is minimal.

That was not the case in New Guinea where the use of the decorative arts reaches a peak probably unmatched in other non-literate cultures. Take body decoration. Many Africans too paint their bodies on ceremonial occasions.[63] The list of sixty-five representational designs employed by the South-eastern Nuba consists mainly of animals, but there are no flowers or other plants.[64] In West Africa, elaborate body painting does not play a major part, although

---

[58] I am grateful to Esther Goody for her extensive work on the ethnography of cloth and to Victoria Ebin for enquiries in retail outlets.

[59] Foliage is also used in some savannah societies, for example by the Bobo of Burkina Faso in their *Do* masquerades where the leaves are incorporated in the mythology. But generally the disguises and decoration are of dry material, as C. Poppi pointed out to me.

[60] The wearing of leaves to cover the sexual organs is particularly common in Africa, often more abundantly at the back; in the Andaman Islands of the Bay of Bengal, women wear a belt of *Pandanus* leaf on the front of which they hang a bundle of leaves of the *Mimusops littoralis*. The protection of the back as against the front may have some relationship to notions of sexual approach, position and satisfaction, but on that question there is little information available.

[61] Rattray 1927:72, Figures 67 and 68.   [62] Rattray 1927:181.

[63] Ebin 1979. On permanent body marks, tattooing, see Rubin 1988.   [64] Faris 1972:94–6.

white is often used to distinguish the bereaved at funerals.[65] Among the tribal peoples, festival decoration turns around the use of cowry shells sewn on strips of leather or, at a somewhat different level, on the use of masks, generally of wood, and fibre dresses. In ordinary life men generally wore a covering of skin or barkcloth over their loins or genitals, while women often used a combination of leather bands and leaves.[66] In state societies, some of which have been influenced by Islam, and all by the coming of cloth and weaving, the daily covering was a smock, gown or 'cloth', while festivals involved 'dressing up', much as in clothed cultures generally. In such traditional decoration as there was, flowers were remarkable for their absence.

New Guinea stands out as a partial exception. Of the lowland areas, Gilbert Lewis observes that people 'like to have *bilas*, i.e. decoration – and flowers come in'.[67] This use is often casual and Lewis contrasts the interest of the Gnau in trees and flowers as being that between strong and near-indifference.[68] The use of body decoration is very elaborate and flowers undoubtedly play a part. While the inhabitants practised relatively simple forms of agriculture in the recent past and were generally egalitarian in the organisation of their society, that may not have always been the case.[69] Moreover, the island fell in the same general area of the Pacific as Indonesia and Polynesia where the culture of flowers was highly developed and displays obvious continuities with South and South-east Asia.[70] But quite apart from these considerations, our hypothesis covering the relations of 'advanced' agriculture to the growth and use of cultivated flowers is a matter of trends. It is societies with advanced systems of agriculture that domesticate flowers, not those with shifting cultivation; the role of the wild varieties is affected only in an indirect way.

To return to the problem of low interest in wild flowers in Africa. As we have seen, they appear to be less abundant in Africa than in other continents; partly too the flower is valued for its future rather than for its present, for what it will be rather than for what it is; partly the features of the plant world that interest mankind are largely leaves, roots and bark, the attributes of trees rather than flowers. That apparent lack of interest in some natural products

[65] Goody 1962.

[66] I use the adjective 'tribal' for convenience to indicate societies without organised government as defined by Fortes and Evans-Pritchard (1940), a category which is roughly equivalent to 'tribes without rulers' (Middleton and Tait 1958) and to 'stateless societies'. In anthropological terminology these are usually acephalous or segmentary societies, of which there were many varieties even at a formal level, just as there were with state systems. Numerous morphological gradations are possible within and between the two categories; 'stateless' often includes societies whose political life is dominated by big men, freebooters, or chiefs of a local kind. Nevertheless, the broad distinction serves very well for northern Ghana and for many other parts of the world; it was very clear to early travellers and to the later inhabitants.

[67] G. Lewis, personal communication.

[68] See also the work of Frankel (1986), Goldman (1983), M. and A. Strathern (1971), Sillitoe (1983) and Mead (1940).   [69] Strathern 1982; Golson 1982; Chowning 1977.

[70] For comments on the use of flowers in the Pacific, see Lambert 1878.

was not unique; I was struck among the LoDagaa by a similar approach to both fruit and feathers, which have distinct affinities with flowers.[71] Aspects of the interest in nature seem to be reflexive; it is often those people cultivating domesticated flowers that display an intense concern with the wild varieties, not only as a result of a reaction between the two, or even an opposition between the urban and the rural, but because it is the wild which represents the ultimate source of garden plants. That notion of opposition raises a further possibility. Was there an implicit rejection of flowers, at least of representations of flowers? I raise the question because I have suggested that there is evidence that this happened with some icons in Africa.[72] It turns out to be a critical question to ask in Europe, both as regards flowers and icons which experience periods when they are deliberately set aside, breaching the notion of universality in differing ways, but at the same time suggesting the presence of similar contradictions and ambivalences in these societies. For discontinuities in the culture of flowers occurred in early Europe, among later puritans and among some groups in Asia. That rejection is elsewhere associated with the objection to other images of God's creation, and in particular of the creator God himself. In Africa there does seem to have been some ambivalence about representing the immaterial in material form, despite notions that those societies were dominated by fetishism, but that has not affected the culture of flowers. Africa did not have the same prerequisites for a culture of luxury, let alone its rejection. For the growth and use of domesticated flowers, like their representations in art and literature, in graphic and in verbal media, are part of the growth of 'cultures of luxury' and subsequently 'cultures of mass consumption', consumer societies. It is an analysis, often just an ethnographic description, of those uses of flowers in hierarchical societies to which my enquiry is directed.

THE AIM

All this suggests the situation in Africa can be illuminated by being set against that in Eurasia, and vice versa. In a sense the rest of this book is devoted to pursuing the culture of flowers in the Eurasian continent; regretfully I omit the indigenous societies of America for reasons of space but the contrast between Mexico and the Amazon seems to parallel that between Eurasia and Africa. In Mexico so great was their use that we find specialist traders in flowers known as Xochemanqui and their widespread use for worship and presentation has been connected with 'the genius of the Mexicans for horticulture'.[73] My own enquiry takes two forms, temporal and geographical. I go back to the ancient

---

[71] The interest in feathers exists elsewhere in Africa but is never developed to the same extent as in the Americas and the Pacific, perhaps because of the different resources available. It was after the voyages to South America that the wearing of feathers expanded in Europe, although the ostrich is of course African and the peacock (from India) was used in the Middle Ages.   [72] See Goody 1991.   [73] Lambert 1878:459–60.

world of the Near East and Mediterranean to establish the origins of such cultures in the agricultural developments of the Bronze Age, then to Greece and Rome to seek the beginnings of the European tradition.

In looking at the temporal dimension, I am trying to outline the way the culture of flowers has been elaborated over the long term, as well as the radical transformations that have occurred, mainly as the result of 'revolutionary' movements of a religious or political kind but which exploit contradictions already existing in hierarchical societies with cultures of luxury. For flowers are absent not only for the reasons we have adduced in the case of Africa but because of deliberate rejection. I have attempted to sketch out the decline, then the gradual emergence in Europe of a heightened activity in practice, in representation, and in scientific and poetic discourse, especially in the context of the incorporation of that continent in a world market which for a period it then dominated. One particular feature of this growth was the widespread use of cut flowers in urban life, strikingly so in Holland, but elsewhere too, especially in Paris, leading to the extraordinary development of the Language of Flowers which I consider both as an example of the elaboration of an 'expert system' and as throwing light on the literary expansion of 'symbolic systems'. In this way its study contributes to the understanding of the nature of cultures that include a strong written component. The following chapter examines the way this 'language' was taken up in the United States in the nineteenth century, how it was adapted locally and what impact it made on a culture that, like Puritan England, has in the past often played down the role of flowers. Nowadays their usage is much more extensive than before, but less 'symbolic' than that of Europe. Of this latter I present a general picture, but try to take into consideration the temporal and the hierarchical dimensions in order to modify any notions of a unitary culture persisting unchanged over time and space.

In looking at the geographical dimension I aim to set out some of the similarities and differences between the main societies of Eurasia, including features that cross-cut other major boundaries. In these chapters observation supplements the documents, looking and talking about the present complements reading about the past, for this means we can fill in some of the many interstices in the historical record.[74] In this way both the temporal and geographical dimensions raise problems for the concept of culture and for cultural analysis more generally.

By using the title of the *Culture of Flowers* I am not trying to suggest that it constitutes a rounded topic, a new specialist field. I do want to draw attention to the interrelation between ecology, economy and usages of a symbolic as well as a practical kind, without wishing to suggest that any factor is

[74] While my observations in these countries have been restricted, there is a lot one can learn about the more conspicuous aspects of culture with the eye alone; for the rest I have had excellent collaborators and advisors.

exclusively determined by any other – which is a matter for enquiry rather than assertion. As the example of Africa has already shown, the object of cultural analysis cannot be opposed to the material or utilitarian, much less to the social.

That much is clear in the title of this work. When hearing the phrase the 'culture of flowers', some overlook the ambiguity it contains and resolve in favour of the search for the symbolic system, an overall interpretative schema. But in the vocabulary which English and French alike inherit from Latin, culture also has to do with the cultivation of the soil, with the growing of plants. Indeed, my title might have been *De flori cultura*, on the analogy of the oldest Roman manual in prose by Cato, *De agri cultura*. In a derived sense the word relates to the 'cultivation' of manners, of ways of behaving, especially of elaborated ways, those that have been carefully tended. Often enough, without any qualification it refers to 'high' culture, as in the phrase 'a cultured individual'. In this sense the concept even takes on some of the connotations of 'civilisation', the culture of cities, a word which has been translated into Chinese as *wen hua*, the transformation by written words. That is of course not the way social scientists employ the word 'culture' as a term of art. But it remains a core meaning in ordinary speech. So too, in the minds of many, is the notion of attending to the growth of plants, which is never purely an automatic, material or technological pursuit, being always guided by man's knowledge and by his intentions, requiring a complex social and cultural organisation of production. The growing of flowers is obviously affected not only by utilitarian considerations but by aesthetic demands, by the meanings allotted to them and by the level of horticulture and of 'civilisation' in general.

So, although the culture of flowers may appear to some as a narrow and restricted topic, having more to do with the leisure activities of gardening and house decoration than with the serious things of life, that is to take a very restricted view. On one level, flowers link up with gardens and gardening, with the whole history of post-Neolithic developments after the second agricultural revolution (the first was the move to extensive hoe farming). The flower is also the blossom of the fruit and the maize, as well as that on the ornamental cherry or the horse-chestnut. Flowers are intrinsic to the reproductive processes of the *Phanerogamia* in which their shapes, their colours, their scents and their sweetness all play a part. Their scents lead into the history of perfumes and unguents, their shapes and colours into the history of art, not only the decorative but the creative as well. They are cultivated for display, for their odour (like that of fragrant woods, which are burnt as incense for their scented smoke), for their taste (like herbs), for their sweetness (transformed into honey) and for their medicinal properties (like plants of all descriptions). All these qualities make them eminently suitable for various forms of self-decoration – the flower in the hair, the ring of roses around the brow, but also for offering to others, in friendship (the bunch of flowers), in glory (the chaplet) or in mockery (the crown of thorns).

Flowers may also be excluded from art because certain creeds reject representations not only of divinity but of all of divinity's creation. The influence of such beliefs on world art, especially upon sculpture in the round and the decoration of the temple, was profound and raises the whole question of the icon, of iconoclasm and the nature of divinity. In the account that follows I have given almost as much weight to the absence of images as to the absence of flowers. The reasons are several. Firstly, flowers are frequently incorporated in images, in icons, and the absence of representations certainly affects the knowledge, the enjoyment and richness of flowers. Moreover, in the European tradition, those of puritanical persuasion were frequently against both, partly because they might be thought 'unnecessary', a luxury, partly because they are often characteristic of rites of which they disapproved as 'pagan'.

In this preview I have necessarily stepped ahead of the argument, overlooked the evidence, reduced the complexity; I do so to help the reader through a number of issues and side issues. Now it is time to go back to the beginning.

2 · In the beginning: gardens and paradise, garlands and sacrifice

In contrast to Africa south of the Sahara, the Near East, Europe and the Mediterranean developed flourishing cultures of flowers. In this chapter my aim is to outline the nature of their development and to point to their internal contradictions so as to set the stage for considering what happened in later Europe. From 3000 BC the intensive agriculture of the Bronze Age introduced and spread new techniques and new varieties of domesticated food crops, whose greater productivity permitted the establishment of a significant hierarchy of wealth and culture. One aspect of the consequent growth of luxury production was the development of an aesthetic, non-utilitarian horticulture that involved the transformation of wild into domesticated plants, including flowers, not for what they will become but for what they are.

I have called this horticulture 'aesthetic' and 'non-utilitarian' but I refer to the growing of plants not primarily for food, shelter, medicine and considerations of that sort. The early use of domesticated flowers included decorating the body, an extension of the uses of wild species we have noted in Africa and elsewhere. That form of self-decoration led to the provision of flowers for guests, of which there is much evidence in early Egypt. In addition to this provision for humankind, flowers were extensively offered not only to the dead but to the gods in general, an aspect not of euhemeristic transition but of the anthropomorphic conception of and approach to divinity. Flowers became essential in such transactions but their very centrality to worship could lead to their becoming an endangered species in conditions of religious change, just as their position as luxury items could do so in situations of social transformation. That is mainly a question for the following chapter; in this I want to chronicle the growth of the culture of flowers in the west of Asia and in the Mediterranean.

The second agricultural revolution, that which introduced what I loosely call 'advanced agriculture', began in the vicinity of the two rivers, the Tigris and Euphrates. So did the written and even the extensive visual record that provides us with the evidence for the emergence of a culture of flowers.

What led to their domestication? While flowers were cultivated for their medicinal or culinary properties, their domestication may initially have had other ends in view, though not purely ornamental or aesthetic, but as offerings to men and gods. Nor were they always cultivated in specialised gardens of display, although in Europe we often make that association. In Bali flowers are often grown among other plants to offer to the gods; in rural Japan flowers may be planted in among the vegetables where they will be gathered for household or religious use.[1] At the popular level, outdoor display was not the most important feature, though of course more formal gardens also existed in more public places such as temples and palaces. Nevertheless, the association between the growing of flowers and dedicated places where they are tended (a nursery) and sometimes on display (a flower garden) is strong. That dedicated space was early conceived as a walled, fenced or hedged enclosure, initially a private as opposed to a public space, in which flowers (and sometimes birds and animals) are not merely allowed to grow but are cultivated and improved, natives collected from the surrounding countryside as well as exotics brought in from other cultures, from distant lands. More recently in human history the tendency was for royal gardens to become the property of the state or some 'great organisation' rather than the prince, leading both to botanic gardens for the cultivation of plants, and to pleasure gardens for the enjoyment of the public, while yet others were newly created around major institutions such as universities and hospitals, temples and monasteries, and by municipalities themselves.[2]

The English word 'garden' continues to mean an enclosure in which the soil has been worked over for planting plants of various kinds. It probably comes from the northern French form of *jardin*, but it also links up with the Teutonic roots of the word 'yard'. That term again refers to an enclosed space, being used by Americans for what in England would be a garden and where a yard tends to be an uncultivated plot, a goods yard, a courtyard, and so forth; the Anglo-Saxon term was 'wyrtȝerd', literally wort-yard or herb-yard. That was often seen as walled, which continued to be very much the sense of 'gardin' in Chaucer's *Romaunt of the Rose* dating from the fourteenth century. But the concept goes back beyond the Judaeo-Christian tradition of the walled garden of paradise and the imagery derived from it.

GARDENS IN MESOPOTAMIA

The name of paradise in the Biblical tradition was Persian and the concept was in turn derived from the earlier gardens of Babylon and Assyria which were associated either with temples or with royalty. Some were royal parks for hunting; others, like Eden, were irrigated gardens, of which the best known were the Hanging Gardens of Babylon, built by Nebuchadnezzar II for his

[1] 'Flowers were regularly included in the ancient Roman vegetable garden' (Jashemski 1979:172), as they are today in parts of rural France.

[2] On gardens in the public places of Pompeii, see Jashemski 1979:155ff.; for public parks, which existed earlier in Athens, see p.165.

wife, Amyitis, daughter of the king of the Medes, and declared by Diodorus to be one of the Seven Wonders of the World.[3] To please his wife, who longed for the hills and forests of her native Persia, the king had built a series of terraced gardens beside the palace, with a hoist to raise water from the irrigation canals below. In this way a huge exotic garden was created which overlooked the roofs of the city itself.[4] One major feature of this and other Near Eastern gardens was the palm tree, which was used as a state emblem and in symbolism more generally. For in those parts of the drier regions where some water was available for the roots, the date palm (*Phoenix dactylifera*) was of supreme importance as a cultigen whose sweet fruits could easily be preserved; in Hebrew its name of *tamar* is related to the Arabic word, *thamar*, which stands for fruit in general.

In larger parks or paradises there were ornamental trees as well as fruiting ones, while the immense park of Sargo II in the eighth century BC also included aromatic herbs. In addition wild animals, including birds, were kept in semi-captivity, for sport as well as for sight, as these were hunting grounds where the princes and their followers could amuse themselves. But more tranquil pleasures were also sought there and a well-known relief of King Assurbanipal and his queen in Nineveh shows them dining outside in the garden (Plate 2.1). The surrounding wall providing the private space encapsulated the hierarchical nature of the community, but the fact that the garden was cut off from the world at large was useful in other ways. For the larger enclosures also served as collecting points, as early botanical gardens, for exotic species. They acted as breeding beds, even as experimental stations, since exotics did not automatically adapt to new conditions; and such nurseries played a part in propagating, improving and distributing plants more widely. Finally, they were not only pleasure gardens and science parks but sanctuaries, offering solitude and communion with nature, a place of retreat and meditation, in which guise they were especially suitable for temples and later monasteries, places where intensive horticulture could be pursued away from the immediate demands of everyday farming. So the garden of the religious house could provide produce, flowers as well as food, for worship or for decoration as well as for sustenance.[5]

Gardens, trees and flowers were widely represented in Mesopotamian art and architecture. Even in the prehistoric Al'Ubaid period vases are decorated with 'garlands', showing 'a frieze of circular or lozenge-shaped elements with fringe-like pendants hanging from it'.[6] Later on, a Sumerian seal from Uruk shows worshippers approaching the temple, one of whom is carrying a garland in his hands, no doubt to deck the cult image.[7] While garlands were

---

[3] See Strabo, *Geographia*, XVI.1, 5; Diodorus I.10. On the somewhat earlier 'hanging' gardens of Sennacherib, see Perrot and Chipiez 1884:ii, 30; Joret 1897:384.   [4] Parrot 1961b:176.
[5] Gardens could be presented to the gods in Mesopotamia (Joret 1897:475), as they were in Egypt (pp.82–3).
[6] Parrot 1961a:166.   [7] Parrot 1961a:74.

2.1 Assurbanipal and his queen dining in a garden, Nineveh, c.645 BC. (British Museum, London)

present at an early stage, the wearing of crowns made from plants seems to have developed only with the arrival of Greek influences. Indeed, as also seems to have been the case in Syria and Egypt, an elaborate culture of flowers, as distinct from that of gardens, did not emerge until a much later period. It is true that Assyrian gardens included some flowers, for they are mentioned in a contract of the time of Assurbanipal in the seventh century BC.[8] At death the Assyrians placed food by the corpse, and for women and young girls, bottles of perfume, objects of toilette and, later on, flowers.[9] In Palestine too aromatics were regularly put near the dead body. Certainly aromatics were grown, unguents employed, perfume made and flowers cultivated. All these were used not only for human but for divine purposes. In Nineveh the king is shown at a sacrifice holding the stalk of a lotus, which like other flowers were sometimes presented in vases (Plate 2.2).[10] Divinities themselves hold flowers; a statue

[8] Joret 1897:285.   [9] Joret 1897:482.   [10] Layard 1849:53:II, Plate 8.1.

2.2 King Sargon offers a sacrifice of an ibex holding the 'sacred flower', Khorsabad. (Parrot 1961:3)

from Mari dating from the eighteenth century B C portrays a goddess of high rank smelling a flower.[11] The odour of flowers was plainly an important feature of their early use and perfumes attempted to preserve those scents over a longer period and make them available for cosmetic purposes, for women more than men.[12] But the use was also religious; the word 'perfume' is derived from the latin *per fumum*, through smoke, and included the notion of communicating, even conveying prayers, with the gods above. It was in these dry lands that the manufacture of aromatics, incense and especially perfume flourished, for flowers had more powerful scents than in northern countries.[13]

Apart from the lotus and a species of lily, it is difficult to identify other flowers, at least until the time of Sennacherib (c.700 B C). Most representations of plants are conventional.[14] By and large icons of plants were ornamental while, as in African art, it was animals and men that carried semantic meaning. Two exceptions were clearly the palm tree which in Chaldea was associated both with the supreme being and with royalty, and the lotus which was offered in gifts and sacrifice throughout the Near East. These two plants were used symbolically as well as decoratively.[15] However, it was abstract flower-type designs, such as the palmette and the rosette, which appeared in architecture as well as in craftwork, on clothes and on carpets (Plate 2.3).[16] The characteristic linking of rosette, lotus and palmette motifs (not the palm), which travelled across Asia, was incorporated into the decorative art of Mesopotamia when Egypt established an Asian empire in the time of the New Kingdom.

THE VALLEY OF THE NILE

Like the land between the two rivers, Egypt was a region of sun, fertile soil and well-watered gardens, producing figs, vines, pomegranates and sycamores; in the middle of the garden there was often a kiosk to take one's rest.[17] Under the

[11] Parrot 1953: Figure 132, from the courtyard of the palace.

[12] Perfume was not made by distillation until that process was developed by the Arabs in the eleventh century, but there were other ways available for extracting the scent, such as maceration and absorption.

[13] Lavender and peppermint from Northern lands are prized precisely because they are too heavy in Southern ones. See Rimmel 1865:19.   [14] Joret 1897:432.

[15] 'Lotus' is an awkward word to handle. The Greeks used *lotos* for a number of plants. In the case of the lotus-eaters or lotophagoi, a people encountered by Odysseus on the Libyan coast, this was possibly the opium poppy, since those who ate it were overcome by forgetfulness. But the term can refer to many different plants. The Greeks used the word for the *Ziziphus lotus* of the buckthorn family, a native of Southern Europe whose fruit can be employed for making bread and fermented drinks. The blue variety of the Egyptian lotus (*Nymphaea caerulea*) was dominant in Egyptian art. The sacred lotus of the Hindus and Buddhists (*Nelumbo nucifera*) is an aquatic plant with white or pink flowers; varieties are also found in eastern North America. The Romans wrote of a lotus tree, the Libyan lotus, which was probably *Celtis australis*. The *Lotus* is also a genus of the pea family. Theophrastus has a long description of *Nelumbo nucifera*, under the name of the Egyptian 'bean', recording its practical uses (Needham 1986:135), for the pink lotus was then a food as well as a flower as it is today, at least in China. It was widely used after its arrival and even spread to Europe, being depicted on a Nile mosaic from Pompeii in the Naples Museum (Joret 1897:165ff.; Jashemski 1979:20, figure 19).   [16] Joret 1897:431.

[17] Winlock 1935; on the ceremonial use of flowers in Egypt, see Lambert 1878:464-7.

2.3 A stone carpet decorated with lotus and palmette designs, from the North Palace of Assurbanipal at Nineveh, c.645 BC. (British Museum)

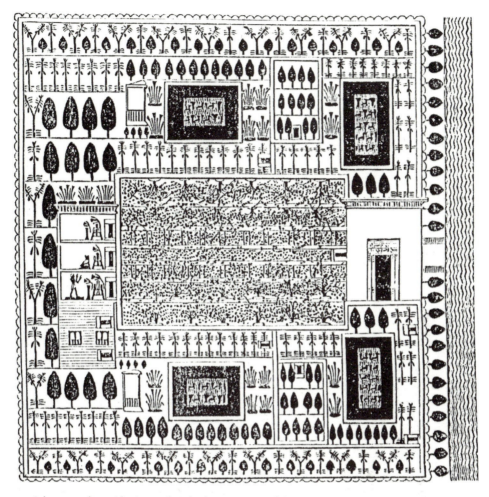

2.4 A large garden with vineyard and other separate enclosures, tanks of water and a small house. Tomb painting, Thebes. (Wilkinson 1837:11, 143)

New Kingdom, beginning about 1570 BC, the town of Thebes, near the Luxor of today, was rebuilt as the capital by the XVIIIth Dynasty (Table 2.1). The decoration of the tombs included many models and representations of gardens. One image shows a royal garden surrounded by an 'embattled wall, with a canal of water passing in front of it, connected with the river. Between the canal and the wall . . . was a shady avenue of various trees' (Plate 2.4). At the back a gate opened to the vineyard and outside its wall palm trees were planted; 'four tanks of water, bordered by a grass plot, where geese were kept, and the delicate flower of the lotus was encouraged to grow, served for the irrigation of the grounds; and small *kiosks* or summer houses shaded with trees, stood near the water and the water overlooked beds of flowers'.[18] Like

[18] Wilkinson 1837:ii, 144.

2.5 A garden by a shrine in the Theban countryside, with lotus and fruit trees and gardeners raising water by means of the *shaduf*. Note the columns of simulated papyrus and the lotus capitals. (Maspero 1895:340)

Table 2.1 *The dynasties of ancient Egypt*

Early Dynastic period	c.3100–c.2686 BC
Old Kingdom	c.2686–c.2160 BC
First Intermediate period	c.2160–2040 BC
Middle Kingdom	c.2040–c.1786 BC
Second Intermediate period	c.1786–1567 BC
New Kingdom	c.1570–1085 BC
Third Intermediate period	1085–656 BC
Late Period	664–332 BC
Macedonian and Ptolemaic period	332–30 BC
Roman and Byzantine Egypt	30 BC–AD 642

the pink Indian lotus (*Nelumbo nucifera*), which was introduced there during the Persian period (525–332 BC), the Egyptian lotus or waterlily (*Nymphaea*) had strong religious connotations and the white and blue varieties were constantly used in offerings to the gods as well as to adorn humans.[19]

The gardens themselves were sometimes associated with tombs when these were situated near water, but they were more usually found near temples established for royal, divine or funerary purposes.[20] They were irrigated by water raised by means of the *shaduf* or swing beam that employed the principle of the lever (Plate 2.5). Perhaps under Mesopotamian influence, fragrant trees from the land of Punt, that is, Ethiopia, to the south, were introduced. Subsequently, in patio gardens, birds with clipped wings joined the colourful array, adding sweet sounds to sweet smells and sweet colours, against a background of cool waters supplied by ingenious machines. During the New Kingdom, the XVIIIth Dynasty defeated the invading Hyksos and greatly extended the empire. The booty of Queen Hatshepsut's sea-borne expedition to the south included over thirty perfume shrubs in baskets which were planted in Thebes.[21] A botanical garden was created, complete with catalogue, consisting of local trees and plants as well as exotics brought from afar. As in Mesopotamia, much of the earlier interest seems to have been in aromatics, perfumes and unguents; carved vases for containing these date from the fourth millennium BC. It was part of a cosmetic culture, a culture of the 'toilette', that used eye-black, henna, mirrors and baths, often by women to enhance personal beauty and attractiveness to men. Odour was an important constituent of the culture of the toilette and this feature of flowers could be conserved even if their appearance could endure only in dried form.

Other Egyptian sovereigns also took a great interest in horticulture.

[19] *Book of the Dead*, p.61.   [20] Perrot and Chipiez 1883:i, 301, 309.
[21] Perrot and Chipiez 1883:i, 426; Hatshepsut was the daughter of Thutmosis I who married her half-brother, Thutmosis II, and ruled after his death.

Hatshepsut's co-ruler and successor, Thutmosis III (1504–1450), extended the empire in Asia and brought back flora and fauna, which are depicted in the festival hall at Karnak, near Thebes. It was not only from the South that new plants were introduced, though it was from there that aromatics came; the bay, the lime and many others came from the more temperate regions across the Mediterranean.[22] According to the Harris Papyrus (i.83f.), some two and a half centuries later Ramses III made 'great vineyards, walks shaded by all kinds of fruit-trees laden with their fruit, a sacred way splendid with flowers from all countries'. Long before Europe was faced with a similar problem in the period of its expansion, we find the cultivation and hence the classification of plants that lay well outside the local repertoire. The shift from a local folk schema to a more inclusive one was not a process first encountered with Aristotle, let alone much later with the Renaissance and the expansion of Europe; the deliberate introduction of plants, including cultivated flowers, was a long-established feature of Eurasian society. So too was the trade in spices and aromatics, that is, in the dried rather than the fresh. Egyptian doctors included some seven hundred ingredients, mostly vegetable, in their pharmacopoeia, and their knowledge of plants extended to those of neighbouring countries, of Syria, East Africa, Arabia and even India, serving as a model for the later studies of Greeks and Arabs.[23] Aided by the use of written records, the collection of exotics meant breaking through the bounds of local classifications and establishing a broader system of botanical knowledge which was a precursor of later 'scientific' schemes of the Renaissance.

At first the gardens of Egypt seem to have been devoted more to fruit and ornamental trees than to flowers, being mainly parks and orchards. In Pharaonic Egypt there were few cultivated flowers apart from the lotus and some flowering shrubs such as *Sesbania aegyptica* and henna. But those they had were widely used.[24] Only with the New Kingdom (c.1570–1085 BC) do we find definite evidence of the cultivation of a wider range of blooms; Ramses III writes of the gardens he had offered to the god of Heliopolis, with their pools filled with lotus and rushes, and 'with flowers from every country, sweet and fragrant'.[25]

Egyptian paintings of gardens are more formal and less realistic than later Roman ones, so that the evidence on flowers is more difficult to interpret. While the ground plan is given from above, plants are individually portrayed in profile, rather as in a Persian carpet. In these paintings not only the lotus but the cornflower, poppy, anemone and chrysanthemum, presumably the crown chrysanthemum, have been identified.[26] In addition, remnants of garlands and

[22] Joret 1897:94–5.
[23] Joret 1897:310–11, based on the Ebers Papyrus. The nature of hieroglyphic writing makes the problem of identification more difficult.
[24] For flowers in Egypt, see Hepper 1990, and the references there to works by R. Germer (1985), V. Tächolm (1974) and F. Woenig (1886). See also, more generally, the excellent illustrated volume by Scott-James, Desmond and Wood (1989).   [25] Joret 1897:98.   [26] Jashemski 1979:346.

collars have been found in tombs, such as that of Tutankhamen (d.1327 BC) which included the lotus, cornflower and mayweed, as well as various fruits.[27] Some of these may have been gathered from the wild but a few were cultivated.[28] While the cultivated flora of Egypt increased progressively with the expeditions and conquests of the New Kingdom, with the Persian invasions and finally with the conquests of Alexander until the Ptolemaic period, it lacked a wide range of garden flowers and herbaceous bushes.[29]

In the earliest times the lotus was the Egyptian flower par excellence. It is represented as early as the Vth Dynasty (2494–2345 BC) and was associated with Upper Egypt just as the papyrus was identified with the Lower Kingdom, the stalks being shown entwined to represent the union of the country that finally occurred during the Ist Dynasty (about 3100 BC). The first of the great Egyptian festivals, directed towards all the gods and goddesses, took place on the opening day of the month of Toth. On the second day was the procession of the Great Lotus. The lotus was central to mythology. One version tells how the sun god, Râ, when he was still submerged in the primordial ocean, was imprisoned in a lotus bud. Responding to the cry of 'Come to me' from Toumou, the inert sun 'before the beginning of the world', he emerged with his solar disc from the blossoming flower, being known as 'the god who rises from the great lotus' (Plate 2.6);[30] the solar disc represented either the body or the soul, depending on the particular theologian. A similar notion applied to the rebirth of humans after death. In *The Book of the Dead* the deceased is reborn from a lotus, an idea associated with the solar cults on the one hand and on the other with the lotus as the womb from which mankind emerged.[31]

The uses of flowers were secular as well as religious. Under the New Kingdom they were gathered for entertainments. As soon as the ceremony of anointing the precious unguents was complete, servants brought a lotus to be held in the hand during the feast.[32] The guests were then presented with necklaces that included flowers, mainly the lotus.[33] A garland might also be placed around the head and a single lotus attached to droop over the forehead; for a lotus bud was an accepted part of a woman's headgear (Plate 2.7).[34] During the festivities attendants brought fresh flowers to replace those given earlier or simply for the guests to enjoy the smell. Flowers would also adorn the table at a feast[35] and were used to decorate houses more generally since we find containers with holes cut in their rims as well as vases and jars of pottery and glass.[36] These rested on wooden stands and may have held cut flowers

---

[27] Hepper 1990:8ff.   [28] Joret 1892:92ff.
[29] Joret 1897:95; see Lindsay 1965:248 for a similar conclusion.
[30] Joret 1897:260–1; Maspero 1895:137–8, 140. On other mythological uses of the lotus, see Lambert 1878:464.
[31] Lindsay 1965:249ff. See the Papyrus of Ani (c.1420 BC) for the transformation of the dead through a lotus (*Book of the Dead*, p.60).   [32] Lambert 1878:466.
[33] Wilkinson 1837:ii, 215ff.   [34] Wilkinson 1837:iii, 370.   [35] Wilkinson 1837:ii, 393.
[36] On the vases used for lotus in ancient Egypt, see Berrall 1969:10ff. But this was hardly flower arranging, and in Greece and Rome there is less evidence, apart from the well-known Roman mosaic, the Basket of Flowers, from the second century. No Greek vases were made exclusively for the purpose of holding flowers.

2.6 Horus, or the young sun, rising from a lotus. (Maspero 1895:136)

(Plate 2.8).[37] In addition, some flowers were even hung around the vases themselves.[38] But their greatest use was for making up into bouquets, crowns and garlands with white and blue waterlilies as well as poppies, daisies and similar wildflowers.[39] Other cultivated flowers and shrubs were used for funerary crowns: *Mimusops schimpei*, which probably came to Egypt in the XXIInd Dynasty, fragments of olive garlands from the XXth, garlands of acacia flowers, possibly of oak and lotus, of sesbania, and crowns of laurel

[37] Wilkinson 1837:ii, 216.
[38] For more recent copies of the paintings on Theban tombs, see Davies and Gardiner 1936.
[39] Joret 1897:121, 131, 144, 151, 152, 154.

2.7 Daughter of Tehoutihotep, crowned with white lotuses and holding a blue lotus. Tomb at El-Bersheh, XIth Dynasty (Foucart 1897:87; Maspero 1895:340)

leaves from the Graeco-Roman tombs of Hawara excavated by Flinders Petrie.[40] Crowns were of great importance not only politically, as in the two crowns of Upper and Lower Egypt, fashioned out of more permanent materials, but as wreaths of vegetable matter used in personal and public rituals. These wreaths were placed on mummies to 'celebrate a just life, full of love towards the gods and one's neighbour'.[41] If the chapter of *The Ritual of Rougé*, entitled 'The crown of justification', was recited over 'a divine crown' and accompanied by an offering of incense to Osiris, that justified a man, whether dead or alive, against his enemies. When Osiris had judged him worthy of entering the Earu fields, where duplicates of these very plants grew, the dead were crowned with the appropriate chaplet consisting of leaves and petals fixed on a strip of palm leaf. Statues of the gods too were crowned in similar ways.

The lotus formed part of the offerings placed on the altar, sometimes as a single flower but often as a bouquet. In the Ptolemaic period the variety increased; now we find the persea and the olive, ivy from Europe, the laurel,

---

[40] On funerary crowns in Egypt, see Pleyte 1885. Herodotus writes of the Magi of Persia wearing a crown, preferably of myrtle, when making a sacrifice (*Hist.*, 1.132).   [41] Pleyte 1885:18.

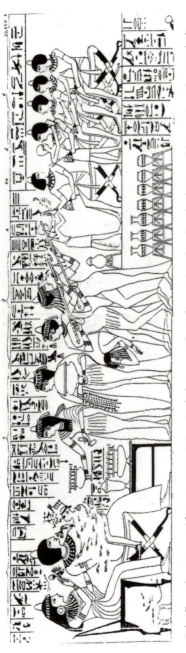

2.8 An Egyptian party with women receiving single lotuses, others flowers in a bowl and others necklaces. Note the stands for vases. Tomb painting, Thebes. (Wilkinson 1837:ii, Plate XII)

myrtle, sambac jasmin from India, the cornpoppy, stock, the mallow, the willow-herb, the crown chrysanthemum (*Chrysanthemum coronarium*), the eastern cornflower, fleabane, Cretan cress, the convolvulus, the Nubian heliotrope, sweet marjoram, the silver cock'scomb, the lily-of-the-valley, the Siberian iris and others too.[42] Above all there was the hundred-petalled rose, which became so important a product of Egyptian gardens but was only cultivated under the Ptolemies (332–30 BC). All these flowers were used to create the bouquets, chaplets and garlands so much admired by the Romans. Garlands were offered to the army after military triumphs. On a domestic level, women placed them in their hair and on their breasts, but men also wore flowers and used perfume, even in war. Being concerned about the physical perpetuation of the body as a condition of eternal life, the Egyptians developed the art of embalming. For treating the dead, as for treating the gods and the living, they needed unguents, incense and perfume, partly to create pleasant odours to combat the foul stenches but more importantly to please the recipients.[43] The trade in spices and aromatics, which was later taken up by Rome, was of fundamental importance to the country.

As well as in daily life, the lotus played a dominating role in architecture, in painting and in poetry. In the XVIIIth Dynasty we find lotiform chalices, one gold example of which is known as the 'lotus of offering',[44] while alabaster ones were used for drinking. The blue lotus (*Nymphaea caerulea*) variety were cult vessels, often appearing in rituals of the dead; the fine Tûna chalices were possibly connected with Hermopolis, the very scene of the Creation story where the sungod appeared on a lotus.[45]

Uses were also made of the papyrus and palm tree, not only in graphic representation but in architecture; the columns of temples were carved as bundles of papyrus or as palms on which the lotus, often truncated, figured as a capital (see Plate 2.5).[46] That flower had already made its appearance on wooden columns in the tomb of Ti (c.2494–c.2345) at Saqqarah, the ancient Memphis, where the capitals represented a half-opened flower flanked by two buds linked together by little bands; one of these bouquets of two or three flowers tied together resembles those held in the hand by figures in the wall paintings.[47] The capitals of stone columns were at first simpler, but they followed the wooden model in borrowing motifs from the vegetable world. In time this type of ornamentation became increasingly elaborate, with the shafts themselves being decorated with garlands of leaves or petals. All three

---

[42] Joret 1897:288–90, essentially from the reports of the Graeco-Roman excavations by Flinders Petrie, 1889a and 1890, which includes a chapter on botany by P. E. Newberry. Elsewhere he mentions peppermint, the immortal (*Helichrysum staeches*), the hollyhock, larkspur, reseda, acacia flowers, safflower (*Carthamus tinctorius*), wild celery and delphinium.

[43] Joret 1897:129; Lindsay 1965:272ff.; and, more generally, see Corbin 1986.   [44] Tait 1963:98, 132–3.

[45] On the blue lotus in wreaths placed on mummies from the xviiith Dynasty, see Pleyte 1885:17ff.

[46] Perrot and Chipiez 1883:ii, 100.   [47] Joret 1897:219.

plants, lotus, palm and papyrus, were used decoratively on capitals, to be joined by rosettes,[48] palmettes, grapes and more abstract elements.[49]

There was clearly a hierarchical component to the Egyptian uses of flowers. It was the upper rather than the lower sectors of society that engaged in extravagant banquets, in elaborate funerals and in complex behaviours that could be seen as not directly concerned with the more immediate processes of sustaining life. Such situations breed conflict of a cognitive kind which becomes more acute with the growing of what to some will appear as 'useless' flowers in preference to edible fruit, in private gardens rather than in public spaces. While the watered gardens of palaces and temples served a variety of purposes they were always manifestations of luxury, places of conspicuous consumption and display, though partly hidden from the populace by their enclosing walls. As such they sometimes became objects not so much of envy as of wider social commentary and a counter-reaction, comparable to that found in the development of luxury cuisines.[50] It was partly as a result of such a reaction that such luxuries were somewhat muted in Egypt under the XIXth Dynasty (1320–1200). It is impossible to detect such reactions without a strong literary tradition but on general theoretical grounds and judging by the examples of later civilisations, such a critique seems to be a potential feature of all culturally stratified societies. The basis of such attacks is sometimes seen as the failure to appreciate the limited span of human existence, for man's worldly goods cannot all accompany him after death, though token attempts are often made in that direction. But even in life there is often a poignant recognition that pleasures are fleeting. Of their evanescent nature flowers are themselves a potent reminder. That has been the theme of countless poets of antiquity such as Anacreon and Horace, and of many moralists like the author of *The Book of Wisdom* who insists that we should 'take our fill of the dearest wines and perfumes, let not one flower of springtime pass us by, before they wither crown ourselves with roses'.[51] There are only intimations of such attitudes in Egypt and their major expression comes later in the ancient world with the expansion of literary activity and of democratic discussion.[52] While this counter-reaction is found as a subdominant theme in many cultures, in some it takes up a dominant position, radically affecting the whole character of the culture of flowers. One such society was that of ancient Israel, whose members lived in both Egypt and Mesopotamia and whose ideology has so deeply affected the later Jewish, Christian and Muslim worlds.

[48] Joret 1897:235.
[49] See the useful discussion in Joret 1897:218ff. These developments may have had a political component. In his history of the lotiform order in Egyptian architecture, Foucart distinguished three phases of development linked to changes in the monarchical system, though his remarks should be treated with some scepticism. At times of change, he suggests, the *vide monumental* was one of the most significant marks of the weakness of royal power. With the return of an active prince, the evolution of the style continued (Foucart 1896:288ff.). The *horreur de vacuité* in provincial Roman art has been regarded as a sign of political decadence, again a suggestion to be taken with scepticism.   [50] Goody 1982.   [51] Jerusalem Bible, p.1008.
[52] On the note of warning in the midst of luxury in Egypt, see Wilkinson 1837:ii, 411ff.

BIBLICAL FLOWERS

The Semitic word for garden, as in the Garden of Eden, was *gan*, *janna* in Arabic, being derived from *ganan*, to protect or cover; the garden was 'secluded from the surrounding country and the incursions of strangers, and concealed by overhanging trees from observations'.[53] While Chinese, Japanese and Indian gardens have all played an important role in the history of flower cultures, gardens as we know them have their mythological as well as their historical beginning in the Near East where the Mesopotamian tradition was undoubtedly the origin of the Garden of Eden, with its fruit and other trees (the tree of knowledge and the tree of life) and its irrigated lands, vital in the more arid regions but needed in semi-tropical zones to raise the productivity of horticulture:

The LORD God planted a garden eastward in Eden; and there he put the man whom he had formed. And out of the ground made the LORD God to grow every tree that is pleasant to the sight, and good for food; the tree of life also in the midst of the garden, and the tree of knowledge of good and evil. And a river went out of Eden to water the garden; and from thence it was parted, and became into four heads. (Genesis, 2.8–10, Authorised version)

So the garden or park was an irrigated area, containing fruit trees as well as trees planted for aesthetic purposes. But it also included animals, especially birds:

And out of the ground the LORD God formed every beast of the field and every fowl of the air: and brought them unto Adam to see what he would call them: and whatsoever Adam called every living creature, that was the name thereof. (Genesis, 2.19)

The rest of the story is well known. God created Eve, who then proceeded to eat of the forbidden, but unnamed, fruit of the tree of knowledge. As a result woman was destined to bring forth children 'in sorrow' and be ruled by the man she had betrayed; while man was destined to labour the fields, and eternally combat those enemies of cultivation, weeds. For just as God had created food plants, so too he created weeds to disturb mankind:[54]

Thorns also and thistles shall it bring forth to thee; and thou shalt eat the herb of the field: In the sweat of thy face shalt thou eat bread, till thou return unto the ground; for out of it wast thou taken; for dust thou *art*, and unto dust shalt thou return. (Genesis, 3.18–19)

---

[53] Whitehouse 1901:1640.

[54] Just as dirt can be seen as matter out of place, so weeds are plants out of place. Or rather they are plants not used for cultivation. I do not think the LoDagaa have a concept of the weed, partly because so many plants have a use, whether wild or cultivated. They do of course clear plants growing around the crops, an essential part of farming, but this is a matter of clearing the 'grass' (*mwo*), the same word that is often translated as 'bush' in the phrase *mwo puo*. This usage is in no sense peculiar to Africa; in France too a weed is a 'bad grass' (*une mauvaise herbe*) which contrasts not only with the good hay (*foin*) for animals but with the better *herbe* (*potagère*) for cooking.

Adam was then thrown out of the garden of Eden lest he eat of the tree of (everlasting) life. That left the search for the luxurious existence he had briefly glimpsed an ever-present feature of man's life, if not on this earth then in the next. These gardens were known in Hebrew of the Persian and Greek period as *pardēs*, paradise, from the Persian word for a walled enclosure.[55] The Greeks themselves borrowed the word from the Persian for a park or pleasure-ground and it was used in the Septuagint, the Greek version of the Hebrew scriptures produced in Alexandria in the third–second centuries BC, to translate the phrase the Garden of Eden. It also passed into ecclesiastical Latin and Tertullian employed the word for the abode of the blessed, so that there was a gradual shift of meaning from earthly to heavenly, from royal park to luxurious garden.[56]

The general statement about God's creation of the world of plants and animals, which were given names by Adam, is accompanied by a declaration that God created a garden. This Near Eastern garden had to be cultivated by hard labour to eliminate the enemies of cultivated plants, namely, weeds. In other words, he created not hunters and gatherers, not even shifting cultivators, but settled gardeners, belonging to 'civilisations' based on advanced agriculture and the growth of cities. The history of the gardens and the history of the city are closely intertwined.

Nevertheless, there was something curious about this Semitic garden. It was without flowers. Despite the later versions of Dante and others of terrestrial and heavenly paradise, there are no flowers in Eden. In fact there are remarkably few references to flowers in the Bible or the Talmud.[57] In the written word the emphasis is again placed on aromatics, on smell rather than sight. Only three flowers are mentioned. These are not easy to identify, but are probably the white (madonna) lily (*Lilium candidum*), the narcissus (*N. tazetta*, the 'lily-of-the-field') and the *Pancratium maratimum*, the lily or rose of Sharon. Only once is reference made to the gathering of flowers: 'My beloved is gone down into his garden, to the beds of spices, to feed in the gardens, and to gather lilies' (Song of Solomon, 6.2). That situation has nothing to do with the lack of flowers, wild or cultivated, in the Mediterranean. It is also one that continues in Judaism today. Flowers and plants are not generally used in ceremonies at the synagogue, the cemetery or even at the house. Gradually some Jewish families are adopting the norms of their host communities, so that in the United States flowers now appear at family events. But traditionally even at funerals and in cemeteries, flowers or

---

[55] From Old Persian *pairidaeza*, enclosure (from 'to form around'), Armenian *pardez*, late Hebrew *pardēs*, modern Persian and Arabic, *firdaus*, garden. The Persian word referred especially to a royal enclosure, associated in mythical tales of the Golden Age with the notion of abundance when fruits and animals offer up their produce without cultivation.

[56] Lindsay 1965:260–1; Tertullian, *Apol.*, 47:13, 'If we mention paradise, a place of supernatural beauty destined to receive the souls of the blessed, separated from knowledge of the ordinary world by a wall, as it were, of that fiery zone.'   [57] See also Lambert 1878:467.

wreaths were absent, and arguments occurred even about the planting of trees in the grounds of the synagogue. Down to today one finds stones not flowers in the cemetery, and then as reminders rather than as offerings. Commenting upon the use of flowers in ancient Israel, one writer describes the Hebrews as 'a simple people without pomp', who employed only sheaves (*gerbes*) and leaves.[58] But, unlike Africa, this refusal to use crowns and garlands was a deliberate rejection, not a lack of knowledge, for they knew well what happened in Mesopotamia and in Egypt where they sojourned. There are several factors at work. One is the way mankind envisages and approaches the immaterial divinities. There are always contradictions, especially in the nature of sacrifice, which may lead to the rejection of material offerings. That is especially true where the sacrifice of humans is involved, as this may raise 'humanitarian' questions in an acute form. In ancient Israel the rejection of garlands was based upon their religious connotations; it represented the setting aside of the *mol'k*, the sacrifice of infants to Ba'al Hammon, which was practised by the Phoenicians and then at a much later date by the Carthaginians. They were not the only ones to do so; such killings were forbidden by the Romans, although they permitted a kind of human sacrifice in the form of gladiatorial spectacle, which remained at the centre of Christian attention.[59] Philosophical considerations were certainly relevant. But animal sacrifice was discounted, although animals were ritually killed. At the same time, the strict austerity of Jewish worship, both in its object ('Thou shalt have no other gods . . .') and in its content (reading and prayer), distinguished the community from its neighbours. According to the Talmud, non-Jews would garland idols at festivals with crowns of roses and of thorns, and it was the absence of such offerings that marked off the chosen people.[60]

Diacritical factors, the rejection of strange gods and the need to worship one's own in a different way, played a prominent part. The lack of the use of flowers by the Israelites is specifically attributed to a rejection of the 'idolatry' of their neighbours by that acute nineteenth-century horticulturalist, Henry Phillips: 'as the gardens or sacred groves of the heathen nations were generally the scenes of their obscene revellings, such public plantations, together with the erection of statues or images, were forbidden by the laws of the country'.[61] It was presumably this rejection of current ways of approaching the gods that led Pliny to declare that the Jews were 'a race remarkable for their contempt of the divine powers'.[62]

---

[58] Blondel 1876:12; on the relative absence of the use of flowers in Israel, see Lambert 1878:467.

[59] Charles-Picard 1959:268. Human sacrifice continued occasionally under the Romans, in Gaul in the third century, in Roman Africa, although the *molchinon* was a deliberate substitution of animal for human. In Carthage the *mol'k* did not appear to involve the use of garlands but there are many motifs using palm bundles, strictly palmettes.

[60] There has been much discussion about the possible role of garlands in first fruit rituals. Certainly there are general references to flowers in early Jewish sources but largely in the context of the acts of other peoples. A woman married as a virgin wore a myrtle wreath, a fact that was related to the amount of dowry she received (Lambert 1878:467-70).   [61] Phillips 1829:i, xxvi-xxvii.   [62] Pliny, *Nat. Hist.*, XIII. ix. 46.

Nor did the problem of flowers and other natural objects lie only in the nature of offerings to God. Jehovah's Commandments were strict not only about monotheism and morality, but about representation as well. 'Thou shalt not make unto thee any graven image, or any likeness of anything that is in heaven above, or that is in the earth beneath, or that is in the water under the earth' (Exodus, 20.4). This injunction might be seen as qualified by the next verse, 'Thou shalt not bow down thyself to them', which specifically refers to the fashioning of images for religious purposes. But taken literally the commandments would inhibit not only art but most developments of botanical and zoological knowledge. Even as a ritual exclusion, the consequences for Israel were profound. The centres of the decorative arts, of artisanal and architectural expertise, developed outside Palestine itself. For the building of the palace of David and the temple of Solomon, craftsmen were brought in and with them ornamental motifs from the regions around.[63]

Floral themes were not uncommon in other decorative contexts, for similar reasons. The ornamentation on the bowls of the candlesticks took the form of almonds with a knop or calyx and a flower or petal (Exodus, 25.33), while brims of cups were decorated with the lily flowers (I Kings, 7.26) and boards of cedar were 'carved with knops and open flowers' (6.18). Such forms of graphic representation are not always at one with the dominant religious ideology, perhaps because they are considered as ornament without specific meaning (like the rosette), sometimes because they fall into the secular sphere, or because they are created by others – since it is the act of creation that is prohibited. On the other hand, we can perhaps also discern an example of a general tendency to elaborate ritual and to make use of natural objects, despite the formal rejection. That seems to have occurred in a minor way with the actual use of flowers. Later references are made in the literature to the crown worn by the high priest of the form of the calyx of the *Hyoscyamus* flower as well as to floral wreaths. The apocalyptic works speak of floral chaplets being worn by virgins, by those celebrating Tabernacles and by victors in battle, while the Talmud refers to bridegrooms wearing wreaths of roses and myrtle.[64] In other words, some use of flowers, similar to that persisting in the Mediterranean and in Europe today, seems to have intruded, outside the context of the offerings themselves.

The region had of course long seen the development of early gardens of trees, ornamental and fruiting, at Jericho and elsewhere.[65] Aromatics had long been prized throughout the regions bordering on the dry lands where they mainly grew; frankincense and myrrh represented only a small fragment of the total range of available products.[66] But Israel took up specific attitudes

---

[63] Joret 1897:412.
[64] On the Feast of the Tabernacles (Sukkoth), a bouquet of myrtle, willow, palm and the citron or persea was carried (Josephus, 1930:345; 1943:372).
[65] In Carthage, the Semitic tradition began with aniconic grave symbols which gradually took on a human or animal form under the influence of Hellenism.   [66] Joret 1897:397ff.

towards the use of flowers, partly to discourage the worship of false gods, partly for more general diacritical reasons, and partly for wider theological ones that concerned the approach to divinity. In addition, there was the associated question of representations and whether it is right to imitate the work of the creator. Subsequently these themes strongly influenced the later history of the Near East and of Europe since they were taken up in different ways and at different times by the Christian and Muslim religions. In contrast, the major civilisations of the Near East that Israel rejected paid great attention to the culture of flowers, as they did to icons more generally, and to those further developments of the later period we now return. For the culture of flowers took off in the Hellenistic period, both in actuality and in representation.[67] I begin with a consideration of the spread of lotiform and related designs in architecture and the graphic arts.

THE SPREAD AND FORMALISATION OF DESIGN

Increasing visits to Egypt from about 650 BC gave the Greeks the opportunity to get to know about Egyptian stone buildings, providing the starting point for 'the ultimate development of monumental architecture and sculpture'.[68] The lotiform may have specifically influenced the capitals of the Ionic order which evolved in eastern Greece after the Doric, appearing on stone columns with capitals elaborately carved in floral hoops – 'an Orientalizing pattern familiar mainly on smaller objects and furniture'.[69] In this way Egypt contributed to the Greek architectural forms that constituted what has been called 'the most comprehensive and stable manner of design the world has ever seen'.[70]

The lotiform may also have influenced the design of the capitals on Assyrian columns and Phoenician stelai.[71] As a decorative theme the lotus emerged in Theban tombs of the New Kingdom not only as part of a graphic scene but as a form of decoration which came to be of fundamental importance for the history of Eastern as well as Western art. Three distinct design elements made their appearance in these Egyptian tombs, the lotus, the palmette (a pseudo-flower), and stems in the shape of spirals. Lotus and spirals were joined in borders and across broad expanses of wall, with the occasional addition of palmettes. While these three elements formed designs by themselves, they also acted as frames or borders for other designs.

[67] Joret 1897:400.   [68] Boardman 1985:962.   [69] Boardman 1985:962.
[70] Sir John Summerson, quoted in Gombrich 1979:176.
[71] On the stalks and flowers of the lotus on capitals, not in Syria itself but in Cyprus, see Joret 1897:435. The columns of the temple of Paphos simulated the trunks of palms. The capitals of the temple of Byblos were decorated with lotus petals and palmettes as found in Assyria (p.436). The votive stela of Carthage carried lotus and other vegetative ornaments. The tree of life, on the other hand, appears to have been a transformation of the palm tree in Chaldea (Joret 1897:432) and a cypress in Assyria (p.462), but the general shape and notion extended from Palestine to Eastern Asia and the Pacific; it appears, for example, in the contemporary shadow puppets of Indonesia and South-east Asia (Plate 1.1).

2.9 Lotus and palmette border with arcaded stems, from a Caeretan *hydria*. Etruria, sixth century BC. (British Museum, London; Rawson 1984:215)

With the military expansion and commercial activity under Thutmosis I (1525–c.1512) and his successors, Egyptian decorations spread to Mesopotamia and from there to Syria and the Aegean, including Greece.[72] So the 'ornament developed in the Near East between the sixteenth and the seventh centuries BC provided the vocabulary later exploited in the islands of the Aegean and the mainland of Greece'.[73] The elements now consisted of lotuses, palmettes and rosettes (Plate 2.9). Such motifs appeared as border decoration on Greek vases after the Geometric period in the seventh century, especially in Corinth. To these patterns of lotuses and palmettes bound together by an arcaded stem, the Greeks later added the scroll of acanthus leaf that characterised Corinthian capitals and served either to support the flowers or else to supply a running plant stem (Plate 2.10).[74] Though Egypt remained unacquainted with the undulating scroll of the acanthus, found originally among the Mycenaeans, it was combined with the lotus design to form a motif that was 'infinitely adaptable to any area it is expected to fill'.[75]

The motifs appeared in architecture as well as in painting and sculpture. It was the eastward conquests of Alexander that established provincial forms of Hellenistic architecture in Central Asia from which the practice of decorating Chinese Buddhist caves on the Silk Road 'was derived in its entirety'.[76] As a result elements of certain flower patterns in Chinese art can be traced to ancient Egypt, possibly with some Aegean influence.[77]

The art historian Riegl showed how the leaf-palmette type of border to

[72] Rawson 1984:199ff.
[73] The intermediary in the diffusion of many Egyptian motifs was the trading contact with Mycenae, Knossos and other such centres.
[74] *Acanthus* is a genus of prickly herbs of the Mediterranean region that have spiny-bracted flowers. The last of the three main orders, the Corinthian, made its appearance at the end of the fifth century BC.
[75] Gombrich (1979:184) who cast doubt on the claim that the palmette developed into the acanthus. Goodyear 1891.   [76] Rawson 1984:23.   [77] Rawson 1984.

2.10 Border of lotus and palmettes showing the use of acanthus leaves. From the Erechtheion, Athens, late fifth century BC. (British Museum, London; Rawson 1984: 219)

Oriental carpets was derived from late antique models and those in turn from classical Greek art.[78] The arabesque too can be considered a transformation of the palmette, of which the acanthus has been seen by some as yet a further version. In the beginning Greek decorative themes had been conventional and symmetrical, at least until the fourth century, the period of Pheidias. Roman art made some attempt to come closer to the observed form of plants.[79] Nevertheless, the decorative motifs continued as part of a formal repertoire, a corpus, that was drawn on by different societies, different cultures.

The acanthus was used in Byzantine and Romanesque churches as in Moorish art, and eventually led to the much more naturalistic forms of Gothic leaf work that mark Amiens and other Northern cathedrals. In its stylised ('classical') form the design reappeared in the Renaissance. In this way it spread throughout the continents of Europe and Asia, providing an impressive example of thematic diffusion through the range of complex societies. In the first centuries AD, during the Han Dynasty, it travelled across Asia to China, appearing in India both in Buddhist and Hindu sculpture, spreading from there to South-east Asia and Indonesia, even returning to Europe as a design on Indian cloth. The acanthus leaf made its impact even in the further reaches of the East, moving along the silk routes to the courts of Tang China, of the three kingdoms of Korea[80] and of Japan in the Nara period.[81] But equally Eastern motifs travelled in the opposite direction.[82] By these exchanges the same elements of design came to be used in a wide variety

---

[78] Riegl 1891, 1893.
[79] It was argued by Courbaud that the vast body of Roman bas-reliefs was of Greek or Near Eastern inspiration. While that contention would be no longer accepted, neglecting as it does the Etruscan influence, the Pompeiian paintings of cupids as garland makers, the sculptured putti carrying bouquets in baskets and in their hands, and the cupids on sarcophaguses holding the ends of garlands of fruits and flowers, these were derived directly from Alexandrian models, from the paintings of the Delta region (1899:6ff., 12).
[80] Lee 1984:59ff; Kim 1988:100ff.   [81] Hayashi 1975.   [82] Rawson 1984.

of Eurasian cultures. Of course there was always some degree of reinterpretation. But often only a limited measure was required since so many of these forms were conventional, carrying little specific meaning. While all is recast, the forms themselves take on a largely decontextualised existence. In writing of the Roman heritage from Alexandria and the East, Courbaud remarks on 'the tendency [of all ornamental art] towards schematic representation, the transformation of the animal or vegetable subject into a particular motif, more or less fixed once and for all, the leaf of the palm tree for example into palmette, the rose into rosette or "rose" [*rosace*]'.[83]

Such persistence in pattern over time and space is seen by the historian of art, Gombrich, as due to 'habit', what anthropologists call 'custom' or even 'culture'. These designations in themselves tell us nothing about the reasons for such continuity. On a more concrete level, Gombrich attributes this spread to the capacity of this motif to meet the three basic requirements of decorative design, framing, filling and linking. Doubtless part was played by the prestige of the sources, which continue to influence architecture throughout the world. Religion and trade were important; so too were other forms of power. Partly as a result of military force, which led Greek armies as far as India in the East and Roman troops to Britain in the West, aspects of classical imagery became common throughout large parts of Europe and Asia.

EGYPT AND THE CLASSICAL WORLD

Until the coming of the Persians the Egyptians seem to have had rather few garden flowers, not even the pink or Indian lotus.[84] The Greeks played a major part in extending their repertoire of flowers as well as their use as garlands. The most important of the new acquisitions was the rose which came to dominate usage, literature and popular imagery in Greece and now tended to displace the lotus in Egypt. The Greeks conquered the country in 332 BC and in 30 BC the Ptolemaic Dynasty gave way to the Romans.

For the Romans, Egypt was a land abundant with year-round flowers, by comparison with what was seen as their own less fertile soil. References are made by Pliny to Egyptian chaplets, as well as to artificial flowers in winter:[85] Egypt was also the land of spices and perfumes, although many of these came from further afield.[86] Egyptian florists and gardeners had a high reputation and developed a major industry, for flowers were needed locally for elaborate banquets, as in earlier times, feeding the Alexandrine fashion of what has been described as Garlandomania.[87] They were also exported across the Mediterranean to Rome.

---

[83] Courbaud 1899:13. There is little agreement about what a palmette does represent (see Rawson 1984:202).
[84] Joret 1894.   [85] Pliny, *Nat. Hist.*, XXI.iii.5.
[86] Miller 1969. See also the *Periplus of the Erythraean Sea*, roughly contemporary with Pliny, which suggests that spices used in Rome came from the Yemen and India; the tradition of importation went back to Ptolemy II but Yemen had exported to Egypt long before.   [87] Grimal 1969:281.

With the demand for flowers from both inside and outside the country, the effect on Egyptian horticulture was profound. Consider the nature of the production, manufacture, collection and distribution of flowers and garlands that is implied in the following letter from Roman Egypt:

Roses are not yet in full bloom here – in fact they are scarce – and from all the nurseries and all the garland-weavers we could just barely get together the thousand that we sent you with Sarapas, even with picking the ones that ought not to have been picked till tomorrow. We had all the narcissi you wanted, so instead of the two thousand you asked for we sent four thousand. We wish you did not think us so petty as to make fun of us by writing that you have sent the money [for the flowers], when we too regard your children as our own and esteem and love them more than our own, and so we are as happy as you and their father. [Customary regards][88]

We are dealing not only with great gardens that provided a 'subsistence' horticulture for aristocrats but with a wider market that involved the commercial growth and sale of flowers on a large scale, sometimes on credit, for religious services and for domestic use, including marriages. Flowers were grown both for the market place and directly for the workshops where garlands were made. The sale of flowers was but a small part of the larger market in fruit and vegetables that supplied the urban population. The land on which this produce was grown, some of which was owned by women, was subject to a complex system of taxation and transactions, of sale and purchase, of leasing and sub-leasing. On this elaborate tenurial base, 'market-gardening stands as a link between the pleasure-garden and the festival or party with its wreaths and scattered flowers, and the feast or banquet at which food was served'.[89]

The horticulture and the floriculture of Greece and Rome depended heavily upon the earlier achievements of their Oriental neighbours. At different times both these states occupied Egypt and invaded Asia, putting them in close touch with the cultural achievements of those extensive regions. Such contacts affected not only the parks of the very rich but the smaller gardens of the towns and the commercial horticulture of farmers. It has been suggested that the Roman garden, especially the commercial version, developed by the adoption of Hellenistic influences from Egypt through Campania.[90] Certainly Egypt had close trading ties with Pompeii and other centres on the coast, but the strength of this Egyptian mediation has been questioned by those who see the Greek influence as being crucial in southern Italy.[91] In any case it appears to have been in the Alexandrine period that commercial horticulture reached its zenith and became capable of supplying year-round flowers, for religious as well as purely social reasons.[92]

[88] Oxyrhynchos Papyrus, 3313, quoted in Lewis 1983:80.
[89] Lindsay 1965:284.   [90] Grimal 1969:297.[91] Jashemski 1979.
[92] Grimal 1969:60, 63. Lindsay writes: 'The market gardens that grew up around Rome and other large Italian towns were based to a considerable extent on those of Ptolemaic and Roman Egypt: the *paradeisoi* named in the *Nomoi Teloikoi* or Tax Regulations' (1965:284).

THE GROWTH OF GARDENS

The earlier gardens of the ancient world had been mainly a creation of the centres of socio-economic power, namely of the royal courts, the aristocracy and the temples. These centres were also the foci of artistic representations associated with the high culture; so that in both literature and the graphic arts – the decorative as well as the creative – this garden and its contents became a major theme. The tradition continued in the classical world of Greece and Rome. In the *Odyssey*, the palace garden of Alcinous was planted with fruit trees, vines and evergreen herbs (VII), while the garden of Calypso included a vine with purple flowers and grassy meadows with violets and wild parsley (V). But the garden culture extended beyond the court with the development of Greek democracy, the partial disappearance of royalty and the increased wealth of society. In the fifth century BC wealthy Greeks deliberately imitated the royal gardens of Persia, especially the paradise of Cyrus at Sardis. The practice expanded during the Hellenistic period, both in the religious and secular domains. A formal layout of shrubs and trees surrounded the Agora at Athens, contrasting with the more natural ambiance of the sacred groves, of Antioch-Daphnae for example, that were such a prominent feature of the religious life. Urban domestic gardens are mentioned in written sources but there is little archaeological evidence on the form they took.[93] Water was scarce, space crowded; unlike Rome, the area within the peristyle, that is, the colonnaded open space, was more or less barren of plants, although gardens producing herbs and food were sited outside the town walls. Potted plants were found within the city but mainly for the festival in honour of Adonis when fast-growing seeds of fennel, lettuce or barley were planted in pots by mourning women to represent the rebirth of spring.[94]

Religious gardens or parks were of two main types, the cultivable, which could be rented out, and the rustic shrine, 'where statuary and trees coexisted without definite planning'. In addition, public places such as gymnasia or philosophical schools were connected by parks and shaded walks which often included a shrine to a deity or the tomb of a hero. Cemeteries too were provided with trees and flowers, even with wells and dining pavilions, being places where the living could commune with the dead. These religious settings perhaps formed one of the antecedents of the Roman garden.[95] But there were others yet more important.[96]

---

[93] Ridgway 1981:28. A series of garden pots with holed bottoms were found *in situ* around the Hephaeston in the Agora.   [94] D'Andrea 1982:46.   [95] Grimal 1969:63.

[96] On gods and gardens, see Grimal 1969:70ff., Jashemski 1979:115ff. and earlier Gibault 1901. For sculpture in gardens, see also Dwyer 1982 and Ridgway 1981, who points out that the gods especially associated with Greek gardens were 'the gods of life', Aphrodite, Dionysus, Eros, Asklepios, Herakles and Adonis; de Caro (1987) notes the combination of gods and humans in the gardens of Pompeii, remarking that the Romans were vague about their identification of the statues.

By the time of the late Republic, the aristocracy and the rich had extensive pleasure grounds.[97] At least as an 'art form', the garden developed quite late in the history of Rome, only after the imperial expansion in the second century BC and it was the generals who had conquered Asia who were the first to establish large parks. The animal paintings on the walls of Pompeian gardens recall these great estates which the rich filled with wild animals and which were first described by the Greek writer, Xenophon, who had himself witnessed the *paradeisa* in Persia.[98] When Alexander conquered the East, he assumed control of the parks which were in turn taken over, copied and developed by the Romans when they came to dominate the Hellenistic world.

In Rome gardens were created by a larger segment of the population than in Greece but were nevertheless regarded as emblems of luxury.[99] The extravagances of the lavish suburban villas and gardens of Rome, originating in the first century BC and known as *horti* because of the earlier use of the area, led moralists to cry out against them.[100] And not only moralists. Their very ostentation made the gardens open to personal envy as well as to political predation. In 82 to 81 BC their possession could bring upon the owner 'the dreaded publicity of proscription under the rapacious dictator Sulla', who also introduced a number of other sumptuary rules.[101] Lavish gardens are often an obvious public manifestation of great wealth and as such are likely to attract envy.

THE CHANGING CULTURE OF FLOWERS

Whatever the contribution of Egypt and the Orient, the rise of Greece and Rome altered the culture of flowers in important respects. There was, firstly, the changing shape of gardens, dominated by statuary in Greece and by topiary in Rome. Secondly, our knowledge of their achievements is greatly extended by the large amount that was put down or developed in writing, both in the outstanding botanical treatises such as that of Theophrastus and in more discursive works such as *The Deipnosophists* (The Gastronomers) of Athenaeus. Thirdly, the power of prince and priest was less in evidence and the culture of flowers took on a more secular, bourgeois and perhaps demotic aspect, owing partly to the extension of knowledge, partly to the diffusion of

[97] The classic account of Roman gardens is by Grimal (1943, revised edn 1969), although the strong form of the 'Oriental' thesis has its critics. For more recent work see MacDougall 1987 and Jashemski 1979.
[98] Xenophon, *Anabasis*, I.ii.7; *Cyropaedia*, I.iii.14; *Hellenica*, IV.i.15. See Jashemski 1979:72.
[99] Grimal 1969:24; Littlewood 1987:10.   [100] Purcell 1987:203, *horti*, see below pp.57–8.
[101] Plutarch, *Sull.* 31.10; Littlewood 1987:11. 'Even the murderers began to say that, "his fine house killed this man, a garden that, a third, his hot baths"' (*Plutarch's Lives, Sulla, The Dryden Plutarch*, revised by A. H. Clough, vol. 2, Everyman's Library, London, p.172). While Pliny drew special attention to these depredations of Sulla, most emperors in fact confiscated property, and not only from those with *horti*; for example, *bona caduca*, which included the property of anyone unable to make a will or failing to do so, automatically fell into the imperial *fiscus*.

wealth, partly to the advent of some democracy and partly to the growth of technology. Fourthly, there was a proliferation in the kinds of flowers being cultivated in the Eastern Mediterranean at this time.

In these areas north of the Mediterranean it was the rose rather than the lotus that came to dominate both in life and in art, both in gardens and in literature. In literature the rose was the most beautiful of flowers, the joy of gods, the pillow of Cupid, the garment of Aphrodite.[102] It rapidly made its mark on the standard imagery of poetic language, 'rosy-fingered Dawn', as well as in prose and presumably in common speech. In painting, a five-petalled variety was represented very early on in the Blue Bird fresco of the second-millennium palace of Knossos in Crete (which was also the home of saffron) and it was woven into fabric, a double purple web with rose design being part of the cloth that Andromache was making at the time of Hector's death at Troy.[103]

Roses in turn became symbols of luxury. Zeus had slept on a bed of saffron, lotus and hyacinth, but it was a bed of rose petals that became the epitome of the good life in Rome.[104] However, the rose had its more melancholy side, not only because it had a place in funerals, not even because of its thorns, but because, like other cut flowers in later cultures, it represented the evanescent nature of pleasure. So the flower not only stood as a symbol of luxury, but carried a message of warning about life itself; a canker lay within the rose.

THE PAINTED FLOWER

Our knowledge of the Roman culture of flowers does not depend upon literary descriptions alone, nor yet upon the careful work of garden archaeology that has been carried out in recent years, especially under the shadow of Vesuvius. The gardens of Pompeii were planted with some evergreens that remained in leaf all year round. Larger gardens would have had examples of the topiary art favoured by Pliny and many had copies of Greek sculptures. While actual flowers played only 'an incidental role', their representations were common.[105] For the inhabitants of Pompeii decorated the walls of their peristyle gardens, which formed the centre of the house, with paintings of the flowers that they purchased or grew, partly in order to extend their size by a kind of *trompe l'oeil* (Colour plate II.1).[106] A favourite flower was the oleander but birds and sometimes wild animals and mythological

---

[102] Anacreon, *Odes*, 35, 1–2; 53; 55, 1–10, translated by Thomas Moore.

[103] *Iliad*, XXII.441. Hurst 1967; or is it more generally 'broidering flowers of varied hue', as in the translation by A. T. Murray in the Loeb edition (1976:ii, 487), and which is the sense of *thròna* in Liddell and Scott, 'flowers embroidered on cloth' or 'herbs used as drugs and charms'.

[104] Cicero, *Tuscu. quaest.*, v.26; D'Andrea 1982:80.

[105] Rose, lily and violet were most frequently mentioned; in addition there was myrtle, flowering ivy, viburnum, the daisy chrysanthemum, the Madonna lily, the poppy, the iris and the oleander (Jashemski 1979:47, 54).

[106] Jashemski 1979:273. In Greece there appear to have been few or no plants in the peristyle houses (p.18).

figures appear. In this way flowers were eternalised, providing a permanent backdrop even to bare courtyards, just as empty ponds were sometimes painted with fish and plain walls with statues and garlands.

Paintings of flowers were not confined to the garden. One of roses, bachelor's buttons and other flowers against a dark background was executed on a framed panel inserted in the ceiling of a house. Like mosaics and other forms of Roman art, such paintings were perhaps attempts to reproduce in less costly and more permanent ways the achievements of Hellenistic cities such as Alexandria and Pergamum.[107] Was this painting a graphic version of the kind of reversible ceiling by means of which the Emperor Elagabalus smothered the guests in flowers in the course of dinner?[108]

These paintings from Pompeii illustrate very clearly the objections that some held, not only puritans, to representation as deception, whether in the theatre or in art. There is a wreath on the wall of the *lararia* which represents a permanent offering to the tutelary deities. It has the same character, and raises similar objections from some, to plastic flowers on a grave. An offering of something impermanent, a flower or vegetation, is made in a permanent form. What may be acceptable as a type of decoration loses value as a gift to others, especially to the dead who cannot immediately respond; for some, that is cheating or deception. Of course the creators of the wreath did not look at it in that way, but the view, the puritan view, remains not far from the surface of human action.

THE MARKETING OF FLOWERS

In Athens itself the philosopher Epicurus was one of the few to have established a garden and that was in connection with his philosophical school. But by Roman times there is ample evidence of the extent of private gardens, for example, in and around the town of Pompeii. In early Rome the *hortus* had

---

[107] On the role of painting on walls as a cheaper substitute for hangings or carpets, see Gombrich (1979:173) who relates it to skeuomorphs, to the tendency to pattern new objects (for example, the car) on the model of the old (the carriage), a Greek sense of the word 'metaphor'. In Rome such reproductions were not confined to the less costly mansions.

[108] Littlewood 1987:25–6. On the flowers from the ceiling and other extravagances of the effeminate boy Emperor Marcus Aurelius Antoninus, alias Elagabalus, see Hay 1911:245. His large expenditure on flowers was not only for decoration. At the table dormice were baked in poppies and honey; a cup known as mulsum was prepared from white wine, roses, nard, absinthe and honey; beds were strewn with flowers and perfume and his path was covered in lilies, violets, roses and narcissus (pp.254–6). See the painting *The Roses of Heliogabalus* (1888), by the Victorian artist, Sir Lawrence Alma-Tadema, who vigorously portrayed women and flowers in classical times; as a result he has been called 'The Painter Who Inspired Hollywood' (Ash 1989). Certainly he represents the end of puritanism in many ways. See also Lucretius, *De natura rerum*, II.624–8, for a shower of roses on the goddess Cybele as Mother Earth; and Claudian, *Shorter Poems*, 35, 116–19, for the nuptial chamber treated in a similar fashion: 'Soon as they reached the doors of the marriage-chamber they empty baskets full of red spring flowers, pouring forth showers of roses and scattering . . . violets gathered in Venus' meadow.' According to Coats (1970:163) the hanging of a rose over the dinner table is a related practice, one that gave rise to the phrase *sub rosa*, indicating the hearer should respect the confidentiality of the hospitality he was given. *The Oxford English Dictionary*, however, suggests a German origin for the phrase, while Thomas (1983:230) places the custom in the sixteenth century.

been primarily a kitchen garden, flowers being cultivated in the courtyard house. However, the remarkably preserved remains of Pompeii, dating from AD 79, provide firm evidence for the extent of the culture of flowers in this fertile area of Campania, whose roses were praised by Pliny. The Roman aqueduct brought abundant water to the town, allowing pools, fountains and irrigated beds, so that outside the town gardens were no longer confined to evergreens like the myrtle, oleander and the ivy but were enlivened by the colours of seasonal flowers.[109] Even today the climate and soil enable three crops, one of flowers, to be grown each year and the region produces plants for many large European seed companies. In addition, carnations, roses, gladioli and tuberoses are grown for the extensive market in cut flowers.[110]

In antiquity flowers were grown in Pompeii for two main purposes: for garlands (*coronae*) and for perfume (*odor*). The making and use of garlands is illustrated in a number of drawings and paintings. Flower dealers made garlands as well as selling the flowers to others for their manufacture, very much as in flower markets in India today. Indeed, the corona (Greek *stephanos*) seems to have been created out of garlands (*corona longa*; Greek *hypothymiades*, 'the perfume rising') in the Indian style, being wound round the heads of men and the necks of animals. Leaf coronae also existed and are abundantly portrayed with their leaves sewn together. Excavations have shown the frequency of gardens in the town, a few of which may have produced flowers for the market as well as for household use. But most flowers seem to have come from farmers living near the cities on land owned by rich proprietors.

The oldest piece of continuous Latin prose is the work by Cato (234–149 BC) entitled *De agri cultura*. There he describes an estate divided into nine parts of which the second, after the vineyard, is the watered garden. If near a town, this should contain vegetables and chaplet flowers for garlands.[111] The statement about the proximity to the town suggests that we are not simply dealing with a 'surburban' rural retreat (*villa pseudourbana*, as Vitruvius called it), but with the opportunity to supply both a town house and the market.[112] Varro had the same advice about location: 'And so it is profitable near a city to have gardens on a large scale; for instance, of violets and roses and many other products for which there is a demand in the city.'[113] The area outside Rome was in fact well known for the development of market gardening.[114]

In Ptolemaic Egypt, especially Alexandria, in Greece and in Rome of the later Republic, flowers were marketable commodities requiring not only

---

[109] D'Andrea 1982:4.   [110] Jashemski 1979:287–8.
[111] Cato, *De agri cultura*, 8.2.   [112] Littlewood 1987:12.
[113] Varro, *Rust.*, 1.16.3; Purcell 1987:188. The cultivated violets were probably stock (Jashemski 1979:54).
[114] 'C'est en Egypte . . . qu'il faut chercher l'origine des cultures florales "industrielles" qui prospère à côté de Rome et fournissent les roses, les violettes et les autres fleurs aux fabricants de couronnes et aux convives des banquets' (Grimal 1969:60).

growers, who were necessarily specialists, but sellers. Sale took place in four main ways, much as in later Europe, that is, in the market, from flower shops, from semi-permanent stalls and by travelling flower sellers (Plate 2.11). In Alexandria, 'la ville des fleurs', the making of chaplets was carried out by women in a special quarter of the town, suggesting the presence of an occupational group.[115] The paintings of Pompeii show little cupids acting as flower sellers as well as makers of wine and unguents (Plate 2.12).[116] The real-life florists were tougher in various ways. The Greek dramatist, Aristophanes, writes ironically of a widow with five children who is trying to maintain the family by 'weaving chaplets for the gods' in the myrtle market.[117] This she succeeds in doing until a tragedian, Euripides, persuades the public that there were no gods, since when her sales have dropped by a half. Even so, she has twenty votive chaplets to deliver. The passage brings out the close connection between flowers, the gods and hence icons of the gods; it is difficult to offer anything to the 'invisible god'.

Other sellers, no doubt of lesser status, peddled their wares in the streets,[118] while a third tier were florists of greater accomplishments. One of them, the garland maker Glycera, was the lover of the Greek painter, Pausias, who tried to represent her creations in his own medium.[119] But these arrangements she was always changing to test out his skills, so that 'there was a duel between Art and Nature'.[120] Apparently flower girls, as later in history, were often objects of delight, partly because they were selected for their looks, partly because of the attraction of their wares, and partly because of the nature of their commerce, which brought them into direct relations with their clients. For the sellers were largely female. 'It's always the girls', wrote Sappho, 'who weave the garlands of flowers';[121] elsewhere the garland weavers are not exclusively female, but the sellers often were and the weavers too. The much later *Greek Anthology* (V.81) contains a poem attributed to Dionysius the Sophist: 'You with the roses, rosy is your charm; but what do you sell, yourself

---

[115] Courbaud 1899:12.   [116] In the House of the Vettii, see Jashemski 1979:268, Figures 397, 399.

[117] *Thesmophoriazusae*, 450.

[118] In the story of Lucius' transformation into a donkey he can only become human again by eating the petals of roses. He first tries in a garden but discovers they are oleanders. Eventually he finds someone passing by in the street who is carrying crowns and garlands of flowers of all sorts, including fresh roses. When he eats them, he turns back into his former self (Lucius of Patras 1822:90); the magical quality of the rose made him human again.

[119] A modern version of the painting of Pausias known as the *stephaneplokos* is the *Pausias and Glycera* of Rubens, painted in collaboration with a flower painter, probably Osias Beert. Freedberg regards this painting as not only implying a recasting of the traditional art–nature theme (the painted being superior to the natural) but as 'a statement of the newly acquired status of a traditionally lowly genre, flower painting' (1981:121). In the National Museum of American Art, Washington, DC, there is a statue of Nydia, 'the blind flower girl of Pompeii', by Randolph Rogers, modelled in marble between 1855 and 1856, the source of which is Bulwer-Lytton 1834.

[120] Pliny, *Nat. Hist.*, XXI.iii. On the use of courtesans as models for painters in the Tang Dynasty in China, see Laing 1988:35.

[121] Forty-one in Saklatvala 1968:72; in these fragments there are other references to necklaces (47), garlands (49) and, in Ovid's 'Sappho to Paon', to perfumes brought by the Arabs (p.194).

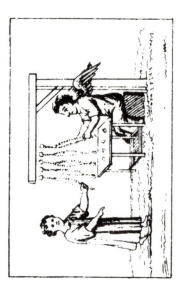
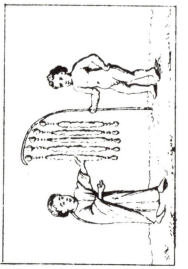

2.11 Roman pictures of flower dealers, with stands and itinerant garland sellers. (Jashemski 1979:268)

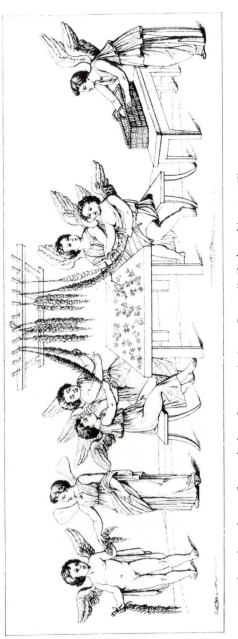

2.12 Cupids and psyches as flower dealers, from a painting at Pompeii. (Jashemski 1979:268)

or the roses, or both?'[122] Both the wearing and the selling of flowers were associated not only with sex, but with the sale of sex, making *hetaerae* more attractive to the buyer.[123]

Crowns of course were used by both sexes but mainly males. While some people made their own and others brought them in the market, the houses of royalty and of the rich had their own employees for this specialist work. The Egyptian craftsmen of Alexandria were especially valued, but floral weavers also practised in other countries. When Alexander's conquering army took possession of the household of Darius III of Persia, it was found to include 46 men employed to weave chaplets and 14 perfume makers, besides many other specialists, including 329 concubines who were also musicians.[124]

THE LUXURY TRADE AND ITS CRITICS

Horticulture often contained a mixture of the commercial and the aesthetic. In the next century we find Pliny reinterpreting Cato's remarks solely in the latter terms, suggesting that he encouraged people to include 'chaplet flowers' among their garden plants 'especially because of the indescribable delicacy of their blossoms'. These are to be prized not for their utility (*usus*) 'but blossoms and their perfumes [Nature] brings forth only for a day – an obvious warning to men that the bloom that pleases the eye most is the soonest to fade',[125] touching again upon that very general theme of philosophy, religion and the arts we have already encountered. On the other hand, the first chaplets, he claims, were made not of flowers but of the branches and leaves of trees for use in sacred contexts. Indeed, Pliny speaks of the crown of grass having the highest honour among military and civilians alike,[126] an idea that 'exists even today among the Germans'.[127] The notion of a decline from simplicity and the reference to the purer customs of the Germans forms part of a more general critique of luxury and decadence of which Tacitus' account of family life in *Germania* is another example. Only later, Pliny asserts, were flowers used, including 'what are called Egyptian chaplets, and then winter ones, made from dyed flakes of horn at the season when the earth refuses flowers'.[128] The employment of artificial flowers outside the season and for purposes to which fresh flowers are inappropriate has as long a history as the use of cultivated ones, both in the West and in the East. Pliny writes of 'the latest form taken by the luxury of our women' being chaplets 'made of nard

---

[122] 'Garland sellers' was indeed the title of a lost work by the poet and dramatist Eubulus, possibly the original of the *Corollaria* of Naevius, although that seems to mean the play about 'a Garland' rather than 'The Garland-Girl'. Garland sellers seem to have enjoyed a reputation for low moral character but Hunter (1983:191) rejects the suggestion that these characters were prostitutes. In the *Anthology*, the aged and painted women of Fragment 98 are *hetaerae* who have passed their prime; they may either be garland sellers themselves or belong to a group contrasted with them. Fragment 104 appears to refer to a garland seller saying to a (male) customer, 'for who would forbear to kiss a girl wearing this (thyme)?' (D'Andrea 1982:84).
[123] Athenaeus, *Deipn.*, xx.679.   [124] *Deipn.*, xiii.607.   [125] Pliny, *Nat. Hist.*, xxi.i.1.
[126] Pliny, *Nat. Hist.*, xxii.iv.6.   [127] Pliny, *Nat. Hist.*, xxii.iv.8.   [128] Pliny, *Nat. Hist.*, xxi.iii.5.

leaves [*folia*]'[129] or of 'multicoloured silk steeped in perfumes';[130] even fresh flowers were sometimes drenched in perfume. Foreign origin, unseasonal behaviour and changing fashion occur as underlying themes in his critique. No chaplet, he declares, was fashionable 'except those stitched together with genuine petals only, presently only those fetched from India and even beyond'.

While the trade in dried and artificial flowers and in perfumes is discussed as part of the luxury trade with Egypt and the East, little is said about the nature of commerce in fresh flowers. Since the Romans grew very few kinds of chaplet flowers in their gardens, 'practically violets only and roses',[131] the demand must have been there. The iris was useless as a flower, Pliny declares, since it was no good as a chaplet, but its roots were employed to make an unguent and medicines. It was roses from Cyrene in north-west Libya that were said to have the finest perfume, while Spanish varieties were praised for their year-round blossoms.[132] So flowers from other parts of the Mediterranean world and beyond were known and used in Rome; Virgil writes of Syria's roses and Horace of Persian garlands, in the same way that today people speak of French clarets and German hocks.[133] But Egypt stood out as the main producer in this trade, which was a continual target of criticism.[134] Martial writes of this commerce in an epigram that I quote in full because of its general relevance to the culture of flowers:

> Her winter roses Nile hath sent to thee,
> Caesar, in boastful mood and deemed them rare;
>
> But now her envoy marvelling to see
> Thy gate, holds Pharos' garden poor and bare;
>
> He marked sweet Flora's treasure everywhere
> And splendour from the Paestan rosaries;
>
> Where'er he turned there met his wandering eyes
> A street ablaze with wreaths, a flower-clad Rome.
>
> Egypt, thou canst not match our Roman skies,
> Send us thy sheaves and take our roses home.[135]

The comment on flowers has a critical edge; once again we are exchanging necessities for luxuries instead of the reverse. These imports consisted not only in out-of-season flowers for ordinary use (perhaps in pots rather than as garlands) but, after the incorporation of Egypt as a Roman province, of the

---

[129] Indian spikenard (*Nardostachys jatamansi*). Blondel compares this product with what was formerly known in France as *fleurs italiennes*, which 'industry imitates as well in our day' (1876:84).
[130] Pliny, *Nat. Hist.*, XXII.viii.11.   [131] Pliny, *Nat. Hist.*, XXII.x.14.   [132] Pliny, *Nat. Hist.*, XXII.x.19.
[133] Virgil, *Eclogues*, IV.29: 'Assyrian balm shall fill the land' (see Royds' translation, n.d.:25).
[134] Blondel (1876:70) on the authority of Saumaise says that every two weeks the fleet of boats called *Kataplus* from Alexandria arrived at Ostia, the port of Rome, loaded with flowers of all sorts. I know of no other authority for this statement.   [135] Martial, *Epigrams*, VI.80; Pott and Wright n.d.:189.

particular flowers needed for the 'Oriental' cults which had been introduced there.[136] For example, the cult of Isis, goddess of fertility, required crowns of lotus as well as branches of palm and roses.[137] The amarynths of Alexandria were much prized because of their durability, and they too may have been imported, for Pliny states that they can be revived when moistened.[138]

The Romans themselves developed techniques for forcing the growth of flowers, if not in hothouses at least by the use of heat.[139] That process eventually made them less dependent upon outside supplies, but it also drew down criticism against unnecessary interference with nature in the search for luxury.[140] The French horticultural historian, Gibault, describes 'culture forcée' as 'la culture de luxe' which could only develop in periods of very advanced civilisation.[141] We have abundant evidence of such horticulture in Rome as elsewhere in Eurasia. Vegetables such as asparagus and artichokes were grown out of season by using hot water or steam, as in a hypocaust, as well as by using greenhouses fitted with transparent stone (*specularia*) rather than glass, or by growing plants on wheeled trollies (*horti pensiles*) that could be moved into the sun. Such activities were not widespread and were condemned by the Stoic philosophers who recommended sticking to the vegetables of the poor. But among the nobility the consumption of these luxury products was spectacular, especially of roses, which were needed for every great banquet. Suetonius writes of a friend of Nero who threw a feast where the roses cost 4 million sesterces. To meet this huge demand, they had to be imported from Egypt and Campania to add to the local production of forced flowers.

PERFUMES FROM FLOWERS

While chaplets were certainly their main use, flowers could also be strewn on floors and used as food, frequently for the medicinal purposes which Pliny discusses at length. But they also entered into the manufacture of perfumes, using oils as a base, colouring and a gum or resin to delay evaporation.[142] The scents were often associated with different localities in a more concrete sense

[136] I have placed 'Oriental' in inverted commas because, as others have argued in other contexts, it is an established concept that needs to be treated with great caution. At one level it means simply 'coming from the East' but many writers on the classical world endow it with the further implications of strange, mysterious, irrational. That notion will emerge again in nineteenth-century discussions of the Language of Flowers. My own theme runs in quite the opposite direction. In many contexts the oriental was a civilising force for the West but except in specific contexts there is little to be gained by substituting one dominant direction for another. At the most general level I am trying to call attention to points of convergence in all literate, advanced agricultural societies.

[137] Apuleius, *Met.*, XI. Courbaud writes of a candelabra in the Vatican decorated with lotus flowers (1899.12); an Indian lotus appears in Nile mosaic in the House of the Faun at Pompeii (Jashemski 1979:20).

[138] Jashemski 1979:273.   [139] Joret 1892:41; Littlewood 1987:20.

[140] 'Do not men live contrary to Nature who crave roses in winter or seek to raise a spring flower like a lily by means of hot-water heaters and artifical changes of temperature?' (Seneca, *Epistolae morales*, 122; Purcell 1987:190).   [141] Gibault 1898b:1109.   [142] Pliny, *Nat. Hist.*, XIII.

than crowns. Iris perfume came principally from Corinth, the attar of roses from Phaselis, oil of saffron from Soli in Cilicia, vine-flower and cypress scent from Cyprus, marjoram and quince-blossom from Cos; in addition there were almond and narcissus scents and numerous others. Some of the ingredients for perfumes and unguents (known as 'foreign essences') came from further afield. Together with all that was involved in the making, the distant origin made them very expensive, 'the most superfluous of all forms of luxury', used by both women and men to attract attention.[143] Like incense, perfumes formed part of offerings, and the eagles and standards of the army were anointed on holidays – bribing the eagles to conquer the world, as Pliny put it.[144] Like crowns, perfumes were not entirely linked to gender.

Oil had long been used not only for anointing and for cooking but as a base for perfume and unguents in order to preserve and adapt the 'essence' of flowers. That use throughout the ancient world was a manifestation of fashion or 'la mode' in two senses. Since the ingredients were largely exotic and expensive, their use set the rich apart from the poor, or rather some rich, the fashionable rich. It was also possible to be well-off but object to extravagant expenditure, that is, to be puritanical in the manner of Pliny when he wrote of attempts 'to dye even linen so as to adapt it for our mad extravagance in clothes'.[145] Such sentiments were readily taken up by early Christians such as Tertullian. Secondly, the practices were fashionable in another related sense in that preferences were always changing; as Pliny remarks, perfumes come in and out of fashion, just as the place of their manufacture shifts, or as the manufacturers in the same place change, to adapt to fashion.[146] The constant change is again likely to draw the fire of critics as a sign of a lack of serious purpose.

The greater the areas and energies devoted to the cultivation of flowers, the less were available for the growing of grain, a shift of emphasis that once again fed the critique of luxury. Send us the grain, it seems to say, that we ourselves should be growing. But the external contrast reflects internal divisions. The growth of the culture of flowers represents a growth of the standard of living of the rich. It begins as a matter of differentiation, of luxury, which involves the diversion of limited resources and human energies to producing goods and services for the minority. The contradictions of class-restricted consumption in a society where so many are poor become particularly clear when the practices themselves are recent, regarded as of foreign origin, and where there is an awareness of land being shifted from essential to non-essential uses, from the utilitarian to the 'aesthetic'.

Pliny's complaints are neither entirely idiosyncratic nor a purely literary

[143] Pliny, *Nat. Hist.*, XIII.iv.20. The main occasions when men used perfume were at symposia, after bathing and exercise and at their wedding. See Hunter 1983:194, commenting upon Eubulus, Fragment 100, for references. [144] Pliny, *Nat. Hist.*, XIII.iv.22. [145] Pliny, *Nat. Hist.*, XIX.v.22.
[146] On the manufacture of perfumes, see the paintings at Pompeii (Jashemski 1979:268). Aristophanes (*Eccles.*, 841) speaks of perfume-selling girls in the same vein as florists.

exercise, for as with gardens themselves, the widespread use of coronae seems to have been a recent practice of the empire. Before that, crowns were awarded for bravery. They could be worn during the festivals to Flora but not at dinner and certainly not in public.[147] The expansion of their use came with the conquests of the East and with the freer adoption of Hellenistic models. It was seen as a sign of affluence, of civilisation, but by some critics as a potential contributor to the weakness and possible downfall of the state.

THE USE OF CROWNS AND GARLANDS

Some indication of their importance is suggested by the number of classical authors who wrote specifically on the subject of flowers, crowns and perfumes. In his *Natural History*, Pliny devoted one chapter of his massive survey to discussing 'crowns', both those of flowers and those of foliage. As a source he claims a book by Claudius Saturninus, and other references are made to works on the subject by Eschinus, Paschalius, Asclepiades, Apollodorus, Philonides and Hephaestion. The general topic was clearly one of great literary interest.

The actual uses of crowns were many, largely for joyful occasions. They were never worn for funerals, although the crowns of the deceased were placed on the bier. While we hear of peasant chaplets, for even some wild flowers were used, it is their role at the higher levels of society that we discover from art and literature. Chaplets were already in use in Homer's time, for the shield of Achilles, made by Hephaestus, was decorated with a scene showing youths and marriageable maidens dancing with hands on one another's wrists, 'the girls in fine linen with lovely garlands on their heads'.[148] On the other hand, this single instance suggests that the use of crowns was not yet well developed in Achaean Greece.[149]

In classical Greece secular uses were accompanied by religious ones; the sacrifice demanded a garland both for victim and for officiant, and sometimes for the statue of the god to whom the offering was to be made. According to Athenaeus, the first use of crowns among the Greeks was to wear on the head in honour of a divinity. Sappho implored Dika to weave herself a wreath of fresh green leaves:

For the graces, we may believe, look with greater blessing on those who're adorned with flowers, than on those who wear no garland.

In a comment Athenaeus adds that she enjoins the wearing of wreaths in sacrifice 'because the more decked with flowers, the more acceptable a thing is in the sight of the gods'.[150]

---

[147] Blondel 1876:60ff.   [148] *Iliad*, XVIII.352.
[149] Referring to the Homeric period, Clement of Alexandria writes, 'The ancient Greeks never made use of wreaths' (*Paid.*, II.vii.72), but he was of course anxious to make a case.
[150] Athenaeus, *Deipn.*, XV.675.

In Rome too flowers were extensively used in religious contexts.[151] Funerals demanded masses of blooms. The corpse was adorned as 'an expression of honor and affection'. The funeral urn was similarly decorated, flowers were scattered on the guests at the funeral banquet, and wreaths of dry or artificial flowers were placed in the tomb.[152] A marble relief from near Rome of late Flavian, early Trajanic origin shows a woman laid out for burial, above whom stand two tall vases garlanded with fruit and flowers. Her hair is surrounded by a light wreath of blossoms and a man stands ready to place a heavy flower garland around her neck.[153] On the left an acanthus leaf may represent the foliage that is placed in front of the door to show the presence of a corpse. Nor were the dead abandoned after the funeral. Fresh flowers, especially roses, lilies and violets, were widely used to deck out tombs as a memorial, and show that the dead were still remembered.[154] Both individuals and burial clubs arranged for flowers to be provided. At the Parentalia, celebrated from 13 to 21 February, each family brought flowers and food to its tombs where banquets were often prepared. At the Rosalia and Violatio, roses and violets respectively were placed there.[155] The tomb itself was sometimes surrounded by a garden, and the income from the sale of the produce of this plot might be used for its maintenance or *tutela*.[156] Some of the walls and vaults of tombs were even painted with pictures of 'counterfeited flowers' as a pledge of everlasting life.[157]

Flowers were also offered to the household gods. In the prologue to *The Pot of Gold* Plautus even writes of the daughter of the house who prays constantly to the familial shrine, *lar familiaris*, and makes daily gifts of 'incense, wine, or something: she gives me garlands'. On the other hand, Cato declares they are offered on holy days, which seems more probable.[158] Hooks for hanging these offerings have been found in Pompeii, as well as garlands painted on the walls of the shrine rooms or *lararia*; once again flower painting, so popular in the Low Countries in the seventeenth century, is the epitome of the artificial flower.

In secular life, crowns were provided for guests at banquets and for

[151] See Lambert 1878:470–7 for further examples from Greece and Rome. She observes that they dedicated particular flowers to individual deities, the poppy to Ceres, the anemone to Venus, the lily to Hera, the myrtle to Artemis.

[152] Jashemski 1979:151. See the corona of everlasting flowers found in a Roman tomb in Hawara, Egypt, in the British Museum, London.   [153] Toynbee 1971:44–5.

[154] Euripides, *The Phoenician Maidens*, 1632–3; Sophocles, *Electra*, 894–6; Virgil, *Aeneid*, VI.883–6; Tibullus, *Elegiae*, II.iv.47–8; Propertius, *Elegiae*, I.xvii.22; Alciphron, *Epistolae*, IV.ix.5; Lucian, *De luctu.*, 11.

[155] Jashemski 1979:142, and 350 for further references; Toynbee 1971:63. Rosalia was held in May and June.

[156] On the use of funerary gardens for productive and commercial purposes in Roman Egypt, going beyond mere maintenance, see Lindsay 1965:298ff. He sees funerary gardens and their banquets for the dead as originating in the East (p.303).   [157] Toynbee 1971:63.

[158] Cato, *De re rustica*, 143.2. Of the housekeeper he notes: 'on the Kalends, Ides, and Nones, and whenever a holy day comes, she must hang a garland over the hearth, and on those days pray to the household gods as opportunity offers'. In the later fourth century BC Theophrastus satirises those superstitious Greeks who hung myrtle wreaths on their household gods on the fourth and seventh days of each month and spent 'the livelong day doing sacrifice to the Hermaphrodites and putting garlands about them' (*Characters*, XVI.10).

drinking. They were commonly placed not only on the heads but round the cups themselves; at times the leaves or flowers from the crowns were even placed inside the cups, a practice known as *coronas bibere*.[159] The use of floral arrangements was extended to decorating ships, and the tyrant Dionysius sent a ship decked in garlands to meet Plato, 'the high priest of wisdom'.[160] Whole cities might be garlanded for special occasions such as the 'marriage' of 'Aphrodite', when purple robes and garments, roses and violets, were scattered in the path of the bride.[161] Lovers would put crowns on the doors of the house of their beloved, which was also a sign that a child had been born. 'Crown your door with garlands, now that you are at last a father'.[162] In Greece when a child was born a family ceremony was arranged for the eighth day and a crown of olive leaves hung on the door if it was a boy, a band of wool if it was a girl.[163] The associations are obvious. A crown of olives was placed on the head not only of Olympic victors but also of poets. However, Homer and Pindar were said to have worn crowns of laurel, which was also worn by priests and some victors as well as by those consulting the oracle of Apollo.

It is about the foliage crowns of victors in war games and poetry we hear most. But crowns of flowers were worn for public speaking and presented to those departing on an expedition.[164] They were also awarded to artists and authors for theatrical performances, a practice that Herodotus claims came from the East. In the ancient world even jewels and items of clothing might be showered upon the successful individual. The offering of flowers continues today, having been deliberately revived after the rebirth of the theatre in Europe in the sixteenth century.

Given this widespread and varied use of chaplets, it is not surprising to find their composition tended to depend upon the context. In the Olympiad, victors often wore a crown of olive branches: with lovers it was roses. Lovers might exchange these crowns or send one as a gift, together with a bitten apple. Crowns of pine may have been associated with virginity while ivy, linked with Bacchus and the vine, was worn at dinners and thought to be good at warding off headaches and hangovers. But roses were also used on these, and indeed on many other auspicious occasions.

While I have given no separate treatment to the uses of various kinds of crowns in classical times, we should keep clear the different roles of those made of leaves and flowers, partly because of the importance of this distinction in later periods.[165] Although such an association is not exclusive in the classical period, leaves tended to be woven into victor's crowns, while

---

[159] On the use of crowns in feasts and drinking, see Blondel 1876.
[160] Pliny, *Nat. Hist.*, VII.xxx.110.   [161] Lane Fox 1986:139.
[162] Juvenal, Satire IX.   [163] Blondel 1876:29.   [164] Aristophanes, *Eccles.*, 148.
[165] For an extensive discussion of crowns in antiquity, which I encountered too late to use, see Baus 1940.

chaplets of flowers were used for pleasing social occasions, for love and marriage, for spring, for dining and drinking.

Rich victors made copies of crowns in gold and silver, and there was obviously a conceptual link between the royal crowns of other cultures and the crowns of victors in Greece.[166] A two-way process was at work. Historically chaplets of flowers and leaves may have preceded those of precious metals. Once royalty started using crowns, restrictions were likely to be placed on their use by commoners, except in situations of deliberate reversal, of the paper hat, or of a non-political nature where enhancement is required, as with the bridal crown. But the proliferation of the uses of the crown in Greece and Rome stems from none of these because it arose in a context where hereditary rulers had been set aside. It is true that the widespread use of valuable crowns in Hellenistic Greece and imperial Rome can hardly be taken as manifestation of the triumph of democratic rule. On the other hand, it provides some evidence of the extension of wealth and power to a larger segment of society, and to the part played by criteria of achievement in the system of stratification. There was no absolute contrast to the ascriptive ranking of their Eastern neighbours, but achievement was central to the working of their societies, whether in the peaceful arts of poetry, the soldier's feats of arms, or perhaps most typically, most emblematically, in the athlete's victory in games. For this end, the award of a crown for achievement contrasted with its ascription by inheritance.

Attempts have been made to establish a comprehensive code for the significances of different types of crown. Certainly some continuing associations did exist. Writing at the end of the nineteenth century, Blondel even claims that the use of crowns was as firmly coded as the Language of Flowers so much in vogue in his own day, with lovers using colour to indicate a place of meeting. He goes on to state that the system goes back much farther 'coming from the East, where this silent language dates from earliest times'.[167] In both cases the suggestion, which is exactly the claim of nineteenth-century writers on the Language of Flowers, overturns the notion of a culturally specific code. But the evidence from Greece and Rome suggests that while some general significance attached to various flowers, leaves and branches, there was considerable flexibility in usage and nothing, except agreement in advance about a particular meaning in a particular context, that would count as 'language' in any useful sense.

The names by which different chaplets were known display another feature associated with the later Language of Flowers. Part of what Athenaeus himself calls his 'wreath-laden lecture'[168] consists of listing a series of named wreaths, the Naucratite (after the Egyptian town), the Isthmian, the Antinoeis

---

[166] The Roman 'crown' gold was a tax, the proceeds of which went to the emperor, as the champion of his people.   [167] Blondel 1876:78.   [168] Athenaeus, *Deipn.*, xv.686.

of Alexandria. Many of these names are drawn from other literary sources. In the context of the dinner around which his book, *The Deipnosophists*, revolves, this listing emerges as a game, a kind of challenge to produce further examples, no matter how exoteric, how far removed from actual behaviour. Even the framework of the games at dinner seems a largely literary device. In ordinary life the meanings of different crowns are not exclusive but overlapping, as is often the case with codes of practice. The names of the crowns are precise but literary inventions of minimal significance, as is often the case with written codes.

BLOOD AND FLOWERS AS OFFERINGS TO THE GODS

The culture of flowers is always in some sense threatened by its internal contradictions of this kind, which turn around riches and poverty, excess and restraint. But aside from intrinsic internal contradictions, the culture of flowers had put down deep roots in most societies of the Mediterranean and the Near East, being rejected only by ancient Israel. As we have seen the Israelites accepted neither the sacrifices made to their neighbours' gods nor the garlands that accompanied these offerings.

In earlier times blood sacrifice had been one of the main ways of approaching the gods as it continued to be until recently among most non-literate communities. It took the form of the killing of an animal to a deity and the consumption of its flesh by the congregation in the manner classically but somewhat idealistically described by Robertson Smith as a communal meal or communion. On the other hand, where Buddhism, Hinduism and Jainism prevail, flowers constitute a major element in offerings to the gods, substituting for the animal sacrifice which predominates in Black Africa in rather the same way that in the Biblical story Jacob was ordered to kill a sheep instead of his son, Isaac, that is, to replace the human with an animal offering.[169]

There was no such generalised substitution in Bali. Though some offerings are vegetarian, others are not. Nor was that the case in most of the Near East where flowers accompanied animal sacrifice rather than acted as a substitute. Nevertheless, there too the extensive use of flowers was already a move towards the replacement of blood sacrifice, which is perhaps an indication of an implicit contradiction. The garland, including painted and sculpted ones, gradually became more significant than the offering; only occasionally is an animal sacrifice depicted on the paintings in the *lararia* of Pompeii.[170]

While garlands accompanied blood offerings, there is evidence that they were seen as more appropriate to the *sacrificium incruentum*, the sacrifice without blood. Offerings both to the gods and to the dead continued till the

[169] The same substitution occurred in Roman Carthage, the shedding of blood remaining central to pagan *molchinon* but only metaphorically to Christian worship.   [170] Jashemski 1979:120.

end of antiquity, the two being combined in the temples of deified emperors such as Divus Julius or Divus Augustus, but they tended to change in emphasis. Those offerings included garlands which were at times substituted for the shield,[171] a shift from the icons of war to those of peace. Indeed, garlands are at times specifically opposed to the bloody part of sacrifice. In late antiquity some images of emperors in public cemeteries even had garlands incorporated in them, while portraits were decorated with vegetable elements, including flowers, garlands and acanthus.[172]

Like the total rejection of sacrifice, this shift seems to build on a continuing contradiction that lies near the surface of these rituals. In the first place food is being offered to the gods, yet eaten by men. In Greece the problem was made explicit by Hesiod who recounted how Prometheus tricked Zeus by getting him to choose that portion of a great ox which consisted of bone covered with shining fat;[173] it was for this deception that Zeus denied men access to fire.[174] The competition for food divided even the gods; the material and immaterial are always in some kind of tension in the case of concrete offerings made to spiritual beings, who clearly do not enjoy that offering in the manner of humans. At the same time, the notion of blood sacrifice was criticised on different philosophical grounds. The fifth-century philosopher Empedocles saw all the taking of life as defilement, but especially sacrifice, a view connected with the idea of transmigration: 'Their altar was not drenched by the (unspeakable) slaughter of bulls, but this was the greatest defilement among men – to bereave of life and eat noble limbs.'[175] Much later in the third century AD the Neoplatonist Porphyry condemned Christians for eating the flesh of animals in any circumstances.[176] These notions are humanitarian in the literal sense of the word; they treat animals as human, at least in terms of the shedding of blood. A similar ambivalence is pithily expressed by the fisherman in *Śākuntalā*, a Sanskrit drama of the fifth century AD, when he is exercising his profession:

> a priest
> doing his holy rites
> pities the animals
> he kills.[177]

These views build on and extend a widespread aspect of man's attitudes to the killing both of other men and of animals, namely, an ambivalence about wielding the knife and shedding blood, as well as hesitation about the problems involved in offering material gifts to an immaterial divinity. One partial resolution of the first can lie in the use of flowers as a substitute. But in

[171] This was the shield of the *victor* and later of the *pater patriae*, the father of the people.
[172] I am indebted to Salvatore Settis for his help with references to late antiquity.
[173] Hesiod, *Theog.*, 540ff.   [174] Brown 1980.
[175] Fragment 118, see also 120, 122, 124.   [176] Porphyry, *De abstinentia.*   [177] Miller 1984:145.

the ancient world they often appear as an addition and are therefore seen by some as 'contaminated' by their role in sacrifice to the gods of others. Even where no such contamination is present, we have discerned an undercurrent of ambivalence that criticises the aesthetic as being not only a luxury but one which softens the moral fibre and fails to fill the peasants' rice-bowl. In this chapter I have tried to point to the origins of the culture of flowers in the Near East and the Mediterranean, leading to the highly elaborate practices of ancient Rome and the internal criticisms to which this gave rise. These views were already present in Europe with the coming of the barbarians on the one hand, and the rise of Christianity on the other. Despite these events, Rome provided a continuing focus for later Europe and the decline and later renascence of the culture of flowers was largely played out against a classical backdrop. The results of this conjunction for the cultural history of Europe will be explored in the next few chapters.

3 · The decline of flower culture in Europe

The fall of Rome had a devastating effect on both the knowledge and the practice of flower culture in Europe. Not only did botanical learning fail to increase, it actually declined. The same was true of other forms of knowledge related to plants. The medical profession almost disappeared, although herbal medicine was kept tenuously alive by Christian monks who preserved the manuscripts of Dioscorides, Pliny and Galen.[1]

GARDENS AND FLOWERS

So too was the case with the cultivation of flowers itself. The classical gardens of Greece and Rome did not immediately vanish. Sidonius Apollinarius (c.431–86), a Gallo-Roman aristocrat from Lyons who became bishop of the Arverni people, had a villa near Clermont with an elaborate garden. A number of the Gallic nobility in the fifth century preserved porticos and gardens in their villas. Sidonius describes a friend near Nîmes as:

walking in his secluded gardens which are like those that bloom on honey-bearing Hybla [Sicily] or those others, the joy of the old man of Corycus ... or there among his violets, thyme, privet, serpyllum, casia, saffron, marigolds, narcissus, and blooms of hyacynth ... or he may have chosen to rest in his mimic grotto on the edge of the hill ... Who would now bring into comparison the ancient orchards of the Indian King and the golden vines?[2]

Gardens also survived partly because the barbarians who conquered southern Gaul and the rest of the Roman empire in the West welcomed romanisation. For while their culture was largely antipathetic to such luxuries, the ruling elite was introduced to a number of the ways of the civilisation it had conquered. But for a variety of reasons such gardens did not in general endure, except in Byzantium. When the attempt was made to revive the structure of Roman gardens in the Italian Renaissance they were reconstructed with difficulty

---

[1] D'Andrea 1982:21.
[2] Sidonius, *Carm.*, 24.56ff. The reference to Corycus is to Virgil, *Georg.*, IV.125ff.; that to the Indian king is to the legend of the fabulous gardens of King Porus' palace. I am indebted to Dick Whittaker for this and other references in this and the previous chapters.

from written works, a reminder of the hiatus created by the disappearance of the empire in the West. One historian comments: 'with the collapse of the Western Roman Empire, gardens and garden art dwindled to such an extent that we may say, without exaggeration, that they virtually disappeared'.[3] Another writes of the general neglect of flowers in Europe as compared with the Near and Far East.[4] Or as an art historian more poetically puts it, 'In the early Middle Ages much of Europe had returned to wilderness.'[5]

That may indeed be something of an exaggeration. But while the ideology and the practice of the conquerors might adjust to luxury, the economy could not maintain its earlier affluence and the life of towns declined. The rich garden culture of Pompeii with its paintings, statuary and commercial crops disappeared. So too did the related horticultural techniques; the practice and even the knowledge of forced growth seems to have been lost for centuries. The country too changed. At first some gardens lived on in the face of the increasing fortification of large houses.[6] With uncertainty and unrest, considerations of defence came to dominate land use as well as domestic architecture. However, these changes were not a matter of bread alone. The culture of flowers might well have continued in some form or even revived in another had not elements in the early Christian church actively discouraged the use of pagan practices in many religious contexts. Acts that smacked of 'idolatry' were prohibited and, as in Judaism, these included the garlanding of the statues of gods, of the beasts to be offered and of the suppliants themselves. For the West the prototypical pagan scene was that depicted in John Keats' nineteenth-century poem, 'Ode on a Grecian Urn':

> Who are these coming to the sacrifice?
> To what green altar, O mysterious priest,
> Lead'st thou that heifer lowing at the skies,
> And all her silken flanks with garlands drest? (v.iv)

In secular life, especially in Byzantium where the influence of the East was stronger, their use lived on. The *coronatio urbis*, the decoration of the city with flowers for imperial appearances, continued under the Christian emperors.[7] In some sense that prepared the way for the decoration of churches, though the borderline between secular use and that of worship itself would remain a constant problem to theologians over the centuries. Flowers are mentioned by Gregory of Tours in relation to the worship of relics, which were sometimes treated like triumphal emperors.[8] Relics of saints became the

---

[3] Thacker 1979:81.   [4] Gorer 1975:4.   [5] Stokstad 1986:177.   [6] Littlewood 1987:26–7.
[7] Prudentius, *Contra orationem symmachi*, 2.727–8, writing in AD 395. 'What flowers shall I scatter and in what wreaths set my halls?' (Loeb edn.) In 837 the Emperor Theophilus ordered the children of an Asian city to decorate it with wreaths of flowers (*Imp. exp.*, Bonn, 508.2–5), and in 879 Byzantium welcomed the usurper Basil I with floral wreaths (*Imp. exp.*, 498.17ff.) See McCormick 1986:149 and 155, for these and other Eastern triumphs. For Western equivalents see Van Dam 1985.
[8] Greg. Tur. *Liber in gloria martyrum*, 90.VI.36.

focus of therapy in Gaul and were the object of pilgrimage and worship. But this practice had its early critics and a priest named Vigilantius accused Christians who acted in this way of being 'ashmongers', of taking over pagan ceremonies. In the sixth century relic cults became yet more popular and enhanced the prominence of local aristocratic families who provided so many bishops of the church and therefore became the descendants of saints. Their installation in a particular place could be compared to the *adventus* ceremony which celebrated the arrival in a city of an emperor or of the imperial image. But in commenting upon the bringing of relics to Rouen in the late fourth or early fifth centuries, Bishop Vitricius called attention to the great differences between the two practices. In the Christian ceremony the royal cloak becomes 'the garment of eternal light'. In this and other ways the traditional rites were given metaphorical interpretations. However, not all was metaphor, not all garlands were heavenly diadems. Flowers were gradually incorporated into secular and religious performances, as we will see in the following chapters. But not as in classical times and with much more ambivalence, especially on the part of the Fathers of the church. The use of flowers clearly diminished as did their cultivation together with knowledge about them. In certain contexts their use was strongly condemned by the more radical Fathers because of their role in pagan ceremonies, especially as garlands or in other forms accompanying offerings to the gods, and crowning alike the priest, the sacrificial animal and the statue of the god that was often set in the surroundings of a garden.

CROWNS

The use of flowers in crowns or garlands, especially on statues of pagan gods, was roundly condemned. Indeed, crowns of all kinds were rejected by some Christians. As I have noted, their deep significance to the classical world is shown by the number of works written on the subject of *coronae* and by the attention devoted to it in the more learned studies of authors such as Theophrastus and Pliny. Their meaning for many in early Christianity is equally strongly brought out in a work of that Father of the Christian church, Tertullian, written after he had broken with the Catholic branch and embraced the extreme doctrine of Montanism. In *The Chaplet* (AD 211), Tertullian's starting point is the story of a Roman soldier who, as a Christian, refused to wear a crown of laurels on his head at the time of a *donativum*, in this case the gift of money made on the death of Emperor Septimius Severus. As a result he was arrested and thrown into prison. Tertullian's problem is to justify the refusal to wear crowns, even though such a prohibition has no Biblical authority. In the end he has to appeal to custom (*consuetudo*), which he says some Christians wish to ignore, and goes on to produce an argument 'from silence' since there is no mention of this practice in the text.

His own rationale is, firstly, that wearing crowns on the head, as distinct from the use of flowers in a bouquet, is contrary to nature. Note the opposition of forms. Secondly, according to Greek mythology the invention of crowns was the work of the Devil for idolatrous purposes. For the 'crown is made to be an offering to idols' (10.5); 'crowns adorn the very doors, victims, and altars of idols; their ministers and priests wear them, also' (10.9). On the other hand:

No crown ever rested upon the head of a patriarch or prophet, levite, priest, or ruler; nor, in the new dispensation, do we read of an Apostle, a preacher of the Gospel or bishop who wore a crown. Not even the Temple of God, I believe, nor the Ark of the Covenant, nor the tabernacle of testimony, nor the altar of sacrifice, nor the [seven-branched] candlestick was ever adorned with a crown. Now, if a crown were worthy of God, these surely would fittingly have been so decorated both in the ceremony of their first dedication and in the jubilation of their restoration. (9.1)

So the sacred history of the Jews is adduced to confirm the custom of Christians for whom all crowns are to be avoided, including the marriage crown worn by the groom (which is 'why we do not marry pagans', 13.4), the crown on the door, the special crowns of magistrates, even the crown into which a woman's hair may be skilfully arranged (14.2). Christ was forced to wear a crown of thorns, but in Heaven he wears a crown of gold. As a Christian you should 'not demean your brow with a little chaplet and a twisted headband, when your destiny is to wear a diadem' (15.2). Following Christ, the earthly crown is exchanged for a heavenly one. Another pre-Constantine ascetic leader, Clement of Alexandria, specifically linked his objections to crowns to the Christian story, declaring it to be 'inconsistent for us who celebrate the holy suffering of the Lord, who know that He was crowned with thorns, to crown ourselves with flowers'.[9] A third component in these objections elaborates one common to the imagery of many cultures, namely, the impermanence of flowers, 'a crown of pride' in Isaiah's words, as compared with the 'crown of glory' obtained through worshipping the Lord, a contrast that the New Testament phrases as the pagan garlands that wither away and the 'incorruptible' crown of the Christian.[10] Here the crown is not heavenly but spiritual, perhaps even metaphorical.

These objections to floral crowns around the head are embodied in the work of the early Christian Father, Minucius Felix, whose sometimes strange argument rejects crowns but not flowers or garlands in themselves. He makes Caecilius, the supporter of paganism, attack Christians because of their objections to garlands: 'You do not wreath your heads with flowers; you do

---

[9] Clement (1954): 156 (2, viii.73.3). See Kronenfeld 1981:291.

[10] Isaiah, 28.1–5; 1 Peter, 5.4; 1 Corinthians, 9. 24–5; Kronenfeld (1981:291), to whom I am indebted for discussions and references, points out that the New Testament largely maintains the distinction between *stephanos* or corona as wreath (though also used metaphorically for a spiritual *victory*) and *diadema*, originally a filet of cloth, which is a sign of royalty.

not grace your bodies with odours; you reserve unguents for funeral rites; you even refuse garlands to your sepulchres.'[11] His objections, recalling those of Pliny to the Jews, go much further, to the absence of altars, temples and 'acknowledged images', so that their God 'they can neither show nor behold ... he runs everywhere'. The associated problem of the aniconic trend in early Christianity will be discussed later, but it is significant that the absence of images is seen as linked with the absence of offerings and with the invisible, omnipresent and omnipotent nature of God.[12]

To this attack Octavius responds, at length. We gather flowers in spring, especially the rose and the lily, for their odour and colour, and use them scattered loose and free as well as for garlands round our necks. But 'Pardon us, forsooth, that we do not crown our heads; we are accustomed to receive the scent of a sweet flower in our nostrils, not to inhale it with the back of our head or with our hair. Nor do we crown the dead', for they can smell nothing. Rather than 'a withering garland', 'we wear one living with eternal flowers from God'.[13] This defence of the Christian approach relates to a specific objection to crowns on the head. Yet underlying the discussion is not only a different perception of God (he is 'everywhere', invisible) and of offerings to God, but also a consciousness of the passing beauty of flowers in comparison with his lasting glories, a contrast between frivolity and luxury on the one hand and gravitas and restraint on the other.

Explicit use is made of metaphorical interpretation as a way of 'explaining' aspects of the writing of the Old Testament or of classical authors, or indeed of 'practice' itself; that technique was a great resort of the early Christian apologists. 'A beautiful crown of flowers that never fades awaits those who live well ... only heaven holds the secret of bringing it to blossom'.[14] Or even more extravagantly, 'The crown of the woman must be considered the husband.' Of course what is metaphor for the observer may well appear as truth to the actor. For such interpretations are forced upon practitioners who hold the text to be sacred and all-important, but cannot reconcile themselves to a literal reading, a reading 'by the letter'. As Lane Fox remarks, 'Christianity had a particular relationship with texts.' Several paintings in the Roman catacombs show Christians arriving at the Last Judgement clutching their books, and the book remains a constant theme of Christian iconography. The text, in the shape of the conventional papyrus codex, replaced a religion based 'on oral culture of myth and conjecture'.[15] Roman society was hardly devoid of the written word, but the Christians applied writing predominantly and extensively to their religious ends. Some of this application consisted of

---

[11] See Clarke's note giving further references to wreaths. 'The early Christians eschewed wreaths both for the living (worn at festivals, celebrations, as a mark of honor, used at sacrifices by both celebrant and victim ... etc.) and for the dead.' He sees the basic reason for rejection as their heavy religious connotations. The Jewish tradition seems less different than the note suggests but it did change over time (Clarke 1974:238–9.).

[12] Minucius Felix 1869:465 (cap. 10) and 468 (cap. 12); Pliny, *Nat. Hist.*, XIII.ix.46.

[13] Minucius Felix 1869:514–15 (cap. 38).   [14] Clement, *Paid.* II.8, 73, 71.   [15] Lane Fox 1986:304.

reinterpreting earlier Hebrew texts to suit later situations of practice and doctrine, that is, to the use of what might be seen as allegory, metaphor and kindred tropes. In these tropes, references are made to flowers, especially in flowery passages modelled on classical authors. Look for example at the letter 10 of Cyprian of Carthage who finds among the blossoms of the church both the lily and the rose: 'Let each man now strive for the highest honour in either estate. Let them win crowns – white for good works, crimson for sufferings. In the heavenly fortress both peace and warfare have their own flowers, so that with them the soldier of Christ may be garlanded in glory.'[16]

The range of flowers used for the forbidden chaplets covered the whole of the floral kingdom: 'you will see that there is not one beautiful flower, not one luxuriant leaf, no sod or vine-shoot that has not been consecrated to the head of someone or other' (7.7). All were in this sense suspect. However, Tertullian's objection to chaplets did not go so far as to condemn the use of flowers as such, or even as chaplets providing they were carried and not worn, that is, providing they were bouquets, not placed upon the head. For Tertullian, it was specifically the crown or chaplet that was condemned:

An extraordinary mode of using a thing, however, is no hindrance to its ordinary use. Use flowers, then, when they are tied together and twisted [into a crown] with thread and rush, just the same way as you would when they are free and loose, that is, things to be looked at and smelled. Count it a crown, let me say, when a bunch of flowers is tied together in a series, so that you can carry many of them at the same time and enjoy them all at once. If they are so pure, then lay them on your breast; or spread them on your bed, if they are so soft; or even dip them in your cup if they are so harmless. Enjoy them in each of the ways in which they affect the senses. (5.3)

Nevertheless, although he does not have the same objection to other uses of flowers, the whole tenor of his injunctions, here and in *The Clothing of Women* and in *Spectacles*, is against luxury or display of almost any sort, an attitude of extreme puritanism that led him to condemn the theatre, the wearing of jewelry, the use of cosmetics and the wearing of coloured cloth, justifying the latter ban on the bizarre grounds that if God had wanted us to wear such garments he would have sent us red and blue sheep. We cannot take these views as typical. Tertullian's work was written in his Montanist period, in a society before the conversion of Constantine when Christians were in the minority. So too that of Minucius Felix. But while such comments may seem particularly far-fetched, they were not unique and more measured criticism was often applied to other aspects of Roman life on the grounds of their

[16] In an informative footnote Clarke remarks that the white and crimson is a cliché of Latin verse, especially that of the lily and the rose. This imagery was taken over by Cyprian, Paulinus of Nola, Satirus, James and Jerome. He also refers to a liturgical convention whereby a blessing was pronounced on fruits and sometimes on the rose and the lily. There are some iconic representations; in the catacomb of Domitilla, Christ presented the saints with crowns of roses for they are presumably martyrs. (Clarke 1984:1, 75, 236–37.).

luxury. Once again the link with Roman moralists is clear; the difference lay in the relation of the writer to his audience.[17]

STATUARY

In the Roman world, crowns and garlands had their place in both secular and religious spheres. They were used to adorn the statues of gods as part of worship and sacrifice. So statues too were suspect, especially as they were not simply symbols of the gods' presence but themselves able to work 'good deeds of power'. Secret rites could be performed to 'animate' them, following Egyptian precedents: 'far into the Christian Empire, papyri still prescribed the spells which could be written on a slip and posted into a statue in order to "inspire" it'.[18] While the object itself was a manifestation of the god who, from Homeric times down to the late empire, was capable of appearing to humanity in a variety of forms, the statue itself also had power. Not long before the victory of Constantine, the Emperor Maximin in the East told how the people of the cities came to plead for a renewed persecution of the Christians, bringing with them the images of their gods.[19]

The significance of statues was sufficient for some Christians to see in their very presence the work of demons, opposed to the true religion. 'If you believe in your gods' miracles through man-made statues', asked Theophilus, 'why do you not believe in God's resurrection of the body?' 'Far into the Byzantine period', comments Lane Fox, 'Christians eyed their cities' old pagan statuary as a seat of the demons' presence. It was no longer beautiful: it was infested.'[20] Many early Christian bishops condemned even paintings inside the church, which were prohibited at the Council of Elvira in Spain.[21] At times they also encouraged the breaking of statues. On the other hand, some survived as decoration, in Constantinople for example, being left as 'demonic' survivals in the new centres of religion.[22] On the whole, three-dimensional statuary became very rare, although there were a few Biblical statues in Constantinople. In secular contexts some images of the emperor persisted in Byzantium where garlands of flowers were standard features. Nevertheless, even secular statues were looked on with suspicion by some Christians who, following the Judaic tradition, saw all as 'man-made' and opposed to the work of God, whether as regards his act of creation or in the resurrection of the body. These were both divine attributes.

One of the greatest achievements of the ancient world was the statue – the representation in the round of man, god and hero. From the fifth century, it

---

[17] A similar thought is expressed in Virgil, *Eclogue* IV.49–50. 'the living ram Shall softly blush with purple fleece' (Royale n.d.:26).
[18] Lane Fox 1986:135.   [19] Lane Fox 1986:612.   [20] Lane Fox 1986:136–7.
[21] Lane Fox 1986:66; they also condemned the theatre and the races.   [22] Lane Fox 1986:674.

virtually disappeared. There was little Byzantine statuary in Constantinople, Syria or Egypt.[23] The same was in effect true of the West. Sculpture lived on in other forms but not the statue. As in the case of flowers, rejection of paganism combined with earlier Judaic objections changed the face of European culture, of three-dimensional representation in Europe. There were of course some exceptions. But the stark contrast remains and it arose not so much from a loss of technique or the decline of the economy but rather from a deliberate rejection, the roots of which lie deeper than any one religion.

SACRIFICE

So, from the standpoint of the new church, classical gardens and their statuary were suspect. They were linked to acts of worship to other gods. Roman and Greek temples were hung with garlands at sacrifices, and so at times were private houses. These cult centres continued to be active until the time of Constantine, and the willingness to participate in their sacrifices was a critical distinction for both sides, pagan and Christian, becoming a matter not only for theology but for persecution. While offerings to the gods took a variety of forms, blood sacrifice remained central to most cults, despite the comments of philosophers and other critics: moreover, 'a sacrifice was the one recognized occasion for consuming meat in the diet of the Greek (but not the Roman) cultural area'.[24] In his attempt to revitalise the empire and give it a new stability, in AD 303 Diocletian issued an edict requiring sacrifices to be made to gods, state and emperor; both the nature of the offering and its recipients caused grave difficulties for followers of those religions, Christians, Jews and others too, who believed in one invisible God to whom prayer but not material objects should be offered.

As we have seen, ambivalences about the theory and practice of blood sacrifice were already present in classical society, and not among the moralists alone.[25] That was also the case in Judaism. Obedience to God's Commandments is better than sacrifice (1 Samuel, 15.22) and prophetic criticism was directed to the aspect of outward conformity that overlooked inner attitudes. In addition there was the outright rejection of sacrifice, by Judaism after the Destruction of the Second Temple in the year 70, by Christianity, and by Islam, at least in principle.[26] That rejection was of two kinds. Firstly, there were the offerings of the pagan which had to be avoided. While the consumption of sacrificial meat was held by pagan emperors to be a sign of

---

[23] There is a head of Theodora (?) from Ephesus, and a large statue of Justinian once stood in Constantinople. One problem is that we do not know how much existed before the destruction of the iconoclasts, but Grabar and Pelikan tend to play down that factor.   [24] Lane Fox 1986:70.

[25] Apollonius of Tyana also rejected animal sacrifice (Philostratus, *Life of Apollonius*, 1.31–2) and advocated vegetarianism (1.31). The Hermetists stressed mental sacrifice through praise and adoration and were much admired by the Christian Lactantius.

[26] 'It is not their flesh and blood that reaches God but the purity of your heart' (Qurʾan, Surah 22.38).

compliance, the Christians thought of it as internalising demons and involving the rejection of the faith. So when Christian emperors banned sacrifice, 'they were aiming at the living heart of pagans' cult acts'.[27] Secondly, neither blood sacrifice nor indeed other material offerings were to be made to the invisible God. Complex reasons were sometimes given for this rejection. Minucius Felix has Octavius ask if 'I should throw back to Him His own gift', a theme which is repeated in seventeenth-century poetry and one that obviously applies to all kinds of offerings to God – it is impossible to give anything to the giver, the creator, of all.[28] So part of the meaning of the notion of sacrifice was transferred to other objects and to other actions. Christ sacrificed himself for mankind, a reversal of the normal role of a god; and according to the Epistle to the Hebrews, the blood of bulls is contrasted with that of Christ, which far surpasses it:

Neither by the blood of goats and calves, but by his own blood he entered in once into the Holy place, having obtained eternal redemption for us. For if the blood of bulls and of goats, and the ashes of an heifer sprinkling the unclean, sanctifieth to the purifying of the flesh: How much more shall the blood of Christ . . .[29]

Meanwhile the early church divested the imagery and language of sacrifice 'from blood offerings for the demons to the Christians' own offerings of alms and first fruits to their bishop'.[30]

It is true that the notion of the sacrifice of the 'Lamb of God' was found among Christians in North Africa where the idea was inherited from Saturn–Ba'al worship. But the Donatist church continued this tradition only in a metaphorical way;[31] indeed, the practice of blood sacrifice was viciously denounced by authors such as Lactantius.[32] Nevertheless, the Donatist saw the modified sacrifice as saving both the victim and the sacrificer, whereas elsewhere the sacrifice and adoration of the Lamb of God was a metaphorical act of a different kind. Of course the rejection of blood sacrifice occurred in more radical forms in South and East Asia. A number of factors promoted this general development, both ideological[33] and socio-economic,[34] which related to the emergence of full-time religious specialists (priest and monks) and of a partly independent ecclesia which required offerings for its own maintenance rather than the communal meal shared among the congregation; indeed communion or eucharist now becomes symbolic in quite another way, although different for different Christian sects.

The discussion in the Acts of the Apostles about whether converts needed to be circumcised according to the Law of Moses agreed that the Gentiles should be dealt with differently. James suggested that they should impose no irksome

[27] Lane Fox 1986:67, 70, 72.   [28] Minucius Felix 1869:504 (cap.32).
[29] Hebrews 9.12–14.   [30] Lane Fox 1986:89.
[31] In the Near East in recent times, some Christian groups actually perform a blood sacrifice of the lamb at Easter time.
[32] Lactantius, *Divine Institutes*, VI.i.5.   [33] Goody 1986:13ff.   [34] Goody 1982:149.

restrictions on those who were turning to God, but 'write unto them that they abstain from pollution of idols, and from fornication, and from things strangled, and from blood'.[35] Blood was of course often polluted by idols, although this phrase has also been interpreted to refer to all ingestion of blood. But offerings of flowers too were endangered by such contact. According to St Augustine, the culmination of a month-long series of rites addressed to Libar, the god presiding over liquid seeds including semen, was when a matron placed a wreath on a penis.[36] Practices that included offerings to pagan deities whether of blood sacrifice, or of food or of garlands, were anathema to members of the new sect, whose invisible and omnipotent God required praise and adoration. Gifts were for his church, not for himself.

At the level of practice some immolations still persisted, some goods continued to be placed in tombs. Following an ancient custom, that close companion of man, his horse, was sometimes killed when he died. In Islam, and perhaps in Christianity, the notion existed that he could ride to paradise, as Ibn Fadlan writes of the Oguzians he visited about the year AD 920. Such a practice was reported from Germany as late as 1781, even though it had been condemned by Pope Gregory III and the rejection of the killing and consumption of the horse was, according to Grimm, the distinctive mark of those who had converted to Christianity.[37]

OTHER OFFERINGS

Flowers were only part of what was forbidden to the gods and to the dead. Equally condemned were other forms of offering. No animals were slaughtered, no food was offered to the gods. Pagan deities were automatically made irrelevant by conversion and to the God of the new dispensation one gave prayers not material gifts. Indeed, there was at first no material manifestation to whom offerings could be addressed. Early Fathers had emphasised the fundamental divergence between Christian worship paid to the invisible God and every form of idolatry paid to visible representations of deity.[38] It was the pagans, the Greeks, who were identified with the view that man was nothing more than 'the visible form of the body', a heathen notion of those who worship idols, whereas the Christian emphasised the rationality of the soul. 'The perception of the senses' (*aisthēsis*) was opposed to 'reason' (*logos*).[39] The pagans engaged in sensual worship which consisted 'in smelling the "fragrance" of incense or seeing the sight of the "blood or fat of sacrifice"'. The 'bloodless sacrifice' of the Christians did not depend on the senses.[40] In the words of John Chrysostom, theirs was 'a worship without

---

[35] Acts 15.20.   [36] St Augustine 1949:284–5.
[37] Letter written about 732, *MGH, Epistolae*, III, p.279; Salin 1959, text 290, p.483; Grimm 1844:625ff; McNeill and Gamer 1938:40; Salin 1959:27.   [38] Pelikan 1990:68.
[39] Athanasius, *Against the Heathen*, XXX.4, XXX.2, quoted by Pelikan 1990:104.
[40] Athenagoras, *Embassy for the Christians*, XIII.2, quoted by Pelikan 1990:104.

anything that is bodily or gross or entangled in the life of the senses'.[41] Even incense was excluded from early Christian worship as part of this denial, although aromatics had earlier played their part in Jewish ritual. Only in the early sixth century do we find references to its use in the Eastern church, to be followed much later in the West.[42]

The use of incense offers a prime example of the way that the rejection of the practice of 'others' was employed to define ritual identity. Widely used in China, India and the ancient Near East it was part of the culture of flowers, aromatics and perfumes in all the major civilisations. In ancient Israel it was reserved for Yahveh, and in Psalm 141 is likened to prayer, though its use for secular purposes is indicated in the Song of Songs (3.6). In Islam it is burnt in places of worship to create a pleasant odour but has no special significance. However, early Christian Fathers, Cyril of Alexandria and John Chrysostom, condemned its use because of the association with pagan practice, though Clement of Alexandria thought it could be included in ritual. Christians became identified by their refusal to offer incense to a statue of the emperor and some were martyred as a result. Those who compromised to escape death were known as *turificati*, burners of incense. Until the time of Constantine incense played no part in the public worship of the Christian church but by the ninth century it was being used in a number of churches, later to be more widely adopted in the East and then in the West.[43]

It was the treatment of the dead that was the real problem, since the dead, our dead, family as well as martyrs, are always with us. Conversion may change the form in which they are conceived and addressed but not their existence. To them the Romans had offered sacrifices and gifts, especially flowers, and had accompanied their departure with goods buried in the grave. Even with cremation, which was a common way of disposing of the dead, gifts and personal possessions would be placed on the funeral pyre, itself often garlanded, and the eyes of the deceased were opened so he could see his presents. Sacrifices took place in the very making of the grave, goods placed inside, and the tomb itself often decorated with roses.[44] In the Greek East the festival of roses, or Rosalia, was occasionally preferred as a way of honouring a dead man.[45]

Under Christianity all material offerings to the dead were forbidden, just as they were to divine beings. Taking food and drink to the graveyard was a sin, although the practice continued down the ages, as we learn from a number of sources.[46] To make such offerings was to treat the dead as if they could

---

[41] Chrysostom, *Homilies on Romans*, XX.2; Pelikan 1990:125.   [42] Pelikan 1990:109.
[43] Rahim 1987. For the rare word *turificatus* see Clarke 1986: III, 167.   [44] Toynbee 1971:50–2.
[45] Lane Fox 1986:39. The Rosalia is not very well testified in Rome, though it occurs.
[46] These sources are not all that plentiful. The early Irish penitentials (Bieler 1963) have little about 'pagan' practices, apart from condemning the belief in witches (*striga* and *lamia*, 'witch' and 'vampire'), the use of magic (*maleficium*) and apart from a passage in the 'Second Synod of St Patrick' on offerings to the dead (*de oblatione pro defunctis*) which asks: 'For he who did not in his life deserve to receive the sacrifice, how shall it

influence human affairs, whereas one should approach them only through God. Even the burying of grave goods with the body, whether to honour the deceased or to accompany him to the other world, was prohibited. Such goods gradually disappeared from cemeteries in Anglo-Saxon England in the seventh century, although for a time there was a period of overlap when the emblems of Christianity might be buried with the dead.[47] The practice that ensured the survival of the magnificent Anglo-Saxon treasures from the Sutton Hoo ship-burial, not to speak of the superb goods that graves have produced right across the old world from ancient China to ancient Egypt, gave way to the strict asceticism, the material emptiness, of the Christian tomb.[48] When flowers returned to the tomb, they were more acceptable than food, drink and grave goods, since they could be construed as decoration or a memorial, rather than as sacrifice, communal meal or 'ornament'.

Nevertheless, Christianity took its time to get a firm grip on Western Europe, at least in terms of funeral architecture and especially in rural areas. Early Christians had used the palm and garland as designs on their tombs in the catacombs, partly for concealment, partly for tradition and partly because not all of the early Fathers were equally strict in their prohibitions on icons and practices.[49] Elsewhere in Europe the process of Christianisation went more slowly. Gallo-Roman society was disrupted by the 'torrents' of AD 407 and 451 when major invasions occurred. That society may have been nominally Christian at the time but it was only with the conversion of the Franks that much changed in the course of 'a very gradual process'.[50] By the end of the seventh century grave goods disappeared, except in some princely burials and except for what was worn by the deceased.[51] While church-oriented burials occurred earlier, it was not until the eighth century that most burials took place in churchyards, 'as near as possible to the holy building, under the drops of water that fall from its roof – *sub stillicidio*'.[52] The churchyard was now the graveyard, which became holy ground in a very specific sense, subject to priestly supervision of the most direct kind. Nothing went on there without the approval of the church. Only with the Puritans of seventeenth-century New England were graveyards secularised once again and placed under municipal control.[53]

Offerings of food and drink were nevertheless difficult to eliminate entirely.

be able to help him after death?' (XII, 189). In these penitentials the sacrifice is to be understood as the host. Otherwise the punishments are predominantly for sexual behaviour (even child abuse), drunkenness, theft, bodily harm and the treatment of the host (for example, letting it be eaten by worms, taking it outside the church, etc.) The continental penitentials are more outspoken on magical activities. An eighth-century source lists thirty superstitions and pagan practices of which the first consists 'of sacrilege at the graves of the dead' (McNeill and Gamer 1938:419). The list makes clear the continuing fear of 'idols', offerings, fires, amulets, divination, etc.; there was a threatening pagan world out there which had to be kept at a distance.

[47] D. Wilson 1984:12.   [48] Bruce-Mitford 1972.
[49] Le Blant, *Inscriptions chrétiennes de la Gaule*, Paris, 1865:ii, 429.
[50] James 1988:128.   [51] Salin 1959:448, 453–4.
[52] Clovis was buried in a church in 511 and the aristocracy followed (James 1988:145). Salin 1959:455.
[53] Geddes 1976.

In the sixth century St Caesarius of Arles (c.470–542) protests at both Christians and pagans who take 'food and wine to the tombs of the dead, as if souls departed from the body had need of earthly sustenance . . . But those who claim they are offering a feast to those who they hold dear, devour it themselves; that which pleases their bellies they attribute to charity.'[54] The critique was characteristic, taking up the themes of earlier commentators, Christian and pagan. The new dispensation demanded that charity should be offered through the church. Nevertheless, some earlier practices persisted. In the region of Toulouse, feeding the dead as well as feasting and performing the *danse macabre* continued for a long time, despite the constant attacks of the church.[55] Not only the laity were involved in these transgressions. Around 748, St Boniface complains about sacrilegious priests who offer sacrifices of bulls and bones to pagan gods, the eating of which is followed by sexual orgies.[56]

The attempt to stamp out 'pagan' practices continued for many centuries, demonstrating that they had never been completely suppressed. The eleventh-century penitential of Burchard of Worms strictly forbids sacrifices to the dead, pagan funeral rites, wakes and feasts at the burial, as well as condemning drinking and merry-making. His questions about witchcraft and sorcery have a very African-sounding ring.[57] Even the use of herbs was seen as potentially dangerous since it involved magical beliefs, so that medicinal plants had to be gathered while reciting the Creed and the Pater Noster.[58] But the ritual shedding of blood was particularly worrying to the church since any such sacrifice was necessarily being offered to other gods.[59] The only blood to be shed in sacrifice was that of Christ himself, which was drunk in the mass, not even symbolically but substantially; the church became the locus of the 'communion', the sacrificial meal being elsewhere forbidden.

This attitude to offerings of all kinds to divinity and the dead is forcefully expressed by St Augustine in *The City of God*, a constant theme of which is the rejection of the sacrificial varieties. Who has heard, he asks, of any sacrifice to a martyr? 'Sacrifice', understood in a spiritual sense, is offered only to God. We can emulate the martyrs 'in winning like crowns [*coronae*] and palms'. Offerings to their shrines, however, are acceptable only when their aim is purely 'ornamental', when they 'are intended as acts of respect to their memory, and are not sacred objects or sacrificial offerings [*sacrificia*

---

[54] Migne, *Patrologia latina*, xxx.ix, App., Sermo 190, col. 2101; Salin 1959, text 296, p.486.

[55] Bordenave and Vialelle 1973, esp. p.257.

[56] Pope Zacharius, May 748? *MGH, Epistolae*, iii, p.358; Salin 1959, text 295, p.486.

[57] McNeill and Gamer 1938; Gurevich 1988:87. 'Hast thou observed funeral wakes, that is, been present at the watch over the corpses of the dead when the bodies of Christians are guarded by a ritual of the pagans; and hast thou sung diabolical songs there and performed dances . . . and hast thou drunk there and relaxed' (p.333). [58] McNeill and Gamer 1938:330, the Corrector of Burchard of Worms.

[59] Ingesting the blood of any animal was condemned. The prohibition seems to have weakened around the fifth century but became stronger in the sixth and seventh centuries when missionary activity began among the Germanic peoples (Gurevich 1988:239).

mortuorum] made to the dead as if they were gods'.[60] He describes a practice, 'not done by Christians of the better sort', whereby people bring food to the shrines of the dead, as at the Roman Parentalia and as had long been the custom of Africa. However, the intention and the treatment were different. They 'say a prayer when they have laid the food down by the shrine, and then take it away to eat it or to bestow some of it also upon the needy'. Apparently this custom was practised by Christians in North Africa for when Augustine's mother Monica first came from Carthage to Milan, she took food to the martyr's shrine, not knowing that it had been prohibited by St Ambrose. Augustine condemned such offerings, as did later writers, for 'we honour our martyrs neither with divine honours nor with human crimes . . . nor do we offer sacrifice'. Offerings are translated into charity, which is administered through the church for its own support and for the support of others. In this way what God has given directly is returned to him indirectly through his church.[61]

The absence of offerings, therefore, especially blood sacrifice, became a diacritical feature of Judaism and Christianity where it was linked to the absence of even abstract representations of God in Judaism. The objections to sacrifice and other offerings to God extended to the garlands that were given, to the gardens in which the flowers were grown and to the statues of gods who received them. For even gardens like the Forum contained the statues of satyrs which, according to Pliny, were 'dedicated as a charm against the sorcery of the envious'. As a result, items connected with sacrifice to pagan gods were looked upon with suspicion by Christians and the term 'sacrifice', like many others, was given a new interpretation. So too in a parallel way gardens below were sometimes exchanged for those above. Paulinus of Nola once declared that he had not abandoned Ebromagus, his estate in Aquitania, in order to cultivate a little garden; 'instead of my inheritance and my native city I have preferred the Garden of Paradise'.[62]

ASCETICISM AND LUXURY

For the ascetic, Christian paradise was to be found in the Elysian fields above, not in the royal garden below. A similar view is expressed in the course of the conversion by the Persian prophet, Mani, of a Mesopotamian prince who was a great gardener and opposed the Manicheans' rejection of working the soil and pruning plants and trees. One day Mani entered the prince's garden and

---

[60] St Augustine, *City of God*, VIII.xxvii.

[61] I have earlier argued (Goody 1983) that the retention of property by the church had an important effect on the whole kinship system, as it did upon the economy and the tenure of land. The thesis has been criticised as paying too much attention to material factors. In this chapter I have tried to bring out certain theological aspects.

[62] Paulinus, *Ep.*, 11.14. There is a later tradition that Paulinus passed himself off to a barbarian prince as a gardener, while Christ was also so described but in metaphor rather than in disguise.

was asked, 'In this Paradise you preach; will there be a garden as good as mine?' Whereupon the prince was given a tour of the gardens of paradise and became converted.[63] Mani's objections to gardens were related to a profound respect for plants and animals but in his strong opposition to hunting and to gardens there seems to have been a condemnation of the luxurious ways of the rich.[64] The potency of the appeal of such rejectionism should not be understated: Cyprian saw his conversion to Christianity as linked to his distaste for displays of rank and riches.[65]

These objections to luxury appear in the writings of many of the Fathers of the church, whose works were based not only on Holy Scripture but on classical moralists and satirists. In a book much read in the Renaissance, Clement of Alexandria condemns luxurious behaviour of all kinds in a manner that offered ample models for later puritans. He raised objections to the use of perfumes by women, to men removing their hair, to excessive eating and drinking. He rejected even baths which men, as distinct from women, could take only for reasons of health, not pleasure; hence they had to be taken cold. In his extensive catalogue of undesirable behaviour, he condemned not only the wearing of crowns but the picking of flowers:

It is good in springtime to linger in meadows soft and humid with dew, in the midst of fresh flowers of different species, drawing nourishment like the bees from their pure and natural scent; but the wise do not 'weave a floral chaplet from flowers gathered in the field' and take it back to the house; it is not done to cover the hair let down for pleasure with rosebuds, violets, lilies and other flowers, in robbing nature of her own.[66]

Flowers can be enjoyed with the eyes in worshipping God and not by making them an instrument of worship, for they soon fade and one has plundered nature for nothing. Crowns, which he claimed were not indigenous to the Greeks, are to be enjoyed metaphorically; in reality, they are dedicated to idols.[67] For this reason crowns are the main objects of his attack. Flowers and their perfumes are not in themselves harmful; they can be used as medicines and even, in certain cases, for wise and moderate relaxation. For flowers and aromatic plants are there to help us in need, not to lead us into ostentation and luxury. Enjoy the scent of flowers, he concludes, but do not use them for crowns.[68] In other words, the medicinal use and passive enjoyment of flowers is permissible; what is deplored is their use in festivals, for domestic pleasure or even for ritual and religion.[69]

Such criticisms of luxury were not confined to Christians for just as some

[63] Lane Fox 1986:566.
[64] The same asceticism did not always apply within the sect itself which produced lavishly illustrated manuscripts.   [65] Lane Fox 1986:15.
[66] Clement, *Paid.*, II.8, 70, 1–2.   [67] Clement, *Paid.*, II.8, 72, 2.   [68] Clement, *Paid.*, II.8, 76, 4–5.
[69] The rejection of crowns as luxury also appears in the work of Minucius Felix and of the Greek Senator Ambrose who condemns the lack of moderation in the festivals of the pagans (Lambert 1880:819–20).

earlier Roman writers criticised the displays of wealth, others the logic of sacrifice and killing, so festivals too were decried for their licence. In some of these festivals flowers played a prominent part, which led to their condemnation by early Christian writers. For the Roman festival of Floralia, the very goddess of flowers, had earlier included the spectacle of prostitutes undressing at the invitation of the spectators.[70] In this way flowers were associated with the fruits of fertility, with randy animals and with a public display of sexuality that provoked the censure of moralists and satirists such as Juvenal and Seneca, though defended equally strongly by Ovid and Martial.[71] It was a theme the Christians took up with vigour. The writer, Lactantius, converted to Christianity about AD 300, condemns Floralia, and in a curious piece of mythological deconstruction, of euhemeristic invention, argues that the celebration of the goddess of flowers was a deliberate attempt to cover up its impure origins associated with a girl of disrepute called 'Flower'. 'How great must that immortality be considered which even harlots attain? When Flora had gained great wealth through her prostitute's ways, she named the populace her heir and left a certain amount of money, from the annual interest of which her birthday was to be celebrated by the display of games which they called the Floralia.' In order to conceal the shameful origin of the festival, he claimed, the Senate decided to add dignity by associating the celebrations more closely with the name itself. But wantonness still reigns. 'For, beside the license of words with which every obscenity is poured forth, the harlots also take off their garments at the insistence of the people.'[72] Flowers, and their festival, were associated not only with offerings to the wrong gods but with immoral behaviour that was encouraged by their own divinity. It was a story that was revived in the seventeenth century by the Puritans of Old and New England in their objections to the rites of May. Indeed, both the attack on festivals and their defence resemble the later controversies of that period.

THE ROSE

The opposition to offerings, to pagan rites and to luxury meant that, while some allowances were made and some liberties taken, huge inroads were created in the culture of flowers. The use of crowns and garlands in particular came under pressure. And what happened with garlands also happened with that flower of flowers, the rose. Writing on its history, Joret remarks: 'Its culture, which had been so developed throughout the Roman empire, if not abandoned altogether, was neglected because of continual wars.'[73] But not

---

[70] Hild 1896:1191.
[71] Martial, preface to *Epigrams*; Ovid, *Fast.*, IV.945, V.331, 352; Seneca, *Ep.*, 97; Juvenal, Satire VI.250, XIV.262.
[72] Lactantius, *Divine Institutes*, I.xx.5; Prudentius, *Contra symmach.*, 1.266.   [73] Joret 1892:141.

wars alone. Christian writers condemned the role played by that flower.[74] For them the rose was in disfavour because of its connection with Venus. Only gradually did it make its appearance in Christian iconography.[75] Clement of Alexandria (150–211/15) forbade the use of crowns of flowers, especially singling out those of roses and lilies,[76] while Prudentius (348–c.405), the Spanish poet whose work was so influential later in the Middle Ages, boasted of using neither roses nor aromatic plants.

> Hic mihi rosae spolia,
> Nullus aromate fragrat odor.
> Here no plunder of the rose,
> No scent of spice smells in my nostrils.[77]

He praises Eulalia for despising crowns of roses, ornaments of amber and necklaces of gold.[78] Even bridal wreaths at weddings were repudiated by some because of their connections with pagan feasts.[79] At the beginning nuptial crowns too were absent.[80]

So the rose suffered a partial eclipse because in Rome it had become 'a symbol of voluptuousness and debauchery', although it was commonly used at funerals.[81] Even in that context the flower was not immune from criticism as an extravagance, a waste of resources which could be better employed. Jerome drew a contrast between the violets (*violas*), roses and lilies that other husbands place upon the urns of their wives, and the works of charity by which Pammachius honoured the memory of Paulina.[82] The moral was clear. Give to others, through the church, rather than incur such wasteful expenditure. While Clement is not altogether set against the employment of flowers, they should be used only for needs, not misused as luxuries; since needs have to do with health, it is their medicinal uses that were to be encouraged.[83] Flowers can be enjoyed outside in a meadow, but to wear garlands indoors is not done by 'men of good sense'.[84] The crown of flowers was thus seen as unnatural, a luxury, but above all identified with idols and not to be brought into the house.

On the other hand, flowers that were rejected as the means of influencing the dead or the divinity could become acceptable as decorations. Intentions count and there is a shift, as it were, from meaning to design. So some allowance was made, on the more moderate wing of early Christianity, for the use of flowers in secular life and for other decorative purposes. Augustine quotes Christ's speech on the lilies of the field, as well as referring to the words

---

[74] 'The coming of Christianity dethroned the rose' (Coats 1970:163).   [75] Haig 1913:71.
[76] *Paid.*, II.8.78.   [77] Prudentius, The Daily Round, *Cathemerinon, Hymnus ante cibum*, 21–2.
[78] Prudentius, Crowns of Martyrdom, *Peristephanon, Hymnus in honorem Eulalia*, 21–2.
[79] Lambert 1880:812.   [80] Baus 1940:99, referring to Schrijnen 1911:316.   [81] D'Andrea 1982:72.
[82] *Epistola ad Pammachium*, Letters LXVI.5 and LXXVII.10. (Migne, *Patrologia latina*, XXII, cols. 641, 697).
[83] *Paid.*, II.8.76.   [84] *Paid.*, II.8.70.

of the Neoplatonist, Plotinus, in which 'the beauty that is seen in tiny flowers and in leaves' comes under 'the mighty hand of God's providence'.[85] Such sentiments provide for the use of flowers not as a substitute for the sacrifice of animals and the offering of food and drink, but as a totally different kind of prestation, one that decorates and shows respect, not on the model of a gift to the dead but as a gift for the dead, a 'true' gift, expecting no return. Or better: they were a decoration rather than an offering or ornament, for decorations did not carry meaning, at least in the same specific sense, while ornament, in the ecclesiastical context, refers to accessories essential to the ritual.

The practice of putting flowers on the tomb had at first been condemned by St Jerome, St Ambrose and others. But there was ambivalence as well as disagreement; the practices of the saints did not always tally with their words and a tendency to memorialise the dead with flowers emerged. In a letter to Heliodorus, St Jerome refers to the practice but metaphorically, the sprinkling of flowers of eloquence over the tomb of Nepotian.[86] On a more concrete level, Prudentius advises the young to gather violets and saffron for the altar of St Eulalia, who had despised crowns of roses, after her martyrdom:

> We shall care for the entombed bones
> With violets and green leaves in plenty,
> And with perfumed essence sprinkle
> The cold stones that bear the epitaph.[87]

Like St Augustine, who also testified to their presence, they were both against the use of flowers in other contexts.[88] The same was true of incense. While perfume for humans was wasteful luxury, and women who used it displayed an 'extreme vulgarity', Clement of Alexandria thought the use of incense permissible in worship because its meaning had quite changed; it was no longer a sacrifice but 'the acceptable gift of love'.[89] So too with flowers. In the sixth century a poem by Fortunatus, bishop of Poitiers, sang the glories of spring flowers, especially when used to decorate the churches: 'Then do men decorate their doors and houses with flowers, and women adorn themselves with sweet roses. But you, not for yourselves, but for Christ, gather these first fruits; and you bear them to the churches, and wreathe the altars with them till

---

[85] Matthew 6.28–30.
[86] 'Super tumulum eius Epitaphi huius Flores spargare . . .', *Epistola*, LX, 'Ad heliodorum, epitaphium nepotiani'. Migne, *Patrologia latina*, XXII.331 (p.590).
[87] *Cathemerinon*, x, Hymnis circa exequias defuncti, v.169–72, Migne, *Pat. lat.*, 59, 363–4 (p.888). *The Poems of Prudentius* 1962:77, The Hymns, 10, 169–72.
[88] For an earlier discussion of the Christian uses of flowers, which I encountered only after having written this chapter, see Lambert 1880.
[89] On the rejection of perfume (and coloured wools) see Clement, *Paid.*, II.8.65, referring to Plato's *Republic*, II.37A: 'There are women who always exude extreme vulgarity; they keep scenting and sprinkling their bed covers and their houses, and in their daintiness, stop short only of making their chamber-pots fragrant with myrrh' (64). 'If any one object that the great High Priest, the Lord, offers up to God incense of sweet odor, let this not be understood as the sacrifice and good odor of incense, but as the acceptable gift of love.' (*Paid.*, II.8.67).

they glow with colour.'[90] The emphases of individual churchmen differed; some were themselves ambivalent; a number found a solution in metaphor. But little contributed to a flourishing culture of flowers.

ART AND AUSTERITY

Similar problems of rejection and attraction of the Roman 'pagan' model occur in literature and art. Some early Christian writers, including those who attacked Ambrose, deliberately avoided quoting from classical authors.[91] Others followed the tradition of adapting the words of poets such as Virgil to Christian thought, a mode that became dominant after the fourth century. After the initial criticisms there were certainly fewer references to flowers although there was a greater continuity in literature than in art, perhaps because of the continuing relevance of floral metaphor. However, in art there was a wider problem affecting visual representation as a whole, especially three-dimensional but also in two dimensions, and especially religious but also secular.

There was one obvious problem with existing religious art, as with classical authors, namely the pagan origins. It was essential to set aside such practices, the idols Gregory finds, 'fashioned out of the creatures of the woodlands and the waters, out of birds and beasts' or that his uncle Gallus destroyed at Cologne, narrowly escaping with his life.[92] But another important strain in early Christianity went further and condemned the creation and worship of all divine images, not simply pagan ones, for theological reasons.[93] That this element was not always dominant and gradually lost out in the Orthodox and Catholic churches is true. Two-dimensional images of Christ appear in the late antique art of both the West and the East, often taking the place of the emperor in ceremonies such as *adventus*, in the Bassus sarcophagus of the late fourth century, the Barberini diptych of the fifth and the Ravenna mosaics of the sixth.[94] That imperial ceremony made use of floral decorations. In 311, when Constantine arrived at Autun, the streets leading to the palace were decorated. Nevertheless, the trappings of the *adventus* were rejected by other Christian writers as being inappropriate for the new religion;[95] there was always some explicit tension.

---

[90] Lambert 1880:810; *Venantii Fortunati*, misc. Lib. vii. Caput XII. Migne, *Patrologiae cursus completus*, CXXXVIII.267, Ad eamdem de floribus super altare. Fortunatus also sends a poem (p.286) to Queen Radegund with a floral offering (Caput XI, de violis). See also Fortunatus, *Carm.*, VIII.7; Van Dam 1985:292.

[91] Ambrose, *de Fide*, III.i.3, Migne, *Patrologia latina*, XVI.427 (pp.589–90).

[92] Gregory, LH II.10; *Life of the Fathers*, VI.2.

[93] In Anglo-Saxon art there was no consistently competent representation of the human figure until the tenth century, which D. M. Wilson sees as a possible trace of 'a pagan taboo against the naturalistic representation of the human form' (1984:27). I do not know of any other evidence of such a taboo except in the Judaic and other Semitic traditions, although implicit doubts about human attempts to recreate the creation are found more widely.

[94] MacCormack 1981; Baus 1940, Plates 8–10, 13.   [95] MacCormack 1981:28, 24.

The North African tradition of Roman mosaics, which flourished between the second and fourth centuries AD, continued on the floors of Christian churches, although compared with its predecessors, the impression is of 'iconographic poverty'.[96] The great episcopal churches are paved with geometric or floral patterns. Part of this iconographic poverty was due to a reluctance to place on the floor anything which might be regarded as a sacred 'image', a widespread prohibition throughout the empire.[97] Especially in the early period before the Vandal conquest, the decoration of the basilicas was restrained; it became more adventurous after the Byzantine reconquest, as in the nave of the great Justianic basilica at Sabratha. The East was definitely richer in images than the West. There the symbolic tradition largely takes over from earlier North African realism. The main feeling was at first 'still that of a rich and flowering paradise', but it is subjected to an organisation which becomes 'more formalized and decorative with the passing of time'.

Nevertheless, for the first two centuries, according to the historian of art, Grabar, Christianity was aniconic, traditionally so, like the Jews.[98] It began to provide itself with an iconography in the first half of the third century, beginning with the catacombs of Rome for funerary purposes. In the earliest period, before Christians could freely practise their faith, their art inevitably tended to make use of classical themes, endowing them with a concealed Christian meaning. Backgrounds of foliage, birds and flowers set in architectural frames were copied by artists and suggested the Christian soul in the gardens of paradise.[99] In this case existing symbolism was given added rather than alternative meanings, providing a necessary ambiguity under the persecutions; for example, the palm was an emblem of victory offered to a martyr who died but triumphed 'as an athlete of God',[100] while Bacchus and the vine leaves represented the wine of the eucharist. With the coming of official Christianity, meanings no longer had to be *double entendres* in the same way; on the other hand, some classical themes continued to be employed by rich Romans, as in the mosaic roof of the church of Santa Costanza at Rome (c.358) which includes foliage patterns with putti working in vineyards.

The reign of Septimius Severus (193–211) also saw the emergence of a Jewish and Christian iconography on the walls of places of worship in Dura-Europos on the Euphrates frontier between the Roman empire and Persia. Shortly afterwards the sect newly founded by Mani expressly utilised images in the process of conversion, including images of God and of the prophet himself.[101] These developments of the use of images for cult purposes appear to be interrelated, for this centre was marked by the worship of Roman, Greek, Semitic and Persian deities. The walls of the Mithraeum and the

---

[96] Dunbabin 1978:188.   [97] Dunbabin 1978:189, 193.
[98] Grabar 1968:23ff.   [99] Stokstad 1986:11.   [100] Stokstad 1986:12.
[101] Four centuries later St Augustine used images of the Last Judgement in his efforts to convert the English. That is only the second reported use. The existing examples of Manichean images are much later in date and were made for a manuscript written in Turkistan 'showing strong Chinese influence' (Grabar 1968:28).

temple of Bel were covered in wall-paintings of Persian inspiration; that was also true of the Jewish synagogue and the Christian baptistery, which have been described as 'oriental forerunners of Byzantine painting'. For the content was clearly influenced by the Orient, just as the introduction of the paintings was probably a question of conforming to local custom, which was very different from the continuing Greek artistic tradition of a city like Antioch. Indeed, the members of the Dura congregation may have been making a conscious decision between '"graven images", statues and cult images that were regarded as embodiments of the deity and actually worshipped, and paintings which conveyed messages of Jewish unity and redemption'.[102]

As Eastern Christianity became hellenised in the second and third centuries AD, it adopted some representational art.[103] Small sculptures illustrating the Jonah story have also been found from the mid to late third century. All the earliest Christian images, which appeared about AD 200, Grabar calls pictorial signs; the majority of these relate to situations of divine intervention and are often associated with the desire for eternal life.[104] The edicts of tolerance issued by Constantine appear to be followed by a period of minimal figuration. There is strikingly little religious iconography at a time when one might have expected a great expansion. The emperor was not averse to secular art, including representations of himself. On the other hand, in the context of religion he adopted the letters chi-rho on the imperial standard as a sign of Christ, but no images. Indeed, it has been suggested that 'Having broken with idolatry, Constantine could easily have wished to dissociate representational images from the religion of Christ.'[105] Even when the Roman empire became officially Christian in the fourth century, some of its leading members continued to be apprehensive about the arts. 'Only the practical value of art as an instrument of instruction and the inherited taste for monumental commemoration gave license for images that would otherwise have been considered too worldly, too ostentatious, and too reminiscent of pagan idolatry. Sculpture in the round was particularly vulnerable to the charge of idol worship, since it encouraged association with the gods of the pagan world.'[106] But more than that – it was too 'representational', too close to reality. This disappearance of statuary, which in classical times was largely nude, may have been reinforced by the ambivalences that Christian writers had about the human body, what le Goff has called 'la déroute doctrinale du corporel' of the Middle Ages.[107] But it was also close to idols and associated with pagans. The same objections did not always apply to two-dimensional forms like mosaics and paintings or not fully three-dimensional ones, like reliefs. Nevertheless, there was an undercurrent of thinking that, looking back to the Mosaic Law and sideways to pagan practice, condemned all iconic activity. That activity continued, but so too did the protests.

---

[102] Matheson 1982:26–7.   [103] For an authoritative account, see Grabar 1968.   [104] Grabar 1968:10.
[105] Grabar 1968:38.   [106] Stokstad 1986:23..   [107] Brown 1988; Le Goff 1985:123.

So while the Eastern tradition of iconography soon revived, this move did not go unchecked. Towards the middle of the fourth century, the church historian Eusebius of Caesarea (c.264–340) associated statues with the ways of the Gentiles who pay them honour indiscriminately.[108] Preference was given to small-scale portable objects since icons could not be placed in the sanctuary. Epiphanius of Salamis tore down an image painted on a curtain, considering it to be idolatrous.[109] The rejection was not absolute, even of religious images; but none were to enter the temple, at least in three-dimensional form. The two-dimensional varieties did appear, not for worship but for instruction. In the East there were the Byzantine icons; in North Africa mosaics; in the West, frescos. In the fifth century Bishop Perpetuus had the walls of the church of St Martin at Tours covered in frescos showing the saint's miracles.[110] That was for educational purposes.

Aside from the aniconic trends, there was the denial of worldly goods as well as the austerity of actual poverty which encouraged the rejection of art and monumental architecture, as distinct from the construction of places of worship, by segments of the Christian community.[111] For whatever reasons, confessional or economic, a similar transformation took place in Anatolia in the architecture of tombs. 'The tender solicitude for the family grave, and for the perpetuation in death of the ties of kinship, which the third-century Christian shared with his pagan neighbour, made way in the sixth century for that 'nudité redoutable du dernier jour'.[112] Such changes were not inconsistent with what was happening in the kinship system and the partial substitution of 'spiritual' for consanguinal kin. But the artistic consequences of this renunciation were devastating.

As we have seen, at one level this asceticism was theological, philosophical, intellectual, related to contradictions in the logic of sacrifice as an offering and to the aversion to the spilling of blood that has been felt in many societies. So too the rejection of images of the deity embodied a different, variant view of the supernatural which meant that it could not be expressed, encapsulated, represented, in material form; the word, the concept, could not be made flesh, given an objective correlative, a physical counterpart. Alternatively, representations are created but restricted; images are excluded from the sanctuary, are two-dimensional or in relief, or they are permitted only for secondary figures. The more radical notion is found among other new or reforming religions before they become 'corrupted' by the world. Early Buddhist sculpture never represented the figure of the Buddha but rather an earlier incarnation, a Bodhisattva.[113] While the contrasts between the early and late phases of Christianity, Buddhism, and to a lesser extent Judaism and Islam, are of the utmost importance from the standpoint of the graphic and plastic arts, these

[108] Eusebius, *Historiae ecclesiasticae VII*, 18, see Migne, *Patrologia graeca*, xx.680.
[109] Weitzmann 1987:3–4.   [110] Van Dam 1985:137.   [111] Stokstad 1986:9.
[112] Calder 1920:55.   [113] Dutt 1962:189.

phases are perhaps less distinct conceptually than might appear. Even in the earlier stages, God is never entirely immaterial, being there in sign and symbol, and as wind, ghost or spirit; equally, even in the later phases, he is never entirely incarnate. Nor could he be, at least in mankind's conception. There is always ambivalence, which as Gilbert Lewis points out in a sensitive essay, opens the way for scepticism as well as for belief.[114] The return of aniconic tendencies was always a possibility given these ambivalences, and given the context of Holy Writ itself.

There were other interesting consequences of this aniconic approach. Because of the virtual absence of standardised images, visionaries claimed to see Christ and other figures in a variety of forms, as child, youth and in middle age.[115] There was nothing like the elaborate religious art of Greece, which has been held to account for the contrast with the Jewish way of conceiving divinity, the former seeing divine beauty as visual and harmonious, the latter as experienced through sound, voice and the effects of light and colour. According to the Jews, God could never be comprehended by mortal eyes, only through the scriptures; so too the Christians and Muslims focused on the text, on the word of God. While writing could in principle have provided a detailed description of the supernatural, the text worked instead through similes and symbols, by implications and even by avoidance.

Part of the problem was that, like any new sect, Christianity at first lacked an architecture and an art of its own, especially of its own prophets or divinities. Some representations of Jesus appeared on sarcophagi around the year AD 200. One group of marginal Christians owned portraits of Christ.[116] But the bishops were against representational art and others were suspicious of it. In the apocryphal Acts of the apostle John, a Greek text from Asia Minor attributed to the second century or later, a disciple of John secretly arranged for a painter to paint his master's portrait. This he placed in his bedroom and crowned it with flowers, setting before it candles and an altar. John condemned the disciple, thinking he was still living 'in heathen fashion', but when he learned it was a portrait of himself, he condemned its inadequacy as a 'fleshly image'.[117]

As with the Jews, this rejection was explicitly theological and at the same time a rejection of the beliefs of others, as were various ritual changes such as the colour of mourning garments[118] and the timing of the sabbath.[119] But there were two other important elements, which have emerged as sub-themes of this discussion. In Germanic Europe the third of a man's property that had gone into the grave ('the soul's third') was now claimed as God's part, Christ's part, which was to come under the church's care.[120] It was this third which, together

---

[114] Lewis 1986.   [115] Lane Fox 1987:397.
[116] They were from the distant Persian town of Dura-Europos where there were even wall paintings in the synagogue (Lane Fox 1987:318). See pp.92–3   [117] Grabar 1968:66–7.   [118] Goody 1962:58.
[119] In the second century Christian writers recognised the Sabbath as the day following the Jewish celebrations.
[120] Goody 1983.

with other transfers over the few centuries following the conversion of Constantine, enabled the church to gain so strong a position in European society, constructing vast buildings of great beauty and owning lands of immense extent. So rapid a growth could only be assisted by the abandonment of gifts to the dead and indeed to the divinities themselves. Gifts were no less welcome but they had to be mediated by the church and its priesthood, to whose support they were so necessary. It was they who were now the recipients of 'sacrifice', not in this case the sacrifice of Jesus but the sacrifice of the congregation in the form of offerings, part of which was also channelled to the needy.[121]

The second theme is one implicit in Gregory's denunciation of idols 'fashioned out of the creatures of the woodlands'. That theme has nothing directly to do with the rejection of paganism nor yet with the use of religious icons but with the creation of any representation of natural creatures. At this juncture, aniconic tendencies affect very much the culture of flowers, since they render impossible any of the fine secular painting that we find at Pompeii and, in the extreme, any of the representations that are so valuable for botanical purposes. Such traditions take a long time to recover and it is characteristic that when icons do appear, it is in the religious rather than the secular sphere, more concerned with the life of saints and the Biblical story than with the life of plants, especially flowers.

EFFECTS ON BOTANICAL KNOWLEDGE

The decline of the culture of flowers in the West was associated with Christianity's desire to set aside other religions, to limit luxury and to encourage charity, as well as to follow the injunctions of the Old Testament and to adopt a different view of divinity and how it should be approached. It was also linked to the invasions of the barbarians in the West, who became in time the mainstay of Western Christianity. But Asia suffered from constant invasions by similar groups of nomads from the steppes and from the deserts which did not have the same effects on the culture of flowers. That can most clearly be seen in developments in the study of plants itself. In summarising the history of botany, Joseph Needham concludes: 'as so often before . . . that in China there was a slow and rather steady growth in knowledge about plants, with no Dark Age at all'.[122] The foundations of botany, he argues, were laid in Greece and China at roughly the same time. But in the West the great achievements of Aristotle's pupil Theophrastus of Eresus (371–287 BC)

---

[121] A contemporary leaflet of the Mariannhill Fathers of Dearborn, Michigan, asks Catholics to remember poor souls in Purgatory during November. 'So . . . pray . . . do penance . . . make sacrifice [usually in almsgiving].' On receipt of a 'sacrificial offering' the Fathers will pray for the dead friends; the offering is 'my personal sacrifice'. This redefined notion of 'sacrifice' is closely linked to the giving of alms to or through the church.

[122] Needham 1986:xxv.

had no real successor for sixteen centuries. Not only that, but knowledge actually fell away, so that while the Peripatetic's list of plants ran to six hundred, in the twelfth century the number described had dropped to seventy-seven, to rise very steeply at the end of the fifteenth century.[123] As with gardens, garlands and roses, botany itself suffered a drastic decline, partly as the result of invasion and hardship, but partly with the rise of Christianity and the diversion of the written tradition for religious ends. It is some indication of the state of knowledge in medieval Europe that Dioscorides' work of the first century AD, which divided plants into culinary, aromatic and medicinal, and was the first treatise to be illustrated, remained crucial to medical botany in Europe for the next fifteen hundred years. Its illustrations, like its information, were passed down as the received truth.[124]

This stationary quality of knowledge is not altogether unusual, especially in manuscript cultures, those of the hand rather than the machine. One of the problems about knowledge in such cultures is that, following oral precedents, there is a tendency to merge the processes of reproduction and accumulation, the distinction between the role of copyist and that of author. Sacred texts have to be copied exactly by individuals and any subsequent additions have to take the form of commentaries which are necessarily of an inferior status. But other texts too have to be copied word for word by hand, if they are to be circulated or even preserved. In this process there is no room for improvement; the job of the 'writer' is to repeat, so that even non-sacred texts may take on something of the quality of the sacred or the ritual. The process by which any text is to be preserved and transmitted by being constantly copied by the hand of a 'writer' is highly conservative. The text of Dioscorides continued to be reproduced in this manner over a very long period of time because there was no alternative available. The failure to improve the illustration was part of this repetitive tendency of manuscript cultures, which in the context of botany resulted in copying the master-work rather than observing nature itself. Only printing, mechanical reproduction, made clear the differences in role between 'writing' and writing, that is, between copying and composing, in effect by virtually eliminating the 'copywriter' as far as scientific or literary works were concerned.

ROME AND THE WESTERN PERIPHERY OF EUROPE

Two currents that came from Rome affected the culture of flowers in Western Europe in very different ways. Firstly, as part of their cultural baggage, the Southern invaders of Celtic and Germanic Europe brought with them many of their preferred plants and foods. In this way the Romans transformed the

---

[123] Needham 1986:2–4.
[124] *De materia medica* is known from a Byzantine copy in Vienna, dated about AD 512 and illustrated with coloured pictures probably taken from a yet earlier work by Crateuas.

nature of British horticulture and gardening. The list of cultivated plants introduced, domesticated or established by the invaders gives some idea of life before and after; these included the vine, mulberry (*Morus nigra*), walnut, fig, plum, damson, cherry, almond, Italian stone-pine, olive, Spanish (or sweet) chestnut, mustard (white), radish, dill, parsley, fennel, coriander, opium poppy, pea, turnip, pear, cucumber, cabbage, carrot, celery, strawberry, raspberry, blackberry and apple. Of these, the last seven items existed before the coming of the Romans, but probably only as wild species.[125] The imports consisted not so much of flowers as of flowering fruits and other foods, including herbs which greatly widened the range of the local diet by acclimatising cultigens from the Mediterranean, many themselves acquired from further east, to the harsher weather of more northerly Europe. They represented the extension of central aspects of Mediterranean horticulture into the periphery.

The barbarians followed, so too did Christianity with its prohibitions and exhortations. It further diffused a system of writing (Roman) together with a language of the written word (Latin) which gave the periphery access to wider sources of knowledge than the local society provided. The food plants were accepted, including the vine required for cultic as well as for secular purposes. But the 'barbarians' on the one hand and a reforming religion on the other pushed the culture of flowers into the background. Of course some use was undoubtedly made of flowers both before and after the coming of the Romans. What disappeared from the repertoire was the kind of 'higher' cultural activity that we have seen developing in Mediterranean societies that were stratified in complex ways, economically, politically, religiously, intellectually. For these cultures of antiquity were far from homogeneous, so that different segments of the population did different things with flowers, giving them different meanings in the process. That 'higher' culture was sorely afflicted by the coming of a religion that rejected the idea of offering material gifts to God, whether of flowers or of other more tendentious objects, rather than to his church, which rapidly became a wealthy competitor.[126] In particular, as we have seen, it was the use of crowns and garlands to which objection was made and the prohibition on such behaviour reached out from religious to secular use. In the pre-Christian world, the sacrificer, the gods and the animal sacrifices themselves were all garlanded. The first Christians, according to Blondel, 'rejected with horror the pagan use of crowns, as if they feared these profane ornaments would dishonour the brows that had been sanctified by baptism'.[127] At the same time, there was a specific reason why early Christians should be disturbed by the use of crowns and that was the obvious opposition between the crown of roses and the crown of thorns. Roses and thorns may in some sense have stood for pagan and Christian, but

---

[125] Cunliffe 1981:98–9.   [126] Van Dam 1985.   [127] Blondel 1876:94.

both belonged to the same plant, and one is inconceivable without the other. Gradually, through the course of the Middle Ages, Europe experienced a revival of the garden and the garland, as well as of botany and of gardening.

This opposition between Christian and pagan ideas and practices followed along the same lines as the earlier one between Hebrew and pagan; it referred back to the same sacred text which discouraged not only material offerings to God but any representations of him, and in the extreme form any image of any part of his creation. That prohibition profoundly affected the practice and conceptualisation of art. We have seen that the question of images was not simply one of rejecting neighbouring religions but of reformulating religious thought about the nature of divinity and the act of creation. The attempt to prohibit graphic representations of God and his creatures left little room for the artist to work, except in abstract, formal or geometric terms. Even flowers were largely excluded. It was not visually but in words that God became incarnate, in conformity with the devotion to the book that marked Judaism, Christianity and Islam. Reading the works of the early Christian Fathers, as well as reading the Talmud and the Ḥadīth, one is struck by the great stress on the book, the continual reference to the scriptures, the pulling apart of every passage, in other words, both by the sacredness of the text and by the analytic scrutiny it was given. 'In the beginning was the Word', not only of God but of his prophets, his disciples and their commentators. Hence the importance of the written word even in Britain, the western periphery of Eurasia.

The objection to the use of flowers had been quite specific, at least from many of the Fathers of the church. While their use may well have continued at a popular level, in art and literature their absence must also be seen as part of a more general attitude towards nature, the *contemptus mundi* of the monastic view, which influenced the world at large. Nature was subordinate to the divine, and even to man himself. Not until the later Middle Ages do we find any profound or extensive appreciation of landscape in the arts.[128]

The effect of Christianity on man's view of nature was not limited to a hesitation about flowers and garlands. The world itself had to be seen and understood in spiritual terms that in principle excluded the secular; in the arts, above all in the visual arts, nature was to be interpreted in a 'symbolic' rather than a naturalistic fashion. That of course was at a level of 'higher learning' which affected but did not always control more popular practices and beliefs. Even at the level of higher learning a more secular view gradually established itself, although largely in opposition to the religious. The revival of Latin meant reading classical texts; but selectively. Even on the threshold of the growth of the universities out of the earlier schools, a Provincial Council of Paris in 1210 forbade reading or teaching Aristotle's books on natural science

---

[128] Pearsall and Salter 1973.

under pain of excommunication.[129] That incident reflects the distance that secular learning in Europe had to travel, even after fifteen hundred years.

It was a similar story with the arts, with all of which, save perhaps architecture itself which was needed for the construction of churches, Christianity displayed ambiguous relations. Music was seen by some as distracting attention from the words of the service and from worship itself. Even when the use of music in the form of plain chant borrowed from the synagogue was established in the sixth century, it was justified as an enhancement of the audibility and meaning of the words. So too with the visual arts. Even when icons were permitted, the realism of Roman painting and sculpture was deliberately abandoned in favour of more abstract, spiritual forms borrowed from Eastern art, and vigorously taken up in Ireland. At the same time, there were pressures to use painting, frescos, illuminations and mosaics as the books of the illiterate, as means of instruction that concentrated on the person of Christ in majesty, the Virgin and the apostles. There was some representation of Biblical scenery, though very rarely with anything that can be seen as approaching a realistic landscape. That was the Romanesque style which changed only with the coming of the Gothic. It was the same with drama. In the later empire that had degenerated into mimetic and athletic *ludi* which were associated with the mocking and suffering of Christians and strongly condemned by Fathers from St Chrysostom to St Augustine and St Jerome. The barbarian invaders of the sixth century did away with what the Fathers had been unable to stop. Only in the course of the eleventh and twelfth centuries did 'Christian society [feel] ready . . . to approach dramatic art as a teaching instrument in the service of the faith.'[130] By the end of the twelfth dramatic art had established itself again throughout Christendom.

The return of the rose, the development of botany, the rebirth of naturalistic painting, the acceptance of three-dimensional sculpture, these were aspects of a long, slow and much debated process; the closer it touched upon religion, the lengthier it became. In this return, the Muslim East played an important part, for the contrast with the West in terms of culture of flowers was enormous, not in representations (for Islam followed the Biblical tenets) but in use and in literary reference.

---

[129] Southern 1953:220; Pearsall and Salter 1973.   [130] Wickham 1987:23.

4 · Flowers without representation in Islam

At the time of the decline of Rome and the rise of Christianity, the Near East did not suffer the same setbacks as Europe, either politically or economically. Attacks from outside, economic and urban decay within, were less marked than in the West. The material conditions for a culture of flowers were not threatened in the same way, at least until the time of the Arab invasions.

At the same time Eastern Christianity was less harsh on representations, and, as we have seen, an iconic tradition, with some Persian influences, already manifested itself in the third century in the wall paintings of Dura-Europos, found in the Jewish synagogue as well as in the Christian baptistery. Nevertheless, prohibitions against images were embodied in the Holy Book that was common not only to Judaism and Christianity but to Islam, which expanded from Arabia to become dominant in virtually the whole area after the seventh century. Indeed, Islam was stricter about the enforcement of the ban on images, both sacred and secular, criticising the others for their lapses, so that there was little room for the development of any iconography, especially representations of nature, of God's creation. But on the level of gardens and the growing of flowers, the situation was very different from the West. Despite some falling away in the economic life of the Near East that took place at the time of the Arab invasions and which led to some initial neglect of the irrigation canals and terraces, there was not the parallel loss of knowledge that occurred in the West. On the contrary, Islam constituted one of the major channels by which classical learning returned to Europe, for Arabic scholars had translated many texts partly in the search for what they considered profitable information.[1] After the Sāsānian empire of Persia had been defeated by the Arab armies in AD 636/7, the ʿAbbāsid caliphate was eventually established in Baghdad in 750, leading to the growth of Persian influence in the Islamic world. Translations were made of works of Indian provenance as well as others from Byzantium. Islamic civilisation was essentially formed in that city in the eighth and ninth centuries. When the invading Arabs with their reforming religion adopted Iranian culture, including that of the court, they maintained more of the achievements of their

---

[1] Burkhill 1965:2.

predecessors than Christians did in the West. This is clear from the continuity of the culture of flowers. Even though they were yet stricter about religious icons and the representation of natural objects, the practice of gardening did not fall into desuetude, as we see from the splendid Moorish gardens of southern Spain.[2] Flowers continued to be cultivated and used in secular life. Despite the attachment of Islam to the aniconic traditions of Israel, the ban on images did not adversely affect practice. As a conquering as well as a missionising power, Islam did not see itself as opposed to a surrounding pagan culture in quite the same way as early Christianity or Judaism. It was not in the same position of political inferiority. Indeed, its opponents were often the followers of those two creeds themselves. Moreover, when it conquered Cairo, Damascus and Baghdad, its rulers adopted the luxurious secular styles of those courts, which were richer than anything in the experience of contemporary Northern and Western Europe, while the culture of much of the South had been severely set back by the barbarians from without and the Christians within.

GARDENS

The Far and the Near East became major resources in the later rise of the culture of flowers in the West; the whole of Asia supplied plants – and later representations of plants on paper, cloth and porcelain, as well as artificial flowers and perfumes, aromatics and spices, while the Near East continued to provide a model for the enclosed garden. That model was also present in the Biblical account of the Garden of Eden, but it was brought closer to the West not only by the circulation of literary works and by the influence of the returning Crusaders, but by the implantation of Islam in southern Spain, in southern Italy, and subsequently in Eastern Europe.[3] The paradise gardens of Iran and of earlier Mesopotamia were the direct ancestors of the gardens of Islam, not only in myth but in actuality. The continuity is evident. A palace set within a garden of paradise is reported from the second-century stronghold of Qaleh-i Yazdigird in Parthian Iran.[4] The tradition continued under the Sāsānian rulers and with the advent of the ʿAbbāsid dynasty to power, when the centre of Islam shifted from Damascus to Baghdad, the form of the Persian garden was carried to the Mediterranean, to Egypt and to the Maghreb.[5]

Along with the civilisations of South and East Asia, Persia had one of the most developed cultures of flowers. Situated on a dry plateau above the region between the two rivers of Mesopotamia the country has an average rainfall of 30 centimetres a year. The coast south of the Caspian sea is part of that continent-wide band of temperate climate in which fruit trees and other

---

[2] Dickie 1976.   [3] For an extended discussion of Islamic gardens see Lehrman 1980 and Brookes 1987.
[4] In the palace some of the decorative motifs are definitely Mediterranean, for 'artistic ideas were as mobile as the trade' (Vollmer *et al.* 1983:42).   [5] Pinder-Wilson 1976:73; Marçais 1957a:235.

flowering plants flourish. In the rest of the country, irrigated water was essential to most cultivation and the walled garden was not only an oasis but a microcosm divided into four quarters (*chahar bagh*), with a pool or kiosk in the centre.[6] In Arabic, paradise is simply *al-janna*, the garden. While later Persian gardens did not follow the pattern of Eden in any close way, they were often constructed around a watercourse at right angles to which the secondary axis might consist simply of paths, bordered with aromatic shrubs and herbs, with a pavilion in the centre.[7] The plot would be largely decorative in the middle, with covered walks, but increasingly functional towards the periphery, forming not so much a garden, which some see as a concept of the Renaissance, but a *hortus* in the Roman and Levantine sense.[8] In contrast to European gardens, the importance of water arose from the fact that these were situated in arid lands where trees and vegetation were sparse and needed to be carefully nourished and protected. In Europe the watercourses tended to be replaced by paths giving a four-square design that was perpetuated in the first botanic gardens of the West, the establishment of which followed upon the discovery of the new world[9] (Plate 4.1). The four quarters, earlier divided by the four rivers, were now looked upon as the four continents, Europe, Asia, Africa and America.

Close attention was given to flowers as well as to food crops. In the garden roses (*gul*) dominated all other flowers and even had their own specialised space, the *gulistan* or rose garden. In the early nineteenth century one visitor remarked that 'in no country in the world does the rose grow in such perfection'.[10] The petals were used to make rosewater which was sprinkled on guests, just as garlands of roses had been offered in the ancient world, while the flowers constituted an ingredient for flavouring desserts, including sherbets and pastries. As in early medieval Europe, there seems to have been little use of chaplets, or even of garlands, for personal adornment. The man's head was covered with a turban, part of a complex code of status, the woman's with a veil or headcover. The personal use of flowers and foliage is obviously linked closely to the way in which the body is covered with cloth and ornamented with jewelry, and this in turn to considerations of propriety before man and God. In the Near East the covering of the head with a cloth took on a greater importance than the wearing of crowns, while the use of necklaces and other forms of jewelry as part of a woman's dowry outweighed that of less permanent adornments. Only in India do we find the continued use of the garland that was so prevalent in pre-Christian Egypt. Personal decoration apart, the culture of flowers flourished, predominantly in the shape of gardens as they played no part in worship.

---

[6] For a discussion of an alternative meaning of *chahar bagh*, see Pinder-Wilson 1976:79.
[7] Harvey 1976:21.   [8] Dickie 1976:93.
[9] Pre-eminent among these botanic gardens were Padua, Leyden and Montpellier established in the sixteenth century, and Oxford, the Jardin du Roi in Paris and Uppsala in the seventeenth (Prest 1981:1).
[10] Wilber 1979:71, quoting Porter.

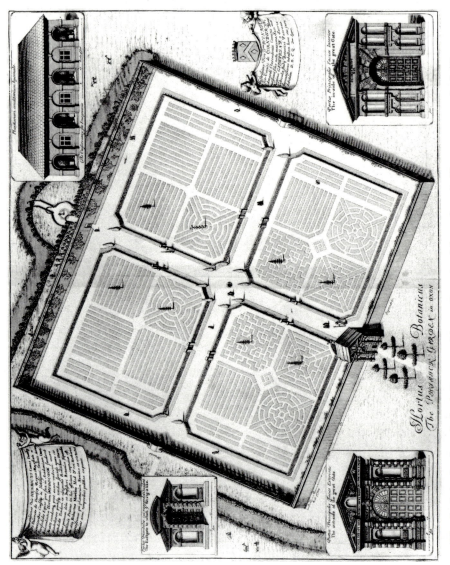

4.1 The Botanic Garden, Oxford. (Loggan, 'Hortus Botanicus' from *Oxonia Illustrata*, 1675, Oxford)

From Iran the culture of gardens and flowers spread both west and east. The Islamic garden made its appearance in Tunisia by the ninth century, from whence it passed to Spain.[11] Archaeological evidence shows gardens with oranges, roses and dwarf trees confined in basins, such as Pliny reports for Rome, such as appear in later Indian miniatures and such as are found in the contemporary bonsai of East Asia. The lowered beds needed for irrigation increased the geometrical dominance of the paths and provided a floral carpet on which to walk.[12] Such gardens were first confined to the courts but they gradually became adopted by the richer citizens themselves, a feature that was remarked upon by Leo the African in Tlemcen at the beginning of the sixteenth century. Their number and luxuriance greatly impressed European visitors of the time. About 1470 a Flemish traveller to Tunis claimed there were four thousand individual, irrigated, gardens around the town, full of fruit and with flowers perfuming the air. In many cases such estates were maintained by Christian captives and provided their owners with alternative residences outside the town during the hot summer months. So the model of aristocratic and later bourgeois gardens was available to visitors from the North well before their establishment in those lands.

The enclosed garden of the Near East retained much of its character until recent times. Walls protected its valuable property from other men as well as from animals; in the polygynous societies of Islam women as well as flowers were shut off from the outside world. In the early eighteenth century Lady Mary Wortley Montagu described the Sultan's garden in Istanbul in the following words:

the Women's Apartments are all built backward, remov'd from sight, and have no other prospect than the Gardens, which are enclos'd with very high Walls. There is none of our Parterres in them but they are planted with high Trees, which give an agreable shade and, to my fancy, a pleasing view. In the midst of the Garden is the Chiosk, that is, a large Room, commonly beautify'd with a fine fountain in the midst of it. It is raised 9 or 10 steps and enclos'd with Gilded Lattices, round which Vines, jess'mines and Honey suckles twineing make a sort of Green Wall. Large trees are planted round this place, which is the Scene of their greatest Pleasures, and where the Ladys spend most of their Hours, employ'd by their Music or Embroidery. In the public Gardens there are public chiosks where people go that are not so well accommodated at home, and drink their Coffe, sherbet, etc.[13]

Spreading a carpet under a tree by a river in order to sit and drink coffee and listen to music was one of the divertissements of 'the most considerable Turks' at that time.[14] The cities were surrounded by such areas and 'for some miles round Adrianople the whole ground is laid out in Gardens', not only for pleasure but for profit;[15] the gardeners, who were mainly Greek, supplied the

---

[11] Marçais 1957a:236.   [12] Jellicoe 1976:111; Dickie 1976:100.   [13] Montagu 1965:343–4.
[14] Montagu 1965:331.   [15] Montagu, letter to Alexander Pope.

city with fruit and vegetables. The ambiance was not essentially different from *Le déjeuner sur l'herbe* in the Bois de Boulogne outside Paris in the late nineteenth century, although the pleasure garden was combined with the commercial.[16] Such gardens represented a more or less continuous tradition going back to the earlier Near East which was only then being widely taken up in the West, not just because of the inclemency of the weather, but because of the slower development of public gardens for the populace at large, or private ones for domestic use, except for those of the clerics and the aristocracy.

LITERATURE

From the beginning the garden under Islam played a central part in literature because it represented paradise. Indeed, the study of Arabic gardening is essential to the understanding of Arabic poetry in which the literary genres of *nawrīyāt* and *rauḍīyāt*, of flowers and gardens, were two of the most popular among Hispano-Arab poets, providing another potential model for Christian Europe.[17]

As in English, and as with the original Greek *Anthology* (the *logos* of *anthos*), a gathering of flowers came to stand for a collection of 'flowers' of speech, of poetry.[18] In the same way *peristephanon*, the 'crown', had been used by Prudentius as the title for his lives of the martyrs.

Flowers pervade Persian literature as nowhere else except China, and in the works of occasional individuals in the later West such as Robert Herrick. When Firdausi, the national epic poet of Iran, wrote *The Book of Kings* in AD 1010 in order to provide for his daughter's dowry, he included many descriptions of nature, mainly domesticated (Colour plate IV.1). Of the banks of the Caspian, the fertile area where fruit and flowers flourish, he says:

> Mazanderan is the bower of spring . . .
> Tulips and hyacinths abound
> On every lawn; and all around
> Blooms like a garden in its prime,
> Fostered by that delicious clime.

That secular literature also flourished in Andalusia where the work of writers like Ibn Ḥazim (994–1064) in *The Ring of the Dove* is thought to have influenced the lyric poetry of southern France, in particular that of the troubadours and the tradition of courtly love.[19]

In the celestial arena, the Qur'an promises the faithful the blessings of eternal gardens, which specifically include flowers, fruit and 'maidens good

[16] Painted by Manet, with a later variation by Picasso.   [17] Dickie 1976:89.
[18] The word in Latin, *florilegium*, has the same meaning and was later used for collections of excerpts from past authorities on, for example, the relation between the divine and the human nature in Christ.
[19] See for example Menocal 1987.

and comely'.[20] But flowers are also present as images and in metaphors, which might be used to present an opposition to the actual culture of flowers in a rather similar fashion to the way the metaphorical transformation of 'crowns' took place in Christianity. For the sensual descriptions had their early critics among philosophers and mystics, some of whom spiritualised the notion of paradise, finding the proper way to worship God to lie in the contemplation of his works.[21] The Sufis in particular discovered complex analogies between different aspects of God's creation. Man himself is seen as a spiritual garden, while the bud, Mary, gives birth to Jesus, the rose. But the rose, a favourite of the Prophet, stood for others too; it was connected with 'almost all the great religious figures as bearers of Divine Revelation', with Abraham, Moses, Joseph and with Solomon.[22] There was no single key to unlock this symbolic displacement of luxury to the spiritual.

CREATION AND CRITIQUE

Critiques of earthly gardens come from yet another direction, since theologically their perfection could challenge the uniqueness of God's creative powers. It is told that an attempt was made by one king of southern Arabia to imitate paradise on earth in the Garden of Iram. As a result his creation was destroyed by God.[23] The legend became a focus of literary and moralistic attention. Man's creations cannot be allowed to rival God's. Gardens may come close, filled as they are with beautiful flowers. The extreme position held that making a garden fell into the same category as creating other representations, for all were imitations of God's handiwork, of his initial unique act of creation, in this case of Eden, the original walled garden.

While that view of gardens did not prevail, it was a different matter with icons. The objection to them was partly to worshipping images of other gods. Muhammad emptied the Ka'bah of idols and specifically condemned the impurity of idolatry, that is, the representations of the other religions including Judaism and Christianity which were intensively practised in Arabia at that time. But it was not only icons of other gods but of all of God's creations. The Qur'an implies that the creative efforts of the artist or sculptor may be unlawful if they attempt to imitate God's powers. Subsequent collections of the Prophet's sayings, the Ḥadīth, are quite clear that it is blasphemous to usurp God's powers, for artists take on themselves his role as *muṣawwir*, 'creator' or 'fashioner'. These commentators developed the Biblical notion, identifying representations with the attempt to create. A tradition ascribed to the Prophet declared that on the Day of Judgement a person who had made a picture of a living thing would be asked by Allah to

---

[20] Surah 76.   [21] Schimmel 1976:22–3.   [22] Schimmel 1976:33.   [23] Hanaway 1976:46.

'bring alive what they had created'.[24] The related notion that the fashioning of images was a matter of vain pride competing with the handiwork of God took shape during the reign of the Umayyads of Damascus (660–750) who had taken over the Christian workshops of Syria.[25] Some commentators disagreed, and other authorities allowed exceptions which vary over space and time. These exceptions included figural work on cloth, as well as the use of gold and precious stones for some decorative purposes.[26] Nevertheless, the faithful would do better to avoid such things.

It would be a mistake to insist on the total effectiveness of the prohibition on images of nature.[27] Although some elements in early Islam criticised extravagance, the garden itself was normally safe. Even in what little representational art existed, we find some depiction of gardens, not to speak of the later development of carpet design, often mainly geometrical but sometimes realistic. Landscapes with trees appear in the earliest pictorial representations in the Islamic world found in the Dome of the Rock in Jerusalem and the Great Mosque in Damascus.[28] Moreover, pictures of various kinds were tolerated in the private apartments of palaces, especially by the Shiah. However, the more usual emphasis was on formality, with ornament as a means of detracting from the representative qualities of human figures. The framing of a picture by means of the border removes it further from reality, just as low relief was held to be less objectionable than sculpture in the round. Some iconic influences did come from the East, first with the Seljuq Turks, and reached their apogee in the work of Persian miniaturists of the fifteenth and sixteenth centuries working for the Mongols (1220–1500) and the Safavids (1501–1732). It was the illustration of books that gave rise to the miniature tradition; such art arose out of the word, much as in the European tradition of illumination. The production of books had been promoted in Baghdad under the reign of the great Hārūn ar-Rashīd (786–809) after a group of Chinese paper makers had been captured at the Battle of Talas in 751. But there was little development of iconic art, nor yet of those areas of knowledge dependent on representation, until the Safavid period. And that was an exceptional development, influenced by outside factors, especially from China.[29] Otherwise, as a French authority declares, 'l'art musulman ignore la grande sculpture iconographique, la manière de l'art grec ou romain, de l'art chrétien, des arts hindous, ou khmer, ou chinois'.[30]

Whatever images were allowed in secular life, sacred space was virtually without icons. Even in Fāṭimid Egypt, which made greater use of images of the living than most other Islamic societies, including some limited sculpture in the round, no representations are found in the mosques. The same was true of the Umayyads of Damascus, as well as in India where the Mughals developed

[24] Marçais 1957b:70.   [25] Marçais 1957b:75.   [26] Bravmann 1974:15ff.
[27] Marçais 1957b:67ff. and 8ff.   [28] Ettinghausen 1976:7.   [29] Welch 1972:41, 54.
[30] Marçais 1957b:68.

the Persian tradition of secular painting.[31] Images did not appear in religious surroundings. When the Normans conquered the island of Sicily, where the Fāṭimids had established a naval base, it was the Christians who, copying the Persian lions and griffins on silk cloth, introduced them into their places of worship. The famous Capella Palatina in Palermo was built by the Norman kings of Sicily and decorated by Fāṭimid artists; they applied a secular tradition to the religious art of 'unbelievers'. At this time, the Muslim West, as distinct from the East, was intent on removing all representations of men and animals from its decor; the African dynasty of the Almoravids and their successors brought with them the austerity of desert Islam. The Almoravids who entered Spain in 1085 and stopped the Christian advance were a Berber dynasty from the desert. They succeeded the Umayyads and introduced a strong puritanical element into the artistic field, using ornamentation as an end only in the 'minor' decorative arts of weaving and ivory carving. In building mosques they avoided the lavish decoration of the late Umayyad style. Even in the secular sphere, they shunned the building of luxurious palaces and monuments. In the Islamic West generally there was little representation of living things at all after the eleventh century.

Only in the caliphate of Cordova (929–1031) and later in the fourteenth century among the sultans of Granada do we find some continuation of the earlier Persian tradition, for example, in the Fountain of Lions in the Alhambra palace, which also contains the thirteenth-century Garden of the Builder. The orientalisation of the court led to an increasing refinement in the spheres of art and architecture, as well as in the layout and content of gardens, which was to play a part in the changing situation in Christian Europe.

There was another source of criticism, apart from the theological, of these developments in gardens and iconography, and that is associated with the contrast between the nomadic Bedouin and the settled Arabs of the town. This contrast between the simple life of the desert and the luxury of the towns lay behind Ibn Khaldun's analysis of the rise and fall of Muslim dynasties, but it was significant throughout the history of Islam. In particular it centred upon the very compromises that Islam had made with the existing cultures of the Near East when it conquered Damascus and Baghdad.[32]

ROYALTY AND LUXURY

Early gardens associated with the court and with the delights of paradise were the centres not only of prayer and meditation but of revelry and sexuality, some pavilions being 'made expressly for the purposes of love'.[33] The ruler

---

[31] Marçais 1957b:76. On Persian painting of the period, see Gray 1930.
[32] While the point is not directly relevant to the role of the Near East in the revival of the culture of flowers in Christian Europe, it does affect our understanding of later developments within Islam, especially in Iran, in Central Asia and in North India.   [33] Wilber 1979:46.

might disport around the pools where his harem bathed, encouraged by the sexual paintings that in the fifteenth century enlivened the walls of his chambers but were so reprehensible in the eyes of Western visitors. Other paintings show sexual intercourse taking place on a flowered carpet in a garden.[34] These floral carpets both inside and outside the dwelling are a frequent feature of miniature album paintings, above all in India where the genre spread from Persia about 1500 to amalgamate with the traditional Hindu styles.[35]

For the influence of the Persian culture of flowers and gardens was felt as strongly in the East as in the West. The Baghdad caliphate, which had ruled Persia from AD 642, was conquered by the Mongol followers of Genghis Khan in 1220. By then Islamic gardens had been long established in Spain but in the East the great series of royal gardens were created only after the advent to Persia of Tamerlane (Timur) and his conquering Turkish armies.[36] Becoming lord of Samarqand about the year 1369, he moved west into Iran in 1381. Bringing architects from Persia back to Samarqand and adapting their designs to the setting of a nomad encampment, in 1396 he ordered the construction of a garden called Dilgusha, or Heart's Ease, which was to be built on a meadow known as the House of Flowers.[37] Many other gardens followed, including the Gul Bagh or Rose Garden. By the time of the visit of Clavijo, the ambassador of Castile and Leon, in 1404, the town had been quite transformed by the first of the many gardens which the Turkish rulers built there. Of these Clavijo considered the New Garden as the finest he ever saw. But the plans of those built in later centuries were similar, the layout resembling the Mesopotamian and Biblical gardens. 'Most characteristic were the enclosure within high walls, the division of the enclosed area into quarters, the use of a main water axis, the location of a palace or pavilion at the centre of the area, the choice of a natural slope or the creation of an artificial hill in order to insure proper flow of water, and a mixture of the utilitarian vineyard and orchard with the pleasure garden.'[38]

The Timurid empire broke up in AD 1500, but twenty-six years later Babur, who was Timur's descendant of the fifth generation, defeated the rulers of the Muslim sultanate of Delhi (1206–1526) and established the Mughal Dynasty of India. He then tried to adapt the Persian garden for more southerly climes. The main sites were around palaces. But they also surrounded mosques and shrines, as well as mausolea, which was one meaning of the word *rauda* (or *rawḍa*). The greatest of all *rauda* was the memorial that the widowed Shah Jahān (1592–1666) built to his best-loved wife (d.1631). That magnificent building, the Taj Mahal, was intended for public enjoyment as well as for

---

[34] E.g. Mandel 1983:15.
[35] Such books were 'intended to be enjoyed by members of aristocratic households, especially the women'. They were in some measure 'educational, demonstrating what was possible and delightful in sexual love' (Rawson 1977); if part of the education was in the ways of acrobats and prostitutes, they were at least more accessible to those practised in yoga.   [36] Dickie 1976:92.   [37] Wilber 1979:27; Pinder-Wilson 1976:77.
[38] Wilber 1979:29.

private meditation. Even royal gardens were sometimes divided in three, part for the king, part for the harem, part for the public. But the gardens that the Mughals created in India were not only for pleasure but also for income. During the reign of Emperor Jahāngir (1605–27), who was much influenced by his Persian wife and her family, it was claimed that in the Vale of Kashmir there were no less than seven hundred and seventy-seven gardens, undoubtedly a notional number. However many there were, they provided a substantial revenue from roses and bedmusk, probably the musk mallow (*Hibiscus abelmoschus*), the seeds of which give out a musky scent and are scattered among clothes to keep away insects.[39] Once again merchants became heavily involved in the culture of flowers as the demand increased and the clientele widened.

In diffusing garden design and the cultivation of flowers from Persia both to the West and the East, Islam encouraged the secular use of flowers. It differed in this respect from Christianity, even though it suffered from similar invasions and derived from the same Judaic tradition. Influenced by the courts of Damascus and Baghdad, Islam acquired many of the traditions of luxury prevalent in earlier East Asia. Nevertheless, the Judaic commandments on representation had a profound effect, as is clear in the Muslim impact on India. Hindu art had centred largely on the temple with its wealth of sculptures, mostly figures of humans and deities. But flowers and plants, especially the lotus, were part of worship and appeared on many carvings.[40] Despite the accommodation to Hindu culture, the attitudes and iconography of the Mughals remained very different. Hindu sculpture was often literally defaced in the fashion of iconoclasts everywhere. Human and animal forms were not permitted on their own religious buildings, which for decoration tended to use floral elements and calligraphy in abstract patterns;[41] in this context designs were geometric, avoiding the accusation of imitating God's creation. Even with gardens, the layout was often highly formal, as were the water gardens (although not the great parks) that were incorporated into Persian carpets. But these fell largely in the secular sphere where rules were more relaxed, and which permitted such developments as Persian miniatures and Mughal paintings.

CARPETS

Already in the sixth century, the kings of Persia had tried to overcome the seasonal limit of their paradise by having huge carpets made to represent gardens, the form and colour of which provided reminders of more pleasant

---

[39] Jellicoe 1976:115.   [40] Crowe *et al.* 1972:23.
[41] By and large, Islam encouraged flowers, seeing in them the evidence of divinity, even its unity, but they were celebrated in verse and language more than in representations. However, the Ottoman Turks displayed whole tulip gardens on the tiles that decorate the mosques of Istanbul and Edirne (Schimmel 1976:23), the tulip being valued by mystics because its name, *lāle*, contained the same letters as *hilāl*, crescent, the symbol of Islam, and as Allāh himself.

days.[42] So huge was the garden carpet of the Sāsānian king, Khosrau II, who reigned between 590 and 628, that those who sacked his palace divided it into four.[43] Gardens became a standard theme of the Oriental carpet used by nomads, peasants and city-dwellers alike. Few could have gardens; most could have carpets, which do not need watering and flower all year round. Once again, under Islam no copy could ever be perfect, and it is said that some flaw had to be left even in these representations of the world. Only God was perfect, or could create perfection.

The alternative was to go for formal, geometric designs that did not attempt to imitate nature and were especially suitable for the knotted carpet. A specialised variety called 'garden carpets' belongs typically to the seventeenth, eighteenth and early nineteenth centuries. But most Persian carpets of all periods are garden carpets in a wider sense, using floral patterns and often the formal framework of a garden design. These in their turn were copied in actual gardens, though this example of life imitating art may have been a late phenomenon.[44] The simplest plan was that of the Garden of Eden, the gardens of Mesopotamia and of Samarqand. The carpet represented an area divided into four parts by the crossing of two perpendicular axes formed by canals, at the junction of which was placed a building, perhaps a kiosk or a fountain (Colour plate IV 2). Once again, the whole resembled the cosmos, the world divided into the four parts, each with its major river oriented to the four cardinal points, the four 'heads' of the Garden of Eden, and clustered around a central mountain. Thus the carpet represented the garden, which in its turn was the microcosm of the world and of its very origins. The prince's ownership of that magnificently luxurious object of the court (the knotted carpet as distinct from the woven *kelim* of commoner use) was itself perhaps the symbol of his domination of that world.

Formalised flowers constitute an intrinsic part of geometrical carpets, especially Persian ones. Their use relates to technical factors. In the Turkish or Ghiordes knot, the wool is taken over two warp threads and then stands up as a bunch in the middle; in the Persian or Senneh knot only one thread stands up between the two warp threads. Due to the gap between the warps in the Turkish knot this type of weaving did not lend itself to curved lines but rather to straight ones;[45] whereas the Persian knot enabled the weaver to represent flowers more easily, especially as the craft developed towards the end of the fifteenth century.

The fifteenth century was a critical period in many respects, mainly because

[42] Dick Whittaker suggests that a similar purpose was perhaps served by Roman mosaics, where the floral style was so popular in North Africa in the later empire. We have already remarked upon the *trompe l'oeil* aspect of much garden painting in Pompeii.
[43] 'A seventh-century AD manuscript describes a carpet that Khusru II placed in the palace of Ctesiphon. Its purpose was to remind the king of spring during the cold months of winter. It was woven of gold and silver thread and covered with gems on a field depicting a garden with canals, birds, trees and flowers' (Coen and Duncan 1978:4).   [44] Wilber 1979:13.   [45] Schürmann 1979:12.

of the increasing influences from the East, which were instrumental in modifying the Islamic attitude to representation in Persia and in making the Safavid tradition in that country, and subsequently the Mughal in India, quite different from that prevailing in other Muslim areas, whether in book illustration, in carpets or in minatures. Religious art, mosques, architecture and sculpture were little affected; the changes took place in a largely secular domain.

The effect on carpets was striking. At that period, 'Gifted artists adapted the book illustrations and the perfectly executed book covers for the ornamentation of rugs.'[46] Animals were represented but in east Turkestan the carpets included 'such an abundance of blossoms, flowering shrubs, pomegranate trees and rosettes that there is no room left for animal reproductions'.[47] The change was remarkable and was influenced by contacts with China. There the 'naturalistic reproduction of floral ornaments (lotus blossoms, peonies, chrysanthemums) has been carried to stylistic perfection'.[48] Chinese carpets include dragons as well as some symbolic motifs, although frequently the weavers are unable to give any account of their meaning.[49] Some of the designs are even found in Persian carpets. The waving banner of the *qi* appears among the clouds; the dragon fights with the phoenix.[50]

NATURALISTIC INFLUENCES FROM EAST ASIA

Chinese motifs made their mark in West Asia through the trade in textiles, fabrics, metalwork and paintings, just as the demand in turn influenced the design of the supply. For the Iranian peoples were the great mediators between West and East, who once inhabited an area reaching to Chinese Turkestan. While the rise of chinoiserie in Western Europe did not occur until the eighteenth century, one of the extraordinary features of Persian miniatures of the Safavid Dynasty, which followed the Mongols, was the extent of the borrowings of Chinese motifs among the Tabriz school of the north-west, especially as compared with similar work in the Timurid centre of Herat in the eastern region.[51] Tabriz was the capital of Turkman rule which in the fourteenth century had been occupied by the Mongols who brought with them models, themes and motifs from East Asia. But it had long been a major entrepôt in the trade along the Silk Road, dealing in Chinese goods and designs at least since Hellenistic times, as well as those from India and Europe (Plate 4.2). The Turkman style was influenced by Oriental flowers, birds, blossoming trees, soaring rocks and dragons. 'Long yellow-outlined petals

[46] Schürmann 1979:15.
[47] Schürmann 1979:24–5.   [48] Schürmann 1979:25.   [49] Schürmann 1979:27–8.
[50] Marçais 1957a:79. From the ninth century, the ceramic art of Persia had borrowed from the Tang Dynasty of China.   [51] Welch 1972:37.

4.2 *Lions in a Landscape*. Drawing in the Turkman style from Tabriz, c.1480, showing Chinese influence. (Istanbul album in the Topkapi Sarayi Museum, Library H. 2153; Welch 1972:41)

bend and twist, outsize peony blossoms and palmettes seem to expand on the page . . .'[52] Not only paintings but the architecture of the gardens themselves was affected, walls being covered with Chinese porcelain and papier-mâché, interlaced patterns of woodstrips coming from China and marble wainscoting from India.[53]

Persia came to hold a very special position in the Islamic world from the standpoint of art, because of its situation at the centre of long-distance trade routes, its extensive local tradition in the figurative arts, and its barbarian rulers coming from the East. How did these developments affect the representation of flowers? Apart from Persia, the use of design in Islamic art was highly formalised, stylised, even geometric. That was often the case with flowers. Marçais recalls the many occasions on which he saw Algerian craftsmen working in front of a vase containing a flower, or with jasmine or orange blossoms in their fez.[54] But never did they copy them, or become inspired to refurbish their repertoire of decoration, which consisted largely of

[52] Welch 1972:39.
[53] Wilber 1979:31. Of these Persian gardens, Marçais raises the question of whether they originated in China, like the dynasty, only to prefer a local hypothesis (1957b:235).   [54] Marçais 1957b:74.

the classical acanthus and the vine, mediated by Christian artists. Copying of this kind is not unusual; it was a significant element in the artistic traditions of Europe and East Asia. But it is more prevalent with decorative design which dominated Islamic art partly for theological reasons. The fact that such art is decorative rather than representational, sharing the nature of the arabesque rather than writing itself, was perhaps a favourable feature in getting round the proscription, notional or actual, on living things. For they were neither representational nor yet symbolic; they carried no 'meaning' as such. But their range was restricted and a wider repertory of flowers was only to be found in Persian art.

As we have seen, one of the features of Islam, and one that strongly affected the culture of flowers, was the separation between the secular and the religious which was paralleled by that between representation and 'reality'. One did not use flowers in worship, although they played an important role in the culture generally. This separation continues in Iran today.[55] On the other hand, unlike other Islamic cultures, the secular representation of flowers in Persia was not forbidden after the fifteenth century, while almost everywhere the role of the garden, of flowers, of roses in life and in literature was of central importance. Nor were flowers forbidden in domestic rituals or at events such as the New Year (Nauruz) which is of Zoroastrian (that is, non-Islamic) origin. This festival, which is also celebrated by Afghans and by Kurds, has secular connotations; in it the hyacinth plays a prominent part, being one of the seven items beginning with the letter S that are used in the ceremony.

THE IMPACT ON THE CHRISTIAN WEST

Despite the downturn in the culture of flowers in the West, the Near Eastern garden continued to provide a potential model and it was from this and other Eastern sources that many of the component items of the later culture of flowers came to Europe, mediated by the Mediterranean. As a result of internal change, the Arab conquests of Southern Europe and the Crusades, the limited monastic gardens gradually gave birth to the rose gardens of courtly Europe in the twelfth and thirteenth centuries. While the Islamic occupation of Spain lasted until the fifteenth century, from 711 to 1492, its influence continued much longer, especially in the form of the Moorish gardens of the South which maintained the notion of a walled enclosure, with a patio that mediated between house and garden such as was described by Lady Mary Wortley Montagu.

The gardens which Lady Mary saw were the descendants of those

---

[55] Although flowers are not used in worship, they play a part in life-cycle rituals. At weddings a cloth is laid out before the couple, on which are placed many objects that are associated with prosperity, including flowers. At funerals the tulip predominates and has even become the flower of the Islamic Republic as a reminder of the death of the martyrs (Mir-Hosseini, personal communication).

encouraged by the Turkish rulers well before the capture of Constantinople in 1453 and the subsequent construction of the Topkapi Sarayi. Already at Edirne the Ottomans appear to have paid special attention to ornamental gardening, probably having better techniques than anywhere in the West outside Granada. 'Istanbul was becoming a garden-lover's paradise a whole century before its treasures were opened to the European nations through the embassy of Ogier Ghiselin de Busbecq in 1554–1562.'[56] Those treasures included the tulip and possibly the carnation, which entered Europe through the East, while other plants and techniques came from the Muslims in Spain. It followed that works on Spanish horticulture in the Middle Ages were the best in Europe, beginning with the 'magnificent treatises' of Ibn Baṣṣal and Ibn al-'Awwām dating from c.1080 and c.1180 respectively; these volumes provide full details of what the Moors grew in Toledo and Andalusia, including plants of 'purely aesthetic interest'.[57]

The enclosed garden or *hortus conclusus* of twelfth-century Europe looked back to Biblical sources but was modelled in part upon Eastern, and ultimately Persian, examples revealed to the West during the Crusades as well as to travellers in Sicily, North Africa and Muslim Spain. By these means 'the rudiments of the walled garden, pool and pavilion' were brought to France, England and the Low Countries.[58] The same geographical source that had earlier provided the Biblical Garden of Eden continued to influence the West and many similarities of concept inform the descriptions and representations of Europe during the twelfth to the fifteenth centuries, for example, in the shape of the Persian garden, though visual forms of these did not appear until the later fourteenth century.[59] Earlier references speak of trees brought back from Alexandria for the garden of love in the *Roman de la Rose* and one written account of Muhammad's visit to Paradise was available to Europe in the fourteenth century. The role of Sicily and Venice as centres of trade in spices, dyes and textiles from the East was critical and the latter city has been proposed as the original home of the Madonna-in-a-garden pictures of the fourteenth and fifteenth centuries, which were the religious counterparts of the garden paintings with lovers and courtiers.[60] The important *Madonna in a Rose Garden* by Stefano da Zevio may have been inspired by a fourteenth-century Persian painting[61] (Plate 4.3).

One aspect of the decline of the West in comparison with the East was the disappearance of forced cultivation, both of flowers or of vegetables. With the fall of the Roman empire, all horticulture underwent a radical change. Even Charlemagne no longer grew in his gardens the vegetables previously

[56] Harvey 1978:52–3; 1976.   [57] Harvey 1978:47.   [58] Harvey 1976:21.
[59] In Guillaume de Lorris' *Le Roman de la Rose* there is a reference to trees being brought back from 'la terre Alexandrine' to plant in a 'vergier', an orchard (lines 589–92).
[60] Pearsall and Salter 1973:78, referring to Meiss 1951:140–1; also 108.   [61] Clark 1949:29.

4.3 Stefano da Zevio, *Madonna in a Rose Garden*, early fifteenth century. (Museo del Castelvecchio, Verona)

cultivated for the rich, that is, asparagus, artichokes, melons and cardoon.[62] Throughout the Middle Ages we find only one account that refers to greenhouses. A retrospective life of Albertus Magnus tells how the learned Dominican offered a banquet on 6 January 1249, the Feast of Epiphany, to the Emperor William of Holland in his monastery at Cologne. By his art, which was attributed to magic, the banquet hall was decorated with rose bushes covered with flowers and with many fruit-bearing trees. At the same time, the Arabs in Spain, more knowledgeable than the Northern peoples, were using the heat of fresh manure to bring on vegetables. But in the North this practice is found only with the Renaissance when the tradition of forced cultivation began to be re-established.

Under Islam developments were more continuous than in Europe, in the garden arts as in many other spheres. Whatever element of 'puritanism' marked the early creed, it did not lead to an extinction of the culture of flowers in the practical, secular sense, nor indeed in the written word, even if in all but a few instances their representation as icons and use in worship were non-existent. Until the Safavid period in Persia, with its artistic influences from the Far East, this was a culture of flowers virtually without representation.

Why was Islam at once more generous to secular flowers (but only occasionally to their representations) and less to flowers in the religious context? The aniconic strictness was theologically based, and became a diacritical feature that distinguished Islam from the lapses of Christianity and of pagans elsewhere. The desert creed with its deep respect for the word demanded the close adherence of its followers. In neither Islam nor Judaism was there any growth of monasticism and little of any religious hierarchy that was not directly involved in the interpretation of the Book. In Christianity the temptations and opportunities for compromise and elaboration were far greater.

Under Islam, compromise took place at the court, taken over from the earlier rulers of Damascus and Baghdad, together with the sophisticated irrigated agriculture of the Near East. The culture of the court permitted secular representation in the form of wall paintings, miniatures, porcelain and carpets. And it gloried in gardens, being based on more elaborate systems of horticulture than the West, where court life and the economy of the Roman world had suffered so greatly under the combined impact of Christianity and the invaders.

In this chapter I have tried to show that while floriculture in Christian Europe plunged after the Roman empire, earlier traditions were maintained and extended under Islam. Influences from the East contributed to the slow revival of the culture of flowers in medieval Europe, and Turkey, India and China all continued to play a major part in later developments. Those

---

[62] Gibault 1898b:1112, citing Capitulaire, *De villis*, art. 70.

influences were important both for flowers and for icons of flowers. Eastern contributions have tended to be underplayed in the history of Western thought, life and literature. Classical scholars have discounted Semitic influences on the alphabet and on other facets of the classical world. Christianity, like Judaism and Islam, was an Asiatic religion (even if the word for Nazarene in Arabic has come to mean European). Arabic texts of classical authors contributed much to the revival of learning; medieval architects learnt from their Southern neighbours and the troubadours, in Arabic *taralsa*, were also stimulated by Hispano-Arabic poetry.[63] It is very easy to exaggerate these contributions. Nevertheless, it has long been recognised that the renascence of the twelfth century contained many features derived from Islam.[64] The contributions to the history of medicine are well known.[65] So too the influence of Averroes on the history of philosophy. While the walled garden of Europe had other roots, Islamic models in southern Spain, Sicily and the Mediterranean were important for the revival of the culture of flowers in its form, its contents and in its attitudes towards their use.

[63] Menocal 1987.   [64] See Haskins 1927.   [65] Sarton 1951.

5 · The return of the rose in medieval Western Europe

Whether because of puritanism or because of opposition to other cults, significant elements in Christianity had put aside not only blood sacrifice but other features of the religious life associated with material offerings to divinity, namely, statuary, flowers, incense, perfume and icons themselves. In some of these matters their views corresponded to Judaic beliefs, while others ran parallel to those of the Roman moralists regarding luxury.

Blood sacrifice and other offerings to divinity did not return in any significant sense. Their practice was too inconsistent with theological doctrine on ways to approach 'the invisible God'. But the other features did reappear at varying points over the next millennium. Of these the return of the use of flowers is one of the most difficult to assess. We are largely dependent upon literary and artistic evidence, some of which may simply represent a backward glance to earlier times, using the imagery and images of the classical tradition, possibly in a metaphorical or at least in an imaginary way.

The question of metaphor and allegory is central to any discussion. In the spectrum of significances implied by a word like 'flowers', Christianity has often selected the metaphorical. That was especially true of concepts like garland, crown, adoption, sacrifice. This transformation makes some reports difficult to use as evidence; icons (images as distinct from imagery) are more apparent but even their use raises problems, for the garland may continue as an icon when the object itself has disappeared.

It was a comeback rather than a coming, a rebirth rather than a birth. In Western Europe the progression of culture, of social life generally, is sometimes discussed by historians and other scholars as if the growth of knowledge and the development of social organisation in the pre-industrial period – towards complexity at the level of the state, towards simplicity at the level of the family – was a process happening for the first time in the story of humanity. That story is too often seen by European scholars as running ineluctably from ancient society to feudalism to capitalism, privileging the sequence constructed for the West. In a wider perspective, that was rarely if ever the case. As Joseph Needham shows for the history of botany, Europe experienced an enormous falling off in knowledge which did not occur to the same extent in the East. There barbarian hordes are rarely seen as having quite such destructive effects and were perhaps more readily absorbed. In any case developments in Asia were more continuous, less interrupted. At the time of Charlemagne in the eighth century the largest cities in the world were Baghdad and Chang-an (now Xian) at the two ends of the Silk Road. Indeed, one of the strengths of the West in the later process of 'modernisation' was its relative 'backwardness' during the Dark Ages, leaving it freer to select for constructive adaptations to the growth of knowledge, stimulated to greater heights by the advent of printing and the advance of the economy with the development of trade and the physical expansion of European interests.

There were several elements leading to the very gradual revival that occurred. Firstly, the invaders adapted to the pre-existing cultures. But that was of relatively little importance in this context, since they were initially more involved in becoming Christian than in becoming Roman. Secondly there was the weight of 'popular culture'. It is never easy to decide what that weight might be. For the culture of ordinary folk is not immune to change and has at times undergone not simply dramatic changes but sweeping reversals in obedience to the religious or political system. That was so with the advent of the Reformation to Scotland, to New England and at times to England itself. The thinness of rituals, popular and ecclesiastical, in New England in the seventeenth century, was such that even funerals and the commemoration of the dead were bleak affairs, although time and the Episcopalians led to some limited elaboration.[1] The suppression of popular rituals and iconoclasm tend to go hand in hand. How far this affected early Christian Europe is difficult to say, but the potential influence of the church was undoubtedly radical, since popular culture was seen as pagan and hence as something to be destroyed. Priests installed in every parish acted as cultural watchdogs. Developments in the culture of flowers represented a reassertion of popular interests but unless brought under control they often worried the church because of their 'pagan' associations, which it attempted either to ban or to christianise. Just as churches were built on the sites of pagan worship, so herbs and flowers were literally christened, renamed, as Mary's wort or John's weed. Even then the herbs had to be gathered while saying a prayer, just as many other actions in ordinary life were preceded by the making of the sign of a cross. Herbs, leaves and flowers continued to be important for medicinal and related purposes, whatever the church had to say. Their pragmatic use opened a window to the aesthetic as well as to a compromise with the popular. For there is an underlying tendency to elaborate rituals, to introduce material elements like flowers even into the worship of the 'invisible God', which is often more important than any actual continuity of social action.

Thirdly, there was, as we have seen, an ambivalence about some of these excluded features, especially flowers, among the early Fathers of the church,

[1] Geddes 1976.

which rendered possible an early compromise. Although early Christianity was predominantly aniconic, a representational art slowly came into being in the religious domain. By c.330–40 a portrait of Christ was set in a floor mosaic in Dorset. By c.380–400 the shrines of saints occupied a dominant place in churches and were becoming surrounded with works of art. By the following century 'an emergent portrait art' was 'helping to focus the Christians' sense of divine presence'.[2] But in this art flowers played almost no part.

While there was as much ambiguity about flowers as there was about images, some formidable figures of the early church were not against their use. Although crowns were rejected by the early Christians, as early as the fourth century their use was being advocated by Christian writers for a specific purpose.[3] In the special context of an award for virginity, both at marriage and at death, St Chrysostom declared: 'Garlands are wont to be worn on the heads of bridegrooms, as a symbol of victory, betokening that they approach the marriage bed unconquered by pleasure.'[4] The practice of marriage crowns was revived and in the Eastern church the service itself became known as 'the ceremony of the wreath'. That wreath or crown is now made up of citrus sprays, either artificial or natural. To be married and to be crowned with the wreath are synonymous; it is placed on the couple's heads by the priest who asks the Lord to crown them 'with glory and honour', sanctifying the earthly use by a metaphorical one of the spirit. In other contexts too crowns were sometimes used. The Romulus intaglio of the fifth century portrays three laurel-wreathed figures crowned by victories and the chi-rho symbol. And in Byzantium crowns are awarded by Christ and the Virgin, but these may equally stand for metaphorical crowns.

In church too flowers were allowed by some and in Book XXII of *The City of God* by St Augustine, a reference is made to their use. Although flowers were no longer given as offerings but as decorations, their function shifting from the religiously 'utilitarian' to the religiously 'aesthetic', medieval altars were sometimes embellished with flowers, lilies above all, so that a perpetual springtime might seem to pervade the House of God. Paulinus of Nola (353–431) recommended the faithful attending the feast of St Felix that they should advance spring by spreading flowers on the ground and decorating the threshold of the church with garlands.[5] St Jerome praised Bishop Nepotian for putting flowers and foliage in basilicas and in the chapels of saints.[6] In

---

[2] Lane Fox 1986:677.   [3] Lambert 1880:819–20.   [4] *Hom.*, IX.1 Tim. (transl. J. Tweed).
[5] St Paulinus of Nola, 'De S. Felice natalitium carmen', III, *Poema* 12, v.110–12:
Spargite flore solum, praetexite limina sertis:
Purpureum ver spiret hiems, sit florens annus
Ante diem, sancto cedat natura diei.
See *Paulini nolani episcopi opera digesta in II tomos*, Paris, 1685, I. p.43.

[6] *Epistola* LX, 'Ad Heliodorum: epitaphium nepotiani'. Migne, *Patrologia latina* XXII.340 (p.597): Hoc idem possumus et de isto dicere, qui basilicas Ecclesiae, et Martyrum Conciliabula, diversis floribus, et arborum comis, vitiumque pampineis adumbrarit: ut quidquid placebat in Ecclesia, tam dispositione, quam visu, Presbyteri laborem et studium testaretur.

Augustine's *City of God*, a blind woman miraculously recovers sight when the bishop carrying the relics of St Stephen hands her some of the flowers used in the ritual.[7] Gregory of Tours was said to have done likewise and the practice appears to have been widely adopted. Gradually flowers became increasingly incorporated in rituals, especially those directed to tombs of saints. For these marble tombs themselves became objects of worship, whose power could provide the cure for disease and a palliative for misfortune. Graphic descriptions tell of the populace showering them with flowers and foliage in order to acquire their blessing. These offerings were in effect tolerated by the church in a way that gifts of food and the sacrifice of animals clearly would not have been.[8]

These compromises which the ambivalence of the Fathers allowed arose not only from 'popular culture' and ritual elaboration by themselves but also because of the persistence of Roman models in all parts of the West and the constant renascences that called attention to them. It is true that monuments to ancient Rome were to be found in the Germanic areas but obviously not to the same extent as in southern France or Rome itself, where Charlemagne's conquests took him. The remnants of former glories lay physically before the eyes of the inhabitants, and to this actual presence has been attributed the new fascination with ancient Rome in the twelfth century. For those monuments were potentially available as models, as cues, not simply as antiques, as relics.[9] Iconographic traditions of vanished peoples, the objectified culture of the distant past, had a different impact in post-classical Europe than in those societies in Africa who built in earth and carved in wood. The products of Roman civilisation lived on to influence the future in a more direct and enduring way. As a result the past was always present as an object. Indeed, many new buildings were constructed on the sites or from the materials of earlier Roman ones. In the seventh century, some early monastic establishments of Merovingian France were built on the sites of Roman villas that had been granted to them by local aristocrats; Moissac in the south-west may have been one such foundation. Cemeteries were started in the same way, the graves being cut in the mosaic floors; even existing forts were sometimes adapted for these purposes, with their walls providing an enclosure.[10]

In many ways a radical and deliberate break was made. In ecclesiastical as distinct from funerary architecture the Christians were determined to set aside earlier religious forms. When the conversion of the empire permitted a fuller development of such buildings, they rejected the model of the temple in favour of the basilica, the audience hall and the mausoleum. However closely early

[7] *De Civitate Dei*, lib. XXII, Caput VII, 10, Migne, *Patrologia lat.* XLI.41, 766: Ad Aquas-Tibilitanas episcopo afferente Praejecto reliquias martyrivs gloriossimi Stephani, ad ejus memoriam veniebat magnae multitudinis concursus et occursus. Ibi caeca mulier, ut ad episcopum portantem duceretur, oravit: flores quos ferebat dedi; recepit, oculis admovit, protinus vidit.

[8] Gregory of Tours, *De gloria confess.*, L, *Patrol.*, 72, 935 (p.886).

[9] Bloch 1982.   [10] Of the kind described in the life of St Philibert; James 1981.

Christian art was linked to the Graeco-Roman, the content changed dramatically. And not only the content, for there was a virtual absence of monumental public sculpture; the previously dominant form of three-dimensional statuary was now limited to small pieces and to private memorials.

Another important factor was the example of Islam in the South, especially its horticulture, which was reviewed in the last chapter, and finally there was the contradictory role of the church itself in the rebirth of the culture of flowers.

I want to deal with the return of flowers and icons of flowers during the European Middle Ages by breaking the period into two, with the twelfth century as the rough dividing-line: secondly, I want to consider in separate sections the interrelated subjects of flowers in gardens, flowers in literature, flowers in art (the graphic arts) and flowers in architecture.

FLOWERS AND THE MONASTERY GARDEN BEFORE THE TWELFTH CENTURY

If flowers were not to be encouraged below, they were still to be found in Paradise above. One third-century visionary, Saturus, described how he ascended to heaven and found roses and cypress trees inside the heavenly garden.[11] Flowers remained at least in verbal imagery and eschatological visions. So the rejection of flowers for religious performances was only one aspect of early Christianity. An alternative trend saw the re-emergence of their use within the Catholic church. In the early phases, it was mainly the monastic branch of the church that came to advance horticulture and eventually nourished their production and use. The culture of the rose, so strongly encouraged in the secular gardens of the Near East, as it had long been, was not totally neglected in Europe. Monastic gardens harboured not only fruit, vegetables and shade trees, but plants later to be destined for the decoration of altars on holy days. Many of the early monastic gardens concentrated on flowers for their medicinal properties and the related culinary ones. Nevertheless, over the long run the aesthetic aspects emerged in the context of worship, since it was as decoration not as offerings that they were to be used in church. So, as in Roman times, the flowers and fruits from Southern Europe were acclimatised for northern countries like Germany and England in these protected enclosures. But that was a slow process that covered some thousand years.

Appropriately enough, the new tradition began in Egypt with the desert Fathers who followed the lead of St Anthony when he retired to a remote mountain in 286 and made himself a little garden with vines and a pool of

[11] Lane Fox 1986:402.

water. In fact, many of the desert Fathers lived near the benign valley of the Nile and cultivated their own vegetables, and in some cases fruit trees. Hermits apart, monks of the cenobitic or community tradition aimed to support themselves within the bounds of the monastery walls as instituted by Pachomius.[12] The first monastery was founded in Fayum in 305, and from there monasticism spread to the northern shores of the Mediterranean. In the early sixth century another member of the upper strata of society, St Benedict, disgusted at its licentiousness, retired to Subiaco, east of Rome, to become a hermit and established his rose bush, *il roseto*, the flowers to delight the senses, the thorns to mortify the flesh.[13]

Benedict laid out a model on which monasteries should organise themselves, so that they were to become the strongholds of the Catholic religion and of the Latin tradition. It was they who supported the pope both against Byzantine Greeks and against Arian Lombards. But in the mid eighth century Rome had to appeal for military aid to the Carolingian Franks, resulting in the defeat of the Lombards, who had nevertheless spared the church, and in the creation of the papal states, partly out of former Byzantine territory. Earlier in the century, in 725, that territory had been racked by disputes over the decree of Emperor Leo III condemning the cult of images, signalling the beginning of the Iconoclastic Controversy in the West. It was the conquest of Italy by the Franks that led not only to the crowning of Charlemagne as emperor on Christmas Day 800, but to the *renovatio imperii*, especially the revival of Latin, at an artistic and literary level.

Interestingly, herb gardens, a general feature of later medieval life, seem to have been absent in the early centuries. The value of herbs as medicine was sometimes questioned by contemporary followers of Christian science, on the grounds that curing lay in the hands of God. Cassiodorus warns monks, 'do not place your trust in herbs or seek cures in human advice.'[14] The serious practice of medicine in monasteries seems to have been a result of the Carolingian revival and it continued until the rise of the medical schools at Montpellier, Salerno and elsewhere, after which it became forbidden to monks.[15] The herb garden was of course a fragrant retreat to which monks could go for pleasure, especially as temperatures were warmer than in Northern Europe so their contents were more varied, and more scented. Nevertheless, there was always a tension between the rejection of worldly things, as practised by the desert Fathers who went into the wilderness, and the search for God among his creations. It was in this latter context that we see the development of lawns and flower gardens or *violaria*, violet beds.[16]

Southern Italy remained part of the Byzantine empire, until the Arabs

[12] Meyvaert 1986:25–7.
[13] *Il roseto* is still to be seen in the Sacro Speco (a cave) at Subiaco where Benedict did his penance; it was a rose bush the thorns of which tore his flesh. On Subiaco, see Egidi *et al.* 1904 and Giumelli 1982.
[14] Cassiodorus, *Institutiones*, quoted Meyvaert 1986:39.
[15] Meyvaert 1986:39–40.   [16] Meyvaert 1986:44–5.

finally occupied Sicily (827–78) and the Normans subsequently conquered both that island (1061–91) and the southern Italian provinces of Puglia and Calabria (1071) in the course of their Mediterranean offensive. Under the Arabs for two hundred years, Sicily had prospered economically. Vineyards were turned into orchards; citrus, sugarcane, dates and mulberry trees (*Morus alba*) for silk were introduced and irrigation developed. The Islamic arts and sciences were encouraged, palaces, mosques and elaborate gardens were constructed. In a sense these developments led the revival of Europe through the extension of trade in the Mediterranean and the growth of horticulture, the sciences and the arts. The Norman kingdom of Sicily that followed maintained the high level of civic life and culture, acting as an intermediary, in all these spheres, between the Muslim and Christian worlds of the Mediterranean, and together with Spain contributing to the gradual revival not only of horticulture but of the culture of flowers, reinforcing and extending the earlier Mediterranean influences.

The development of such 'aesthetic' gardens was slow and there is not much evidence for flowers in the first monasteries in the North. While the early association of monasteries with gardening was strong, their plots consisted largely of edible produce such as vines, fruit and herbs. When flowers appear in a Cluniac list of signs of the end of the eleventh century, designed to allow monks to communicate in periods of silence, the poppy, lily and the rose are listed under the category 'vegetables' (*olera*) as distinct from legumes. Among other flowers, lupins were also widely eaten.[17] There is promise of a shift to 'aesthetic' gardening but the evidence points heavily in the utilitarian direction. The garden contained blossoms, especially of fruit trees in spring, but they were often present for practical purposes, not as flowers in themselves. There is early evidence of a utilitarian garden separated from the open space within the cloister, which as in the famous monastery of St Gall was often modelled after the Near Eastern prototype. The well-kept lawn (or *prau*) was divided into four bypaths (the four rivers), often with a tree at the centre symbolically joining heaven and earth.[18] In the case of St Gall flowering fruit trees were planted at the four corners. But there is little early evidence of special flower gardens, 'paradise gardens' as they were called by later commentators of the nineteenth century. The paucity of flowers, their employment for largely utilitarian purposes, did not prevent them being admired, and that is what happened in literature well before it did so in art.

FLOWERS IN LITERATURE

While the physical relics of Rome remained a potential source of artistic renovation for the future, for the culture of flowers even more important were

---

[17] Meyvaert 1986:37. See the twelfth-century reference to flower gardens in the work of the Cistercian author, Guerric of Igny.　　[18] Gibault 1896b:9; Lenoir 1852:311.

the texts, even the Christian texts. In descriptions of Paradise, roses and lilies were standard components; Adam and Eve walked in the garden 'in the midst of flowers and large clusters of roses', wrote Dracontius, the poet who participated in the literary revival in North Africa in the later part of the fifth century A D.[19] In the same century the miraculous voyage of the Celtic saint, Brendan, took him to Paradise where

> Euerech herb was ful of floures;
> and ech treo was ful of fruyt.[20]

These references may well represent purely literary gestures, as with the later inclusion of flowers in the Garden of Eden. But it provided an incentive for bringing them back into performance.

The notion of the chaplet also lived on in other, literary forms, in particular in the form of the *stephanos* or anthology, which was used for a collection of poems.[21] In early secular literature, references to the use of roses entwined in garlands never entirely disappear, but how much of this belongs to a stylistic tradition is difficult to judge. Whether the unique *Copa*, or the Dancing Girl of Syria, should be attributed to Virgil or to some later imitator, it includes a wealth of references to the use of flowers:

> There's even garlands for you, violet wreath and saffron,
> And golden melilot twining with crimson roses,
> And lilies plucked where they grow by the virgin river.

And later

> Heigh ho, but it's good to lie here under the vines,
> And bind on your heavy head a garland of roses,
> And reap the scarlet lips of a pretty girl.
> – You be damned, you there with your Puritan eye-brows (prisca
>   supercilia)!
> What thanks will cold ashes give for the sweetness of garlands?[22]

The sixth-century poem 'Lovely Venus', possibly from North Africa, refers to the same three flowers as the *Copa*:

---

[19] De laudibus Dei, I.437, *Monumenta germaniae historica, auctorum antiquissimorum*, ser. 1, v.14, *Reliquiae fl. Merobaudis. Carmina Blossii aemilii dracontii. Carmina et epistolae Eugenii Tolenani episcopi*, ed. Fridericus Vollmer, Berolini, 1905.   [20] Horstmann 1887:221.

[21] At the beginning of the first century BC Meleager of Gadara had made a collection of short poems composed in the classic period of Greek literature, from the seventh to the third centuries; it was called the *Stephanos* or 'Crown'. In the reign of Augustus, Philippus of Thessalonica composed another 'stephanos' and in the sixth century the Cycle of Agathias appeared. But these books are lost and what remains is a manuscript of the tenth century collected together by Constantinus Cephalas, a later edition of which now constitutes the *Greek Anthology*. The Greek poems have been translated into English under titles such as *Chrysanthema gathered from the Greek Anthology* (1878), *Amaranth and Asphodel* (1881), *Love in Idleness* (1883), *Grass of Parnassus* (1888), *From the Garden of Hellas* (1891), *Rose Leaves* (1901), all the titles preserving the notion of flowers or plants.   [22] Waddell 1929:2–5.

> Violets wither, 'spite of dew,
> Roses shrivel in the sun,
> Lilies all their whiteness stain.

Ausonius of Bordeaux (c.310–c.395) speaks constantly of roses, as did the Epicurian poet, Fortunatus (348–c.405), who wrote:

> If 'twere the time of lilies,
> Or of the crimson rose,
> I'd pluck them in the fields for you,
> Or my poor garden close.

So, whatever the fate of flowers in the religious or secular spheres, they lived on not only in the works of art and architecture left behind by the world of antiquity, but also in the Latin poetry that continued in some form the classic tradition.

While there had been a degree of continuity in the composition of poetry and other Latin works after the collapse of Rome, it was Charlemagne who deliberately encouraged the use of that language in his attempt to provide a unitary means of communication for the empire of the Franks which stretched all the way from Bremen to Brindisi. The earlier use of Latin in the Roman church had inevitably led to the reading of pagan writers and to some acquaintance with Roman culture and society. But Charlemagne's recourse to those earlier models was a very deliberate attempt by him and his entourage to combine 'ancient high culture with Christian orthodoxy'.[23] Nowhere perhaps is this made clearer than in Theodulf's poem, 'The Books I Used to Read':

> I very often read Gregory and Augustine . . .
> I have often read the writings of the pagan sages
> who achieved eminence in various subjects,
> as well as 'Virgil and wordy Ovid'.[24]

In the body of poetry that was produced at this time, there are a few references to the culture of flowers and gardens that draw in part upon classical models, in part upon contemporary experience. Einhard describes the walls around his hunting park, filled with woods, lawns, meadows, birds and wild beasts.[25] These are royal concerns, with their emphasis on blood sports. But in an 'Elegy on His Life at Aachen', the Yorkshire monk, Alcuin, looked back upon his earlier existence in rustic terms:

> Throughout your enclosed gardens apple boughs smell sweetly,
> and white lilies are mingled with little red roses.[26]

In another poem, Spring was visualised as wearing a 'garland of flowers', an image used more concretely by Florus of Lyons in whose phrase power was

---

[23] Godman 1985:5.   [24] Godman 1985:169.   [25] *Karolus Magnus et Leo Papa*, Godman 1985:205.
[26] 'Claustra per hortos', lines 9–10 (Godman 1985:125).

'like a garland [*corona*] of flowers cast down from his head'.[27] That image relates to the loss of the royal crown[28] and to the decline of the Carolingian empire.[29]

This body of medieval Latin poetry also provides the earliest detailed description of a monastic garden in Walahfrid's *De cultura hortorum*, On the culture of gardens, which was based upon observations of his 'small garden close' as well as upon a wide reading of ancient authorities. But it was presumably from the royal gardens that Charlemagne's daughters get the usual three flowers to offer the emperor:

> Bertha gives roses, Hrothrud gives violets, Gisela lilies . . .[30]

Of the twenty-nine plants mentioned in Walahfrid's poem, which appears to be based on the metre of Virgil's *Georgics*, most are herbs that are included for medicinal rather than for purely culinary purposes. Of 'flowers', we find only four, apart from flowering fruit trees, namely, the iris, poppy, lily and rose. For the last two he presents a set of symbolic associations that are essentially ecclesiastical. Otherwise the literary meanings of flowers are developed only in shadowy fashion.

The enjoyment of flowers was not simply passive for in poems they are strewn in a lover's chamber, which is scented with green herbs.[31] In the much later poem by Sigebert of Gembloux (c.1030–1112), dedicated to the Virgin martyrs, he writes of them 'wandering through the fresh fields':

> Gathering flowers to make them a nosegay,
> Gathering roses red for the Passion,
> Lilies and violets for love.[32]

The three flowers appear together as a cliché. Roses too have now taken on an ecclesiastical meaning, the red standing for the suffering of Christ on the cross rather than the earthly love to which the early Fathers objected; the symbolism has been christianised. But the use of flowers in the religious context is still not without its problems of acceptability. Another poem by the same author ('The Martyrdom of the Theban Legion') vividly expresses the ambivalence of Christian authors in using flowers in worship, since nothing can be good enough for the martyrs, let alone for God:

> I tried to make a garden for the saints . . .
> No lily for me, violet or rose,
> Lilies for purity, roses for passion denied.
> (Lines 1–3)

[27] Godman 1985:14, 6; Waddell 1929:97, 115.   [28] Godman 1985:40, 69–70.
[29] See also the reference to 'crowns [*coronae*] of martyrdom' and to the burial of saints with 'fragrant spices' in tombs encircled with 'images of cherubim' in an anonymous poem (Godman 1985:185).
[30] Theodulf, 'On the Court', line 97; Godman 1985:155.   [31] Waddell 1929:145.
[32] Waddell 1929:159, On picking garden flowers, see 'The Earth Lies Open Breasted', Waddell 1929:209. On strewing flowers on altars, p.217, both from the twelfth-century *Carmina Burana*.

So in their place he weaves 'poor crowns' from privet blossom as a more humble offering, the only virtue of which is the love with which it is offered.[33] His humility rejects the luxuriousness of flowers. These were not simply literary metaphors. The use of garlands was found in popular festivals, especially those at 1 May, when the gathering of garlands was associated with the choice by girls among rival loves and with the selection of festival queens. Nevertheless, the ambivalence towards such behaviour is apparent in its condemnation by Robert Manning of Brunne in 1303 in *Handlyngen Synne*, where he writes that it was against the commandment to cause girls to gather flowers for garlands (the 'floure-garland or couronne') to see who was the fairest when she was crowned.[34]

The return to flowers in literature and art was part of a wider return to nature that we see in the treatment of landscape, the long-term direction of which is clear: 'from an observation of nature which always and systemati-cally subdues natural phenomena to larger philosophical and spiritual meanings, which is essentially symbolic, to an observation of nature which finds the beauty of appearances philosophically explicable and aesthetically satisfying, and which can therefore rest on its actual forms'.[35] Two elements contributed to this process. One was the literary interest in landscape that partly re-emerged out of the post-classical tradition of rhetoric which included an element of *descriptio loci*, description of place, exemplified in stylised spring scenes and gardens which were forerunners of the more elaborate landscapes of the *Roman de la Rose* and were encouraged by the various revivals of Latin scholarship in the Carolingian renascence of the ninth century, the Ottonian of the tenth and the renascence of the twelfth century, as well as by Byzantine influences. The developments of the *plesaunce* landscape were further stimulated by the introduction of Oriental motifs, by ideas of the earthly paradise, by the renewed classical influences in the romances as well as less directly by the appearance of encyclopaedias like that of Isidore, closely associated with notions of secular love as part of the whole rhetoric of love.[36]

FLOWERS IN ART

The revival of interest became apparent in representations as well as in reality. However, rebirth of images of flowers in art and architecture took longer than that of flowers themselves, just as three-dimensional art took longer to re-establish itself than two-dimensional forms. The tradition of classical and Egyptian painting continued in association with the text in the form of illuminating the books that developed at the end of the first century AD. In late

[33] Waddell 1929:160–1.   [34] Lines 996–1000, see Baskerville 1920:44.
[35] Pearsall and Salter 1973:161.   [36] Pearsall and Salter 1973:47ff.

antiquity, that tradition flourished in manuscripts of Homer and Virgil. Scenes of a classical kind appear in the Vatican Virgil (end of the fourth, beginning of the fifth centuries) and in the Roman Virgil of the fifth century. Other illuminations came from the Eastern empire. Particularly important was the version of Dioscorides made in Constantinople in the early sixth century consisting of 400 detailed miniatures of plants, 25 of snakes and 47 of birds. Illustrations to this first-century manuscript continued to be produced until the fifteenth century because there were so few competitors. From the beginning the Byzantine tradition exercised a continuing influence on Western art, at times in the direction of greater realism; the early-eleventh-century manuscript, *Cynergetica* by Oppian, includes numerous illustrations of hunting, fishing, mythological scenes and battles, which combine fantasy with close observation.[37] But in general Western illuminations were intended for educational purposes and took as their topics Biblical scenes, concentrating mainly on human figures.

At the centre of early Christian illumination, produced in the old Mediterranean towns, stands the Bible. Some examples follow earlier illusionistic techniques in painting rich landscapes, some being adapted from mosaics and frescos. The use of icons for the purposes of instruction and conversion did not suffer the same objections as icons in the sacred precincts, which might appear as idols to be worshipped. Bede recounts that when St Augustine landed in south-east England to convert the country in AD 597, an audience was arranged with the king in which they held up the cross and the image of Christ painted on a board. They did the same when they arrived at Canterbury for the first time. A few years later, in 601, further missionaries arrived bringing 'many books'. These may have included the sixth-century Italian Gospel, now in the library of Corpus Christi College, Cambridge, which contains two full-page paintings showing details of the life of Christ. In the East, as in the St Augustine Gospel, the stress on linear design can be seen as the beginning of intentional abstraction, which proceeds more swiftly in the provinces.[38] It was the East too that developed the strong interest in ornamentation, especially of the borders. In the eighth century, with the emerging Middle Ages, we find a new tradition in which 'the composition no longer adheres to natural space' and looks forward to the future illuminations of the West.[39]

The paucity of landscape in the Middle Ages has been attributed to the 'medieval mind' which discarded the Hellenistic tradition in order to exercise its 'symbolizing faculty'.[40] The tardiness in the realistic representation of

---

[37] See Bologna 1988:92.   [38] Weitzmann 1977:22.   [39] Weitzmann 1977:24.
[40] Clark 1949:19, who mentions the continuation of the tradition in the Vienna Genesis executed in Antioch about 560; the ninth-century Utrecht psalter is also full of landscape motifs taken from Hellenistic painting, but the copy made by Eadvine for the monastic house of Canterbury in the mid twelfth century shows the triumph of 'symbol over sensation'.

5.1 The prophet Daniel, from St Cuthbert's stole, Durham cathedral, c.910. Winchester style, using plant decoration, including the acanthus, derived from Carolingian sources. (Wilson 1984:155)

nature was partly a matter of the icon being seen as an attempt to duplicate God's creation, partly because of the virtual absence of a secular as distinct from a religious tradition of graphic arts, and finally perhaps because the nature that appeared in the indigenous art of the Germanic and Celtic peoples was animal rather than vegetable.

The slowness of this revival in the North is apparent in the art of the British Isles. While it was the word that was supreme, it was again the text that provided a crucial focus for the rebirth of the image. The ability to read a text opened up the classical sources that formed the basis of a series of renascences occurring over the centuries. But the text itself, which was at first a plain manuscript, offered an opportunity for developing the icon in a more direct manner (Plate 5.1). In Anglo-Saxon England of the seventh century many ecclesiastical manuscripts were unilluminated, including great service books such as the Stonyhurst Gospel. However, most of the grander volumes began to have 'at least slightly embellished initials, sometimes merely filled with a wash of colour'.[41] At first they were only provided with illuminations of the calligraphic kind, the flourishes of the arabesque, the elaborations of Roman cursive, the 'insignificant' decoration of the Irish manuscripts. Historiated initials make their first appearance in Europe in the Leningrad manuscript of Bede, dated 746, while pictorial narrative does not become widespread until as late as the twelfth century.[42] An underlying pressure towards elaboration led in that direction, away from the sparseness of the Anglo-Saxon psalter towards the luxuriating miniatures of the Books of Hours, towards the return of the rose, or at least to vegetation, although the environmental components long remained the human and the animal rather than the floral.[43] (Plate 5.2)

In Anglo-Saxon art the southern, Canterbury, school was strongly influenced by the art forms of Italian, Gaulish, Byzantine and other missionaries who came with or after Augustine in 597. In Northumbria manuscript illumination was stimulated by the revival of learning of the seventh century in monasteries such as Lindisfarne that were connected with Ireland and its Celtic tradition of curvilinear forms. The Anglo-Saxons followed Germanic traditions in the desire to fill every space (the *horror vacui*) with largely abstract designs, interlace patterns of a zoomorphic kind; flowers and vegetation generally played only a minor part. With the influences from the Mediterranean, human figures were introduced into Hiberno-Saxon art.

Some floral patterns of an abstract kind did appear, mostly as ornaments to the text. Scrolls with leaves decorate the late-sixth-century portrait of St Luke in the St Augustine Gospels[44] and the binding of the Stonyhurst Gospel has a fine plant scroll, but much of the decoration in such manuscripts consisted of

---

[41] D. Wilson 1984:30.   [42] D. Wilson 1984:63.

[43] It was the Bede manuscript of 746 that introduced another element to their manuscript art, the plant ornament (D. Wilson 1984:63).   [44] D. Wilson 1984, Plate 15; Bologna 1988:49.

5.2 St Aetheldreda holding a lily, from the Benedictional of St Aethelwold. High Winchester style using florid acanthus ornament. (British Library, Add. 49598, fol.90v. C. 971; Wilson 1984:167)

5.3 St John Chrysostom, Homilies on the Gospel of St Matthew, Salzburg. (National Bibliothek, Vienna)

interlace, spirals and animals.[45] In the Carolingian period in France, there was
some limited figuration of nature as the background to pictures of saints (Plate
5.3), in Biblical scenes (Colour plate v.1) and in the calendrical sections of
manuscripts depicting the seasons. One image from the first quarter of the
ninth century shows May as a man holding a bunch of flowers in one hand and
some kind of garland in the other.[46] It is possible that such representation was
part of the classic naturalism that referred to earlier Roman practices rather
than to current Carolingian ones, just as astrological treatises continued to
disseminate representations of a wreath or crown in the signs of the zodiac.[47]
The revival in learning had resulted in the introduction of acanthus leaves into
English manuscript art during the early tenth century,[48] though the vine scroll,
another exotic, had already been an element of the tradition;[49] the Winchester
style of the second half of the tenth century, associated with the monastic
revival in England after the Danish invasions, blended both local themes with
those introduced under the Cluniac reforms of the early tenth century.[50] But it
seems more likely that such scenes show what was going on at a popular level.
We find greater evidence for the continuity of the culture of flowers and
foliage in the sculptural forms used on the tombs in which Christians were
wont to bury their distinguished dead. In Gaul between the fourth and sixth
centuries the sarcophagi were decorated with bas-reliefs, although the subject
matter had greatly changed; Christian iconography dominated, but the style
and the decoration included some earlier motifs. In particular cases old tombs
were recycled but in others the workshop traditions would continue to add
baskets and chaplets;[51] on a baptismal font at Tunis, we find a woman with
flowers. The use of these themes provided the purists with good reason to
complain.

Nevertheless, while the rose among other flowers continued to appear on
some early Christian tombs, in a number of early churches in Rome and in
the Byzantine mosaics in Ravenna, as well as a decoration on some garments,
this critical flower largely vanished from the iconography of Western Europe
even down to the period of Romanesque art, with the first examples coming
from Syria, Spain and Italy.[52] Despite the classical precedents, only very
slowly, over a period of more than one thousand years from the beginning of
Christianity, did flowers make any substantial reappearance in the visual arts,
even as a decorative theme.

[45] The Stonyhurst Gospel is also known as the St Cuthbert Gospel. It appears to have been buried with the saint
in 698, and carried around in his coffin for 400 years until his relics were installed in Durham cathedral in 1104
when it was found there (de Hamel 1986:24).
[46] Durliat 1985, Figure 446, (fol. 90, cod. 387, National Library, Vienna).
[47] Constellations, in Isadore of Seville, *De natura rerum*, ninth century (Durliat 1985, Figure 447; fol. 161,
Bibliothèque Nationale, Paris, MS lat. 5543).   [48] D. Wilson 1984:156–7.
[49] Acanthus leaves also appear on the embroidered textiles of the same period, notably those found in the tomb
of St Cuthbert at Durham.   [50] The abbey of Cluny was founded in 910.   [51] Le Blant 1886:x.
[52] Joret 1892:425–6.

ICONS AND ICONOCLASM

The early paucity of flowers as icons was linked to the predominantly religious character of art. Paintings existed in the mystery cults such as that of Isis, but in Christianity their presence was initially suspect, especially the rose. For, as we have seen, icons themselves were roundly condemned by some among the Fathers of the early church, just as they had been by the Neoplatonist, Plotinus, who was concerned with the deceptiveness of imitation. The Christians had additional reasons. In the third century, Origen of Alexandria replied to the criticism of the philosopher Celsus about the hostility of Jews and Christians to images, by referring back to the Ten Commandments that condemn such behaviour and calling for martyrdom rather than submission to pagan pressures. It was the insistence on spirituality as distinct from 'sensuality' (or, better, sense experience) that marked the Christian as against the pagan.

Nevertheless, we have seen that icons, other than those in manuscripts, began to enter into Christian experience. Secular images continued to be made, and they appeared in palaces which it was certainly permissible to decorate with birds and flowers.[53] In the religious domain, illuminations continued to be part of book production, illustrating the written word rather than challenging creation or, above all, acting as 'idols' in the context of worship. But even here the 'Christian idealism' of Clement and Origen came to be supplemented by the development of a 'Christian materialism'.[54] That raised other fundamental issues of the 'world view'. God's visibility was deliberately contrasted by some Christian writers with the invisibility of the God of the Old Testament. John of Damascus proclaimed that 'The ancient Israel did not see God, but beheld the glory of the Lord by means of the face that has been revealed to us.'[55] That was acceptable for instructional purposes. What the book is to the reader, the icon is to the illiterate. The hidden presence in the Burning Bush is set against the concrete sense of revelation.

In this revival a painting became more acceptable to Hellenised Christians than the fully embodied sculptures of the pagan tradition, which they were concerned to reject. In the fourth century, Bishop Eusebius of Caesarea (c.263–340) mentions icons of Christ and other religious figures, at a time when paintings in the church, as distinct from private, small-scale, portable pictures, were often considered idolatrous; as a supporter of the Arian doctrine, he condemned their use.[56]

The problem was not simply one of icons but of their worship. In this development the use of relics to conjure up the presence of the saint has been

---

[53] Runciman 1975:89.   [54] Pelikan 1990:107.
[55] Quoted by Pelikan 1990:113.   [56] Sahas 1986:85, 134ff.; Eusebius is also said to be of Pamphilus.

seen as one of 'the roots of future image worship'.[57] When St Helena, the mother of Constantine, found what she claimed to be the true cross in Jerusalem, she sent one part to the emperor to be enclosed in his own statue.[58]

The return of the icon in holy places did not go unchallenged. It is significant that the Umayyad Caliph Yazid II issued an iconoclastic edict in 724 that was carried out with considerable rigour. Only three years before the famous decree of Leo III he ordered the destruction of all icons found in the Christian churches under his dominion, an event that some authorities, especially Islamic ones, see as crucial in the explosion of the Christian controversy.[59] The Emperor Leo was apparently following a local tradition expressed by his soldiers against the cult of the icons, which were being paraded around towns in the belief that they would ward off misfortunes of various kinds. The Monophysites, prominent in Syria and Egypt, took the view that Christ's nature was solely divine, so they could not accept that he be portrayed. Leo's son and successor added to iconoclasm a loathing for Mariolatry, for relics and even for the title of saint.[60] While Leo was accused of being semi-Muslim (he had in fact warded off attacks by their armies), his objections were rooted in Eastern Christianity. However, the iconoclastic movement was not against all representation of God's creation, as was the case in Islam. Ultimately it can be seen as based on the Mosaic proscription against idols, which it was wrong to make and worse to worship. But the argument displayed a specifically Christian character. On the one hand, objections were made to depictions of Christ because his divine nature was not 'capable of circumscription'. But the iconoclasts also objected to the icons of saints and Leo ordered their removal from churches, although the provision had little effect in southern Italy and some other parts of the Byzantine empire.[61]

So the outbreak of iconoclasm in AD 726 led to attacks on representations of saints and devotional scenes in every medium, whatever the scale, including coins.[62] Church Fathers were forced to defend their images, arguing that it was the human not the divine nature of Christ that was portrayed. Attitudes towards representation differed and were influenced by theological doctrines about the nature of Christ, for if his divine and human natures were distinct it was possible to paint one and not the other. Arian doctrine denied the contemporaneity of father and son, while the Monophysite churches, such as the Coptic church of Egypt and of Abyssinia, initially took a stand against the representation of Christ because they did not accept the notion of the distinct divine and human natures. Nestorian churches too did not fully recognise the separation of his two natures.

That situation did not last. It was with the second Council of Nicaea in AD

---

[57] Kitzinger 1977:10.   [58] Pelikan 1990:27.
[59] Sahas 1986:18ff. for a bibliography of the extensive literature.
[60] Runciman 1975:83.   [61] Pelikan 1990:150.   [62] That also occurred in Islam.

787 that images and their worship became orthodox and God-pleasing.[63] Early Fathers had emphasised the fundamental divergence between Christian worship paid to the invisible God and every form of idolatry paid to visible representations of deity.[64] The orthodox interpretation of the Incarnation, much developed by the Iconodules, asserted that Christ had a nature that was both divine and human, so that divinity became visible. Five centuries later John of Damascus was defending the use of images for the instruction of those who could not read. On the other hand, icons were still not admitted within the sanctuary itself.

One element in this rejection had nothing specifically to do with paganism and was wider than any specific doctrinal controversies. That element was linked to the broader problem of whether one could address or even represent any divinity in material form, in other words to the very possibility of religious art. The problem was particularly acute with three-dimensional forms, since these more nearly approach material reality. Such forms were largely rejected by Christianity during the earlier Middle Ages. But that was not specific to Christianity. Intimations of such a conceptual change in notions of divinity were found in the classical period. In early Greece and Rome the worship of gods had mainly focused on the statue in the temple; for private worship replicas were placed in a niche in a room of the house or garden. During the third century AD sculpture tended to be replaced by flat relief, and then by paintings, especially in the mystery religions. These changes have been seen as resulting from a transcendental outlook which found a 'more appropriate expression for the Deity in the dematerialized rendering of the human body'.[65] The swing between icons and iconoclasm relates to wider human concerns.

THE RETURN OF SCULPTURE

In the earlier periods a variety of materials were employed for icons, mosaics, metals and sculpture too, although a flat relief was usually preferred 'in order to subdue the impression of pronounced corporeality'.[66] In the middle Byzantine period we find groups of figures and the representations of great feasts.

But the development was in no sense unilinear. Continued attempts to 'dematerialise' the human body in the eleventh and twelfth centuries led to another decline in the incidence of sculpture, since idolatry continued to be associated with marble figures in the round. A few statuettes were carved, probably for niches, while bas-relief was used on screens and balustrades. So, while statuary was not specifically forbidden in the post-Nicaean period in the Eastern church, painting predominated and there was little place for free sculpture in the Greek world.

---

[63] Pelikan 1990:1–2.   [64] Pelikan 1990:68.   [65] Weitzmann 1987:3.   [66] Weitzmann 1987:6.

In the Latin West, by contrast, there had not been the same widespread iconoclastic revolt as in the East. Nevertheless, around 599 Serenus, bishop of Marseilles, wanted to destroy painted *imagines* in the churches because they were being worshipped by the congregation. However, Pope Gregory the Great supported the idea of painting the history of the saints in holy places as a way of educating the illiterate. On the basis of this and other texts, the French scholar, Hubert, speaks of the continuation of religious statuary in the early Middle Ages. However, the material evidence for sculpture in the round as distinct from bas-relief is sparse. That situation changed with the Carolingians. It was then that Western Europe finally separated itself from the East on one fundamental question: the nature of their views on the religious image.[67] The West had rejected iconoclasm but the Carolingians did not approve of the decisions of the second Council of Nicaea. In their eyes those decisions came too close to the worship of images by asserting that they could provide a way of entering into communion with the saint who was represented. For the West, images were material objects that played an educational role for those who could not read. Any implication of worship was banished, but under this rubric images could be encouraged.

While the beginning of the revival of free-standing sculpture has been traced to literary sources dating from the late eight century, it was a long and laborious rebirth.[68] A well-known statue, said by some to be of Charlemagne, classical in type, represents a crowned emperor riding a horse.[69] At this period the head crowned with laurels or with a diadem appeared on seals and money. There are other references to statues. The golden equestrian representation of the Gothic King Theodoric was brought by the Emperor Louis from Ravenna to Aachen, where it served as the symbol of tyrannical rule, at least for the ninth-century poet, Walahfrid.[70]

While the West experienced no overt movement against icons, neither was there quite the same development of independent religious paintings. Some frescos are reported, painting on walls being excluded from any ban.[71] There was also one form of statuary that subsequently became widely significant, namely, the crucifix, the figure of Christ on the cross. In the carved oak Gero crucifix in the cathedral of Cologne, dating from before 986, the body of Christ clearly stands out from the cross itself and is surrounded by a nimbus, a kind of heavenly crown originating in ancient Egypt.[72] The carving reveals a measure of realism that would be developed in the renewed sculptural tradition of Western Europe. The spiral column showing the life of Christ in St Michael's, Hildesheim (c.1020), is an example of Ottonian art, the

[67] Durliat 1985:174.   [68] Forsythe 1972:91.   [69] Hubert 1970:224–5.
[70] *Ad serenum massiliensem episcopum, S. Gregorii Pop. I cognomento*, Magna Opera Omnia, viii, Venice, 1771, fos. 134 and 242.
[71] Bernard d'Angers, *Liber miraculorum sanctae Fideis* (ed. Bouillet and Servières), 1900:472–3.
[72] See also the Anglo-Saxon ivory crucifix from the Victoria and Albert Museum, London (Durliat 1985:172).

art of the Saxon successors to the Carolingians as rulers of the Holy Roman empire, who also encouraged a classical revival. On the one hand it looks back to the triumphal columns of Trajan and Marcus Aurelius, and on the other it looks forward to the sculptured elaboration of the great Romanesque monastery of Moissac in the south-west of France, not only to the tympanum over the portals but to the detailed carvings of the cloister capitals.

Reacting to the second Council of Nicaea, the Carolingians defined the images it was legitimate to venerate as the host, which was Christ's body, the cross, the scriptures, the holy vases used in the mass, and finally the relics of saints. Their rejection of other themes was expressed in the *Libri carolini* which attempted to find a middle way between iconoclasm on the one hand, and what they saw as the idolatry of the second Council of Nicaea on the other.[73] Once again the crucifix avoided the problem of representing deity, since the image stood only for the human aspect of Christ and was therefore consistent with the notion of his two natures. Theological considerations dominated notions of representation.

THE DEVELOPMENT OF RELIQUARY-STATUES

One early development in the gradual process of legimating three-dimensional representation was the reliquary-statue. Here too the ban on the worship of idols was initially seen as circumvented by the presence in the statue of a relic of the saint, so that the worshipper was in fact addressing the saint himself, since part stood for the whole. The cult of relics, which had swept through Europe during the sixth century, did so again when the Crusaders returned with booty from the East. It fitted well with iconoclastic tendencies, for one worshipped not an image but the real thing, whether that was a bone of St Christopher or the foreskin of Christ. It has been argued that one of the functions of the reliquary-statue was to legitimise the return of sculpture to the European tradition.[74] This thesis is discounted by others, for the enthroned *Maiestas*, the seated statues of the Virgin, are by no means all reliquaries. However, the first known example, the golden Madonna at Clermont-Ferrand from the late ninth century, was certainly of this kind; so too were others from the Carolingian period.

Such statuary emerged in France in the last quarter of the ninth century; that of St Maurice at Vienne in the Rhône valley, a crowned figure, dates from 879–87, that of Sainte-Foy (St Faith) at Conques in Rouergue from about the same time (Colour plate v.2).[75] Once again the use of these reliquaries in the south did not go unchallenged, especially by the orthodoxy of the north. Some hundred and twenty-five years later, in 1013, a cleric from the Loire, Bernard of Angers, made a pilgrimage to the Auvergne and expressed surprise at the

[73] Schmitt 1987:274.   [74] Forsythe 1972.   [75] For a general discussion, see Forsythe 1972.

'viel usage' and 'antique coutume' of that region.[76] He was quite unambiguous about his initial reaction to the statues of patron saints made out of precious metals that were to be found there, in Rouergue and around Toulouse. 'This practice was looked upon by learned men, without any intention of offence, as a superstition; such a rite was, in effect, the survival of cult directed to the gods, or rather to demons.'[77] He himself saw the cult as 'absolutely opposed to Christian law' and when he first encountered such a reliquary at Aurillac he turned to his companion and said, in Latin, 'Brother, what do you think about this idol? Would Jupiter or Mars have thought the statue unworthy of them?' For as northern clerics they had been taught that 'since the highest form of cult was due only to the one true and sovereign God, it was improper and absurd to make statues of stone, wood or bronze, except to represent Our Lord on the cross'. Sculpture or metalwork should be used only for the crucifix, the one exception; to represent the saints one had to be content with the written word or with painting on walls. 'We tolerate statues of saints only because of the antiquity of the abuse and the difficulty of reforming the minds of simple folk.'

Three days later the two men visited Conques where the crowd prostrated itself before the statue of St Faith and Bernard was again amazed that people could address themselves to a material object that was incapable of speech and intelligence. He even referred to the names of Venus and Diana. Nor were such references entirely out of place for a very literal reason. Recent research has shown that the reliquary of Sainte-Foy was built up on an earlier Roman mask of gold crowned with laurels, which represents an emperor of the late empire (Plate 5.4).[78] But on this second occasion Bernard set aside his doubts and was suddenly 'converted', partly because the statue was also a reliquary, partly because of the miracles (the 'games') associated with it, but above all because he realised this figure could not be seen as 'an oracle one consulted or an idol to which one offered sacrifices, but was simply honoured in the memory of the holy martyr, in order to glorify the Supreme God'.[79] One worshipped God by honouring, by memorialising, the saint.

The distribution of reliquary-statues in the Auvergne was regarded by Hubert as the result of the Norse raids that terrorised the lowland areas accessible by the rivers flowing into the Atlantic, leaving only the remoter hills safe from plunder. That author rejects the idea that they represent 'a return to human representation after centuries of oblivion'. Nor does he see a France divided into two zones, the north hostile to images, and a laxer south. The West was, he argues, very little affected by the iconoclasm of the East and there was continuity in art forms from the later empire.

While this argument avoids a dichotomy between North and South, between town and country, between high and low, it draws too strong a line

[76] Bernard d'Angers, *Liber miraculorum sanctae Fidis*. See also Durliat 1985:233.
[77] Bouillet and Servières 1900:472.   [78] J. and M. C. Hubert 1985:358.
[79] Bouillet and Servières 1900:473.

5.4 Mask of gold, with laurels, of an emperor of the late empire, which forms the basis for the reliquary-statue of Sainte-Foy of Conques. (Hubert 1985:358)

between East and West. The tendency to iconoclasm was not simply a matter for the Eastern church to deal with; it was located at the heart of the Jewish, Christian and Islamic traditions. While such ideas were under constant pressure from socio-cultural forces favouring an expansion of images both in two and three dimensions, they always remained a potential clamp on those activities because they were embodied in Holy Writ, expanded in the comments of the early Fathers, and related to wider doubts about the worship and representation of an immaterial God through material means.

The earlier doubts of Bernard of Angers represent a strong current of thinking even in the West. The case of Serenus of Marseilles was 'followed by the influence of the adoptionist heresy, condemned by the Synod of Frankfurt in 794, on the activities of Claudius of Turin, who condemned not only images but the cross, since Christ was only a human, adopted by God not divinity itself'.[80] Later on a number of manifestations of similar iconoclastic trends occurred in Western Europe, especially during the attempts to restore

[80] Schmitt 1987:278.

sculptural forms. A fascinating example is to be found in one of the earliest episodes of religious dissent to follow the millennium, the account of which comes from an orthodox source. One Leutard, a peasant from the Marne, dreamt about a swarm of bees which he interpreted as a revelation from God. He went home, divorced his wife, proceeded to the local church where he 'ripped down the cross and smashed the likeness of Christ'.[81] Subsequently his fame spread and he gained a local following whom he told 'not to pay tithes' and declared that in his view the Biblical prophets had inserted 'falsehoods' among their 'useful statements'. As Stock points out in a valuable discussion of 'heresies', his views represent more than an early instance of Cathar dualism or simply a sign of opposition to nascent feudalism; there is a case for looking at Leutard as 'an illumined layman, a self-styled interpreter and propagator of Scriptures, who is "called" to perform the Lord's work'.[82] In other words, he has to be considered as one who was bound to God's word, written down over fifteen hundred years earlier and preserved for posterity in a fixed text. Others have seen this incident as an example of publicity seeking, which undoubtedly motivates some individual destroyers of paintings at the present day.[83] But religious considerations, including the whole problem of the representation of divinity and the sacredness of the holy text, were undoubtedly of underlying importance in generating such notions. For this manifestation was far from the end. The controversy flowed like a submerged stream, always ready to be brought to the surface.

THE CAROLINGIAN REVIVAL

Of course, a measure of continuity was present, especially in Mediterranean Europe; Roman models, in literature and in material remains, continued everywhere, making possible the revival of classical forms and images. Since these were of either pagan or secular provenance, they tended to threaten the total domination of the religious. But such renascences were nevertheless constant features of cultural history, not only of Western Christianity. In the Eastern church a classical revival followed the end of the Iconoclastic period (726–842), possibly in an attempt to escape its strictures by freeing art of the religious image.[84] That meant turning back to classical models in the ninth century. The same iconoclastic controversy was one factor in causing the papacy to call for support from the Franks, leading to Charlemagne's creation of what later became the Holy Roman empire, as well as to the related cultural *renovatio*, a name by which the revival was known to intellectuals at his court. One of those declared, 'Our times are transformed into the civilisation of Antiquity. Golden Rome is reborn and restored anew to the world.'[85] There

---

[81] Stock 1983:102.   [82] Stock 1983:103.   [83] Freedberg 1985:44.
[84] The Council of Nicaea had already declared against the doctrine in 787.
[85] Moduin of Autun, Egloga: Poetry and the New Age, 26–7, in Godman 1985:193.

were of course earlier returns to the past in Italy, where the reminders of the greatness of Rome were obviously stronger than elsewhere and where economic and social activity was more vigorous than in Northern Europe. Early medieval Italy was never a totally enclosed economy. Its many markets required the use of money, and in the Byzantine South relations with the East were active, with Amalfi possessing colonies and warehouses at Constantinople and elsewhere in Asia.

Owing to the political conditions that obtained in Italy at this time, it fell to the lot of bishops, whose seats were necessarily in towns of importance, to act as local princes in the civil as well as in the secular realm. They did something to conserve the civic and civil traditions of Rome, including the principles of Roman law, and in Carolingian times many became masters of the cities. It was then we find the most deliberate attempt to date to resurrect the glories of Rome. The interests of the new empire combined with the devotion to ancient learning displayed by its scholars, not only those in the church but those called upon to run the bureaucracy.

The reference back to Rome was always ambivalent on the socio-cultural level. On the one hand, the empire had been pagan, the opponent of the true faith, committed to the worship of the dead, to the garlanding of statues, and to the offering of animals and other goods in sacrifice. On the other hand, it was the home of civilisation and of secular learning. If there was to be any such learning in medieval Europe, it had to refer back to the classics, whether in rhetoric, botany or in astronomy. The *Leiden Aratea*, a major work of Carolingian art, was a ninth-century copy of an astronomical and meteorological treatise written in the third century, the thirty-nine miniatures of the constellations, the seasons and the planets being presumed to be copies of a late antique manuscript, now lost. Like the script of rustic capitals, not only the model but the origin was Roman.[86] One of the illustrations consists of a garland of the classical kind, entitled *Corona Borealis* (Colour plate v.3). Apart from being used as an astronomical term, corona meant literally a crown, a chaplet. It stands there, in the sky and on the page, as a reminder of ancient custom, as a potential source of imagery and even practice. That was true of the Heavens themselves. For although Christianity had established a new eschatology, had suppressed or reinterpreted pagan shrines and gods, it did not succeed in changing the previous names for time and space, in particular heavenly space; though the Puritans were later to refer to the Lord's Day in order to avoid the term Sunday, the traditional name never disappeared. For the measurement of ritual time, the church imposed its liturgical calendar, embodying in the year the life-cycle of the prophet; and it changed the whole reckoning of the era, inaugurating the one that now dominates all others. But days and months proved resistant, partly because

---

[86] More strictly, it was based upon the *Phaenomena* written by the Greek poet Aratus (c.315–240/39 BC), see Katzenstein and Savage-Smith 1988.

they were tied into the mapping of heavenly space by astronomers and astrologers. The constellations of the zodiac, derived from Babylonian science, remained as a perpetual mystery, a potential source of mystical attraction, for future generations. Nor were the constellations of the Greeks and Romans renamed, so they continued to provide a reference back to classical mythology. 'Who was Orion?', his belt leads us to ask. While some clusters had local, vernacular names such as the Plough or the Morning Star, to the learned they were Ursa Major and Venus of Latin parentage; so the sky continued to display reminders of a pagan mythology, even for the 'unschooled'. These were the potential links which figures in the Carolingian renascence sought to expand, as we have seen in the account of flowers in literature and art.

THE LATER PERIOD

At least in a limited way, by the twelfth century flowers had returned in monastic and royal gardens, to popular usage and to poetry. While they had never altogether vanished, they were now part of the efflorescence of higher culture, and presumably of popular culture too. But still little room was given to them in the visual arts, on which no great stress was placed, especially statuary in the round. That further revival was to take place after nearly a thousand years of Christianity which had come to dominate so many of the intellectual horizons of Europe and its artists. It began during the period that saw the coming of the Romanesque, but yet more vigorously at the time of the emergence of the Gothic architectural traditions, though these developments were only the most visible examples of a series of changes, not only in architecture and the arts but in society at large.

THE ROMANESQUE

In the revival of monumental sculpture in the West, Apulia and Sicily became early leaders, providing a congenial meeting place for ancient, Byzantine and Islamic art. These influences merge in the great church of St Nicola at Bari, which was started in 1089 to accommodate the newly acquired relics of the saint as well as the pilgrims coming to venerate them. Columns rested on the backs of lions while the archbishop's marble throne was supported on the shoulders of three figures representing the peoples of the world.

In the North the revival of monumental stone sculpture took themes from manuscript illumination, the book again serving as a model, as well as from Ottonian gold and bronze work. But it was in the Romanesque churches that monumental sculpture began to return in strength, with the sculptors often taking their inspiration from the illuminators, as in the tympanum of the Cluniac priory of Moissac.[87]

---

[87] Stokstad 1986:242.

Another great Romanesque tympanum of this period in the south-west was created at Conques, one of four major churches standing on the pilgrimage routes through France to the shrine of Santiago (St Jacques) of Compostella in northern Spain, and the eventual resting place of the relics of St Faith. Following the discovery of the tomb of St James in the ninth century, Compostella came to rival St Peter's itself. The other major Romanesque churches on that pilgrimage route were St Martin at Tours, St Sernin at Toulouse, and St Martial at Limoges; all probably employed some of the same craftsmen. In these buildings monumental sculpture developed in the attempt to get the Christian story across immediately and forcefully to the numerous pilgrims. It was part of the educational process that led to the revival of narrative art. That already existed on some earlier frescos, but arising out of the calendar icons of the eleventh century, the end of the twelfth saw the development of narrative paintings of the lives of saints.

The Muslim influence on Romanesque architecture took a number of forms including the ornamental corbels with large flowers framing the portal of St Sernin at Toulouse.[88] The introduction of the floral design from the South was paralleled by the floral imagery which marked the Muslim influences on Provençal poetry, the secular poetry of the troubadours, as well as on actual flowers and gardens. Architecturally of greater significance, however, was the pointed arch and other decorative features that developed in the Gothic period.

THE GOTHIC

In the graphic arts, the Byzantine East had a continuing influence on the West long after the Carolingian period. The key channels for this influence were Venice, which maintained relations with Constantinople, and southern Italy, reconquered by the East around 970, although Sicily remained in Muslim hands until taken by the Normans at the beginning of the twelfth century. The Norman kings then made it a centre of cultural development, importing craftsmen from Constantinople and Fāṭimid painters from Egypt to decorate their new cathedrals. At the same time, the Byzantine influence made itself particularly felt in Ottonian Germany, the heir to the eastern Carolingian empire.[89] That was a dominating force in painting until the appearance of the Italian masters of the fourteenth century, *i primi lumi*,[90] when Italy began to match the position France had held, especially in the art of the illuminated book, over the previous hundred and fifty years.

The influence of Byzantine image-making on the Ottonian court began to change attitudes which had earlier been ambiguous.[91] During the following

---

[88] Stokstad 1986:27; a corbel is an architectural feature projecting from within a wall as a support for some object of weight.
[89] Otto I reigned from 936 to 973; the authority of the dynasty declined until it became extinct in 1125.
[90] Panofsky 1972:114ff.   [91] Schmitt 1987:282.

two centuries the Western church adopted the very positions it had earlier condemned among the Greeks. The cross became the crucifix, sometimes containing relics and always emphasising the humanity of Christ. Already in France at the end of the ninth century we have seen how reliquaries developed from containers to three-dimensional statues, which were later followed by statuary itself.[92]

Once again these developments raised protests. The beginning of the eleventh century saw the appearance of popular heresies directed against these 'artificial' forms of mediation between God and man. The rejection of the cross was explicit in the acts of the heretic, Leutard of Vertus, around AD 1000, and that was often accompanied, as among the later Cathars and the Waldensians, by an inclusive rejection of images.[93] As with the Iconoclasts, this movement led to a defence and elaboration of images on the part of the orthodox. Among those justifications were the writings of Abbot Suger, builder of the first great Gothic cathedral at St Denis, near Paris, in the late eleventh century and those of St Thomas Aquinas, whose 'conception of the religious image is contemporaneous with the multiplication of paintings, offered by the faithful and new to western art'.[94] In Italy such paintings included those masterpieces of the thirteenth century by Pisano, Cimabue and Giotto, together with the icons that arrived from the East after the capture of Constantinople by the Crusaders in 1204. It was at this time too that images were promoted by the new religious orders, the Franciscans and Dominicans, and by the lay confraternities attached to them. For the church required every aid to defeat heresies and to defend itself in the first age of feudalism.[95]

For two-dimensional images, the development of the full-page manuscript illustration and eventually of panel painting in the West were inspired to a significant extent by the Eastern tradition of icons.[96] Those illuminations were in turn taken as models by Romanesque sculptors. But the progression was again challenged. St Bernard of Clairvaux (1090–1153) persuaded the Cistercians not only to reject the idea of statuary and of visual representations in their buildings but to give up full-page illuminations and even historiated initials in their texts. All these were distractions from the word, from the reading in the cloister: 'We are more tempted to read in the marble than in our books.' St Bernard went on to add that if men are not ashamed of these follies, they should at least be ashamed of the expense. The visual arts were anathema to him, partly as distracting, partly as luxury, feelings that extended to architecture as well as to art.[97]

During the period from 950 to 1050, improved methods of construction, the grand scale, the assured design, the increasing mastery of masonry vaulting and the rich use of foliate and figural sculpture, all these considerations

---

[92] 'La tridimensionnalité était traditionellement attachée aux idoles païennes' (Schmitt 1987:286).
[93] Schmitt 1987:286.   [94] Schmitt 1987:297.   [95] Schmitt 1987:300.   [96] Stokstad 1986:158.
[97] Stokstad 1986:246; Panofsky 1946:25.

contributed to the development of the Romanesque style of architecture that came to dominate Western Europe. But with painting and sculpture, so with architectural decoration. The Cistercian order was strongly opposed to decoration of any kind and its churches, such as that at Fontenay (1139–47), were built with elegant simplicity that set aside both painting and sculpture.[98] The reaction of the Cistercians against representation was extreme, for they were even worried about illuminated books. Their statute of 1131 declared that initials should be made of one colour only and not illustrated.[99] Bernard himself protested strongly against the exuberance of early-twelfth-century Cluniac art, part of the attempt to prevent the importation of secular themes into religious art.[100] That call for separation and restraint repeatedly emerged as part of the theme of *contemptus mundi* and had wide-ranging effects. Two centuries earlier the movement for ascetic reform, which spread from the monastery of Cluny in France throughout Western Europe in the first half of the tenth century, had discouraged churchmen from writing for the laity. For the next century little was composed in the vernacular.

With the coming of Gothic in the form of the abbey of St Denis (1081–1151), that restraint disappeared. The abbot and architect, Suger, took a very different attitude. The 'anagogical movement' saw 'the dull mind' rising to truth 'through that which is material'. Indeed, jewels and coloured glass were perceived as able to transform 'that which is material to that which is immaterial'.[101] Craftsmanship was the gateway to understanding divinity.[102] The west front was developed as a frame for sculpture, while the lighter walls arising from the newer forms of construction made possible the introduction of stained-glass windows, whose narrative content served to educate the illiterate. Included in this development was the rose window itself. Examples of circular windows existed in the Romanesque period, for example at Santa Maria in Pomposa, Italy, dating from the tenth century. But the rose window as a rich decorative feature appeared around 1200 only after the Crusades, when it became a feature of many transitional and early Gothic churches, first in France and subsequently in England, Italy, Spain and Germany.[103]

The opposition between the high-born St Bernard, abbot of Clairvaux, the mentor of the Holy See and the greatest spiritual force in Europe, and the oblate, Suger, abbot of St Denis, successor to Abelard, adviser to the crown and the greatest political power in France, represented the continuing struggle between different conceptions of the approach to the divine, that mediated by the word and that by the object, between the contemplative and the active, between the self-denial of the one and the luxuriousness of the other. By reforming his abbacy in a bureaucratic sense, Suger helped accumulate the finances needed to rebuild the church dedicated to St Denis, apostle to the Gauls, the first major Gothic building in Europe and one adorned, elaborated,

[98] Shaver-Crandell 1982:24.   [99] de Hamel 1986:97.   [100] Randall 1966.
[101] Panofsky 1970:162.   [102] Panofsky 1946:47–9.   [103] Cowen 1979:8.

created, in quite a different spirit from the plain Romanesque style favoured by St Bernard. The latter had written: 'But we who, for the sake of Christ, have decreed as dung whatever shines with beauty, enchants the ear, delights through fragrance, flatters the taste, pleases the touch – whose devotion, I ask, do we intend to incite by means of these very things?'[104] He goes on to pose the question, 'What has gold to do in the sanctuary?' Suger takes quite the opposite view and tries to adorn his church with every available luxury in honour of God and of the saints. Following the writings of Dionysus the Areopagite recently translated by John the Scot, he accepted the view that the immaterial could only be reached through the material. As a result, the whole material universe becomes a big 'light';[105] objects symbolise the word, shed light on the word, as the stained glass of his great church windows open the way to understanding. Once again the problem was one of communicating with the immaterial.[106]

So the return of the rose had an ideological counterpart. It corresponded to the return to Aristotelianism by thirteenth-century philosophers where nominalism 'reinstates the observation and empirical knowledge of the concrete. Thomas Aquinas, Roger Bacon and William of Occam reconciled theological thought with sensation and the experience of nature.'[107] In this way the divine became increasingly realised through its creation, a process of quasi-secularisation that was justified by the church itself as well as being congruent with growing antipathy to direct representations of the holy.

This was the period when the scholarly study of plants made its return. Written work on botany did not disappear entirely in the European Middle Ages, even if it is difficult to recognise the Anglo-Saxon herbals as increasing or even maintaining the sum of that knowledge. The thirteenth century saw the appearance of what Needham describes as 'the only theoretical botany of the Latin West' in the shape of the *De vegetabilibus* (c.1265) by Albertus Magnus, bishop of Regensberg. This work owed a lot to the pseudo-Aristotelian treatise, *De plantis*, now attributed to Nicolaus of Damascus (first century BC), which was one of those many classical studies that entered Europe at this time by way of Arabic translations and were eventually rendered into Latin.[108] Nevertheless, the greatest advance came later with the printing in 1475 of the earlier work of Konrad von Megenberg (1309–74), much of which was a translation of the yet earlier Latin writings of the Belgian, Thomas of Cantimpré (1201–63).[109] A study of Bartholomew the

---

[104] Quoted by Panofsky 1946:15.   [105] Panofsky 1946:19–20.

[106] But in building that church, which set the course of Western architecture for more than a century, Suger had himself destroyed as well as created – 'this destructively creative enterprise', Panofsky called it. For he did away almost entirely with the earlier Carolingian edifice in order to give birth to the 'new light' and this destruction he had to defend in his writings against Cistercian puritanism.

[107] Sterling 1985:7, quoted by Tapié 1987:23.

[108] Arber 1938:4; see also Reeds 1980 and Stannard 1980.

[109] On the relationship between the work of Konrad von Megenberg and Thomas of Cantimpré, see Brückner 1961.

Englishman, written around 1250, listed one hundred and fifty-four plants; this was eventually printed about 1470, shortly before the work of Konrad. But the major achievement of the latter was visual rather than verbal, for it contained woodcuts that were probably the first intended for 'recognition rather than ornament',[110] after which 'things happened rather fast', stimulated in part by the further recovery of classical knowledge with the fall of Byzantium and 'in part by the possibilities of mass diffusion which the newly arrived [Chinese] invention of printing offered'.[111] While written language was essential to the development of most other contemporary systems of knowledge, physical representation was critical to botany and other sciences of nature which depended upon the recognition of objects out there in the world. Symbolic meaning and decorative design were of minor interest compared with realistic representation of the whole and the parts. Similar advances had occurred in China some four centuries earlier, following the development of printing techniques in the ninth century. In these respects late-medieval and Renaissance Europe had to catch up with China and with its own past. The gradual upswing in botanical learning, which began to take shape in the thirteenth and fourteenth centuries and spread throughout Europe, was closely linked to the development of gardens and the growing of flowers. For 'the flower-filled settings of many northern European paradise gardens of the fifteenth century are specifically indebted to Italian botanical studies of the preceding decades.'[112]

Flowers appeared not only in botanical texts but from the thirteenth century were introduced into architectural decoration; representations of nature were encouraged in stone, wood and metal. The urban cathedrals of northern France took their decoration 'straight from nature' and incorporated into their capitals flowers and leaves of many kinds.[113] In the church of St Peter at Lisieux (c.1200), 'more or less naturalistic buds' began to thrust forth from the close-set Romanesque foliage. Then at Laon and in Rouen cathedral they spring to life, becoming yet more naturalistic; at Notre Dame, a watercress frieze with motifs based on celandine leaves and snapdragon flowers. In the early stages the leaves and flowers were those of the small plants of the medieval garden, constituting a much wider repertoire than in the earlier period: columbine, primrose, ranunculus, cranesbill, violet, aconite, pea, rue, broom, saffron, lily-of-the-valley, together with a number of brookside plants; bracken, plantain, wild arum, cress, waterlily, clover and hart's-tongue fern. As the century advanced, all the plants of the gardens of Champagne came to be represented in decorative form. The capitals of Rheims cathedral were carved with more than thirty kinds of plants, including roses. The formal *rinceau* or foliage tradition disappears and simple leaves and trails of flowers are carved 'as if laid upon the stone'.[114] The naturalistic

---

[110] Needham 1986:4.   [111] Needham 1986:4.   [112] Pearsall and Salter 1973:60.
[113] Evans 1931:i, 42.   [114] Evans 1931:i, 45.

5.5 *La Fôret*, Gothic tapestry, c.1500. (Private collection, Paris; Kjellberg 1963:163)

style spread from northern France to England, where maple, bryony, greater celandine, hawthorn, columbine and many other flowers and plants were used. The creators of the dynamic Gothic architecture 'wreathed their capitals with leaves and branches of natural vegetation, and adorned their walls with the growing plants of the garden and the orchard'.[115] No longer do we find only the formal decoration of classic capitals, copied from the previous carver, but motifs based upon the gardens that had become a prominent feature of the domestic environment, at least of the monasteries and the royal

[115] Evans 1931:i, 47. The leafy capitals in the Lady chapel at Ely date from the period 1321–49.

domain, the kind of garden described by Albertus Magnus, aimed not only at utilitarian needs but for the delight of sight and smell.[116]

A similar 'naturalism' touched the graphic arts. It was the twelfth and thirteenth centuries that saw the re-emergence of landscape in the Western tradition, drawing significantly on Byzantine precedents.[117] As we have seen, the previous centuries produced little by way of landscape in painting or in poetry, except for some isolated instances of classical influence in Italy which more than anywhere had before it an abundance of 'physical evidences lacking elsewhere in Europe'. In contrast, Irish and Hiberno-Saxon art was 'totally non-naturalistic', while the tendency in medieval literature was 'to polarize all landscape into symbols of heaven and hell'. Only the Byzantine tradition provided some 'dried remnants' of the tradition of the classical landscape for later revival, although the Arabs in Sicily, who contributed both to decorative themes and to gardens themselves, stood as a reminder of the 'potential presence of oriental non-representationalism in all Eastern Christian art'.[118]

In the second half of the thirteenth century, the illuminators of the manuscript of the Apocalypse written for Edward I or his wife included individual trees. In secular embroidery, the forest flora of the chase was especially favoured. During the later Middle Ages, the carpets (*tapis sarrazinois*, 'of the Saracens'), which were increasingly used as a floor covering and as tapestries (*tapisseries*) for hangings on walls, were themselves sometimes carpeted with flowers as in the Persian tradition (Plate 5.5). In medieval European art and literature, representations of Paradise, of the earthly Garden of Eden and the celestial counterpart in heaven, were seized upon as the occasions for introducing flowers into the landscape.

In this development there was no neat chronology for the different possibilities lay embedded in the very notion of paradise. In the earlier Christian centuries, allegorical expositions dominated, while the more concrete examples appear at the end of the medieval period.

FLOWERS IN PRACTICE

The notion of paradise as full of blooms may even have encouraged the growth of flowers themselves, for monastic gardens were also places where intensive horticulture of an experimental kind took place. However, there were some flowers in what became known as the paradise garden attached to

[116] Alberti Magni ex ordine praedicatorum, *De vegetabilibus libri VII, historiae naturalis pars XVIII*. Editionem criticam ab Ernesto Meyero coeptam, absolvit Carolus Jessen. Frankfurt am Main, 1982 (1867), p.636: Sunt autem quaedam utilitatis non magnae aut fructus loca, sed ob delectationem parata . . . Haec autem sunt, quae viridantia sive virdaria vocantur. Haec autem, quia ad delectationem duorum maxime sensuum praeparantur, hoc est visus et odoratus . . .   [117] Pearsall and Salter 1973:30.
[118] Pearsall and Salter 1973:33, 41, 44; in this respect Icelandic sagas stand out in contrast to other medieval literature in Europe.

the monastery, which was influenced by the Byzantine church, combining Persian garden with classical courtyard, rather than the Grecian garden that contained statues dedicated to the pagan gods or yet the Roman variant which depended more upon topiary.[119] But that development was not an early one for the first use of the term 'paradise' in English was in about AD 1000.[120] The cultivation of monastery gardens was never simply a matter of following tradition but also of innovation. Complex grafting techniques were adopted and developed; under the church as under the Romans, the growing of wheat and grapes, the constituent elements for the bread and the wine, was pushed further and further to the north, becoming adjusted to new climates and to different soils.[121]

The later monastic garden contained plants of all kinds, including flowers which supplied decoration for the altar and church generally, as well as being used for medicinal, spiritual and aesthetic purposes. The garden was a place of repose as well as of beauty; its flowers came to be used in services, in crowning priests,[122] wreathing candles and adorning shrines. So they were required not only for monasteries but for churches and chapels as well, with some having to be purchased for major occasions, creating a secular market.

It was in keeping with the line of anagogical thinking that Durandus, the late-twelfth-century bishop of Mende, held flowers to be emblems of goodness and recommended that on Palm Sunday the people should deck themselves with blooms, olive branches and palms, the flowers to signify the virtues of Christ, the olive his role as peacemaker and the palm a sign of victory.[123] The symbolism now developed was a means of understanding the doctrines of the church, especially for those who could not read. For others, flowers and plants were to be divided into the good and the bad, those that helped or hindered mankind. So flowers acquired additional symbolic significances and additional uses proliferated in church services. By 1366 we hear of Ascension being called the 'festival of the rose' although that title was more frequently given to Pentecost when ecclesiastical practice began to take on some of the luxurious character of Roman festivals.[124] During that feast,

---

[119] McLean 1981:126.
[120] It was present in the Vulgate and appears in a translation of St Luke (23.43) in the Ags. Gospel. In Old English the term was *neorxna wang* (land), as in *The Phoenix*. In England the variant *parvis* was a fourteenth-century usage (Latin *parvisus*, thirteenth century) for an ecclesiastical precinct, but an enclosure, portico or porch in front of a church, especially St Pauls, where lawyers met, and Notre Dame, where books were sold (see Chaucer, *Prologue* to *The Canterbury Tales*, A.310 about 'a sergeant of the lawe'). My statement in the text remains tentative as neither the *Middle English* nor the *Oxford English Dictionary* give sources for the notion of paradise as a monastic garden, though it was later used for secular gardens.
[121] One indication of the predominance of monastic flower gardens in the early period emerges in the story of the visit by Henry I of England to the convent in which his future wife, Eadgyth or Matilda, was being educated. The abbess, her aunt, was troubled by the approach of his knights but the King entered quietly into the garden (*claustrus*) 'as if to look at the roses and other flowering herbs'. Amherst 1896:7; Migne, *Patrologiae cursus completus*, CLIX–CLX. xii, *Eadmes*, p.427.
[122] At these ceremonies the priest would be crowned with 'coronae sacerdotales'.
[123] Haig 1913:17. In England willows were sometimes known as 'palms' in medieval times. A 'palmer', however, was one who had made the pilgrimage to Palestine (Anon. 1863:214, 216).
[124] Joret 1892:393–4.

particularly in France, a profusion of flowers was showered down from a high place to symbolise the descent of the Holy Ghost, rather in the manner of Elagabalus. At the same time, the trumpets sounded and doves flew heavenwards. Coming down to the fifteenth century, records show the purchase of box and palm on Palm Sunday, broom for Easter, garlands (or roses) for Corpus Christi, more garlands on St Barnabas on 11 June, birch for midsummer, and holly and ivy at Christmas.[125] In some places the customs appear to have continued well after the Reformation.[126]

Many rituals of this kind were incorporated into the Catholic church. In Italy red roses were used, so giving Whitsuntide the name of Pasqua rosa. However, abuses of the rite led to it being prohibited by the church although the *immissio florum* was still being performed at Messina in Sicily in the middle of the nineteenth century.[127] In Germany it was the peony that was used at Whitsuntide, being known as the Rose of Pentecost (*Pfingstrose*). At other rites too roses played a part; in Holland it was the Feast of St John, in Belgium that of St Peter. At Rome on 5 August a rain of white jasmine fell from the roof of Santa Maria Maggiore in commemoration of the basilica's origin.[128] The month of May, Mary's month, was a special time for floral celebrations, religious and secular. In Italy roses were kept on the oratory or toilet-table throughout the month, and even the servants bought roses for their own rooms.

Not only flowers but wreaths too were widely found in churches on festive occasions. In 1405 the bishop of St Paul's in London wore a chaplet of red roses (*garlandis de rosis rubris*) at the Commemoration of St Paul and that English custom was remarked upon by visitors from the continent.[129] In Germany, France and Italy, chaplets of roses were worn by many participants in the Corpus Christi procession. Roses were also worn by the clergy at other rites of passage, at Nola when the diocesan priests paid their annual homage to the bishop, the chaplets being passed on to matrons of the city.

RELIGIOUS SYMBOLISM

The notions of Durandus emphasise that this growth in the culture of flowers had its symbolic aspect, above all in the religious sphere where flowers, like painting, were used for instructional purposes. In ecclesiastical architecture the symbolic element was especially elaborate in the devotion offered to the Mother of God. The image of a virgin as a flower in an enclosed garden was present in ancient Israel as well as in Rome.[130] In the art and literature of medieval Europe the Virgin Mary was sometimes visualised as the enclosed

---

[125] Nicols, *Extracts from Churchwardens' Accompts*, 1797, quoted Lambert 1880:816.
[126] Cole 1659, quoted Amherst 1896:19.
[127] J. P. Migne, *Encyclopédie théologique*, 1944, vol. 8, Pentecote, 1010.
[128] Lambert 1880:810–11.   [129] Lambert 1880:816–17.   [130] Littlewood 1987.

garden, sometimes as a rose in that garden; she was a rose (often white) without thorns.[131] The rose, which became so significant for Roman deities, was transformed into a symbol of complex, indeed contradictory, character. In secular contexts, the red rose was the sign of spring, of love, but it also represented the blood of the divine victim or martyr, and because of its thorns, death itself. According to the Christian poets, 'Mary's motherhood enclosed the whole of heaven and earth within her womb, within the space of a single round rose.'[132] The floral imagery was overlapping rather than exclusive, for the Virgin was also seen as a lily and a violet, while, as we have seen, Christ too was represented by a red rose, stained by his blood, which in one story he offers, in a garland, to the sultan's daughter who adores him as a beloved.[133]

The Virgin was associated with living flowers in quite another way. Just as gardens were 'christianised' by being brought into the monastery, flowers were baptised with 'Christian names'. The marigold is one of many flowers linked to the Virgin Mary after the increasing popularity of her cult in the eleventh century. In the great cathedrals, statues of the blessed Virgin were often dressed up in valuable robes which had been presented by grateful supplicants; these dresses were changed from time to time and became especially rich when the figure of Our Lady was carried in procession. To these statues flowers were increasingly offered.

Wild flowers underwent a yet more extensive process of renaming, since the change rendered the wild less pagan, less available for 'magical' cures. At the same time, the teachers of religion in the countryside called upon the flowers as illustrations for their text, bringing them into the service of the church in the same manner as symbolic usages in art and literature. In this way the combined action of church and people, of religion and popular culture, clothed the Virgin in wayside plants. These flowers, now often called 'Lady's' this or that, were formerly 'Our Lady's', but during the course of the Reformation, their names were classed as 'Popish nonsense' and stripped of their religious significance.[134] The list was lengthy and before these later changes took place:

> Black Bryony was Rosaries,
> Alchemilla, Our Lady's Mantle,
> Greater Budweed or Convolvulus, Our Lady's Nightcap,
> Ribbon Grass, Our Lady's Ribands or Garters,
> Meadowsweet or Bridewort, Our Lady's Girdle,   .
> Dodder or Strangleweed, Our Lady's Laces,
> Bird's-foot Trefoil (Slipper Orchid), Our Lady's Slipper,
> Cuckoo-flowers or Milkmaids, Our Lady's Smocks,
> Harebell, Our Lady's Thimble,
> Canterbury Bells (Foxgloves), Our Lady's Gloves,

[131] Joret 1892:249.   [132] McLean 1981:128–9.   [133] Joret 1892:244–5; see also Tapié 1987:26.
[134] Equally, Sweet William was 'Sweet Saint William' before the Reformation.

Kidney Vetch or Lambs Toes etc., Our Lady's Fingers,
Wild Orchids, Our Lady's Tresses,
Cowslip (Primula), Our Lady's Keys,
Thrift, Our Lady's Cushion,
Portulaca, Our Lady's Purse,
Primula, Our Lady's Candlestick,
Solomon's Seal, Our Lady's Seal,
Clematis, Virgin's Bower,
Ground Ivy, Herb of the Madonna,
Mint, Herbae Sanctae Mariae,
Parsley, Our Lady's Vine,
Lungwort, Our Lady's Tears,
Lily, the Madonna Lily.

By renaming these flowers from both the garden and the field, they were brought within the orbit of the new dispensation.[135]

FLOWERS IN EVERYDAY LIFE

The development of the use of flowers and floral symbolism did not only occur in a religious context, but in secular life as well, some indication of which is given in poetry. By the time of the Carmina Burana of the late twelfth century, we find references to the picking of both wild and garden flowers, the strewing of flowers and green herbs in a beloved's room, the giving of a rose to a lover, and above all the association of spring flowers with love, beauty, dancing and the greenwood tree:

> Here come the virgins
> Flower-garlanded.[136]

This is the time when the notion of pleasure garden clearly emerges in aristocratic life. In the Arthurian romance of *Erec and Enide* there is a permanent garden of flowers and ripe fruit with no wall but 'enclosed on every side by air so that nothing could enter it' (line 5739). Nevertheless, the king and Erec ride in to take their 'great pleasure', followed by a throng of people. A more earthly enjoyment is provided in *Cligés*. Fenice tells her lover that 'a garden where I could enjoy myself would be very good for me'. One is created and they go there to make love but are discovered lying naked by a knight, Bertrand, who is out hawking (lines 6347ff.).

One of the major uses of flowers was in crowns, that is, chaplets of foliage or flowers, the use of which had its heyday between the beginning of the

---

[135] For a list of 'Mary' flowers, see Anon. 1863:234 and more especially Prior 1863.
[136] *Acies virginea
   redimita flore.*
   Waddell 1929:209, 217, 236–7, 251, 253 ('Take thou this rose').

thirteenth and the second half of the fifteenth centuries, though it seems to have begun earlier in Germany.[137] These crowns were sometimes built up on a base of an existing head cover, such as a knight's helmet, but they too required a circle made from a flexible leafy branch or stalk, of willow or reed, to which flowers could be attached.

It is in the thirteenth century that French romances such as Renart's *Galeran* provide descriptions of the hero's clothes embroidered with flowers as well as the chaplets of flowers which he wears.[138] In Adam de la Halle's play from northern France, *Le Jeu de Robin et de Marion* (c.1283), the heroine wears a *chapelet de fleurs*, the 'traditional' garland of the shepherd queen, which she then places on the head of her lover as a token of love.[139] In many ceremonies, people wore a *chapeau* or chaplet of roses, nuns in procession, girls when they married. In Germany such a practice at weddings went back to the tenth century but after the Renaissance roses gave way to the crown of orange blossom, except in Russia where red roses continued to be used until the eighteenth century.[140] Those known not to be virgins had to be content with chaplets of straw, while married women sometimes wore the crowns over other headgear.

Men too wore chaplets of flowers or foliage. These consisted of 'crowns' of greenery or herbs to which were attached posies or bouquets of flowers. Worn largely by the nobility, such crowns were made of flowers and foliage, usually aromatic herbs such as rue, mint and armoise. In *Galeran*, a young man wears a chaplet of violets and roses, for the preservation of which there were special recipes. In Florence garlands of greenery were worn by *vicedomini*, the temporal guardians of the bishopric, during the two days of the bishop's initial entry into his town, the first detailed account of which dates from 1286.[141] In *Lancelot de Lac* the future knight finds a wreath of red roses on his pillow every morning, put there by his foster-mother.[142]

But their use was not confined to the nobility or to those in authority. In Chaucer's *Canterbury Tales*, the drunken and lecherous Summoner wore 'a gerland' on his head (line 666). In *The Knightes Tale* (lines 1505–8) Arcite

---

[137] Chaplets are not mentioned in the *Chansons de gestes* and the earliest romances. They are present neither in Marie de France nor in Chrétien de Troyes, although the latter describes the use of a floral crown made of gold and probably precious stones. Shortly afterwards, in his *Roman de la Rose* Jean Renart (better known as Guillaume de Dole) mentions 'chapel' flowers in three places. While the *Roman de la Rose* of Renart does not specify the flowers in the chaplets, in the later *Roman* (c.1280) of Guillaume de Lorris, all are of roses, although by the time Jean de Meung completes the tale, the chaplet and the rose are less prominent. However, mention is made of flowers of silk and gold, as well as of floral crowns being worn in the communal tub (Planche 1987).   [138] Lyons 1965:72.

[139] Axton and Stevens 1971:262, 272. The same gesture occurs in *Galeran*.

[140] According to the *Oxford English Dictionary* this practice only reached England from France in the 1820s.

[141] Giovanni Lami, *Sanctae florentinae ecclesiae monumenta* (4 vols.), Florence, 1758, vol. iii, pp.1709ff. I am indebted for this reference to Christiane Klapisch, who in fact finds very little by way of the use of flowers, even in the chaplets of the new bride on her way to the house of her husband (personal communication). Either there was a lot of local variation or the sources are inadequate.

[142] Shaher, 1989: 220, quoting *Le Livre de Lancelot del Lac*, J. Frappier, *Amour courtois et table ronde*, Chapter 10.

celebrates the month of May by going to the woods to make a 'gerland' of honey-suckle (woodbine) or hawthorn, while Emelye gathers garden flowers to make herself 'a subtil garland for her hede'. Even some servants wore crowns like their lords, for example, a messenger or a carver at table.[143] But above all they were worn by lovers, and by the goddess of love herself (*The Knightes Tale*, line 1962). Consequently they were carried at dances and used as favours.

In the same spirit garlands were awarded to the winners in popular games, in dances and for poetry, a practice that continued in Germany until the sixteenth century.[144] But at the same time as being an award or sign of love, the crown of roses might also be offered by an inferior to a superior as a mark of submission, or as part of a feudal due or rent (*cens*). Examples of this practice are found in France and England dating from 1124[145] and they become especially common in the fourteenth and fifteenth centuries.[146] In both countries charters make mention of the gift of a rose, the equivalent of a peppercorn in terms of rent, and certainly a sign of dependence; it was used as a feudal due, together with gloves, gilded spurs, iron lanceheads and swords.[147] The *baillée des roses* was a feudal obligation owed to parliament by the French peers in April, May and June, when that body represented the king to whom hommage was due. One peer scattered roses in the various rooms of the building and in front of him was carried a silver plate with roses and artificial flowers which he offered to the magistrates. This custom continued until the sixteenth century and analogous practices existed in the parliaments of Toulouse and of Rouen.[148] In the case of Paris some of the flowers originated from noble households where they were made up into garlands. But the roses mainly came from places like Fontenay-aux-Roses on the outskirts of Paris where they were part of an extensive market activity in the *courtils*; one record reports their purchase from 'Marguerite la mercière', the mercer, emphasising the close connection with apparel.

Such chaplets were now mainly freed from their earlier associations, at least for personal use and were even used to decorate the statues of saints. The christianisation of the crown of roses was partly accomplished through the extension of the Marian cult. The queen of flowers became identified with the Queen of Heaven and was used to adorn the new statuary and virtuous girls (les rosières), overriding earlier associations. But the practice was not without its critics, for whom it was essential to distinguish decoration from 'ornament'. When she was being interrogated, Jeanne d'Arc was said to have

---

[143] Joret 1892:408.   [144] Wright 1862:290.   [145] Joret 1892:414ff.

[146] For English examples of the 'quit rent' paid in roses see Amherst 1896:61. A similar practice existed among the Aztecs of Mexico where those who had the temporary use of crown lands, or Tecpantlalli, held these lands 'subject to a tribute of nosegays of flowers, and different kinds of birds, which they were bound to present to the King whenever they visited him' (Lambert 1878:460). Clearly this was not simply a token. The practice was apparently less common in Italy. Could it be in 'les pays du droit écrit', the countries of the notaries, that this form of *traditio*, like the seal, was less important because the transaction was embodied in a document?   [147] Chéruel 1865:409.   [148] Chéruel 1865:1049.

woven garlands, making chaplets for our Lady of Domrémy as well as St Catherine and St Marguerite. The way the questions were framed suggested that her inquisitors perceived a pagan element in such practices, especially when these were associated with an old beech, 'le beau may', said to be frequented by fairies.[149] The greenwood tree or maypole created one problem for Jeanne. The other problem she faced was the thin line between honouring and worshipping the saints with such offerings; it was a matter of the intent behind the communication.

Beginning in the twelfth century, with the growth of chivalry and an increased measure of luxury among the upper groups, flowers served a variety of purposes. Rose petals were strewn in houses as well as in streets on joyous occasions such as marriages when lilies too were used. Houses, and sometimes tables, were decorated, garlands hung on the wainscot and flowers used not only for their beauty but for their fragrance. With roses, the ladies defended and the knights attacked the Castle of Love in a mock battle of flowers of the kind that has continued, or been revived, in other forms down to the present day.[150] Baths were scattered with rose petals and in one manuscript of the *Minnesaenger*, the German poetry of courtly love based on the Provençal troubadours, a knight reclines in petalled water while a lady offers him a chaplet of roses.[151]

Some have claimed that this widespread use of flowers for self-decoration went back to a tradition preserved by the church in its processions,[152] but no evidence is cited and the claim seems doubtful for an earlier period, even though some elements in the church did encourage the use of flowers for Christian purposes. According to the historian of fashion, Enlart, the custom of wearing 'chapeaux de fleurs et d'herbes' was one of the many customs the Middle Ages had taken up from antiquity, its widespread adoption being a feature of the renascence of the twelfth century. The practice, first reported from Germany, was common in France, spreading to England, Italy, Spain and the Slavic countries. It flourished until the second half of the fifteenth century when the word 'chapeau' takes on a different meaning as the hair had to be covered in more complex ways, using artificial flowers or foliage in metal.

SECULAR GARDENS

The rebirth of a wider interest in flowers coincides with that of secular gardens. In the early Middle Ages, few gardeners were to be found outside the

---

[149] Herbermann *et al.* 1907 ; Barrett 1932:54–5, 132.
[150] According to Joret, the first report of such events is from 1214 in Treviso, Italy (1892:403). In the thirteenth-century allegorical work of Robert Grosseteste, bishop of Lincoln, the Chastel d'Amour represents the Virgin (de la Rue 1834:110). In Padua, there was a game of courtship during the rites of spring in which the young girls of the town gathered in a wood-and-cardboard fortress, and young men from various places, dressed in the colours of their town, beseiged it by throwing flowers. (Heers 1971:112–13).
[151] Joret 1892:405.   [152] Lespinasse and Bonnardot 1879:LXXVI.

monasteries where manual work was prized. The monk placed in charge was known as the *hortulanus* or *gardinarius*, a term which in Rome had often indicated a gardener-florist; in this case too one of his tasks was to decorate the church with appropriate flowers.[153] The flower garden of the monastery was supervised by the Sacristan, who at Abingdon had to rent it from the *gardinarius*. The earliest reference to the 'gardinum Sacristae' in England appears to be at Winchester in the ninth century, where the site still bears the name of 'Paradise'.[154]

Partly the insecurity of the feudal period meant that secular gardens were found only among the high nobility. In the thirteenth century a small meadow with trellises of vines was established around the dwellings of the rich. This garden would include small trees, flowers and seats of grass. In the next century more complicated garden structures with pavilions appeared, to be followed by the fashion for labyrinths, for topiary and even grottoes.[155] The variety of flowers was not great, but in the thirteenth century the royal garden at Westminster was noted for its profusion of roses and lilies, while in the earl of Lincoln's garden (later Lincoln's Inn) only roses were named.[156] On the French estate of the duke of Burgundy in 1372, one gardener was paid extra to look after 'le jardin Madame' consisting mainly of roses. There were other flowers and aromatic plants for household use – for making chaplets, to cover floors, for perfumes and toilet water, all essential for such a household.[157] While pleasure gardens were initially confined to the great, that was not the case with flowers themselves. Aside from the aristocracy and the monastery, private gardens seem to have first developed in an urban setting, that is, in the suburbs of the free cities of Italy and Germany in the early Middle Ages.[158] They were also grown along with herbs on window ledges. As early as 1417 the provost of Paris warned people against such pots falling on those walking in the streets.[159] The danger is still there and in parts of Paris the same prohibition holds today.

THE MARKET AND THE GUILDS

Unlike monks, the aristocracy clearly did not themselves cultivate the land but employed others to do so. This work was often inherited from one generation to the next, even by widows and daughters, for in the later Middle Ages many women were employed.[160] Gardeners worked both in private and in commercial gardens. The former supplied large houses, but some of the produce found its way to the market, for the gardeners of the early bishops

---

[153] Gibault 1898a:67; Amherst 1896:10ff.   [154] Amherst 1896:17.   [155] Gibault 1898a:68, 73.
[156] On the flowers cultivated in English gardens in the fourteenth century see Amherst 1896:61–4. These were above all roses, then white lilies, together with yellow flags and purple irises, geraniums and poppies.
[157] There is evidence that Henry III made a Queen's garden, mainly of roses, at Woodstock in 1250 (Amherst 1896).   [158] Hyams 1970.   [159] Gibault 1912:828.   [160] See Amherst 1896:105.

and even of citizens of London, aliens as well as free men, were accustomed to sell their fruit and vegetables to the public near the gate of St Paul's churchyard. No mention is made of flowers. In 1345 the practice of selling became the subject of complaints, but the mayor and aldermen upheld their 'ancient usages' which were clearly essential to the life of the town.[161] In the reign of Edward III (1327–77) they were subject to regulations for the locations for the sale of their goods, while they themselves imposed restrictions on recruitment, taking care to exclude 'foreigners'. Having existed as a mystery or fellowship for centuries, gardeners were eventually incorporated as a Company in 1605, the members being involved in the sale as well as the growing of plants, seeds and presumably flowers, since these appear in their armorial bearings.[162]

In the thirteenth century we find evidence that the emergence of professional gardeners was accompanied by the growth of a market. Evidence of this market is also provided by the royal charters on Parisian guilds which date back to the thirteenth century. These corporations, which were more directly involved in the provision of chaplets, came under the jurisdiction of the provost who regulated a wide spectrum of their activities. There were four guilds of *chapeliers*, that is, of hatters, for while the clothes people wore may have been very similar, they often showed their individual preferences in their headgear. This was made by guilds of *chapeliers de feutre* (felt), *de coton* and *de paon* (peacock's feathers), whose produce was sold in the shops of the mercers in rue Saint-Martin as well as in the vicinity of the court.[163] At this period men wore bonnets underneath their helmets, and these were made by the *chapeliers* of cotton; this rare commodity was mixed with wool for bonnets, gloves and mittens. When these rules were laid down, the *chapeliers* of peacocks no longer used feathers but only headpieces made of gold and stones. Finally, there were the chaplets of fresh flowers, especially roses, made by the corporation of *herbiers* or *chapeliers de fleurs*. In gardens outside the walls of the city they grew the flowers and herbs needed to make the chaplets worn by both sexes, as well as to scatter on the floors of houses. Such families were often both gardeners and florists, making 'tresses' and chaplets during the season and gardening the rest of the time.[164] As in the eighteenth century, there may well have been a sexual division of labour, the men doing the gardening, the women selling flowers. These could be sold on any day except Sundays, although roses were allowed to be sold even then on payment of a forfeit to the king's treasury. Like many of the occupations organised by the guilds, that of florist was part of the luxury trade. Indeed, such headgear as

[161] Amherst 1896: 43–4.   [162] Welch 1890:4–10.
[163] Depping 1837:lxxv. There were also guilds of *fourreurs de chapeaus* (makers of linings) and of *feserresses de chapiaux d'orfois* (the women makers of trimmings), see also Lespinasse and Bonnardot 1896:LXXVI.
[164] In seventeenth-century Holland, at the time of the tulip boom, the bulbs were grown by 'florists' who belonged to companies (Posthumus 1929).

they provided may have been reserved for 'les gentiuz hommes', for the nobility and not the bourgeois.[165]

The corporation of *chapeliers de fleurs* did not last beyond the fourteenth century, although that of florist-gardener did, and its members presumably continued to make some chaplets. For while people still wore 'crowns', they were no longer made of fresh flowers but of ribands and bands of gold or silver cloth. 'The luxury of nature', writes Depping, 'was set aside in favour of the luxury of art.'[166]

With this great demand for roses, it is clear that the seasonality of the flower posed a problem. The religious ceremonies in which they played a part were those of summer. But all weddings could not be confined to June, let alone the countless other occasions for their use. Efforts were made to preserve the buds.[167] But resort had to be made to dried, artificial and metal flowers, as well of course to foliage, *le chapelet vert*.

THE HIGH AND THE LOW

In this chapter I have tried to sketch the cultural history of flowers in the West over the period of the Renaissance, in a way that may serve as a paradigm for the interplay of religious reform, an expanding market and a measure of secularisation over the whole domain of culture. In particular, attention has been drawn to the pressures not only towards the use of flowers but against their use in a number of circumstances, for religious worship, as emblems of luxury and by extreme reformers in a wider range of contexts.

There are two further points to be stressed, now and in the final conclusions, namely, the hierarchical and spatial nature of the boundaries of cultural acts and the reasons behind the change in medieval Europe. In any region the culture of flowers was differentiated in a number of ways. Was the return of the rose, and flowers in general, the result of pressures from below or from above? Most of our evidence inevitably comes from the higher realms of culture, from the aristocracy, from church art and architecture, from the literature largely (but not entirely) of the upper class. At first it was they to whom the market was mainly oriented. There is some evidence of popular usage, not only at marriages and in the semi-official cults that centred around tombs and statues but in the unacceptable, magical activities so vividly described in the eleventh century 'Corrector' (Penitential) of Burchard of Worms which suggests the continued use of crowns for 'pagan' purposes. There the priest enquires of his parishioner: '94. Hast thou eaten anything offered to idols, that is, the offerings made in some places at the tombs of the

---

[165] Depping 1837:247.   [166] Depping 1837:lxxviii.
[167] The fourteenth-century household guide, *Le Ménagier de Paris*, provides several recipes for preserving rosebuds, such as enclosing them in a container of porous clay or wood filled with sand and placed under a current of water. When they were taken out, they had to be placed in warm water (Planche 1987:144).

dead or at springs or at stones or at cross roads, or [hast thou] carried stones to a cairn, or wreaths for the crosses which are placed at cross roads?' The word translated as wreaths is *ligatura*, literally knots or bandages, the word that is used more generally for 'tying' in magical ways, and in the French form of *noeuds* (knots) for small bunches of flowers.[168] Foliage used for such purposes would come from people's fields or gardens rather than the market place.

Popular usages of a more secular kind undoubtedly existed. Although chaplets may ordinarily have been the prerogative of the nobility, evidence from the illuminated manuscripts points to the wider and earlier use of garlands by others. But it seems doubtful if flowers then played a great part at any level of society and when they returned in strength they did so among the aristocracy and the church. The town gardens of the bourgeoisie came later, as did much of the evidence for 'popular' rituals such as the crowning of the May queen. It is significant that usages of crowns at weddings, May revels and in France for *la rosière*, involved acts in which individuals were 'dressed up' to look like those of higher status, as with brides in China, India and the Near East. It would be too simple to conclude that these rites were developed by the high and adopted by the low. But they were often encouraged from above, as we see in the 'paradox of May'. Dramas of Robin were often put on by owners of estates; royalty went maying.[169]

The new culture of flowers emerges in the interaction of high and low. On the one hand, aristocratic and then bourgeois culture became denser, more elaborate. At the same time, the dominant voice of the church changed with respect to representations of all kinds, as is evident in its whole approach to icons and to offerings, to the material aspects of worship. While flowers had never quite disappeared and made a gradual return over the centuries, it was the Romanesque and above all the Gothic of the twelfth century that saw the return of the rose.

Why the twelfth century? This period has been called the medieval Renaissance and saw the growth of Italian trade in the Mediterranean as well as the beginning of the Crusades, involving a new kind of interaction with the East. The century begins with the flourishing of the cathedral schools and closes with the establishment of universities. It sees the study of Roman and canon law in response to changing socio-economic conditions, as well as the full development of Romanesque and then of Gothic, and the flowering of a vernacular literature in Italy and France side by side with that of Latin – there had long been the equivalent in Britain. At the same time, new classics made their impact on European culture, coming especially from northern Spain and Sicily. Significant advances followed in science, in medicine and in philosophy. Politically, the modern bureaucratic state begins to emerge.[170]

---

[168] McNeill and Gamer 1938:334.
[169] See my article, 'Knots in may', to appear in the *Journal for Mediterranean Studies*, 1993.
[170] This characterisation depends heavily on Hoskins' classic study (1927).

Many factors contributed to this renascence, the increase in trade, the opening up of learning, but much was linked to the Islamic world, firmly established in Spain and Sicily, and controlling much of the Mediterranean trade, not to speak of that running eastwards by sea and by land to China, India and the Spice Islands. These developments looked forward to the later Renaissance in Italy and then to the artistic and economic efflorescence of North-west Europe. It was there and then that the return of the rose came to full term.

6 · Icons and iconoclasm in the Renaissance

I want to pursue the interplay between icons and iconoclasm, of flowers and their rejection (or their metaphorical transformation), in literature, in art, in life as a whole, for it takes different forms in all three.

We are not simply dealing with a cyclical movement because these swings have to be seen against the background of the growth of the market which eventually turns cultures of luxury into cultures of mass consumption. This happened with sweetness in the eighteenth century with the large-scale production of sugar. It happened with cotton cloth at the outset of industrialisation, which made possible mass production for mass consumption. It happened with flowers at the beginning of the nineteenth century, with results which I will examine later.

But back to the Renaissance. In thinking of the cyclical movement and the rebirth of the culture of flowers we again find ourselves considering the role of the classical model, of the Near East and beyond, of so-called popular culture. But we will also review once again the religious aspects, the struggle between the orthodox and the heretic, between Catholicism and Protestantism, as it affects both flowers and icons. Those interrelated factors touch upon one other general theme, that of flower symbolism and the nature of its codification.

The revival of the culture of flowers in Europe was part of a rebirth, a renascence, not simply a stage in the development from ancient through feudal to capitalist society. That is to say, one aspect of its cultural achievement, as with the use of writing in the twelfth century,[1] was to reinstate what had fallen away, although of course in a different form, a different context and with different implications, some of which related to the internal critique of the culture of flowers we have already encountered. In this chapter I want to look at that culture at the time of the Renaissance, at the way flowers were incorporated in the literary and iconic tradition, then to see how this was affected by the aniconic, anti-'pagan', 'ascetic' tendencies of the Reformation that followed that rebirth.

Renascences of European culture did not have to await the great

---

[1] See Stock 1983 and Clanchy 1979.

Renaissance in Italy. Even rebirths of classical learning had taken place on a number of occasions since the fall of the Roman empire. The Sixtine Renaissance of the fifth century revived classical learning, especially in the field of ecclesiastical architecture, giving rise to the basilican church of Santa Maria Maggiore in Rome.[2] That was followed by the Carolingian and Ottonian revivals in ninth-century France and tenth-century Germany respectively. Later on, knowledge of the classics was stimulated by the transmission of texts through the Muslims who occupied extensive parts of Europe and even left their language in the Mediterranean island of Malta. Many authors have called particular attention to these cultural attainments, others to those of the twelfth century.[3] All these 'rebirths', as we have seen, contributed to the revival of an interest in the culture of flowers. But the return of the rose in the twelfth century came to its full blossoming in Italy in the fourteenth, the rich and creative Trecento. That return was part of a wider shift to naturalism which has been linked to the decline of the *contemptus mundi* of the monastic worldview, with the delight in nature expressed theologically by St Francis and philosophically by Aquinas, and which was embodied in the carved leaves of Southwell minster and in the detailed descriptions of Albertus Magnus.[4] That is, at one level there was a greater pictorial use of nature, but the use of flowers and their embodiment in icons was part of the culture of luxury against which the Franciscans reacted. At the same time, it constituted a return to earlier, Roman models, as we see very clearly in the revival of the classical crown, when the laurel and the myrtle tend to replace the crown of roses, although in different contexts. What later replaces both are flowers in pots, *fleurs d'appartement*, and cut flowers in vases. These were not entirely new; lilies appear in earlier scenes of the Annunciation, but they are now used on quite a different scale.

CROWNS IN THE ITALIAN RENAISSANCE

By the sixteenth century, the chaplets have disappeared and the word 'chapeau' takes on another meaning. The use of cloth head coverings and of peacock and ostrich feathers took the place of flowers. However, floral crowns are used by communicants, for the *rosières*, at marriages where orange blossom replaced the rose, while fresh flowers decorated the walls of churches and banquet tables.[5] For many other purposes the crown and the garland gave way to the bouquet, not only in the realm of art (the flower painting) and in literature (the posy and the nosegay), but also in practice, the practice of giving and in the associated matter of house decoration. The shift from the crown to bouquet was consistent with early Christian thoughts about the

[2] Panofsky 1972.   [3] Haskins 1927.
[4] Pearsall and Salter 1973:162; Clark 1949.   [5] Planche 1987:144.

crown as well as with the new ideas of sixteenth-century reformers, though this was only one reason for the change. But there was one important area where the classical crown now made its return at the very threshold of the Renaissance.

It has been argued that one of the significant features about Italy in the period of the Renaissance was an urban environment and an intellectual background leaning towards medicine and law rather than the theology and metaphysics characterising France.[6] That is to say, that lent towards the secular rather than the ecclesiastical, looking back to the Codex and Digest rather than to the Bible, to Rome rather than Jerusalem. The full recovery of the corpus of Roman law took place against the background of economic activity and urban growth, in Rome, Pavia, Ravenna and especially in Bologna in the eleventh and twelfth centuries. One of the most prominent of those touched by the new appeal of antiquity was Albertino Mussato of Padua (1261–1329), a poet who wrote in a manner more influenced by ancient models than other Italians and who in 1315 was the first to be crowned with the laurel leaves. This movement hardly represented a revolutionary transformation. There was much continuity with earlier activity in Italy, while France had already seen a revival of writing in Latin which may even have influenced Padua, just as in the arts Pisano and Giotto may even have been influenced by earlier French models. But it was Italy of the fourteenth century that provided the motive force that was to change the course of cultural activity in Europe.

A central feature of the Renaissance, of any return to the past of this kind, was its literary and graphic character. It depended upon non-oral recall, not on memory but on the resurrection of works that live on after all that has faded; it depended upon objects that, once created, are partly autonomous of men in a way that differs from the culture, largely verbal, that is transmitted in face-to-face conversations and in other such communications that leave no extra-mental trace. With the written word as with the graphic arts, interaction may be delayed for a year, a century, a millennium, as in the case of the Renaissance itself.[7]

The movement had general aims. But these were often embodied in specific acts of retrieval, ranging from the revived interest in classical literature and classical themes, down to the use of wreaths and garlands in public life. That critical figure of the early Renaissance, Petrarch, was awarded the same laurel crown of immortality as Mussato on the Capitol in 1341, ostensibly for his Latin rather than his vernacular writings.[8] In accepting this honour he went

---

[6] Hay 1977:71ff.; Hay is summarising the argument of Kristeller (1961) who refers specifically to the universities.

[7] Durkheim brought out the partially autonomous nature of all 'social facts', but written culture is characterised by a special kind of autonomy.

[8] On the installation of Mussato and Petrarch, see Kristeller 1961:158; he regards that coronation ceremony as developing from the public recitals and approbation of books at the medieval universities.

firmly against the decision of Dante who, when it was suggested that he could be crowned at Bologna if he abandoned the vernacular and wrote a poem in Latin, refused to deny Italian for the sake of an academic accolade.[9] But Petrarch was a man whose work had other significances for our argument, since it has been said that with him 'reappears the cultured enjoyment of Nature', where the emphasis is as much on culture as on nature.[10]

In being crowned with laurels in Rome in preference to Paris, Petrarch was aware that an ancient custom was being reborn. In what has been called the 'first manifesto of the Renaissance', he declared that this practice had not merely been lost but was 'reduced to a matter of a strange legendry, and discontinued for more than twelve hundred years'.[11] It was discontinued of course because of its pagan meanings. Even after the lapse of that long period of time, even bolstered by the new-found prestige of the classics, the custom was still not entirely safe. Following a minor republican conspiracy in 1468, the pope had some hard things to say about the paganising trend in poetical studies.[12] Later on, the pagan roots of the Renaissance, at least as far as religious images were concerned, were a theme to be taken up in the sixteenth century by Protestant reformers.

It was not simply a matter of falling into paganism but of the reinstatement of the secular. For the Renaissance saw a widespread change of attitudes towards the doctrines of the church. The monk, remarks Hay, ceased to monopolise virtue;[13] the activities of the merchant and the soldier were now given more ideological weight. Wealth was no longer subject to the 'guilty consciences' that endowed monasteries and churches, since the possession of worldly goods could lead to the exercise of civic virtues.[14] Under the new dispensation, the notions and recipients of *caritas*, of charity, changed drastically. However, the consciousness of unequal distribution and the differential enjoyment of wealth was not so easily banished; riches continued to embarrass, as Schama has insisted for the golden age in the Netherlands when that country took up the cultural and commercial leadership from Italy in the sixteenth and seventeenth centuries, when the focus of trading switched to Northern Europe as the result of the sea trade with the Americas and round the Cape of Good Hope to the East.[15] The use and embarrassment of riches managed to accommodate both capitalism and Protestantism, the one based on the enjoyment of man's worldly goods, the other encouraging their rejection; so the denial of the role of representations in church was accompanied by the bringing of paintings, of flowers and of luxuries of all

---

[9] Hay 1977:79.   [10] Pearsall and Salter 1973:185, quoting Whitfield 1943: 90.
[11] Wilkins 1953:1241, 1245.   [12] Hay 1977:147.   [13] Hay 1977:130.
[14] On accusations of paganism directed at Renaissance scholars, see Kristeller 1961, Chapter 4: 'There was ... a good deal of talk about the pagan gods and heroes in the literature of the Renaissance, and it was justified by the familiar device of allegory, and strengthened by the belief in astrology' (p.71). But 'the rehabilitation of ancient religion' was in some ways even stronger in the hands of scholars like Salutati, the humanist chancellor of Florence, and da Fiano (Baron 1955:270ff.).   [15] Schama 1987; Burke 1974.

kinds into the bourgeois home. Even the earlier phases of the Renaissance were accompanied by an avowed anti-clericalism, by an attraction to the pagan world, and for some by a split between what happened in the secular and religious spheres, manifested in the heavy dependence of artists on both classical and religious themes.

ILLUMINATED FLOWERS

Since the Renaissance was so concerned with representations, both positively and negatively, and therefore provides such abundant evidence, let me turn first to the development of icons of flowers in art, continuing with the example of England which was discussed in the previous chapter. The beginnings lay with illuminated manuscripts and were closely linked to the book. Anglo-Saxon artists developed not only the initial letter but also the frame of the illumination. This frame consisted of a decorative enrichment of interlace, animal and other patterns. In the works of the Winchester school these earlier traditions were combined with the Carolingian, bringing in the classical acanthus. Sometime after the Norman invasion we find the full Romanesque style in the St Albans Psalter (c.1120), showing evidence of Ottonian and Byzantine influences. This style in turn gave way to the greater naturalism of the early Gothic in the later thirteenth century when the production of books was carried out not only in monasteries and at court but at workshops in the new university towns. Already in twelfth-century Italy book production began to pass into the hands of professionals.[16] Late Gothic manuscripts (c.1290–1500), which flourished in East Anglia, were produced for rich lay patrons and showed an increasing concern with naturalistic depiction, influenced by the works of the Italian Trecento, possibly through French artists like Jean Pucelle. Finally models from the Netherlands brought the art in England within the scope of the new realism of the International Gothic.[17]

With this latter style we find the development of new kinds of border, for example, in the works by Lorenzo Monaco of Florence. In the Book of Hours illuminated in 1485, probably for Lorenzo de' Medici, borders include a range of fruit, flower and foliage forms together with *putti*, cornucopiae and candelabra as well as a range of other classical and Renaissance themes. The further development of the border in the fifteenth century seems to have arisen out of the resolution of the problem of representing three-dimensional space on a two-dimensional surface by the use of single-vanishing-point perspective. The illuminated book combined script, which had to be read two-dimensionally, with picture, which had to be interpreted three-dimensionally. Confusion was avoided in the transition of the eye from one to the other by surrounding the text with a wide, mainly two-dimensional border of hair-

---

[16] Alexander 1977:10.   [17] Alexander and Kauffmann 1973.

spray type, creating a kind of neutral zone (Colour plate VI.1).[18] The Hours of Engelbert of Nassau by the Master of Mary of Burgundy (c.1477–90), an important figure in the early Netherlands school, uses a *trompe l'oeil* border[19] creating a 'window aspect'.[20] On many pages the borders appear on all four sides composed of thin hair-sprays in pen with delicate flowers, leaves and fruits.[21]

There is a further use of flowers in the pictures themselves; Mary of Burgundy at her devotions is balanced by a tall bunch of irises in a glass vase. In an Annunciation scene stands a flower pot containing Madonna lilies. Another pair of illuminations includes an unusual border made up of pots, including two of glass and one water jug, all holding flowers, the water jug also adorned with a peacock's feather. The next stage was to abandon 'the anecdotal of the still life and simply to sprinkle the flowers or jewels at random on the coloured ground.'[22] Another contemporary manuscript depicts ladies tipping flowers out of wicker baskets on to the borders themselves; these are shown in great detail to draw them close to the eye of the reader.

So in Europe we see a shift in border decoration from the stereotyped foliage chains and more realistic animals of the early Middle Ages to the more naturalistic flowers of a period corresponding to the emergence of the Gothic. The ability 'to paint flowers in a lifelike way is one of the great features of Flemish art from the very beginning of the fifteenth century'.[23] The border became larger and larger, and finally in the works of the specialist painter, Jan (Velvet) Breughel (c.1568–1642), the flowers step right out of the border and form a garland surrounding the Virgin, the subject of his painting *Garland of Flowers with the Virgin* (Plate 6.1), which takes up the earlier theme of the Madonna in a Rose Garden, with its Persian antecedents. Breughel studied in Italy and had ties with Cardinal Federigo Borromeo, archbishop of Milan, a great patron of painting in the Counter-Reformation, whose instructions to him seem to have created this form for paintings of the Virgin Mary about 1608.[24] As in the later Middle Ages, the Catholic church encouraged the use and depiction of flowers as well as of the Virgin (who was herself a flower), partly as a means of approaching God, partly as a way of distancing the objectives of 'reformers'. Moreover, the dominance of the church was not simply ideological; through patronage it exercised a decisive influence over the subjects that were painted.[25]

Breughel was influenced not only by the Northern illuminators, those of

---

[18] Alexander 1977:15.

[19] Early examples occur in the *Très riches heures* of the duc de Berry. Some of the earliest are Italian from the late fourteenth century.   [20] See the *Rolin Madonna* of Jan van Eyck (c.1435).

[21] Alexander 1977; some of these borders have been painted over with those of the *trompe l'oeil* kind.

[22] Alexander 1977.   [23] Freedberg 1981.

[24] Other commissions were quite as precise; in 1469 Lodovico Gonzaga wrote to Mantegna, 'I desire that you see to drawing two turkeys from life.' Even the quality of colours was specified in the contracts entered into (Baxandall 1972:12).   [25] Freedberg 1981.

6.1 Jan Breughel (with P. P. Rubens), *Garland of Flowers with the Virgin, Infant Jesus and Angels*. (Prado, Madrid. Photo: Anderson, Eemans 1964: Plate 1)

Burgundy and the Low Countries, but by the Southern revival of interest in Roman precedents. It was his pupil, the Jesuit Seghers (b.1590), who extended this garland surround to Christ, to the saints and to portraits themselves.[26] Later the internal window disappears and flowers take over, but usually in the form of a still life, resulting in a vase painting rather than a garland or festoon. That was the beginning of the tradition of flower painting that flourished in the Low Countries in the early part of the seventeenth century, becoming one of the main genres of still life.

STILL LIFE IN THE LOW COUNTRIES

The tradition of still life painting represented another important contributor to the development of flower painting. The great creators of illusionist borders were the late Flemish manuscript painters of the Renaissance, sometimes known as the Ghent-Bruges school, who flourished after 1475 under the patronage of the Burgundian court whose domain stretched as far as Switzerland. Illusion in itself harked back to antiquity, where effects of perspective and *trompe l'oeil* were already incorporated in paintings. The illuminators in their turn had been influenced by the panel painters, for Jan van Eyck and Hans Memling had worked in Bruges and Hugo van der Goes and Joos van Ghent in Ghent.[27] These painters paid detailed attention to material objects, which included garlands of flowers in the case of Memling. But while, as we have seen, flower painting flourished in the Catholic environment of Flemish Antwerp, it was further north in the Netherlands that the great development of still life, of *nature morte*, took place at the end of the sixteenth century.[28]

The germination of the idea of this genre lay in introducing 'dead things', such as the wheel of St Catherine, into religious pictures.[29] Raphael (1483–1520) became a significant contributor to the tradition by employing a painter to detail the musical instruments at the feet of St Cecilia. About the middle of the sixteenth century Biblical design became 'a pretext for displaying kitchens and market-places with vegetables and hunks of meat unashamedly occupying the foreground'.[30] The genre took a firm root in Holland where 'the broad stratum of the middle-class . . . provided a market for an astonishingly

---

[26] Delenda 1987:18. The flower painting of Seghers had considerable influence in Spain, thanks to the close relations of that country with Flanders.   [27] Kren 1983; Panofsky 1958.

[28] The earliest known example of this genre may be a painting in Munich dated 1504 by 'a degenerate and deracinated Venetian', Jacopo de' Barbari. But it is possible to seek the origins of the genre even further back, for instance, in the frescos of Taddeo Gaddi around 1337 in the niches of the church of Santa Croce in Florence, as well as in the work of his contemporary, Giotto, possibly following a classical model (Tapié 1987:22). 'Dans leur ensemble, les décors floraux des fresques antiques qui pouvaient subsister ont constitué pour les artistes des xve et des xvie siècles un répertoire de formes inépuisables' (p.24).

[29] Following the discovery of Nero's grottoes of Domus Aurea, grotesques were sometimes included in paintings in the fifteenth century, though that development was arguably not in the main line of still life.

[30] Friedländer 1963:279–80.

wide range of profane pictures – genre-paintings, landscapes and also still life'.[31] In no other Protestant country did the latter enjoy the same popularity; France and Germany had their eyes on different artistic forms, although together with Spain and Italy they made a contribution to flower painting. However, despite the interest in flowers and gardens, the genre was virtually absent in Britain.

The prevalence of more realistic paintings in the Low Countries had much to do with the patrons. 'It is a commonplace in the field of Dutch art history', remarks Montias, 'that the importance of this clientele in shaping market demand, steered the fashion in subject matter away from mythologies drawn from classical literature to realistic landscape, still-life, and genre.'[32] In Delft this clientele was one of master-craftsmen and small merchants as well as the burgher noblesse, providing 'a more or less anonymous market demand' in contrast to earlier traditional and ecclesiastical patronage. The shift in subject matter was gradual, beginning at the end of the sixteenth century, with ecclesiastical and mythological themes giving way during the course of the seventeenth century to more realistic forms.[33]

Flower paintings came to form part of this still-life tradition, following the earlier Italian practice of including flowers in vases in religious paintings.[34] In 1565 Ludger tom Ring (b.1522) in Germany produced what is probably the earliest example of the genre;[35] from there it was introduced into the Low Countries by the Flemings, Roelant Savery at Utrecht and Jacob II de Gheyn (b.Antwerp, 1565) at The Hague. In the seventeenth century, still life flourished in the Low Countries, partly as a decorative art in which flower paintings played a major part. But in the Catholic South as distinct from the Protestant North, more was involved. In the Middle Ages, much of the symbolism of flowers was derived from literary sources, firstly from the Bible, from commentaries and especially from the *florilegium*, collections of literary fragments, maxims, quotations and explanations of the Bible that were seen as flowers in a basket. In these works the garden stood for the church or the scriptures, in which all types of plants were used to illuminate the word of God. Towards the end of that period works of devotion proliferated under the name of *Hortus* or *Hortulus*. That represented the gardens of the spirit and at the same time the 'enclosed garden' of the Virgin, which was sometimes also identified with the Garden of Love of Venus as well as with the monastery garden surrounded by cloisters. Written mainly by members of the orders of minor and preaching friars, such books were produced at many diverse centres in the fifteenth, sixteenth and seventeenth centuries, but especially at Antwerp. In the hands of the Jesuits, these works developed the notion,

---

[31] Friedländer 1963:278.   [32] Montias 1982:332.   [33] Montias 1982:242, Table 8.3.
[34] For works on flower painting, see Hairs 1965 and Bergström 1956, as well as additional references in Freedberg 1981:136.   [35] Pieper 1980:314.

already present in the approach of Suger, that flowers (and nature as a whole) revealed profound religious truths.[36]

In Antwerp, from where most of the masters born in that century came, Seghers adorned altar pieces and devotional pictures with garlands of flowers. The association of flowers with the Madonna was elaborated in the Counter-Reformation, and took on important theological and political meanings. Images of the Virgin were surrounded with garlands by the new school of flower painters in order to enhance the standing of the Virgin whose very representation had been attacked by the Protestant iconoclasts. On the eve of the great anti-icon riot in Amsterdam in 1566, it was her venerated icon that was pelted with stones and mocked. Such iconoclasm led to a pictorial as well as to a theological response, the specific impetus for which may have come not only from paintings of the Madonna in a garden but of her surrounded by the rosary, then by roses, then by garlands of flowers, which were representations of the actual wreaths that often decorated her image from at least the mid-fifteenth century.[37]

The flowers in these Catholic garlands are often provided with complex symbolic interpretations.[38] The painting of *The Virgin and Child in a Garland* attributed to Frans Yvens and Gérard Seghers has been analysed in the following terms:

The roses evoke the love of the Virgin, the lily, her purity, her triple virginity, and her majesty, the carnation, her perfume as well as the redemption. The orange blossom symbolises the mystical engagement of Mary, such as the Fathers of the Church described it inspired by the *Songs of Songs*. The chestnut again means purity (the fruit is preserved by its spikes from original sin) as well as chastity (chestnut and chastity have the same etymological root, *casta*). The fig, like the hazel-nut, is a symbol of salvation, of resurrection and of charity. Attribute of luxury in antiquity, the fig became the fruit of the Virgin, known as the new Eve. By the sacrifice of her son, Mary participated in the redemption.[39]

The commentators on this painting go on to point out that 'the meaning of each flower belongs to the tradition, found in all the holy texts, in literary works or in collections of emblems', which mix religious and secular meanings and become superimposed in the course of the passage of time. So flowers do not carry distinctive meanings since there is so much overlap. In other words there is 'no message in the linguistic sense of the term'. In my view symbolic usages are generally more contextualised than this statement implies, with the rose window of the cathedral being seen as clearly distant from the rose in the Garden of Love. Nevertheless, there is an overlap, and

---

[36] See especially Le Roy Alard 1641.
[37] Freedberg 1981:123ff. See p.146 for references to recent research on the origin of the rosary.
[38] For references to the literary and pictorial uses of flower symbolism, see Freedberg 1981:146–7.
[39] Tapié and Joubert 1987.

there is both avoidance and redefinition. Even Catholic painters like Jan Breughel and Daniel Seghers never mention symbolism in their writings. One may argue that the meanings were already implicitly present for the audience. However, they were using flowers not in the deliberately didactic way of some Jesuits but rather for their form, colour and more commonplace significances of luxury, vanity and the passing beauty of earthly things (Colour plate VI.2.). So their paintings were imbued with some of the *vanitas* symbolism as well as with the wider range of meanings that we find in emblem books or in the *Iconography* of Ripa.

Italy was the ultimate source of these books which soon became popular throughout Western Europe, in Protestant circles as well as Catholic.[40] But their use embodied moral considerations arising from two different theological views about nature, and specifically about flowers and their representations. Many Calvinists and even many Catholics thought that the beauty of the natural world could distract from the significance of the word of God. An alternative doctrine, essentially Catholic in origin and at this time strongly associated with the Jesuits and with the circle of Federigo Borromeo in Italy, saw the beauty of the physical world as a means of understanding the wisdom of God.[41] However, it is not always easy to see which of these views is embodied in a particular painting, for an artist like the German Georg Flegel (b.1566) may represent both at the same time. What happened in the course of the seventeenth century was a gradual loss of the religious symbolic element in flower painting, so that the *Basket of Flowers* (c.1630) of Johannes Bosschaert, son of the Protestant painter, Ambrosius, has nothing of the symbolic about it – flowers are just flowers.[42]

The great vogue for flower paintings proper began with the seventeenth century when the rich Protestant merchants of the Low Countries were no longer commissioning votive paintings with garlands but shifted their interest to flowers, real and pictorial, for the adornment of the house. While floral painting was carried out in Amsterdam and Antwerp, the main centre was the seaport of Middelburg where Ambrosius Bosschaert the Elder (1573–1645) had moved from Antwerp to escape Catholic persecution. There the Catholic *couronne* gave way to the Protestant, or rather the secular, bouquet. Together with his sons and brother-in-law, he devoted himself to flower pieces, starting about 1610, being strongly influenced by botanical studies.[43] His *Basket of Flowers* (1614) has blooms spilling out on the table, with a butterfly and a dragonfly which follow closely the line of illusionist border painters.

Although still life held a lower status than historical painting, it was much in demand. A flower piece would fetch more than many a large religious

---

[40] Tapié 1987:26–28.   [41] Wheelock 1989:17–18.

[42] The painting is in the Louvre, Paris. The possibility of an alternative symbolic significance underlying genre paintings is discussed in de Jongh 1968–9. Rembrandt painted his first wife as Flora; the painting is in the Hermitage, Leningrad.   [43] Friedländer 1963:283.

painting by Rubens, and a garland of flowers surrounding an image of the Madonna would heighten its value.[44] These new Madonnas in Flower Gardens followed by a few years the full acceptance of the independent flower piece at the turn of the seventeenth century. It should be added that in both Catholic and Protestant countries, flowers were also used to celebrate the Roman goddess Flora. Her representations became common in European art, receiving attention from Botticelli, Rubens, Jan Breughel, Giordano, Rembrandt and Poussin, as well as in masques. Indeed, it was the English queen dressing up as Flora that occasioned the criticism of Puritan writers against theatricals.[45]

Painting interacted with life both on the level of commerce and of science. Flower paintings became valued at enormously high prices at roughly the same time as the inflation in tulip bulbs. These bulbs arrived when botany was making exciting advances and when many new plants were being imported into Europe. Indeed, some early paintings may even have been made in response to requests to see what 'new wonders the botanists had developed.'[46]

At this time botany was making remarkable progress, partly because of the advent of new species, partly because of the development of means of recording and identifying the old. In Europe the age of deliberate botanical exploration began in the sixteenth century, first with the travels of Pierre Belon in the Levant in 1546–8 and then with de Busbecq's appointment as the imperial ambassador to Turkey from 1554 to 1562, which was followed by 'a sudden flood of species' to Vienna, Antwerp, Paris and London, often brought by merchants who had been encouraged by the success of his mission.[47]

But it was also a question of identifying and classifying the old. The rising interest in botany was stimulated by the advent of printing, especially in Germany and the Low Countries, and the capacity to reproduce drawings, so that herbals, books on plants with illustrations became popular reading. Thus both in painting and in botany developments have to be seen in the context of the botanical illustrations of the sixteenth century in the works of Fuchsius, Clusius and others. This activity resulted in an enormous increase in plants both in art and literature as well as in actuality.

If one compares the number of flowers appearing in early-sixteenth-century manuscripts with those in printed herbals later in the century, the difference is staggering. There are 59 in the margins of the Grimani breviary in Venice, then 515 plants, the majority flowering, in *De historia stirpium* by Leonhard Fuchs (1501–67) and 840 in *De stirpium historia* by Rembert Dodoen (1617–85).[48] These included old plants newly incorporated as well as new plants from abroad whose cultivation was initially restricted to a small circle of aristocrats and to the scholars in their service. Gradually such knowledge

[44] Freedberg 1981:126.   [45] Poussin's *The Triumph of Flora* is to be found in the Louvre, Paris.
[46] Wheelock 1989:14.   [47] Harvey 1976:21, quoting Coats 1969:11–13.   [48] MacDougall 1989:27.

extended to professional botanists and an important market developed among the bourgeoisie.

The painting of floral still life in the Low Countries contrasted with the narrower decorative use of flowers in Italy and was connected not only with the nature of the mercantile economy and of the bourgeois society, with the requirements of smaller urban houses rather than great *palazzi*, with Protestantism and the dethroning of religious art from its central position, but also with the circulation of botanical texts, stimulated by the mechanical reproduction of printing, as well as with practical and intensive gardening adapted from Italy, and with the enormous popular demand for flowers of all kinds.[49]

FLOWERS IN LITERATURE

The uses of flowers in literature developed in a parallel fashion to those in art, although in general it had a more secular audience. In the *Divina commedia*, Dante made many references but largely in a religious context. For him the Terrestrial Paradise resembles the flower gardens that appear in the works of Fra Angelico and Benozzo Gozzoli – following the Florentine rather than the Biblical mode. But the number of species is not numerous and there is little trace of any knowledge of plant-lore, although he knew that of the 'bestiaries'.[50] Of those he mentions, the rose, rather than the lily, is undoubtedly queen, representing the Virgin Mary, 'quel bel fior', 'la rosa'. But he also uses the snow-white rose to describe the army of saints.[51] More concretely, the heads of saints are crowned with lilies and especially roses, 'che tanti ardesser di sopra da i cigli', 'all on fire above their brows'.[52]

At this time the crown and the garland ceded place to the bouquet. It is in the seventeenth century too that we hear of flower arranging in Europe; though some kind of aesthetic of display had obviously existed earlier, it was not consciously developed until the great period of flower painting. It had been slow in coming, for in China it appears with Buddhism and was already adopted by the Japanese in the seventh century, where it developed into a highly specialised system of expert knowledge at a much later date.[53] In fourteenth-century England, Chaucer describes the rich and elaborate employment of flowers in aristocratic clothing as well as their display in gardens themselves. In the *Romaunt of the Rose* Love is painted in the following terms:

> For naught y-clad in silk was he,
> But al in floures and flourettes,

---

[49] For further discussion of flower painting as a sub-genre of still life, see Schneider 1980 and Pieper 1980.
[50] Paget Toynbee in Cotes 1898:8 and 15.   [51] *Paradiso*, XXXI.1.   [52] *Purgatorio*, XXIX.146.
[53] For the history of flower arrangement and its modern development in seventeenth-century Holland, see Berrall 1969.

Ypainted al with amorettes . . .
His garnement was everydal
Y-portreyd and y-wrought with floures,
By dyvers medling of coloures.
Floures ther were of many gyse
Yset by compas in assyse;
Ther lakked no flour, to my dome,
Ne nought so much as flour of brome,
Ne violete, ne eek pervenke,
Ne flour non, that man can on thenke,
And many a rose-leef ful long
Was entermedled ther-among:
And also on his heed was set
Of roses rede a chapelet. (Lines 890–2, 896–908)

This garden of love had obvious links to the notion of paradise. As Giametti remarks, 'The image of the earthly paradise haunts the *Roman de la Rose* and the *Roman* haunts the literature of succeeding centuries.'[54] However, the Tudor, Elizabethan and Jacobean ages employed much floral imagery, which corresponds to developments in religious and secular art as well as to the growth of gardens and of the flowers they contain. That was especially true of the works of Shakespeare and later of those of Herrick and other Cavalier poets. Two specific questions arise, both of which take up earlier discussions. The first is the social and political significance of this growth to the people themselves, which forms the subject of a later section on iconoclasm. The second has to do with that of symbolism raised in a previous chapter. How far was this imagery related to an underlying code of more general significance? We have noted the emergence of a limited but overlapping set of religious meanings. Was secular usage more or less systematic? If more so, how far did this represent a common cultural code of ordinary social life, outside the sphere of literature?

One of the classic points of reference is the deranged Ophelia's speech in *Hamlet*:

OPHELIA. [to Laertes] There is rosemary, that's for remembrance – pray you, love, remember – and there is pansies, that's for thoughts.
LAERTES. A document in madness, thoughts and remembrance fitted.
OPHELIA. [to the King] There's fennel for you, and columbines. [to the Queen] There's rue for you, and here's some for me, we may call it herb of grace o'Sundays – O, you must wear your rue with a difference. There's a daisy. I would give you some violets, but they withered all, when my father died – they say a' made a good end. (IV.5. 174–85)

Ophelia's distribution of flowers has been a puzzle to scholars. What did she mean by allocating this flower to that person? And how do we determine,

54 Giamatti 1966:66.

decide, the symbolic meanings either for her as speaker or for us as audience? Of the first two mentioned, rosemary and pansies, Laertes accepts what a recent editor calls 'an emblematic meaning'; the associations with remembrance and thoughts were certainly of common occurrence. That editor then goes on to claim that an intelligent audience, more accustomed to such 'emblematic usages', would be able to interpret the remaining flowers in a similar way, with the proviso that their meanings should be sought not in herbals but in popular beliefs: in the words of the dramatists Beaumont and Fletcher, 'What every flower, as country people hold, Did signify'.[55] The writer goes on to regret that much 'has not survived' while records of the 'mystic language' give different significances, raising the problem of 'selecting the meanings which are applicable to the play'.[56] While such a selection should be based on 'popular beliefs', the evidence of usage is in fact drawn from emblem books, herbals and other literary works. The status of these works with regard to popular or general usage is clearly problematic, since emblems and herbals often drew more widely upon European sources and were the product of a literary culture of non-local dimensions that often looked towards the formalisation of highly selected notions.

Another editor of *Hamlet* tells us that fennel means flattery, columbines, adultery, rue, unhappiness and regret, the daisy, dissimulation, and the violet, faithfulness. While these equivalences may make some specific sense in the context of *Hamlet*, they do not all constitute elements in an enduring pan-European code. Nineteenth-century French books on the Language of Flowers give quite a different set of meanings. Take the listing of Charlotte de Latour, who played such a significant role in these developments:

> fennel, force
> rue, 'moeurs'
> violet, modesty

The agreement is only of a very limited kind. Nevertheless, to many the passage from Shakespeare suggests an accepted code, perhaps not generalised throughout society, but at least representing the practice of one segment. It is sometimes quoted with this idea in mind, as if it revealed some general meanings of flowers current at the time. Ault, the editor of a standard anthology of Elizabethan lyrics, writes of Shakespeare 'quoting' from a lyric, possibly by Hunnis, that was printed in Clement Robinson's *A Handefull of Pleasant Delites* in 1584. It runs:

> A Nosegaie, lacking flowers fresh,
> To you now I do send. (Lines 1–2)

The nosegay includes the following flowers whose meaning is spelt out:

---

[55] Beaumont and Fletcher, *Philaster*, I.i (ed. A. Glover, Cambridge, 1905, p.88).
[56] H. Jenkins, notes to *Hamlet*, 1982.

> Lavander is for lovers true . . .
> Rosemarie is for remembrance. . .
> Sage is for sustenance. . .
> Fenel is for flaterers. . .
> Violet is for faithfulness. . .
> Thyme is to trie me. . .
> Roses is to rule me. . .
> Leliflowers is for gentlenesse. . .
> Carnations is for graciousnesse. . .
> Marigolds is for marriage. . .
> Penniriall is to print your love. . .
> Cowsloppes is for counsel. . .

The poem concludes,

> I pray you keep this Nosegaie well,
> and set by it some store.

The significances attached to each flower are clearly ruled by the desire for assonance, for the initial letters of flower and meaning to conform; hence 'marigolds is for marriage', 'rosemarie is for remembrance'. In actual practice the bride and groom gave rosemary to friends at weddings, perhaps for remembrance, and the same plant was widely used at funerals, together with other evergreens, as symbols of immortality.[57] The public placed great credence in the virtues of rosemary and that continued to be the case for some time to come. Looking back at popular usage, one nineteenth-century commentator remarks: 'It was used at weddings, gilt, like oak-leaves on King Charles' day; and was hung about the porch and door-posts, to bring good luck into the household. It kept off thieves, and, best of all, it could make old folks young again.'[58] In other words, the range of actual meanings was much wider than either Hunnis or Shakespeare suggests. The written code is largely a literary conceit in which the meanings are shaped or constructed to fit the poem's form. And while some relate to wider experience, it is mainly these literary significances that are taken over by Shakespeare in this critical passage.

What strikes one in the literature of the Renaissance is the great emphasis given to flowers as sources of smell and of sweetness. Of sweetness, because sugar was still an expensive import.[59] Sugar did not reach the culture of the masses until the late eighteenth century. So where the bee sucked was important to all. Of smell, partly because of the relative lack of alternative perfumes, especially in Puritan circles, but partly too because flowers had been

---

[57] T. Middleton, *The Old Law* IV.1.36 and R. Herrick, *Hesperides*, The Rosemary Branch, quoted by Seager 1896:263. Rosemary was sometimes gilded and on occasion put in sack as a wedding drink.

[58] Anon. 1863:241.

[59] In 1597 Breton enumerated 'Four sweet trades in a Citie: Sugar-men, Confit-makers, Perfumers and Nose-gay-makers'.

less subject to forced growth and genetic manipulation and their odours actually did play a greater part in one's life, especially as that was more likely to be a rural life. By contrast there appears to be little regard for the scent of flowers in the Middle Ages and early Renaissance, where they are valued for colour and form.[60]

It was in the Elizabethan period that the use of perfumes expanded. They were not unknown earlier in England; the Crusades had reinforced the repertoire by bringing back Near Eastern cosmetics. But it was in the sixteenth century that they came into widespread circulation, predictably meeting the opposition of Puritans who preferred the real to the artificial.

FLOWERS AND GARDENS

Representations in art and references in literature were aspects of a growing development in the culture of flowers that influenced society at all levels. The growth of formal gardens among the nobility has received adequate treatment from many hands. Suffice it to say that their rebirth in Europe is closely tied to the rebirth of knowledge, formal knowledge, in the Renaissance, as well as to the shift from defensive castle to country house.[61] There was also the attempt to revive classical forms. But, as MacDougall had remarked, when men wanted to construct gardens on the classical model, they had nothing to turn to except the literary and graphic sources which stood at some remove from reality. The gardens themselves did not survive. There were no plans. Even the detailed description of Pliny, the most prolific classical writer on gardens, has led to proposals for many alternative layouts. So much had to be left to the imagination of the new gardeners, while artists either built upon the later medieval models of the enclosed garden or constructed imaginary landscapes of quite a different kind. This activity involved not only a growing specialisation but a change in the status of the practitioners.

In the late Middle Ages the cultivation of flowers had developed not only in palaces and monasteries but also in the gardens of rich merchants such as those of Swabia, Bavaria and the Rhine valley, and later in the town gardens of Augsburg, Ulm, Nuremberg, Basle, Cologne as well as in the Low Countries. Bourgeois gardens in Paris are mentioned in the fourteenth-century *Menagier de Paris*; and these would have contained roses, violets, lavender and carnations as well as herbs, possibly with window boxes of marigolds.[62] It was not until much later, in the reign of Louis XIV, that the forced cultivation of flowers began again in any major way.

[60] Plutarch writes of flowers but says little of their odours and that is the case even with Erasmus writing in 1522. There is a specific use of odour (sometimes said to resemble flowers) in the Middle Ages in the concept of the 'odour of sanctity' that issued forth when a tomb was opened after death and was held to be one of the proofs of sainthood. This is a highly specialised image.

[61] There have been so many intelligent and interesting discussions of the shift from the standpoint of social, technological and political history that it is only necessary to draw attention to recent sources. See Girouard 1978.   [62] Gibault 1896b:7; *Menagier* (1981), II.2, pp. 118–24 (which does not mention marigolds).

Simple procedures were employed in the sixteenth century and in 1600 Olivier de Serres in his *Théatre d'agriculture* advocated the use of glass cloches for growing melons in the north. However, it was early peas that drew most attention, the expense being remarked upon by a Dutch visitor in 1657, by Mme de Maintenon at the end of the century and by many other writers as a costly and unnecessary luxury. The construction of orangeries and conservatories, bringing the garden indoors, was an achievement of the country house that could hardly be envisaged in the medieval castle. It represented quite a different ambiance, a different attitude to and use of flowering plants. At court, dining rooms and ballrooms were all decorated with flowers, and beginning in January, gardens produced a succession of hyacinths, anemones, narcissus, crocus, tulips and primroses. The growing of flowers had at first been an indulgence of the rich who could afford the huge prices commanded by indigenous gardeners and by the rich exotics that began to come in from all quarters of the globe. Gradually the market enabled the middle classes to establish flower gardens, and from there the practice spread to rural folk as well. In 1677 one observer notes that scarcely a cottage is without; about the same time a book on flower growing is produced for 'plain and ordinary countrymen and women'.[63]

The major flower remained the rose. In the whole of central Europe, writes Joret, there were from now on no gardens, however humble, without some rose bushes.[64] In England roses were used for the purpose of decoration from the thirteenth century, following which their cultivation spread and the number of varieties grew.[65] Medical and herbal use would tend to call for the protection of established varieties; but predominantly aesthetic considerations stimulated the search for new specimens. Some of these came from abroad. The expulsion of the Moors from Spain, where Toledo in particular was noted for its blooms, left their gardens in the hands of the Christians, resplendent with different varieties of the rose.

The name 'paradise' was now sometimes applied in a lay context, part of the process of secularisation. That was the case with the Dutch gardens in the sixteenth century.[66] In the following century the English diarist Evelyn wrote of Hampton Court where there was 'a parterre which they call Paradise, in which is a very pretty banquetting house set over a cave or cellar'.[67]

REACTIONS TO THE CULTURE OF FLOWERS

It was the Tudor period when the growing of flowers in England achieved so rapid an expansion that Keith Thomas is led to speak of a Gardening Revolution in early modern times. The increased demand for flowers was

---

[63] Thomas 1983:228.   [64] Joret 1892:186.   [65] Wright 1862:243.   [66] Hellerstedt 1986.
[67] *The Diary of John Evelyn*, ed. W. Bray, Everyman's Library, London, 1907, vol. i, pp.371–2. There is a paradise garden at the royal palace in Prague.

critical. They were now valued for their appearance and especially for their scent. 'Flowers, herbs and even whole branches of trees were brought into the house and kept in pots. Sweet-smelling plants were strewn upon the floors; nosegays were placed in bedrooms; in summertime hearths were adorned with boughs, wreaths or flowers; and women wore chaplets and garlands on their person. Fritillaries, as the herbalist John Gerard observed, helped further to beautify "the bosoms of the beautiful". . .'[68] In his *Herbal* Gerard mentions garlands of crow flowers (the wild marsh-gillyflower), of columbines and of saffron, the first also being used for crowns, the second in the house. Other flowers were placed on new graves.[69] All were subject to market transactions and to market fluctuations. In 1603 the price of flowers, herbs and garlands rose during the plague year, presumably because of the lack of labour, the excess of deaths and a reluctance to transport flowers to the city.[70]

This demand prompted the rise of the professional nurseryman and a huge expenditure on plants and seeds, much imported from the continent, an activity which centred upon the metropolis; 'the first recognisable commercial nurseries appeared in Tudor times, multiplied in the early seventeenth century and increased sharply in scale thereafter'.[71] Books on gardening multiplied in the same way as the nurserymen and gardeners. In the sixteenth century there were some nineteen new titles on botany and horticulture; in the seventeenth one hundred were published and in the eighteenth six hundred.[72] At the same time England saw the appearance of luxurious books of flower illustrations. Real flowers proliferated as well as reproductions; in 1500 there were perhaps two hundred cultivated plants in England, whereas in 1839 the figure was put at eighteen thousand. 'Nearly all our garden flowers arrived during the intervening years; in the sixteenth century tulips, hyacinths, anemones, crocuses; in the seventeenth michaelmas daisies, lupins, phlox, virginia creeper, and golden rod; in the eighteenth sweet peas, dahlias, chrysanthemums, fuchsia. There were auriculas from the Pyrenees, fritillaries from France, lilies from Turkey, marigolds from Africa, nasturtiums from North America.'[73] The floral landscape was dramatically altered by these new acquisitions.

Many of these developments, especially in neighbouring East Anglia where their ancestors, the Friesians, had settled, were influenced by the Dutch. In Norwich, immigrants from Holland had stimulated flower growing in

---

[68] Thomas 1983:224.
[69] See the well-known passage in Webster's *White Devil*, v.iv.95–8.

> Call for the robin-redbreast and the wren
> Since o'er shady groves they hover,
> And with leaves and flowers do cover
> The friendless bodies of unburied men.

(*The Selected Works of John Webster*, ed. J. Dollimore and A. Sinfield, Cambridge, 1983).

[70] Dekker, 'The Wonderful Year 1603', quoted Seager 1896:263.
[71] Thomas 1983:224.   [72] Thomas 1983:225.   [73] Thomas 1983:226.

Elizabethan times. To these refugees have been attributed the development of market gardening, the growth of roots as a farm crop, and an improved culture of flowers. Many of these immigrants became well-off and were called upon as specialists to advise on gardens in other parts of the country. Norwich became famous for its flowers and gardens, and 'florists' feasts' were held there as early as 1637. According to Moens, it was from there that the cultivation and love of flowers spread to other manufacturing towns, especially the weavers of Spitalfields, Manchester and Bolton, who were said to retain the same attachments in the late nineteenth century.[74]

Flowers abound in accounts of Renaissance Europe, especially at marriages and other secular festivities. At Epiphany of 1513, the great occasion for royal masques, a pageant presented a golden mountain with broom plants and 'riche flowers of silke', the first referring to the Plantagenets, the second possibly to the white and red roses of York and Lancaster.[75] One hundred years later the French artist Jasper Isaac depicted Comus, the god of banquets, at a feast where ladies dressed in classical attire and wore chaplets on their heads. Likewise Vincenzo Cortari shows Comus wearing a chaplet after a wedding, with the floor scattered with flowers.[76] Revels were the time for flowers, both the real and the artificial, and their presence was no doubt part of the classical influence on such performances. That influence extended to the impersonation of 'pagan' gods, with royalty itself taking part in a masque as the goddess Flora and other classical deities.[77]

FLOWERS IN THE HOUSE

Parisian window boxes and forced cultivation are examples of the proliferation of flowers inside as well as outside the house, influencing domestic arrangements, including furniture on the one hand, and the nature of flowers on the other. In the course of the shift from garland to bouquet, the vase emerged as a vessel specifically designed to hold cut flowers, though there were other containers for growing plants. In earlier paintings the 'vase' was often a water jug rather than a special container for holding flowers, although such containers had long been available in China.[78]

Baskets and bowls appeared earlier than vases. In Giotto's frescos in the

---

[74] Moens 1887–8:84, referring to Norfolk Tour, xlv and to Loudon 1822:84.
[75] Orgel 1981:28.   [76] Orgel 1981:152.
[77] For a seventeenth-century compendium of religious flower symbolism, see Picinelli 1694.
[78] Similar doubts about the early uses of vases are expressed by Lambert (1880:812) since they are absent from old churchwardens' accounts. Certainly in post-Roman Britain we find little evidence of any container for flowers. The tradition of Anglo-Saxon pottery continues from the earliest settlements in the fifth century AD through to the Norman conquest and beyond. Much of the earliest surviving pottery is funerary in origin with stamped, incised or bossed decoration mostly of a geometric kind but with some human or animal motifs or rarely runic texts. With the abandonment of the pagan burial tradition, the pottery becomes purely domestic, though sometimes still decorated, but there are still no 'vases'. (I am indebted for help to Leslie Webster, Deputy Keeper of the Department of Medieval and Later Antiquities at the British Museum, London.)

Scrovegni chapel at Padua, dating from the first decade of the fourteenth century, some of the women in the marriage scenes wear hair bands of plain cloth or crowns of foliage.[79] Among the virtues, the figure of Charity not only has a floral crown but holds in her right hand a bowl of flowers and fruits which seem to be painted from nature.[80] Flower vases first appear in illuminations at the beginning of the fifteenth century.[81] The word itself is from the French 'vase', one important sense of which is a flower vase, otherwise known as a *bouquetier* (sixteenth century) or *porte-bouquet*.[82] Already by the sixteenth century the bouquet (cognate with *bosquet*, a little wood) meant a bouquet of flowers.[83]

A vase figures in one of the earliest paintings done in the new technique of oil, the *Annunciation* by the Flemish artist Robert Campin (active 1406 – d.1444), an older contemporary of Jan van Eyck. In this highly domestic interpretation, the lily, standing for chastity, is not presented to the Virgin by the Archangel Gabriel, as is often the case, but stands in a jug on the table.[84] These vases, which are sometimes very similar to apothecaries' jars, appear in the paintings of the Bruges artist, Hans Memling (c.1430/5–94), who had also worked with Rogier van der Weyden. In his hands too the Annunciation takes on a much more domestic, less mythological, air, with the flowers standing in a vase rather than being presented (Plate 6.2).

The growth in the domestic use of flowers in the Low Countries was part of the wider shift of artistic culture from church to house; just as the painters ejected from the Protestant churches found new patrons among the merchants, so too did flowers, at least during the intensive phases of reform. Their use in places of worship gave rise to suspicions. In any case, the chaplet was giving way to the bouquet, the bunch of flowers that could be presented as a gift and arranged in a vase. From the fourteenth century the corporation of *chapeliers de fleurs* of Paris disappeared and became the new '*communauté*' *des maîtres jardiniers* (also known as *maraîchers* or *préoliers*), while the bouquetières in charge of selling the flowers had their own organisation.[85] Apart from the bouquetières, there were the *grainiers-fleuristes* established as a guild in 1595, and who also sold salt.[86] The gardeners of Paris flourished in the sixteenth century, especially with the importation of new species from overseas. But at the end of the seventeenth century the ability to sell produce

[79] See the *Marriage at Cana* and the *Bridal Procession of the Virgin Mary*.
[80] Gnudi 1959:173.   [81] *Hours of the Duc de Berry*, 1413.
[82] Vase is cognate with *vaisseau* (vessel), Latin *vas*, a container. In French it has a wide range of meaning from *un vase grec*, a Grecian urn, to *vase de nuit*, chamberpot.
[83] In the sixteenth century Olivier de Serres distinguishes between the four following forms of gardening, 'potager, bouquetier, medicinal et fruitier'.
[84] In the Metropolitan Museum of Art, New York. In the painting of the Annunciation by the Master of the Vyšší Brod Altarpiece (c.1350), the lily is growing in the ground (National Gallery, St George's Convent, Prague).
[85] Gibault 1896b:7; the first mention is 1467, the first police ordinance 1473, following complaints of fraudulent sales.   [86] Gibault 1896b:18; *Guide des marchands*, 1766:268.

6.2 H. Memling, *Flowers Sacred to the Virgin* (reverse of his *Portrait of a Young Man in Prayer*). (Collection Thyssen-Bornenisza, Lugano)

was granted to others and the corporation fell on evil days until in 1776 some of those other *petites professions* were further opened up, not only the work of *jardiniers* and bouquetières but that of dancing masters and basket-makers.

The use of cut flowers spread rapidly, like the flower paintings and flowers themselves, being introduced in France through the salon, 'the living room', of the Marquise de Rambouillet in the reign of Louis XIII (1610–43). With cut flowers it is not only a question of the vases but of where to stand them. Special demands are made on domestic space; tables, sideboards, fireplaces, shelves, window sills are the obvious places for their display. In traditional African surroundings none of these supports exist and even in early European paintings, vases are often placed on the floor. Later on, the window sill became a prominent focus, not only for cut flowers inside but for those planted in pots and pans of various kinds. All these forms of display proliferate in the genre paintings of window scenes by the seventeenth-century Dutchman Gerrit Dou.

In its origin the use of sills for the display of potted plants or window boxes is essentially an urban phenomenon, as indeed are cut flowers themselves. For the countryman flowers grew, if at all, in the garden, not in the house. Their presence on sills, in pots and boxes, was linked to the intensive raising of plants in the city and its outskirts. This development occurred at approximately the same time among the merchants and bourgeoisie in Western Europe and in Japanese towns such as Kyoto, although yet earlier in China. It arose partly from the restricted space available in these particular living environments, then as now. This house-plant culture was important to horticulture in three ways. Firstly, great care and attention meant that plants were able to adapt rapidly to new conditions. Secondly, such an 'aesthetic' interest encouraged the continuous introduction of exotic species. Thirdly, the proliferation of new varieties was hastened through human intervention, a process of manipulation that had many implications for food plants as well as for decorative ones. All three aspects of the new culture of flowers emerge from the remarkable history of the tulip in Holland.

TULIPOMANIA

The name 'tulip' was derived from the Turkish, *dulband*, a turban, and the flower was also known in English as the 'Turk's cap'. It was seen growing in that country by de Busbecq, ambassador of Emperor Ferdinand I to Istanbul, who brought its bulbs back to Vienna in 1554.[87] Agents and merchants took these back to the gardens of courtiers, scholars and bankers in Antwerp, Brussels and Augsberg in the 1560s, reaching Holland in 1578 where the soil proved especially suitable. Among others, Clusius (the Frenchman, de l'Ecluse), who had been director of the emperor's garden in Vienna between 1573 and 1589, experimented with different hues and sizes – and not only of bulbs, for Clusius also helped to spread the cultivation of the potato throughout Europe with far-reaching effects on world history.[88] But it was the manipulation of the varieties of tulip that attracted so much attention and led to the eventual establishment of the Dutch bulb industry. By 1629 Parkinson, author of *Paradisus*, enumerated one hundred and forty varieties in English gardens, where it was not only considered beautiful but medicinal; if drunk with harsh, that is, red, wine it was good for curing a crick in the neck.[89]

France was a little late in receiving the tulip, about 1608, but soon afterwards women were wearing them tucked into their low-cut dresses, and

---

[87] This does not appear to be the first introduction of the tulip to Europe, for it is present in the (restored) *Basket of Flowers* mosaic from Rome (see also Chapter 2, n.36) as well as in later paintings. But north of the Alps it had made no mark until the later imports of the sixteenth century (see Berrall 1969).

[88] See Salaman 1985:89.   [89] Blunt 1950; Parkinson 1629:45–67.

bulbs were changing hands for extravagant sums. One groom was prepared to agree to a single bulb, appropriately called 'Mariage de ma fille', for his wife's dowry. From France the craze spread northward to Flanders and then to Holland. New forms of the flower arise through sports as well as through breeding and it was partly this fact that led to the colossal speculation that developed, not only among the richer merchants but among the whole population. In the great emporium of Amsterdam, which had profited from Antwerp's unfavourable position in the war against Spain at the end of the sixteenth century when the River Scheldt was blockaded, the demand for flowers and the tools of the capitalist market combined to provide the conditions for a boom. People won and lost vast amounts of money gambling upon the colours of their new bulbs, which were always somewhat unpredictable. It became the very model of speculative attempts to calculate the profit and the loss.

Speculation took place not only on unpredictable colours but on unpredictable prices. At the end of 1634 many non-professional buyers were attracted by the chance of big profits. The following year prices rose rapidly, with weavers and even labourers buying on credit. By 1636 much of this buying was organised by unofficial 'colleges' that met in inns and often traded in non-available bulbs (the trade was in bulbs rather than flowers), speculating on the market in futures. In February 1637 the bubble burst; prices fell through the floor and buyers and sellers were left with enormous notional debts and heavy actual losses. In the eyes of contemporary moralists (and it was a field day for the Puritan concerned about the embarrassment of riches) the incident became the epitome of capitalist financial operations and the iniquity of the unregulated market – though in the end florists, local authorities and eventually the state had to intervene. Their disapproval was all the stronger because the commodities were seen as part of the luxury trade. Some modern writers have seen this process as an early example of the workings of the business cycle, long preceding the South Sea Bubble.[90] The elements of modish luxury, subjected to the whims of fashion, certainly meant that flowers were subject to later booms as well; in Istanbul in the early eighteenth century, in hyacinth bulbs in 1734, in gladioli in 1912, but nothing of quite the same scale.[91] Nevertheless, despite this setback, the production of bulbs took off commercially and their great attraction was reflected in the paintings of the period.[92]

The collapse of the bulb market was only one aspect of the culture of flowers calculated to upset many reformers. The sight of the queen of England performing the role of Flora in a masque had been another. Little wonder the Puritans, with their republican sympathies, their rejection of luxury and their

[90] Posthumus 1929.   [91] Blunt 1950; Coats 1970:195ff.; and especially Schama 1987:350–63.
[92] Schneider 1980:310.

suspicions of images and imitations, condemned the lot. Masques were particularly open to Puritan objections because they were courtly, extravagant and ephemeral. 'Pompous vanities', the Devon diarist Walter Yonge called them.[93] In 1633 the barrister William Prynne attacked all theatrical performances in *Histrio-mastix*, or *The Players Scourge*, and had his ears cut off by the public executioner for a presumed aspersion on the part played by the queen. When the Puritans came to power, words were translated into deeds. Nine years later Cromwell closed the theatres, as well as attacking the arts by selling off the collection of royal pictures and ordering statues to be defaced.[94] The very act of imitation, in drama as in art, usurped a divine prerogative.[95]

While it would be too facile to suggest that the return of flowers as a consumer luxury led to a reaction against display, there is a sense in which the point is valid in a wider cultural perspective. During the twelfth century the use of flowers expanded in Europe, the period when Gothic buildings ushered in a lavish style of church architecture, with greater use of statuary, with stained glass windows, with more images of all kinds. That development was accompanied by learned defences of their proper employment in the works of Thomas Aquinas and others. More decoration now made its appearance, both in the secular and in the religious domains. Ritual expanded, within the church and outside.

While flowers in the house met with the puritanical objections to luxury and unnecessary expenditure, it was the presence in the churches of what they saw as distractions from the worship of God that aroused such righteous anger. There was plenty to be condemned. Inside the church, the ornate rood screen separated the nave from the chancel, the congregation from the priesthood. Above the screen was affixed the great rood or crucifix, and often above this, in the boarded chancel arch, there was a painting of the Last Judgement. The churches were filled with decorations and with paintings, with embossed roofs and with gilded towers. The paintings represented Christ, the saints and even God himself as 'a bearded old man with tiny Christ on his lap and a dove representing the Holy Ghost on his breast'.[96] All the earlier inhibitions about portraying the divine in places of worship had long since disappeared. Crosses were everywhere, lights and candles abounded, statues could be dressed in expensive cloth, and images beautified with curtains, flowers, colouring and gilding, while on feast days 'the churches were filled with the scent of fresh boughs and floral decorations'.[97] At Christmas there were holly and ivy, palm and box on Palm Sunday, roses on Ascension Day, flags and woodruff on Corpus Christi and boughs of birch at

---

[93] Underdown 1985:127.
[94] Not all 'Puritans' reacted against the theatre. Nevertheless, many did so and the effects were radical. See Heinemann, 1980.   [95] Orgel 1975:60.   [96] Phillips 1973:27.   [97] Phillips 1973:28.

midsummer.[98] The floor was strewn with green rushes or straw to kneel upon, and in season, rose petals, lavender and rosemary would be substituted. It was the same with ecclesiastical dress.

In Italy a priest wore a crown when he said his first mass, after which he sent it to his nearest relative. In Germany in the late nineteenth century a similar custom persisted. In the contemporary Church of England, a priest may bring flowers to his first eucharist, giving them to his mother, wife or fiancée, a custom revived by the ritualistic movement rather than displaying any actual continuity with the medieval past. For the use of flowers has continued to reflect swings in theology and patterns of worship, with reformers taking a similar stance to that of the early Fathers. For example, in Mainz at the beginning of the seventeenth century 'the walls, houses, every place available for decoration was ornamented with flowers and foliage and all the road-ways were strewed with them'.[99] The bishop of Mainz was a Jesuit, Serarius, who was a prolific polemicist against Luther, Calvin and Zwingli. In the spirit of the Counter-Reformation he laid down the way flowers should be used in processions and at the same time defended that use against the reformers who had strong objections to such rituals.[100]

All this complexity of acts and objects, including the mass itself and the clothing worn by the priests, became identified as images by those who attacked their proliferation and their use. From their very beginning in 1098, as strict interpreters of the Rule of St Benedict, the austere Cistercians took up these themes which were also central to the movements of Lollardy, the Hussites as well as to some later Humanists. During the course of the twelfth century, the Cistercians successively proscribed the use in churches of sculptural decoration, manuscript illumination, stone towers and stained glass. In other words reform, including a measure of iconoclasm and the advocacy of poverty, formed a constant sub-dominant motif in the ecclesiastical history of Europe, for it grew out of the search for the right way of worshipping God and of seeking salvation. The notion of Purgatory and prayers for the dead had already been rejected by the Waldensians of the twelfth century, who had so influenced later heresies. In the first half of the fifteenth century, during the Hussite wars in Bohemia, monasteries were destroyed because they were seen as examples of the unjustified wealth of the church. But reactions were more specific. For at the same time the radical wing and even some moderates condemned pictures in churches as idols. They were associated with the cults of miraculous images and relics which in turn were

---

[98] Pendrill 1937:61.
[99] Lambert 1880:817. On the use of the flowers of diverse colours, and the doves at Pentecost, see E. Martène, *Tractatus de antiqua ecclesiae disciplina in divinis celebrandis officiis*, Chapter 28, *De antiquis ecclesiae ritibus*, Antwerp, 1764, vol. 3. p.195.
[100] *De processionibus opusculorum theologicorum*, Mainz, 1611, vol. 3, pp.142–3.

accompanied by donations to the altar. At the same time, according to St Bernard, they were manifestations of luxury which contrasted with the poverty of the congregation. And they were material objects that diverted attention from the spiritual.[101]

As the direct heirs of Wycliffe and the Lollards and of the Hussites of Bohemia the Protestant reformers adopted and elaborated the critical attitude to performance and representation. The service was no longer viewed as a sacrifice, and no longer known as the mass, rather as a 'thanksgiving'. Meanwhile the altar became the Holy Table and attacks were mounted on outward signs, on the use of ritual objects, of church art, of incense, even of the eucharist. These trends were pushed much further in Calvinist churches, among Puritans and other 'Non conformists'. Indeed they often rejected the separation of religious and secular domains and objected not only to church rituals but to public performances of all kinds, popular as well as theatrical.

One danger feared by Puritans was of images distracting from the worship of God. But some took the wider theological view of icons associated with Islam. As in the twelfth century the Cistercians had come out against illuminations and sculptural decoration, so the Lollards of the late fourteenth and fifteenth centuries rejected all images, relics and saints. Their argument declared that 'art should be true to earthly fact' because the human imagination was suspect;[102] so they had a clear preference for 'real objects' (good works) over simulated ones (works of art). 'If the late sixteenth and seventeenth centuries showed a developing aesthetic consciousness for works of art [that is 'artifice'] among gentry and intellectuals, a Puritan "counter-aesthetic" developed at the same time'.[103] It was not just a matter of religious images but an attitude that 'clearly rejected the view of man as an independent creator'. At the same time, throughout the long period of English iconoclasm that continued over one hundred years from 1525 to 1660, we find evidence of that other theme common to moralists in many societies, the objection to luxury combined with the desire to make better use of expenditure, the argument of the necessity for charity and redistribution, though this was seen as a religious duty.

While the second Commandment was interpreted quite literally by some Protestants as rejecting all representation, there were Catholic theologians who avoided its implications and argued that such prohibitions applied only to the Jews.[104] On the other hand, most of the moderate reformers, including Erasmus, objected only to the way images had come to be worshipped, that is, to their misuse rather than their use. But while Luther's attitude towards images was tolerant, that was not the case with Zwingli. He was responsible

---

[101] Kejř 1988:134.   [102] Phillips 1973:xii.   [103] Phillips 1973:xii.
[104] Among the earliest of the literalists was Ludwig Hützer, *Ein Urteil Gottes*, Zurich, 1523; see Freedberg 1988:34.

for the outburst of iconoclasm in Zurich in 1523 that initiated a whole series of outbreaks in and around Switzerland in the following decade.[105]

When Henry VIII of England finally broke with the church of Rome in 1534, some clergy, including Hugh Latimer, objected to abuses of images, saints and relics, and two years later the Convocation was persuaded to issue a declaration putting images, including the crucifix, outside the church. It went on to draw up the Ten Articles, possibly influenced by Luther's Wittenberg Articles of the same year;[106] the sixth article prohibits the idolatrous worship of images, although not their correct use. In a sense the compromise was undone by Henry VIII's desire to dissolve the monasteries, whether for financial or political reasons; these institutions were eliminated as the 'chief supporters of pilgrimages, images and superstitious cults', the inessentials or abuses of religion.[107] In this way some of the romantic ruins of England were created not by the hand of time but by the attacks of the iconoclast who provided the ideological justification for the massive despoliation and dispersal of objects of all kinds, including ancient manuscripts.

Iconoclasm was widespread during the following reign of Edward VI and in 1550 shiploads of religious statues were exported to France. With the restoration of Catholicism under Mary such attacks ceased but during the Elizabethan period (1558–1603) the fires of Protestantism were fuelled by the return from Geneva of the Marian exiles of the previous regime. Many Puritans refused to participate in the historical compromise. And even in 1559, the wooden rood images from St Peter's and other churches in London were burnt in two huge bonfires. That experience was repeated a century later under Cromwell when the great cathedrals of Exeter, Canterbury, Winchester and Ely suffered terribly at the hands of the Puritan iconoclasts.

In the early seventeenth century a profound controversy arose over the *Book of Sports* issued by King James, permitting Sunday amusements, such as May games and maypoles. Royalists considered festivities as a way of binding the kingdom together, while Puritan radicals like Stubbes condemned May Day and similar celebrations as pagan. Where the latter came to power, in Scotland, in Massachusetts and in Cromwellian England, many secular performances were suspect; the theatre was forbidden, dancing restricted and a negative attitude taken to the arts in general, even to organ music in church. In England the statues in the Lady Chapel at Ely cathedral were beheaded under the instructions of Edward VI and iconoclasm became rampant. The most extreme sects of Protestantism had little ritual or art – all attention had to be directed to the word, not only in church but outside.[108] For Puritans and indeed for other Protestants, discourse was closely linked with the notions of

---

[105] Freedberg 1988:50.   [106] Phillips 1973:54.   [107] Phillips 1973:63.
[108] The particular conceptions of Protestant or rather puritanical iconoclasm have been extensively treated by Kibbey (1986), Phillips (1973), Freedberg (1985, 1988) and others.

'naked truth', 'decent and comely apparel', 'plainness', and 'speech alone' as distinct from their paradigmatic contrasts in ornamentation, the 'externals' of worship, and 'visible signs'. Although some held to the distinction between worshipping an idol or image and worshipping God through such an image, Calvin saw both as idolatrous.

The objections to the worship of images, whether accompanied by the offering of flowers or in any other way, was already incorporated into the articles of the Church of England which were directed against contemporary practice in Catholic rites as well as appeasing the Reformers. The article 'Of Purgatory' was concerned to reject not only the doctrine of Purgatory, but the worship of relics, the invocation of the saints and the granting of pardons. Hence All Saints' and All Souls', while not abolished from the liturgical calendar, were given much less importance, since they implied that one could assist the dead in the other world, as well as gaining assistance from them.[109] That was contrary to Protestant doctrine. So that what became one major focus for the use of flowers in Catholic countries was rejected by all Protestants, not simply the Puritans.

Nevertheless, it was the Puritans who were most engaged in the wholesale attack on religious images (and in Britain did much to discourage the secular ones). Suffolk and Cambridgeshire emerged as the extreme sufferers of later Cromwellian iconoclasm, as that is described in the *Journal* of William Dowsing. There he records his achievements acting on commission from the earl of Manchester following the Long Parliament's Ordinance of 1643 concerning images. For iconoclasm like puritanism was not solely the ideology of the masses. The ordinance passed by both Houses of Parliament demanded that in all churches and chapels, altars of stone were to be taken away and demolished, rails and communion tables removed; all this paraphernalia was too like that required for a pagan sacrifice as well as separating the congregations from the intermediaries. The ground raised for the altar was to be levelled before 1 November, by which time all tapers, candlesticks and basons were to be removed and 'all crucifixes, crosses, images, pictures of one or more persons of the Trinity or Virgin Mary, and all other images and pictures of saints, or superstitious inscriptions were to be taken away and defaced'. The destruction was vast in scale. At Clare in Suffolk, a thousand 'pictures' (panels of stained glass) were destroyed, although nearby King's College escaped for political reasons; the coloured glass obscured the true light of God.[110] On 6 January of that year, Manchester writes: 'We broke down about an hundred superstitious pictures, including pictures of God and Christ, and a great stone cross on a church.'[111] Even this central symbol of Christianity was not exempt. In Herefordshire in 1641

[109] See Art. 22, Of Purgatory.   [110] Cheshire 1914:77–8.
[111] Freedberg 1985:40–1; Dowsing 1885; Cheshire 1914.

crosses were beaten to pieces in 'a hectic orgy of image-smashing'.[112] Nor was this behaviour confined to England. German, Swiss, French and especially Netherlands examples of similar actions exist, beginning with the Zurich riots of 1523, over that same period; the phenomenon was widespread throughout Europe and not the preserve of a small sect.

There was another aspect of the Reformation that affected the culture of flowers. This had to do with the memorials to the dead. In 1560 the queen attempted to limit the effects of this movement by defending these memorials against the attacks of the reformers, which had a decisive effect on the development of tomb sculpture. In the first place devotion could no longer be shown in the same ways as before, through adorning either churches or tombs. But it was the form as well as the offerings to which objections were raised. Some memorials erected in the late sixteenth century were still extravagant celebrations of status but instead of being adorned with religious themes, they were decorated with personifications of the abstract virtues, faith, wisdom, hope and charity, as well as with a variety of symbolic ornaments; Indians, skulls and crossbones, scythes, urns, weeping cherubs.[113] Reform resulted in the secularisation, and to some extent the egalitarianism, of the cemetery.

In sixteenth- and seventeenth-century England strong objections were made about the nature of the existing rituals surrounding the disposal of the dead. The rejection of the notion of Purgatory had of course been central to Luther's protest against indulgences; the efforts of kith and kin could make no difference to the fate of the soul which had already been predetermined. Moreover, the way the soul would eventually be resurrected in the body was of little concern. Ritual surrounding burial was decreed to be 'popish', a notion that culminated in the statement in *A Directory for the Publique Worship of God* in the mid 1640s that the dead should be immediately interred 'without any Ceremony' for these have proved 'hurtful to the living'.[114] That meant the abandonment of All Souls' Day which according to one disaffected Protestant, could not now be mentioned; for 'we must leave the dead with the dead. Previously our burial places were covered with flowers, now there is nothing so wretched as our tombs.'[115] So the culture of flowers was once again drastically affected by the attitudes of Puritans towards ritual. Flowers were removed from the graveyard, both at the annual ceremony for the dead and at funerals. While flowers returned for funerals by the middle of the nineteenth century, and for some before that, tributes to the older dead remained conspicuously scarce in many Anglo-Saxon cemeteries.

The main objections were directed against religious images in churches,

[112] Underdown 1985:139.   [113] Phillips 1973:118.   [114] Stannard 1977:101.
[115] The comment is published in Pierre Muret's *Cérémonies funèbres de toutes les nations*, published in Paris in 1679 and in an English translation in 1683. See Stannard 1977:105–6.

and outbreaks of iconoclasm, of cleansing of churches for worship, occurred soon after these ideas were first formulated. Attacks were especially strong against statues; the distinction between statuary in the round and two-dimensional painting, which was not seen as having the same substantial reality, had been of great importance in the early Greek church, and indeed in Christianity as a whole.[116] The Netherlands, possibly the major centre of painting at the time, was also a great centre of religious iconoclasm;[117] some of the destruction of images was even carried out by painters themselves, while others fled and some gave up their profession altogether. For those who continued, the movement of reform affected what they painted in a number of ways, often polarising them according to their religious beliefs since these influenced the content of their work. The Adoration of the Golden Calf became a common theme in the Netherlands early in the sixteenth century; Lucas van Leyden's picture of this title was painted in the late 1520s.[118] In such pictures, the use of flowers, feasting and dancing is associated with the worship of idols.

The story of the Golden Calf epitomises the history of Reformation iconoclasm. God appointed Moses to build a tabernacle and gave him two 'tables of testimony' 'written with the finger of God'. While Moses was away, the Israelites went to his brother, Aaron, to ask him to 'make us gods'. So Aaron collected their gold earrings, made a molten calf and 'fashioned it with a graving tool'. Before this idol, as the King James version describes the statue, the people offered sacrifices, ate, drank and danced naked. On seeing what was happening, Moses cast down the tables on which the word of God had been 'graven', and called upon his people to follow the true God. The Levites agreed to do so, and so he instructed them to go through the camp slaying 'every man his brother'. As a result three thousand fell, but Moses had saved the remainder from sin, consecrated them to the Lord, obtained a duplicate of the tables and was promised a land 'flowing with milk and honey'.[119]

This story is relevant to our theme in a number of ways. The Israelites are taught to worship Jehovah and to eschew all other gods. Secondly, the graven word is opposed to the graven image, rather in the fashion that Bernard of Clairvaux was opposed to Abbot Suger; that opposition continued to be a general theme of European cultural history. Thirdly, three thousand perished in this earliest account of a religious persecution where the object of worship, the religious image, is itself destroyed. And that object is associated with blood sacrifice and with luxury (as indeed was the Tabernacle itself), but also with feasting, drinking and with dancing, nude dancing, licentious behaviour.

The same theme was central to Poussin's painting of *The Adoration of the Golden Calf* of 1626, one hundred years after Leyden (Plate 6.3). Garlands

[116] Campenhausen 1968:197; Freedberg 1988:11.   [117] Freedberg 1988.
[118] Others are listed in Freedberg 1988:187ff.   [119] Exodus 32.1–35; 33.1–3.

hang round the calf's neck and belly as well as around the plinth itself;[120] in the wilder revels of the later and finer painting of the same title in the National Gallery, London, this feature is less emphatic. Poussin made much use of chaplets not only in classical pictures, such as *The Arcadian Shepherds*[121] and extravagantly so in *The Inspiration of the Epic Poet*,[122] but also in Biblical scenes such as *The Triumph of David*.[123] That he was highly conscious of the implications of decorations of foliage and flowers is clear from *The Kingdom of Flora* of 1631 where the themes of flowers, sexuality, garlands, classical statues and gardens are closely interwoven (Plate 6.4).[124]

Iconoclasm occurred throughout Europe. Let us recall what these puritanical progenitors of modern European capitalism, according to the Weberian thesis, did, not in the Netherlands, England or Massachusetts, which were to remain Protestant, but in France, even in a region as remote as Conques in the hilly region of the Rouergue in south-west France. The abbey had to become a secular college, but that was not all. The Calvinists made their first appearance in Rouergue in 1558. By 1561 they felt strong enough to attack Conques. The treasure, including the statue of Sainte-Foy, was hidden. But the carved woodwork of the choir was pulled down, piled against the columns of the apse and set on fire in order to destroy the church itself.[125]

Much later, at the time of the Revolution in 1790, the seizure of ecclesiastical possessions was pursued officially. The church of Conques itself did not suffer but centuries of archives were publicly burnt. The valued treasure was saved by the commune in a dramatic series of incidents in which the attention of the Convention's perquisitioners was distracted so that the contents could be dispersed among the inhabitants by night. Once again a popular movement was directed towards the confiscation or destruction of religious images.

When art is largely religious, or involved with religion, then the question of the representation of deity and the nature of the divine is inevitably present either implicitly or explicitly. The evolution of distinct realms of secular and religious activity, which was furthered during the Renaissance, partly resolves the problem for the artist since he can now concentrate on the human form and avoid the divine. Secular portraiture supplements, even takes over from, the religious. Such changes were partly a matter of re-establishing the differentiation of the 'great organisations' and the accompanying fragmentation of the conceptual universe (not all was now sacred). At the same time, alternative sources of patronage emerged, merchants, secular colleges, independent scholars and others, depending on the relative balance of

---

[120] In the M. H. de Jong Memorial Museum, San Francisco.
[121] In the Devonshire Collection, Chatsworth, Derbyshire.
[122] In the Louvre, Paris.
[123] In the Prado, Madrid.
[124] Staatliche Kunstsammlungen, Dresden. See also *Bacchanal Before a Herm*, National Gallery, London
[125] Bouillet and Servières 1900:115–16.

6.3 N. Poussin, *The Adoration of the Golden Calf*, 1626. (M. H. de Jong Museum, San Francisco)

ideological, political and economic power. With the Renaissance the balance of artistic activity in Europe finally swung away from the church; in Islam a distant tradition of secular art had taken root in Persia in the Safavid period, and in India after the Mughal invasions.

The establishment of a secular tradition meant that, at least in Holland, the painting and enjoyment of flowers could take place outside the domain affected by the reformers. Iconoclasm affected the use of flowers for religious purposes by eliminating the statues with which they were adorned, even if only in decoration or reverence, and in ridding the church of images of all kinds. But the movement to reform Christian worship affected the culture of flowers in other ways because it often radically altered attitudes to ritual and to performance generally, even those held outside the church. In England, as in France, the mystery and miracle plays died out in the early Elizabethan period. Other elements of popular culture came under attack by the Puritan wing as we see in the controversy over *The Book of Sports*. In Essex there was a distinct decline in festivals and festivity at the very moment of the rise of witch-hunting;[126] even traditional displays of hospitality at Christmas were

[126] Hunt 1983:136.

6.4 N. Poussin, *The Kingdom of Flora*, 1631. (Staatliche Kunstsammlungen, Dresden)

viewed with suspicion. Community rituals, both secular and religious, tended to be associated with flowers; Protestants, especially Puritans, emphasised the individual's approach to God and society, often unmediated by others. That view had its effects on festivals of all kinds.

FESTIVALS AS RELIGIOUS AND POLITICAL TOOLS

Christmas was a celebration that was intimately involved with the question of the divinity of Christ and how to represent and worship him. As Christianity became established in the Roman empire, it was led to define its own doctrines more precisely. Was Christ a prophet or was he God himself? Was he both at once? And if so, did he develop from one to the other or were both natures in existence from the very beginning? The doctrine of Christ's dual nature was established at the first Council of Nicaea in 328, but only at Ephesus in 431 was it established that he was God from birth. In opposition to the Nestorians, Mary was declared 'God-bearing'. As a result the Nativity became an all-important date in the religious calendar. While the feast was mentioned in 336, the earliest crib was recorded between 432 and 440 in the first of many Western churches to be dedicated to Mary.[127] That was the doctrinal context

[127] Murray 1986.

in which the household and public celebrations emerged, based no doubt on local precedents, and which later involved the decorating of the house with greenery, that is, with holly, ivy and mistletoe.

For some Reformers of the sixteenth century these festivities not only had an aura of paganism about them but were characterised by an excess of joy. Supposed continuity from the Roman Saturnalia or from the northern Yule were beside the point, for the celebrations were antipathetic to some reforming Protestants, especially the Puritans and Presbyterians of England, Scotland and New England, on a number of contemporary grounds. In the 1580s the attack on excess was set out by Philip Stubbes in *The Anatomie of Abuses*. A further objection arose from the fact that while in the late medieval period Christmas had been subordinate to Easter, the conflicts of the sixteenth century gave it an increased significance in the eyes of Catholics of the Counter-Reformation, partly because of the emphasis on the role of Mary as mother and of the icon of the Christmas crib.[128] So for some Protestants, Christmas was both pagan and Catholic at the same time.

The division of opinion about Christmas and other 'sports' separated not so much Catholics and Protestants but Anglicans and Catholics on one side and various dissenters or 'Non-conformists' on the other.[129] While festivals continued in the early seventeenth century and were indeed encouraged by the *Book of Sports*, the 'Morris book' as it was contemptuously known, Puritans strongly objected to such activities or sought refuge in alternative celebrations of a determinedly secular character. In 1606, following the attempted conspiracy to blow up the Houses of Parliament, that body instituted Gunpowder Treason Day, Guy Fawkes' Day as 5 November became popularly called, as a national holiday. The move was strongly supported by Puritans who rejected all 'papist' festivals, including the nearby All Saints' and All Souls' of 1 and 2 November for which it became a deliberate substitute, leading to an exchange of fireworks for flowers. Saints' days, mystery plays and revels were associated with 'popery and superstition', quite apart from being occasions for licentious and disorderly behaviour. They were also great occasions for the use of flowers, which once again became associated in the eyes of some with paganism, Catholicism and with excess.

The most severe attack on religious festivals in England came during the Civil War. Questions were raised as to whether one should fast or feast on Christmas Day. In 1645 the *Directory for the Publique Worship* denied that festival days, 'vulgarly called Holy days', had any warrant in the word of God. Some two years later, after Parliament had gained its victory over Charles I in 1646, an ordinance abolished those feasts, providing regular holidays for students, servants and apprentices on the second Tuesday of every month. As

[128] Durston 1985; Bossy 1985.   [129] Marcus 1986.

in other areas they dominated, Puritans did away with images, condemned the maypole in particular as 'a painted calf' or 'idol', broke stained glass windows, burnt altar rails, sold church organs, banished Christmas and Easter, instituting Days of Thanksgiving in their place.[130] Instead of visual symbols they relied on the word, the plain word, and on rational discourse.

But English culture remained, unlike that of New England, heavily split between the views of reformers who cleansed the churches of all extraneous features and who pulled down the maypole, and the conservative forces that decked the churches in flowers, as was the case before the Civil War,[131] that interpreted paganism as proto-Christianity following the doctrines of Hermes Trismegistus,[132] and that saw flowers, like images, as means of communicating with the divine.[133] On the Anglican side, the work of the poet Herrick (1591–1674) has affinities with the Greek anthology, itself a collection of flowers. Herrick was the most original of the 'sons of Ben [Jonson]', who revived the spirit of the classical lyric. His life spanned the whole of the period of the abolition of the monarchy, the Commonwealth and the Restoration. His flower poems have been compared to Dutch flower pieces of the *vanitates* type, in their insistence on *memento mori*, on the inevitability of death.[134] It is sometimes difficult to locate him in the spectrum of belief and accommodation, for during the Commonwealth 'Laudian ritual and tolerance of ungodly sports could all too easily be interpreted as signs of Catholic sympathies'.[135] That was true of May Day celebrations; at Ditcheat Richard Allein declared 'a maypole was an idol'.[136] So when birds and flowers display 'a natural May Day piety' in Herrick's poem 'Corinna', they aligned themselves against the Puritan cause. Some supporters such as Marvell and Milton wrote magnificently of gardens. But for more extreme partisans the use of both flowers and gardens carried political statements. In *Lucasta* (1659), part of a pastoral by that ardent royalist, Richard Lovelace, Aramantha retreats to the peaceful countryside, away from the Civil War, and enters a garden where the flowers themselves crown her Flora, queen of the May, a ritual banned in the nation at large.[137]

While the interest in classical wreaths and chaplets was revived during the Renaissance, the contrast persisted between the perishable garlands and enduring crowns, preferably spiritual, and became especially relevant to seventeenth-century controversies. At the same time, the garland of roses, as a symbol of ease, luxury and even damnation is opposed to the crown of thorns.[138] The worth of flowers may even be diminished by the fact that they are a prelude to fruit. To remove the flowers is to leave a barren tree, a vine

---

[130] Underdown 1985:55, 51, 78.　　[131] Marcus 1986:222.　　[132] Marcus 1986:223–4.
[133] On the doctrine of signatures or phytognomy, that plants exhibit some outward sign of their properties, see Hunt 1983:1.　　[134] Fowler 1980:247.　　[135] Underdown 1985:129.
[136] Underdown 1985:77.　　[137] Marcus 1986:218.　　[138] Kronenfeld 1981:291.

that does not 'bear fruit' in Christian imagery. So that in his poem 'The Coronet', Marvell remarks:

> I gather flow'rs (my fruits are only flow'rs).[139]

The wreath, especially the laurel wreath, is given a partly Christian embrace, being offered to those achieving moral virtue, though the reference is often to the metaphor rather than the material; the metaphor and the image were always acceptable even though the original could be considered pagan.[140] The main but not the exclusive interpretation of the garland and the wreath, especially in Protestant circles, was as a prize, a reward, for literary achievement or more usually for moral virtue, as typically in George Wither's *A Collection of Emblems, Ancient and Modern*.[141] Once again, even as metaphor there is a potential contradiction in making any offerings to the divinity as opposed to men, for 'the paradox of all religious poetry' is that the honours paid to the creator God by mortals can never add anything to his immortal glory, let alone to his store of material things. So that when Marvell thinks of offering to the Lord a coronet, variously referred to as a garland, chaplet, crown and diadem, he ends by crushing the flowers under his feet.[142]

THE RESTORATION OF FLOWERS

Such provisions of the *Directory* failed to stop popular celebrations. At Christmas, visiting still took place in various parts of England while literary defences were offered in support of ancient law and custom. The old order, remarked one commentator in 1645, demanded 'the meritorious maypole, garlands, galliards and jolly Whitsun-ales'.[143] Like the maypole, which became an obvious symbol of royalists, garlands formed part of the folk traditions that had developed, elaborated and proliferated, with the culture of flowers, since the thirteenth century. One such local ceremony consisted of 'carrying the garland' and led to fighting between the men of nearby villages to seize possession.[144] To the Puritans these activities smacked of heathenism. On May Day 1648 in Oxford, the soldiers even confiscated garlands and fiddles. In 1657 a man took a garland from some children and crowned his companion as a political protest. The garland carried an obvious association with the crown and therefore with royalty. After the Restoration on Coronation Day in 1661, the wife of the mayor of Bath led four hundred

---

[139] Line 6. See Hardy 1962:47.
[140] See 'The Coronet' by Andrew Marvell, 'The Garland' by Henry Vaughan and 'La Corona' by John Donne.
[141] Third book, 1975 (1635):135; see also p.258.

> The Garland, He alone shall weare,
> Who, to the Goale, doth persevere.

[142] Hardy 1962:46.   [143] Underdown 1985:178.   [144] Underdown 1985:96.

maidens in white and green, carrying 'gilded crowns, crowns made of flowers, and wreaths made of laurel mixed with tulips'.[145] Flowers had made a dramatic return. Wells like that at Droitwich were often decorated annually with greenery and flowers on the day of the patron saint, a custom that still persists. But such activities were prohibited during the Civil War and the well dried up; the next year the custom was revived and the water returned.[146]

Some activities were kept alive, like music and drama in a few country houses. Many others like the maypole vanished but made a dramatic return with the Restoration. In May 1660 the streets of the Dorset town of Sherborne were decorated once more with flowers. With the return of the monarchy in 1660 Christmas festivities came back, reinforcing the association of the Restoration with the maypole and with Merrie England. But in other parts of the world, in Scotland and New England, it was many years before Christmas was to become a significant event in the Christian year. Even in England much disappeared, never to return except in nineteenth-century revivals, for there was continuing apprehension about festivals and images in some levels of society. Where they occurred festivals were viewed as part of the traditional community based on the participation in joint rituals and revelry, in contrast to the newer approach that valued individual piety and sobriety.[147] At the local level much was lost throughout the country. Conflicts over maypoles and festivals continued, for Nonconformists did not disappear overnight, even if they had lost political domination. Performances centred more on church and chapel than had earlier been the case.

The further attacks of the Reformers inevitably led to further defences by the Counter-Reformation. In 1570, not long before Jan Breughel started painting flowers, the theologian Molanus produced a treatise on Christian iconography in which he insisted on the role of the painted image. He was not alone in discussing iconography nor yet in holding that works of art, like sermons, poetry, emblems or the theatre, were ways of instructing the people and of permitting them to approach the verities of the faith. Following their founder's injunction 'to look far and find God in everything', the Jesuits made much use of images for this purpose, placing particular value on flowers as a way of revealing the truths of religion.[148] Their symbolic association with the Virgin Mary was developed in the face of Protestant criticism, and after the Council of Trent (1545–63) the rosary prayer, addressed to Mary, 'took on the aspect of a crusade'.[149] Catholic writers like Henry Hawkins developed the notion of the Virgin Mary as the enclosed garden planted with flowers,

[145] Underdown 1985:283.
[146] Underdown 1985:261. Well-dressing continues in the English Midlands to this day and makes great use of flowers.
[147] Underdown 1985:275. As the author shows, the contrasting approaches were connected with regional cultures associated with ecological differences.   [148] Delenda 1987:16.
[149] Delenda 1987:19, referring to work of Giovanni Pozzi and Marzia Cataldi Gallo.

especially the lily, rose, violet and sunflower, as emblems of the heart.[150] Such elaborations were connected with the sodalities encouraged by the Society of Jesus for the purpose of projecting the faith. In medieval Latin lyrics the Virgin had appeared as the lily among thorns, the Rod of Jesse, the Burning Bush, the mystic Rose. In Hawkins' work, as in other emblem books of the period, such epithets were accompanied by an engraving of the theme which might then be further elaborated in poetry.[151] Flowers were employed as verbal and visual images as a way of approaching divinity and bringing out the truth, whereas the Protestant aim was generally to strip away imagery and decoration in order to concentrate on 'plain words'.

Although many of the popular rituals never returned to those areas where the reformers had held sway, flowers eventually regained some of their earlier favour, even in the Church of England. At the annual feast day at St Paul's in London, the dean and chapter wore garlands of red roses. In Staffordshire on St Barnabas Day in 1750 everyone was wearing white roses.[152] Roses might be planted on the grave and flowers deposited annually, especially those sweet-smelling varieties standing for purity, while French or African marigolds were in bad taste.

However, among dissenters and in the 'low' Church of England, flowers continued to be regarded with some suspicion in a religious context. That was also true of the related question of aromatics and perfumes. The use of incense distinguished Catholic from Protestant worship. Even the use of perfumes took on similar dimensions. They were considered as luxuries under the Commonwealth, in the Puritan regime of America and even in the Victorian period. As in the culture of flowers, and fashion generally, it was France that led the way until the First World War; even today that country has not lost its lead in 'la mode', in apparel and accoutrements for women. The reasons are not hard to find. Long after the Restoration, a bill was introduced into the British parliament with the following provision:

That all women of whatever age, rank, profession, or degree, whether virgins, maids, or widows, that shall, from and after such Act, impose upon, seduce, and betray into matrimony, any of His Majesty's subjects, by the scents, paints, cosmetic washes, artificial teeth, false hair, Spanish wool, iron stays, hoops, high heeled shoes, bolstered hips, shall incur the penalty of the law in force against witchcraft and like misdemeanours and that the marriage upon conviction, shall stand null and void.

The same male-oriented law was adopted by the state of Pennsylvania; perfumery was literally witchcraft.[153]

The return to favour of flowers was partly due to the increasing separation of the religious from the secular sphere on the one hand, and to the

[150] Freeman 1978:179, on Hawkins, *Partheneia sacra*, 1633.
[151] Strictly speaking the emblems were the words which were illustrated by the drawing.
[152] Thomas 1983:223, 230.   [153] See Piesse 1879.

development of the market and of consumer society on the other. One aspect of this development that led to the domination of flowers in the lives of ordinary people lay in the consequences of the expansion of Europe and the growth of trade with the East. While that expansion led to a spectacular increase in the number of plants available to Europe, with consequences, Atran has argued, for the nature of botanical classification, representations of flowers often preceded the actual objects themselves in the shape of imports from the East, both of Indian cotton and of Chinese porcelain.[154]

That is a fitting point at which to pause, since the impact of Indian cottons presaged the Industrial Revolution itself. With the increasing wealth and increasing secularisation, the undercurrent of opposition to icons had less force and took less obvious forms. Like other types of rejectionism, it lives on in times of radical political change when the monuments of the old regime are toppled in favour of the new, or under revolutionary governments that attempt a drastic turn-about in the direction of human activity, throwing out religious action and filling the peasant's rice bowl by discouraging activities that may detract from the production of 'necessities'. And there is still a wing of Islam, as of the other religions deriving from the Near East, that clings to former attitudes, though even here the advent of mass media and the growth of the market have inevitably made their inroads. But essentially it was the expanding market that dealt the blow to extreme forms of puritanism; the development of mass consumption of cars, for example, makes the Amish and their horses increasingly archaic, increasingly marginal. The attack on pollution is in part a reformulation of the rejection of 'luxury', as was more directly the counter-culture of the 1960s; that movement reacted against the culture of abundance, the hope of which had provided America with an alternative to the socialist path, just as it has done in Eastern Europe from the late 1980s.[155] Part of that culture of abundance is the growth in the market of flowers from a local to a world scale which I examine in the next chapter.

[154] Atran 1990.   [155] Susman 1984.

7 · The growth of the market

In writing of recent times, there are several points I want to elaborate. The first has to do with the growth of the market and its effects on the use of flowers which, when this was a luxury, was subject to ambivalence, criticism and opposition. Some elements remain that manifest themselves in current Anglo-American usage; others take the form of a personal resistance to expenditure on funeral flowers ('ni fleurs ni couronnes'), and yet others manifest themselves in the practice of some socialist states. But, as the example of Holland convincingly shows, the growth of the market can still most of these protests, partly by playing off the need to give on days like St Valentine's, which the florists themselves promote, against religious and ethical worries. Secondly, I want to develop the theme that a large part of the formal culture of flowers is urban in origin, connected with processes seen as 'civilising', whether by priests, by florists or by authors and their publishers. As such it is encouraged from above or from outside, especially in rural districts where in the earlier Middle Ages the penury of public rites acceptable to the church may have made it welcome by the populace at large. That raises two other problems, that of the meanings of flowers and the composition of popular culture. In Chapter 8 I look at the Language of Flowers that arose in Paris in the early nineteenth century and spread throughout Europe and, as discussed in Chapter 9, to America. While this language can be considered part of 'popular culture', it is largely a product of the urban literary world that is 'imposed' upon or taken up by the rest of society. Other, more 'popular', elements I examine in Chapter 10, but here too we are faced with problems that are related to what I call the 'paradox of May Day'.

The development of the economy in Europe was accompanied by a growth in the market for flowers and exotic plants, in the range of species, in the demand, especially for cut flowers, the shift from crown to bouquet, and in the complexity of the mechanisms for their supply. That market was stimulated by the increasing predominance given to flowers in the internal decoration of the home. I do not only refer to the tradition of flower painting that except in the Low Countries touched mostly the rich, although the invention of colour printing in the nineteenth century enabled merchants to produce coloured catalogues for flowers, artists to make coloured prints and virtually everyone to hang reproductions on their walls. Van Gogh's *Sunflowers* decorated many a living room, even if the original could only be acquired by a rich patron of the arts for personal enjoyment, a museum for public consumption or a pension fund or corporation as a material investment. In the decorative arts the important change, the democratisation of the flower, came earlier with the development of printed cottons and wallpaper, both of which were inventions of the East based on painted prototypes. Earlier we touched upon the influence of the East on European culture, in particular the culture of flowers and their representations. Reference was made to architecture, to painting and to literature. But it was later with the domestic arts that those influences were dominant, especially in the sphere of cotton from India and porcelain from China. In the first part of the twentieth century, virtually every other home in Western Europe displayed flowered curtains, flowered wallpaper, flowered bed-covers, flowered women – at least in their summer dresses. Flowers entered what was largely a woman's domestic world but one that played an enormous role in the development of the market, first in Asia, then later in Europe as the production of cotton cloth expanded in the prelude to the Industrial Revolution. Only with that Revolution was Europe able to reverse the terms of trade which, since Roman times, had been in favour of the cloth-producing East (Colour plate VII.1).

The fall of the Roman empire diminished but did not stop the importation of silks and cottons. These materials continued to be used as prestigious clothing for churchmen and kings, eventually being produced in the West. But trade with the Far East declined, although to the Near East contacts were maintained by the Baghdad caliphate. Western Europe had to wait until the revival of the economy, the renewed activity along the Silk Road to China in the thirteenth century and the increase in the Indian trade by land and sea.[1] Silk production was for long a monopoly of China, although in the West the fabric was unravelled, rewoven and dyed. Production only began around AD 550 when the Byzantine emperor, Justinian I, is said to have persuaded two Persian monks to smuggle silkworms from China to Constantinople in the hollow of their bamboo canes. Palermo in Sicily became the centre of textile production after the Arab conquest which began in AD 827.[2] With the invasion of the French in 1266 many of the silk weavers fled to Lucca. When Florence captured the town in 1315 many of the Sicilian weavers were removed. From there the culture spread to France about 1480, where weaving was centred on Lyons, with production taking place in the region of Montpellier and the

---

[1] The Silk Road to the Near East and Europe had been open since the second century BC.
[2] Under Arab rule, Palermo became one of the greatest cities of the world, with a population larger than any other Christian town except Constantinople. See Finley, Mack Smith and Duggan 1986:52.

Cévennes, later dominated by Protestants, some of whom brought the industry to England as a consequence of the Revocation of the Edict of Nantes in 1685.[3]

While the main thrust of Indian exports lay to South-east Asia, and in smaller quantities to East Africa, there was also an important trade by sea to the Near East. By whatever route, the Portuguese were importing painted cloth (pintados) from India even before their voyages around Africa, and soon selling it to Africans on the Guinea coast where it was much in demand.[4] However, for Europe the major change, that first affected the rich but eventually touched a large part of society, came with the direct participation in the Indian trade of the nations on the Atlantic seaboard, and with the consequent shift of the centre of mercantile activity from Venice to Antwerp and Amsterdam, from Italy to the Low Countries situated at the mouth of the Rhine.

The effect of the imports from the Far East in the sixteenth and especially the seventeenth and eighteenth centuries was to enliven the homes as well as the gardens of the West with flowers. First of all it was their representations that adorned the cloth, the porcelain and the furniture brought back in increasing quantities following the discovery of a direct sea route to the East in the fifteenth century, which culminated in the capture in 1511 of the crucial entrepôt of Malacca in present-day Malaysia. Silks, muslins, spices and perfumes had earlier been imported in such quantities that a threat was seen not only to the moral and military virtues of Rome but also to the economy itself. Both themes appear in the works of moralists like Seneca. The problem was slow to go away. A very similar objection to the use of silk is made by T. Mouffet in about 1584, when he criticised the English desire for silken habits. 'But time will make them forego this wantonness, when they shall observe that their moneys are treasured up in Italy.'[5] For the same reasons spice was said to be 'a thief', taking wealth outside the country for the sake of luxury. Expenditure on these, especially on items of personal adornment, generated its own critique.

Judging by the references to nudity and to the evidence of wall paintings, the preference in Rome appears to have been largely for silks and muslins rather than for multi-coloured cottons. Heavier embroidered fabrics were associated with the Coptic tradition and with the later princes of the Christian church (the silk stole of St Cuthbert of Durham, for example) and with the

---

[3]   These were the Huguenot silk weavers of Bethnal Green and elsewhere. In France artificial silk flowers used in the clothing industry continued to be known as *fleurs italiennes*.

[4]   See the letter of the officers of Casa de Guiné to King Manuel concerning São Jorge da Mina, 27 September 1510, referring to the demand for *pimtados* or *pintadoes*, which the editor observes are 'a sort of printed chintz or callico, from the East Indies'. Without such cloths, 'gold cannot be obtained from the merchants'. It is possible that those goods came from India where a base had been established ten years earlier, but we know that Indian cloth also reached Europe through the Near East (Blake 1942).

[5]   T. Mouffet, *Theatre of Insects* (c.1584), p.1033, quoted Seager 1896:288.

more northerly climes where thick clothing on the body and weighty hangings on walls were in greater demand rather than carpets on the floor.[6] Some of the patterns used by the Palermo weavers, and later in Lucca, were floral in design. Silk was in many ways a much more attractive material than wool for this reason.[7] Some cotton cloth was imported into Europe, but like the coloured beads of Venice, much seems to have been directed to the African trade where European imitations, waxprints from the Netherlands, Britain and France, are still in great demand today, complete with peacocks, 'mangoes' and other traditional Indian motifs depicted in all their bright colours.

The overland trade through the Near East was always limited by the nature of the terrain, the length of the journey, the modes of transport and the exactions of both states and bandits. An active sea trade existed from Egypt to India, vividly portrayed in the fragmentary documents from the Cairo Geniza, but it was only with the emergence of the Portuguese caravels in the Pacific in the sixteenth century that goods from the Orient began to be available to a wider market in Western Europe, in greater quantities and at better quality and prices. Small as these boats were in comparison with the Asian craft they encountered, their holds could carry significant quantities of precious goods and with the advantage of their superior armaments the Portuguese were able to play a substantial part in the extensive sea-borne trade of the Indian Ocean and the China seas. A further breakthrough came at the end of the sixteenth century when the nations of north-west Europe were able to break the monopolies of the Spanish and Portuguese and develop their own independent trade links. Liberated by the adoption of Protestantism they disregarded the papal restrictions that had favoured the merchants of the Catholic monarchies.

DECORATED FLOWERS FROM THE EAST

At the time of the Renaissance, the creating of highly patterned cloth was difficult and expensive, whether for clothing or for the house. Furnishing materials were generally heavy and expensive, usually consisting of tapestries woven in wool.[8] Lighter woven materials were mostly plain, although contrasting weaves, as in damask, could produce subtle patterns. Some fabrics could even be printed with a pattern by means of hot plates placed against a wooden block to create 'printed paragon'. Linen was little used for

---

[6] Henry VIII was painted standing on a Turkish carpet, indicating the existence of a luxury trade in the early sixteenth century.

[7] Contrasting the woollen goods with the attractiveness of silk sold in the new department stores of nineteenth-century Paris, Zola wrote: 'mer montante de teintes neutres, de tons sourds . . . sol noir de décembre' (Gaillard 1980:15).

[8] Flowers made their appearance on wool cloth very early, among the ancient Egyptians, but as embroidery (Joret 1897:240ff.).

decoration, being normally left white. Silk damasks from Genoa and Lyons had bolder patterns, some being brocaded. Even plainer silks might have small patterns known as *tabis de fleurs*.[9] But decoration was limited, the cloth expensive and the processes laborious. It was only at the end of the sixteenth century that colourful printed cottons from India began to be imported in greater quantities through Marseilles, and later Lisbon, Antwerp and London.[10] That changed the nature of decoration. By 1609 the East India Company had built up a lively trade, whose effects were rapidly and widely felt. By the end of the century, 'from the greatest gallants to the meanest cook maids, nothing was thought so fit to adorn their Persons as the fabrick from India! Nor for the ornament of Chambers like India Skreens, Cabinets, Beds, or Hangings, nor for Closets like China and lacquered ware.'[11] By the 1680s 'plenty of these colourful materials were to be seen in every grand house in England, Holland and France'.[12] 'Painted calico' was widely used for wall hangings, window curtains, table-covers and bed hangings. Colourful porcelain was found not only in priceless collections such as that of the Topkapi palace in Istanbul, but in the larger mansions of Europe, and later the United States, Brazil and wherever the China trade penetrated.

As mercantile capitalism gave way to industrial capitalism the market expanded, in terms both of supply and demand, and what were at one time luxury goods were seen as objects of increasingly wide-scale usage until they eventually became items of mass consumption. They were then no longer characteristic or emblematic of a 'class', moving from the category of 'luxury' to that of 'necessity'. These riches became less embarrassing and objections such as those of Pliny carried less weight. On the other hand, despite the increased circulation of commodities and the development of redistributive taxation, even among the richer nations such sentiments still emerge when belts have to be tightened and choices made, especially regarding the import of goods from overseas.

Within a short period these Eastern imports had a marked influence on tastes not only for foreign products but even for the local decorative arts. For example, the patterns of the English crewel embroideries came to derive from the printed cotton palpampores of India. So great was the demand that copies of many of these goods began to be produced in Europe. In 1625 an English company was founded to weave hangings with Indian figures and in 1676 Sherwin received a patent to print on broad cloth in 'the only true way of East India printing and stayning such kind of goods'. But imports continued to dominate and local prints, made first with wooden blocks, did not come into their own until after 1730. That printing was on imported cotton, and for clothing and decorative purposes. It was the same with Chinese imports. In

[9] Thornton 1978:107ff.   [10] Beginning in the 1570s and 1580s (Irwin and Brett 1970:4).
[11] Evans 1931:ii, 61, quoting Pollexfen.   [12] Thornton 1978:116.

1614, Wytmans obtained permission to make 'porcelain' at The Hague, and shortly after 1642 Chinese blue-and-white ware was being imitated in faience at Delft. Early painted pottery in the Netherlands followed the style of Italian majolica but in the early years of the seventeenth century, captured cargoes of Chinese porcelain, mostly blue-and-white export wares of the Ming dynasty, were taken to Holland. Known as 'carrack porcelain', they inspired the production of the tin-glazed wares that became known as delft, since production was concentrated in that town.[13] Imitation did not stop there, for polychrome ware of the *famille verte* and *famille noire* was copied as well as Imari wares from Japan. 'Nanking' porcelain, which is often confused with the Blue Willow made at Ching-te-Chen, was exported from that town, while polychrome ware was shipped through Canton. From Delft production spread to England leading to the tradition of the willow pattern at the end of the eighteenth century. That was invented in Shropshire in 1779 although like other variants it followed the Chinese taste. As a result of the entrepreneurial skills and consumer orientation of Josiah Wedgwood, the design penetrated every British home.[14]

The tin-glazed techniques employed for delft had been reinvented in the Near East in the ninth century. It was at the beginning of that century, about the time of the crowning of Charlemagne, that the great caliph of Baghdad, Hārūn ar-Rashīd, was presented with a number of Tang porcelain bowls. Pottery then became an artistic medium, and remained important to the thirteenth century. Because of the richness of their decoration large amounts were imported and imitations made, initially in painted pottery, spreading to Spain and Italy in the form of majolica. While Islam largely observed the ban on representations in the mosques, in the secular domain, floral patterns often escaped censure, as they later did in illuminations.

For wall hangings themselves paper already began to be substituted in the seventeenth century.[15] In Europe the placing of handpainted or stencilled paper on walls is found soon after the introduction of papermaking in the later fifteenth century. Painted Chinese papers, known as India papers, began to arrive towards the end of the seventeenth century, especially produced for the European market. Their studied dissimilarity of detail made them greatly prized and copies began to be created locally in the eighteenth century. Based on Eastern models, they were produced at a factory in Rouen but only became of more general use in the following century, not only in France but in England, where a tax was levied in 1712 in an attempt to discourage such imports. The industry developed using new design motifs, such as chintz, and the first machine for printing wallpaper was invented in France in 1785,

[13] Syria was producing copies of blue and white ware in the fourteenth century.
[14] McKendrick 1960, McKendrick *et al.* 1982.
[15] For examples of Chinese floral wallpaper imported to New England following the opening up of the China trade after Independence, see Nelson 1985:84–5.

followed by the introduction of endless rolls. In England machine-printed wallpaper began in 1840 and was revolutionised from 1862 by the designs of William Morris and the Arts and Crafts Movement which popularised many floral patterns.[16]

Such Eastern models provided an alternative to academic classicism, as Evans remarks, an art of glowing colour, of rare materials, of exquisite finish. 'The curiously complete break made in the seventeenth century with all the decorative traditions of the Middle Ages, even in peasant art, is perhaps partly due to this discovery of an art that met the same needs as the medieval tradition . . . Bright colour, engaging narrative, natural observation, and skilful stylization were all to be found in the wares of China; and the illuminations, the enamels, and the embroideries of an earlier day were soon forgotten.'[17] This is not surprising, since the art of illuminated manuscript, the tapestries and other features were expensive to buy, laborious to create and essentially features of a minority rather than a mass culture. The imports of cloth from India and porcelain from China derived from a manufacturing base, proto-industrial in character but capable of large-scale if not mass production, that is by block printing as well as by painting. Block printing of fabrics employed the same techniques as block printing on paper, and so the Chinese printing of books, where the process of stamping out logographic script, already well established by the early Middle Ages, was similar to that of stamping out non-linguistic designs. The process resembled the use of stamped as distinct from rolled seals.

The impact of the Indian cloth on the domestic landscape was as strong in East Asia as it was in Western Europe, and occurred about the same period. It was the Southern barbarians, the Portuguese and Dutch merchants in the middle of the sixteenth century, who brought to Japan the first chintz, called *sarasa*, from what was known to that country as the 'Middle West'. Fragments of cloth preserved in the eighth century imperial collection at Nara show that much earlier motifs from Persia, China, India and even Greece made their way to that country. The transfer of classical patterns along the Silk Road is well known and from China they were adopted in Korea and Japan. One Japanese commentator, Wada, is even led to ask whether there were indeed many designs that originated with their own ancestors.[18] When chintz arrived in quantity, it was not simply destined for a royal court but for a bourgeois market. A revolution took place because of its brilliant colours and the nature of the patterns. These affected the whole development of textile design, including the kimonos of the highly 'traditional' Nōh plays and the costumes of the period up to the end of the seventeenth century, 'opening the eyes of our ancestors to the nature of design'.

The bright colours that so struck purchasers in the East and West resulted

---

[16] Havard 1887–90.   [17] Evans 1931:ii, 65.   [18] Sanzo Wada 1963.

from the greater speed of absorbency of cotton, which allowed them to run into one another at the edges. So popular did Indian painted and printed cloth become that in Europe in the late seventeenth century measures were taken to restrict imports and to encourage native products. The French government banned its importation because it threatened the market for locally woven silks and woollens.[19] The ban was also consistent with the attempts of Louis XIV's minister of finance, Colbert, to encourage the local production of luxury objects through the establishment of manufactures such as Les Gobelins in Paris. Colbert followed a policy that was the aim of many but was bound to fall into difficulties in the long run, of making the country at once self-sufficient in every sphere and at the same time an exporter to others.

In 1701 similar regulations were applied in England. As in France, Spain and Germany, the result was to encourage local imitations together with the import of the raw cotton needed for their manufacture.[20] It was the development of the cotton industry that played such a key part in leading up to the process of mass industrial production that dominated Western Europe from the 1780s, encouraging the growth of towns and the depopulation of the countryside. The industrialisation of cotton cloth mechanised the production of chintz, of printed patterns, using many natural objects, especially flowers, which became such a common theme of domestic design. That culture was influenced in other ways. The Industrial Revolution changed the nature of the market for real and artificial flowers as well as the nature of their representations.

FLOWERS FROM THE EAST

The range of actual flowers increased enormously and flower gardens became more popular, fuelled by the advent of luxurious exotic blooms from both East and West which followed from the expansion of European trade and colonisation. Some flowers like the tulip came from the Near East. Many cultigens, including flowers, were brought from America in the seventeenth century but the great period for their importation from the East began in the eighteenth century with the growth of popular gardening, and then with the larger urban markets for cut flowers that developed in the nineteenth.

As we have seen, the search for exotic plants had already existed in the ancient world as well as in China itself. Among other plants, the pomegranate had travelled there from the West where it was characteristically prized as much for its blossom as for its fruit.[21] But the main movement of flowering plants was in the other direction. While the transfer of flowers such as the

---

[19] Vollmer *et al.* 1983:2.   [20] Evans 1931:ii, 68.

[21] China received many cultigens from the West at an early period; Laufer (1919) lists a variety of plants, including indigo, jasmine and narcissus. Meanwhile in the other direction went rhubarb and the hollyhock (*Althaea rosea*).

lotus, the rose and the tulip had already taken place over many centuries, the deeper and more intensive contacts of the world-wide colonial encounter meant that flowers were introduced in increasing numbers. From South America Jesuits brought the passion flower for which they had constructed an elaborate didactic 'symbolism' as a mnemonic for Christian catechists. India produced her riches but it was from East Asia that many domesticated plants arrived. Camellias, chrysanthemums, peonies, magnolias, forsythia, wisteria, the gardenia, all came from China as well as new varieties of roses and pinks. Plant hunters were dispatched to comb the world for new varieties to fill the gardens, nurseries and greenhouses of the West.

It was the scale that was quite different from earlier transfers and affected botanical knowledge as well as the market. Increasing numbers of Westerners were stationed in far-off countries where one of their first intellectual tasks was to make sense of the flora and fauna of their new environment. That and the demands of the administration, of agriculture, of teaching, led to the production of systematic treatises on plant life. These works followed the lines taken earlier by botany in Europe where it has been argued that the sheer number and variety of imported plants created the need for a more organised understanding, a need that eventually resulted in the comprehensive classificatory scheme of the eighteenth-century Swedish botanist, Linnaeus. The Italian Renaissance and the German Reformation had already loosened the structure and content of knowledge systems. But botanical knowledge was also promoted by the development of more intensive communication about science, especially the unprecedented output of books and papers, both in numbers and in copies, that followed the invention of printing, that is, of movable type for use with an alphabetic script. For such knowledge one of the most important features of the printing press was its capacity to reproduce accurate drawings of plants in large numbers, at a time when artists in Northern Europe were turning away from the public painting of the South, both religious and secular, towards a more domestic art of smaller scale. That was the case with the work of the *Kleinmeister* who followed Dürer, and with the compact paintings of the Low Countries that were designed to adorn a burgher's home. Much of this production was for decoration as distinct from worship, but it had strong links with the new sciences which were then making such great strides forward.

THE URBAN MARKET

That same setting developed the demand for cut flowers, not petals to strew upon the floor of public buildings, but long-stemmed herbaceous plants to fill a vase, to decorate a room, to make a suitable gift for its inhabitants. Gardens too developed, not only the great formal gardens of the Renaissance that attempted to renew the glories of Rome, but the smaller flower gardens of lesser folk in an urban setting. Later on, in the late eighteenth century, came the flower beds in cottage gardens that are considered so typical of England.[22] These were followed by the allotments that were especially created for the nineteenth-century working class where its members could grow their flowers as well as vegetables for competitive display. Gardening was encouraged by such display, first among the middle class and later among the working class. In Bristol in the mid eighteenth century there were two flower shows a year, one for auriculas, another for carnations. Once they had reached an affordable price, it was possible for the poor to give plants as much attention as the rich. Competitions were much encouraged, since it was thought that the spread of gardening would have a civilising effect upon the working man and woman, rather like the deliberate spread of the tea ceremony in Japan or of competitive football in the nineteenth century.[23]

In these small plots on the outskirts of town, today so visible around Warsaw, Berlin, Prague and Amsterdam, city people could get a taste of country life. They could grow their own flowers, but for many that was not possible. The rapid urbanisation that industrialisation promoted often meant dense conglomerations in small spaces, even for all of the bourgeoisie. It was in this atmosphere, stimulated by the general interest in the advances in scientific botany and by the travel literature that world-wide contacts threw up, that we find in eighteenth-century England a great development in flower painting for illustrating books and for reproducing on calico prints. Nineteenth-century Europe gave birth to that bizarre feature of the culture of flowers discussed in the next chapter, namely, the Language of Flowers. That was just one aspect of the growing volume of books, including coloured prints, on flowers and on the planting of flowers, inside as well as outside the house, that grew up in the first half of the century. But above all the urban scene was marked by the sale of cut flowers and their use by a wide segment of the inhabitants of the major cities. Their usage was not confined only to the larger towns (although these tended to set the fashion). In the 1830s, the Countess of Blessington paid a visit to a small hotel in Arles where the large antique fireplace was filled with fresh flowers.[24]

THE SELLERS OF FLOWERS

The market in flowers in Europe developed nowhere more rapidly than in Holland where the density of cities, the richness of the alluvial soil, the many overseas connections, especially with East and South-east Asia, but also with South Africa and the Americas, led to a lively trade not only in cut flowers but in bulbs of various kinds, especially the tulip.[25] The early domination of the Netherlands, commercially and culturally, was epitomised in its vigorous

---

[22] See Hyams 1970; Clayton-Payne and Elliott 1988.   [23] Thomas 1983:229, 234.
[24] Blessington 1842:31.   [25] Schama 1987.

tradition of flower painting. In many spheres its position as a commercial power was taken over by England, while culturally it was often France whose urban life provided a model for Europe as a whole. Certainly that was the case with the Language of Flowers, for, while the Dutch retained a lead in the production and even consumption of flowers, it was Paris that tended to set the fashion in their use.

The opening up of the market in France, its proliferation into a variety of outlets for flowers, was a direct result of the abandonment of the earlier monopoly that had been granted to the bouquet-makers of Paris and confirmed by the parliament of Louis XV in 1735 when it established a corporation on their behalf. But in 1776 and 1777, like many other corporations, the profession of *marchandes bouquetières, fleuristes, chapelières de fleurs* had its privileges withdrawn. The sale of flowers and the manufacture of bouquets was opened up to all and sundry. As a result, in 1789 a petition was addressed by the profession to the newly convened States General asking for a restoration of those privileges on the grounds that the quality of work and the level of income had dropped dramatically following the lowering of prices. That fall in income had led to the practitioners seeking 'in dissolute behaviour and the most shameful debauchery the resources they need'.[26]

As a further consequence more police were required at the market place because 'women without principles' threw themselves at the produce brought by the growers (*jardiniers-fleuristes*), damaging some and buying the rest at arbitrary prices. These women were *colporteuses, filles non marchandes*, who went in for practices 'contrary to good order' such as pinning artificial flowers to branches of orange flowers or putting several carnations (*œillets*) together on cards and selling them as a single item. These free vendors would stay for the whole night at the Halles, especially on the eve of the days of patron saints, waiting for the arrival of the gardeners so that they could buy before the usual time, sometimes even going directly to the country to take flowers from the parterres and orangeries of nobles and others. Because of these outcomes the former *journalières-bouquetières* asked for the return of their ancient privileges, declaring that 'liberty is the enemy of licence'.[27]

The 'freedom' permitted to all and sundry to enter the market led to the ensuing conflicts between regulated traders and enterprising freelances. It resulted in a proliferation not only of numbers but of types of seller. Even in 1789 the bouquetières were not the sole 'community' of women dealing in flowers; another petition (*doléance*) was directed to the States General by the *marchandes de mode, plumassières, fleuristes de Paris*.[28] The grievances of this group were more technical in character, and concerned with apparel rather than with flowers as such. Flowers, especially artificial ones, played an

[26] Rebérioux 1989:53.   [27] Rebérioux 1989:54.   [28] Rebérioux 1989:45.

increasing part in personal decoration where they were constantly linked with the use of feathers, especially when these became more available following the opening up of trade with South America. This association between the two was common in many parts of the world, both being gaily coloured and portable additions from the world of nature to the human form.

The activities of the closed corporations in the eighteenth century gave way to a broader and more loosely structured spectrum of producers, wholesalers and retailers after the Revolution. That period saw the final destruction of the system of guilds, leaving the way open for the great change in retailing that occurred in the 1830s. Even before the Revolution there was some division of labour between those who produced in the periphery and sold in the market place, those who peddled flowers in the streets and those who made use of flowers for apparel. The major change in retailing was the emergence of the boutique and the store with the gradual diminution but never the disappearance of purchases direct from the flower market, from street stalls and from perambulating hawkers. In the nineteenth century in Paris there were the 'bouquetière au panier' at the bottom of the hierarchy (Plate 7.1), then the 'bouquetière ambulante' (Plate 7.2), followed by the new 'kiosque de fleuriste' (Plate 7.3), and at the top the 'grande maison' established in a boutique. Independent of the bouquetière au panier, male hawkers profited from the bargains when the market in Les Halles was coming to an end, buying the remaining stock at a low price, loading it into baskets which they carried on their backs and appearing at street corners with a basket of violets, of narcissus, carnations, and even of cress.[29]

The impact of the boutique profoundly affected social life. While purchases elsewhere never entirely disappeared and exist in the larger towns even today, a large part of the booming trade was now in the hands of the bouquetières des boutiques who were selling flowers in the new shops in main streets lit up by the magic of gas, as Paul de Kock describes these novelties in *La Grande Ville, nouveau tableau de Paris, comique, critique et philosophique*, a remarkable account of Paris in the 1840s produced with the help of Balzac, Dumas and others.[30] Such boutiques were not altogether new, except in their lighting and their arrangments. But the growing prosperity of the 1830s led to a proliferation of *magasins*, of which many of the most prominent catered for la mode, a hierarchy of shops occupied by the *modiste* (selling *chapeaux à fleurs*), the *couturière* and the *cordonnier*.[31] In addition new restaurants opened, and for groceries a new kind of store arose, selling dried goods and

---

[29] Maumené 1897:38. The account is from the last decade of the century but the situation seems to have changed little over the previous fifty years.

[30] De Kock's works were well known to his contemporaries. They appear in the reading of Karl Marx who compares Balzac and Paul de Kock in a letter to Jenny, 17 September 1878; Engels refers to one of his plays in a letter to Eduard Bernstein, 21 July 1884, and again in a letter to Laura Lafargue, 13 June 1891, he speaks of him jokingly, as a 'great authority' on 'the origins of marriage and the family'. An obvious pun is made on the name in Molly's long monologue in James Joyce's *Ulysses*. [31] See for example Blessington 1842.

7.1 Flower girl with basket, Paris, late nineteenth century. (Mauméné 1897:35)

7.2 Flower girl with handcart, Paris, late nineteenth century. (Mauméné 1897:37)

7.3 A florist's kiosk, Paris, late nineteenth century. (Mauméné 1897:41)

known as *magasin de nouveautés*. A few decades later, in 1869, Aristide Boucicaut laid the foundation stone of Bon Marché, the first department store in Paris, possibly in the world, although parallel developments were taking place in America and in England at about the same time.[32] The growth of the shop was not only a matter of supplying the wants of customers; it also created a demand that the temporary market stall never could. In earlier society the phenomenon of fashion was also present. Demands for certain commodities were rapidly created and extinguished. In Shakespeare's *The Winter's Tale*, Autolycus' tray carried trifling objects of adornment that were undoubtedly subject to such swift changes; hairstyles, song and dance display the same features in many African societies which have certainly been less static than the word 'traditional' often implies. In the modern period in Europe the difference lay not in the existence but in the pace of change and in the range of items subject to 'fashion', to 'la mode', and those sold by 'les marchands de nouveautés'.

Flowers participated in this expansion of the domestic economy and of retail outlets. De Kock speaks of the great consumption of bouquets, the main customers being 'les petites-maîtresses, les artistes, les lions et les dandys'. There were no workers, no 'grisettes', no men of the people, for these strata bought their flowers, when they needed them, at the markets.[33] The clientele, he declares, are mainly men, who are giving to women other than their wives, a situation that gave rise to a paradox.[34] 'Women in Paris use an enormous amount of flowers but what is strange is that the women buy few and their husbands never.'[35]

The 'dandys' and 'lions', men about town of various ages, would send flowers as gifts to ladies on various occasions, for example, if they were going to the theatre. The ladies would then throw the bouquet to an actress who had pleased them for her performance. Since it was a mark of esteem to receive flowers in this way, it was sometimes arranged that enough tributes should be showered at her feet to swell her pride and improve the takings. De Kock tells the story of one mother who made sure that her daughter's performance was well received, then gave the show away by going backstage to count the bouquets to check she hadn't been cheated by the florist. The practice is not unknown to producers of plays and to the relatives of performers in more recent times.

With the development of flower shops went a change in status of some flower girls. In earlier days they went about with *un éventaire*, a hawker's basket, carrying the bouquets which they offered to passers-by. 'When the flower girl was pretty, one might be tempted by her eyes as much as by her flowers; everything is intertwined and one thing often leads to another'.[36] Later some of them took up stalls at the corners of streets and boulevards. But

---

[32] Miller 1981.   [33] Kock 1843/4:35.   [34] Kock 1855:7.   [35] Kock 1843/4:40.
[36] Kock 1843/4:32.

by mid century, there were also boutiques selling flowers which quite changed the character of those who worked there. In the old days, they wore a simple bonnet and used terrible language. 'But the flower girl in a shop is an attendant at the counter, with her hair as well dressed as a seller of fashions, as well got up as a haberdasher, and expressing herself with as much taste as a seller of perfumes.'[37] The comparisons are instructive since they all refer to women's clothes and accoutrements, which was one major use of flowers, real and artificial, at this period. By moving in from the pavement to the booth, from the street to the shop, from the outdoors to the indoors, the nature of the occupation changed from the rough to the smooth, from the dirty to the clean, from the despised to the respectable.

Not that everyone had altered. In the first place, the 'petits marchands ambulants' of the period before the Revolution, practising their colportage, did not disappear; they were still present at the end of the nineteenth century when the historian of horticulture, Gibault, was writing. He describes the bouquetières as young and beautiful but speaking a slang ('la langue verte'), and standing under their umbrellas on both sides of the Pont Neuf which crosses the river at the western end of l'Ile de la Cité.[38] In fact boutiques and shops were added to the other retail outlets for flowers, girls with stalls and those who walked through the streets crying:

> A mon pot d'Oeilletz!
> Il est plantureux,
> Pour faire bouquetz,
> Pour les amoureux.

After dark the sale of flowers was much as it is today, except that now the sellers are often men. 'La bouquetière des établissements de nuit' only appeared in the evening. The senior ones sold their flowers expensively inside; the flowers were carried in small baskets and arranged as little bunches for the women and as buttonholes for the men.[39] According to the season, they carried bunches of roses with long stalks, mimosa or carnations. On the terraces of the cafés, those bouquetières who did not have the right of entry sold a greater variety of the most common flowers, including some wild ones, at cheaper prices. They and their male counterparts still haunt the restaurants, streets and metros of Paris after dark. They increasingly visit the restaurants even of provincial towns such as Cambridge, peddling Colombian roses, just as they do in metropolitan Washington and in West Berlin.

THE ROLE AND MYTH OF THE FLOWER GIRL

Apart from the Language of Flowers, there is one particular aspect of the spread of the use of flowers in Europe that is embedded in the myth and

---

[37] Kock 1843/4:34–5.   [38] Gibault 1906b:66.
[39] Kock 1843/4:38. Today one can pay at least five times as much for flowers in a restaurant as from a stand.

symbolism more than in other parts of the world. This is the role of the flower girl which is closely related to the expansion of the market, the epitome of the female who is called upon to perform personal services to dominant males, and one that has developed its own mythology. I have spoken of Pliny's tale about one called Glycera who acted as model to a Greek painter, or rather it was her flowers that supposedly acted as models. Perhaps she did too, but in any case the bond was intimate in a variety of ways. The painter-model relation is closer than that between the buyer and seller of flowers but the element of personal service by women for men is crucial to both.

In Paris the typical bouquetière stood at a busy street corner selling bouquets and single flowers for the buttonhole, *la boutonnière*. Her cry was, 'fleurissez-vous madame. Pour un sou, embaumez-vous', for in reality buyers were mainly women. The bouquetière was lower class but not necessarily marginal. While Eliza Doolittle came from the working classes and spoke with a formidable Cockney accent, she was certainly not marginal, either in her London origin or in her later status. Selling luxury goods had always been a ladder of mobility for women. Nell Gwyn, mistress of Charles II, peddled oranges in the streets of London in the later seventeenth century. Many a dressmaker (*coutoumière*) followed in Carmen's footsteps; actresses too, but, like modistes, they have now become high status in themselves. Those who work more closely with their male bosses, secretaries and nurses, are even more likely to marry or befriend them. Some flower sellers, like Isabel Brilliant during the imperial period, acquired great popularity and a certain renown of their own. Isabel was admitted to the Jockey Club and sold her flowers in the enclosure of the racecourse where the *petits vernis* paid more than ten francs for bouquets worth ten sous. During the period of her decline, she sold flowers in chic cabarets and theatres in the evening. Some flower girls were even members of the upper classes who had hit hard times; a story relates how the comtesse de Pathé, a friend of Napoleon III, sold flowers, mainly violets, outside Père Lachaise, the main cemetery of Paris.[40] In a different guise the theme of poor girl, rich girl, runs through this mythology, especially of the nineteenth and early twentieth centuries, but with some interesting changes.

Flower girls play an especially prominent part in the works of that dramatist of boulevard life, Paul de Kock. In the play *La Bouquetière des Champs-Elysées* (1839), Séraphine, an orphan from a poor home but of a good family, sells flowers secretly in order to help her friend, Daligny. He had come to her rescue in difficult circumstances but could no longer earn a living by painting since he had been wounded while fighting a duel to defend her honour. The plot, such as it is, turns on the fact that flower selling is a 'low', public occupation, where attractive girls receive much attention from their high-status customers. In this instance, both hero and heroine turn out to be of

[40] Mauméné 1897:36.

good families and so in the end they marry. Another flower girl appears in de Kock's novel, *La Bouquetière du Château d'Eau* (1855), where Violet, a young girl brought up in a poor family, sells flowers in one of the stalls (more a booth than a boutique) that had recently been allowed to be set up in this part of Paris. She is often approached by gallants whose advances she rejects with replies such as: 'I cannot stop my customers from saying stupidities.'[41] Once again her true, 'high' status is revealed in time for her to make a proper alliance. The plots of these plays are highly predictable. In Nicholas Mullen's *Janet, the Flower Girl* (1880), an English lord visits France and falls in love with a beautiful girl selling lilies-of-the-valley. He buys her whole stock for his buttonhole at an exorbitant price. Later the girl turns out to have been his cousin, stolen as a child by a gypsy, so a marriage is arranged.[42] This theme of the revelation of a beloved's true class position, always a matter of raising the girl's status, is a variation of the hypergamy theme. While that was desirable in Europe, it was essential to societies like India where one has to marry a person of the same (or possibly adjacent) caste. In two of the three fifth-century Sanskrit dramas of Kālidāsa the lowly heroines, Śākuntalā and Mālavikā, are in the end discovered to be of high rank, fit brides for the king.

The social position of flower girls, both in and out of the boutique, was similar to that of other female vendors. They provided dating material for men of all ages, though primarily the younger ones. De Kock has a story of 'une brodeuse' (an embroiderer), Mlle Anastasie, who hired 'un bain à domicile', a bath that was delivered to the house and filled with hot water. But she allowed the bath water to run down the stairs, to the consternation of the other inhabitants. She is described as a responsible girl, 'here and there she received a visit from a young student or a barrister, but these gentlemen always left before midnight'.[43] Dressmakers were game for students throughout Europe. As in Schnitzler's play, *Die Liebelei* (1895, English translation, *Playing with Love*, 1914), the students were often of higher status and the affairs rarely led to marriage. By this time realism had crept into the story which tells how two girls of modest means meet two young men of higher status, one a medical student. One of the girls, Christine, comes to dinner bringing some roses which are scattered over the table as if they had fallen from the ceiling, Roman fashion. In contrast, her own home has a vase of artificial flowers which her suitor remarks always look dusty. 'There must be real flowers in your room, which smell sweet and are fresh.' The contrast in styles of life, of fresh and artificial flowers, lay at the roots of the insoluble problem of the liaison that led to tragic results.

De Kock describes men of various ages hanging about outside the new

---

[41] 1855:i, 83. Kock also wrote *La Jolie Fille du faubourg* (1840), *La Demoiselle du cinquième* (1856), and *Les Demoiselles de magasin* (1863). His was a drama of the urban scene, of the boulevards of Paris.
[42] On finding this play in the Widener Library at Harvard, I predicted to my companion that the girl would turn out to be well born. So it proved.   [43] Kock 1843/4:26.

boutiques waiting for the employees to be released so that they could entertain them. Flower girls, especially those working in the street, had a particularly close relationship with their male clientele. In the fantasy world of the nineteenth century marriage took place, but to someone who turned out to be a member of the same class. By the end of the century, as in Schnitzler's play, the discrepancy in position is shown to make marriage impossible.

The theme of the flower girl as a partner continued to play a central role in the cinema between the two world wars. Nor is the myth confined to Hollywood; indeed the films of Europe are much richer, as one might expect, from the richer culture of flowers. Once again the flower seller is almost invariably a poor girl who falls in love with or is loved by a man of higher status. The theme is strongly international. In the Dutch-Belgian film, *Angela* (1973), a flower girl tries to find love but her quest, the résumé says, 'is shattered by prejudice and conformity'. In the British film, *Good Night Vienna* (1932), entitled *Magic Night* in the United States, a Viennese captain 'has the tragic misfortune of falling in love with a poor flower girl . . . who fails to receive the respect of his peers'. The Hungarian film, *Love and Kisses, Veronica* (1936), shows a flower girl falling 'in love with her boss, which leads to a series of misunderstandings'. Flower girls were lower class, like the Cockney Squibs in the early British silent film, *Squibs Wins the Sweepstake* (1922), but they were very attractive. Even a Russian officer, in the Italian romance, *I Choose Love*, falls for a Venetian flower girl and decides to defect; in Chaplin's great movie *City Lights* (1931), she is blind and beautiful. But the prototypical flower girl, in the cinema as on the stage, was the Cockney Eliza Doolittle in Shaw's *Pygmalion*, a girl who has to be re-educated in order to make her fit for society, and for her husband, a self-satisfied and bigoted academic.[44] Flower girls are no longer hidden members of the bourgeoisie, nor is marriage any longer impossible, but they have to be transformed before they can be accepted. Only later did upper groups see cross-status marriage as possible without such a transformation, and even then the difficulties tend to receive more attention than the advantages.

For certain commodities the role of the boutiques, and hence of those who worked there, was radically changed by the coming of the department store after the middle of the century. *Les grands magasins*, the department stores, depended upon rapid turnover which enabled them to buy cheaper and sell cheaper, 'à l'américaine'. They raised fear and hostility among the boutiquiers who could not afford to meet their prices nor offer their 'primes', such as the giving of bunches of violets (a Napoleonic symbol). Meanwhile some moralists objected to the temptations being offered to 'la petite bourgeoisie' who might overspend on luxuries, such as silk. For the mass consumption of luxuries was the aim not only of the new proprietors but of the Second empire

[44] The source for this information and for the quotations is Magill's Survey of Cinema on the Dialog Data Base.

itself which saw Paris as becoming the capital 'de la mode et du luxe', just as London was of finance and trade. With the construction of the grands boulevards by Haussmann the stores abandoned the back streets to boutiques and took up a dominant stance towards Paris and the world.[45] Nevertheless, smaller shops persisted for clothes as distinct from fabrics, and while flowers were sold in department stores, their perishability and the nature of the demand gave those little advantage. Florists' shops proliferated, although itinerant sellers played an increasingly marginal part in the market.

Today the hierarchy of flower sellers itself remains much as in the last century, but the demand and outlets for flowers have enormously expanded. Not only the trade in cut flowers but also that in plants for indoors and outdoors, especially flowering plants. The expansion of the trade in outdoor plants is obviously more a suburban than an urban phenomenon, while the attempt to turn every room into a conservatory is increasingly characteristic of both city and suburb. The retail trade in plants has long existed, sometimes in connection with a florist's shop, more usually at nurseries or at growers. But the numbers and the scale have expanded greatly with the creation of garden centres. In contemporary England some of these have developed into attractions for family outings on Sundays, since they are one of the few kinds of shops allowed to open on the Sabbath. The old-time nursery has fallen into obscurity, a resort of the specialist rather than the wider public.

Garden centres themselves do not set out primarily to sell cut flowers, although some may do as a sideline. That remains the job of florists and individual flower sellers, especially in the bigger towns. In the country people largely grow their own, and in the smaller towns buy in the market. Some years ago in small towns like Gramat in the south-west of France, flowers would also be sold by the grocer. Today it boasts two florists; even the smaller centre of Bagnac nearby now has two, with the man looking after the nursery (*pépinière*) while the woman sells the garden plants, cut flowers and artificial flowers.[46] In the country florists often combine flowers with the sale of funeral decorations, plaques for the graves, with inscriptions such as 'à notre Mémé', made in porcelain and decorated with flowers, more permanent than artificial and dried ones such as *les immortelles*, which are much favoured in the region for house decoration in the winter. Death provides one of the main outlets for flowers, fresh, dried and artificial, although it is rare to have a florist sited right next to the cemetery, as so often in Italy.

In Paris, shops are more specialised, and the kiosks and the bouquetière ambulante have largely but not entirely disappeared. So too have the flower girls standing at the corner of the road, partly because of the domination of the streets by the motor car. However, the bouquetière au panier has been replaced by the bouquetier du métro, catering not to the day-time rush of

[45] Gaillard 1980.   [46] Now is 1991.

humanity along the pavements (the buttonhole is no longer daily wear even among the rich), but to those who have forgotten to buy some flowers to take to their hostess at dinner. At festivals the peripatetic evening trade is supplemented by day-time hawkers.[47] One thing that has changed since the late nineteenth century is that most or all of these flower men, salesmen rather than flower sellers, are outsiders in a way that was not true for earlier flower girls. These occupations of the lower class have been largely taken over by immigrants.

This gamut of flower sellers represents current practice, with the florists' shops themselves varying from the everyday to the grand whose window displays elegant and expensive sprays of rare blooms. What has changed is partly the increase in demand, especially in country districts which television, the cinema and greater mobility have induced to follow more closely the ways of the city, partly the nature of the retailing, but more dramatically the extent and variety of the supply.

FLOWER PRODUCERS AND THE TOWN

In the past, and to some extent still today, flowers were produced on the outskirts of big towns. That situation is well represented by contemporary Ahmadabad in Gujarat, India, where local producers, sometimes specialist horticulturalists of the Mali caste, more usually local farmers planting, say, marigolds in part of their fields, dispatch the flowers overnight to a central market in town to which they are transported at the slow pace of the cart drawn by a camel or an ox. In São Paulo, Brazil, the huge daily flower market is supplied by the trucks of the individual producers, many of them Japanese who originally came as indentured labourers on the coffee plantations, others recent immigrants from Portugal. At these central markets flowers are sold in bulk to the various retailers in the city.

Flowers were sometimes supplied by more distant growers, as in ancient Rome. That depended upon the nature of the transport. The trade from Egypt was by boat. The market in Paris was greatly changed by the advent of the railway to the Mediterranean which brought 'les fleurs du midi' overnight;[48] indeed, the Riviera remains the major concentration of floriculturalists in France, that stretch of perpetual spring from Menton to Toulon, and extending further to Toulouse for violets and previously for chrysanthemums. In England the railway also meant competition from the provinces, especially

---

[47] On one Good Friday I met two men walking down the rue Dauphine selling daffodils, no longer from a reed basket but from a plastic tray. Later that same day, a man came selling flowers (and a woman cigarettes) in the Procope, possibly the oldest surviving restaurant in Paris, while on the pavement outside another man and woman with small bunches were discussing where they should go next, having been refused admission to sell.

[48] Perfumes as distinct from flowers had long come from the Mediterranean area of France.

from the Isles of Scilly with their daffodils.[49] However, writing at the end of the last century, Mauméné observes that the big shops preferred the forced flowers of Paris, mainly from around Versailles which was known as the 'Gant français'.[50] Ghent in Belgium was another major source of flowers for the Paris market, especially of azaleas and orchids. With the aid of the railway the European market was already international; cut flowers from the Midi and forced flowers from Paris were exported in winter to Germany, to England, even to Russia.

To this southern competition the northern growers, who had worked around Paris since the Middle Ages, responded by entering the market for out-of-season flowers which even the south could not supply. At the end of the nineteenth century Vilmorin recalled the time when Parisians gaped at the sight of a bouquet of roses in January, or of the perpetual carnation or camellia worn as a buttonhole by the smartest men-about-town. By the time he was writing such miracles were happening everywhere owing to the practice of forcing flowers in glasshouses that had grown up on a large scale in the outskirts of Paris, with orange blossom and cyclamen at Grenelle, camellias at Montreuil and roses at Santeny. As many as twenty growers were engaged in forcing lilacs, fifteen roses, twelve bulbs, fifteen ferns.[51]

The flowers produced in this way were costly, so their use was confined to the well-to-do. Even marriage bouquets varied by social class. The less well-off had to content themselves with 'an artificial bouquet that was kept as a souvenir under a glass globe', the middle group got orange blossom from Nice as their 'symbols of virginity', while the upper classes bought orange blossom which had been forced by a specialist near Paris.[52] This type of bouquet was especially expensive when many buds were wired together on a single branch to make it light for the bride to carry; the end was then wrapped in lace and presented by an uncle of the bride, at a price of 25 louis.

The market dealt with more than cut flowers alone. Each of the floral products were in their turn affected by the successive changes in transport, the cart and boat, the train, the truck and the steamboat. Colporteurs from various regions of France, Germany and especially Holland took bulbs, seeds and simply catalogues as far afield as the south of Russia and Brazil, aided by the railway and the steamboat, to sell wares on behalf of growers. In this way distant parts of the world were supplied with annuals and other plants from the more temperate areas of Europe. There breeding and commerce combined

---

[49] The export of daffodils from the frost-free gardens of Tresco, one of the Isles of Scilly, seems to have begun in 1867 when Augustus Smith received the sum of one pound for a small box of cut daffodils sent to Covent Garden. The business was expanded by his nephew Thomas Smith Dorrien. See King 1985.

[50] Mauméné 1897:25.   [51] Vilmorin 1892:5; Yriarte 1893:25.

[52] Yriarte 1893:47; for examples of *le bouquet sous globe*, see *Objets civile domestique*, Inventaire général des monuments et richesses artistiques, Paris, 1986, pp.504–5, and *Le Mobilier domestique*, II, Inventaire général, Paris, 1987, pp. 962–3.

to establish this overseas export industry, one that continues to this day, especially with Dutch bulbs which reach most corners of the world.

The next step in the transformation of the market was the coming of the aeroplane which has widened the trade even in cut flowers from one between adjacent nations into a transworld network. These are now shipped around the world like manufactured goods, and I have bought Colombian carnations in the United States and England, American roses in Hong Kong and English carnations in America. In this trade the Netherlands is the hub, both from the standpoint of production in the rich alluvial soil of the estuary of the Rhine and for sales and distribution through the computerised auctions of Aalsmeer, Westland and other centres which dispatch blooms throughout Europe and much further afield.

In the world market in flowers, by far the greatest volume of imports, representing 67.7 per cent in 1987, is directed to the European Community, well over half of which goes to Germany. Many of the largest exporters are also from Europe, with Holland being the dominant force with 70 per cent of the market, followed at a great distance by Italy (fourth), Spain (fifth) and France (seventh). The other major exporters are largely from the Third World, with Colombia second, Israel third, Thailand fifth and Kenya eighth.

While the country had long been a significant exporter of plants and bulbs, the great growth of the Dutch market in cut flowers is more recent. In the early part of the nineteenth century growers in Aalsmeer, south of Amsterdam, switched to the cultivation of flowers. In 1871 the first heated glasshouse was built, roses were grown 'commercially' at the beginning of this century and the first Dutch auction in cut flowers was established there in 1911. Of these, roses continue to be the most important, followed by chrysanthemums and carnations. Exports account for a large part of the produce, 63 per cent in the case of cut flowers, 51 per cent of pot plants. The main outlets are Germany, which takes nearly half, then France, Britain and Italy, mostly dispatched by truck. But flowers are sent much more widely afield by air, to the United States, Hong Kong, Japan, Liberia and elsewhere in the world, where they are offered for sale within forty-eight hours of leaving the Dutch market.

The world trade in cut flowers has shown a dramatic increase over the past twenty years. In 1970 exports represented a value of 179 million dollars. By 1987 this figure had risen to 2,088 million dollars.[53] For England in 1974 the most important supplier was France, the principle import from that country being carnations, followed by anemonies, roses and mimosa. More recently countries of the Third World have been making significant inroads into the market, especially Kenya and Colombia. In 1972 France supplied 347 tonnes

---

[53] SITC figures 292.7 of the UN Department of Economic and Social Affairs. I am indebted to Partha das Gupta and Andrew Cornford for their assistance.

of carnations, followed by the Netherlands with 185 tonnes, Kenya with 165 and Colombia 67, the latter a huge increase over the 1971 figure of 1 tonne.[54]

This increase in exports from the Third World has been achieved despite the application of 'antidumping' legislation by the United States, of protectionist tariffs by the EC and of administrative and sanitary restrictions by Japan.[55] As a 'luxury' crop flowers are very sensitive to the level of economic activity and to the rates of exchange. Especially successful have been the exports from Colombia to the United States and from Kenya to Europe and the Near East. In the Colombian case the growth of exports has been spectacular. From less than 1 million dollars' worth in 1970, these reached a value of 200 million in 1988.[56] Nevertheless, flowers account for only 5.9 per cent of that country's total agricultural income and only 3.7 per cent of the total income from exports. Guatemala is higher, at nearly 9 per cent of exports, Kenya much less. So that despite the significant rise, it can hardly be argued that Third World countries are rendering themselves vulnerable to shortages by producing flowers for foreign exchange. Indeed, the foreign exchange enables them to buy cheaper grain from abroad.

I have touched upon the growth of the market in flowers and its impact on the life of towns. Clearly that growth is related to the wider economy of Western Europe and in particular to the increase in the volume and range of consumer goods and to the related phenomenon of 'consumerism' and the 'mass consumption' of material goods previously considered to be luxuries for the few. Behind the supply side lies the immense complexity of the social organisation of production to which I have given little explicit attention. Behind the demand side of the market lies the pressure of personal and cultural dispositions. At a very general level one can relate these dispositions to changes in attitudes towards the use of flowers that have occurred in Europe since the fall of the Roman empire. The market benefited from the greater purchasing power of the population, from new species from abroad, especially from the East, from more scientific methods of breeding, from more intensive methods of cultivation and from the general interest in botany, in colourful design and in the meanings of flowers.

The development of this market and of the whole culture of flowers was influenced by the major transformations of society, by the changes of the twelfth century, by the Renaissance, by the mercantile expansion of Europe, by the growth in industrial capitalism. But we have to be careful of accepting, at least for this aspect of consumer culture, too tight a link with the unilinear periodisations often set out for the development of the economy in Europe. Whether we concentrate on the supply side or the demand side, on production

---

[54] AGREX report 1974:8.   [55] La industria de las flores en Colombia 1988:40.
[56] La industria de las flores en Colombia 1988: 31–43.

or exchange, the tendency is to look, after the year 1200, for junction points at which the major changes took place that led to the present achievements of European society. The tenor of my analysis has been that we need to see these changes in a much wider historical and comparative perspective in order to avoid foreshortening historical developments and interpreting them in ethnocentric terms. That does not mean a relapse into an ahistorical relativism. Historically the culture of flowers followed upon the emergence of Bronze Age societies, the high degree of economic stratification and the development of intensive agriculture. The two combined to allow for the development of 'aesthetic' gardening, the production of flowers not only for the adornment of the rich but as offerings to the gods. The beginnings of consumer culture in flowers have to be pushed much further back in time but also further afield in space, to the Near East, to South and East Asia, and to Central America. The luxury cultures that accompanied the early development of 'civilisations' were marked by a limited consumerism that was largely restricted to the highest classes. Its subsequent extension has been from the court and nobles, to merchants, the wider middle and even the working classes, so that in the end one can talk of mass consumption. That process has obviously experienced some major breakthroughs at the level of supply, though these have rarely had the sudden, 'revolutionary' effects of shifts in the political domain, for the developments of material culture have often been marked by cumulative changes over the long duration. At the level of demand, attitudes are certainly capable of sudden if incomplete reversals, as in the case of the early Christians. But I follow Braudel at least part of the way in believing that, at least since cultural stratification made emulative behaviour possible on a societal scale, 'there is always a potential consumer society';[57] it is the supply of many, but not all, luxuries that is problematic.

In this chapter I have outlined the growth of the market in Western Europe, one factor in which was a broadening of the range of flowers available to the consumer as the result of the introduction of new varieties from East and West. In line with my earlier argument, few of these came from Africa, with the exception of the temperate regions of the South. The growth of cut flowers was at first largely an urban or suburban affair, only later spilling into country districts. The market was highly dependent upon communications, that is, upon changes in the mode of transport, in order to bring the perishable product into the major towns, although that was obviously less true of seeds, bulbs and to some extent plants. In these towns a complex hierarchy of sellers provided the customer with a variety of cut flowers and plants, in a variety of conditions at a variety of prices. Initially the trade depended mainly upon local markets and hawkers, but the nineteenth century saw the expansion of flower shops and the flower girls at the street corners, an occupation that

---

[57] Braudel 1982:177.

attracted much attention in the popular literature of the period which created a myth of sexuality, of the hypergamous attraction of the rich for the poor, the Cinderella story to gladden the hearts of the less-well-to-do. Since the flower trade dealt in luxuries, the market expanded with rising standards of living and with the coming of train, truck and aeroplane. These helped bring about the present world-wide patterns of commerce in cut flowers and plants, which in turn had their effects on choice and use. It was this urban culture of flowers in the nineteenth century that gave birth to that long series of publications devoted to the Language of Flowers which attempt not to unravel their social significance but to determine their symbolic meanings in a very precise and particular context.

8 · The secret Language of Flowers in France: specialist knowledge or fictive ethnography?

A picture of the nineteenth century would be incomplete without an acknowledgement of the role of flowers, and of the expansion and democratisation of their culture in so many ways. In art there was the middle-class lady with her easel, the classical subjects of Alma-Tadema, the medieval romances of the Pre-Raphaelites, the perfection of late Victorian English water colourists and above all the vigorous sensations of the Impressionists.[1] This was the era of horticultural societies, the flower shows and competitive displays, of the universal gardener and of the literary garden into which Tennyson invited Maude. So much took place with flowers and gardens that for Baudelaire flowers became evil symbols of a world he had rejected.

But many people in Europe, when they hear the phrase the 'culture of flowers', immediately think of the 'Language of Flowers'. By this, they refer to two interrelated sets of meanings: firstly, the significance that flowers have in the variety of symbolic contexts in which they appear in any culture; secondly, the specific form this took in the numerous nineteenth-century books that attempted to analyse the Language of Flowers.

This language was often claimed by its more serious exponents to be a 'universal language', even part of the structure of human thought. Many people today, especially in Western Europe, continue to think of such a language as an established part of their culture, but one of which they are largely ignorant.[2] The existence of symbolic meanings attached to flowers is well known from religion, heraldry, painting, literature and everyday life. But in the early nineteenth century a new literary product presented a set of highly formalised lists of meanings together with a whole semiotic analysis of the 'language'. Was this the discovery or the invention of tradition? For tradition it certainly became, at least for those who thought these manuals presented knowledge which their mothers or grandmothers had known but of which they themselves knew little.

My interest in this field is partly ethnographic; I was drawn to the

---

[1] See Bumpus 1990.
[2] Such has been my experience in talking to people throughout Europe and America, and the notion is documented in the book by Curcio (1981) discussed later in this chapter.

phenomenon as part of European culture subject to the influences of the East, whether in the shape of Orientalism or in other forms. But I am also concerned with the nature of 'culture' in complex societies, and especially with the role played by written schemata. The use and meaning of flowers in human interaction raises the question of the relationship between general and specialist knowledge, especially when the continuity of the specialist system does not depend upon being held in and processed by the mind of one or more individuals. That is, when it takes a distinct literary form. In this chapter, I want to look at the literary forms taken by the Language of Flowers in nineteenth-century Europe partly as a system of human knowledge and communication.

The notion that a language of flowers existed in the Orient became known to Europe largely through the letters that Lady Mary Wortley Montagu, friend of Alexander Pope, wrote from Turkey early in the eighteenth century. Previous travellers had referred to the use of flowers and other objects as 'a mysterious language of love and gallantry . . . to express the most tender and delicate of sentiments'.[3] But it was the Lady Mary who brought it forcibly to people's attention in 1718.

What she reported was a manner of communicating by means of objects, and she gives an account of it to a lady friend who had asked her for a 'Turkish love letter'. She sends her a purse containing a series of objects. 'The first piece you should pull out of the purse is a little Pearl, which is in Turkish call'd ingi, and should be understood in this manner':

> Ingi, Sensin Uzellerin gingi
> Pearl, Fairest of the young.

Here the verse containing the 'meaning' rhymes with the name for the object. Similar verses follow for the other objects, a clove, a jonquil, paper, pear, soap, coal, a rose, a straw and so on. 'There is no colour, no flower, no weed, no fruit, herb, pebble, or feather that has not a verse belonging to it; and you may quarrel, reproach, or send letters of passion, friendship, or civility, or even of news, without ever inking your fingers.'[4] A few years later Aubry de La Mottraye gives other examples of these verses which 'the young Girls learn by Tradition of one another'.[5] Slightly earlier the French historian, Jean Dumont, had written of a love letter consisting of 'Trash, wrapt up in a Piece of Paper'.[6] These reports stimulated the interest of Europe in the Orient and its secrets. That developed throughout the eighteenth century and at the beginning of the nineteenth was expressed in Goethe's *West–Oestlicher Divan* (1819), which included poems on 'Secret Writing', or a code, on talismans and on flowers:

---

[3] Hammer 1809:346.   [4] Montagu 1965:388–9.   [5] de La Mottraye 1723–32:i, 254, ii, 72.
[6] Dumont 1694:268.

> With fruit and flowers I regale
> These captivating tables,
> And if you want a moral tale
> I serve the freshest fables. ('Four Favours')

At the time that Goethe was writing, the status of the 'langage des *harems*' was investigated by the Austrian Orientalist, Hammer (also Hammer-Purgstall) who called attention to its uniqueness, despite the use of flowers in Persia for love (the rose and the nightingale) and in India for religious offerings. But he notes the contradiction in the claim made by Lady Mary (and by many subsequent promoters in the nineteenth century) that this was a means whereby those shut away communicated with the outside world. 'A language known by everybody would be of little use for two lovers when the least suspicion costs them their lives.'[7] This being the case, should we consign the language to the category of Oriental tales? No, replied the Orientalist, who spent many years in Istanbul and collected verses from those working in the harem. While they are not used for communicating between men and women, they do constitute a language known only to women, who 'invented it in the leisure of their lonely life, and who employ it as an amusement, or as a code for lesbian attachments.'[8] What we have done for colours, they amused themselves to do for plants, fruits and so on, creating a language which Lady Mary brought back together with the practice of inoculation. It is a language constructed not on the basis of the relations which the imagination can find between flowers and ideas or sentiments, but rather like the Elizabethan equivalent of choosing words that rhyme with the names of the objects and then composing appropriate verses:

> Tel – Bou ghed je gel
> Bread – I want to kiss your hand

The English translation of other such verses runs:

> A wire – Come tonight, my dear
> Salt – Day and night I am desperate for you, o cruel one
> Hair – Take me away, if you wish
> Mouse – Is your husband at home?

Books aiming to elucidate a language specifically of flowers appeared in Paris not long after the end of the Napoleonic wars, at a time when interest in new botanical discoveries ran high, when many exotic flowers were reaching Europe from the East and when the urban retail market was rapidly expanding, especially in 'la mode' and in 'nouveautés'. Their background lay in the growth of the culture of flowers in France. Their literary forerunners were the traditional flower poetry of the *Guirlande de Julie* (1634), making use of emblematic clichés like the modest violet. The eighteenth century had

---

[7] Hammer 1809:348.   [8] Hammer 1809:549.

developed new types of floral imagery, as in the work of Malherbe, though much is buried in the remnants of the pastoral tradition. Flowers get 'discovered' in the middle of the century in works such as Thompson's *Seasons*, or in the prose of Rousseau's *Julie ou la nouvelle Héloïse* (1760) with its commitment to rustic nature and sentimental botany.[9] More frequently we find references to the 'flower poetry' of Cowley and Rapin.

Other contributors to the genre were botanical treatises such as those of Linnaeus and Jussieu, and allegoric 'games' such as those of le père Sautel. All these and more are referred to by E. Constant Dubos, professeur au Lycée Impérial, Paris, in his book, *Les Fleurs, idylles morales, suivies de poésies diverses* (1808). That volume consists of fifteen poems (*idylles*) on various flowers starting with the rosebud and ending with the *immortelle* (everlasting), together with a note on each poem offering horticultural and historical information as well as references to other poets. There are also some remarks about current usage, such as the 'naive childhood game' played with the *petite marguerite* or *paquerette* (the daisy). But apart from phrases like 'the everlasting is the flower of friendship' and 'the rose is sacred to the Mother of Love', there are few of the kind of highly specific, highly structured symbolic associations that we encounter in the Language of Flowers a few years later.[10]

Contemporaries generally attributed the Language of Flowers to Charlotte de Latour, in a book first published in Paris in 1819 by Audot.[11] In 1811, B. Delachênaye, who described himself as a military pensioner of the government, dedicated a book to S. M. l'Impératrice-Reine, very appropriately given her interest in the great garden at Malmaison, outside Paris. The book was entitled *Abécédaire de flore, ou langage des fleurs . . .*, and set the pattern for what was to come. About the same time appeared Mme de Genlis' *La Botanique historique et littéraire* (Maradan, 1810) and Mme Victoire M(augirard)'s *Les Fleurs, rêve allégorique* (Buisson, 1811). Mme de Genlis was a prolific author, a number of whose books were translated into English. This interesting volume contributes little to the emerging 'language' but it does discuss at length the usages connected with particular flowers in many countries. An anonymous publication printed in Paris in 1816 presents a more closely related history of flowers and their significances. The title of this pamphlet of thirty-one pages gives its complete contents, a conjunction of symbolism and botany in the form of a crib for students. The title runs: *Les Emblèmes des fleurs: pièce de vers, suivie d'un tableau emblématique des fleurs, et traité succinct de botanique, auquel sont joints deux tableaux contenant l'exposition du système de Linné et la méthode naturelle de Jussieu.* The book contains no introductory remarks, except in the form of two poems, one called 'les Emblèmes des fleurs', and the second 'Hommage à la rose', the

---

[9] Knight 1986:13ff.   [10] Dubos 1808:72, 102, 74.
[11] See Seaton 1985a:74. She also calls attention to Mollevaut (1818) and to publisher Janet's *Oracle de flore* (1817). Another volume is listed for 1819 in the catalogue of the British Library as *Le Langage des fleurs, ou les sélams de l'Orient. Ouvrage orné de douze bouquets*, Paris, 1819, p.176.

latter being an apology for neglecting that flower in the first. The opening poem addresses itself to the specific meaning of flowers:

> To depict his burning flame
> The lover whose ardours were too timid
> Created this precious art
> Of hiding the secrets of the soul
> Beneath ingenious covers.

There is no mention here of a 'universal' language of flowers, with its roots in the Orient, which became so common a justification from 1819 onwards. In fact the author claims that he will 'point out new emblems'. Throughout the poem the numbers placed above certain words refer to the *Tableau emblématique des fleurs* that follows, one hundred and forty-two items in all, and begins:

1 Absinthe	Amertume
2 Acacia	Inquiétude
3 Aconit	Remords

This list is precisely the same as the one that appeared two years later in the collection of poems by C. L. Mollevaut, *Les Fleurs: poème en quatre chants* (Paris, 1818); again there were one hundred and forty-two items in all, each one numbered. Indeed, Mollevaut too presents Linnaeus' classification;[12] for learning was to be awakened with entertainment. He makes very similar remarks about how flowers can be 'le courrier charmant' for the shy young girl. But in addition he refers specifically to the 'langage des fleurs' and its Oriental origin:

> Get to know the language of flowers;
> Learn it in the East,
> Where Love uses it for sweet purposes.[13]

Both these themes were to receive an elaborate development as the century wore on.

Who was this anonymous author of the earlier volume? The answer is given in a much larger work by Ch. Jos. ChXXXXt (Chambet), a member of 'several literary societies', which claims to be a second edition, 'revised and augmented', published in Lyons in 1825 under the title *Emblèmes des fleurs ou parterre de flore, contenant le symbole et le langage des fleurs, leur histoire et origine mythologique, ainsi que les plus jolis vers qu'elles ont inspirés à nos meilleurs poètes...*[14] M. Chambet is quite clear about his priority with regard to Charlotte de Latour:

---

[12] Mollevaut 1818:136.   [13] Mollevaut 1818:87.

[14] Knight (1986:286) lists a volume by 'G.' Madame's of 1816 entitled *Le Bouquet du sentiment ou Allégorie des plantes et des couleurs*, which is listed in the *Bibliographie de la France* (1810–56). The Bibliothèque nationale gives *Les Bouquets du sentiment, ou manuel de famille pour les fêtes* ... under the authorship of C. J. Ch. (Chambet) 3rd edn, Paris, 1825. There appears to be no entry for G.

We think we should point out to our readers that the first edition of his collection appeared in 1816, and that the work published by Mme Latour on the same subject has existed for only two or three years [in fact six]. So we have priority over her, although her work is the product of a remarkable talent; we lay claim to a date, without wishing to diminish in any way the merits of our kindly imitator.[15]

While this was formally the case as far as the list of symbolic associations was concerned, M. Chambet had now written a completely different book which was wholly influenced by the work of Mme de Latour. For example, the second edition is now 'destiné aux Dames' and the notion of the oriental origin has been added. 'In the Orient, the captive beauty has recourse to the ingenious Selam.'[16] As in de Latour, the meaning of flowers is discussed in a paragraph or two which offers some justification for that meaning by reference to mythology as well as by reprinting poems, often enough taken from E. C. Dubos, that support the general theme. However, while the list has remained basically the same in form, the significances have in many cases undergone a sea-change: at the head of the list absinth remains 'bitterness' (*amertume*), but acacia now signifies 'platonic love' as opposed to anxiety, attributed to 'the American savages' (*les sauvages de l'Amérique*) while other entries are now derived from classical mythology, such as acanthus ('indissoluble knots', from Rome) and almond ('carelessness', from Greece).

So much for the controversial beginnings of this literary genre. Let me turn to the content of the work generally conceded to have started this tradition. But first, who was this Charlotte de Latour? The aristocratic surname was a pseudonym: she was in fact one Mme Louise Cortambert.[17]

Mme Charlotte de Latour's *Langage des fleurs* runs through the seasons month by month, giving the names of flowers and any 'significances' she has discovered, together with selected anecdotes. At the end of the volume is a formal listing of the meanings a person may wish to convey and the flowers to be used for doing so, in the shape of a *Dictionnaire du langage des fleurs avec l'origine de leurs significations pour écrire un billet ou composer un sélam*. For we are not dealing so much with a list of meanings derived from earlier usages in poetry or in life itself, as with a language in a much more specific sense, a method of writing a letter using these partially hidden meanings or by offering a bouquet of flowers in which they were incorporated. The significance of each offering had to be translated in both directions, so a second list was entitled *Dictionnaire des plantes avec leurs emblèmes pour traduire un billet ou un sélam*; this gives the name of the plant or flower and its significance,

---

[15] Chambet 1825:10.   [16] Chambet 1825:7.

[17] There is no entry for Louise Cortambert in the *Dictionnaire de biographie française*, nor yet in *La Grande Encyclopédie*. There are entries for the first half of the nineteenth century for three closely related Cortamberts: the brothers Eugène (1805–81) and Louis (1809), and Richard (1836–84), son of Eugène, who produced innumerable books of geography and travel; into this family she was married, but even productive women received less recognition than men in these encyclopaedic sources. Or was it that the type of book she wrote was not considered sufficiently academic?

reduced again to one word: absinth is 'absence', for instance, acacia 'platonic love', rose acacia 'elegance', acanthus 'arts.'[18] The word *sélam* comes into use at this time as a 'bouquet whose symbolic arrangement forms a code' (according to *Robert*) and which is therefore 'emblematic'. In this sense, and with the stress on secret wisdom coming from the East, the word was employed by that extensive commentator on the Paris scene of the first half of the nineteenth century, Paul de Kock.

The formalised attributions of symbolic meaning do not end here, for there are yet other lists showing how to indicate the time (for example, of a rendezvous) by means of flowers: a 'table showing the attributes of each hour in the ancient world' assigns a 'bouquet of blooming roses' to the first hour, a 'bouquet of heliotrope' to the second, and so on. In addition a curious entry under 'language' on the use of rings indicates the formalising, classifying and 'imaginative' quality of much of this work. Whatever the status of such associations in actual life, whether in England, in Greece, in Rome or in the East, they are paradoxically presented both in some concealed mode of conducting social intercourse (especially when we want to hide our intentions from others, from parents, suitors or from the world at large) and at the same time as part of some 'universal' set of symbolic meanings. While there is certainly some meaning attached to the use of rings (as of precious stones), nothing in ethnography suggests anything so complex as is indicated in the comment on ring-wearing practices – attributed, as so often, to a foreign country, in this case England, where a man is supposed to carry a ring on his first finger if he wishes to get married, the second if he is engaged, the third if he is married, the fourth if he wants to remain single and so on.

Charlotte de Latour sees flowers primarily as a means of communication between the sexes. 'It is above all for those who know love . . . that we have brought together a few syllables of the language of flowers.' But other ends too can be served. 'This language also lends its charms to friendship, to gratitude and to filial and maternal love.'[19]

As with any other language, one can manipulate the flowers in order to elaborate one's meanings. So the author provides a few 'rules' (*règles*) 'to run through the dictionary'. Firstly, 'a flower held upright when given expresses a thought . . . it is enough to hold it the other way to make it mean the opposite . . . for example, a rosebud with its thorns and leaves means "I fear, but I am in hope"; if one turns the bud upside down, that means: "One mustn't fear or hope."'[20] Secondly, one can modify the emblem in other ways: stripped of its thorns, the rose means 'there is everything to hope for', while stripped of its leaves it means 'there is everything to fear'. A flower can be combined with others, rather in the spirit of Chinese characters; it can be made meaningful by its position on the body ('A marigold [*fleur de souci*] on the head means

---

[18] Latour 1819:199.   [19] Latour 1819:4.   [20] Latour 1819:5.

1.1 A temple offering in Bali. (Ramseyer 1977)

11.1 Peristyle garden with wall painting, in the house of Venus Marina, Pompeii. (Jashemski 1979:62)

IV.2 Persian garden carpet, seventeenth to eighteenth centuries. (Wagner carpet, Burrell Collection)

IV.1 The poet's picnic from Firdausi's *The Book of Kings* (*Shab-nameh*), Safavid period, sixteenth-century Iran, in the Turkman style from Tabriz. (Welch 1972:83)

v.1 From the Moutier-Grandval Bible, Tours. (British Museum, London)

v.2 The reliquary of Sainte-Foy, Conques.

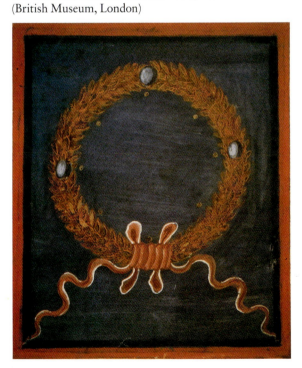

v.3 The corona of the Aratea, ninth century. (Rijksuniversiteit, Leiden)

VI.2 Jan Breughel, *A Vase of Flowers*. (Fitzwilliam Museum, Cambridge)

VI.1 The opening of St John's Gospel from Lady Margaret Beaufort's Book of Hours, fifteenth century. (St John's College, Cambridge)

VII.1 Seventeenth-century flower-tree hanging. Trade cloth produced in India for the European market. (Victoria and Albert Museum, London)

X.1 Funeral flowers in their wrappings, outside a house in Bethnal Green, London, 1987. (M. Goody)

XI.2 Marigolds in the flower market, Ahmadabad, December 1986.

XI.3 Garlands on a flower stall, Ahmadabad, December 1986.

XI.1 Woman in Persian costume, Mughal school, first half of eighteenth century. (Bibliotèque Nationale, Paris, MSS Or., Smith-Lesoüf 247, f.13)

XII.1 The altar of a Buddhist nun, Xiaolan, China, 1988. Living flowers must be used for the deities. (H. F. Siu)

XIII.1 Bringing home the tangerines for New Year, Chencun market, Guangdong, 1989.

XIII.2 The family peach tree, Hong Kong, New Year 1989.

花開富貴

迎春接福

恭喜發財

XIII.3 'Flowers, Blossom, Prosperity', Chinese New Year Banner, San Francisco, 1988.

XIII.4 A grower at the Chencun market, Guangdong, showing off a prize bloom, New Year 1989.

trouble to the mind, on the heart the pain of love, on the breast ennui'); it can even be made meaningful by the use of direction ('the pronoun *moi* is expressed by leaning the flower to the right, *toi* by leaning it to the left').[21]

The enormous popularity of this work is demonstrated not only by the controversy which surrounded the circumstances of its publication but by the fact that the French version went into eight impressions between 1858 and 1881, the ninth edition of the London 'translation' appeared in 1843; two years earlier a version on engraved cards was published in Birmingham. The first German translation, *Die Blumensprache, oder Symbolik des Pflanzen-reichs*, was published in Berlin in 1820. Such popularity meant that booksellers were competing for the publication of this and similar works, Philadelphia versus New York, Edinburgh versus London. By 1884 an edition with illustrations by the famous creator of children's books, Kate Greenaway, was produced in London.[22]

Not only the editions but the printing attained international status; in 1890 an edition was printed in Germany for the English market. Meanwhile, other authors were willing to adapt Charlotte de Latour's compilation for different publishers, adding not only illustrations but appropriate quotations from French, English and classical poetry.

Volumes on the Language of Flowers increased in popularity during the nineteenth century. Apart from the many reprints there were continual attempts by authors to produce new versions. Some of these were no doubt set in motion by publishers, and any new version tended to require a criticism of previous works, or at least a justification for redoing what had been done before. But other writers had stronger reasons, some wanting to add a more scientific (botanical) or even practical (horticultural) element, others a more moral, less mundane, interpretation. Among the latter were Christian apologists who viewed the meaning of flowers as coming from God rather than man, and especially not the pagan man of mythology; part of their justification lay not only in the use of flowers for worship but also in the many 'popular' names of Christian origin given to plants with curative and other properties, of which the Abbé Magnat gives a long list (1855), approving some, disapproving others.

But the Orient from which the *Sélam* was supposedly borrowed was not that of Palestine but of Turkey, not of Christianity but of Islam. From the

---

[21] Latour 1819:6.

[22] One of the most remarkable successors to this work of Latour was a book published anonymously in Berlin in 1821, only two years after the original and one year after the German translation. This volume addresses itself more particularly to the Oriental element under the title of *Selam, oder die Sprache von Blumen*. Written by J. D. Symanski, it is very different from any other work in this tradition employing as it does a full array of German scholarship, footnotes, references, the lot, in order to trace the history of the genre. A section on 'Die Bäume' is followed by one on 'Die Blumen' and a third is entitled 'Die Blumensprache'. Here the author refers to the sélam (a concept that never made it into English in this sense), as well as to the legend of the slave and the sultana needing a means of secret communication, stressing the Oriental origins of the code.

beginning the messages which it communicated were secret rather than open. Thus another aspect of the tradition that developed lay in Orientalism, occultism, cryptography and their various associated crafts, leading to yet more specialisms, such as selamography and hierobotany. Already in 1817 an anonymous volume was entitled *Oracle de flore*, and the notion of a pagan Oriental origin is deeply embedded in the early tradition. But as the nineteenth century went on, these various strands tend to produce their own variants.

It is not clear how soon a translation of Latour appeared in English. One version translated by Shoberl came out in 1827 and another was published by Saunders and Otley in 1834, entitled *The Language of Flowers*, specifically acknowledged as a rendition of her original. The preface notes, 'This work is founded on the French, though from the alterations . . . which have been introduced it could not be said to be a translation.' In possibly the same year the second edition of a work with a similar title, *The Language of Flowers, or Alphabet of Floral Emblems* was published in Edinburgh, and in the United States in New York; it is dated 1834, but an entry in the Library of Congress catalogue suggests it may have been 1827.

The tradition was elaborated at the hands of Mme Leneveux, who develops the grammar, adds to the various lists, gives some botanical information but above all incorporates poetry and other embellishments from the English who 'have seized the language of flowers'. For 'this ingenious art, which was born in the austere harems of the Orient, has come to perfection in the gay boudoirs of Paris and London'.[23] Her work had a curious sequel in that of Albert Jacquemart. This writer began with a scientific book and then proceeded in a second work to try to botanise the 'langage des fleurs' itself. Like many of those who took up this genre, he too was a prolific author of books on other topics, including histories of porcelain, ceramics and furniture, all of which were translated into English. Published in Paris in 1840, *Flore des dames: botanique à l'usage des dames et des jeunes personnes* made a serious attempt to provide instruction in botany, in the form of walks with a friend, who had had to quit Paris for the country. It was followed a year later by a further volume, addressed to the same noble lady who had asked to be initiated into the Language of Flowers, and claimed to be a new edition 'entirely revised and considerably augmented: completed by a floral grammar and a treatise on the composition of the *sélam*'. To the study of the Language of Flowers, he added quite a new dimension of linguistic analysis. The author criticises 'the pages signed with the pseudonym of Mme Charlotte de Latour' as being too literary. The book of Mme Leneveux he recognises as attempting to fill the gap 'by some principles that make it easier to use flowers as signs of thought', but it is nevertheless too laconic. Moreover:

---

[23] Leneveux 1837:vi. She had already published *Les fleurs emblématiques* in Roret's *Encyclopédie* in 1827.

she made . . . the serious mistake of not understanding that she had in her hands the elements of a language as old as the world, of which only the grammar needed completion, but where each sign had an unchanging value. (p.5)

Her account destroys the most sublime feature of 'the alphabet of the fields', its simplicity. So Jacquemart then proceeds completely to set aside his earlier scientifically oriented treatise in favour of one that incorporates and elaborates, especially on the 'grammatical' side, the work of his two predecessors. Sections on 'the fundamental principles of the language of flowers' and 'different ways of using flowers emblematically' are followed by paragraphs headed 'substantif', 'adjectif', 'verbe', 'pronoms', the grammatical categories of the word which teach one to deal with the 'conversation florale'. This he exemplifies in the form of a discussion with 'an old man', elaborating earlier themes in a manner that develops the linguistic aspect more systematically than any other. It is an extraordinary attempt to apply linguistic concepts to this other 'language'.

Apart from his grammatical interests, Jacquemart introduces a professional element into his horticultural comments as well, most unusually it should be said, as giving some concrete information on the actual uses of flowers, the *couronne blanche* for first communion (*la rose blanche*); the bouquets that help choose a husband; the *fleur d'oranger*, with its virginal significance, for the marriage crown alone, never in a bouquet; at the marriage banquet, 'the heads of all the ladies are decorated with flowers'; the children's bouquets of (wild) flowers for their mother's saint's day; the wreaths (often of 'everlastings') at funerals; the displays of flowers on Corpus Christi (Fête-Dieu) and at Rogations, when hawthorn (*aubépine*) has its part. It is not often that everyday use plays any part at all in these treatments of the Language of Flowers. But here we also find a whole series of culinary uses, apart from medicinal ones. The *capucine* (Tropaeolum), imported from Peru to France at the end of the seventeenth century, is used in salads (as are the leaves of the thistle), soups and even as purée; leaves of the dandelion (*pissenlit*) serve both for salads and for divination. In Japan, at marriages, the cherry flower is made into an infusion which is given to the guests to drink and symbolises the happiness of the new couple.

The tradition established by Latour was continued in the works of Fertiault (1847), Zaccone (1853), Francal (1860), Mme Anaïs de Neuville (1866), Mlle Clarisse Juranville (1867), Poisle-Desgranges (1868) and Mme Emma Faucon (1869). Of these the most interesting is the volume by Juranville who describes herself as 'institutrice', 'author of many works relating to teaching'. In this she was highly successful; her book, *Le Premier Livre des petites filles*, appeared in seventy-three editions between 1886 and 1919. She was one of those authors who sustained and profited from the extension of reading and writing in France in the second half of the nineteenth century, especially with the introduction of compulsory schooling in 1882 and the massive increase in the circulation of educational books that followed. Her declared intentions are consistent with this role and therefore different from those of de Latour, aiming at teenage girls rather than the boudoir. Hence she wanted to transform 'les fleurs en moralistes' and so eliminates or changes references such as 'white rose bud, Heart that knows not love'.

New techniques of mass colour printing made it possible to use visual representations of flowers in quite another way. Such colour printing, as distinct from the colouring of prints or woodblock printing, began with the invention of chromolithography by Alois Senefelder in the 1820s; it spread throughout Europe, reaching Boston in 1840. Paris soon became a centre of special importance. The volume by Mme Emmeline Raymond, entitled *L'Esprit des fleurs, symbolisme, science* (Paris, 1884), is a beautifully illustrated version, featuring each flower mentioned in the text, and turning its back on the earlier tradition. 'The present generation', she writes, 'is perhaps unaware that there was once a certain number of volumes devoted to the language of flowers', which gave the translation 'of the symbol represented by each flower'. But the present age has less time for symbolism and poetry, so any new version needs to add 'a little solidity' to a symbolism 'which one might justly reproach with being at the same time too superficial and not chaste enough; it was necessary to remove everything that might trouble the imagination of a young girl, and to make an effort to popularise the science of botany under an elegant and pleasant aspect'.[24] For this purpose good coloured reproductions, which contemporary technology had made possible, were essential. Science is better for the morals of a young girl than symbolism, and offers a more solid and moral way of passing the time.

Raymond's own contribution takes the form, exploited earlier by Mme Leneveux, of a 'congrès de fleurs', that is, an assembly of flowers that speak. The only relic of the traditional book is an 'alphabetical table of plants and their synonyms', which includes all those illustrated, together with a few meanings.[25]

THE RELIGIOUS TRADITION

Thus the Language of Flowers became more than merely a game 'destiné aux Dames'; in a minor way at least, it was a means for their instruction, in morality as well as in botany. The morality was given a specifically religious emphasis in the works of a number of nineteenth-century French writers. In a more general way flowers had long played an important part in religious

[24] Raymond 1884:2.
[25] Raymond's work was followed by that of Riols (1896) and Dugaston (Dujarric) (1920).

symbolism, not only in worship and in iconography but also in instruction.

The 'Flowers' of St Francis referred of course to the 'flower' (the essence) of his teaching, but the specific use of flowers for instruction in the doctrine of Christianity is also quite frequent. One example from the nineteenth century was the *Flore mystique de Saint François de Sales ou la vie chrétienne sous l'emblème des plantes* (Paris, 1874), which consists of a series of quotations from the writings of the saint, mentioning flowers by way of imagery. However, other works drew more heavily on the Language of Flowers itself. Despite the title and the author, the Abbé Casimir Magnat, who published his *Traité du langage symbolique, emblématique et religieux des fleurs* in 1855, has rather little to say about the religious side. His elaborately produced book owes more to the main line and even to the 'scientific' traditions. He combines the scientific (he is described as 'ex-professor of botany') with a comprehensive treatment of the Language of Flowers taken from Jacquemart (1841), who had also been a professor of botany. In addition to the standard account of the composition of *sélams* and the grammar of the Language of Flowers, Magnat includes a look at the use of flowers around the world, not only historically ('mythologically') but in other civilisations, and concludes that Northern Europe was singularly backward in this respect. Despite the usual bows to the universality of the Language of Flowers, he notes that 'the Gauls and the ancient peoples of the North never concerned themselves with the culture of flowers'.[26] During the Middle Ages, the culture of flowers was 'almost entirely abandoned', picking up again only when trade put Europe in touch with the Orient. That touches upon one of the major themes of this study, although in the literary context of the Language of Flowers the extensive contributions from the East are more usually seen as romantic and even as barbarous and primitive.

Subsequently we are given as comprehensive a series of lists as appears in any other source, together with a full explanation of the grammar of the Language of Flowers, that is, the uses of nouns, adjectives and verbs. This grammar is taken straight from Jacquemart but with a few additions and some different examples. Indeed these examples are elaborated, from any point of view extravagantly, to show the use of flower 'meanings' in the 'translation' of prose, an activity one would have thought somewhat removed from either the abbé's pedagogical or his religious roles. Here is one example of this translation by means of a code of flower names:

La Pensée du Cyprès nous donne de l'If, mais la Pensée de notre Asphodèle Blanc et de l'Armoise promise à notre Menthe Sauvage que nous avons cultivée dans la Luzerne, doit nous donner du Peuplier Noir pour ne plus commettre d'Aconit envers la

---

[26] Magnat 1855:9.

Gyroselle et avancer avec beaucoup de Gouet ou Arum Commun dans le sentier de la
Lobélie Cardinale et de l'Ananas.

Translation: The thought of death makes us sad, but that of our future resurrection
and of the happiness promised to virtue in this life should encourage us to commit no
more sins before God and to continue with enthusiasm along the path of virtue and
perfection.

There can hardly be a more extravagant example of developments in the
Language of Flowers than this contribution by a professor of botany who is
also an abbot of the church. But the Christian interpretation of the Language
of Flowers achieves its apogee in the two-volume work, anonymous but
apparently by the Abbé F. Nöel, published in 1867. The title reveals its
contents: *Le Véritable Langage des fleurs, interprété en l'honneur de la plus
grande dame de l'Univers, par l'un de ses plus dévoués admirateurs, ouvrage
formant une série de bouquets, couronnes et guirlandes symboliques, suivi de
l'Ecrin de Marie*. The author is well acquainted with the secular tradition
which he criticises for its frivolity and worse. He then proceeds to adapt that
tradition in a quite radical fashion for his own ends.

A further example of the same genre is the book by Mme Marie XXXX,
entitled *Voyage autour de mon parterre: petite botanique religieuse et morale,
emblème des fleurs* (Paris, 1867), but which is of a very different inspiration
from the general run. She begins by posing the question, 'I said to the flowers,
Tell me what God told you to tell me'.[27] To understand the meaning of
flowers is to understand God. She starts with *aubépine*, continues with the
orange, the first being 'the symbol of innocence', the second a 'virginal
emblem', a fit offering for the Virgin Mary. Thus she travels through the
garden, giving each plant a moral significance. The bay (*laurier*) is the 'symbol
of glory', especially valuable to Christianity because France is the 'eldest
daughter of the Church'.[28] Acacia, as elsewhere, is 'the symbol of platonic
love', the everlasting, 'flower of the graveyard, symbol of sorrows and
regrets'.[29] In this aspect of the tradition the emphasis is placed on the heavenly
rather than the earthly referents of floral symbols.

THE SCIENTIFIC TRADITION

The use of tables such as Linnaeus' 'Horloge' and the employment of Latin
names marks many of the works in the main tradition, but it is worthwhile
drawing attention to those volumes that tended to give greater stress to
botanical and other scientific elements.

This 'scientific' tradition, the instructional trend that characterised
Jacquemart's earlier work, is continued in that of another professor,

---

[27] Marie xxxx 1867:32.   [28] Marie xxxx 1867:181.   [29] Marie xxxx 1867.

J. Messire, who published in Tours in 1845 *Le Langage moral des fleurs, suivi des principales curiosités de la Touraine*. He begins by enumerating various flowers, such as the rose de Provence for which he adds not only a meaning but also some appropriate poetry, some history and even some instruction about growing. At the end there are various lists, mixing the 'Horloge des fleurs' and 'Emblèmes des couleurs' with one of 'Plantes annuelles'.

When Mme la Baronesse de Fresne published her version of *Le Nouveau Langage des fleurs des dames et des demoiselles, suivi de la botanique à vol d'oiseau* in 1858, she had already written for the same series, *Bibliothèque des salons à l'usage des gens du monde*, a book entitled *De l'usage et de la politesse*. Her volume is addressed to her nieces and attempts to cover, in short compass and now conventional fashion, both the outlines of botanical classification and the Language of Flowers itself. The latter consists of modified paragraphs on each flower topped off by a 'Calendrier de flore' and the 'Horloge des fleurs', the latter on a twenty-four hour basis.[30]

The emphasis of a series of works on the scientific side of botany reflects the general development of the field during the century as well as the feeling that this knowledge should be widely shared and form part of informal as well as formal education. Parts of this scientific corpus were included in the majority of the volumes considered, even in some of the religious ones. But it stood at odds with the notion of a universal, secret language of Oriental origin as well as with the final element, that which concentrated upon the occult.

THE OCCULT TRADITION

From the beginning the Language of Flowers claimed its origin as a product of the Orient, from the *sélam* of the Turks (or Persians or Egyptians). On the other hand, some writers declared the language to be universal (usually with little sense of contradiction) but again pointed to pagan rather than Christian roots. Indeed, the very nature of a secret system of communication brought it close to other forms of 'hidden' knowledge – to divination, occultism and the like. We see this trend stressed early on in the work of Blismon, a pseudonym for Simon Blocquel, who first published a mainstream version entitled *Nouveau Manuel allégorique des plantes, des fleurs et des fruits, des couleurs* . . . (Paris, 1851). He includes a certain number of tables of 'meanings' which had nothing to do with flowers, for example, a table of emblems drawn from the lives of famous men (Abel signifies 'innocence') as well as tables relating to ancient peoples and to pagan gods, ending with a 'jeu des fleurs' played with a pack of fifty-two cards. Seven years later he produced a new edition in which he introduced the science of 'Selamography', under a new and more

---

[30] Other volumes in this tradition are *Le Parfait Langage des fleurs* (Anon. 1862), *Des jardins* (new edn 1886).

appropriate pseudonym of Ana-gramme Blismon. The title of his new book is: *Nouvelle sélamographie, langage allégorique, emblématique ou symbolique des fleurs et des fruits, des animaux et des couleurs. . .*

But it is in the work of a much later writer, Sirius de Massilie, that this tradition reaches its peak. His first volume, published in 1891, was fairly mainstream, although it displays a considerable degree of ingenuity. In *Le Nouveau Langage des fleurs*, he stresses two elements in their meanings: colour and scent. The strongest sentiments are expressed by the most penetrating perfumes and the brightest colours. White is purity, with orange blossom symbolising the virginity of those who have pledged themselves in love. Red is ardent love, blue the colour of tender souls, violet of widows, green of hope, yellow of marriage, of a long-established marriage as well as of 'cuckoldry'. Combining various shades, he produces an elaborate set of 'meanings'; twenty-one for red alone, including 'amaranth red' ('long-standing desire'), 'cardinal red' ('sublime desire') and 'carmine' ('deceitful desire').

His 'Vocabulaire du langage des fleurs' is much like previous ones, but to it he adds an 'alphabet of love' by which, in a 'bouquet cryptogramme', you can spell out your name in roses: 'A. Grande Alexandre (rose de Provins)'. In addition he offers another method of corresponding secretly with a loved one by enclosing a note behind the bark of a stalk of *saule* (willow). However, it was in his next volume on flowers, published in 1902, that Massilie really exploited this penchant for the cryptogram and for the development of new meanings. The title of this volume is *L'Oracle des fleurs: véritable langage des fleurs d'après la doctrine hermétique: botanologie, hiérobotanie, botomancie*. The year previously he had published a book under a parallel title, *L'Oracle des enfants: prédiction du sexe des enfants avant la naissance*, of which a new edition appeared in 1911 entitled *La Sexologie: prédiction. . .* This literary activity again emphasised the oracular and the mysterious, in the guise of a new science. Note the shift to oracle, the insistence (as before) on truth, the recourse to the hermetic doctrine as a source of authority, the invention of new (pseudo) scientific disciplines (like Blocquel with his Selamography) and the assumption of a quasi-Oriental identity.

Botanology is defined as 'the Science of the mystical language of flowers,' and is seen as closely connected with magic, that is, with 'the Supreme Science whose secrets the Magi kept so jealously in the impenetrable temples that sheltered their religious mysteries'.[31] To this end he tries to set aside those aspects of earlier versions that were marked by 'an ignorant charlatanism' that 'favoured and exploited human passions without the protection afforded by custom', and that 'prostituted the admirable hieratic language of flowers',

---

[31] Massilie 1902:1.

making them 'the messengers of sentiments that are often libidinous and an invitation to debauchery'. The moral sentiments of this occultism met with those of orthodox religion, resting upon the sense given by 'tradition, in other words, the hermetic kabbala which is the sacred tradition', and is based on 'analogy'.

As a result of his 'research', the dictionary of the Language of Flowers is very different from others and is firmly announced as such:

A dictionary of the hermetic language of flowers, a unique work, essentially different from all others in which error and unfounded legend are always allied to superstition and often to ignorance.

His first entry shows one significant difference:

> Abricotier Blanc rose ♀ C.
> Je vous aime et vous n'aimez pas
> Insensibilité du coeur, amour qui n'est pas payé de retour

The interpretation of the apricot as insensitivity of heart remains the same as in his previous volume. But in addition we now have the cabbalistic symbol, a new component that runs throughout the dictionary.

These volumes represent a trend that is at once old and new. The Language of Flowers from the beginning was 'secret' or else a 'discovery'; it was a means of communicating clandestinely or at least semi-openly between lovers, and it was a way of revealing the morality behind nature. The morality was given a more explicit Christian turn by ecclesiastical authors, even though the language was supposed to be Oriental in origin. But flowers and other plants had significances, medicinal and occult, that were not known at all, which reminds us of the organisation of knowledge in the herbals of the Middle Ages. These books continue to be available even today. Culpeper's herbal is still published in London, just as the Language of Flowers still appears in Paris, New York and indeed in many other parts of the world.

THE CONTEMPORARY SCENE

Works giving lists similar to those we have examined continue to be published in a variety of forms. One is given in an encyclopaedia published in 1930 under the title of *Larousse du XXème siècle*. But it demonstrates that the equivalences posited by the works on the Language of Flowers did not remain stable over a very long period. The list starts with *abricotier*, which does not appear in Latour, and continues with absinth ('bitterness') and acacia ('desire to please' instead of 'platonic love').[32] The next four are absent from the

---

[32] *Larousse du XXème siècle*, 1930:520–2.

earlier collection and we then come to almond ('sweetness' instead of 'thoughtlessness') and amaranth ('immortality' rather than 'unending love'). The As continue in similar manner, some absent, all disagreeing.

Once again, a few entries have a general (though not universal) relevance. The rose means 'love', the violet 'modesty', just as colours have their 'natural' meanings, red, 'love', white, 'innocence'. But the 'tableau synoptique', like all others, goes much further, giving every flower not only a 'signification emblématique' but another entry in which the meaning differs with the colour of the flower: for example, rose amaryllis means 'you are too flirtatious' while red amaryllis means 'you are too sought after'.

The most recent volume available in the bookshop of Bon Marché was *Les Fleurs et leur langage* of J. C. Lattès. The listing offers a variation on many earlier editions. It begins with absinth, under which we have two entries, 'Signification: you heap bitterness on my head and your reproaches hurt me. Symbolism: absence, bitterness,' 'Absinth' is now the emblem (here symbol) both for 'absence', and for 'bitterness', with obvious associations (bitter, 'sans douceur'), some of which are detailed in the commentary (as in the work of Mme de Latour and others). There are other variants. Acacia follows with the significance, 'your love passes into my soul with your kisses'. The symbolism is also much stronger, white, 'penetrating love', instead of 'platonic love', and pink, 'elegance'. But the *Achillée* (*Achillea millefolium*), herb of St John, formerly 'war', has become 'healing and comfort', for Jesus is said to have used it to cure a wound of the carpenter, Joseph.

The end of the book produces yet more of the kind of structured equivalences that we found in Louise Cortambert's original volume and which were developed throughout the century that followed. There are lists on the significance of colours ('Thanks to the colours of flowers, you can express all the shades of your feelings and of your passions'); on the flowers that in the occult tradition symbolise the signs of the zodiac, each month and each day of the week, as well as on the flowers for each hour of the day ('The botanist Linnaeus having observed the hour at which each flower blooms'); on the flowers that symbolise the various nations; and on the love meanings of flowers ('if you wish to express surrender, offer anemone'). In this final list we return to the earlier meanings assigned by Mme Cortambert, in contradiction to the 'meanings' given in the previous section.

Books specifically devoted to the Language of Flowers are still published in England and France, partly as a sort of *recherche du temps perdu*, as a souvenir of the more leisurely life of the urban bourgeoisie of Victorian and Edwardian England. In France, perhaps in England too, that life exists in books of what we call, following the French, books of etiquette, in books which are known as *manuels du savoir-vivre*.

Of these books, the *Guide du protocol* by former préfet, J. Gaudouin, was aimed first of all at the quasi-administrative audience who wanted to know what to do on public occasions. But not entirely: he suggests that in giving gifts one should not forget the meanings of flowers.[33] His list has a closer relationship to people's stored knowledge than the earlier dictionaries since the aim is practical knowledge. Moreover, he is aware of taboos as well as of injunctions. For instance, he notes that some people are troubled by receiving gifts of heather or carnations; for others 'the marigold meant jealousy'.

His information and suggestions about the occasions for giving gifts (for which flowers are the first choice) are more precise, namely, births, baptisms, communions, marriages, gold and silver weddings, saints' days, birthdays, Christmas, New Year and Easter. In addition, he remarks that 'les fleuristes, chemisiers et parfumeurs' have added 'la fête des mères', 'la fête des pères' and St Valentine's (14 February, 'fête des amoureux et de l'amitié'). The day of St Valentine has long been celebrated in Europe, at least from the fourteenth century and even then was the occasion when women could demand the hand of a man in marriage. But it seems to be only recently that it developed as a major occasion for giving flowers. Apart from these points in the human and annual cycles, flowers should also be offered to friends in hospital, at dinners for 'distinctions honorifiques' accorded to relatives at retirement and when colleagues, either one's equals or superiors, have received promotion.

The listing of the Language of Flowers in the *Manuel du savoir-vivre d'aujourd'hui* of Michèle Curcio (1981) is word for word that of Charlotte de Latour-Cortambert. The only exception is for roses which are given a more pagan and stronger meaning: the rose 'belongs to Venus'.[34] In the earlier dictionary it is not characterised as meaning 'violent passion'; the moss rose means 'love and delight', it is the carnation that signifies 'lively and pure love'. But for Curcio, the red rose is the emblem of the deepest passion, while a white rose 'carries a message of innocence and virginity.'

Despite this list Curcio displays even less personal commitment to the Language of Flowers than Gaudouin. Her explanation is interesting:

I was quite young when my mother taught me what flowers a boy could send a girl and what that might mean. 'But', I said, 'that's old-fashioned. People are no longer interested in the language of flowers!' 'One never knows', she said in a dreamy voice. 'Perhaps when you are married and another man sends you red roses, you will understand that something lives on' . . . This language of flowers has perhaps no longer any place in works officially recognised as modern, but, in the bottom of people's hearts, there always remains something and it is so charming that one would not want it to fall into oblivion.

Moreover, you need to know it for fear of upsetting parents and those superstitious ones who fear the carnation in the home.

---

[33] Lindon n.d.; Curcio 1981; Gosset n.d.; Roger n.d.; Bernage and de Corbie 1971; Gaudouin 1984.
[34] Curcio 1981:46.

THE INVENTION OF TRADITION

One interesting aspect of these contemporary handbooks is that they accept as 'traditional' what the early writers of the nineteenth century thought of not perhaps as 'invented', but at least as 'discovered'. Curcio writes of it as what her mother knew, Gaudouin of a form of communication on which people need guidance. But for both it is an aspect of traditional patterns of behaviour. All tradition is of course invented. In this case the invention, while not widely accepted in anything like its entirety, nevertheless had some influence on other facets of social life. In literature we have references to the Language of Flowers and even to the work of Charlotte de Latour in the works of Balzac. It was incorporated in his novel, *Le Lys dans la vallée*, where the aspiring lover, Felix, noticed there were no flowers in the vases in the house of his beloved and went out with the intention of making ('composer') two bouquets with which to express his innocent love. 'Love too has its heraldry, and the countess will decode it secretly.' In this way he discovered for her 'a knowledge lost to Europe where flowers on the desk replace the written words of the East with fragrant colours'. Later on Felix refers specifically to this bouquet as his *sélam*, and Balzac was clearly making a reference to the current vogue.

The Language of Flowers had its impact in other ways. French poetry in the nineteenth century was deeply impregnated with floral images,[35] although this had a plurality of sources including the interest of the Romantics in nature. In 1820 Hugo spoke of these 'doux messages / Où l'amour parle avec des fleurs'. Musset addresses a flower sent to him as a 'mysterious messenger'. Sainte-Beuve refers to the Language in 1824 and Gautier writes that 'Chaque fleur est une phrase.'[36] Senancour sees the Language of Flowers as comparable to poetic usage, and many others of the period make reference to the associations of their colours and their perfumes, not only as a code but in relation to music. However, a more creative usage lay in rejecting or modifying the symbolic structure of the language of everyday. For Mallarmé the blood-red rose of *Les Fleurs* stood for something quite different, 'rose / Cruelle', and his new language, which was to ignore the real, was 'destructive of conventional discourse'.[37] It was the 'langage des fleurs du mal'. So while references were made in other literary forms the Language of Flowers itself was hardly the stuff of poetry. Commentators have attributed the use of the 'language of flowers' to both Joyce[38] and Senghor,[39] but in both cases the reference is to the flower imagery in general, not the specific language developed in France. Baudelaire's *Les Fleurs du mal*, published in 1857, was a deliberate rejection of 'the more flowery provinces of the realm of poetry' in an attempt 'to extract *beauty* from *Evil*'.[40]

[35] See Knight 1986.   [36] In the introduction to Le Sélam, a keepsake of 1830, see Knight 1986:254.
[37] Knight 1986:214.   [38] Saldivar 1983.   [39] Spieth 1985.
[40] Preface to the volume of translations edited by Marthiel and J. Matthews (revised edn), New York, 1963.

Of course, many other authors (and many Impressionist painters) employed the symbolism of particular flowers, but here references are being made to part of the whole 'dictionary'. Apart from creative writers, the other category of people to make selected use of the language is the florists. I have come across excerpts from the Language of Flowers not only in a florist's in the rue de Buci in Paris (1986), but in a simplified form to do with roses in New Haven (1987), in an alley climbing up the steep slopes of Hong Kong and even in a shop in Guangzhou in the People's Republic of China (1989). The commercial reasons behind such use require no more explanation than the search for structured 'meaning' by the writers. But there are more general ways in which the language impinges on people's behaviour by creating a feeling that such 'expert knowledge' was constructed out of 'tradition', a tradition that is disappearing, whereas it would be nearer the truth to say that it was invented. This language has been described to me by native speakers as a specific feature of Czech, Hungarian and German culture. In fact, the opposite is nearer the truth: we are in the presence of a deliberately created addition to cultural artefacts, a piece of initially almost fictive ethnography which takes on an existence of its own as a product of the written rather than the oral.

THE STATUS OF THE LANGUAGE

The lists in the Language of Flowers represented a formalisation of common usage. As such they recall Renaissance (and earlier) attempts at the classification of plants. One characteristic feature of many of such lists, at least in the early phase, is their use of the alphabet as a means of grouping and of retrieval. But while formalisation may increase our understanding of the world, it may equally obfuscate things. Such is the case with the Language of Flowers. These formalised statements of nineteenth-century writers, which spread throughout Europe, produced an extensive literature parallel to that of cookbooks but having a different normative status, a different role with regard to behaviour. The relationship between the two depends upon the domain. Cookbooks are frequently accounts by cooks or gastronomes of a series of recipes, programmes for action. People consult them to know what to do. Books on letter writing and books on etiquette served a similar but more restricted purpose. With the coming of greater informality, together with increased formal education, they have largely disappeared – but not entirely; the former are still available in shops in rural areas of south-west France (as well as in the Third World) and books on etiquette form a significant section of the output of a number of publishing houses.

Books on the Language of Flowers never seem to have had this normative pull. There was and is a sort of practical language of flowers, richer in some ways (because buried in contexts) and less elaborated in others (because not formulated in tables and charts). Very little of this seems to have been written down in treatises either for the actors or for observers (except marginally in books of etiquette). On the other hand, one significant indication of the state of the Language of Flowers even in its heyday was the comment by Paul de Kock in his account of social life in Paris in *La Grande Ville* (1843/4). 'We do not understand the language of flowers, as in the orient; but without knowing how to make a *sélam*, we know quite well what it means to send a bouquet.'[41] In his later novel, *La Bouquetière du Château d'Eau* (1855), de Kock takes up the theme in his description of a rather foppish young man who wants to give his father a bouquet for his saint's day. He explains to his mother: 'for a bouquet in the hand, you make a choice of different flowers, which, placed one next to another, take on a deeper meaning. . . the Turks call this a *sélam*. . . I want to offer a *sélam* to my father'.[42] While the mother pours scorn on this foreign custom, it is also clear that Violette, the flower girl, knows nothing about such *sélams*; in any case, men do not offer them to men. Nevertheless, the incident shows how this fabricated language did feed back directly on to one level of society at least, limited as this was, and hardly 'popular' in any of the usual senses of the word.

We may speak of the Language of Flowers as an expert knowledge 'system' or 'structure' in the manner of cognitive scientists. It has some particular characteristics. Most of the 'systems' studied transmit knowledge that is assumed to have some general application and can provide a measurement of what is correct and what is incorrect. Simply working in terms of the information contained in books on the Language of Flowers, it is possible to make some such assessment of people's knowledge. But the knowledge contained there has little to do with what is contained in memory and with the symbolism used in other written contexts (for example, in novels), not to speak of the more 'objective' knowledge contained in botanical classifications and handbooks. It is a constructed 'language', a knowledge system that has minimal reference outside itself. It is one of a number of such systems which produce highly structured codes, for example, the religious and the heraldic. The art historian Baxandall made an interesting comment on this multiplicity of codes in relation to colours. Assembling symbolic series of colours was a late-medieval game still played in the Renaissance. He contrasts a theological with an 'elemental' code, red signifying 'charity' in the first and 'fire' in the second. There were also astrological and heraldic codes. 'There were others too and, of course, the effect is that they largely cancel each other out. Each could be operative only inside very narrow limits. But unless reference to a code was prompted by special circumstantial clues . . . it could not be part of the normal digestion of visual experience. Symbolisms of this class are not important in painting . . . There are no secret codes worth knowing about in the painters' colour.'[43]

[41] Kock 1843/4:36.   [42] Kock 1855:28.   [43] Baxandall 1972:81.

While some of the symbolic meanings are related to ones found in the orally held knowledge systems of people, the Language of Flowers deviates from these in the following ways. Firstly, it assumes homogeneity over time and space; it proclaims itself a universal system. Secondly, it has, by its format, to disregard contextual usage and choose one symbolic equivalence, for example, for the red rose, plus (possibly) certain systematic variations (when the flower is offered upside down). Thirdly, it has to fill empty boxes and construct significances for flowers that had none before. These three characteristics are those of written lists in general as I have suggested in *The Domestication of the Savage Mind*.[44] But fourthly, there is the question of its relation to other levels or arenas of knowledge about the uses and meanings of flowers.

The broad character of these other levels or arenas will be discussed elsewhere.[45] All that has to be said at this point is that the books refer to a single aspect of flower behaviour and the actual symbolism of flower use is much more fragmentary, localised and complex. There is some feedback from the elaborated, written system, at least in terms of providing a semi-official 'code' which has been incorporated in books of protocol as 'approved behaviour', although the pull that these more general schemes have on the actual behaviour, say of a rising urban bourgeoisie, is certainly very limited. This tradition of knowledge, while it displays a certain overlap and even continuity, is very different in its implications from the related tradition of botanical classification and analysis. The latter is accepted (in the relevant circles), it is cumulatively instead of additionally productive, and is related to the external world in a relatively contingent rather than a relatively arbitrary manner. But an interesting feature of people's knowledge of flowers is that a large number thinks there exists a 'code', perhaps not in the highly structured way of the Language of Flowers, but nevertheless a systematic use of which they are ignorant. In this sense, they are wrong; the structure is absent, but its felt absence is possibly the result of the appearance of these constructed codes which purport to reveal the hidden 'truth' that lies behind surface diversities.

[44] Goody 1977a.
[45] I have touched upon some of the general points in an essay, 'Culture and its boundaries: a European view', in the *European Journal of Social Anthropology*, 1992.

9 · The Americanisation of the foreign mind

In the first edition of his famous work, *An American Dictionary of the English Language* (1828), the puritanical lexicographer, Noah Webster, made a deliberate attempt to set out a distinct linguistic usage for a new nation. He had begun many years before, with *The American Spelling Book* (1783), which has sold some one hundred million copies to date. Making a critical use of Dr Johnson's famous dictionary of 1755, he spurned what he regarded as the affected ways of Londoners and preferred spellings such as 'jail' for 'gaol'. Indeed, he was largely responsible for institutionalising the differences that exist today between English and American spelling, differences that were established with a particular purpose in mind and which have served as diacritical features ever since. A tradition was invented and effectively maintained.[1]

The story of the Language of Flowers in the United States displayed some of the same features. Taking a specifically European creation, already a prime example of the invention of tradition, some minor and indeed some more far-reaching adaptations were made to the local scene, but most of the published versions consist of European plants and English poetry fitted to the French model of Charlotte de Latour. One reason had to do with the arrangements for distributing books, since English editors normally made agreements with American companies for their products to be published locally. But there was also the question of deliberate cultural borrowing and adaptation for a particular audience that was still oriented in the direction of Europe.

The nature of this process of transmission is indicated by the speed and thoroughness with which this line of publishing was developed in the United States. A volume central to this history was *The Language of Flowers: With illustrative Poetry: To Which is Now First Added the Calendar of flowers...* revised by the editor of *Forget-Me-Not*, published in Philadelphia, the first edition of which seems to have appeared in 1827.[2] *Forget-Me-Not* was a revue published in London and edited by Frederic Shoberl, who was a prodigious

---

[1] See Baron 1982.
[2] The title I take from the third edition of 1830. I have not discovered the dates of the earlier ones from the *National Union Catalogue*, although a clue is perhaps given by the volume called *The Language of Flowers*, (New York 1834), an imprint on the cover of which refers to a publication of 1827 in New Haven.

translator from several European languages. It was he who produced the first version of Latour's book in English and added to it in the various ways suggested by Louise Leneveux in her comments on the contributions of English authors. It was then published in the United States without any apparent alterations.[3] Edition followed edition both in Britain and in the States. For example, the eighth American edition of 1848 is taken from the tenth British edition, both essentially following the text of Charlotte de Latour.

At the same time as this book went into its numerous editions, an Americanisation of the tradition began to take place, starting with the work of Dorothea Lynde Dix published in 1829 and entitled *The Garland of Flora*. Dix was a remarkable woman who, among many other activities, campaigned for asylums for the insane. Her book shows considerable originality, although she resorts to some much used verse, including that of Percival:

> In Eastern lands they talk in flowers
> And they tell in a Garland their loves and cares,
> Each blossom that blooms in their garden bowers
> On its leaves a mystic language bears.

Essentially it is an anthology of flower poetry, widely chosen, with comments on ceremonial usages drawn from all parts of the world, 'a storehouse', as she calls it, 'of poetical sentiment and imagery'. 'Flowers! – What can be said of flowers, that has not been said and sung in verse and prose, by poet and poetess, thousands and thousands of times . . .'[4] Its language is universal, even if the dialects are different.[5]

To France does thy vagrant spirit guide thee? Long mayst though roam their 'fields Elysian' – crowded with most luxuriant plants; little suspecting that full oft beneath their fragrant shade repose the mortal relics of the dead.[6]

The stilted 'poetic' language is as archaic as the accompanying sentiments are claimed to be.

Between the poetry Dix provides snippets of information on ceremonies and uses of flowers in different parts of the world. She is especially drawn to the May Day of England when youths went off to the woods and remained there till dawn, smelling the flowers according to Old John Stow, making nosegays, wreaths and crowns, according to others,[7] though no mention is made of Stubbes' complaint that 50 per cent of the girls came back pregnant. She saw it as a communal festival in which both court and populace participated in Tudor times, as earlier described in *The Court of Love*, attributed to Geoffrey Chaucer:

---

[3] I have so far found no earlier version in the British Library or elsewhere.   [4] Dix 1829:1.
[5] Dix 1829:4.   [6] Dix 1829:2.   [7] Dix 1829:9.

And furth goth all the Court, both most and lest,
To feche the floures fressh, and braunche and blome;
And namly, hawthorn brought both page and grome.
With fressh garlandës, partie blewe and whyte,
And thaim rejoysen in their greet delyt.

Eke eche at other threw the floures bright,
The prymerose, the violet, the gold.[8]

The custom of Maying was well established in Europe in the sixteenth century. A codex probably emanating from Bruges in about 1515 includes an illustration of 'Boats in May'. In the boat a lady is being entertained by the playing of a lute and a flute; fresh boughs of greenery have been collected. In the background four riders are returning from the woods carrying similar branches.[9] In the *Shepherd's Calendar*, the Elizabethan poet, Edmund Spenser, also writes of May-buskets (an anglicisation of 'bousquet', bouquet) and of 'Hawthorne buds'. The hawthorn or may was the special object of attention at May Day ceremonies that centred on the woods, the maypole and the May queen. Even today in parts of Britain it is considered bad luck to bring the hawthorn indoors;[10] in contrast to Christmastide greenery and Easter willow, it is a plant kept outdoors, associated with unregulated love in the fields rather than conjugal love in the bed. The hawthorn was however brought into Catholic churches in May and Marcel Proust, who described perfumes in so concrete a way, was reminded by its sight and odour of kneeling before the Virgin during 'le mois de Marie'.[11]

May Day festivities have been interpreted as the descendants of earlier 'pagan' rites, whether of Celtic, Germanic or Roman origin. Wickham writes of the church gradually coming to terms with such customs in many places: 'By 1445 "pageants, plays and May-games" had become the responsibility of the Guild of the Holy Cross at Abingdon, Berkshire.' Church wardens' accounts from various parts of the country include entries for expenditure and income in connection with performances of this kind. However, in the thirteenth century other bishops such as Grosseteste at Lincoln and Chanteloup at Worcester tried to control them, partly because of the sexual licence involved in going to the woods overnight.

There is little to show that such customs, at which Robin Hood plays were

[8] Lines 1432–7, W. W. Skeat, *Supplement to the Work of Geoffrey Chaucer*, vol. 7, 'Chaucerian and other pieces', Oxford, 1897; pp.419ff.   [9] *Book of the Hours of the Virgin* (Bologna 1988:159).
[10] In a *Prospect of Flowers* Andrew Young writes that 'people seem to have been half afraid of Hawthorn blossom, they were careful not to carry it into their homes, but left it outside, on the door and windows'. The reason, he suggests, may be that it had a deathly smell (1986:64–5). May blossom wine is still made from hawthorn flowers. It is also said that to bring the snowdrop or willow catkins indoors is to invite bad luck (Jones and Deer 1989).
   The song 'Gathering Nuts in May' probably refers to gathering 'knots', that is, flowers or branches of hawthorn. Indeed, a London Maying song runs 'Knots of May we've brought you. / Before your door it stands.'   [11] Proust 1954: 137, 139, 167–72.

sometimes performed, existed prior to the thirteenth century. It is certainly doubtful if they could have withstood the onslaught of early Christianity and the barbarians any more steadfastly than Roman drama and *ludi* themselves. On the other hand, they possess a relative unity in their structure – in the maypole, the queen (and king), the visit to the woods – throughout Europe, whereas in purely oral cultures one would expect much greater divergence over such a wide and differentiated region. Are they to be seen as an accompaniment to the development of sacred drama, to a secular version of the rites of May performed for the Virgin?

Given her general temperament, more akin to writers like Stubbes than to poets like Herrick ('Corinna's going a Maying'), it is not surprising that Dix reluctantly admits that 'The celebration of May-day in New England is not very general.'[12] As with medieval scholars looking back towards ancient Rome, the society she read about, and in many ways admired, was very different from that in which she lived and to whose values she subscribed. The gap between literature and life was acute. Indeed, what remained of May Day was essentially pre-pubertal and she describes children going out to gather May boughs and May flowers (Plate 9.1).[13] However, early New England was not altogether barren of maypoles. On 1 May 1627, Thomas Morton, described as 'author and adventurer',[14] had an eighty-foot pine (24 metres) erected at his plantation, Mare Mount, to the sound of drums, guns, pistols and 'other fitting instruments' while a pair of buck's horns were nailed near the top. Beer was brewed, an enigmatic poem was fixed to the pole, and the company, including Indian women, danced around singing a song 'to Hymen' and engaging in revels.[15] That was not the first time the maypole had been seen on the coast, for in 1622 'men on ships' had set one up, partly as a landmark. But the practice, permissible to Anglicans like Morton (who reported to Archbishop Laud in England), was anathema to the 'precise Separatists' of Plymouth colony. In addition, Morton was accused of having instructed Indians in the use of firearms, thus breaking that essential monopoly of the settlers. He was arrested and sent to England. During his enforced absence the governor had the pole cut down and the name of the community changed to Mount Dagon. What is interesting are the terms of the condemnation of these rites. Governor Bradford stigmatised the pole as an idol and saw the celebrations as connected with the Roman goddess Flora, whose origin he claimed (following early Fathers of the church) lay in the celebration of a

---

[12] Dix 1829:11.

[13] The custom continued in Minnesota until the first half of this century; children came to school bringing May bouquets of flowers. In the nineteenth century, Swedish immigrants set up maypoles (*maja*) for their children but for Midsummer rather than 1 May. In Germany at midsummer there was dancing round the 'St John tree', a pyramid decked with garlands and flowers (Miles 1912:269).

[14] In the *National Cyclopaedia of American Biography*.

[15] For Morton's account, see his book, *The New English Canaan*, first published in 1637, reprinted in Boston, 1883.

9.1 Planting the may. Coloured engraving of the nineteenth century. (Musée National des Arts et Traditions Populaires, Paris)

whore. In the Biblical context it was referred to as 'the Calf of Horeb'. But for Morton it was a trophy erected in honour of 'Maja, the Lady of Learning', which his enemies despised.[16] However, 'the old English custome' he hoped to establish, thinking perhaps politically and religiously as well as of revelry itself, was firmly suppressed by the dominant Puritans as it was later by their colleagues in Old England. The main difference between the two lay in the Restoration but, as we have seen, that affected popular 'customs' in Britain only to a limited extent. Many were never to be revived, owing partly to the continuation of Nonconformist beliefs and practices. The terms of the debate are interesting. Morton refers to classical precedents, Bradford to pagan scenes from the Old Testament, one justifying the use of flowers and garlands, the other condemning them. It was a debate that went back a millennium and a half, and more.

The very absence of such festivals for adults forced the new state to promote its own, less orientated towards the countryside, more towards the town. Political components in the organisation of ceremonies are widespread.

---

[16] Morton 1883:17, 18, 276ff. Dagon was a god of the Philistines to whom sacrifices were made when Samson was delivered into their hands (Judges, 16.23); Horeb was the place where Moses saw the burning bush (Exodus, 3.1); the calf was presumably the gold calf (Exodus, 32) which Aaron created and worshipped by sacrifice and dancing, though the Bible does not refer to it in these terms.

I refer not only to the great official parades, like the Anniversary of the October Revolution, nor yet their unofficial equivalents, the protest marches that often hesitate between the carnival aspect of the celebrations of 14 July in Paris and the contestatory attack on the original Bastille itself. I also mean that the celebration of May Day in the seventeenth century became a matter of politics, while even something as intimate and familistic as Thanksgiving in America, built on the Puritan alternative to existing festivals, was formally ordained by an Act of Congress, first in 1789, and at its present date in 1863. So too many other public holidays in other countries are held at the pleasure of the government, at least initially – that is, those festivals that were not originally imposed on Christian and non-Christian alike by the Catholic church. Like Webster's dictionary and the work of Dix, the rejection of May Day and the establishment of festivals such as Thanksgiving and Labor Day, were part of the delicate process of defining the new socio-cultural unit and the identities of its members.[17]

Dix's long introduction is followed by a short section of poems entitled 'Nosegays – Posies'. These two English words have now been largely replaced by the French 'bouquet' (Spenser's 'buskets'), but they recall the intertwining of verse and flowers, the word and the image, in Elizabethan literature. For one meaning of posy is poesy or poetry. It may also stand for 'an emblem or emblematic device' and more specifically 'a short motto, originally a line or verse (French *vers*) of poetry, and usually in patterned language, inscribed on a knife, within a ring, as a heraldic motto, etc.'[18] In itself the word provides a summary statement of the Language of Flowers, bouquet as emblem, verse as motto, both being condensed statements of an epitomising kind where meaning is often meant to be hidden from the uninitiated or from the unintended listener.

The third and major part of Dix's book consists of the vocabulary of flowers itself, beginning with the almond, giving the name in Latin, Italian and French, and going on to explain the meaning: 'The almond is the emblem of *hope* and *promise*. It also tokens *vigilance*', a statement that is followed by quotations from the poets (Moore, Dryden's Virgil, Spenser) as well as from Sanskrit and from prose sources. And so we run through the alphabet until we reach Willow, the Weeping Willow. In all this discussion the emblems have a more direct link with the metaphorical and actual use of flowers than in many other cases. In the first place, the poetical illustrations are chosen from among the English poets; in the second, some reference is made to the actual use of flowers in ceremonial. But while most of the poets are English, most of the usages are continental or drawn from the world at large. There is very little reference to the use of flowers in America, where as we have seen even May

---

[17] The right of Congress to do so was recognised by the Episcopal church in 1789 but by the Catholic church not until 1888. Protestants were more willing to surrender their sovereignty over festivals to the political authorities, especially when it concerned a rival to Christmas.   [18] *Oxford English Dictionary*.

Day was of minimal importance. One reason for such an absence has to do with the 'iconoclastic' tendencies of the Puritans who settled on the coast of New England, and whose priorities, particularly regarding the disposal and commemoration of the dead, ran in stark contrast to those of Catholic Europe and of Asia.

Puritan funerals deliberately rejected the more elaborate rituals of Catholic and even Anglican services.[19] They rejected, too, many of the non-religious aspects. But, given that certain specific procedures had to be carried out in order to dispose of the body, there was always a tendency for these actions to become formalised and elaborated, that is, ritualised, possibly by adapting earlier practices. This was true of the transportation of the corpse to the graveyard as well as of the gifts supplied to those who attended.

As in other cultures, some individuals objected even to the limited expense occasioned by such bare-bone ritual as existed in the early days. The Reverend Joshua Moody included a section in his will 'strictly inhibiting those profuse expenses in mourning or otherwise so frequently wasted at funerals'.[20] Cotton Mather regarded such expenditure as leading to the ruin of the family, and in 1721 and 1724 the province of Massachusetts brought in legislation 'to Retrench the Extraordinary Expenses at Funerals', especially the handing out of scarves.[21] In this way the tendency towards elaboration was now restrained by the equivalent of sumptuary legislation, as it had earlier been by ideology and by social sanctions. Even what was common practice was not necessarily approved and, like many other reformers, Cotton Mather called for people to cut out the 'needless expense' of such occasions, and to give the money for charity schools instead.[22] The ideology persisted to the nineteenth century (and in many cases exists today). A typical admonition of that period urged Americans to remember that 'we are members of a republic and that costly and high decorative monuments and sculpture that may be seen in some of the cemeteries of Europe are not fit subjects for our imitation'.[23] Europe provided a model to be rejected as well as to be followed.

There seems to have been little or no use of flowers at funerals, which were deliberately simple and secularised affairs. The corpse was buried in the graveyard, not usually the churchyard of England but a burial ground owned and operated by the town, consecrated only by the dust of the saints who lay there.[24] It might even be used as grazing land, so the model of a field or park was always more appropriate than that of a garden or yard. People were sometimes buried in graveyards and in the churches themselves;[25] on the other

[19] On the elaborateness and hierarchy of some English funerals even after the Reformation, see *The Diary of Henry Machyn, Citizen and Merchant-Taylor of London, from AD 1550 to AD 1563* (ed. J. G. Nichols), The Camden Society, London, 1848.   [20] Geddes 1976:256.

[21] This practice was brought from England. Gloves, ribbons and a 'love-scarf' are reported from Virginian funerals in the seventeenth century, when great expense had to be laid out for drink (Bruce 1927:226–7).

[22] Geddes 1976:256.   [23] Quoted by French 1975:81.   [24] Geddes 1976:261.

[25] French 1975:70.

hand, in the South the sparseness of the population often led to individual family plots on private land. Because of the general approach, burial grounds would fall into a bad state of repair. This neglect was often deliberate. At the turn of the nineteenth century, the Reverend Bentley of Salem, Massachusetts, remarked of the dead: 'Let their memories live but let their ashes be forgotten.' In his poem, 'The Burial Place' (1818), William Cullen Bryant, the poet of the Berkshires, explained that the Puritans did not bring from England the custom of decorating graves and adorning graveyards with vegetation. Instead we find:

> Naked rows of graves . . .
> Where the course grass between
> Shoots up its tall spikes, and in the wind
> Hisses. . .[26]

Simple wooden headboards or tombstones were erected, while the funeral itself consisted of little more than the tolling of the bell, the procession to the burial ground, the handing round of rings, scarves and gloves, and the provision of liquor.[27] No flowers were involved, either cut or planted.

The contrast with Catholic Europe, and to some extent High Anglican England, is deliberate and striking. In her references to the use of flowers around the world, Dorothea Dix wrote of France's Elysian fields, 'les Champs Elysées', where mortal remains lie unexpectedly below the fragrant shade of the most luxuriant plants.[28] Today French cemeteries abound with flowers throughout the year, some in porcelain, some artificial (depending on the region), but always fresh at particular times of the year.

The French, perhaps, more than any nation, cherish the memory of their dead by ornamenting their places of sepulture with the finest flowers, often renewing the garlands, and replacing such plants as decay, with vigorous and costly ones . . . in some of their southernmost towns, the inhabitants long preserved the custom of rearing flowers on the graves of their friends; they planted only the sweet scented, – but had the deceased been regarded by any with an evil eye during his life, they expressed their hatred by sowing around the graves the seeds of such plants as were for some reasons or other regarded as obnoxious.[29]

In the cemeteries of the Lot at the present day, the flowers are largely plastic, fabric or majolica, except around new graves and except at All Saints' (Toussaint) when chrysanthemums appear throughout. France is not the only country that celebrates this ceremony, in fact the Day of the Dead, or All Souls', that is, 2 November, the day following All Saints', and instituted

---

[26] French 1975:71.
[27] The use of scarves and gloves at funerals appears to be derived from English practice. Chambers (1869:274) quotes a book called *The Virgin's Pattern* which describes a funeral in Hackney, London, where the sheet was held by six of the deceased's schoolmates, dressed 'in mourning habit, with white scarfs and gloves'. All the mourners wore white gloves and were given wine to drink.   [28] Dix 1829:2.   [29] Dix 1829:13.

between 1024 and 1033.[30] The festival spread rapidly throughout the Christian church. In southern Italy, in other parts of the Mediterranean, as well as in Latin America, the celebrations took a more active form. 'It is a custom at Naples on All-Souls' day', wrote a nineteenth-century observer, 'to throw open the charnel houses, light them with torches, and deck them out in all the flowery pageantry of a May-day; crowds follow crowds through these vaults, bearing flowers, which they throw around the niches in which the dead are fixed.'[31]

The contrast with nineteenth-century America was stark and remains so today, for Protestants celebrated neither the living in May nor the dead in November or any other month. England, however, was different, according to Dix, even flowers for the dead being considered as one of 'those customs now in some places almost fallen into disuse'. In earlier times the use of flowers at funerals was a common theme of poets. Because her suicide was doubtful, Ophelia was entitled to her 'virgin crants' and 'maiden strewments', the crance being a garland or chaplet, worn as a sign of maidenhood, which was placed upon the bier at burial and afterwards hung up in the church (Plate 9.2).[32] The 'strewments' were scattered on the grave, in this case by the queen, Hamlet's mother.

> Sweets to the sweet. Farewell!
> I hoped thou shouldst have been my Hamlet's wife:
> I thought thy bride-bed to have deck'd, sweet maid,
> And not have strew'd thy grave. (*Hamlet*, V.i.236–9)

Plants were used to mark rites of passage both in the human and in the annual cycles, as well as to decorate and to symbolise. But in New England, as among other Puritans, such uses were minimal, and indeed that was so in parts of England until the mid nineteenth century.

---

[30] Le Goff 1984.

[31] Quoted by Dix 1829:13 from 'Times Telescope'; this information, and more, is included in Chambers' *The Book of Days*, 1869, p.538; the inhabitants feasted on the previous evening and spent the night at the cemetery, leaving the thieves to make 'a harvest of this pious custom'.

[32] The word is from the Germanic root. According to H. Jenkins, editor of *Hamlet* (1982:555), the practice was widespread in Elizabethan England and continued in various parts to the eighteenth century and later. He claims that the original floral wreath for the burial of a maiden came to be replaced by 'a less perishable artificial structure . . . For women of rank this might be a chaplet of pearl or gold and silver filigree, but surviving and recorded items show characteristically a frame of wood shaped like a crown twelve or more inches high, covered with cloth or paper, adorned with artificial flowers (or occasionally black rosettes), and hanging from it ribbons, a pair of gloves, and sometimes a collar or kerchief. The practice of bearing such a symbol of virginity before the coffin and then hanging it in the church seems to have extended throughout northern Europe'. Virgins' garlands were well known in English churches in the nineteenth century. Burne reports them made of two wire loops placed transversely, covered with many coloured ribbons, inside which is a pair of gloves. In the mining village of Minsterley in Shropshire, seven garlands hang from wall brackets, containing cut-out paper gloves; the loops, wood in this case, are covered with linen on which are sewn lilies and roses made of pink and white paper (1883:310–13). The practice was not confined to England, appearing also in Livonia and Courland. In the church of Abbott's Ann in Hampshire there were 39 garlands, some for young men, the last dating from 1896. Gilbert White described them as 'the marvels of chastity' (1789). While the practice continued in the country, it was disappearing in London by the middle of the seventeenth century (Cuming 1875:194).

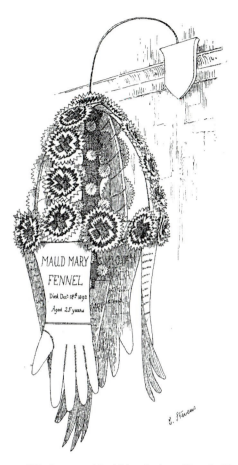

MAUD MARY
FENNEL
Died Dec: 18th 1892
Aged 25 years

9.2 'Virgin crantz' in Abbott's Ann Church, Hampshire, nineteenth century. (Burne 1833)

The contrast with Europe was great, primarily because of that Puritan past. But it was now time to modify this tradition by adapting the culture of the Old Continent to that of the New. Books about the Language of Flowers were one way to do this and the growth and publication of this genre of writing was rapid, in America as elsewhere, often by women. In 1833 Fielding Lucas of Baltimore published *Flora's Dictionary* by a Lady, in fact Mrs Elizabeth Washington (Gamble) Wirt. Her preface shows the same mixture of interest in botanical science, aesthetics and communication that we find in the main French tradition; even the sentiments are borrowed, except that there is a rejection of artificial, courtly behaviour in favour of the simplicity of the 'primitive and interesting people' of the East:

Travellers . . . assure us, that the people of the East see something more in them [flowers] than mere objects of admiration. In the hands of these primitive and interesting people, they become flowers of rhetoric, and speak their feelings with far more tenderness and force than words can impart. With them, there is something sacred in this mode of communication. It is a kind of religious worship – an offering of the fruits of the earth; and, though addressed to an earthly object, it still retains something of the sanctity which belonged to the rite from which it was probably borrowed, and is accompanied with a devotion far more true, and deep, and touching, than the artificial homage which distinguished the courts of Europe, even in the vaunted age of chivalry. Compared with modern manners, either in Europe or in America, what is there that can vie, in picturesque beauty, with the Persian youth, gracefully presenting a rose to his mistress? What language can convey a compliment so delicate and exquisite? and if a communication of a still more interesting nature be intended, how much more refined, poetic and affecting is the mute eloquence of the eastern lover, than those awkward and embarrassing *declarations* which are in use in other countries! How much easier is it to present a flower than to make a speech!

The appeal is to a simple and universal code, and the book is essentially an attempt to reconstruct 'this mystic language of the East'. This she sets out to do, like others, by examining the words of British poets, the name of the flower and its various properties. A few meanings have been '*arbitrarily* assumed . . . from the necessity of giving sufficient range and variety to this symbolic language', a fact she excuses on the grounds that even in spoken language the connection between sound and symbol is just as arbitrary.

The work itself starts rather than ends with a botanical section on the 'Structure of Plants', after which comes 'Flora's Dictionary':

Acacia, Rose	*Friendship*	If I do a vow of friendship,
Robinia Hispida		I'll perform it.
		(Shakespeare)

followed by a series of further quotations which have to do with sentiment and nothing with flowers.

At the end of the book we find a list entitled 'Dedication of Flowers', taken from Hone's *Every Day Book*, which gives the days of the year, the Saints' Days, with the flowers attributed to each saint.[33] Finally the 'Index' presents the 'Sentiments' or 'Significances' together with the appropriate flower (Sentiments and Emblems are key words throughout); this is the equivalent of the French lists of the Language of Flowers.

Absence	Zinnia
Activity	Thyme
Affection beyond the grave	Locust, etc.

A more typical work, one following closer in the French tradition, is that by Catherine H. Waterman (Esling), entitled *Flora's Lexicon: An Interpretation of the Language and Sentiment of Flowers: With an Outline of Botany, and a Poetical Introduction*, published in Philadelphia in 1839. The opening

---

[33] London, 1826.

'advertisement' speaks of the Language of Flowers having 'recently attracted so much attention, that an acquaintance with it seems to be deemed, if not an essential part of a polite education, at least a graceful and elegant accomplishment'. Hence a volume furnishing 'a complete interpretation of those meanings' becomes a valuable part of a gentleman's or lady's library since such knowledge has become a desirable part of social intercourse, in America as in Europe:

> There is a language in each flower
> That opens to the eye,
> A voiceless – but a magic power,
> Doth in earth's blossoms lie;

The Lexicon begins with Acacia, giving the botanical name (*Robinia pseudacacia*), the Linnaean classification. This entry is followed by a comment which is taken straight from the French of Charlotte de Latour but sounds more bizarre, published as it is in Philadelphia. Once again, the deeds of silent 'savages' are to be preferred to the words of the sophisticated:

The savages of North America have consecrated the Acacia to the genius of chaste love; their bows are made from the incorruptible wood of this tree, their arrows are armed with one of its thorns. These fierce children of the forest, whom nothing can subdue, conceive a sentiment of delicacy: perhaps what they are unable to express by words, but they understand the sentiment by the expression of a branch of blooming Acacia. The young savage, like the city coquette, understands this seducing language perfectly.[34]

While the East was looked upon as the main source of this language, there was much reference to primitive people; the concept did not emerge from the ethnographic museum. Yet it was the East, apparently included among these so-called primitives, which not only supplied the symbolism but the flowers themselves, with tulips from Turkey, chrysanthemums from China and Japan, jasmine from India. What is interestingly presumptuous about Europe as well as the United States, even before any major industrial transformation, is the deeply ingrained feeling about the inferiority or primitiveness of these major cultures. The Chinese were lumped with the aboriginal Americans, although the US was vigorously engaged at the time in trading New England ice for the sophisticated products of their export trade. As today, all those 'others' belonged equally to what came to be called the Third World. In principle the categorisation was little different from the Japanese attitude to Southern Barbarians (*namdam*) or the Chinese to Foreign Devils (*yang guizi*). In each case such views distort the nature of cultural understanding and of understanding cultures.

The comment on acacia is followed by the usual quotation from Moore:

---

[34] Waterman (Esling) 1839:13.

> Our rocks are rough, but smiling there
> *Acacia* waves her yellow hair. . .

Once again the poem contains no indication of the supposed sentiment; while the next quotation on chastity expresses a sentiment which has nothing to do with the flower. Although formal correspondences are sought, the treatment of the material leaves many a gap, many an inconsistency, much room for the imagination.

So we make our way through the alphabet to the final entry, Zinnia, absence, which is followed by a few pages on Botany, ending with the usual 'Index of Flowers':

Acacia	Platonic Love
Acacia Rose	Elegance

as well as giving the complementary 'interpretations':

Absence	Wormwood
Absence	Zinnia

Towards the end we find:

> You are my Divinity   American Cowslip,

indicating a further attempt to domesticate the foreign product.

The process of Americanisation, the domestication of the foreign mind, continued with Mrs S. J. Hale's *Flora's Interpreter, or the American Book of Flowers and Sentiments*, first published in Boston in 1832. The aim now became more explicit. The authoress says of her work, 'Nothing new attempted, except in the arrangement, and in the introduction of American sentiments. Flowers have also been symbols of the affections probably ever since our first parents tended theirs in the garden of God's own planting. They seem hallowed from that association.'[35]

The attribution of a special Christian 'virtue' to flowers through their link with the Garden of Eden is a common one, even if somewhat in contradiction to the Turkish roots. However, in Genesis, the garden contains the tree of knowledge and the tree of life, together with weeds, those 'plants out of place'; as we have remarked, it makes no reference to flowers at all. That notion is more appropriate to Paradise, derived from the Persian.[36]

Mrs Hale begins with five pages of Botanical Explanation before going on to 'Flora's Interpreter' which lists the flowers and their meanings ('Significations', for example Acacia, Yellow, Concealed Love), followed by the authority of a poet, in this case Moore, then continuing with a section on SENTIMENTS established with quotations culled from local poets. However, the legitimation of the meanings themselves comes largely from outside, from Europe. As in France, the status of meanings attached to individual flowers is

---

[35] Hale 1832:iii.
[36] The Christian notion of a walled garden has its roots in the Song of Solomon – 'A garden inclosed is my sister, my spouse . . . A fountain of gardens, a well of living waters, and streams from Lebanon' (4.12, 15).

dubious. That they do not belong to any single enduring cultural code is indicated by the differences between lexicons, and of this Mrs Hale is aware. Like others, she claims to have 'carefully searched the poets and writers on Eastern manners where flowers are even now the messengers of the heart'.[37] Since these meanings vary according to the authority, she has selected those appearing to her the most appropriate, which are largely based on the volumes by Dix and Wirt, her American predecessors.[38] A tradition was being established.

In the preface she explains her procedures as follows: 'The authorities for the significations affixed to each flower are usually from European writers. . . They are an elder people . . . But for the sentiments I have preferred . . . American poets, I think it is time our people should express their own feelings in the sentiments and idioms of America.'[39] She concludes: 'To the Youth of America I commit my book. May it inspire our Young Ladies to cultivate their virtues which can be truly represented by the forest flowers, and our Young Men to cultivate their minds, till our land shall become beautiful by the creativeness of Genius.'

The book ends with a section on 'The Poesy of Flowers' which includes one poem entitled 'With Wild Flowers to a Sick Friend' and contains the following lines by Mrs Sigourney:

> Should the green-house patricians with gathering frown,
> On your plebian virtues look haughtily down,
> Shrink not . . .[40]

Yet another is entitled 'To a White Chrysanthemum', beginning 'Fair gift of Friendship!', and taken from the *Ladies Magazine*. In the first of these poems there is some recognition of the hierarchical aspect of the culture of flowers, an acknowledgement that takes the form of the need to apologise for giving wild rather than cut flowers. While this sentiment is perhaps an early indication of sales pressure from the florists' trade (who have many such inventions to their name), the poem is also a comment on the class aspect of the conspicuous expenditure on flowers. The poem on the chrysanthemum indicates that the negative value placed upon it as a gift to the living, which marks its use in France and Italy, had not reached America or indeed England, partly because of the demolition job done by the Protestants on All Saints', in an attempt to revert to the austerity of early Christianity. Finally the book ends in the usual way with an 'Index of Flowers' and one of 'Interpretations', in a sense a summary of what has gone before and an *aide mémoire* for the young ladies she is trying to educate.

Local examples of this genre proliferated. In 1842 Lucy Hooper edited *The*

---

[37] Hale 1832:iii.   [38] The American quotations are from Cheever 1831.
[39] Hale 1832:v.   [40] Sigourney's collected poems were published in 1846.

Lady's Book of Flowers and Poetry; To Which are Added, a Botanical Introduction, a Complete Floral Dictionary and a Chapter on Plants in Rooms. Flowers, she declares, are 'the alphabets of angels', which can 'brighten the dim eye and ease the wearied mind'.[41] Once again the book includes contributions by a number of authors and attempts to cover poetry, botany, as well as the language, for which the usual floral dictionary is offered, including:

> African Marygold – Vulgar Minds. . .
> American Elm – Patriotism,
> American Linden – Matrimony,

a set of meanings that sums up the trend to local values, including perhaps an element of 'racism', though the lexicon is in no sense confined to the United States.

Many more works appeared in the States on the Language of Flowers and related topics.[42] They represent the same general trends we have observed in Europe, that is, the scientific, the religious and the occult, but giving a greater emphasis to issues of morality.[43] A scientific element is already included in many of these volumes. The religious is stressed in Margaret Coxe's book, *Floral Emblems: Or, Moral Sketches from Flowers*, published in Cincinnati in 1845, though it is obviously directed not to the Virgin Mary but to Christ himself. The opening sentence sets the tone: 'Our Saviour, when on earth, sent his disciples to the flowers of the field, for some of the most precious lessons He designed to impart to them.'[44] Her intention was 'to lead the youthful

---

[41] Hooper 1842:8.

[42] In 1848 John S. Adams published his *Flora's Album*, the introduction to which is dated 1 October 1846. It is again a highly derivative volume, following through both the Paradise and Eden themes (p.3), then turning once again to those 'Eastern lands'.

[43] I have only examined a selection of the more widely available. In 1836 a volume appeared with an interesting title *Flora and Thalia, or Gems of Flowers and Poetry: Being an Alphabetical Arrangement of Flowers, with Appropriate Poetical Illustrations, Embellished with Coloured Plates. By a lady* to which is added a botanical description of the various parts of a flower, and the dial of flowers . . . Philadelphia (this was listed in the library of the University of Michigan, Ann Arbor, but was not then available). Others include: Frances Sargent Osgood (Locke) (ed.), *The Poetry of Flowers and the Flowers of Poetry*. New York, 1840; Sarah Carter Mayo (Edgerton), *The Flower Vase*, Lowell, 1844 (in the same year she edited *Fables of Flora* by John Langhorne (1735–79)); Anon., *The Bouquet: Containing the Poetry and Language of Flowers*. Boston, 1845 (repr. 1846); Anon., *The American Lady's Every Day Hand-book of Modern Letter Writing; Language and Sentiment of Flowers; Dreams, their Origin, Interpretation and History; Domestic Cookery*, Philadelphia, 1847; Pliny Miles, *The Sentiments of Flowers in Rhyme, or the Poetry of Flowers Learned by Mnemotechnic Rules*, New York, 1848; Henrietta Dumont, *The Floral Offering: A Token of Affection and Esteem, Comprising the Language and Poetry of Flowers*, Philadelphia, 1851; Anne Elizabeth (pseud.), *Vase of Flowers*, Boston, 1851; Anon., *The Floral Forget Me Not: A Gift for All Seasons*, Philadelphia, 1854.

There was a dearth of new publications in the 1860s but after the Civil War the line continued with the usual batch of anonymous publications and new authors, such as: C. Seelye, *The Language of Flowers and Floral Conversation*, Rochester, 1874; Martha Ewing, *The Language of Flowers and Poetry of Flowers*, Rochester, 1875; Cordelia Haris Turner, *The Floral Kingdom: Its History, Sentiment and Poetry*, Chicago, 1877; Anon. *The Language and Poetry of Flowers, and Poetic Handbook of Wedding Anniversary Pieces, Album Verses, and Valentines, Together with a Great Number of Beautiful Poetical Quotations from Famous Authors*, New York, 1878; Fannie Frisbie (ed.), *Songs of the Flowers*, Boston, 1885. By the end of the century (1899), the Language of Flowers had even been incorporated in the *Vest Pocket Webster Dictionary and Hand Manual: Including a Dictionary of the Language of Flowers*, Chicago.   [44] Coxe 1845:5.

subjects of our country to the study of the works of Nature, on Christian principles'.[45] In fact the volume differs greatly from others on 'Floral Emblems', being in prose, aimed specifically at the young and teaching morality through a series of incidents many of which came from her own experience.

The occult tradition too has its representative in America, in the shape of the work of Samuel A. Binion on *Phyllanthography* (1909). The author, who translated Sienkiewicz's *Quo Vadis* and other of his works from Polish, had already written *Ancient Egypt or Mizraim* (1877) as well as *The Kabbalah* so he was well qualified to embark upon the task of expounding 'a method of leaf and flower writing'.[46] He tells of giving a lecture on the invention of writing when a lady member of his audience commented, 'It would be a good plan . . . if one could invent a picture alphabet for decorative purposes.'[47] Instead of offering a complete floral alphabet, Binion selected the rose alone and used this plant to create twenty-six different combinations, which could then be used to translate language, as in the name 'Mary' (Plate 9.3). While his work was hardly occult in the same way as the French, it nevertheless had recourse to cryptography to propose a new form of knowledge, albeit for purely decorative purposes.

This interest in the Language of Flowers may appear ephemeral but it is nevertheless persistent. In France, England and the United States at the present time new volumes appear, incorporating the versions of floral equivalences which people peruse even if they do not use.[48] Not only did it spread to many lands but people came to regard it as their own, adapting it slightly to the locality, but keeping the main textual form and content.

THE PROCESS OF AMERICANISATION

Europe as 'an elder people', the East as 'primitive', the Youth of America as the promise of the future, these are some of the themes found in the nineteenth-century Language of Flowers in the United States. Youth needs to be cultivated in the ways of the world, in its 'languages' as well as in nature itself, and for this we need to borrow from abroad. At the same time, these European practices have to be Americanised, and there is a continuing insistence on the cultural needs of a new country, of which the adaptations to the Language of Flowers are as much a part as the institution of festivals and the reform of spelling. Independence meant divergence, the invention of tradition, or rather the invention of its adaptations. That tradition was strongly influenced by the Puritan heritage. While it is unlikely that the Language of Flowers would have originated in a country that paid them so little attention at that time, Americans seem to have taken it more seriously,

[45] Coxe 1845:6.   [46] Binion 1909:i.   [47] Binion 1909:iii.   [48] See for example Ohrbach 1990.

9.3 The name 'Mary' spelled out in phyllanthography. (Binion 1909)

more morally, than Europe, stressing its use to promote virtue, to stimulate education and to define the values of the new nation. At the same time, the use of the flowers themselves remained very much in the background. Their relative absence is even more marked in American practice, and remains so down to today; it was perhaps more congenial to keep the Language as a purely literary exercise, and to enlarge the gap between life inside and outside literature.

The moral lurking behind the bouquet partly resolved the tension that existed between the local Puritan tradition, on the one hand, and the adoption of current European modes, on the other. Even the passage of the seasons is thought of as not only ordered by the gods, or by nature, but as having puritanical virtues as well as aesthetic attractions. As Henry remarks in

Breck's *The Young Florist* (Boston, 1833), 'Had we a perpetual summer and a continued succession of flowers, we should perhaps soon become indifferent, and esteem them of little value.' The strength of the Puritan heritage and the problems to which this gave rise for the creation of a tradition of high culture are difficult to exaggerate. The Puritan axe stopped public theatrical performances in England during the Commonwealth and closed down the theatre in Edinburgh for two hundred years. In America public performance was strangled at birth. Not until the middle of the eighteenth century do we find theatre companies touring Virginia, though there were some earlier amateur productions in that colony.[49] New England took longer to adapt and the first performance of *Othello* in that region was billed as 'a moral dialogue in five acts'. The beginning of local authorship took a predictable turn. In 1787 the play *The Contrast* displayed as its theme Yankee honesty winning over foreign affectation. But the culture of flowers was associated with those very foreign affections as well as with luxury, with high culture and even with paganism. Its emergence in North America was the result of a long, hard journey.[50]

AMERICAN PRACTICE

Gardens

Flowers were not a notable part of social life in early New England;[51] at first it was difficult enough to grow the essential crops, especially the wheat and barley to which the colonists were used. However, in the 1630s Lady Fenwick at Saybrook is reported to have cultivated a garden of flowers and herbs, while Johnson claimed in 1643 that 'on village home lots it was not long before the flower garden became companion to the vegetable garden'. But the gardens and their flowers of the seventeenth century were primarily 'for Meate or Medicine', as Ann Leighton points out. Gardening was a serious business, not marked by flowery tributes, although plants were often given a mystical significance. For the population at large flowers were at once utilitarian and didactic, but rarely decorative and symbolic in a secular sense.

What effect did protestantism have on gardens and the culture of flowers?

---

[49] Amateur play-acting began much earlier in the South, where shortly after the Restoration, a play was performed in 1665 by three men on the Eastern Shore. Even then they were hauled up before the justices, who ordered them to appear in court wearing their costumes and bringing with them a copy of the play (Bruce 1927:191).

[50] On the American theatre, see Agnew 1986:150. There was no professional theatre in Boston until 1792. Even 'those colonists who might have used the drama as a means to display their Cavalier affiliations with British culture' were constrained by the 'ascetic legacy of the original religious settlements', which of course also went back not only to Britain but to early Christianity.

[51] See for example Blanchan (1909:49) who finds few flowers in the gardens of New England before the Revolution. There seems to have been more activity in the Dutch and French colonies, even among Protestants. The first commercial nursery was established in 1730 to cater for Huguenot immigrants. But the difference was not all that marked.

Leighton attributes the relative lack of interest to the fact that the English of the period differed from the French in thinking that personal pleasure was an insufficient reason for any undertaking, especially the pleasures of royalty and nobles. In England printed books about gardening were aimed at a bourgeois audience, ready for the democratisation of the garden, or anyhow for its adoption by other social groups. In other words, she sees the effects as being highly contextual, a matter of resentment at the culture of luxury which in fact the objectors were only too willing to acquire. But the ideology of puritanism had perhaps a firmer base and was not so easily to be won over.

In early Massachusetts part of the justification for flowers was that they were largely for medicinal purposes. Not until much later in the eighteenth century do we hear of women gardeners in Vermont who were 'great florists' producing 'flowers worthy of Paradise', in uniform beds rather than in variegated knots.[52] At this time it was the well-off inhabitants of Philadelphia, following the traditions of William Penn, who took up gardening in the 'formal European style'.[53] As for the rest of the country, an early-nineteenth-century writer, Bernard M'Mahon, claimed that 'America has not yet made that rapid progress in gardening' that might be expected from an intelligent and wealthy people.[54] While the heritage of puritanism still lived on, together with the attachment to more utilitarian goals, these attitudes were beginning to be modified throughout the country.

The change in the culture of flowers in the eighteenth century is expressed in the subtitle of Ann Leighton's second volume on American gardens, *For Use or for Delight*, a quotation from John Parkinson's *Paradisus*. But these gardens were mainly located in the colonies south of New England where both attitudes and climate were rather different. In the first place, the immigrants were not in the main Puritans. The difference can be seen in early reports from Virginia, where, as distinct from New England, the Anglican church was dominant. True, Genevan influence was initially strong for there was a Puritan party within the church, so that strict emphasis was placed on conformity. But the ambience was different and when Lord Delaware, the first governor, went to church in Jamestown in 1610, a sexton called the inhabitants by tolling the bell in the steeple. The governor sat in state, the preacher spoke from a pulpit, the church included a baptismal font and the interior was 'kept passing sweet and trimmed up with diverse flowers'.[55]

At the same time, they retained stronger links with England, being involved in the exchange of plants and seeds in a much greater way. At the beginning of the century Robert Beverly observed that while English plants such as lavender and 'july-flowers' have a difficult time in New England, nothing 'miscarries in Virginia'.[56] The physical contrast was quite explicit. At least

---

[52] Leighton 1986:371–2.   [53] Leighton 1986:376.   [54] Leighton 1986:381.
[55] Brydon 1947:16–17, quoting a contemporary report by William Strachey. See also Fischer 1989:233.
[56] Leighton 1986:34.

among the ruling class, Southern gardens included beds of flowers where humming birds licked the dew and honey from the tender leaves. Colonel Byrd's garden, 'the finest in the country', had a summerhouse set round with Indian honeysuckle 'which all the summer is continually full of sweet Flowers.'[57] That aristocratic Quaker William Penn sent flower seeds back to 'a Person of Quality . . . for a Tryal' but also made his own attempts at domestication to add to the roses that had been brought from England.[58]

Similar efforts were made elsewhere, but always with limited results. In 1709 John Lawson wrote: 'the Flower-Garden in Carolina is as yet arriv'd, but to a very poor and jejune Perfection. We have only two sorts of Roses, the Clove-July-Flowers, Violets, Princes Feather, and *Tres Colores*. There has been nothing more cultivated in the Flower-Garden, which, at present, occurs to my Memory: but as for the wild spontaneous Flowers of this Country, Nature has been so liberal, that I cannot name one tenth part of the valuable ones.'[59] It was this abundance of native flora, not only of flowers, that led to such an interest in the plants of America by members of the Royal Society and by many others.

The present situation in American yards and cemeteries in the East does not only derive from the puritanical background of New England. Their cemeteries were well known abroad for their ordered grace, but as paying more attention to trees and grass, than to flowers. That is also true of gardens. In European eyes, beds of flowers are not a dominant feature. Physical factors play a part, with the hot summers and long winters. Many have a touch of the secondary forest about them, their flowers suffering from the ravages of wild animals and smaller pests, so that cultivation demands a great expenditure of time and energy. At times, except among the rich, there are perhaps some lingering feelings that the cultivation of flowers represents an indulgence in private pleasures at the expense both of the public good and of personal salvation. Civic virtue as well as religion was involved.

The influential nineteenth-century gardener, J. Scott, who enjoined the suburban houseowner to throw open his 'front grounds' and to avoid hedging as being 'unchristian and unneighborly', also looked upon flower beds as the lace on a woman's dress: 'Too much decoration, ill-placed, destroys the refinement of the gown.'[60] Similar sentiments pervaded other uses of flowers. One Boston florist incurred the wrath of local ladies when he furnished a bullock's head in flowers at the funeral of a butcher; they protested at the 'floral mess'.[61] Such objections reflect doubts about the 'excessive' use of flowers. Despite the advent of so many immigrants from Catholic countries, those doubts have laid a heavy hand on the culture of flowers. Not to the commercial growing of flowers, in which America has come to excel, both in quality and in price – in January 1989 a florist in Happy Valley, Hong Kong,

[57] Leighton 1986:35. [58] Leighton 1986:49–50. [59] Leighton 1986:63.
[60] Scott 1870, quoted in Leighton 1987:255–6. [61] Leighton 1987:113.

preferred to buy her cut roses from America rather than Holland on both these grounds – it is in the uses in gift-giving and in rituals that there is noticeable restraint compared with much of Europe. A sophisticated American, brought up in Los Angeles and New York, remarked, 'Americans are not tuned into these things like Europeans.' There was a measure of self-deprecation here, for that view is partly dependent upon unfounded notions about what Europeans know. But similar observations are often made about flowers for the dead. Noting the continuity between modern and ancient cemeteries in Pompeii, the American archaeologist Jashemski writes: 'what most impresses the visitor from the United States is that, no matter when one visits the cemetery, each tomb is decorated with a fresh bouquet of flowers. In the hot Campanian sun this means that fresh bouquets must be brought several times a week.'[62] However, there are major differences even between New England and Protestant England, as well as within the United States itself.

Images in cemeteries

The Puritan ideology had a particularly strong and enduring effect in those areas where the sects achieved political power, notably in New England. That was the case not only for festivals and flowers but for images, especially those that attempted to represent divine beings. Samuel Willard, the president of Harvard College at the beginning of the eighteenth century, had much to say about the relations of language, symbols and icons to divinity. The word was favoured; the icon discouraged:

Hence how very unsu[i]table it is to represent the Divine Nature by any Corporeal similitude: I mean in Pictures or Images of any visible and bodily substance, and that whether it be for civility or devotion, *i.e.*, either merely as Ornamental, or as some pretend, to encreate devout Affections in any; how is it possible to rightly shadow a Spirit? Who ever was able rightly to decypher the form or shape of a being which is invisible! It is folly to pretend to afford us the Portraiture of an Angel, but it is madness and wickedness to offer any image or Representation of God: How many solemn cautions did God give his people against this by *Moses*, besides the express forbidding of it in the second Command; and God declares it to be a thing *Idolatrous*.[63]

In practice such iconophobia was limited to the meeting house itself.

It was in the rituals surrounding death that image-making re-emerged in New England. Even early on the corpse was taken to the graveyard in a horse-drawn hearse draped with robes painted with winged death's heads and other symbols. Gloves were sent out as an invitation to the funeral (as they were in the case of marriages) and certain attenders were given gold mourning rings

---

[62] Jashemski 1979:15.
[63] Willard 1726:54 (published posthumously by his students), quoted in Ludwig 1966:33.

representing a death's head. The only music was the tolling of the bell. Ritual was kept to the minimum and differentiation among the dead was eliminated. English burial customs were the subject of a treatise published in 1631 by John Weever, entitled *Ancient Funeral Monuments*, which is directed at the puritanical vandalism against monuments to the dead. Such monuments and the place in which they were erected were tailored to the position the dead person had held in the social system. In New England, as among their co-religionists in Old England, such differentiation was largely abolished in favour of uniformity of treatment, so that the graveyard looked rather like a military cemetery. However, ministers began to be given more elaborate headstones than others and different styles gradually emerged. In England itself classical themes were adopted and Weever deplored the statues of nudes that were then being imported. Urns, garlands and similar motifs dominated urban churchyards and were even to be found in the remote cemeteries of Massachusetts.[64] This development was part of the avoidance of specifically Christian iconography which the Reformers had effectively discouraged. Despite their ambivalent attitude towards the 'pagan' emblems of crowns and wreaths, towards those symbols of which early Humanists and later scholars made so much use, some Protestants were forced to resort to them in preference to religious (that is, Christian) imagery.

These symbols began to be used among the English aristocracy around 1560 to avoid the desecration of their tombs by the Reformers.[65] But at the time of John Weever's massive survey of the images and inscriptions of the remaining tombs in England, it was also the case that 'virtually no religious iconography is reported as remaining extant', even the ostensibly 'acceptable themes' such as the skull and crossbones. So far did their iconoclasm go, according to Weever, that these 'puritanicall' Reformers would choose to exercise their devotions 'in some emptie barne' rather than in a church 'which they hold to be polluted with the abominations of the whore of Babylon'.[66] But it was not only that Puritans were opposed to representation and to ritual. They also rejected existing burial practices exhibiting differentiation. In death, all are equal. But in life too ideas approaching those of the Levellers were relevant to the conduct of earthly affairs.

From about the year 1668, that is, after the fall of Puritan power in England, the tombstones of New England were frequently engraved with all manner of objects, including souls and angels. Nevertheless, they were frequently plain affairs in which, as in the churches or meeting houses, even the cross is used very sparingly. The development of decorated gravestones and the abandonment of the stricter Puritan approach to death seems to begin earlier in New than in Old England, a fact that Stannard attributes to the inward-looking character of the community which led it to pay so much attention to its

---

[64] Ludwig 1966.   [65] Stannard 1977:107.   [66] Stannard 1977:107–8.

founding fathers.[67] However, it cannot be said that there was a massive development of iconography or ritual compared with Catholic countries. In due course the same complaints against urban neglect were put forward, as in England (and in some other parts of Europe), to be taken up by the rural-cemetery movement of the 1830s. Mount Auburn cemetery in Boston was founded in 1831 to provide 'perpetual homes' and became a great commercial success; by contrast only certain tombs in French cemeteries are marked 'concession perpetuelle', the rest being rented from the municipality.[68]

The continuing severity of New England graveyards is proverbial. Even in Catholic cemeteries in the East, floral offerings are few except around new burials. For Protestants and even for Catholics the festivals of All Saints' and All Souls' Days are of little significance, and as in Scotland Hallowe'en is reduced to a secular children's performance with pagan overtones. But Catholic places of burial did not show any great differences. Only in the West of the United States with the dominance of Mexican immigrants do we find any significant family visits to the cemetery at this period, though these are very much part of rural life in Italy and in France.[69] There too an interesting regional variation of culture occurs in the cemeteries, for some Californians decorate their graves at holiday periods, Christmas with fir trees and poinsettias, St Valentine's Day with red roses and other emblems of love, incorporating the dead into the festivals of the living in ways that much of New England would disapprove even today.

The Puritans, and to a lesser degree other Protestants, objected to the Catholic attitude to the cross, just as they did to the use of statuary, relics and images of all kinds. The cross was little used publicly as an early Christian symbol until, together with the chi-rho symbol for the name of Christ, it was promoted by Constantine who had abolished crucifixion as a punishment. Early crucifixes show the victory of Christ over the powers of evil and death, but by the late tenth century it is the suffering figure that begins to be portrayed. While Romanesque crucifixes place a royal crown on his head, on Gothic ones it is a crown of thorns.[70]

At the time of the Reformation the iconography changed. While Lutherans retained the ceremonial and ornamental use of the cross, other reformed churches resisted its use until the twentieth century. The sign of the cross (except in the Anglican baptism) and the crucifix became marks of the Roman Catholic faith rather than of Christianity as a whole. As a consequence the

[67] Stannard 1977:135ff.   [68] For example, in Arfons, Tarn.
[69] I am indebted to Luisa Ciammitti and Martine Segalen for descriptions of their experiences, to James Banker for an introduction to the cemetery at Raleigh, North Carolina, to David Sapir for visits to the cemeteries of Charlottesville and to Emily Martin at Baltimore.
[70] Southern (1953:237) maintains that the idea of the suffering Christ, the human Christ, characterised above all the eleventh century, the century of Anselm, when humanity too became more directly involved in its salvation. Others have detected the trend already in the ninth century.

funerary architecture of Protestant cemeteries favoured the plain headstone rather than the cruciform variety more common in Catholic areas. In general its use in New England, especially as a sculptural feature, still provides a contrast between Catholic and Protestant cemeteries, just as it does between their homes.[71]

Flowers in cemeteries

In New England, cemeteries generally came under the town government and later under private companies who placed firm restrictions on what one could and could not do. The cemetery, as we have seen, is more of a park than a garden, consisting basically of grass and inscribed headstones. Nowadays the flat stone set in the soil, covered with grass cuttings or fallen leaves, reinforces that impression. In the interests of inexpensive maintenance, the large mowing machines keep the grass well trimmed but they put paid to any growing plants, while cut flowers remain on the tombs only between the weekly cuttings.[72]

But here too it is not simply a technical matter. Cemeteries with standing tombstones present a similar appearance. Moreover, notices at the entrances to cemeteries often announce that flowers will be cleared away after a limited period. 'All flowers removed each Wednesday', declares the Calvary cemetery at Santa Barbara, which also forbids artificial flowers, potted plants and wreaths – only permitting cut flowers in regulation vases. But on Wednesdays they become 'dirt', rubbish to be carted away. That was the same in the St Lawrence cemetery at New Haven, which was also Catholic. New England town cemeteries are even more severe, partly because of imposed regulations for reasons associated with tidiness and the cost of maintenance, partly from internalised attitude towards the use of flowers in such a context (Plate 9.4). Nowadays flowers cover new graves. Otherwise there are few. The older graveyards present a monotonous appearance, the green grass providing a rural background for the slabs of grey stone.

Even at festivals, little is done to commemorate the dead. In the West of the country this is changing, partly it would seem at the instigation of the florists, although the influence of the Spanish tradition and the mild climate cannot be overlooked. At the traditional celebrations of All Saints' and All Souls' in New England, the occasion on which French and Italian cemeteries are full of flowers, little is done even in Catholic cemeteries to brighten up the graves; indeed by and large these are kept clean by functionaries rather than by

[71] The image did appear on a few tombstones in New England (Ludwig 1966:128) and is found on soldiers' tombs.
[72] Elizabeth Colson reported that in her childhood in Minnesota plants could be planted on graves but that this had become impossible with modern techniques of maintenance.

9.4 St Lawrence Catholic cemetery, New Haven, 1988.

individuals. In California, more attention is paid to graves at this and other times of the year, but the difference with Italy remains massive.

To make some rough comparisons, I counted the graves of those who had died over the course of the last fifty years, the percentage with flowers providing some kind of measure of the 'depth' of the culture of flowers. These results emphasise the staggering difference between Southern Europe and the United States:

Place of burial	Flowers
Western Massachusetts (early reconstruction)	None
New Haven, Whitneyville Congregational	1%–3% (mainly fresh-cut flowers)
Raleigh, Oakwood, North Carolina	5% (mainly artificial)
California	20%–25% (fresh, plus tinsel)
The Lot, France	100% (90% artificial, except for All Saints')
Bellagio, Italy	100% (90% fresh-cut flowers)
Berlin, Germany	100% (90% plants)

To some of the corollaries of this enormous difference I will return in the next chapter. Here it is worth adding that the present situation is partly the result of the nineteenth-century movement to create cemeteries out of town, partly for aesthetics, partly because of overcrowding, mainly for health.

The florist

In California flowers are more prominent in the house as well as the cemeteries. Throughout the year they are available in shops and gardens. Florists abound. The flower stall at the weekly market in Santa Monica does a roaring trade, crowded with customers, mainly women, making purchases for home and office. The cemetery at Forest Lawn even has its own florists, while flowers are also sold at many supermarkets.

That is also true of supermarkets in the East. There too street sellers form another element of the urban market. In New Haven in the autumn of 1987, there were four around the old campus of Yale, some working till late at night, one oriented to businessmen, two to students and the fourth to a more general public. The student sales were largely of roses of New England origin; many of the business sales were from imported cartons of carnations from Europe and elsewhere by way of Miami. The presence of these street sellers argues for a steady market for everyday purposes.

The highlights of the florist's business, on the other hand, were the major holidays. According to a handbook of the 1930s, the favourite cut flowers were roses and chrysanthemums for Thanksgiving;[73] Christmas was especially busy as it was a 'universal day for gift giving'; St Valentine's Day had been 'assuming greater scope', with married couples giving flowers to each other, as well as children to mothers. Since that time, St Valentine's Day has become the major occasion for buying cut flowers, having extended its symbolism well beyond the realm of sexual love.[74] 'Easter is proverbially a money-maker', especially for 'bulbous plants', with corsages of Easter lilies for the Sunday. Mother's Day was 'becoming of greater value each year', 'despite the encroachment by other trades'.[75] Part of this general growth had to do with promotion, known as 'educating the public'. That involved transforming tastes. 'The education of the public to the wearing of any flower, instead of the traditional carnation, has made matters easier. In fact, many florists avoid the sale of carnations altogether.'[76] So a deliberate effort was

---

[73] Laurie 1930.

[74] In 1991 the estimated sales of flowers on St Valentine's Day in the United States were 400 million dollars. (*Washington Post*, B.1, 14 February 1991, quoting *Floral Index* (Chicago)). That is the biggest day's sale of the year, equalling the week before Mother's Day though less than for the month-long Christmas period. Of the flowers, 70 per cent are roses, purchased by men; mostly these are red, but some are yellow (said to stand for friendship), others white for purity and pink for happiness. The extent of this demand, and its concentration on a particular day, doubles the price to as much as 100 dollars for a dozen.

[75] Mother's Day has largely taken over from Mothering Sunday, the fourth in Lent, which was instituted as the day parishioners visited their 'mother' church, the cathedral of their diocese. Only in the seventeenth century did it become associated with honouring mothers, often with a gift of flowers. It became a day when country girls in service were allowed home to greet their mothers.   [76] Laurie 1930:70.

made to exclude the traditional and less expensive carnation in order to maximise sales, using the emotions generated by the day for that purpose. 'The psychological effect of mother love', writes Laurie, who was professor of floriculture at Ohio State University, 'is a great stimulus to buying.'

Memorial Day, however, 'is of no great value to the city florist', but some business is done at shops near cemeteries, especially for wreaths and bouquets for the graves. This ceremony was established to commemorate those who died in the Civil War, and the survivors of other wars paraded through the streets to the local cemetery. Subsequently people used this day, at the end of May, to remember all the dead, not only the military dead. In many places, rather than flowers, miniature versions of the national flag (much used and of great significance throughout America) are often placed on the graves at this time. However, in parts of America the flowers were used to decorate graves of family members. In Minnesota, for example, the parade ended at the cemetery, where in the morning people had taken flowers gathered from their gardens or from the fields; hence the lack of significance for the florists' trade. Such attention to the graves of family dead depends upon some descendants remaining in the area, to whom kin may send an annual sum to provide flowers on their own behalf. But the same service can also be provided by a professional florist.[77]

Many of these uses of flowers are relatively new, even for funeral flowers: 'today the major mourning symbol, and a huge item of national expenditure, [they] did not make their appearance in England or America until after the middle of the nineteenth century, and only then over the opposition of church leaders'.[78] In fact, flowers were used in Elizabethan times; although Puritans were not in favour of such offerings, such attitudes became of decreasing public significance. Today funeral or 'sympathy' flowers account for more than half the dollar volume of all sales by retail florists in the United States.[79] The extensive use of flowers, still forbidden at orthodox Jewish funerals, was part of the commercialisation of death of which America was the foremost exponent, with the undertaker transforming himself into the 'funeral director'. The close co-operation between the two professions of florist and funeral director expressed itself in a joint interest in 'memorialisation', described as 'traditional American practice'. For 'it is only one step', declared a president of the Society of American Florists, from 'no flowers' to 'no funeral'.[80] That possibility of no flowers is sometimes inserted in funeral notices as PO, Please Omit (Flowers), but such notices have been the subject of great conflict between florists and newspapers. Many newspapers have been

---

[77] E., personal communication.   [78] Mitford 1963:198–9.

[79] Mitford 1963:40, 110, 191. The estimate was 65 per cent of 414 million dollars sales in 1960, that is, 246 dollars for each funeral; the comparable expenditure in England was 60–70 pounds, with relatively more being spent by the working classes. For the United States, another source gives the total figure for 1954 as 1.25 billion dollars, of which 85 per cent was for funerals and weddings.   [80] Mitford 1963:107–8.

pressed to refuse such statements altogether, as Jessica Mitford dramatically recounts. And there continues to be some tension between the professional organisers of funerals and the clergy or clients, who would often prefer *caritas* to *luxuria*, opting for the simple burial rather than the lavish ceremony. It is more frequently the Protestant clergy that express themselves against elaborate funerals, talking of 'pagan display'. These differences link up, on the one hand, with earlier Puritan traditions and, on the other, with Catholic views on the fate of the soul.[81] But they also bear out the way marketing pressures have tended to overcome earlier hesitations about luxury.

For particular occasions, Laurie counsels, special emblems should be produced. Floral pieces can be made for meetings of the Masons or the Odd Fellows, though such confections were then getting rarer, because 'the florist is gradually educating the public away from the set piece', probably because of the amount of work involved. That was especially true of funerals, when little profit could be made. A new opportunity opened up when the use of rapid communication provided a method of increasing the effectiveness of the injunction, 'Say it with Flowers.' Already in 1892 the Florists' Telegraphic Delivery began to replace the direct delivery of flowers by post, and the business of Interflora and other agencies has expanded ever since. Today there are few florists who are not involved in enabling people to send flowers they have never seen.

In these various ways the process of profit maximisation promoted the sale of flowers both at ceremonies and for personal celebrations. At the same time, it cut away at traditional uses when these conflicted with gain, namely, in discouraging set pieces at funerals and carnations at Easter. Another remarkable injunction occurs in connection with Laurie's attempt to improve bookkeeping. Prior to 1917, when the government introduced an income tax on business profits, books of account in small retail stores were 'conspicuous by their absence'. Bookkeeping, he argued, helps calculate costs and hence reduce them. Record the sales and don't give extra measure: 'It is no kindness to yourself or the patron to place an extra rose in the dozen.'[82] In his search for profit Laurie seems to be unaware of the European custom that people do not give even numbers of roses, only uneven ones.[83] Indeed, today this custom has little force in the United States, although some flower sellers still provide thirteen roses for the dozen. Once again the pressures of profit, like the earlier pressures of puritanism, tended to thin out the symbolic aspects of the culture of flowers.

At the same time as florists modify some traditions, they cling to other aspects (indeed they invent new ones) in order to promote their product. For

---

[81] Mitford 1963:252.   [82] Laurie 1930:60.
[83] In Chinese flower arranging every effort is made to avoid pairs of blooms.

example, one Italian florist in West Haven produced a card purporting to give the meanings of the Language of Roses in order to assist his customers:

Red   I love you forever
White   Innocence, purity, loyalty
Pink   Perfect happiness
Yellow   I'm sorry . . . disappointed.

The first two of these meanings are embedded in popular consciousness. But others belong to a fabricated Language of Flowers, the equivalent of which is found in florists' shops in many parts of the world. Laurie himself refers to the use of flowers in the sacred rites of primitive society, which 'encouraged a taste for horticulture even among the uncultured tribes'. Calling particular attention to flowers as 'symbolic emblems' at the same time he offers interpretations that derive from this highly literary 'language', from the invented cultures of the elite, rather than popular practice, past or present.

The Language of Flowers was a creation of the French bourgeoisie, adopted for the amusement and edification of the middle classes in nineteenth-century America as part of the process of domesticating the foreign mind. While it had only a minimal relation with contemporary practice, it did have some influence on commercial culture. In this way it assisted the growth of the market and helped transform the puritanical attitudes that marked not only New England but much of the rest of the country. Even today, outside California the ritual uses of flowers are little developed. But if the American culture of flowers was decidedly thin, except at the commercial level, what was the practice among the 'elder people' of Europe, especially in those areas where puritanism left little permanent trace?

10 · The popular culture of flowers in Europe

Looking at the European past we have found a variety of 'codes' which involved the symbolic use of flowers, the religious, much elaborated from the thirteenth century onwards, at the same time the heraldic, again visible to all but potent to few, the Language of Flowers, an even more deliberate creation than the others. Few of these codes, which were largely pan-European, had any profound influence on the popular mind, except for some aspects of the religious. The culture of flowers that was actually practised, whatever the class, differed considerably from any of them, although all had some relation to 'popular' actions and beliefs.

We have already seen that writings on the Language of Flowers provide a misleading account of the symbolic codes of flowers in Europe, let alone of what people actually do, even though that language still has a limited currency among florists and in books on *savoir-vivre*. Other literary sources pay considerable attention to plants and gardens but little to the role of flowers in human interaction. For recent times some of the most useful sources are the surveys produced by professional associations interested in the sales of cut flowers and potted plants. Nevertheless, their information on use remains restricted and of course omits the whole range of garden and wild flowers, concentrating exclusively on the commercial.

For the recent past I have turned to the material provided by folklorists, for the present to the observations of anthropologists and others. My aim is to show something of the range of the culture of flowers in Europe but more specifically to direct attention to the varying boundaries of such behaviour, which often tend to disregard what we think of as societies and cultures, at times cutting across such socio-political units, but sometimes marking smaller collectivities, sometimes wider sets of relationships, sometimes individuals themselves within larger units, and in some cases representing half-formulated notions of a sub-cultural kind. In my view a consideration of this varying range of 'custom' should modify ideas of the holistic and particularistic nature of 'a culture' as it is often conceived.

It would be impossible, for the reader, for myself and for the publisher, to provide a comprehensive review of the role of flowers in contemporary Europe. Instead I want to concentrate on three facets that take up earlier themes and develop a new one.[1] First of all I look at the use of flowers in one ritual context, that of death, since that topic links more closely with other sections of the book. Secondly, I examine the significances of two flowers, the chrysanthemum and the rose; while the broad variations in the meanings of the chrysanthemum are largely confessional, those of the rose are historically complex, domain specific and exhibit a multitude of boundaries, partly transnational, but not mainly because of the influence of the written Language of Flowers. Thirdly, I return to aspects of the heritage of puritanism, to account for some larger differences within Europe, including the socialist countries; I also treat of flowers in the village in order to point to differences at a local level. Finally, I return to discuss the contemporary market and what that tells us about the culture of flowers in Europe.

FOLKLORE AND THE RECENT PAST; RITUALS OF DEATH

Leaving on one side the uses of flowers and foliage in church services, which we have already looked at, the records of folklorists provide what literature and formal documents rarely do, some indication of their uses at the major annual festivals, as well as at those connected with the rituals of the human cycle, especially rituals of love and marriage, and those of death and the dead, both sets of which suffered the adverse attentions of early Christians and later Reformers.

   Death has its rituals that focus on both the individual and collective levels. In the post-Elizabethan period in England the tributes at funerals, as at marriages, were evergreen rather than floral; they were also marked by class. Writing in 1656 during the Commonwealth, a herbalist notes that 'cypress garlands are of great account at funerals among the gentler sort, but rosemary and bays are used by the commons both at funerals and weddings.'[2] Rosemary sprays continued to be used in the early eighteenth century,[3] but from then on flowers came increasingly back into favour, although much less use is made of them at funerals and in cemeteries than in France. Nowadays wreaths of whatever type are usually the products of the florist's shop rather than the hands of local people. In the Lot in south-west France it is burials that draw many to the church who do not go there at other times and that is the time, apart from All Saints', when most flowers are purchased, especially the big arum lilies that are not found in cottage gardens. Even in our secular age it is difficult to die, or at least be buried, except in a religious mode. At funerals the

---

[1] On the advice of the publisher I have excluded not only sections on rituals of love, but also a chapter entitled 'The shapes of flowers' dealing with the different forms in which they are used, a chapter on Japan, a general theoretical chapter and short appendices on 'The classification of flowers', 'Heraldic flowers', 'Artificial flowers', 'Flowers in New Guinea' and 'Flowers in Polynesia'. I mention this only to draw attention to the fact that these topics were not neglected and I may publish on them elsewhere.

[2] For Elizabethan literary references to the double usage of rosemary, see H. Jenkins, editor of *Hamlet*, 1982, pp.537–8.   [3] Litten 1991:144.

provision in France is greater than in England, where with the increasing popularity of cremation, flowers are less in demand. Moreover, announcements of 'No flowers by request' are becoming more popular, at least among the middle classes where they may be seen as a waste of money that might go to worthier causes.[4] A recent survey showed that 29 per cent of funeral notices in *The Times* mentioned a charity and 17 per cent said specifically 'no flowers'. The sending of flowers is still very important, especially in working-class households, though there is some shift from traditional wreaths to sprays (Colour plate x.1). Even with cremation, which now accounts for two-thirds of all burials, flowers continue to be sent by many and are often recycled to hospitals and residential homes, where flowers have an ambivalent meaning; recycled flowers are rarely welcomed, being viewed as premonitions of death.[5] As a result, large amounts are spent; the average attendance at funerals was thirty-eight persons, the average cost of flowers 23 pounds, so that some 500 pounds is spent at the florists.[6]

Similar developments and similar class differences appear in France. However, flowers, especially wreaths, are seen as more essential for a grave – certainly of the recently dead – than for an urn containing the deceased's ashes. The mode of disposing of the dead is clearly affected by eschatological beliefs and in turn affects the accompanying gifts. There is a certain finality about a burning that is not altogether consistent with the more physical ideas of resurrection, which have in any case been threatened, not only by the secularisation of belief and the spiritualisation of religion, but also by medical requirements for spare-part surgery. All of this, among the middle class, makes flowers for the dead less imperative than flowers for the living.

Death also had its communal rituals linked to the annual cycle. While one major use of flowers centred round love and 1 May, the other, exactly six months later, focused on death and 1 November, especially in the Catholic church with its celebration to the dead at All Saints' and All Souls'.

In the cemeteries of France at ordinary times, flowers continue to be important even after the funeral itself. But in the south-west the tombs are then adorned with artificial flowers in ceramic or plastic. It is usually women who look after the graves, cleaning off the moss and seeing to the decorations, just as they provide the flowers inside the church both for the altars and for the statues of saints. In some cases the women from a family will all gather at the grave of a close relative. But for most people, including those living at a distance, it is All Saints' and All Souls' that provide the occasions to visit the cemetery. Even more than the rites of May, the rituals of death bore the mark of extra-community interests for they fell almost entirely within the orbit of the church, where they largely remain to this day. Indeed, nowadays some

---

[4] *The Market for Flowers*, 1982, p.23.   [5] Wilmott 1986; 15–16.
[6] *Families, Funerals and Finances*, report of the Department of Health and Social Security, and *Which*, November 1982, quoted by Wilmott.

rural churches are only open for this one occasion, the Day of the Dead, to receive the relatives living elsewhere.[7] Residents and relatives eye each other carefully to see what flowers have been brought and who has not come, for it is inevitably a time when family disputes tend to surface.[8]

In the Lot today, Toussaint is the great festival for flowers. The local market places are full of chrysanthemums during the previous week. Writing at the end of the nineteenth century, one French author speaks of the avalanche of flowers, of roses, chrysanthemums and *immortelles*, that descends upon the cemeteries on 1 November, when the bells ring for the feast of the dead.[9] While many different flowers are used at funerals, roses and *immortelles* have become less common at All Saints', when it is the chrysanthemum that dominates.

All Saints' provides an important part of the sales of flowers in France, amounting to a 1,000 million francs in 1984, one-quarter of the amount spent annually for cemetery flowers. More than one-half of the households (54 per cent) placed flowers on tombs, each spending an average of 100 francs (10 pounds or 15 dollars).[10] In 1986 a local nurseryman in Bagnac, Lot, planted large numbers of these flowers so that they would mature at the right time of the year. To profit from this market he had to calculate the moment of planting and the moment of cutting, taking into account the vagaries of the weather. On this occasion that let him down. While flowers grown for any festival may bring higher profits, the grower is also subject to greater risks since he has to work to a precise timetable. Success brings good profits, but flowers specific to a festival like chrysanthemums are worth nothing the next day. Of the flowers that are bought on this occasion the great bulk (75 per cent) is chrysanthemums in pots. There is nowadays some tendency to enlarge the range of plants offered, especially among the young. While these latter are at first less committed to tradition, in the course of the life-cycle they come to take their responsibilities more conservatively. People buy their flowers from the market, from the florist and increasingly from supermarkets, which organise their sales towards this special occasion. In addition, a significant proportion of people grow their own chrysanthemums for the cemetery.

The festival of All Saints' on 1 November had its origin in the conversion of the Pantheon at Rome into a Christian place of worship in the seventh century and its dedication by Pope Boniface IV to the Virgin and all the Martyrs. The anniversary was first celebrated on 1 May but was later moved to its present

---

[7] It was the complaint of a curé of Causse, Lot, in 1989 that people confused All Saints' with All Souls' (Le Jour des Défunts), giving all their attention to their family graves.

[8] In one recent case in the region a man was about to divorce his wife and marry a younger girl when he was killed in a car crash. At Toussaint the new fiancée brought a huge bunch of flowers to his grave. But she was followed by the wife who threw out the tribute of her rival. His sister, who is fully informed about these happenings, now puts a name-tag on her offering to make sure they are not removed. I am greatly indebted to Pascale Baboulet for letting me share the results of her research.

[9] Mauméné 1900:140.   [10] *Toussaint 1984: l'analyse du marché*, CNIH, 1985.

date. It is followed by All Souls' Day which was introduced in the early eleventh century when it had clear affinities with the doctrine of Purgatory developed in the two centuries that followed. It is at All Souls' in particular that prayers are said in order to release the souls of the faithful from that twilight zone.[11] In Catholicism attention after a person's death can influence the fate of his soul; for the Protestant the dead is already damned or saved – there is no intermediary stage.

That festival is still retained in the Anglican calendar, though not in that of other Protestant churches. Such behaviour was sheer paganism to Protestants. With the rejection by the Reformers of the notion of Purgatory, burial places were looked upon with very indifferent eyes. One could no longer help the dead with one's prayers, nor could the dead intervene on behalf of the living. All Saints' lived on only as a secular festival, largely for children, for it was the occasion for the development of Hallowe'en, the Eve of All Hallows or All Saints, on 31 October. Writing in the nineteenth century, Chambers remarked that there was a remarkable uniformity in the fireside customs of this night all over the United Kingdom, but his examples come mainly from Scotland, Ireland and the north of England.[12] It is the time when spirits walk abroad, especially those of the dead, and give the living an opportunity to consult them. So it becomes the time for divination, especially the playful divining for partners in marriage by means of a series of games, as we learn from Robert Burns' poem, 'Hallowe'en':

> The auld guidwife's weel-hoordet nits
> Are round an' round divided,
> An' mony lads an' lasses' fates
> Are there that night decided. (lines 55–8)

Nuts provided only one way of telling one's fate, which could also be discovered by ducking for apples, pulling the 'kailstocks' (or stalks of colewort), putting one's finger, while blindfolded, in the twee luggies or dishes and by looking in a mirror. The first two were still practised in Aberdeenshire in the 1930s, as games rather than as fortune telling. But in England the celebrations of Hallowe'en were virtually eliminated by the anti-Catholic celebration of 5 November, the day in 1605 when Guy Fawkes plotted to blow up the Houses of Parliament in the abortive gunpowder plot. Today, fireworks are let off, bonfires built and the 'guy' burnt. For days beforehand children used to accost passers-by asking for a penny for the guy to spend on the celebrations, but increasing affluence has led to its virtual disappearance.

[11] All Saints' may have had its roots in earlier festivals of the dead, but in its present form it was the invention of the Catholic church. Since the development of these festivals took place after the beginning of the establishment of the Western church as a partially independent body, it is absent from the Orthodox world. The equivalent was the commemoration of the dead at Psychosavato, the main ceremony of which takes place on the eighth Sunday after Easter. It is especially on the eve when people take flowers to the cemetery.
[12] Chambers 1869:519.

In Scotland and Ireland, which had less interest in the fate of the English parliament, the old celebration on the eve of All Saints managed partially to escape the axe wielded by the puritanical Protestants of the kirk. The festival continued, but in the form of the mild familial occasion, whereas in England itself simply the occasional telling of ghost tales remained.

On the other hand, in South America, the celebration of All Saints' Day, and especially All Souls', is an even more elaborate occasion. Julian Pitt-Rivers speaks entertainingly of the Vispíra de los Difuntos, the day on which he delivered his inaugural address:

And I can see in my mind's eye what is happening at this very moment in some hundreds of Mexican cemeteries where parties of celebrants are repairing, burdened with sweet sticky foods and demijohns of rum, to sit upon the tombstones for the next few days and nights, strumming tipsily on their guitars, letting off rockets (and sometimes pistols too) and uttering periodically that piercingly defiant drunk's cry, so uniquely Mexican, that inspired one of the finest passages in the writings of the poet Octavio Paz.[13]

The use of flowers is not simply an import from the West but a continuation of the elaborate flower culture of pre-Columbian Mexico.[14]

The festival of Hallowe'en is widely celebrated in the United States, especially by children as well as by young adults. However, outside Louisiana, even American Catholics pay little heed to All Saints' Day itself and less to All Souls', at least for visits to the cemetery. As a Catholic acquaintance from North Carolina remarked, 'that would be a very spooky thing to do'. The predominantly Protestant ethos of the North swamps any movement to celebrate in a manner recognisable to Mediterranean Catholics.[15] In the east of the United States, the general thinness of ceremonial, including the ceremonial use of flowers, stands in great contrast to the tradition that developed in Catholic Europe after the twelfth century and the difference was often remarked upon by visitors to Italy, where as distinct from the south-west of France, it is fresh flowers that are found throughout the cemeteries. Such abundance of gifts that fade mean the graves receive constant care and

---

[13] Pitt-Rivers 1974:1.

[14] I am specially indebted to Christine and Stephen Hugh-Jones and to Elizabeth Reichel. While I have not been able to discuss the significant role of flowers in pre-colonial America, wishing to concentrate on the old world, it is worth noting that this efflorescence occurred within a complex horticulture of the general kind found in Europe and Asia; it seems to be absent among the indigenous peoples of North America and those in the Amazon region to the south.

[15] Irish Catholics behave differently. People go to the church for the Feast of Holy Souls where they say prayers for the poor souls and are given a plenary indulgence for their attendance. But while some may go to the cemetery, they do not take flowers. That is not the result of an aversion to placing flowers upon the grave since this they do at Christmas time, and during the rest of the year they carefully tend the graves, planting flowers and decorating them in an 'Italianate' fashion, with Holy pictures and sometimes with photographs. With Catholics in the United States a similar mass is held, followed in some cases by a procession to the cemetery, but little is done with flowers either on that day or on any other.

attention, which are associated not only with religious doctrines and familial attitudes, but also with the temporary occupancy of the grave sites and the associated cult of bones.[16]

MARKED FLOWERS

The ceremonial meanings of flowers at rituals of love and death are linked to their wider use in social life, to their 'symbolic' significance in other forms of interaction and especially to their continuing role as gifts. One of the most striking features of the culture of flowers in Europe, developed in the Netherlands at the time of the Renaissance, has been the use of cut flowers as gifts, gifts which can then decorate a room or mark a grave. I will again focus on those flowers connected with death, on the one hand, and with love, on the other, especially the chrysanthemum and the rose. I consider cultural variants of the gross or external sort, as well as the more subtle internal definitions of meaning by the context of social intercouse, that is, by differing 'codes' which are variously subject to changes over time, and whose very co-existence inevitably provides some dynamic for change.

The chrysanthemum is a flower of the autumn, which affects its practical and symbolic uses in Europe and elsewhere. In France, Italy and southern Germany, it is closely linked to autumnal rites for the dead, to the rites of All Saints'. So closely are chrysanthemums identified with the offerings to the dead in those countries that they cannot be offered to the living. On one occasion when I was about to present a Chinese colleague with a bunch of yellow chrysanthemums (a pot would have been more appropriate), an Italian friend pulled at my arm, saying 'You can't do that, they are *fiori dei morte*, flowers of the dead.' In 1991 I visited a florist in rue Daguerre, Paris, where pots and vases of chrysanthemums were labelled 'Marguerites'. When I asked the proprietor, he smiled, saying, 'Otherwise no-one would buy.' A customer approached and wanted assurance that they really were marguerites as she wanted them as a gift. She was promptly reassured.[17]

This is not the case throughout Europe. In the first place, the Western church had largely separated itself before this ceremony was established. On the other hand, the Protestant church decisively rejected these ceremonies. So neither in the areas dominated by the Orthodox and the Protestant religions does the chrysanthemum carry any funereal meaning.[18] In fact, even Catholics in predominantly Protestant America and Jews in predominantly Catholic France generally accept the symbolic status of the flower as defined in the

---

[16] See 'Flowers and bones: the approach to the dead in Anglo-Saxon and Italian cemeteries' by J. Goody and C. Poppi, forthcoming.   [17] In botanical terms marguerites are members of the chrysanthemum family.
[18] In the Midwest of America during the fifties, different coloured chrysanthemums were worn by the supporters of opposing football teams – another use for an autumnal flower.

dominant religion. But that meaning extends well beyond the religious sphere, into the secular one of gifts to the living.

Since its introduction to Europe there has been a radical change in symbolic status of the chrysanthemum from a flower of fertility and longevity in China to one of death in Catholic areas of Europe. The word 'chrysanthemum' comes from the Greek for the golden flower. The name was applied, by herbalists at least, to the wild corn marigold, as *Chrysanthemum segetum*.[19] The history of this process of naming reveals something of the changing conceptualisations of flowers. The common name, marigold, refers to the bright-yellow colour and like many other flowers, it is sacralised by association with the name of the Virgin Mary. This name was in no way specific, for the word 'marigold' was used, like many other English plant names such as forget-me-not, 'corn' and 'millet', for a number of plants not only over time but at one and the same time in different regions. In this fluid system of classification there was but little of the 'scientific' use posited by devotees of 'ethnoscience', nor yet in the more usual sense of 'systematic knowledge', except perhaps at a very local level.

That situation was changed by herbal specialists who produced a 'learned' Greek name to include in their texts. These practitioners adopted a more systematic approach to properties and identification in their books on plants, which were usually created for the guidance of the specialist rather than the public audience. That audience was limited but nation-wide, often continent-wide, so the names for plants had to be taken out of specific local contexts to be applicable throughout Christendom in an unambiguous fashion. Finally, in a further development in the structure of knowledge, Linnaeus and other botanists created a new system of classification, though related to that of the herbalists which in turn had its origin in common usage. The new systematics compared the structure of plants using a wider range of data and made more precise genetic assumptions about their relationships. The resulting system was standardised, accepted by the developing community of scholars in Europe, and broadcast throughout the 'world system' by virtue of the colonial expansion of that continent.

The chrysanthemum in question, the *Chrysanthemum sinense*, was

---

[19] There were a number of other forms of chrysanthemum found in Europe. The *C. coronarium* was the crown daisy or garland chrysanthemum, known to Parkinson as the chrysanthemum or corn marigold of Candy, that is, of Crete, which had therefore been introduced before 1629 when he was writing. The Paris daisy (*C. frutescens*) came to France from the Canaries in the late sixteenth century, being associated with Marguerite de Valois and so sometimes known as the marguerite. The name of Marguerite, which means 'pearl', had already been linked with an earlier Margaret of Anjou, whose heraldic device contained three daisies. Then there is *C. parthenium* or feverfew, possibly indigenous and used, as the name suggests, for medical purposes. Later more complex forms developed which were held by Parkinson to be used for women's diseases 'to procure their monthly courses chiefly and as a special remedy to help those that have taken Opium too liberally. In Italy some used to eat the single kind among other green herbes . . . but especially fried with eggs' (Parkinson 1629:289).

brought back to Holland in 1688 but did not long survive.[20] It reached England in the middle of the eighteenth century, in 1764, but the flower was only successfully introduced following its importation to Marseilles in 1789 by a merchant, M. Blanchard. Further varieties were imported from China and its cultivation caught on; during the next twenty years eight new types were introduced from that country.[21] Only in the middle of the nineteenth century was the flower developed for commercial purposes in the vicinity of Toulouse. In England it was grown in Kew Gardens in 1790, where it had been sent from France. The flower soon attracted the attention of the East India Company which at once began importing other varieties, including Japanese. In that country techniques of breeding had created chrysanthemums whose large size, fantastic forms and a range of colours were to prove a great attraction to European gardeners. Many of these flowers were first introduced to England by Robert Fortune following his successful plant-hunting expedition to China from 1843 to 1846 for the Horticultural Society of London, from where he sent home the Chusān daisy, the ancestor of the pompons. However, already in 1825 the first chrysanthemum exhibition was held in this country and from then on it became, together with the rose, the dominant exhibition flower. One great attraction in the capital was the annual display held in the Temple and Inner Temple Gardens from 1850. Gradually such competitions moved down the social scale from the aristocracy and the bourgeoisie (or their gardeners) to the working class; in 1880, there is a reference to a 'working men's chrysanthemum show', with the name of the flower itself being abbreviated to 'mums'. In France, the otiose president of the Third Republic was referred to as 'an opener of Chrysanthemum shows', a phrase that has become a proverbial expression for the ritual activities of the holders of high but empty office.

A shift in meaning from China to France is hardly surprising, especially given the character of the intermediaries, those plant hunters who snatched the flowers from their cultural habit and brought them back to a European public whose demands for the exotic were constantly increasing. Neither party was interested in the symbolic meanings given to them abroad. What is surprising, on the other hand, is the speed with which this change happened. In becoming the flower of the dead, the Chinese chrysanthemum seems either to have filled a void or to have created a niche. Other representatives of the species, such as the corn marigold, were native to Europe but apparently were never given this significance. In England no flower was uniquely associated with offerings to the dead in the same way (not even *les immortelles*, rosemary or lilies). However, in Southern Europe white carnations were associated with funerals and in parts of Italy the periwinkle was earlier known as the flower of

---

[20] On the early history of the chrysanthemum in Europe see Gorer 1978:72ff.   [21] Emsweller 1947:26–7.

the dead since it was woven into funeral garlands, especially for children. But that practice was disappearing in 1880, at the time the chrysanthemum was taking over.[22]

In France there is some local evidence of flowers that one did not offer because of their association with the dead. In the north of France, 'white pansies, which are a symbol of death, should not be included in bouquets that are offered to the living'. In a similar vein, we are told that in Marseilles people do not present fresh flowers to small children because it brings to mind those that are put on their coffin.[23] That ambivalence towards flowers is sometimes found in hospitals. The restricted range of these practices deserves further comment, but both are indices of the tendency to forbid as gifts for the living those flowers that are linked to death, a very different notion to that involved in the commemoration of the dead in East Asia where the dead are offered those items, food, drink and flowers, that most pleased them in life. So there is no dichotomy between flowers with bad and those with good associations, 'les fleurs du mal' and 'les fleurs du bonheur'.

So the symbolic meaning has been totally transformed from that current in China or Japan where the flowers came from. There they are also used as autumnal offerings to the dead, as part of an offering that includes food and wine, all elements of which are positively valued. However, in the relatively short time the plant has been imported into Europe, it has acquired a deep significance of the opposite kind, enshrined in the song ('Le Testament') by Georges Brassens:

> Effeuillant le chrysanthème,
> Qui est la marguerite des morts.

Here we have a neat juxtaposition between the flower of death and autumn, on the one hand, and the daisy as the flower of love and spring, on the other, the cultivated against the wild, and perhaps the adult's wreath against the child's daisy chain, daisies and buttercups being, as a friend remarked, the silver and gold of children. They are made up into the simplest form of the Eurasian garland, or the petals may be plucked off one by one in a divining game.[24]

Wild flowers are essentially the play things of children, the domesticated varieties for adults. Grown-ups do not normally give wild flowers as gifts, but children gather them for their mothers. These flowers they are allowed to gather on their own; as children we went into the woods of Hertfordshire to gather armfuls of bluebells, and bunches of primroses, cowslips and violets. Such behaviour would have been forbidden in the garden, and is now

---

[22] Lambert 1880:825.   [23] Sébillot 1906:iii, 471.

[24] On buttercups and gold, see Beals 1917:66ff. On daisy chains and College rites in America, see pp. 83ff. The daisy is known as bairnwort, the children's flower, in Scotland. In different parts of Britain there are a number of taboos surrounding the daisy which often relate to children (Jones and Deer 1989:19).

becoming increasingly so in the wild under pressure from ecologists to protect rare species.

The games that children play with wild flowers remain in the memory and are transmitted from one generation to the next, often in similar forms all over Europe. The favoured flowers are particularly those that grow in grass, especially in grassy lawns where they represent the available wild or weed in the midst of forbidden cultigens. So foremost among these is the daisy which, while the younger children make into daisy chains, the older ones use as a 'devinette'. The game is played both in England and France but with some slight differences. In England, the code is usually binary: 'she loves me, she loves me not'; in France the choice is often from four or more possibilities, 'il m'aime, un peu, beaucoup, pas du tout' (Plate 10.1).

A similar kind of game is played with the familiar dandelion, after its yellow flower and salad leaves give way to a ball of reproductive fluff.[25] To divine you count how many puffs it takes to blow away the seeds, thus carrying out the wind's task of dissemination. Any subject can be divined in this way; in some places whom you would marry, tinker, tailor, soldier, sailor, in others to discover what trade you would follow. Both types of divination were marked out for children by the very use of wild flowers which they can pick without fear of the stern voice of adult authority.

In contrast to the chrysanthemum, the red rose stands for ardent love or martyrdom. In urban Europe as well as among the dominant populations of South and North America, which in this respect represent cultural outliers of Europe, the rose is the gift *par excellence* from a man to a woman he is courting. At one level it is universally understood.[26] Nevertheless, there are regional differences. In Europe, as has been mentioned, it is preferred to give in odd numbers and often one rose will suffice; that is also true in Brazil. But in the United States and Colombia a dozen means a dozen, not thirteen; one of the reasons is given in the previous chapter.

Timing also carries important meanings, both for courting gifts and for flowers brought by guests. In 1982 a professional survey of the uses of flowers in England contained the following comment; 'in the words of the psychologist who led our group discussion, "If a man gives a girl roses, she thinks tonight's the night". In one of these discussions an attractive young teenager told a story of how a man she knew sent her a dozen red roses *after* a date – this struck her and indeed struck the other members of her group as being extremely odd.'[27] In fact in upper circles, both in London and Paris, the practice would always be to send flowers after the meeting, possibly as an indication of intimacy achieved, possibly of intimacy devoutly wished for.

[25] Beals 1917:38.
[26] A French acquaintance regarded the gift of a white rose as being a particularly intimate gesture; more usually they are wedding flowers. These personal understandings reflect individual experience and may initiate more comprehensive changes of meaning.   [27] *The Market for Flowers*, 1982.

10.1 Flowers and the daisy: an elaborate form of 'She loves, she loves me not' on a French postcard, early twentieth century. (Love and the Daisy, Carte postale, Collection Belle Epoque, editions Postcard Selection, 75 rue Amsterdam, Paris, 74008)

10.2 Political use of the rose: the Labour Party emblem. (*Financial Times*)

However while sexuality and courting are primary references, as for St Valentine's and similar occasions, these by no means represent the unique significance of the red rose, for meaning depends upon the domain of discourse. The political use of flowers (and colours) as emblems is of as great importance today as it has been in the past. In France the red rose became the symbol of socialism only recently, picking up the colour of the flag: 'The people's flag is deepest red', stained of course with the blood of martyrs. These very strong associations have been tempered by the red rose in M. Mitterand's buttonhole, where it has become the emblem of a centrist political party, just as it has recently become for the British Labour Party (Plate 10.2). So too in the nineteenth century and much further back in the fifteenth, it was used as a marker of political factions in France and England respectively. In the Wars of the Roses, opposing sides took roses of different colours. In the past, as we have seen, flowers would take on a political significance of another kind. When they are growing in other people's gardens, especially the gardens of the rich, a flower such as a rose might be seen as an emblem of luxury, of class, of feudal dependence.[28] That was true of other species. In the province of Quercy

---

[28] Other flowers have played a notable political role. The violet was adopted by the Imperial Napoleonic Party when Napoleon, known to his followers as Caporal Violette, was exiled to Elba. French conscripts to the army were sometimes given flower names in the eighteenth century, though elsewhere such names have usually been associated with women.

(now the Lot) at the time of the French Revolution the decorative horse-chestnuts, aristocratically useless in comparison with the productive chestnut, the *marronnier* as opposed to the *châtaignier*, known as *marronnier d'Inde* to stress its foreign origin, were felled by the local peasantry of Fons along the drive leading up to the château. Such actions lead back to problems of 'class', creativity and change that mark not only in the Christian attitude to flowers but in Eurasian cultures generally.

In the religious domain the red rose stood for agape rather than eros, sometimes for the blood shed by Christ, less frequently for his mother, the Virgin Mary, of whom the rose was usually white. The domains are distinct and individuals can use them without any great sense of contradiction. Nevertheless, they are not walled gardens, let alone prisons, and at times meanings transgress boundaries. Moreover, meanings themselves are generative, especially in the work of poets who are more creative in their use of imagery and in their manipulation of symbols. Once again there is no hard and fast boundary between poet and peasant; one may be more agile and adept in his use of language but that is no unique privilege of intellectuals. Creativity is a characteristic of all human cultures, and of many individuals, at least in the use of language.

Given the different domain-specific meanings, given the changing political or religious scene that leaves a palimpsest of significances, it is not surprising that even in the simplest case of the red rose, meanings are multi-faceted and subject to change. These variations we find within the international culture of the red rose. With interpersonal gifts there are several dimensions of difference apart from the question of odd or even numbers. In France there is some tendency to view large gifts between persons as 'American'; a single rose is a sufficient token. Secondly, as we have seen, there is a class factor in the use and timing of floral gifts, especially of roses.

Apart from the chrysanthemum and the rose, a number of other flowers are strongly marked, mostly in the context of display. The most prominent of these is the carnation.[29] Its most obvious use is as men's buttonholes at weddings, especially for ushers, the use of which has spread to Japan and to Indian ceremonies in Leicester, England. But it was a flower of the buttonhole in a more general sense, formerly worn by city businessmen and men-about-town, plucked from their own gardens or bought from some flower girl at a street corner, now sported only by elderly gentlemen.[30] In Southern Europe it can also be used as a sexual challenge (and it even has a flavour of such in Northern buttonholes), for in many ritual ways carnations are the Iberian equivalent of roses. The carnation has been described as 'the symbol of the woman in Andalusia'. At the *feria* she will dress in the colourful clothes worn

---

[29] French *oeillet*; though with modifiers the word connotes a wide range of flowers of several different species.
[30] In England between the wars smart young men might wear carnations to a dance. I am indebted to Julian Pitt-Rivers, to Maria Pia di Bella and to other friends for comments on these topics.

by gypsies for dancing the flamenco, with her hair done in a low chignon on the neck and decorated with a red carnation, which is sometimes placed in the low-cut front of a dress.[31] Indeed, it has been said that the flamenco costume itself represents the petals of the carnation.[32] At bull fights these flowers are worn behind the ear, on the left if a girl is available, on the right if she is not;[33] that is the kind of semi-secret code which it is important to understand yet not to be aware of. At the successful conclusion of the fight the red carnation, which Julian Pitt-Rivers sees as symbolic of menstrual blood, is thrown into the bull ring like bouquets in the theatre. On the Greek island of Chios it is red carnations that a girl's suitors will leave on her doorstep during Carnival and she will pick up the gift of the one she favours.[34] In general it is a joyous flower.

Although carnations are worn and used in bouquets, in England they were rarely given, anyhow not as bunches; to do so was considered vulgar among the high bourgeoisie. In France too the carnation is not for giving and is even said to bring ill luck; in Italy, the white variety is used in funeral wreaths, and some see them as connected with the evil eye.[35] Similar associations are found in Brazil where white carnations are known as 'cravos de defunto', cloves or 'nails of the dead'; they are never given as gifts for that reason. Everywhere the flower is strongly marked, the direction of the marking depending upon its colour. Although rarely given as a gift, they are nevertheless widely used, forming one of the main floral products of Poland, of exports from France to Britain and from Colombia to the rest of the world.

The carnation carried yet other meanings in the religious domain. From the time of its appearance in Europe, that is, at the beginning of the fifteenth century, the Virgin and Child were sometimes painted with this flower, the significance of which emerges from its botanical name in latinised Greek, dianthus, the flower of God, giving rise to the French name, *oeillet de Dieu*.[36] At the same time, when a person is depicted as holding a pink in the hand, a

---

[31] The association of flowers with gypsy costume is strong. In Mérimée's story, from which the libretto was adapted, Carmen first meets the young soldier, Don José, when she was wearing a bouquet of acacia at the opening of her blouse and held another at her mouth. This she tossed at him, hitting him between the eyes, whereupon he picked up the bouquet and kept it in his jacket pocket (*Carmen*, translated by W. F. C. Ade, New York, 1977).

[32] Pitt-Rivers 1984:252-3.   [33] Compare the use of single earrings, left and right, in gay circles.

[34] Carnival is the time when marriages take place and orange blossoms are worn as a crown by both bride and groom. But it is also the time when visits are paid to the graveyard to take flowers for the dead, on the last two Saturdays of Carnival and the first Saturday of Lent.

[35] Gaudouin (1984) warns that superstitious souls in France may not appreciate carnations or heather as gifts.

[36] In many European languages carnations were called after the spice clove, because of the similarity of scents, hence clove gilliflower (1535) for the early domesticated varieties appearing in the fifteenth century. The shape of the spice had given rise to the name of clove, or nail, *clou de girofle* in French, giving *giroflée* for the wallflower, although in English the name was later applied to the carnation as well (sometimes transformed into July flower). In German a similar notion is attached to its name, *Nägelein*, which again provides a link with the passion of Christ because of its supposed resemblance to a nail of the Cross; in Van Eyck the wallflower provides yet another symbol of Christ. The complicated history of the carnation and its names is thoroughly examined in Harvey (1978). The English name 'carnation' does not seem to be connected either with the fleshy colour of the flower nor yet with the passion of Christ but possibly with its Turkish origin, though why this should have only been taken up in English is puzzling. The variety of *Dianthus plumarius*, known as 'pink' in English, gave its name to the colour rather than vice versa.

betrothal is signified. As with the rose, religious and secular imagery occupy different channels, whereas with the chrysanthemum, new as it is, a single significance dominates the whole range of social intercourse.

The process of marking flowers can be rapid in cultural terms. Another flower, wild rather than domesticated, became strongly marked as the result of a set of specific historical events earlier in the twentieth century. This was the Flanders poppy, proliferating in the churned-up soil of the battlefields of northern France, which became a symbol of the dead of the First World War, a sign of Remembrance Day, that the martyrs, those who have shed their blood for their country, are not forgotten.

Equally some flowers are marked by personal experience: laburnum has for me some of the magic of childhood about it because we often played under such a tree in the garden I first thought of as 'home'. For the first garden, or rather the garden in which one grew up, has a special significance so that the flowers and the garden of orientation (or birth) are not the same as those of the garden of procreation (or marriage), to adapt the phraseology of Lloyd Warner and at the same time apply the notion of the developmental cycle to the understanding of cultural matters. The garden that one establishes as a householder takes on a different quality; it embodies planning and work, and represents the position one has or hopes to attain in the world, being seen in the context of the neighbourhood one lives in, the neighbours one has, the wealth one can display. Whereas the garden of childhood one is born into represents pure pleasure, the scene of numberless games and adventures rather than space for work, competition and show. Such personal meanings may and often do become utilised in literature, especially as there is no single overarching 'code' or 'language' to which reference can be made. Such was the case with the 'catleya', the commonest of the orchids, in the works of Proust.[37] For him the image refers to sexual intercourse, a personal metaphor that he imposes on the work and on the reader.

Finally, the fifth of the marked flowers is the marigold, marked as its French name of 'souci' (trouble) would suggest, though the word derives from an earlier form, 'soulsi', indicating an association with the sun.[38] In France it is not a flower for giving, especially to someone about to depart on a voyage, but rather for growing in the garden.[39] Part of the problem of meaning lies in its golden colour. In Europe yellow flowers are sometimes considered to carry negative implications of infidelity and jealousy. In the Language of Flowers that is the significance, explicitly recognised by some people in France, in the gift of a yellow rose. Indeed, some families never give flowers of this colour

---

[37] 'Mais non, mon petit, pas de catleyas ce soir, tu vois bien que je suis souffrante.' Proust 1954:272; for the origin of this personal euphemism, see p.234.

[38] Beals 1917:151ff. In Mexico marigolds are said to be the flower of death, used in churches but not on festive occasions. See E. Carmichael and C. Sayer, *The Skeleton at the Feast*, London, 1991, p.10.

[39] In the Middle Ages, the marigold, one of the many flowers called after the Virgin Mary, was used as a bitter herb for culinary purposes.

and this was the situation reported by the ethnographers of Minot in Burgundy.[40]

This negative association is by no means universal, even in France, being rejected by many well-informed, culturally 'competent', persons. For while some meanings are quite personal, others are very local, perhaps growing out of personal experiences. Other meanings differ externally, as with the poppy, which never took root in France as the annual symbol of the Somme. Yet others like the carnation differ across groups of countries, as well as contextually. The chrysanthemum, the newest arrival, differs on a con-fessional basis, while in the domain of love, the red rose is widely accepted as a common symbol throughout the Western world, although differing locally in certain details as well as in different domains of social action, political, religious or in personal relations.[41]

FLOWERS IN THE VILLAGE

In the Burgundy village of Minot, as elswhere in France, and in other rural situations we have noted in Japan, Bali and India, flowers are not central to the garden in the physical sense, being planted 'on the perimeter, along the walls and on the edge of paths'.[42] Consistent with this peripheral position is a certain utilitarian or even 'puritanical' ambivalence. 'Too much time should not be spent on flowers', it is said. That is having it both ways. In fact a great deal of time is spent on cultivating them, on exchanging cuttings and on using them in various rituals, secular and religious. The author writes:

Garden flowers are also included in the exchanges that take place among members of the village group. They are given, in white bouquets, to the bride at weddings; and, arranged in country-style wreaths, they are placed on the coffins of the dead in church. They are the last offerings of the community to its daughters and its dead.

What is more important is that flowers establish a link between the living and the dead, between the sacred and the profane. Indeed, all through the year, flowers from the gardens are carried to the church. Lilac decorates the main altar in June; Madonna lilies adorn the statue of the Virgin; yellow flowers are laid in front of Saint Joseph. In the old days the girls of the choir were responsible for the church flowers. Nowadays Mass is no longer sung and the girls have no spare time; an old lady does

---

[40] Zonabend 1980.

[41] The woman who sells her home-grown vegetables and flowers at a stand in the local markets of the Lot seemed surprised at my question, 'Are there any flowers you cannot give a woman?' She laughed. 'Yellow ones?' I persisted. 'No, you can certainly give them if you know her well.' Then, on reflection, she remarked that there are some who don't like to give 'oeillets', carnations, as they spell trouble. My companion agreed. Her German mother did not relish carnations, and it seemed there was an ambivalent feeling about them in Malta where her father came from. I continued in my query. 'Up in Burgundy, they say, people don't like yellow flowers, even in the garden?' She laughed again, louder than before, 'Are they afraid of being "cocu" [cuckolded]?'. This meaning seems to be recognised by local florists as having been recently imported.

[42] Zonabend 1980:24. This study was one of four carried out in the village by Tina Jolas, Marie-Claude Pignaud, Nicole Verdier and Françoise Zonabend.

the job. She looks in gardens for roses that have hardly bloomed, half-opened peonies, dahlias in full flower, and she asks for a 'bouquet for the church'. The request is never refused. Garden flowers are also cut to decorate the little shrine at home set up on the refrigerator or dresser, where photographs of the dead parents and the statuette of the Virgin stand next to each other. Then, on Palm Sunday and All Saints' Day, primroses, pansies and chrysanthemums grown in the garden are carried to the cemetery to be put on the family tombs.

Garden flowers offered to protective saints and placed in the church establish a link with the sacred. By decking the church with the harvest of the home one assures the protection of the whole household. Placed on the little shrine in the parlour or on the family tombs, flowers perpetuate the memory of the dear dead, are part of the care one should bestow on them and help to secure the bonds between living and departed relatives.[43]

Those churchyard practices are widespread in Catholic France. Nevertheless, in the more scattered settlements of the Lot in the rural south-west, life has harsher edges. A few flowers are grown in the gardens around farmhouses for display or cutting, but it is around the new suburban villas, many inhabited by retired couples, where floral display overwhelms the passer-by. In secular activities fresh flowers play a peripheral role and it is artificial ones that often predominate. At weddings blue and white paper flowers decorate the bushes of evergreens, usually juniper, that are cut down and placed outside the houses of the betrothed pair, at the west front of the church and around the doors of the mairie. More rosettes decorate the cars in which the principals are driven to the ceremony. On the other hand, the church itself does benefit from the constant attention of its faithful who provide fresh flowers for services, as in Burgundy, though this represents not so much an 'exchange' of flowers among members of the village as one-way flow to the church.

Country people in the Lot rarely if ever give flowers to one another, either from their gardens or from the florist, though they may exchange cuttings and vegetables. In many of these respects the rural Lot resembles urban Paris rather than idyllic Burgundy; it is not the exchange of household produce that is at the root of village sociability, but rather the mutuality of services, paid and unpaid, together with joint participation in local pursuits. For it is predominantly in the framework of practical activities that interaction occurs, although the annual fête, the weekly markets, the Sunday mass and the occasional *meschoui* or outdoor meal provide more formal occasions.

The comments on Minot are a reminder that gardens and their contents are highly stratified. Formal gardens were always those of the upper groups containing the latest imports from abroad. In England too, before the nineteenth century, flowers in cottage gardens were generally adjuncts to the vegetables. Before the village became the playground of the commuting bourgeoisie during the last fifty years, country gardens contained characteristically different flowers from that of a town dweller, let alone the gardens of the gentry. There were long-standing varieties, like hollyhock and Sweet William, but by and large the flowers were not for cutting but for external display. However, as in Minot one major use of flowers from the garden, not from the florist, became the decoration of the church, at least after the mid century. In the country parishes of the Church of England, ladies of the village take on the responsibility of providing and arranging flowers from their own gardens or from those of others. Most books on flower arranging are devoted to the home but the church came to provide a great occasion for the display of one's talents and some manuals are devoted exclusively to this aspect of the art. Since the flowers are taken from local gardens, they follow seasonal patterns, although red and white blooms are preferred at Whitsun time. The subject of flower arranging and of flowers more generally is a pervasive theme of Barbara Pym's novel about an Oxfordshire village in the seventies, *A Few Green Leaves*.[44] The flowers in the church were provided by a rota of middle-class women from their own gardens. Once a year a flower festival was held in the church which was elaborately decorated for the occasion, again from local gardens. We do hear of a visiting florist who is employed to provide flowers for the tomb of the local gentry no longer living there, but by whom is not revealed. On some of the graves stood vases of artificial flowers, 'surely a disgrace in a rural area', comments the doctor's wife, asking the rector if there were not rules against that sort of thing.

While this aspect of life in rural England appears to resemble that in rural France, the convergence is both recent and partial. In the first place, in Nonconformist chapels flowers would often seem out of place, and certainly against the original spirit of those bare meeting halls of New England, where even the cross was associated with the papacy and no icons of any kind graced the walls. But in the Church of England too the widespread use of flowers in church is far from traditional, for many elements of the puritan reaction to flowers lived on.

THE PERSISTENCE OF PURITANISM

In earlier chapters I called attention to the fact that the extensive use of flowers may be accompanied by worries about their non-utilitarian nature; their beauty is evanescent and the investment of time, energy and money in them may be at the expense of less transient, less luxurious alternatives. At the level of popular culture such ambivalences emerge in conversation with individuals who cannot simply be regarded as 'peculiar' or 'deviant'. That underlying trend is institutionalised in various forms of puritanism, of socialism or types of charitable endeavour where other needs are given priority.

[44] London, 1980.

In any case earlier notions did not disappear overnight and there was an active continuation of puritanical ideas, especially in America. At a general level those ideas emerge in the preference of Loudon, the great English nineteenth-century designer, for 'garden cemeteries' without flowers as well as in the objections of others to the continental decoration of graves.[45] It is in 'Continental churches', remarks an English writer in 1863, that all manner of flowers are found in the month of May, Mary's month.[46] More generally yet the attitude continues in the notices inserted in newspapers in Europe and America asking for contributions to a favoured fund rather than flowers for the dead. In this way such ideas continued to influence the culture of flowers, especially the religious culture, in Anglo-Saxon countries, long after puritanism itself ceased to be so central.

Dramatic instances of the persistence of these notions occur in the nineteenth century where prosecutions could be brought in the ecclesiastical courts for superstitious innovations in the services of the Church of England under the Public Worship Regulation Act of 1874 and under earlier acts. In *Elphistone* versus *Purchas*, the Reverend J. Purchas of St James's, Brighton, was accused of causing vases of flowers to be placed on the holy table as a devotion, an act 'being intended by you and constituting a ceremonial and symbolical observance'.[47] Fortunately for Purchas, the learned judge disagreed and found there was no evidence that 'the flowers were used as an additional rite or ceremony, or as an ornament . . . They appear to me an innocent and not unseemly decoration.' The difference between ornaments and decorations had been laid down in an earlier judgement, as indeed had the distinction between inert objects and those actually involved in ritual, for the distinction between worship and reverence was a constant theme of Christian theology and lay behind the question put to Jeanne d'Arc. In this case, the flowers were judged to be on a par with the branches of holly at Christmas and of willow blossom on Palm Sunday.

Many thought otherwise and considered the decision had 'suffered flowers to creep into the ceremonial of the Church of England'. Opponents drew attention to the fact that the use of flowers had grown in importance with the rise in influence of the Oxford Movement, with their teaching of the Real Presence in the eucharist, and with their general attachment to rituals associated with the earlier Catholic church.[48] The Oxford Movement had begun in reaction to the reforms of 1828–32 in the relations between church and state, following the abolition of the Test and Corporation Acts and the emancipation of Roman Catholics, together with the widening of the vote in

---

[45] For example, Minns 1905.   [46] Anon. 1863:234.
[47] Lambert 1880:814, quoting 3 *Law Reports*, Admiralty and Ecclesiastical, Cases 66.
[48] *Pall Mall Gazette*, 2 January 1875. On an elaborate 'high' Anglican floral calendar giving flowers appropriate to Christian feasts see Cuyler, 1862. In the preface her brother, an ordained priest, denies that such usages smack of superstition; flowers rather recall the life of Christ (*Pall Mall Gazette*, 20 April, 1878).

1832. Some looked back to the high-church, Caroline divines of the seventeenth century and sought to maintain the position of the Church of England by seeking authority in the teaching of the earlier undivided church rather than in the Bible alone, like the 'popular Protestants', or in the Council of Trent, like the Roman Catholics. After the secession of the intellectual teacher J. H. Newman to Catholicism in 1845, the movement spread quietly through the country, becoming associated with the search for 'more reverent worship and ceremonial in churches' based upon antique models. While there were conflicts over ritualism in parishes in London and elsewhere, the effects were widespread, leading to the establishment of monastic communities, the adoption of hymns and especially carols and to the slow but dramatic elaboration of ritual.[49]

Part of this process led to the reincorporation of flowers in worship. The use of flowers in church, certainly as ornaments but even as decorations, had been considered to be against the practices of the reformed church. But the return to ritual brought changes which were in tune with important elements in public opinion that welcomed their use. One observer in 1878 comments on the 'extraordinary spectacle' of Covent Garden Market which shows the general adoption of floral decoration at Easter in the London churches. These decorations were supplied both by a very active market as well as by flowers from the gardens of country gentry, giving a substantial profit to the growers as well as to the shopkeepers. Also elaborate floral tributes were not introduced, or reintroduced, at English funerals until the late 1860s. It was in 1889 that one observer commented on the fashion of sending costly wreaths to cover the coffin, as new in Paris as in London. Porcelain flowers beneath glass domes, mostly imported from Germany, made their appearance in the 1890s.[50]

A book on *Flowers and Festivals*, first published in 1867 with the subtitle of *Directions for Floral Decoration of Churches*, aimed to be a 'hand-book for those who wish to know how to set about decorating their Churches . . . for the various Festivals of the Christian Year'. An attempt was made to evaluate 'the various symbolical forms to avoid misunderstanding or creating the impression of "dark or dumb ceremonies"'. The book begins with the quotation, 'Let the old customs stand firm' and claims to show the virtually universal use of flowers and green boughs throughout the world but especially in Christianity. Examples are given of decorating the churches not only at Christmas and the great festivals of the liturgical year, but at those for local saints and even on May Day. Nevertheless, 'There are many persons who condemn the custom of so decorating the Church, as if there was something idolatrous in the simple and poetic practice.'[51] But such 'ancient customs of the church were more or less smothered by Puritanism'.

[49] Chadwick 1973.   [50] Litten 1991:170; Davey 1889:110.   [51] Barrett 1873:11.

The activities of the Oxford Movement led to a closing of the gap between Anglican and Catholic practices and beliefs, at least in the high church. They also led to wider changes in the rituals, including the use of incense and candles as well as the adoption of the mitre and the crozier by bishops, now accepted as intrinsic to their role. These changes can be regarded either as borrowings from Catholicism or as the restoration of practices of the earlier church. In any case, they represent a return to more elaborate ritual which includes the use of flowers, although such practices were still not immune from criticism from the evangelical or 'puritan' wing.

We have to separate the religious and ceremonial uses of flowers, which had such confessional implications, from the personal gifts of flowers, which, like domestic flowers and flower paintings in Holland, were less affected by these considerations. But affected they were in a certain measure. Especially in Scotland puritanical views overflowed into the secular domain and flowers were looked upon by some as unnecessary luxuries, as the products of an 'aesthetic' horticulture that distracts from the real aims of life, much as stained glass distracted men from the word of God. That view has also been an important theme of secular reformers too, who aim to improve the standard of living of peasant and worker by cutting out luxuries and redistributing riches. Before discussing the giving of gifts in Western Europe today, where these considerations are of marginal importance, I want to look at the fate of flowers in the socialist countries of the Eastern half.

THE ROSE UNDER SOCIALISM

How then have these notions affected the formerly socialist countries of Eastern Europe? Did those nations undergo any of the same transformations as the Chinese in the Cultural Revolution? Flowers were certainly widely used in Russia before the First World War. Mention has been made of the demand for flowers in rural Ukraine, which was catered to by the annual visits of part-time flower traders from Germany. Visitors to Moscow described the proliferation of flower stalls around the Kremlin, for they were also used extensively at all levels of urban society.

The ambiance for flowers certainly changed, both for representations and reality. The public art of the post-Revolutionary period stressed utilitarian production; a woman was more likely to be pictured holding a hammer than a flower and at times the motor tyre to replace the garland. Photographs of gatherings of the period show little use of flowers, except for funerals.[52] Certainly ecclesiastical uses all but disappeared. Nevertheless, after the initial radicalism, the secular uses of flowers remained high. Guests continued to take them to dinner and people offered them to friends and relations on other

---

[52] See Tolstoy *et al.* 1990; Razina *et al.* 1990.

occasions. The production of flowers continued partly on collective farms but mainly on private plots.[53] Flowers were flown to Moscow from the southern republics by private entrepreneurs where they found a ready market. Later on there was some importation of flowers mainly from their Eastern neighbours but even from further afield, since one French exporter had an agent in Moscow in 1986.[54] But on the whole the import trade fell away as the result of the managed economy. So too did the expensive boutiques, since the more opulent flowers of earlier times such as the heliotrope and the tuberose, which were favourites of the aristocracy and the bourgeoisie, disappeared after 1917. The result was a dual process of the centralisation and the democratisation in the use of flowers. The state employed large quantities for national events as well as for town gardens. They were provided in abundance for the funerals of the country's leaders. In particular favour were red blooms, especially carnations of which a new variety came into fashion, large, firm and without scent, suitable for every occasion, especially public ones. For the individual, choice and quantity became more restricted than before. But the demand remained strong and was never altogether suppressed by the kind of puritanical view of flowers that took hold in China. A recent visitor described the Moscow cemetery of Novochevichy (New Virgin) as 'a cheerily animated place' with flowers available for purchase at the gate. Visits continue to be made to the tombs of Soviet heroes and other citizens, including to some extravagant expressions of the individual spirit. 'Flowers act as a kind of afterlife popularity poll. . .', with the largest number being found around 'the breathtaking statue of a young girl mortally wounded, her cropped hair swept back to show where an ear was cut off during torture, and one breast exposed to Nazi bullets'. Excursion groups lay red flowers all around or fix red ribbons to the nearby branches.[55]

The years leading up to perestroika have undoubtedly improved the situation for flowers. There were times during what Hann calls the '"messianic phase" of the new "secular theology"''when such rituals would not have been permitted.[56] Nevertheless, flowers for personal use seem to have been one outlet where individual production made a substantial contribution. Today the range of outlets has increased. Old ladies from the country sell flowers under many an overpass and at street corners. The market has come into its own to such an extent that a distinguished Soviet economist reported a saying in Moscow that flowers are the one success of the free market to date.[57] That should cause little surprise in view of the Dutch experience, including the boom and bust of seventeenth-century Tulipomania.

[53] On the Soviet Union, I am grateful to Aaron Gurevich, Roslan Grinberg, Christel Lane and to a number of recent visitors to that country.
[54] Barjonet 1986.   [55] 'The talk of the town', *New Yorker*, 30 July, 1990, pp.26–8.
[56] Hann 1990 and for references to other works on Soviet and Eastern European rituals.
[57] The place, Berlin; the date, April 1990.

The culture of flowers persisted in the rest of Eastern Europe after the establishment of socialist regimes in the wake of the Second World War. These regimes were established as the result of invasion by an outside power rather than by internal revolution, so the use of flowers in religious and other activities continued to display greater adherence to the norms of earlier times, when the flower culture of the Bohemian region, for example, had been very close to that of the West. Religion was a potent factor. Chrysanthemums are no more welcome as gifts in Czechoslovakia than they are in Italy or France, and for similar reasons. The earlier symbolism which had been embodied in Christian iconography varied little over the continent. The same was true of nineteenth-century developments in the Language of Flowers which was taken up as vigorously in Budapest and Prague as in London and Edinburgh.[58] Those similarities arise out of a 'high', written, culture. Even at the popular level, the same largely Christian festivals were celebrated throughout, often in similar ways, although with local variations as well. These endured under some constraints. While religious services were not approved by the ruling Communist Party, both church services and popular ceremonies continued to be performed with some of their floral accompaniments. Today Easter in Prague brings out the catkins as well as the lilies, which take the place of olive twigs. Girls decorate eggs with floral designs, together with 'whips' which the boys use to force the girls to give them the eggs. Both eggs and whips are displayed on stalls in the Old Square of Prague where they attract many customers.

The cemeteries of that town are especially full of flowers around Eastertide. As in Germany, many of the graves of those who have recently died are carefully tended at all times and decorated mainly with potted plants or dried wreaths, though such tributes were considered 'common' in comparison with fresh flowers. Outside the main Olšany cemetery a cluster of flower shops and individual producers were busily selling potted plants, cut flowers, catkins, but above all a series of Easter 'confections', either pots, sprouting with green shoots, among which are placed a mixture of artificial and fresh flowers, or little wreath-like sprays, also decorated with fluffy yellow chicks.[59] For the house, pots are planted with barley or other grain earlier in the year and kept inside until this sprouts, then decorated with chicks and painted eggs; there is a similar practice in Bologna where grain is also planted for Easter, but blanched by being kept in the dark. As in California, the major ceremonies of

---

[58] On the Language of Flowers in Czechoslovakia, see Macura 1983.

[59] There is a middle-class feeling against the use of 'plastic' flowers. In April the florists had more of these than the fresh variety, which some local residents were quite surprised to have pointed out. I was also told that artificial flowers should not be put in the cemetery, but in Olšany they appear on 8 per cent of the newer graves. This is a rather similar percentage to that I have found in Britain and the United States but very different from Southern France, where they appear on some 80 per cent, and from north Italy, where they are virtually unknown.

the living are celebrated together with the recent dead, to whom one makes seasonal offerings.

The Jewish cemetery of Prague provided a dramatic contrast with the Christian burial places, not only at this but at all times of the year. The old cemetery in the centre of the town operated from 1439 to 1787, and was the site of 12,000 burials, in some places in layers twelve deep. Neither the bones nor the upright tombstones were ever moved, new burials simply being added on top of the old. The stones themselves bore written inscriptions but had only a few icons such as the crown, the pine cone and a bunch of grapes. The word reigned supreme, as it did in the adjacent Old–New synagogue, the oldest in Europe, in which there were no pictures and but few symbols apart from the Star of David. In a Christian cemetery as old as this, one would hardly expect flowers, for there would be no active descendants to decorate the graves. But here grew no blade of grass while the only offerings were small stones, placed on the tombs as a signal of respect and a record of attendance, under some of which a piece of paper had been stuck containing a prayer. The absence of flowers has nothing to do with its age, for the contemporary Jewish cemetery in East Berlin presents a similar appearance. So too do Jewish cemeteries in other parts such as the United States, Hong Kong and Britain. For orthodox Judaism is even stricter than early Christianity about any semblance of 'worshipping' the dead rather than God. Moreover, the Biblical association of offerings of flowers with pagan rites still persists; it is the word not the image or the offering that counts.[60]

It was not only church ceremonies that were celebrated with foliage or flowers in much of the Catholic continent but secular festivities, including May Day. In Czechoslovakia boys cut a tall maypole of spruce or birch, leaving a bunch of leaves at the top, together with an evergreen wreath to which streamers were attached. This pole was erected in the garden of the beloved, very much as at contemporary marriages in the Lot, where it remained until the end of the month. As well as these personal poles, another 'May' was planted in the middle of the village for all the unmarried girls. In Czechoslovakia it retained the name despite the fact that the nationalist movement renamed all the months with Slavic names.

Flowers marked the popular culture of the Czechs in many other ways. On the feast of St Barbara on 4 December, boughs of cherry blossom were cut and kept in the house so they would come into bloom by Christmas Eve.[61] The

---

[60] This same placing of pebbles on tombstones occurs widely in the United States, as it does in Europe. The absence of flowers is again characteristic of Jewish graveyards, although in the States the practices of the surrounding culture have had some influence on the provision of flowers at the funeral itself, where people are increasingly in the hands of the funeral director.

[61] St Barbara was possibly an apocryphal maiden, martyred after she escaped from having to make an arranged marriage. She was very popular in the Middle Ages, being associated with dangerous professions, with firework makers and artillerymen as well as with architects.

girls would then take them to midnight mass under their cloaks when the boys, their prospective suitors, would attempt to steal them. As with May customs, it was a mode of mate selection within the village community before the days of discos and parties. For Christmas, potted plants, especially hyacinths, were grown to decorate the house, and on New Year's Day the four-leafed clover was supposed to bring good fortune for the coming twelve months. At another major festival, the Christian celebration of Corpus Christi, small girls took part in the procession wearing crowns of artificial flowers, white, blue and rose, scattering small leaves from the baskets they carried.[62] Such celebrations were common before the Second World War and persisted at Vinohrady in the middle of Prague until the mid-1950s with young children of both sexes strewing flowers in the street. Then all but the procession was forbidden by the government, although even now the customs persist in some country areas, displaying once again a number of common or overlapping elements in the popular culture of Europe.

Life-cycle ceremonies too had their flowers: death of course, but also weddings, where white carnations were worn by men and roses by women rather than the orange blossom of the West. Often singly rather than in large bunches, flowers played their part on non-ceremonial occasions, both religious and secular. In the week before Easter 1990, many people in Prague, mostly women, could be seen carrying flowers, some to take home, some to place before altars in the churches, others to give to their hosts at dinner. The private use of flowers remains widespread, even if the choice is limited and money scarce.[63] Inside houses, many window boxes are to be seen, while the tables of the more expensive restaurants are always decorated with fresh flowers. Flowers also formed an ubiquitous decorative motif in popular art. The designs on Easter eggs are largely floral, as are those on the magnificent painted and inlaid furniture.

In Eastern Europe from the 1960s, even the official doctrine began to allow for the use of flowers in rites of passage. In the handbook recommending the rituals for the Bulgarian people, issued in 1986, which followed the patterns developed in the Soviet Union in the 1960s, it is suggested that at naming ceremonies the room should be decorated with flowers with the women wearing 'elements of stylized national costume'.[64] This proposal was part of

---

[62] Under the Catholic dispensation of Mary in the sixteenth century, processions were held in London on Corpus Christi Day in which individuals carried torches that were 'garnysyd in the old fassyouns' with flowers. There is evidence from Mainz and elsewhere in Germany of 'clergy and laymen, girls and boys, all wearing wreaths and garlands composed of roses and various other flowers, and oak and ivy' (Lambert 1880:812, 817, referring to *The Diary of Henry Machyn, Citizen and Merchant-Taylor of London, from AD 1550 to AD 1563* (ed. J. G. Nichols), The Camden Society, London, 1848, p.63 and *Serarii opus theol.* vol. iii). In the Roman ritual, boys scattered rose leaves before the Blessed Sacrament. Virtually all processions were marginalised at the Reformation.

[63] There is a difference between Prague and Bratislava in the 'packing culture' of flowers. In Bratislava flowers are packed in the manner common in Vienna and Budapest, whereas the Prague manner is simpler.

[64] Roth 1990.

the adaption of Soviet-style life to nationalist sentiments at a time when the regime could produce less than many had hoped. But it was also a more general reaction against the thinness of rituals at the individual or family level.

One striking feature of the countries of Eastern Europe, which relates more to the culture of gardens than that of flowers, is the proliferation of small plots, mainly on the outskirts of town, with little summerhouses of varying degrees of elaboration. In Czechoslovakia the plots measure some 25 metres square and are planted with a few fruit trees, grass, vegetables and, to a very varied extent, flowers. These holiday retreats are not new; they are found in West Berlin as well as in East, but it is in the Eastern countries that they proliferate, being deliberately encouraged by the governments and welcomed by the citizens as a chance to get away from the tight accommodation provided by the grey blocks of workers' flats.[65] Around Warsaw, Berlin, Prague, Belgrade and other major cities, whole estates are set aside for this purpose. In the first two cases, more flowers are on display; in the South fewer. Ordinary country gardens tend to be even more functional, with flowers being grown among the vegetables for cutting rather than display. There was little evidence of that downward transmission of an aristocratic garden culture of flower display that occurred in England from the eighteenth century. For flowers are often grown for commercial purposes privately as well as by co-operatives; in the valley of the Elbe, for example, some fields are devoted entirely to daffodils for sale in the Market Hall in Prague that is patronised mainly by private growers.

Although there was some retrenchment in the Soviet Union after 1917, the culture of flowers continued vigorously in those countries that came under its influence after the Second World War. The earlier range of product was certainly restricted by exchange controls, some varieties disappeared altogether, the domestic economy stumbled; nevertheless, money, time and energy continued to be put into the use and production of flowers. Of nowhere was this more true than Poland, where the consumption of flowers in 1977 was on the same scale as that of countries like Denmark, Holland and Switzerland. In the following year about 1,100 million commercial blooms were produced, with one-quarter going for export, mainly to the Soviet Union, the German Democratic Republic and Czechoslovakia. That left a consumption of nearly 31 flowers for each individual, 2 a week for every household, or nearly 3.5 for every urban household which constitutes the main market.[66] Ornamental plants were high-value crops: while they occupied only 1 per cent of the area under horticulture, they contributed 17 per cent of the value, partly because they could be grown intensively under glass for out-of-season use; the standard output of carnations under glass was 120 per square metre, with specialist growers cultivating from 1,000 to 2,000 metres. A policy of cheap

[65] In Czechoslovakia the practice was started well before the Second World War as part of the 'log cabin' phenomenon, but these retreats were usually far away from the city. [66] Morgan 1985:340.

energy made this a paying proposition, whereas the market-oriented West has
found it increasingly more advantageous to have its flowers grown in the
natural warmth of the tropics rather than in the artificial heat of the
greenhouse. The impact of the world market is bound to have an adverse
effect on the hitherto successful activity in this sector, not necessarily on
marketing and consumption, but rather on production.

The situation seemed much the same in East Germany and Czechoslovakia
in the period following the Second World War. In both these countries the use
of flowers was widespread, not only for official purposes but privately in town
and country. In the spring of 1990, the florists were well patronised and a few
old ladies were selling flowers in the towns, even bunches of wild flowers at
Easter.[67] However, the shops themselves provided a great contrast with the
West in their range of blooms, for these came either from local sources or else
within the Eastern bloc. The public display of flowers was extensive, but they
were used against as well as on behalf of the state. For the political use of
flowers is as prevalent today as it was in pre-war Czechoslovakia, where the
Socialists adopted the red carnation while members of the Czech National
Socialist Party identified themselves with the mixed white and red variety.[68]
But even under one-party rule flowers were used by the opposition, as well as
by the state, and they became one of the most important 'weapons of the
weak'. In Wenceslas Square in the spring of 1990 both the monument to the
prince and the spot dedicated to Jan Palach, the anti-Soviet martyr of 1968,
were covered in flowers. Such tributes were offered even before the dramatic
political changes of that year. For at the same end of the square two florists in
pavement huts catered especially to those who wished to give flowers to the
dead heroes – those of the past and of the resistance, who stood opposed to the
living collaborators of the present. In 1990 those memorials were being
constantly tended; notices told of Palach's sacrifice, candles were burning and
flowers abounded, informally so in contrast to the layout of the municipal
flower beds that fill the centre of the avenue.

However, although the culture of flowers never disappeared, it is now
undergoing some rapid changes. Hitherto the predominant colours used to be
red and white, now they are mainly yellow. Red had become of less
importance both here and in East Berlin. Not only the preferred colours but
also the occasions for their use are undergoing some uncomfortable shifts. A
friend's uncle had worked in a co-operative in north Bohemia which has
specialised in growing flowers for many years, some of them for export. This
work a co-operative could carry out only with government permission, for
which one had to have the right connections in the ministries. Since the

[67] See the photographs of pre-war Prague in Sitenský, nd: plates 59 and 61.
[68] The term 'radishes' was employed by the Communists for those who had joined to further their careers, red outside and white within. Hann notes that the 'radish' metaphor is also used in Poland to describe their nation-state in the post-war period; the red is always easy to scrape off.

flowers were often for public occasions, they had to be grown to a timetable.[69] One of these was the International Women's Day on 8 March for which the co-operative had been growing fuchsias on a large scale. But with the Velvet Revolution, that celebration had been set aside in preference to 'Mother's Day', that is, the earlier religious festival. The shift from party to church had meant that the co-operative suffered a loss of half a million crowns, since the flowers for Mothering Sunday were not fuschias but lilies-of-the-valley.

The other major change in the culture of flowers occurred during the days leading up to the collapse of the Communist governments. For while flowers were widely used for official purposes, in their personal use they were also symbols of resistance, partly of a resistance to a utilitarian approach to horticulture, a reminder of more spacious days for the middle classes, but more importantly as personal offerings to those who had died for a cause or as a mute appeal to those whose power lay in the gun rather than the vote. That symbolism has been pervasive in contemporary cultures, from the flower people of San Francisco to the Portuguese rebellion against the Premier Caetano in 1974 when carnations were placed in the barrels of the soldiers' rifles. It has been pervasive too in struggles against authoritarian regimes of a socialist kind. In April 1990 the sole protester in Beijing's Tiananmen Square tried to place a bunch of flowers on the monument where the death of Hu Yaobang had been celebrated the year before and which had formed the initial focus of the students' protest. The offering of a flower was not only a significant way of commemorating the martyrs of the resistance, but a symbol of the moral strength of the people as against the arbitrary power of the gun. When permission was granted to Romanian citizens to make a temporary crossing into the Soviet Republic of Moldavia on 6 May 1990, crowds crossed the border taking flowers to give to relatives and to throw into the river that divided them. A few days later when the Soviet army wanted to display its peaceful intentions on a parade in Moscow, the tanks were decorated with flowers. A dramatic picture of the 'velvet' revolution in Prague shows a girl offering flowers to the armed guards (Plate 10.3). Once again the gift of flowers stood opposed to the blood sacrifice, flower power against fire power, and love against war and authority. But even the provision of flowers for these 'revolutionary' situations may have a commercial aspect. The flowers given to soldiers at the Berlin wall were specially provided by a Dutch company who sent a fleet of vans accompanied by flower girls. In this generous gesture the company was simply supplementing its normal routine since it is from Holland that most cut flowers in Berlin already came. The Dutch traders were celebrating the occasion at the same time as gaining publicity for their products.

---

[69] Another such fixed occasion is the end of the school year when women teachers are given flowers by their pupils. Gifts of flowers also play their part in the final rites of the American school, but between boys and girls.

10.3 Girl offering flowers to soldiers, Prague, 1989.

THE GIVING OF GIFTS

Eastern Europe was in many ways a special case, even though the culture of flowers showed some surprising continuities. In the West, in recent years, there has been less interference with horticulture, and the rising standard of living, increasing overseas trade and the gradual weakening of the puritan heritage, has led to increasing consumption all round, mainly as gifts and for decorating the house. As gifts flowers have to be metaphorically 'transplanted' from one place or person to another. Some actual transplanting takes place, which is of importance botanically and agriculturally. But in the vast majority of cases the transfer is of cut flowers or of potted plants.

Just as there are many different categories of garden – kitchen, flower, herb – so too with flowers. In English the most obvious division is between wild and cultivated. As gifts, apart from those of children and except to the intimate, one should not simply give cultivated but purchased flowers, that is, flowers that have not been grown in one's own garden. Indeed the most valuable, orchids, are the most difficult to grow in European gardens.

The urban hierarchy of gift giving runs: purchased, garden, wild. There is a further distinction between the cut and the potted. Cut flowers from the florist are the ultimate extravagance. They are attractive, carefully wrapped but fade fast. Until recently potted plants were rarely given as gifts, except to someone known very well. Today, with the extraordinary growth in house plants, partly associated with the extension of central heating, with conspicuous waste (especially of living space) and with conspicuous consumption, the situation has changed, turning the house into a greenhouse or conservatory, the outdoors indoors. But in many circumstances a potted plant would still be a misconceived gift.[70]

In addition to fresh flowers there are the dried, not for gifts to others so much as for oneself; a long tradition exists of drying flowers to last through the winter. And finally we have the artificial, which constitute the least acceptable gift among the bourgeoisie.[71] A gift to others should be ephemeral and costly, so the orchid ranks higher than the rose, the rose higher than the marguerite.

I have earlier discussed the use of flowers in the liturgical cycle of the church and in the human cycle of birth, marriage and death. It is a third area of occasional gifts that dominates interpersonal relations, of giving to the living. Apart from annual festivals, these occasions are by and large anniversaries (especially of birthdays and weddings), lovers' meetings and visits to friends, especially for a meal. In all these cases, it is largely men giving to women rather than vice versa. It is not only that women do not in practice give flowers to men; in some Italian circles such a gift would carry sexual overtones. 'It would be like touching a man's tie or commenting upon a woman's dress', said Marcia, 'it means you want to undress him or her' – an overt sexual act.

Flowers remain the preferred gift of a woman. In a recent survey by Gallup Poll for Interflora, on the eve of the Chelsea Flower Show, 65 per cent of women thought flowers were the most romantic gift, 18 per cent preferred lingerie, 9 per cent theatre tickets, 5 per cent chocolates. It is commonly supposed that most cut flowers are purchased by men for women; that was the idea of Mauméné for Paris in 1897 and de Kock earlier in the century.[72] A recent survey in England shows that it is not the case. Most cut flowers are bought by women, sometimes for other women but usually for table decoration where even today a potted plant, although filling every other corner of the house, would be considered inappropriate.

A major occasion for presenting flowers is to a hostess at dinner. The custom was widespread among the upper bourgeoisie in urban France and Germany. It has filtered down in the social scale of urban life. In England and especially the United States bottles of wine or spirits have achieved an equal importance, stimulated internationally by the rituals of the 'duty free' that overwhelm the social space of airports and even of aeroplanes. However, in bourgeois households taking flowers to dinner was never the smart thing to do. On this Michèle Curcio is very clear in her manual of *savoir-vivre*. 'You

---

[70] In Bologna a joke circulates about the son-in-law who gave his mother-in-law a potted plant.
[71] When I recounted the story of a gift of artificial flowers to a friend in Paris, she said it was enough to make her hair stand on end at the very idea, 'c'est à faire dresser les cheveux'. [72] Mauméné 1897:15.

should not go to dinner with flowers in the hand or a pot of greenery under the arm. That will only embarrass the hostess. Flowers should be sent before or afterwards.'[73] If you are given flowers, she notes, take them (and any present) out of its wrapping and arrange them straight away in a vase. Norms differ in this respect. In England the gift may be put aside to be opened privately; in France even flowers should be offered wrapped but in Germany they are usually unwrapped before being offered.

Flowers for the sick have special significances. Wherever hospitals of a modern Western type have spread, so too has the custom of bringing flowers to friends or relatives receiving treatment. In newer hospitals in Britain, a florist's shop is often incorporated in the building itself; in Tokyo flower sellers abound outside the hospitals. However, there is a widespread belief that plants should not be left in rooms at night because, it is said, of the competing demands for oxygen. In some hospitals flowers with a strong perfume are unacceptable; in one London hospital white and red flowers were considered unlucky. Undoubtedly some of these local variations are connected with events that have struck the minds of those in a particular institution, but they also reflect the uncertainties that surround the giving of flowers to hospital patients, some of whom get better, others worse. Situations where the outcome remains largely beyond human control provide a fertile field for the development of such beliefs.

THE PURCHASE OF FLOWERS IN BRITAIN AND FRANCE

While the giving of gifts of cut flowers is widespread throughout Europe, even where the history of confessional differences makes for a greater and lesser use in religious and other ceremonies, the levels of sales differ considerably. In 1974 the British figure was 3 pounds sterling per head in value as compared with six in Germany and seven in France,[74] yet in 1977 consumption in the Netherlands was double that of France.[75] The purchase of cut flowers in that country was the highest in the world at 73 guilders per person compared with 68 in Switzerland and Italy and 63 in Germany.[76] The difference can be spelled out in other ways. In the most favoured part of Britain, namely Brighton, there was one florist to every 5,700 inhabitants in 1974; in Glasgow and West Scotland it was 23,200, in France the average was one to 3,200 consumers in 1982. Confessional and economic differences undoubtedly contributed to this great discrepancy, but other factors too.

Attitudes

We have seen that while European men are the main givers of flowers, women are not only the main receivers but the main buyers. But the difference

[73] Curcio 1981:323.   [74] AGREX report, 1984:11.   [75] CNIH 1982.
[76] Ministry of Agriculture and Fisheries 1988.

between them also extends to attitudes.[77] Men's attitudes are not quite what they are perceived by women to be. The more solid masculine type is often thought to be embarrassed to be seen carrying around flowers. It is the ladies' man, the wolf, who is described as the regular giver. In fact, most men do not display quite the level of embarrassment that women expect. They are more calculating in their purchases, seeing flowers as expensive luxuries but ones that mark a special occasion for women. However, some men, especially the young, do get embarrassed at carrying a bunch of flowers, no doubt a function of their role in courting. As one commented,

If anyone wanted me to carry home stuff from the allotments, I'd make someone else carry the flowers, and I'd pick the vegetables. I suppose it's an innate masculine sense that regards carrying flowers as sissy. It's all tied up with the fact that you have bridesmaids carrying bouquets and that sort of thing. Though judges still carry flowers at Sessions, that was originally supposed to ward off smells in court. I must say they look pretty self-conscious and embarrassed about it too![78]

Although flowers are often seen as being given by a man to a woman during courtship, such gifts by no means always carry sexual significance. The gift may be made to a woman as an individual, implying affection rather than love. With the expansion of the market such gifts have an increasing importance within the family, especially on religious festivals such as Christmas and Easter, and commercial ones such as Mother's Day. What differentiates courtship gifts from others is the kind of flower offered, and in this the popular non-literary symbolism of flowers that we have discussed earlier in this chapter plays a limited part.

The division of labour

The difference in male–female attitudes towards the purchase and use of cut flowers does not apply in the same way to the division of garden labour, at least in suburban gardens. In the past there has tended to be a division in the country between the garden for women and the fields for men. On the other hand, professional gardeners, like professional cooks, have been largely but not exclusively male. In suburban gardens, the allocation, or assumption, of tasks, as between house and work, inside and outside, flowers and vegetables, is less fixed than before, especially in the domain of vegetables. The work of cutting the grass (the grass has in effect become 'the lawn' rather than the field in suburban English), chopping trees and digging the ground tends to remain in male hands. This is not so in the flower garden, the care of which represents an option for the suburban male, even if the cutting, like the purchase, of cut flowers tends to have specific gender connotations.

[77] Considerable interest in the purchase of flowers has recently been displayed by horticultural organisations in various countries and I draw on two surveys, one carried out in England, one in France, to fill out the data derived from my own enquiries.　　[78] *The Market for Flowers*, p.13.

The occasions for purchase

Festivals and gifts are by no means the only reasons that flowers are bought; 36 per cent of the population in Britain make purchases at times other than a special occasion, more women (44 per cent) than men (26 per cent) and more in better-off (52 per cent) than in poorer (28 per cent) homes. In addition, 48 per cent bought flowers only for special occasions and 16 per cent never did so at all. In the figures there was little regional variation, despite the great differences in the access to florists' shops as between north and south.

Of the special occasions, the most frequent was a woman's last birthday (52 per cent), Christmas and New Year (44 per cent) and Easter (35 per cent). In addition, 38 per cent of married women had received flowers on their last wedding anniversary and 53 per cent on Mother's Day. The largest volume of sales take place at Christmas, followed by Easter and Mother's Day. In France the best day is All Saints' and in America St Valentine's Day. It would be facile to take such purchases as indicative of the preferred celebration of love in America and of death in France, but if one includes ordinary occasions, more flowers are undoubtedly offered to women in France; it is flowers for the dead that account for the major difference.[79] However, most purchases of cut flowers (70 per cent) are for use inside the person's own household, where the class aspect is evident. 'Working class people buy flowers proportionally much more to put in a church or lay on a grave ... if an AB [better off] person buys flowers other than for home use, four times out of five it is to give to friends or relatives. There is no doubt about the product being more built into the everyday life of the middle class home.'[80] As the authors insist, flowers are still considered something of a luxury, an idea sustained by their high price relative to artificial flowers. It is largely people of the higher income groups (AB) who reject artificial flowers (45 per cent) as compared with 18 per cent in the lower ones (DE). Nevertheless, these are found in 40 per cent of the homes of the top group and are predictably more popular in the north than in the south.

Similar distinctions are found outside the home. Of restaurants, 29 per cent had real flowers on the tables, and 13 per cent artificial ones; the comparable figures for offices were 24 per cent and 5 per cent. In both cases the use of fresh or artificial flowers is seen as indicating a hierarchy. The better restaurants have the fresh variety; offices with flowers were preferred as places of work over those without, and the firms who provided them were thought to be better to work for.[81]

In France too women receive flowers, as distinct from flowering shrubs or green plants, from men more frequently than any other gift, even though it is

---

[79] Figures from the wholesale market of Covent Garden. In 1973, 4 million boxes were sold, valued at 14 million pounds. Of these, 100,000 boxes were sold at Christmas and 85,000 in Easter week and for Mother's Day.
[80] *The Market for Flowers*, p.17.   [81] *The Market for Flowers*, p.20.

perfume, that product so closely associated with flowers, that they prefer to be given.[82] The occasions on which these gifts are offered are primarily birthdays, then on welcoming invited guests, on Mother's Day and on 'fêtes', depending on the age of the recipient. It is friends, followed by relatives, who provide flowers more often than husbands or even oneself. However, there is an increasing tendency, especially in the region of Paris, for women to buy flowers for themselves. In this and other features, there are regional variations. While in that region women tend to buy for themselves, in the high-consumption area further north it is relatives ('la famille') and in the Mediterranean, the husband.[83]

Contrary to expectations, in the north-west of France sales are greatest and florists more frequent. The difference in the sales of cut flowers between the north and south of France may be partly due to the fact that in the south more are grown in pots and window boxes, less used in the house. Farmers' houses may have dried flowers in the winter but are rarely decorated with cut flowers, in contrast to the practice in 'villas' that surround the towns. Commercial production is largely concentrated in the south-east ('les fleurs du Midi'), which in 1986 produced 87 per cent of the total number of carnations and 68 per cent of roses in France. Of these the country exports some, but it imports five times more giving rise to a deficit of two milliards of francs. The Dutch are more successful in raising flowers under cover, for they utilise natural gas, while the French Riviera is very dependent on the price of petrol. That is not the only reason for their success; nor is the terrain. Dutch efficiency is such that they act as advisors and entrepreneurs in many other countries, in Botswana as well as in the south of France.

In contemporary France, the two main outlets for cut flowers are the florist's shop and the market stall. It is usually to the former one goes to buy flowers for gifts, partly because of the better packaging. Flowers for oneself are purchased mainly from the market stall, with flowers for the cemetery being approximately divided between the two.[84]

In this chapter I have tried to sketch out some of the uses of flowers in Europe, both at the present day and in the recent past. Such enquiries have brought home how dangerous it is to talk of the 'language' of flowers except in a very broad metaphoric sense. Some usages are bounded in a fairly precise way, certainly for particular areas (for example the Lot) though these hardly constitute 'cultures' in the larger sense. On the other hand, some practices, such as the use of orange blossom at weddings, extend much more widely throughout the continent. But in interpersonal gifts, the fixed points of meaning are few and the variations wide. In France some competent participants will deny any pejorative significance to the yellow rose, others will prefer the white over the red, while the significances of carnations and

---

[82] It is not clear that the British sample were given this choice.   [83] CNIH 1981.   [84] CNIH 1982:1.

marigolds bring yet more widespread disagreement. Nearly everybody recognises certain strongly marked flowers, but other emphases depend upon personal experiences. Such individual associations may merge into 'social facts', especially when they acquire a collective dimension in the hospital ward or on the battlefield.

The facts at our disposal point to processes pulling ritual in opposite directions, towards diversification and convergence. Similar processes apply to all forms of repetitive social behaviour, the only specific feature of ritual, as I understand the term, being that behaviour so described is not entailed with externally defined activities in the same way as agriculture for example. That is another way of saying that for the observer, but not of course for the actor, the means–end relationship is 'a-rational'. Those two processes are, firstly, the diversification of ritual activity, which I have argued is a recurrent characteristic of oral societies, arising out of man's inventiveness and his search for 'truth', and, secondly, the process of convergence that marks the popular ceremonies, for example, of May Day and of Corpus Christi.[85] One process entails separation from neighbours, the other communication. With the similarities in church rituals over a wide area there is no general problem since not only is the common source quite clear, but authority and communication within the ecclesia leads to the maintenance or adoption of ceremonial appropriate to the occasion; of course many variations occur but within a general framework defined by the text, by precedent and by the authority and solidarity of the church.

No such pressures seem to exist in the case of May Day, which presents something of a paradox since we find some strikingly similar usages throughout the continent. One answer is to attribute such similarities to a common origin in a pre-Christian source, the general heritage of the Indo-Europeans. Such an explanation is profoundly unsatisfactory as, firstly, it accounts for similarity in one area by neglecting diversity in another; why should one rite linger on while another disappears, the perpetual question that is rightly posed by a functional approach. Secondly, the process of the Indo-European expansion, whatever shape it took, was hardly one likely to encourage ritual continuity, especially as the population consisted of different linguistic and ethnic groupings. Thirdly, there is little specific ritual commonality with other Indo-Europeans of the present day that live outside, in India rather than in Europe, except at a very remote level. While there is plenty of diversity, the May celebrations of Europe did display much more uniformity than one would expect in the absence of the kinds of ritual directives that are to be found either in secular China or in a written religion. The rituals in Western Europe may more likely have a common origin either in some general tendency to celebrate the turning-points of the year or in the

85 See also Barth 1987.

10.4 Crowning *la rosière*. Engraving of the nineteenth century. (Musée National des Arts et Traditions Populaires, Paris. Photo: A Guey)

activities of the centralised empire of Rome, rather than being the outcome of a hypothetical commonality among diverse Indo-Europeans. But neither would really account for the highly specific nature of the similarities. If we assume the conjunction of the interests of the ruling aristocracy suggested by King James and the desire of the populace to celebrate turning-points in the year, political and even literary factors may have established and maintained a certain unity of cultural performance. There seems to be little evidence for these specific rites before the Middle Ages, when they may have been encouraged not only by political factors but by the church, which by this time regarded May as Mary's month and which promoted the crowning of virtuous girls as in *la rosière* with maiden crants[86] (Plate 10.4). In each of these cases 'popular culture' promotes diversity, but the common elements may derive from hegemonic sources, rather as in carnival.[87]

Given this flexibility of usage, changes in the use of flowers are inevitable,

[86] In Catholic churches in the Chicago area, a parallel practice existed. In May a girl was chosen to be crowned with roses as the Virgin Mary, though in fact peer competition induced parents to provide crowns for other girls as well.

[87] On the empirical level such an account is clearly speculative, perhaps unwarrantably so. However, more substantial evidence may well be available in the detailed sources.

especially in the political and religious spheres. Naturally the development of sectarian differences means there is no universality embodied in attitudes to flowers associated with the Virgin Mary. But the speed with which a flower like the chrysanthemum or the poppy can acquire deeply felt significance is a reminder that, in any discussion of cultural phenomena we need to take into account the temporal, the spatial and even the personal dimension (since preferences and prohibitions start at this point). Like many other observers and even some participants, anthropologists try to lay down explicit 'rules' to facilitate their understanding of implicit 'norms', that horsemeat is not eaten in the United States or that the French do not eat salted butter.[88] There are some general trends in these directions but to see them as 'rules' on the analogy of grammar is to misconstrue their nature. While some flowers are more highly marked than others, such markings rarely have the compelling and universal quality of language. For the actor that may seem to be the case when he is asked to make his implicit understanding explicit; he may then be tempted to generalise his personal compendium of meanings to a 'cultural' perspective. But looked at from society's standpoint, socio-centrically, internal variations are large, boundaries variable, contexts multiple and changes over time more frequent and radical than one might expect from most concepts of culture, tradition and the social system, especially when we are dealing with behaviour that is not held in check by written 'codes'.

[88] See Sahlins 1976, and my comments in *Food and Foodways*, 1989.

11 · Garlands in India: the marigold and the jasmine

Europe was not the only setting for the culture of flowers. As we have seen, it drew much upon the experience of Asia. This was partly because in many parts of that continent the production and use of flowers was more elaborate than elsewhere. This elaboration had its roots in an intensive agriculture that supported courts and temples, as well as the long-standing urban cultures with extensive mercantile activity, all of which encouraged the breeding of plants of all types. On this and many fronts Asia was more successful than Europe during the Middle Ages, a fact demonstrated in the growth of her population, in trading networks by sea and land and by her cultural and political expansion into the Pacific, the Indian Ocean as well as into Africa and Europe. Notions of 'stagnant Oriental societies' that unlike Europe lacked the elements of growth are quite inappropriate for these dynamic societies in which cultures of luxury were much in evidence, not to speak of knowledge systems that depended heavily on the use of the written word. While no less open to attack from northern barbarians, culture in general, and the culture of flowers in particular, was less adversely affected by such incursions than in Europe. It was less affected too by internal attacks, for while the contradictions in the cultures of luxury were present, they did not in general take the same religiously backed form as in the West, certainly not with regard to flowers. For under the later Indic religions these were seen as substitutes for the slaughter of animals, at least in worship where they formed an important constituent of proper gifts to the gods.

Let me then extend the enquiry to two of the major societies of South and East Asia, that is, to India and China, partly to reinforce the contrast with Africa, and partly to relate the culture of flowers to the advanced agriculture of literate and stratified societies.[1] Apart from demonstrating its elaborateness in cultivation, in usage and in knowledge systems, I want to point to some particular contexts in which flowers were employed. In such large and diverse polities, many differences occur, some highly local, some broadly regional. The tropical South offers more encouragement than does the drier North, so

[1] I had originally written a chapter on Japan but exigencies of space compelled me to exclude it.

321

that it is in Dravidian India and in South China that women are more likely to wear flowers in their hair. While religions that reject blood sacrifice tend to use flowers in its place, the differences are significant. In Hinduism the adoration of gods and men often takes the form of offering garlands. With the support of the sutras, Buddhism is seen as promoting the use of individual flowers in worship. And while, as we have seen, Islam with its origins in the Semitic Near East excludes flowers from worship and from iconography, it encourages their use in everyday life.

Apart from the dimensions related to locality and to religion, there are other, hierarchical, ones. The culture of domesticated flowers developed in societies that were literate (in the sense of possessing a system of writing) and stratified (in relation to productive resources), both of which facts had hierarchical effects upon culture generally and upon the culture of flowers in particular. Notions of luxury and deprivation were more developed than in Africa and flowers were often an item acquired by the rich, while gathered or cultivated by the poor.[2] They were also used by many more of the inhabitants in a kind of democracy of worship. Nevertheless they were the subject of ambivalent attitudes, being forbidden to Buddhist priests, while in Islam they were excluded from all worship and often even from representation; there it was the same with all nature, for it was forbidden to recreate the creation, to repeat God's unique act. And those objections to images were sometimes found even in the highly iconic cultures of Hinduism, Jainism and Buddhism, especially in relation to the highest level of deity, or religious figurehead. But ambivalence about flowers also rose out of the very nature of cultures of luxury so that in the East too we find echoes of the complaints of Roman philosophers about excess in the midst of poverty.

Not only these varied religious influences bore on the culture of flowers in India, but so too in the secular sphere did the period of British rule. Nehru himself adopted the wearing of a buttonhole, using a rose rather than a carnation and so adding a Kashmiri twist to a European fashion. As with religious changes in India, between Buddhism, Jainism, Hinduism and Islam, so in the secular sphere practices within the culture of flowers have a temporal dimension as well as a local one. In a brief survey such differences cannot always be given their full weight; it is the general features to which I want to draw attention.

---

[2] While I accept the argument of John Iliffe (1987) that poverty existed among the disabled and disadvantaged in Sub-Saharan Africa, I do not agree with the contention that the notions or the actuality of riches and poverty were comparable with the major societies of Europe and Asia in their impact on social life. The difference seems to me apparent in the nature of relationships that people had to the land, even in situations where slavery was involved. While slaves constituted a stratum in many states, over time each cohort acquired substantial rights in land. The neglect of fundamental differences in the mode of livelihood and of communication is characteristic of many writers of the 'nationalist' histories of the post-Independence period, as it still is of those development economists who regard the differences as 'technological' in a limited sense without paying sufficient attention to the social organisation of production. Both these approaches tend to foreshorten the historical process to the increasing detriment of the local population.

FLOWERS IN EARLY HINDU SOCIETY

A rich flower culture was already in evidence from the earliest literary and graphic sources, the first of which are largely Hindu but refer to secular life, the second largely Buddhist and relate to religious practice. In the *Rāmāyaṇa*, floral decorations were common, as were references to gardens and parks. An attractive woman's apparel was hardly complete without 'buds, flowers, wreaths, blossoms and tendrils'. Picking flowers was one of Sitā's pleasures; her fondness for lotuses, which she placed 'in her hair', gave the title of *priya-paṇkayā*.[3] Men too wore flowers, especially as garlands which were a favourite bed-time adornment. They were used not only to decorate individuals but for chariots, roads, houses, palaces and even cities. They could be purchased from stalls in the town and their use was closely linked to that of scents and the taking of baths, while it was customary for Brāhmaṇas to gather flowers after bathing.[4] The gift of garlands was connected with courting and marriage, carrying a strong sexual significance; according to the *Laws of Manu*, it was permissible to send a woman flowers or perfume providing she was free. In one form of marriage, known as *Swayamvara*, garlands were exchanged between bride and groom, the implication being that they had either chosen one another or had at least given their consent to the choice of others.

These early references are largely secular, often sexual, but indicate a wide range of usage. In the first centuries AD, the proper behaviour for men and women was laid out in texts which elucidate the 'aphorisms of love' (*Kama Sutra*) and 'the arts and sciences subordinate thereto'. These arts, which are sixty-four in all running from 'Singing' to 'Making figures and images in clay', bring out the central role of flowers, both fresh and artificial, in aristocratic life. Included in the list are:

7 Arraying and adorning an idol with rice and flowers.
8 Spreading and arranging beds or couches of flowers, or flowers upon the ground.
15 Stringing of rosaries, necklaces, garlands and wreaths.
16 Binding of turbans and chaplets, and making crests and top-knots of flowers.
26 Making parrots, flowers, tufts, tassels, bunches, bosses, knobs, etc., out of yarn or tweed.
40 Gardening; knowledge of treating the diseases of trees and plants, of nourishing them, and determining their ages.
47 Art of making flower carriages.
63 Making artificial flowers.[5]

---

[3] IV.1.67, III.63.14, III.64.26–7. See Vyas 1967:219.   [4] III.11.52; Vyas 1967:221.
[5] *The Kama Sutra* of Vatsyayana 1963:108–11. It is also said that a wife should plant a vegetable garden but may also create a flower garden for jasmine and other blossoms (Mulk Anand's edition, 1990, p.165).

One social diversion consisted of men and women 'decorating each other with the flowers' sometimes impressed with the marks of his teeth and nails;[6] bunches of flowers are gathered, flowers placed on the bed with perfumes and more flowers nearby. A courtesan may present her lover with a garland or send her female attendants to bring the flowers he employed on the previous day in order that she may use them herself 'as a mark of affection'. Little is said of the role of particular species; it is flowers in general that delight the hearts of men and women, not only fresh but artificial ones created out of yarn, thread and other materials. Because plants are seasonal, emblematic of a woman's fading beauty and of mankind's short span of life, the absence at other seasons is deeply felt, leading to their early supplementation by dried and constructed specimens. In the use of garlands, of the artificial and of the market, the extensive role of flowers is reminiscent of the Mediterranean world at about the same period. In both areas they had already entered into commerce; in India too we hear of 'flower sellers' as well as of 'perfumers'. Purchased in a commercial transaction, flowers may later be exchanged in a sexual one, or used for decorating a house or a person (Colour plate XI.1).

Further evidence of early flower use is given in poetry, especially in the rich anthologies in the classical Tamil of South India (c.100 BC–AD 250) where the hair of women is described as scented with jasmine flowers, where men wear chaplets even at bull fights and in war itself, where a flower may serve as the emblem of a clan, and where lovers offer each other floral gifts. Different flowers, like different deities, stand for the four regions of the earth, as well as representing the state of relationships between lovers, aspects of the interior landscape. The *akam* or love poems (untitled) are especially replete with references:

> The women wear
> wreaths of buds
> Fingered and forced to blossom
> so they smell differently,
> Wear garlands
> from the pools on the hill
> all woven in chains.[7]

A bride under the wedding canopy, divested of her robe,

> cried Woy!
> in shame, then bowed, begged of me,
> as she loosened her hair
> undoing the thick colourful wreath
> of broken lily petals
> and, with the darkness of black full tresses,
> hand-picked flowers on them

---

[6] The sexual role of these acts is described in the *Khama Sutra*.   [7] Ramanujan 1985:234, 242, 226, 110.

still luring the bees
hid
her private
parts.

Some centuries later, in the work of the great Sanskrit poet and dramatist of the fifth century, Kālidāsa, flowers again abound. One story tells of how the author himself had originally been a foolish cowherd who was called to the court and told to offer flowers to the king. These he gathered every day for the king's daughter and presented them to his goddess, Kali.[8] During the Gupta period flowers were important for both humans and gods in the form of garlands, although they were also used as body decoration mainly by women.[9] The fifth-century account of the Sanskrit stage, the *Nāṭaśātra* by Bharata, includes a garland maker in the typical theatre company. As today, dancers, like royal persons of both sexes, were expected to wear crowns, necklaces, rings, bracelets, armbands, earrings and garlands.[10] But throughout early literature women are as closely associated with flowers as with jewelry (though not exclusively so), with one form substituting for the other. The prologue to Kālidāsa's play *Śākuntalā*, sung by an actress in Prakit, runs:

Sensuous women
in summer love
weave
flower earrings
from fragile petals
of mimosa
while wild bees
kiss them gently.[11]

In his other work, *Mālavikā and Agnimitra*, much of the action takes place in the gardens where the king's gardener and a 'flower-maid' make their appearance. Meanwhile the queen sends a present of red amaranth blossoms to her reluctant husband, inviting him to join her in the 'pleasure grove'. In *Śākuntalā* the heroine is discovered by the king as a young ascetic caring for trees on behalf of the master of a hermitage, wearing a flower in her ear: 'You're as delicate as a jasmine', he declares, 'yet he orders you to water the trees.'[12] Later on the king draws a picture of his beloved, but is dissatisfied by its incompleteness:

I haven't drawn the mimosa flower on her ear,
its filaments resting on her cheek,

---

[8] Miller 1984:3–5.
[9] A love letter is hidden in a flower which is delivered to the king on the pretext of bringing an offering to the deity (Miller 1984:115). The elephant comes 'garlanded with branches' (p.101), the king is garlanded with wild flowers (p.102): Śākuntalā's friend makes a garland of mimosa for her when she departs to her husband's house.   [10] Gitomer 1984:69.   [11] Miller 1984:90.
[12] Mango trees (Miller 1984:155), the male emblem corresponding to the female jasmine.

or the necklace of tender lotus stalks,
lying on her breasts like autumn moonbeams.[13]

The ascetic's grove with its austerities is constantly contrasted with the pleasure garden dedicated to love and hunting. 'One should not enter an ascetic's grove in hunting gear'.[14] The opposition between riches and ascetisim is paralleled not only by that between jewelry and flowers but between all decoration and simplicity, the rejection of luxury.

In Indian legend, as in many notions of sacred royalty, the king is credited with the ability to master the seasons and to control time, including the blooming of plants. In *Urvaśī Won by Valor* and *Śākuntalā*, the control is sometimes deliberate on his part, and sometimes the result of his wrong-doing or omission: 'do my sins stunt the flowering vines?'[15] However, the flowering of plants is especially responsive to the entreaties and the touch of women; the plot of *Mālavikā* turns on the heroine's success in bringing into bloom the flowering *aśoka* tree. There is even a precise term, *priyaṅgu*, for a creeper that puts forth its blossoms at a woman's gentle touch, a gender-based version of 'green fingers'.[16] Fertility as well as sexuality are associated with flowers and those mainly with women.

As in Europe the everyday use of flowers in literature and life was paralleled by scholarly developments in botany which rested on intensive cultivation and the presence of writing. Treatises on the subject are known to have existed and provided a basis for Aiyurvedic medicine. But they mostly disappeared with the destruction of Indian scholarship as the result of Muslim and other invasions (and possibly because of the preference given to the memorisation rather than the copying of texts). One work by Agniveśa on the 'Science of plants and plant-life' was compiled at the request of the Ṛsis or seers in order to present 'an account of the herbs and plants that were beneficial to mankind'.[17] A contemporary, called Parāsára, possibly in the pre-Buddhist period, composed a surviving manuscript which begins, 'Today I will narrate before you the Vṛkṣâyurveda, a subsidiary branch of the Artharvaveda, which is a direct revelation of Brahma. Ṛsis, please give ear to it.' The fifth chapter classifies flowers (*puṣpam*) into four types linked to the position of the gynaeceum in relation to the thalamus and other floral organs, plus two additional ones connected to the formation of the corolla.[18] That is to say, the author presented a scientific scheme for organizing botanical information based on observable structural features.

While these developments illustrate the importance of flowers in secular life, they were yet more important in religious action. The lotus (*Nelumbo nucifera*) in particular was associated with Vishnu, Krishna and Lakshmi, being one of the four emblems of the first two deities. Now the national

---

[13] Miller 1984:156.   [14] Miller 1984:91.   [15] Miller 1984:136, 221.   [16] Gerow, in Miller 1984:373.
[17] Quoted in Sircar 1950:123.   [18] Sircar 1950:129; the technical vocabulary is clearly extensive.

flower, it has a large variety of names, indicating its centrality to Indian culture, and these names are applied to gods and humans, to males and females in various forms. As in Buddhism and in ancient Egypt, the lotus is associated with the birth of the divine. Its symbolic meanings proliferate. 'The lotus has ever been conceived as the symbol of purity and charm. It is the source of Brahmā, the abode of Śrī, the sprout from the navel of Vishṇu to signify him as *rasa*, the symbol of the water of Gaṇgā on the *jaṭās* of Śiva, the sportive flower in the hand of every goddess. Sūrya ["the sun"] as the lord of lotuses, *abjinīpati*, carries a pair in both his hands. The red lotus is a symbol of Sūrya as the blue lily that blooms as the moon rises is his symbol'.[19] In Nathdvara, Rajasthan, Krishna in the form of Shrinathji is shown in paintings on cloth and paper as holding two buds and a full-blown lotus on long stems as well as wearing a garland of lotus buds, setting off his dark appearance.[20] The goddess Lakshmi is seen standing on a lotus, calling to mind pictures of the birth of Buddha.

FLOWERS AND SACRIFICE

Most of these references come from the period when post-Vedic Hinduism adopted notions of the non-violent 'symbolic' worship of gods, along with vegetarianism, from the Jains and the Buddhists. Blood sacrifice virtually ceased with the coming of these literate religions and their critiques of violence (*ahimsa*). Official dogma may have continued to consider the offerings of flowers, incense and lighted lamps to the Enlightened Ones as a form of religious practice inferior to the fierce and violent practice of the monk, but Hinduism of the *bhakti* ('devotion') kind raised that approach to the supreme model of spiritual salvation. In its reformist phases *bhakti* was both egalitarian and anti-ritualistic. Much later, in the fifteenth and sixteenth centuries, its practitioners in northern India waged an 'unending war against obstinate orthodoxy and meaningless ritualism', even rejecting icons of gods; they were deeply 'hostile to all idolatrous practices and caste distinctions'.[21] Consequently, both in the temple and the house, *bhakti* traditions of worship deliberately moved away from the 'living' sacrifice of the self or of others. Flowers thus became a major item which one used as an offering to god, not merely to praise or propitiate him but to honour and love him. Today only in the lowest groups, to village 'mother' shrines or on exceptional occasions do offerings include blood sacrifice.[22]

The 'wooing' of Hindu gods is normally carried out with clothing, jewels, perfumes, music, dance, betel, fruit and flowers but especially with the

[19] Sivaramamurti 1980:11.   [20] See the account by Ambalai (1987).   [21] Rizvi 1978:i, 372.
[22] T. N. Pandy tells me that, among the Tharus of Gonda, flowers, milk and homa were offered in rituals for vegetarian gods, while goats, sheep and chickens were sacrificed to other deities. Note the conception of a vegetarian god, though not all Sanskriticised deities refuse meat; these are in general 'lower', local, female shrines.

coconut and vermilion powder (*sindhur*) which substitute for sacrifice. These items do not simply replace the killing of the animal, although that suggestion is made in some sacrificial texts, but involve a theory of worship that stresses the common enjoyment of the aesthetic. They are seen as a gift to be enjoyed, of the same kind that one would offer to humans. For this reason fruits and cooked foods are given, but not raw foods. The texts call for one to offer to god only food proper to man. In this flowers are the food of the spirit, a sign of respect and of love.[23]

The negation of the flower garland, gaily coloured and sweet-smelling, is the garland of pats of cow dung strung together on a string that is created for the festival of Holi occuring at the time of the harvest moon. On this occasion, as Marriott has vividly described, the world is turned upside down. Juniors play tricks on seniors, covering them with coloured powders and drenching them with the pink fluid in which flowers of the flame of the forest (*Butea*) have been soaked. Disorder reigns, licence is the order of the day. And youths run around in imitation of Krishna as a cowherd having fun with one and all, including placing these garlands of dung around their necks.[24]

THE FLOWER IN BUDDHISM

The use of flowers in Hinduism, the dominant religion in India today, was greatly influenced by Buddhism and later by Islam. Representations of animals and men pervade the iconography of prehistoric India, the Harappan seals being the most prominent example.[25] As elsewhere, early representational art portrayed animals, sometimes humans, but rarely vegetation.[26] That is broadly true of China, although it has been argued that the lack of vegetative motifs can be overemphasised.[27] In India, the early use of flowers in architecture and sculpture is largely associated with Buddhism. In the north-eastern kingdom of Gandhāra sculpture, particularly statuary, was strongly influenced by classical European forms coming through Central Asia and these influences included formal vegetative motifs from the Near East. In contrast, near Bodhgayā, the scene of the Buddha's enlightenment, no sculptural features appear inside the early caves, and very few outside. At other sites religious representations did begin to include flowers. In the third century BC, rosettes, 'honey-suckle' and palmettes appear on the drum of a capital at Rāmapurvā, the bottom of which takes the form of the 'lotus-bell'. A pillar from Vīdiśā dated between 120 and 100 BC provides a further example of a 'lotus-bell' capital and is carved with a garland which may have imitated one hung on the stone itself.[28] These architectural forms may well derive from

[23] I am indebted to Amrit Srinivasan for her assistance with this section.
[24] There are many local differences in the performance and some general similarities depending upon whether it occurs in town or country. My account is taken from Marriott 1966, but the cowpats and colours I have seen in Ahmadabad in 1991.   [25] S. Huntingdon 1985:18ff.   [26] S. Huntingdon 1985:8.
[27] Cheng Te'kun 1969.   [28] S. Huntingdon 1985:58.

the Near East where a different 'lotus', the waterlily, played a similar role in religious life and was also incorporated into artistic and architectural motifs. But the subsequent diffusion of these themes throughout East Asia was connected with the spread of Buddhism.

The Vīdiśā pillar shows a more abundant use of flowers. At the same site another carving depicts a bunch of flowers in the hands of a female figure, while *Yakṣīs*, the female nature spirits associated with fertility, are entwined with flowery trees, illustrating the theme that budding plants long for the touch of a beautiful woman. From that time iconography portrays gods and humans in close association with flowers, which were readily incorporated into acts of worship as well as of representation.

While the Buddha had refused the use of garlands for himself and for *bhikshus* (monks), on his death his disciple, Ānanda, instructed the village people to treat him as a great king, rather as under Constantine Christian worship took on some imperial trappings: 'one constructs a tumulus [stupa] for the bones at a cross-roads, and honours it with parasols, banners of victory, flags, scents and garlands, perfumes, powder and music'. The very objects the Buddha had rejected were brought back to honour him.[29] Many stupas were built as foci of veneration; in a second-century relief from Bhárhut, one is shown adorned with garlands and flanked with *śāla* trees, while heavenly beings offered presents of flowers. In a later relief from Amarāvatī, it is kneeling elephants that offer a floral tribute, as in some contemporary temples in South India.[30]

The placing of flowers before the Buddha may be differently interpreted by monk and by layman. While the ordinary person may regard it as a kind of request or prayer, the learned set another interpretation on the offering as conferring merit on the giver. That difference is brought out very clearly in C. G. Jung's account of his visit in 1938 to the Temple of the Holy Tooth in Kandy, Sri Lanka:

Young men and girls poured out enormous mounds of jasmine flowers in front of the altars, at the same time singing a prayer under their breath: a *mantram*. I thought they were praying to Buddha, but the monk who was guiding me explained, 'No, Buddha is no more; He is in nirvana; we cannot pray to him. They are singing: "This life is transitory as the beauty of these flowers. May my God [*deva*] share with me the merit of this offering".'[31]

By the first century flowers and garlands were widely employed in offerings to the gods, as well as for decoration and gifts. But, as with icons, their use in Buddhism was marked by some ambivalence, being associated with the popular religion of the nature spirits: like those sensuous figures themselves, it contrasted with the ascetic ways of the *sangha*, the community of monks.

At about the time of Christ, the influence of the Hindu devotional cult

[29] *Mahā-parinirvāṇa-suttā*, quoted Snellgrove 1978:19.   [30] Snellgrove 1978:32.   [31] Jung 1961:264.

(*bhakti*) of personal gods like Vishnu was on the increase. Then too the Mahāyāna branch developed the notion of *bodhisattva*, an enlightened being such as Padma pani, 'the lotus in hand', who has not yet entered nirvana but helps others out of compassion. That notion of devotion to a compassionate being placed greater emphasis on figurative sculpture, not only in South but in East Asia. The tide had conclusively turned, with figurative and sculptural art calling for devotional offerings that included the flowers the Buddha had once rejected and left behind.

In the scriptures too the connection of Buddhism with flowers became very close. When the Buddha was born, his first seven steps were said to have been made on lotus flowers (Plate 11.1). Whenever anything extraordinary happened to him, the flowers bloomed out of season, a theme that is developed elsewhere in Asia.[32] When he was about to die, the *sal* trees came into bloom. 'And heavenly Mandârava flowers, too, and heavenly sandal-wood powder came falling from the sky.'[33] In the contemporary iconography of the market place the Buddha himself is pictured as emerging from a lotus. When he had done so, Brahma Shampati, Lord of a Thousand Worlds, insisted that he teach. In his vision, he saw a world of nothing but lotuses in different stages of growth and it was revealed to him how mankind could grow out of the mud towards enlightenment. The metaphorical status of the lotus was central. When the Buddha was asked to ordain his aunt and foster-mother, he at first refused. But then his attendant interceded on behalf of the women and he agreed. Getting permission, it was said, was like placing a wreath of blue lotuses (*utpala*) on one's head.[34] While flowers were associated with the life of Buddha and were used in worship, in the scriptures they became an important source of metaphor, simile and symbol. A whole section (*phulla bagga*) of the *Dhammapāda* employs flowers in this way, where the emphasis is placed upon their scents, for colours are more likely to deceive:

53 As many kinds of wreaths can be made from a heap of flowers, so many good things may be achieved by a mortal once he is born . . .

55 Sandal-wood or Tagara, a lotus-flower, or a Vassiki, among these sorts of perfumes, the perfume of virtue is unsurpassed.[35]

The Chinese text, *Avatamsaka* (Flower Adornment Sutta), and the Pali text, *Saṃyutta Nikāya*, provide more information about the use of flowers in Buddhism, again stressing the symbolic meanings.[36] The most basic offerings consist of the flower, candle and incense. The first stands for impermanence,

---

[32] See Chapter 13.

[33] *Mahâ-paribbâna Sutta*, p. 86 in Buddhist Suttas, transl. T. W. Rhys Davids, and *Dīgha Nikāya*.

[34] *Vinaya Texts*, part 111, transl. T. W. Rhys Davids and H. Oldenberg, *Sacred Books of the East*, New Delhi, p.325, originally published in Oxford in 1885.   [35] Müller 1881:17–18.

[36] *The Great Expansive Buddha Flower Adornment Sutra*, with commentary by Tripitaka Master Hsuan Hua, transl. by Dharma Realm Buddhist University Buddhist Text Translation Society, Talmage, California; *The Book of Kindred Sayings – Saṃyutta-nikāya – or grouped suttas*, transl. Mrs Rhys Davids, assisted by Sūriyagoda Sumangala Thera (F. L. Woodward), 5 vols., Pali Text Society Translation Series, 7, 10, 13, 14, 16, London, 1917–30.

11.1 *The Buddha Emerging from the Lotus*: Tibetan tangka. (Victoria and Albert Museum, London)

the central teaching of the Dharma, being sweet-smelling one day and foul and withered the next;[37] the second stands for light of the wisdom discovered by the Buddha, the third for the fragrance of the pure life of the Sangha, those practising the Buddha Dharma. In the *Saddharma Pundarika Sutra* (White Lotus Sutra) the effect of the Buddha Dharma on men is likened to that of the rain and the sun on plants because it touches everything that grows, that is, on people of all castes, enabling them to reach their full potential as human beings.[38]

Apart from their association with luxury, there was another reason for doubts about the appropriateness of offering flowers which was connected with their association with the doctrine of non-violence. For such offerings are seen by some not only as a substitute for more violent forms of worship but as a violent act itself. To cut a bloom is to destroy a living thing. Such an act fulfilled a demand of popular Hinduism for a 'sacrifice'; at the same time it did not offend orthodox Brahminism because no blood was spilt and the plant continued to produce blooms.[39] Nevertheless, there were doubts, especially among Jains with their great stress on the notion of *ahimsa*. On the one hand, they are not hostile to the use of flowers in worship. When the mother of Mahavira was about to give birth, she had fourteen dreams. One of these was about a garland (*mala*). At the pilgrimage centre of Shatankar, special gardens grow flowers for visitors. After the *puja* or offering, the image is dressed up and on its silver breastplate are placed saffron and flowers. For such purposes Jains make special endowments. While Jainism embodies renunciation, especially for its monks, it is good to give valuable things to the 'divine'. However, it is recognised that flowers are living beings and when an offering is made the garland cannot be sewn together, which would involve piercing, but tied with a thread. Indeed the best flowers to offer are those that have not been picked at all but fall from the tree and are gathered in a cloth before they reach the ground.[40] Such offerings are impractical on a large scale, and that involves commerce. Nevertheless, Jains still display some ambivalence, despite the assurances of the learned that the life of a flower is so short that they make appropriate offerings to the divine, who enjoys beauty. I have already noted the existence of some ambivalence in 'high' Buddhism. Thoughtful Hindus sometimes express similar sentiments. Indeed, Gandhi avoided the garland of flowers which ran contrary to his beliefs in simplicity and non-violence; instead he advocated a garland of spun cotton or even of sandalwood beads. The garland of the living was set aside for the necklace of the inert.

The use of flowers in Buddhism was often lavish, especially in Sri Lanka.

---

[37] The same notion of impermanence attaches to the clay figures of deities that are thrown in the river after their day in the temple.
[38] *Scripture of the Lotus Blossom of the Fine Dharma* (the Lotus Sutra), transl. L. Hurvitz, New York, 1976, Chapter 5.   [39] C. and S. Bayly, personal communication.
[40] As in the flowers that form the backcloth of many paintings of Krishna and the milkmaids in the Shrinathji tradition.

The great extent of flower usage in that country is attested by the national chronicle, the *Mahāvaṃsa*, which tells of the early history of the kingdom and the conversion of the dynasty to Buddhism. While the date is subject to much discussion, the chronicle covers the period up to the beginning of the fourth century AD. In this there are references to the offer of a lotus to a brahman, to the city of begonias (Pāṭaliputta, now Patna, also called the 'city of flowers'), to garlands for the *viharas*, of homage done with gifts of flowers, of pleasure gardens and royal parks; above all there were the religious buildings (*cetiya*) whose courtyards were dense with lotus flowers, and round the city sufficient jasmine flowers were planted to cover a whole building, over 80 metres high.[41]

The repercussions on secular life were considerable, in advancing horticulture, especially of the 'aesthetic' kind, in the ownership of land and in the acquisition of a luxurious surplus by the ecclesia. Buddhist ceremonial, one authority argues, gave 'a singular impulse to the progress of horticulture', including the provision of fruit trees for the traveller. 'Flowers and garlands are introduced in its religious rites to the utmost excess. The atmosphere of the viharas and temples is rendered oppressive with the perfume of champac and jessamine, and the shrine of the deity, the pedestals of his image, and the steps leading to the temple are strewn thickly with blossoms of the nagaha and the lotus.' This abundance already impressed the Chinese writer Fa Hian, in the fourth century AD, who marvelled at the way flowers and perfumes entered their worship. Well he might, for the demand was enormous, the regulations of one temple in Sri Lanka stating that 100,000 flowers (probably petals) should be offered each day. In order to satisfy the demand, the capital was surrounded by flower gardens and, even after the British occupation, the priests owned the most fertile lands in every district, land that was even free of taxes. The influence exercised on the system of production by the demands of the church and by the generosity or acquiescence of the layman and the state was far-reaching.[42]

AMBIVALENCE ABOUT ICONS

There were problems about the use of both flowers and images. The richness of religious iconography of India, which includes humans and gods as well as nature, might seem to set aside any parallel with the ambivalence that marked Europe and the Near East, and which in turn affected the culture of flowers. Nevertheless the Indic religions that emerged around the fifth century BC, Buddhism, Jainism and Hinduism, did not at first create images of the major personalities of their cults, not until the first century AD when all three religions took an iconic turn.

The paradox of religious art – and religion was the major focus of both art

---

[41] Geiger 1950:241–2; Tennent 1859:367.   [42] Tennent 1859:366–7.

and architecture in India – lay in the belief that the truth could never be entirely realised in images since it was by nature formless. An image could never be more than a tool, a metaphor, in the search.[43] Consequently the possibility existed that figurative images might be totally rejected as a way to understanding. As in the Near Eastern faiths that dwelt primarily on the word, all three of these Indic religions emerged about the time that current scripts were being developed, though the scriptures that were handed down were not created until later. In every case the core of the religion (the 'canon') was formulated in the written word. Images and even offerings came later. Those of the major cult figures appeared only after several centuries, possibly as the result of popular pressure. As in Christianity, it was the illiterate, those who had no direct access to the scriptures, who were likely to favour concrete images that they could see, address and comprehend.

Early on Buddhism had adopted an aniconic approach towards its central figure. During the first five centuries there were no images of Buddha, only abstract emblems and biographical scenes in which that figure was absent.[44] Such inhibitions seem to have been more characteristic of the Hīnayāna (Smaller Vehicle) of the South than the Mahāyāna (Greater Vehicle) sect which was especially important in the northward spread to China, Korea and Japan. But all Buddhism initially faced the classic dilemma discussed in earlier chapters, the problem of representing the immaterial in material form. A similar reluctance to portray the high 'divinities' was initially found among the other Indian religions, suggesting that what was involved was more than doctrinal particularities. In Buddhism it was not a question of recreating either the creation or the creator but part of a more general aversion to portraying the highest manifestations of the divine, to representing the absence of being.

When a change of direction did take place in Buddhism and Jainism, when the intellectual doubts had been stilled, at least for the multitude, a further problem was now posed for the patrons and the craftsmen creating the new sculpture, that of how to represent those objects of reverence or worship who had long since departed, or who had never had earthly shape at all.[45] The same problems concerned some of the early Christians. The pre-Constantine Father, Minucius Felix, defended the absence of 'empty statues' in contrast to 'pagan' practice by mocking 'the making of gods' and asking, 'what image of God shall I make, since, if you think rightly, man himself is in the image of God?' He concludes it to be an advantage that 'the God whom we worship we neither show nor see'.[46]

---

[43] S. Huntingdon 1985:xxvi.

[44] An alternative view proposed by S. Huntingdon (1985) and J. Huntingdon (1985) disputes the absence of icons in early Buddhist art, but that idea is not widely accepted and depends largely on argument *ex silentio* as far as the images themselves are concerned.

[45] Snellgrove 1978:47ff.   [46] Minucius Felix 1844–66:490 (cap. 24), 504 (cap. 32).

The early reluctance of Buddhists to create such representations was particularly strong as a result of the belief in Śākyamuni's attainment of enlightenment. That state was described as one of 'nothingness' (*akiñcana*), implying the transcendence of all worldly conditions. So instead of figurative images we find symbols connected with his passage through his human existence – the *bodhi* tree under which he achieved enlightenment, the wheel of law, his footprints, an empty throne. In the Ajanta cave the 'lotus in hand' (*padma pani*) stands for an aspect of the *bodhisattva* of compassion, symbolised particularly in the red lotus.[47] When the Buddha had to be given a material form, much use was made of the lotus, a symbol of transcendence. It appears on a medallion from Bhārhut in the second century BC where Lakshmi, the goddess of fertility who represents the birth of Buddha, holds a lotus in her hand.[48] Like other symbols, the flower stood for the divine object being addressed, just as it formed the offering itself, a substitute for more violent forms.

It was a matter not only of the Buddha's enlightenment but of creating material icons or places in which to keep them. The ascetic, *sanyassi*, tradition established by the Buddha rejected the luxuries of this world while the monks themselves were mendicants, moving from one place to another without permanent shelter. Only later did monastic life emerge, with the mounded burial reliquary or stupa as the centre of the community. In the Mauryan period (325–185 BC) when that development took place, the art was essentially symbolic rather than figurative.[49] Representational art was associated at first with the laity rather than with the monks or *sangha*, often as the result of sponsorship by royalty as well as by merchants and traders, householders and housewives.[50] But a certain contradiction continued. The detailed carvings on the entrance gateway of the stupa at Sanchi, created in the second century BC and enlarged around 50 BC, look back at what the Buddha had left behind at his father's palace, at the peacocks, elephants, horses, bulls, lions and flower vases.[51] What was rejected in his life becomes embodied in art. But the subjects of representation are material objects, rather than human or divine beings. That begins with the lesser divinities, and later gateways are adorned with voluptuous *yakṣīs* who were especially worshipped by merchants to gain protection in their travels. These beings are closely associated with flowers; they wear garland-necklaces and clasp flowery trees that their touch brings into bloom.[52] The lotus itself appears, though largely in abstract form, as in the decoration on the stupa rail of Sanchi. That was to change with the advent of statues of the Buddha. Eventually statuary became part of the architectural

---

[47] The Ajanta caves date from the fifth and sixth centuries; flowers frequently appear in the headdresses of female figures (Berkson 1986).

[48] Snellgrove 1978:26–7.   [49] Hyers 1989.   [50] Dehejia 1989:16.   [51] Hyers 1989:5.

[52] Hyers 1989:4; Dehejia 1989:17, Figure 6 (and especially the reverse). For Mathura, where a woman holds a wine cup to pour over a flowering *bakula* tree, see p.19, Figure 7.

and spiritual environment of the monasteries providing permanent altars for the resident monks. With the advent of the Kushan rulers of Northern India in the first century AD, figures of the Buddha were produced under royal patronage in order to acquire merit.[53] Subsequently every *vihara* would abound with such figures.

AMBIVALENCE ABOUT FLOWERS

Over the following centuries the aniconic trend largely disappeared and the ascetic tradition was modified in a number of ways. While flowers could be seen as emblems of the luxurious life of the palace, they can carry quite the opposite meaning in worship.[54] In movements of reform they may stand for the simplicity which is sought in the approach to divinity. For the attainment of simplicity involves stripping down the complexities of worship and making it possible for each and all to address the deity, a denial of hierarchy in the religious domain where all are equal before god. Revolutionary movements make possible this paring away, both in conception and in execution. Under many forms of Protestantism, the churches were emptied of ritual objects and objects of ritual. The altar no longer received flowers, even as decoration, but only prayers. As George Herbert wrote in 'The Wreath', 'Give me simplicitie, that I may live' (line 9); for complexity represents 'deceit' and 'crooked winding ways'. In the *bhakti* movements in India, simplicity of worship consists in presenting a flower to the divinity, for this offering is available to all. No need for the elaborate sacrifices which only the rich, or the collectivity, can afford; with a flower all are equal as individual supplicants. A similar development took place in the parallel Buddhist cult, that of Chan or Zen. The contemplation of flowers was widely accepted as a mode of reaching understanding. The tradition of Chan starts with the Buddha simply holding up a golden flower before his followers. One of the disciples, Kashapa, smiled faintly and the Buddha noted that he had understood.

Nevertheless, flowers were not completely exempted from the critique of luxury; there remained some residual ambivalence, at least at the implicit level. The *Dhammapāda* makes it clear that flowers, like other beautiful objects, are potential temptations or distractions. Mâra the tempter lets fly a flower-pointed arrow, a notion borrowed from Kâma, the Hindu god of love. More explicitly, it is written, 'Death carries off a man who is gathering flowers and whose mind is distracted, as a flood carries off a sleeping village.'[55] Is it for the same reason that the cutting of flowers or the wearing of garlands is forbidden to Buddhist monks? Or because they accept the Indian notion that devas used to dwell in flowers? The monks are not even allowed to sniff a

---

[53] Dehejia 1989:23–4.
[54] I am grateful to André Beteille for stressing this point, and for help with others.   [55] Section 47.

flower, because that involves taking what is not freely given, taking away from the flower deva. Indeed when a Buddhist or Hindu gives flowers, he too should avoid smelling them, for that removes some of their essence. But the rejection of luxury is also a critical element as the life of the Buddha showed, since among his many ascetic avoidances were 'garlands, perfumes, cosmetics, ornaments and adornments'.[56] These things of the world should be shunned by all ascetics. And not only by ascetics, for the avoidances of a monk may be voluntarily taken on by a layman, as for example with the rejection of garlands, scents and unguents. This ascetic tendency does not mean that cut flowers are unsuitable as offerings to the Buddha, for laymen are encouraged to give a flower or to plant a bo tree. Flowers are also given to monks on special occasions. When their monk attains a certain grade, Thai villagers approach him with flowers. When a man dies flowers are placed in his hands.[57] So that while they may represent luxury in the secular life, and hence be rejected by ascetics, they are also regarded as an appropriate offering in the religious sphere, partly because of their simplicity, partly because one is giving them to the divine or to the semi-divine.

ISLAM, GARDENS AND FLOWERS

The impact of Islam on India, especially on Northern India, affected the culture of flowers in two main ways, at the level of the court and at that of religion. Since the Mughal emperors had strong links with Safavid Persia, they brought with them a secular tradition of miniature painting in which flowers played a prominent part. That tradition was unusual in Islam which was in general averse to any representations. But the construction of great gardens was a feature of Islam where the earthly and heavenly paradise served as models one for another. Gardens such as that of the Taj Mahal were constructed throughout Northern India by the emperors and their followers. This secular culture of flowers continues today in the annual festival of flowers held in Delhi.

However, although they appear in myth, in worship flowers normally played no part at all, for Allah was addressed by the word alone, that is, by prayer, reading and preaching. Some adaptation to local circumstances did take place in India. Together with incense, flowers were offered at the tombs of saints (*pirs*), who were usually renowned Sufi mystics, especially on the celebrations of the day of their death (*uws*). In the miracle literature on saints (*malfuzat*) references are made to the odour of flowers hanging over their tombs;[58] in some cases their remains disappear leaving only flowers. Together with sweets, rose and jasmine petals entered into the ceremonies associated

[56] *Dīgha Nikāya*, transl. M. Walshe, London, 1987, p.69.   [57] Tambiah 1970:90, 94, 110, 124.
[58] The notion appears to be similar to that of the 'odour of sanctity' attached to Christian saints.

with the Muslim year, such as the Birth of the Prophet, as well as the ones in the human cycle, such as weddings.

This adaptation to Hindu practice drew the adverse comments of Muslim reformers, especially the Naqshbandiyya Sufis of the seventeenth century (wrongly called Wahabis) who attempted to purge Islam of 'innovations'. The Indian branch of this Sufi order traces its spiritual descent to Kwaja Ahrar from Tashkent who, though a man of astronomical wealth, lived like the lowliest dervish;[59] all of his wealth went into a religious endowment. His teaching claimed that 'the transient was effaced when the reality of love appeared from the heart and entirely burnt out the imaginary existence of things other than God or His attributes'. It was the duty of disciples to attain colourlessness, which is Pure Unity or the Absolute. Sufi leaders condemned the Indian Muslims for sacrificing animals at the tombs of saints, genuine or fictitious, or even for caring for their graves; yet those graves remained of central importance to village Muslims who approached them using the same forms of prostration as the Hindus.[60] Like other purist sects in India, notably the Barelvis, these Sufis denounced the use of flowers by Muslims as well as the offering of prayers to Krishna. Their puritanical objections resembled those of the Western reformers. Nevertheless, petals and sugar continue to be offered at the shrines of saints in both North and South India, a practice that closely resembles the Hindu *prasad*, the grace of the Lord, a gift that is presented and then partly taken back after it has been blessed by the act of offering.[61] But while Islam recognised the tombs of saints, since the dead are virtually everywhere commemorated in some form or other, it had no images at which to make offerings and was strongly opposed to the 'idols' of others. Consequently when they conquered the north, Hindu sculpture was defaced as vigorously as that in Europe by the Puritans. Their trust lay in the word rather than the icon; even their 'magic' centred upon the use of names, especially the ninety-nine names of God, on zodiacal divination, on numerical squares and formulae, all developed and embodied in writing. In the Indian religions we have noted some ambivalence about icons, especially in the practice of ascetics and in some *bakhti* movements, but not total rejection. In Islam, as in early Judaism and Christianity, these objections seemed to stem not only from the opposition to other religions but from a devotion to the word, especially written, as a mode of understanding and address (the image was the wrong way of approaching God) and from a puritanical preference for restraint as against excess and luxury.

But there was much luxury (and some formal restraint) in the secular tradition of Mughal gardens. Display gardens were also found in pre-Islamic

---

[59] Rizvi 1983:i, 177–8.
[60] Rizvi 1978:ii, 260, 432. In Kashmir, irises are planted on graves; in other Muslim areas it is propitious if wild flowers grow on the grave, but not planted ones.
[61] Eck 1983:12. I am indebted to Susan and Chris Bayly, and they in turn to Dr Muzaffar Alam of the History Department, Jawaharlal Nehru University, New Delhi. For references to Sufi objections, see Rizvi 1978.

India, centred particularly on the courts as great consumers of flowers. Many of these seem to have been supplied not only from the royal gardens but from the market or direct from the fields of a service caste (the *mali*) who was allocated land specifically for the purpose.[62] That also seems to have been the case with Hindu temples. One does not normally see gardens attached to them, although some flowers may be grown in their vicinity.[63] That is understandable, partly because Hinduism is largely a religion of temples rather than of monasteries (so they were without resident labour), and partly because the caste division ensured that priests and Brahmins generally supervised rather than cultivated. Unlike monks in Europe, they gained no virtue by taking over the work of the gardener.

In the towns merchants had water gardens in which the lotus and the waterlily flourished. Some plants were cultivated outside the dwellings for use inside. The *tulsi* plant (a kind of basil) is found in the courtyard of most homes and plays its part in daily worship, especially for Krishna (indeed some argue that it was itself worshipped). But except for the gardens of royalty and their rich followers, flowers were mainly grown in fields, as is the case today, then delivered to the temples and houses of customers or sold in the market and at wayside stalls.[64] In the past there seems to have been little extension of gardening to the bourgeoisie, as occurred in China or Japan. In those countries monasteries too had gardens, although these might contain no flowers at all. Formal Chinese gardens of the elite often consisted of rocks, water, miniature plants and statuary; that was also the case in the gardens in Zen monasteries which were dominated by rocks and sand, with little or no vegetable component. But neither Islam nor Hinduism were monastic religions, so that cultivation by the ecclesia itself largely vanished with the virtual disappearance of Buddhism (except in Sri Lanka).[65] City dwellers bought their flowers in the market and virtually only the rulers developed private flower gardens.

CONTEMPORARY FLOWERS

Today the culture of flowers in India is dominated by the garland that decorates the shoulders of everyone from the politicians to statues, to married couples and the dead. The first practice is recent and scarcely in the Gandhi tradition, though it was the downfall of a later Gandhi. Formerly the garland was mainly for the gods, but there is divinity in us all. Nowadays the success of

[62] In parts of India a sub-caste of *phulmali* specialised in the cultivation of flowers; the *malabars* were also gardeners.

[63] We have walked with young men to the River Temple in Nandol, Gujarat, while they picked flowers planted in the hedges bordering the path to present at the temple, but no flower gardens were cultivated in the precincts.

[64] Today the Hari Krishna temple being constructed at Madaipur has a garden in which flowers are grown for its use, but that is a new cult with many Western components.   [65] Crowe *et al.* 1972:19.

a politician is measured by the number and kinds of garlands he is offered, roses being the most prized. It marked the reverence with which the politicians were received, especially during the long struggle for Independence, as well as contrasting with the formal dress of the British rulers bereft of flowers (except for their wives) or other signs of popular approval. On the other hand, European divinities and Catholic saints were garlanded, as in the cathedral of San Thomé, Madras, indicating their local incorporation. Today honoured guests may be welcomed with anything from a single flower to a massive garland. At public meetings of a religious, political or similar kind, members of the audience bring garlands to mark their desire to welcome the visitor, occasionally even a garland of banknotes. A large pile of flowers builds up, from which some who have not brought their own offering may even take a garland and recycle it. Between individuals, fruit is the most common offering, although garlands are sometimes given at the coming and going of family members on a long journey. In South India, lengths of woven jasmine and *kanagambaram*, a pinkish flower, are sold in the street and kept in the better-off households so that a small piece can be offered, together with betel and raw tamarind, to women guests (but not to widows) to wear on their long hair or bun.

Garlands are woven from red roses, spider lilies, frangipani, *paras*, jasmine, and especially marigolds for weddings, though in the South a lighter yellow chrysanthemum (*javanthi phoo*) is preferred, the marigold being linked by many with inauspicious occasions and with Muslims (though it is used in some villages). The festival of *Dassera* is especially associated with the offering of garlands of marigolds. Some of those who have a tool or vehicle on which they depend for their livelihood decorate it with a garland on this day, recalling the worship of weapons in the *Rāmāyaṇa*. Garlands may also be used for the initiation of a new activity, such as the acquisition of a vehicle or piece of machinery, or placed over the doorway of a new house. Breaking land for new building calls for a *bhoomi puja* when a garland of flowers forms part of an offering together with incense and a coconut. Garlands also serve for any modern anniversary, for the birthdays of young children, to hang around the photographs of dead parents (sometimes in fibre), especially on the anniversary of the day they died, though they are never used for images of the living. Death brings out a further display of flowers which are scattered over the corpse before it is cremated.

In the human cycle marriage is the major occasion for floral displays. Their particular role depends on colour, white standing for purity and being used by bride and groom; red garlands and damask roses (*gul*) with their strong scent also play a part, as well as at anniversaries, and between lovers; yellow ones, mainly marigolds in the North, are prominent as background decoration at weddings and at other ceremonial occasions. Even overseas communities, like the Gujarati of Leicester, England, make much use of flowers for both secular and religious purposes. At a wedding in May 1989, in the Sree Sanatan Mandir, an old church hall transformed to a Hindu temple, the silver canopy above the bride and groom was hung with alternating garlands of red carnations and white roses. These were artificial, and other representations of flowers appeared on the women's saris and on the back of chairs on which the couple sat a lotus was engraved. But real flowers too were abundant, both on the person and in the ritual. Many women, including the principal participants, had their long hair tied in a bun and decorated with a circle of white jasmine flecked at the quarters with red petals; jasmine is the main flower used for the hair because of its strong fragrance but it is replaced by others without scent when not in season.[66] The red and white of these wedding flowers were repeated in the men's buttonholes, for the bride's party had been supplied with red carnations and the groom's with white. As has been mentioned, this adaptation of the European custom, the wearing of carnations in the buttonhole at weddings, is given an additional twist by colour-coding the two sides brought together by marriage, where some guests indicated their relationship to the two families by sporting both flowers. The groom himself, sumptuously arrayed in a red shirt and gilded shoes, wore a garland of pink and white carnations and held a bouquet of the same flowers. At a certain point in the ritual, similar garlands were handed to the couple, the bride placing hers around the groom's shoulders and the groom following suit. These garlands were typically made up of the heads of flowers sewn on to a strip of material decorated with silver paper. Finally, in the ritual itself, the imported Brahmin priest used the petals of yellow and white chrysanthemums in the *pujas* offered to the parents of the bride and to the couple themselves.

The exchange of garlands also constitutes the critical act of marriage for the neo-Buddhists of Maharashtra.[67] This ceremony was adapted by recent Hindu reformers from the ancient form of 'free' marriage, also known as *gandhara* after the north-eastern kingdom. When the bride and groom have completed the exchange, the guests shower them with red petals. In earlier times this population of former scheduled castes was reluctant to use flowers in such ceremonies since the higher castes would have seen this as an attempt to imitate their rites and so raise their status. But now, with increased wealth and decreasing constraints, flowers abound.

Despite the demands of politics and of increasing 'consumerism', flowers and garlands still form a central feature of worship. The very term for offering, *puja*, refers to a gift of flowers or fruit, more usually the former. The

[66] There are a number of varieties of 'jasmine', some more fragrant than others. I have heard both that the fragrance attracts snakes (Madras) and that it protects humans from them. A specially elaborate hair ornament is prepared for the southern rite (*Simantham*) carried out in the third, fifth, seventh or ninth month of a woman's pregnancy. Garlands in the South sometimes include fragrant herbs such as mint and *tulsi*.

[67] In her study of a neo-Buddhist Mahar section of a Maharashtran village, Neera Burra (n.d.) notes that the marriage ceremony, essentially Buddhist, consists of the simple garlanding of bride and groom before the pictures of Ambedkar and Buddha. Though not altogether legal, this is widely practised.

tailors working behind a house in Ahmadabad where we stayed came to the garden almost every day to collect a flower to offer to their shrine to Vishwakarma, the creator god who was patron of craftspeople generally.[68] Garlands are particularly prominent in Vaishnavaite worship. At the twice-yearly decoration of Manikarni Devi in the Holy City of Benares, a 'rectangular wooden frame is positioned over the water and adorned with garlands of marigolds and nosegays of juniper and flowers'.[69] But they are also used by other Hindu sects. At the spring festival of the Great Shivarātri, every visible *linga*, or penis-shaped altar, in the city is heaped with flowers. The next most important festival is the decoration day of Vishvanātha, in the same month, when again the *linga* is decorated with sandalwood paste, leaves, flowers and red powder.[70]

Flowers play a part in Hindu rituals in other, more complex, ways. They were used by the deities (especially the bull, Basava) in Rampura, South India, to send messages to their followers at the time of a drought or during other calamities, a process of flower-asking or flower-divination known as *hu koduvudu*. Told in advance of their coming, the priest washes the deity, sticking water-wet flowers all over the image. When *puja* has been performed and burning aromatics offered to the god, the deity is asked to give a flower. If a flower on the right side drops off the answer is favourable; if on the left, unfavourable. If nothing happens, then the deity does not wish to answer or has abandoned the shrine.[71] In order to be sure a 'stale' flower was sometimes asked for on the following day.

Some floral varieties are used only for worship, while particular gods are offered specific varieties. For Ganesh it is the pink *kanare*; *akra* is given to Hanuman, the *akika* and *tulsi* to Krishna, the purple and white *dhatura* to Śiva. Other flowers may be avoided; the hibiscus is not to be found in any Krishna temple for it has a tongue which Kali put out when she stepped on Śiva; purple irises are prohibited for other reasons, said by some to be related to the use made of this flower by Muslims and Jews at funerals; champac is never used in worship. That is the case in Gujarat. As in Europe religious usage tends to be more widespread and more constant than the secular, where local and hierarchical differences are more common. In Tamil Nadu, brahmins do not use deep red roses (grown around Bangalore) for auspicious purposes, although they are employed at funerals and by other castes.

THE FLOWER MARKET OF AHMADABAD

Today the flowers offered at temples come from a variety of sources, some from the fields and gardens of the faithful, as was the case with our friends in

---

[68] On the first of every lunar month a special *puja* is carried out, entailing the purchase of sweetmeats which are then passed round as religious gifts (*prasad*).   [69] Eck 1983:247.
[70] Eck traces the Hindu puja (*pūjā*) back to the worship of the *yakshas*, the 'first' anthropomorphic deities in India, with blood offerings or *bali* being replaced by the practice of smearing the stone or icon with vermilion.
[71] Srinivas 1976:324–8. Similar rituals occur in eastern Uttar Pradesh.

the English town of Leicester. But garlands are generally bought from garland makers who in turn buy the constituents from the local market which is also the source of supply for large occasions, such as weddings.

A visit to the daily flower market in central Ahmadabad is an extraordinary experience for a European used to the notion of cut flowers. The market opens early in the morning and continues until about 10 am, although some dealers sit around until mid-day, selling flowers at diminishing prices. Except at a very few specialist stalls, there were no cut flowers to be seen, only masses of heads of marigolds, jasmine, red roses and spider lilies. Brought in large baskets by growers from the surrounding countryside, they are emptied onto pieces of cloth for the inspection of the clients. In the first place these are the brokers or middlemen who supply the makers of garlands. The brokers sit at their desks in open shops, an account book set before them on a low table, calculating the prices they can offer the growers and what they can accept from the buyers (Colour plate xI.2). Each shop is surrounded by a number of growers working with a broker on a regular basis. If they think they are not getting a good deal, they will change. But they depend on the help of a broker to find regular customers from shops, factories and temples, and to make daily payments for their produce, even if the middleman has to extend credit to his regular customers. The flowers are highly perishable and one cannot afford to wait around to search for purchasers and get involved in the details of selling. It is the broker's assistant who is responsible for weighing the flowers on the scales, for making up bags for steady clients and for attracting customers to come and buy. For these various services the broker takes a 10 per cent commission, while the grower gets his 300 rupees, perhaps more, for what he has brought along.[72]

On the pavement in front of each wholesaler's shop sat a group of women making up garlands out of the older flowers, while others retailed small quantities to individual customers. The bulk of garland making is done in little shops and stalls that are scattered throughout the city (Colour plate xI.3). These stall-holders do not necessarily belong to the *mali* caste, though they do the same work. Each day they estimate their requirements, buy these in the open market and then sit making up the garlands. Some customers may come to place an order a few days in advance, perhaps to give to their in-laws at a wedding; some need their garlands early in the morning, which means they have to be prepared the previous night and kept damp. Larger orders may be placed at the market but it is to the street garland seller that most people go to make their purchase for religious or secular use. Some of the better-off households buy the 'heads' either for making up their own garlands, or sometimes today for decorating the house by floating the flowers in a bowl of water. In addition some young girls, mostly of the middle classes, buy flowers

---

[72] That was approximately 20 pounds. I visited the flower market in January 1987, and later in March 1992, when much of the marketing had been transferred to a new building on the outskirts of town (as in many other cities there and in Europe).

daily to put in their hair, a practice that is more common in South India where, as in China, the floral vegetation is more lush in character than in the North.[73] Flowers in the hair are especially characteristic of auspicious occasions such as weddings, when even the groom may wear them.

A small section of the market was devoted to flowers imported by train from Bombay and Madya Pradesh in baskets capped one by another. From Bombay came some cut flowers with long stalks, intended for table use; these are sold in European-type florists, or at stalls situated at international hotels, which nowadays provide major outlets for flowers throughout the East, especially in Japan and China. The same florists make up the tributes for Christian funerals, especially Catholic ones, which again follow European models. One of these dealers in imported flowers combined the role of broker and contractor. Under the supervision of a designer, he provided the flowers needed for offices, for marriages, for banquets and even for special temple festivals.[74]

The flower market is supplied by local horticulturalists who devote part of their farm to a field of flowers such as marigolds. One grower came to the market each morning on his motor scooter from his farm 40 kilometres away, bringing his *paras*, a white flower used instead of jasmine to decorate the hair, wrapped in cloth; he was of course growing food crops as well. Marigolds (*zendu*) are in constant demand but especially at Divali, that is, at the New Year. Such special demands create problems for buyer and grower alike. In view of the prospect of a good market and higher prices, some aim to produce a crop for that particular occasion, a risky decision in view of the vagaries of weather and of the market. But larger-scale commercial growing is on the increase, though there is as yet little export trade outside the country. For example, the last fifteen years has seen the rapid growth of the cultivation of red roses in Dholka, near Ahmadabad, initiated by the relatives of a lecturer at an agricultural college. In 1990 there were 118 hectares under cultivation bringing in a revenue of between 60 and 70 thousand rupees a hectare. The farmers pick the roses after midnight and catch a bus to reach the Phul Bazaar (Flower Market) early in the morning; one future aim is to establish a cottage industry producing rose perfume and rose water (*gulab jal*) which are long-established Indian products.[75] The country favoured strong scents and aromatics, which were exported to Africa and West Asia.

Another branch of the Ahmadabad market deals in cotton cloth, mainly factory made but some hand-printed. One major use of flowers is as motifs on cloth, by painting, embroidery, block printing or by machine. They also

[73] Before she was married, Ranjana picked flowers from the hedges in Pune to decorate her hair. Now she buys them each morning from hawkers. This is a *veni* (Hindi) as distinct from a *mala* (garland).
[74] In Pune one florist kept books with photographs of his floral creations for weddings, which included extensive murals and decorated automobiles. Such extravagances are particularly associated in people's minds with modern Bombay weddings.   [75] *The Times of India*, 28 March 1990.

appear on furniture and in a variety of domestic contexts in a tradition of similar peasant decoration that stretches across West Asia and Europe to the shores of the Atlantic. But cloth was the great medium, especially in its influence on Europe, with its brightly coloured chintz, often with a floral pattern. India was in turn influenced by the Near East. Some of the flowers commonly used in textile designs 'seem to have been borrowed from the long-established Persian carpet motif', especially the lotus-palmette.[76] Over the seventeenth century the Mughal craftsman introduced such familiar flowers of Persia and Kashmir as the crocus and the iris. The lotus, the rose, marigolds, Indian chrysanthemums and *Hibiscus rosa sinensis* were also found on textiles as in art, and in South India, saris are woven with motifs of scattered jasmine buds. These designs, as we have seen, had a far-reaching effect not only on Europe but on Africa and the Pacific.

FLOWERS IN INDIA

India is above all the land of garlands, whose use in classical times was also widespread in the eastern Mediterranean. In towns both large and small, one finds little stands of flower sellers where the owner and possibly some of his family are making up garlands. For it is as long garlands that flowers are mainly bought, to be placed around the necks of departing friends, at birthdays, at wedding anniversaries, as well as being presented to the gods. Nowadays they are sometimes used for bourgeois table decoration, the petals of roses or other flowers being floated in bowls of water. Virtually all plucked or marketed flowers consist of the heads alone, not picked with stalks, although some urban shops in big centres will now stock cut flowers for presentation in the European fashion. Nor is this preference confined to the sub-continent but spread with Indian culture into South-east and East Asia. Indeed, the garland culture extends far into the Pacific and flourishes especially in Hawaii where the airport is surrounded by garland sellers and the aeroplanes themselves are equipped to keep the *lei* cool in flight.[77]

As items of worship flowers replaced the blood sacrifice of earlier times and are associated with more egalitarian forms of worship. But they were also items of display associated with wealth and hence largely with the upper social groups. The great educational reformer of nineteenth-century Pune, Mahatma Phule, was a member of the *mali* caste of gardeners whose family provided flowers for the court. It was in this capacity as a florist that he became a man of means able to help his fellow citizens and to provide even

---

[76] Krishna 1967:2.

[77] It has been claimed that this eastward extension may have been the result of missionary endeavours, for the older Polynesian equivalent is tresses of leaves, but given the extent of flower use in Polynesia, that suggestion seems a little doubtful. See Lambert 1878:457ff. See also the collection of Ifeluk songs in Burrows 1963. On the other hand there are some contrary indications in the work of Mrs R. L. Stevenson and others.

today a potent role model for members of the lower castes. Flowers did not play as great a role in the ceremonies of the untouchables, nor yet at the level of the village, at least in Gujarat, although they are more prevalent in South India. This hierarchical aspect to their use gave rise to one aspect of the ambivalence surrounding their role which may be seen in the attitudes of Buddhist monks and in the debates among Muslim clerics. That ambivalence had to do with cultures of luxury as well as in the Islamic case with how to approach the deity, with objects or with words (and deeds); and in the Indic religions another problem concerned the destruction of the flower when an offering is made, for that too was a living being. The general nature of such ambivalences, in the present and in the past, will become clearer in looking at the role of flowers in the culture of China.[78]

One of the reasons that India, which earlier on so influenced the floral culture of Europe with its chintz and *indiennes*, has played little part in the recent world wide trade in cut flowers is precisely because it belonged to a garland rather than a bouquet culture, preferring many blooms to long stems. Bouquet flowers are increasingly sought after but India's slowness in entering the export trade, for which they were so well equipped, may also have been due to the socialist puritanism of the post-Independence ruling class which also dominated in China, particularly during the Cultural Revolution.

---

[78] I came across some minor use of modern plastic flowers in India, though it is increasing. Their use was largely a matter of class. If you were well enough off, or well enough educated, then you normally used fresh flowers whose rapid deterioration (fading) was an intrinsic aspect of their value. Artificial flowers maintain their glory, such as it is, over a longer period but are less valued except on clothing. However they existed from earliest times.

12 · The 'four gentlemen of flowers' in China

The significance of flowers in the culture of China is encapsulated in one of its more ancient names, Hua, 'flower', while the modern term, Zhonghua, means the 'Centre of Flowers'.[1] Outsiders have long agreed and the country was described by one of the many Western plant explorers to work there since the eighteenth century as 'the mother of gardens'.[2] Another, Robert Fortune, who was appointed botanical collector to the Horticultural Society of London in 1842 and spent the next three years looking for plants in China, referred to 'the "flowery land", the land of camellias, azaleas and roses'.[3] It was a combination of geological and geographical features that were partly responsible for this abundance since, at the time the ice covered the northern hemisphere, China already possessed a great variety of plant life, much of which escaped destruction. But the abundance of cultivated as distinct from wild varieties is also related to the long-established system of intense horticulture. And horticulture was promoted, intellectually and practically, by literati using painting, the written word and the cultivation of miniature and specialist varieties, as well as by Buddhists, Daoists and the imperial court.[4] That was the case at least from the Han Dynasty, possibly the early Zhou, to the recent past. As Cheng Te-k'un remarks: 'The domestication and improvement of various kinds of plants and flowers are undertaken by gardeners and florists as well as by scholars and artists whose enthusiasm is prompted by a simple desire to enjoy the beauty of nature.'[5] Given the appropriate geographical and social environment, the work of artisan and scholar intertwined to produce the world's most elaborate culture of flowers.

Flowers were grown both in the fields and as potted plants to decorate houses and gardens, though in a very different manner from the herbaceous borders of the West. The Chinese tradition of the quiet secluded garden was encapsulated in poetry by Tao Qian (c.365–c.427) in the period of the Six Dynasties (220–581, see Table 12.1), although he himself was a smallholder, a farmer rather than a gardener. The garden is seen as a retreat from the world of affairs, constituting in itself a critique of the existence and claims of the government yamen, or office. It was the haunt of the hermit and the scholar, of

---

[1] Cheng Te-k'un 1969:251; perhaps a better translation would be 'central floweriness'.
[2] Wilson 1929.   [3] Fortune 1987:13; Dyer Ball 1900:240.
[4] Following Faure and Siu, I use the term 'literati' for higher degree holders, and 'local elites' for those with lower qualifications.   [5] Cheng Te-k'un 1969:252.

Table 12.1 *The dynasties of China*

Shang	Mid sixteenth to mid eleventh centuries BC
Zhou	1111–225 BC
(Spring and Autumn period	770–476 BC)
(Warring states period	475–221 BC)
Qin empire	221–206 BC
Han	202 BC–AD 220)
Six Dynasties	220–581
Sui	581–617
Tang	618–907
Five Dynasties	907–960
Song (Northern)	960–1127
Song (Southern)	1127–1279
Yuan	1215–1368
Ming	1368–1644
Qing	1644–1911

birds and flowering trees. Indeed in the notion of the 'Peach Blossom Spring', the ideal garden becomes a 'timeless paradise'.[6] At the same time, it is a kind of microcosm of the universe.

The use of cultivated species in social life, the attention they are given in poetry and painting, have a long and continuous history. A wide range of species was produced, many of which were later exported to the West, others imported from Indo-China, India, Persia and yet further afield.[7] The day lily and rhubarb were two early westward exports, being valued for medicinal reasons.[8] Much later on, in the eighteenth century, the merchants and plant-hunters brought back a wide range of plants that transformed the flower culture of the West. The chrysanthemum was one of the most prominent but there were also magnolia, gardenia, rhododendron, forsythia and wisteria, as well as Chinese roses and pinks, all of which were adapted for the climate of Europe where subsequent hybridisation produced a whole set of new varieties that entered the flower world.

In this chapter I want to look at the depth of the culture of flowers in China, historically as well as ethnographically. For evidence of historical depth one turns to the use of floral motifs in design, to painting and to poetry, as well as

---

[6] Barnhart 1983:15. A separate tradition from the *Peach Blossom Spring* of Tao Yuanming goes: 'In the fabulous garden of the Queen Mother of the West, peach trees bloomed once every three thousand years and ripened for another three thousand years. When the fruit was ready it became the fare at a banquet for immortals' (Laing 1988:162; Williams 1941:315–17). See also Siu (1990) for the tracing of current practice to this writer.

[7] Among the 'beautiful plants' imported during the Tang were the jasmines, *Jasminum grandiflorum*, originally from Rome and Iran, and *J. sambac*, together with the *Michelia champaca* from India. The blossoms of the latter were worn in the hair, rubbed on the body and offered to holy shrines (On this and other flowers, see Schafer 1963.) Peaches and dates too came from Persia as did the saffron flower.

[8] Li 1959:109–10.

Table 12.2 *The origins of important garden flowers in China (after Li 1959)*

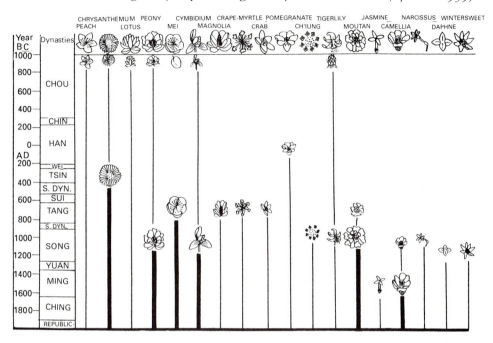

to flower arranging and gardens. These spheres of activity were largely the prerogatives of the literati who developed their own complex symbolism of flowers. To examine more clearly their uses in ritual and daily life, one has to look at recent accounts. As in the case of India, I have tried to indicate the long and intimate association of domesticated flowers with Chinese culture, a fact that is related on the one hand to intellectual developments in botany as in art, and on the other to a certain ambivalence about the use and cultivation of luxury products. An impressive framework of unity was provided within this immense empire by the written and graphic tradition of the elite; nevertheless, the culture of flowers varied in the different localities. One important factor was the ecological difference between the North and the South which influenced the distribution of plants, domesticated and wild.

ECOLOGY AND AGRICULTURE

The evidence from design, painting, architecture and literature reveals an elaborate flower culture dating back to the first millennium BC, at roughly the same time as we find similar developments in the Mediterranean. The enormous historical depth of a rich garden culture is suggested in Table 12.2, but although the early dates are conjectural, many of the flowers could only have reached their present state after centuries of intensive domestication.

One reason among others for China's major contribution to the range of ornamental plants and fruit trees is the fact that plant resources abound in the region. The total number of species in the world is given as around 225,000, the average number in each genus being 18. Out of this total, the flora of China contains some 33,000, slightly more than tropical America, very much more than tropical Africa, although the reasons for these differences are not fully understood. In the northern temperate zone the Sino-Japanese region is far and away the richest, having as many species of trees as all the rest put together. The relative poverty of Europe and North America may have been due to the way in which those regions were affected by the ice ages of the Pleistocene. However that may be, this proliferation of species meant that China's contribution to the repertoire of cultivated plants was potentially much greater. From the northern temperate zone it provided ginseng (*Panax schinseng*), the *Camellias*, the mulberry (*Morus alba*) and the persimmon (*Diospyros kaki*); the south-east was probably the home of the main species of rice (*Oryza sativa*), of tea (*Camellia sinensis*) and all fruits of the genus *Citrus*.

Cultivated flowers in China are largely tree flowers such as the peach, plum, magnolia, camellia and tree peony, whereas before the eighteenth century the West had little but the rose. That was the reason the advent of these species aroused so great an interest in Europe, leading to extensive searches for the wild varieties.[9] Although azaleas and rhododendrons are native to West and South China, it was European plant-hunters who brought them back and improved upon them for garden use. In contrast to the numerous tree varieties, China produced relatively few herbaceous flowers apart from the chrysanthemum, a fortunate chance crossing between white and yellow varieties that doubled the number of chromosomes and gave rise to a range of new types.[10]

The distribution of plant species reflects geobotanical factors in the broadest sense. But the flowers that most interest us are not those of wild species but of cultigens. This domesticated nature represents the product of a highly developed agriculture which achieved a scientific or literate as well as a technological or practical status that until the Renaissance outdistanced most European achievements in this sphere.

On the practical side, Chinese farming differed over the vast and varied regions of the country, but above all between the pastoralism of the northern plains of Outer China, and the agriculture of Inner China. From the standpoint of climate and soils, Inner China is scarcely a unity but can be roughly divided into the North and South.[11] The broad differences between their agricultures rested partly on ecology; the North is an area of dry farming, the South of wet. In the tropical South the growing season is longer, with plenty of water available for irrigation, and where the same techniques of intensive horticulture are applied to flowers as to food. The South is far the richer region. Despite the higher density of population on cultivated land, it

[9] For a more complete list, see Li 1959.   [10] Nakao 1986:II, 2.   [11] Cressey 1955:248.

produced 20 per cent more in grain equivalent. The major crops are rice, tea and silk as distinct from the wheat, millet and kaoliang (sorghum) of the North. Its navigable rivers provided a system of efficient transport that encouraged mercantile activity, externally as well as internally.[12] Moreover, the South has developed 'corporation lineages' which played an important part in manufacture, commerce and in agriculture, as well as possessing a greater proportion of tenant farmers, often holding land from the lineages.[13]

These differences were further widened as the result of the 'Green Revolution' of the Song (AD 960–1279) by which time the economic centre of China had shifted from the dryland plains of the North to the Yangzi region in the South.[14] The balance of the population moved from the North, driven by fear of nomadic invaders and attracted by the government's efforts to increase production by introducing quick-ripening varieties of Champa rice which allowed double-cropping to take place. In this development the bureaucratic state played an important part. Seeds were widely distributed, written instructions circulated, and tax incentives offered. The success of these measures increased productivity and made greater demands on labour. In the event the Southern peasants accepted this burden and farmed the land reclaimed by the landlord and by lineage associations, but they farmed smaller plots, often as tenants, rather than the larger farms of the North.

Increased productivity permitted further specialisation to take place, with different areas concentrating on the production of silk, of sugar or of other commercial crops. 'Cottage industry' expanded, especially in the realm of cloth which was also used to pay taxes in kind. Its production was largely in female hands and the classic method was that of 'putting out', which was also a central feature of proto-industrial activity in the West. These developments did not result in the radical disruption of existing economic relations, possibly because the optimal size of fields for the cultivation of wet-rice is small and there was little opportunity to introduce animal-powered machines or other economies of scale; large livestock were in any case scarce except in Outer China. Even the employment of labour on an estate basis had its disadvantages because of the amount of supervision required. Peasants normally rented small areas of land for a fixed sum, often on semi-permanent tenure.[15]

BOTANICAL KNOWLEDGE

The knowledge involved in the propagation of flowers, especially flowers for ritual, out-of-season, purposes, was closely related to this development of intensive horticulture in which a whole range of fruits and vegetables was

---

[12] Shepherd 1988:406, citing Buck 1937.
[13] On North and South differences in land tenure and tenancy, see Shepherd (1988). For earlier discussions, see Cressey (1955), Wakeman (1975), Gamble (1963), Potter (1970) and Pasternak (1969). On ecology, see Elvin (1973) and Perkins (1969).   [14] Elvin 1973:113; Bray 1984:598.
[15] Bray 1984:605; Blunden and Elvin 1983.

domesticated. Such knowledge was scholarly as well as practical, taking a variety of written forms, not only of textbooks on agriculture and gardening but of more abstract treatises on botany. As Needham points out, at the time of the great contributions of Theophrastus and other classical authors, Chinese knowledge of botany was more or less equal to that of the Greeks. As with other forms of knowledge, China did not suffer the same long-term setbacks and even decline that occurred in the West, so that for many centuries it outshone the rest of the world, until Europe rediscovered and then rapidly built on its earlier achievements.

That position is clear from the monographic literature, for 'in the days when Western botany was struggling in the depths with Isidore of Seville, Thomas of Cantimpré and Konrad of Megenberg, Chinese scholars were devoting elaborate treatises and elegant tractates to particular genera of cultivated plants, both useful and ornamental, recording the results of hybridisations and naming varieties literally by the hundred'.[16] For example, the earliest Chinese monograph on the chrysanthemum dates from the beginning of the twelfth century, and lists twenty-five cultivars; in a botanical thesaurus published in 1708, nearly three hundred were described.[17] Large encyclopaedias of agricultural and horticultural knowledge were already being produced by scholars in the Song dynasty, around the tenth century. General works on gardening followed, the earliest manual being *The Craft of Gardens* by Ji Cheng, published about 1631.[18] While Chinese woodcut illustrations were imperfect, they were superior in quality to those of the West and assisted true identification of plants and the accumulation of knowledge.

These achievements in the botanical sciences are themselves linked to another human invention that, in most parts of the world, accompanied the development of an advanced agriculture, that is, of a productive system able to sustain the type of differentiated, urban-centred culture that prehistorians speak of as civilisation, the culture of cities. That invention was writing, which provided mankind with the potential to identify, classify, describe and record a much wider array of vegetable life than is the case in an oral society. Nor is this simply a quantitative matter; it is also a question of the development of summae, thesauri, encyclopaedias and textbooks that allow for ease of reference and lay the basis for an increasingly rapid accumulation of knowledge, through corrections and additions, through diffusion and instruction. The development of listing, tables and numerical techniques permits types of information to be abstracted and compared. In botany the associated use of the graphic techniques of drawing and painting to represent natural forms (effectively but not entirely limited to societies with writing) helps those processes of collection, identification and the elicitation of similarities because of the greater capacity that a visual correlative provides for recording material of this kind. In this sense the study of botany and the

[16] Needham 1986:11–12.   [17] Gorer 1970:72.   [18] Translation by Alison Hardie.

painting of flowers are closely related. In China it was the woman painter Wen Shu who illustrated the *materia medica Bencao*, which was then copied by two of her students, the Zhou sisters, in the late seventeenth century.[19] While all artists learnt from the masters, there were some painters who went further and adopted a naturalistic style based on observation, for instance, in the album of Yun Shouping (1633–90), renewer of the Changzhou school, entitled 'Flowers and plants sketched from life'. Moreover, the link between science and poetry was close. Chi Han, the fourth-century author of a treatise on the flora of South-east Asia, was also a prolific poet who fancied plants and flowers.[20]

FLORAL MOTIFS AND DESIGN IN EARLY ART

The earliest evidence for the use of flowers comes from graphic sources and that will inevitably continue to be the case until the archaeological study of the remains of the flora themselves becomes more intensely developed and more widely practised. Floral motifs already emerge in the Neolithic and in the early historic period they are found in Shang writing itself (c.1520–c.1030 BC?).[21] The range widens in the Eastern Zhou when the lotus appears both in art and in literature, 'probably the earliest flower to gain the attention of the Zhou horticulturalist and the dictionaries of the following period' which give names for its various parts. The lotus was of course later associated with Buddhism but its earlier popularity may have resulted from its link with 'water', which was adapted by the first emperor as his dynastic power element under the yin–yang theory. For the same reason lotus patterns were used on buildings as a protection against fire.[22] Other plants such as the mulberry are sometimes portrayed and these representations can be seen as the forerunners of the Han tradition of painting.

The earliest carving on jade appears in the third century BC, becoming more frequent in the Han (206 BC–AD 220), after which we find sprays of flowers, the *meihua*, plum blossom, the *mudan* or peony, the *juhua* or chrysanthemum, and peach petals.[23] But most of these decorative motifs and designs were conventional. It was not until the seventeenth century that sprays of flowers conceived in 'a rather naturalistic and sophisticated style' were produced, though of course they had long been represented in painting.[24]

Under the Han floral motifs began to overshadow both geometric and animal ones. They also took on a different conceptual dimension, being brought into a closer and more elaborate association with literature, symbolism and mythology. Ornaments of all kinds, including personal

[19] Laing 1988:110.　　[20] Li 1979:11.　　[21] Cheng Te-k'un 1969:308, 310–12.
[22] On the many significances of the lotus as an emblem, see Koehn 1952:136.
[23] By the thirteenth century the last of these motifs, the symbol of longevity, was especially associated with Daoists, for whom the movement of *yin* and *yang* could be symbolised by a whirling circle. 'Life is created with this everlasting rotation like a blooming flower.'　　[24] Cheng Te'kun 1969:296, 304.

12.1 Lotus designs on the ends of rooftiles for Buddhist temples, Unified Silla, Korea. (*Catalogue of the National Museum of Korea*, 1988:69)

ornaments, were decorated with flower designs; ladies of the upper class are depicted wearing a large flower, real or artificial, in the hair over the forehead. Women's facial make-up (*huazhuang*) came to be enriched with an assortment of flowers and petals on the forehead and cheeks.

By the end of the Han Dynasty, Buddhism had reached China from the North and then later from the South. With it came a wealth of Indian plant forms. Buddhism brought not only the Indian lotus (*Nelumbo*), both pink and white, but also the Egyptian lotus (*Nymphaea*), varieties of which were also present in Indo-China, as well as the peepul or *bodhi*, the sacred fig tree under which Gautama achieved enlightenment, the flowering saul tree (*Shorea robusta*) which bloomed as Gautama passed into nirvana, and various unidentified plants, such as '*Nāga*-flowers' and 'Buddha's land leaf'.[25]

[25] Schafer 1967.

Representations of plants can be seen in the temples of the Six Dynasties that followed, but the lotus was particularly conspicuous, reaching outside the context of Buddhism. Deities were enthroned on lotus pedestals and their backs adorned with large lotus rosettes. On Nestorian stone tablets in Quanzhou, Fujian, even the Christian cross emerges from a lotus. In secular contexts, they appear on textiles, pottery and porcelain. Buddhist sculpture of the Tang period (AD 618–907), which is characterised by more natural draperies and richer jewelled ornaments, is dominated by flower rosettes (Plate 12.1). The trend continued in the Song, augmented by Indian and Persian influences, when flower painting developed as an art of the literati.

The elaboration of floral design as distinct from floral motifs starts with simple undulating scrolls as a feature in Buddhist architecture, where they also take realistic forms.[26] They finally come into their own under the Sui (AD 581–618); following that, in the Tang, such patterns appeared on silverware, and in the Song they were used on porcelain, surviving to become the undulating foliage that dominates much recent tableware produced in the West as well as in the East. These patterns travelled to Europe from China and Japan, but they had their origins in the acanthus and the palmette of ancient Greece and the Near East which penetrated East Asia through the spread of Buddhism. This interchange of flower-like patterns largely preceded that of flowers themselves.[27]

FLOWER POETRY AND FLOWER PAINTING

References to flowers appear very early in Chinese literature, especially in poems of courtship and marriage where the beloved, as in later Japanese poetry, is compared to plum blossom, to peach blossom, to beautiful creepers, to slender bamboos, to the pepper-plant, to lotuses, and to the Chinese gooseberry (or goat's peach). Such comparisons are already being made in the *Book of Odes*, dating from the period 800–600 BC:

> In the lowlands is the goat's peach;
> Very delicate are its flowers.[28]

Another poem runs:

> Gay the flower,
> Gorgeous its yellow.

While in his translation of these poems Waley rightly compares the songs and ballads of early China with those of Europe, he claims that the evidence of floral and indeed natural imagery is earlier in the East, as with visual representations.[29] Indeed, from the late Tang–Song, poems were often written on paintings just as paintings were sometimes composed for poems. The arts of painting and calligraphy were closely intertwined.

---

[26] Rawson 1984:14. [27] On plant motifs on Chinese porcelain exported to Turkey, see Krahl 1987.
[28] Waley 1937:16, 21. [29] Waley 1937: App. 3.

It was in the extraordinary development of painting that the culture of flowers achieved its most vivid expression. Chinese painting begins with fragments from around the third century BC; it developed during the Han, spurred on by the invention of paper (1st or 2nd cent. B C). But our knowledge only expands with the Six Dynasties when illusionistic shading was introduced from the West, along with the iconography and doctrine of Buddhism. Under the Tang much emphasis was given to figure painting under imperial or court patronage, but the largest body of works from the period is of Buddhist origin, coming from the caves of the Thousand Buddhas near Dunhuang on the Silk Road to India and beyond. By the ninth century interest had begun to shift from man (and god) to nature, sowing the seed of the later landscape tradition.

Chinese landscape painting developed in the Han from the work of earlier precursors who employed designs of a natural kind, a more pronounced emphasis on nature than in other Asian traditions. Especially with the advent of Buddhism, the subcontinent of India experienced influences from a number of directions, including the West. But Hindu art, mainly sculptural, was centred largely on temples and consisted predominantly of representations of deities and heroes, usually in very 'human' situations; figures crowd the scene. With the Muslims, art was largely secular and even court art concentrated on two-dimensional painting for theological reasons. Importing the Safavid tradition from Persia, which had in turn been influenced by Chinese styles, the Mughals relaxed the prohibition on image making and developed a court art which still focused on human beings, at least in comparison with the prominence given to nature in Chinese paintings. Nevertheless, we find fine examples of flower paintings, not simply in the form of the garlands that adorn many of the royal figures, particularly in their role as lovers, but also as representations of particular blossoms.

That development took place much earlier in China. Though the groundwork had already been laid in the Tang, it was during the Five Dynasties (907–60) that flower painting developed into a distinct branch of art, with depiction of flowers as independent subjects 'inaugurated and influenced by the literati'.[30] Among these was the peony, a symbol of prosperity, which had already been an object of appreciation in the Sui Dynasty (581–617). One of the earliest poems on the flower itself was composed by the Tang poet, Wang Wei (701–61):

> The deep green foliage is quiet and reposeful,
> The petals are clad in various shades of red;
> The pistil drops with melancholy –
> Wondering if spring knows her intimate thoughts.[31]

---

[30] Sze 1956:435. There is in fact a reference to paintings of 'flowers and birds' in the Tang period in Zang Yanyuan (A D 847), see Acker 1954:146.   [31] Waley 1937.

The appearance of the peony as a centrepiece of poetry was followed by its incorporation in paintings in the Five Dynasties of the tenth century.[32] At this time, Huang Quan developed at Chengdu a new technique of applying colours directly, known as *mogu hua* or 'boneless painting', while his rival at Nanking, Xu Xi, drew his flowers in ink in a broad, free style. The first manner was adopted mainly by professional painters, the latter by scholars. But both artists were fine painters of bamboo, a task demanding great technical skill in handling the brush and one that became especially associated with the literati, whose scribal training and activities centred upon the use of that instrument.

Although it was already listed in the Tang (*hua niao hua*) and developed under the Five Dynasties, it was in the eleventh century that flower and bird painting emerged as an important genre. Taken less seriously than other genres, paintings of flowers and birds (and other plants and animals) were encouraged by the interest of the Emperor Huizong who ruled between 1101 and 1125.[33] The painting of flowers could take many forms, some concentrating on meaning, others appearance. Under the Emperor Huizong, realism dominated; under the Mongols, their depiction took on a political dimension of nostalgic protest, evoking the 'lost gardens' of earlier dynasties.[34] The later painters of the Song Academy specialised in still life on silk and paintings of plum blossom were among their most important compositions. At this time, painting was largely a court art organised by the academy, although works also came from the brush of conservative literati and 'smelly monks'. A catalogue of the court's holdings lists 6,387 paintings by 231 artists; of these the largest genre was that of flower and bird painting (2,776), followed by religious subjects (1,180) and landscapes (1,108).[35] These works were copied by artists of the literati school and, during the Ming and Qing, art teachers analysed the masterpieces in order to assemble various type-forms of flowers for the instruction of their students. The result was a variety of manuals, the most important of which was the *Mustard Seed Garden Manual of Painting* (1679–1701).

While flower and plant painting ranked below landscape in the hierarchy of genres, it became highly popular, especially during the Qing. In the sixteenth century a great expansion of flower painting took place in the commercial centre of Suzhou, the wealthiest town in China, whose private citizens

---

[32] Chu (1988:153–5) attributes both the painting of peonies and the boneless technique to Xu Xi.

[33] Cahill 1960.

[34] The interest in such activities took on political significance at a time when the North had been lost to the barbarians. See Barnhart 1983:26, 30, 37. On the political significance of plum poetry and painting in the Southern Song, see Bickford 1985:26, 71. A fine instance of the use of flowers in painting is the attempt of the Song patriot, Zheng Sixiao (active about 1250–1300) to express his feelings about the rape of Chinese soil by the Mongols in paitings of unrooted orchids (Sullivan 1974:31). The reading of political implications into flower poetry is not only a thing of the past. In an account of life in Shanghai under the Cultural Revolution, the author tells how her teacher, Miss Pong, was criticised for painting a branch of the *meihua* hanging down rather than upright to symbolise the downfall of the Communist Party (Cheng 1986:39). In fact this flowery tree was often painted in this manner by the old masters, so may have had no such implication at all.

[35] Barnhart 1983:27, 38.

followed Nanjing of the previous century in creating an urban art. Gardens of the period took a different form from the great estates of earlier times, being walled precincts suitable for a city environment. They were not only the subjects of painting but the place where poets and scholars lived, following the model of Tao Qian at the end of the fourth century. It was the 'symbolic miniature model of and substitute for the world of nature so little accessible to urban dwellers.'[36] Miniature gardens focused on three elements: water, rocks and vegetation; rocks, creating 'artificial mountains', were important in their own right – they were part of the essential furnishings of a retreat.[37] These gardens go back to the beginning of the Tang but have earlier antecedents in the *boshanlu*, incense burners worked in natural stone, sometimes with plants added. These were associated with the notion of the home of the Queen Mother of the West and the island mountains in the sea of the Three Isles of the Blessed: Penglai, Fangzhang, and Yingzhou. Like the incense burners, the gardens served to ward off evil as well as being pleasing to look at, and are closely associated with temples.

In the following century pictures of flowers, birds and gardens became increasingly important. The centre shifted to Yangzhou, the wealthy city of salt merchants, until after the Taiping rebellion in the mid nineteenth century when, like Suzhou, it was devastated and the focus of cultural activities moved to the coastal town of Shanghai.

FLOWERS AND WOMEN IN POETRY AND PAINTING

The Tang was the great period of 'flower' poetry, especially in the *tz'u* which, in its literati form, is said to originate with Li Bo (A D 701–62). This genre consisted of writing lyrics to melodies depicting 'the world of the courtesan and the singing girl, the beautiful "flowers"'. The mid-tenth-century anthology of these poems, *Huajian ji* (Among the Flowers), which was rediscovered in the Dunhuang caves, is dedicated to the celebration of love in all its many stages. Flowers themselves are often mentioned but do not form the main focus of the genre which, though it became associated with the court, seems to have had its roots in the 'Southern singing girls'. The editor of this work expressed his hope that they would learn these new versions and 'stop singing songs of the lotus boat' (the word for lotus, *lian*, puns with a word for love, *lian*). But many of these girls were trained as companions for scholars, not only to sing but also to compose, so there appears to have been a constant interaction between the popular and the literati forms. Indeed, it was the Jiangnan region of the South that saw the great development of this poetry when, at the end of Tang, military struggles in the North brought about the shift of power and of cultural centres to the Yangzi delta.[38] One poem will give the flavour of interplay between the two kinds of 'flowers', the vegetable and the human:

[36] Barnhart 1983:63.   [37] Stein 1990:37.   [38] Fusek 1982 and Wagner 1984.

> Riding the painted boat,
> Passing the lotus banks;
> The oars' song abruptly wakens the sleeping mandarin ducks.
> Adorned with fragrance, the travelling girl leans toward her
>   companion and smiles,
> Incomparably lovely,
> She picks a round lotus leaf to shade herself from the evening sun.

Scarcely a poem in the anthology does not refer to flowers of both kinds.[39]

From early on, the beauty of flowers was interchangeable with the beauty of women. Nearly every written character describing beauty has a female radical and the entire range of terms is applicable only to women, flowers and fruit. As a result 'a strong element of eroticism is built into the depiction of flowers',[40] though obviously more marked in some artists than in others. The work *Tree Peonies* by the seventeenth-century painter Yun Shouping is accompanied by a poem in which the cut flower in his hand is seen as a lovely woman dancing in his palm, a phrase that referred to a favourite concubine. In the work of the former Buddhist monk Shi' tao, the hibiscus recalls the passionate experiences of earlier days which are made explicit in the accompanying poem. In an album of *Flowers* the poetry dwells upon 'the familiar and euphemistic language of love-making', for example, in the classic yin–yang combination of feminine plum blossom and masculine bamboo.[41]

In the later urban centres, Suzhou, Nanjing, Yangzhou and Shanghai, the painters included a number of women. They favoured flowers as subjects, partly because they travelled less than men and so had less experience of the variety of landscapes, partly because of their expertise in embroidery using flower designs, partly because they accepted 'the whole package of girl-and-flower associations perpetuated by centuries of poems, stories and legends, not to mention female names'.[42]

Over the centuries, women painters comprised members of court and gentry circles, daughters of professional artists and courtesans. The latter painted flowers, raised narcissus and appreciated blossoms, accomplishments which might lead to them being taken from the brothel and elevated to the status of concubine or secondary wife. Upper-class men enjoyed patronising and reading books about courtesans and the late Ming saw the compilation of a volume, *The Hundred Beauties of Nanking*, on the subject of the most beautiful singing girls the author had met there. They were ranked in a manner similar to the top hundred candidates in the metropolitan examinations, and each was matched with a particular flower.[43] Not only were women's names frequently floral but matching courtesans with flowers was an accepted compliment. For instance, an imperial favourite was likened by a

---

[39] On the nature of flowers in poetry see Frankel 1976.   [40] Barnhart 1983:84–5.
[41] Barnhart 1983:96. The Buddhist faithful are reborn in heaven through the petals of a lotus (p.91).
[42] Weidner 1988:24.   [43] Published in 1618 in Suzhou; Laing 1988:36, quoting Hanan 1981:89.

Tang poet to the peony, the 'king' of blossoms, a symbol of feminine beauty as well as of love and affection.

Handscrolls also depicted 'one hundred flowers' (*baihua*), progressing from spring to autumn, as in the seventeenth-century work, based on much older models, by the concubine Jin Yue, working in a tradition dating back to the Six Dynasties. Some of these scrolls may be understood as references to courtesans, a more delicate and euphemistic forerunner of the series of beautiful women painted by later Japanese artists and which are also represented in the nineteenth-century Chinese album, *Pictures of One Hundred Beauties of the Past and Present* by Wu Jiayou.[44] Courtesan painters themselves tended to favour the orchid as a subject, as in rock and orchid, just as gentry women did rock and lilies and men rock and pines or bamboo, partly because they were easy to represent, partly because it was a metaphor for a lovely girl living in seclusion which was just how gentlemen described a woman of this kind.[45]

Their participation was justified by the author of the seventeenth century *The Mustard Seed Garden* who remarks that orchid painting was undertaken by some women, most of whom were beautiful and talented courtesans.[46] People might think this fact, he observes, would cast a shadow on the flower. 'However (ever since the two princesses of Xiang were given as concubines by their father to his successor), the orchid fields of the River Xiang have reflected a blush of shame and yet continue to bring forth no ordinary flowers or common grass.'[47] So the art of painting the orchid was not compromised by the participation of women and still remained central to literati culture.

MANUALS ON FLOWER PAINTING

The painting of flowers gave rise to an extensive body of writings. The tradition is interesting partly because of the intensely literary approach of many of the practitioners. Their manuals resemble the painters' books of Renaissance Europe and illustrate the practice of Islamic craftsmen. Students were first taught to copy the 'book' of nature rather than to follow nature itself, and that meant learning and following a long-established tradition. For example, bamboo painting was traced back to Wu Daozi in the middle Tang of the eighth century.[48] Two centuries later Wen Tong (1018–79) was acknowledged as the great practitioner in ink; he was the ideal 'gentleman-painter', a term applied to the Song masters of the Southern school and to the literati who followed them. The tradition was in many ways highly conservative. For bamboo painting was the closest to calligraphy and poetry, the traditional concerns of scholars and gentlemen, and its symbolism stressed

---

[44] Bartholomew 1985; Laing 1988:37; Weidner 1988:114–15.   [45] Laing 1988:37.
[46] Women also painted other flowers and trees but never large landscapes; their expertise was associated with embroidery.   [47] Sze 1956:324; that is, in the legendary past around 4,000 years ago.
[48] On the importance of bamboo in Chinese art, see Barnhart 1983:50–4.

moral character and ideals.[49] Painting was critically evaluated in a similar way to calligraphy, the premier art of personal expression, so that brush movements were held to reveal the character of the artists. As a result, such painting came to be regarded as 'a form of self-portraiture', with bamboo as the great literati subject, frequently used by poet and philosopher as the symbol of a perfect gentleman.[50] Its qualities included subtle strength since it could bend without breaking; remaining green throughout winter, it carried the notion of unfading companionship, as well as longevity and modesty.[51]

Bamboo itself was one of the 'four gentlemen of flowers' which stood for the four seasons. These flowers formed the subject of books of instruction such as *The Mustard Seed Garden Manual*, which is still in current use; the well-known contemporary painter of peasant origins, Qi Baishi (1863–1957), used it to practise painting.[52] This manual draws deliberate attention to the similarities between painting and writing as well as to the embeddedness of graphic art in the written tradition, for the author discusses the representation of another of the four flowers, the orchid, in the following terms:

Mi Cao says: Before attempting to paint finished pictures of the orchid, one should study the works of the ancients. Later one may inject one's own ideas. First, however, one should know the various methods; the rules phrased for memorizing by chanting (*gejue*)[53] should be learned and one may then start with the basic strokes contained in the character *qiu*.

In learning to write, one begins with simple characters made up of a few strokes and proceeds to complicated characters with several strokes. In the same way, in learning to paint flowers, one begins with those with few petals and proceeds to those with many petals, from small leaves to large, and from single stems to bunches. Each division of subject matter is classified here so that beginners may learn them thoroughly, not only beholding them with their eyes but retaining the impressions in their minds. In calligraphy, one first learns to write *qiu*, which contains the eight basic strokes; though there are hundreds and thousands of characters, the fundamental strokes are all found in *qiu*. Likewise in painting flowers: when the beginner has learned the basic steps, he will have started on the way to acquiring experience and skill.[54]

So the similarities with writing are many. Paintings and characters are both analysed in order to isolate the basic strokes, which are practised and learned by heart. Only on the basis of extensive knowledge is it possible to be creative. One begins by copying others, not with individual inspiration; originality eventually comes to crown a career. Historically Chinese writing came before

---

[49] Sze 1956:362.   [50] Robinson 1988:67.   [51] Koehn 1952:134.   [52] Bickford 1985:146.

[53] A note of the editor on the phrase *gejue* has fascinating implications (Sze 1956:323). '*Ge* (sing, chant) *jue* (secret), an expression used here about learning the rules of painting. Chanting by phrases was a common practice in the process of memorizing, applied notably to the classics learned in childhood. *Jue* is also used in terms describing the mysterious and occult, magic formulas, etc., and suggests the relationship with the mantras (the chanting of religious texts), the sounds of which were believed to set up vibrations in a manner that might be described as 'tuning in' with the Infinite. A relevant statement appears in the *Shu Jing* (Book of History): "Poetry is the expression of earnest thought; singing is the prolonged utterance of that expression" (Legge, *The Shoo King*, part II, I, v.)'.   [54] Sze 1956:323–4.

figurative painting. Brush and ink as used in calligraphy dominated pictorial art, especially of the literati, brush strokes being the most important element in painting; as a result 'any literatus, because of his training and experience, could be an artist'.[55]

The art of painting orchids, associated with women, is held to depend entirely on drawing the leaves, for which elaborate instructions are given.[56] On the other hand, attention had also to be paid to the flower, particularly to its heart; Chinese orchids have small, almost insignificant flowers, and are renowned more for their leaves and fragrance:

Dotting the heart of the orchid is like drawing in the eyes of a beautiful woman. As the rippling fields of orchids of the River Xiang give life to the whole countryside, so dotting the heart of the flower adds the finishing touch. The whole essence of the flower is contained in that small touch. How can one therefore possibly neglect it?[57]

The orchid (*lanhua*) is the emblem of refinement and the 'Ancestor of all Fragrances', to be compared with the breath of beautiful women and the fame of great men. The painting of an orchid in a pot suggests 'friendship with perfect men'.[58]

While the plum, the next of the 'four gentlemen' and the emblem of winter, was also of great aesthetic importance, only later did it receive independent status in painting.[59] However, the author of the manual develops the interpretation of plum painting more systematically than for the other flowers, employing the number symbolism based on the *Yijing* (Book of Changes) used for divination:

The symbolism (*xiang*) of the plum tree is determined by its *qi*. The blossoms are of the *Yang* principle, that of Heaven. The wood of its trunk and branches are of the *Yin* principle, that of Earth. Its basic number is five, and its various parts and aspects are based on the odd and even numbers. The peduncle, from which the flower issues, is a symbol of the *Taiqi* (the Ridgepole of the Universe, the Supreme Ultimate, the Absolute), and hence it is the upright form of the calyx. The part supporting the blossom is a symbol of the *Sancai* (Three Powers of Heaven, Earth, and Man) and consequently is drawn with three sepals. The flower issuing from the calyx is a symbol of the *Wuxing* (Five Elements) and is drawn with five petals. The stamens growing in the centre of the flower are symbols of the *Qizheng* (Seven Planets: the five planets with the sun and the moon) and so are drawn numbering seven. When the flowers fade, they return to the number of the *Taiqi*, and that is why the cycles of growth and decline of the plum tree are nine.[60]

This laboured elaboration is in itself evidence of its literary origin rather than of 'popular' roots. In this it resembles the way in which the Jesuit Fathers

---

[55] Lee 1988:18.

[56] On the meaning of the orchid especially as seclusion, see Robinson 1988:74, Barnhart 1983:35 and Van Gulick 1961:92, 102. On urbanisation and seclusion, see Bickford 1985: 3. On painting the orchid as 'the national fragrance', see Barnhart 1983:55.   [57] Sze 1956:326.   [58] Koehn 1952:132.

[59] On painting the plum, see Barnhart 1983:55.   [60] Sze 1956:404.

developed their interpretation of the passion flower of Peru and other species for the instruction of their converts, and no doubt their own delight in 'conceit', except that in their case the process is more explicitly hegemonic.[61] In the realm of gardens, especially miniature ones, elaboration takes a different but equally complex form since the objects are selected and rearranged to conform to particular mythical, theological and symbolic notions.[62]

While the flowering plum appeared in art, literature and decoration before the Song, only with that dynasty did there develop an extensive body of 'plum poetry' which was gathered by a scholar of the Southern Song, Huang Dayu, in his twelfth-century anthology, *Flowering-Plum Garden*. At roughly the same period another poet produced the first botanical treatise on the tree, and painters also offered both technical and aesthetic instruction in their manuals.[63] Achievement in poetry, painting and botany were closely intertwined in rather the same way as the cultivation of aesthetically pleasing flowers and utilitarian vegetables. Plum blossom acquired a special position in flower painting, which in the end led to the new genre of the ink plum, the genre of scholar-amateurs rather than of professional artists whose recourse to colours rather than monochrome brush work they affected to despise.[64]

The paintings themselves suggest a more concrete and less complicated and comprehensive interpretation of the significance of plum blossom than that provided by the manual:

Appearing on gnarled trees early in the new year before other flowers have emerged and when winter weather has yet to depart, plum blossoms have long symbolized renewal and courage. The trees themselves are emblematic of endurance. The white colour of the blossoms and their lonely vigil suggests purity, while the brevity of their flowering brings to mind the fleeting nature of beauty. From such associations came two durable literary images: the flowering-plum recluse and the plum-blossom beauty. Scholarly hermits identified themselves with these lofty flowers by planting plum trees around their retreats and adopting such literary names as 'The Plum Blossom Daoist'. The plum-blossom beauty was the creation of poets who, in reflecting on the transience of life, likened these delicate, chaste flowers to lovely young women.[65]

The flowers of the plum come out before the leaves and are taken to symbolise female chastity.[66] The idea of the plum-blossom beauty goes back to the sixth-century poet Xiao Gang, who compares women with the transient glory of the blossom, but the two aspects become fused in the work of Song writers. It was

---

[61] On the symbolism of the passion flower see Anon. 1863:248, referring to Bosio, *La trionfante e gloriosa croce*, Rome, 1610; Parkinson suggested the flower be assigned to Queen Elizabeth.   [62] Stein 1990.
[63] Bickford 1985:28, 68. In 1260 Zhao Mengjian produced *Three Poems on the Painting of Ink-Plum Blossoms and Bamboo* which contained instructions on how to paint plum blossoms in that particular genre. During the Yuan Dynasty it was followed by the more comprehensive *Pine-Studio Plum Manual*.
[64] Bickford 1985:17, 56ff.   [65] Weidner 1988:139.
[66] Koehn 1952:127. On the combination of plum blossom and other emblems to form punning references, see p.128.

the same with the association of blossom and isolation in the idea of the 'flowering-plum recluse'.

Here the contextual nature of flower symbolism becomes clear; we shift from a philosophical to a poetic interpretation which was created by poets and painters and which was removed from ordinary usage but nevertheless fed back in a variety of ways into 'popular culture' as well as picking up themes from that realm. The connection of plum blossom with the New Year is widespread and long established; in Beijing it was cultivated in greenhouses so that its blossoms would appear for that festival.[67] The trees had an equivalent status to the cherry in Japan. Individuals and parties still arrange to 'view' the blossom of the plum and the cherry in favoured sites, just as they do the changing autumn leaves in the more northern parts. This deep-rooted significance of the plum blossom was expressed not only in poetry and painting but in life itself:

In late winter flower vendors brought the first budding branches to town. These girls stuck plum sprigs in their hair and teased admirers to choose between their beauty and that of the blossoms. Scholars took branches indoors, forcing the cold buds into early flowering and hastening spring. Sometimes they put them into antique bronze vessels; sometimes into a ceramic flowering-plum vase (*meiping*) whose tall body and narrow mouth were designed to show off the elegance of a single 'branch of spring'.

The fourth 'gentleman of flowers' was the chrysanthemum, noted for its great variety of colours and forms.[68] This flower of autumn was a symbol of joviality and a life of ease and retirement,[69] at the same time as being 'defiant of frost, and triumphant in autumn'.[70] Up to the Ming 'only the literati and retired scholars treated the subtle fragrance of the chrysanthemum as a special subject for painting' (Plate 12.2).[71] It is described as 'a flower of proud disposition' to paint which 'one must hold in his heart a conception of the flower whole and complete'. Interiorisation is seen as an intrinsic part even of the process of copying, just as reading a sacred text is often not enough in itself; to 'know' is to memorise, so that one can repeat its words 'by heart', that is, verbatim.

These four flowers represent spring, summer, winter and autumn respectively. They were known to the literati by highly allusive references such as the 'flower whose fragrance lingers along the bamboo fence to the

---

[67] Koehn 1952:127.
[68] The chrysanthemum was particularly associated in painting with a poem by the recluse-poet, Tao Qian (365–427), 'Written While Drunk':

> I pluck chrysanthemums under the eastern hedge,
> And gaze afar towards the southern mountains.

[69] Koehn 1952:143.
[70] Three hundred varieties of chrysanthemum are described in an encyclopaedic work of 1708; now it may be several thousand. See Li 1959:37ff. on the botany of the chrysanthemum.   [71] Sze 1956:435.

12.2 *The Planting of Chrysanthemums* (c. 1550) by Lu Zhi (1496–1576). Hanging scroll, ink and pale colour on paper. Detail. (R. M. Barnhart, *Peach Blossom Spring*, Metropolitan Museum of Modern Art, 1983:77)

east'. These titles, indeed the whole tradition of painting, once again indicate the extent to which the culture of flowers was elaborated by the literati and then, through their members across the country, incorporated as components of local culture. From an early date elegant gatherings of scholars were held in gardens to enjoy painting, poetry, calligraphy as well as music, drinking and sometimes beautiful women, the first recorded occasion being in AD 353.[72] Many literati artists were versed in the three perfections, painting, poetry and calligraphy, so they sometimes supplied their own poems to paintings in their own hand. On other occasions they included a verse from an earlier author that was appropriate to the subject of their painting, while poems were sometimes added by those who acquired and admired the paintings.[73] Far Eastern painting, especially of scholars, is remarkable in allowing ideas and feelings to flow back and forth between the words and picture.[74]

That there was a large market for flower paintings is clear from the number of artists, from the paintings that have survived and from the statements in biographies claiming that individuals turned to painting to support themselves and their families. One reason for this demand was the calendrical significance that these compositions acquired.[75] The practice went back to a calendar in the *Liji* (Book of Rites), in which each month is associated with a variety of natural phenomena. Flowers and birds were firmly associated with specific months, a pattern that, with some variations, became a favourite theme of painters.[76] Chinese garden books included floral calendars (*huali*). In the early seventeenth century Tu Benjun set down a ranked table of vase flowers for the twelve months, the first being of plum blossom and the double-flowered camellia. These associations were echoed on furnishings, ceramics, bedding and clothing.

FLOWER ARRANGING

Apart from the representation of flowers, in design, poetry and painting, their formal uses were elaborated in other ways. The art of gardens was closely connected with the practice of flower arranging, both of which were influenced in turn by painting. In all three we find the idealisation of natural scenery, with gardening as an attempt to bring mountains and lakes to one's own courtyard by an arrangement of rocks and trees; rock gardens were constructed as early as the Han, and grotesque rocks were the subject of long expeditions and fetched high prices. There was a continuous interplay between art and 'nature', gardens being made to copy paintings, just as paintings represented gardens, actual and ideal. The most famous place in

[72] Chu 1988:152.   [73] See Sullivan 1974.   [74] Sullivan 1974:30.   [75] Weidner 1988:21.
[76] Li 1956:38–9; Weidner 1988:123–4.

Suzhou, the Lion Forest, 'was supposedly created in the style of paintings by Yün-lin with splendid rocks and many old trees'.[77]

Palace gardens represented large-scale attempts to realise this ideal. Indeed, the court made an important contribution to gardens, to the cultivation of flowers as well as to flower painting. As early as c.100 BC, the Emperor Han Wudi had a major impact by constructing parks that were designed to help him gain immortality. No doubt using literati ideas and practices, the court was an influence that cannot be ignored.[78] In 740, when Xuanzong encouraged the planting of trees along the roads of both capitals and in the parks inside the city walls, the trees probably came from the great nursery and garden (the Tabooed Park) established near the palace. In addition there was the imperial herb garden directed by the 'Master of the Medicinal Garden', an important centre of study and practice. Some private parks were also extensive and exotic. In one case, the young men of the household constructed a movable garden of wood, mounted on wheels and planted with 'renowned flowers and strange trees' which was displayed in public in the spring.[79] Some of the gardens of the literati and the merchants were large in size, especially in the later period. At the beginning of the nineteenth century the Chen family's Garden of Peaceful Waves in Haining occupied nearly 7 hectares, filled with towers and pavilions, winding lanes and galleries, rocks covered with vines and a thousand ancient trees, 'all of them reaching to heaven'.[80] Such gardens were to be looked upon 'as a beautiful woman handsomely dressed' rather than 'a simple country girl'. There were large gardens too in towns like Suzhou, but we also find a range of miniature courtyard gardens tailored to the urban environment. The same process was carried yet further in the development of tray gardening, known as penzai (Japanese, bonsai), pot or tray culture, or penjing (bonkei), and landscape or scenes in vessels. The process of dwarfing trees is highly specialised, requiring precise knowledge and great patience.[81] In these trays curiously shaped rocks suggest rugged mountains, while dwarfed trees, plants or mosses create the idea of a forest. Little temples, bridges, boats and figures add the human dimension to landscape, following a pattern set in gardening itself and in painted representations.

The arranging of flowers was part of this same process of bringing nature, transformed nature, into the house, a process stimulated by the advent of

---

[77] Shen Fu 1983:136. Ni Can (1301–74) is the more common name for this painter.

[78] This point was made to me by Joe McDermott, who also thinks that I overstress the cultural role of the literati (following their own practice). In any case, the Chinese literati drew not only on Confucianism but on Daoism and Buddhism. They were certainly eclectic. But, whatever the beliefs of most individuals, in terms of institutionalised 'religions' these East Asian traditions seem to maintain varying degrees of distinctiveness, at times of opposition, at others of outright conflict.   [79] Schafer 1967.   [80] Shen Fu 1983:110, 112.

[81] For a description of the process, see Li 1956:57ff. and Shen Fu 1983:56–62. On the 'metaphoric mutability' of Chinese flower images, see Bickford 1985:25. See also Rogers on Lü Ji (ca. 1440–ca. 1505): 'symbolic consistency is not always to be found . . . Sometimes a painting is only a painting' (1988:116).

Buddhism in the first century AD,[82] when monastic gardens provided a new arena for the culture of flowers. But there was a contrast in the use of flowers between Confucian and Buddhist culture. In the temple and for ancestral offerings a mass of blooms was presented in a vase, whereas flower arranging in the house emphasised line, as in much literati painting in ink. Cut twigs and flowers were carefully set out according to a series of established principles, not so rigidly as in Japan but nonetheless subject to considerable written attention.

These indoor uses had a strong influence on interior furnishings. Li lists the many varieties of flower stands, tables and complex devices that were used to display table plants, furniture that was itself often decorated with flower designs. Flower arranging itself necessitated a variety of containers, in metal but especially in ceramics, which became one of the special features of Chinese crafts. The creation of an enormous range of vases for the display of flowers, branches and plants produced its own literature, at least from the time of Zhang Qiande (1577–1643), whose *Pinghua pu* (Treatise on Vase Flowers), dates from 1595. Some pots were for large flowers, others for single twigs, some for particular flowers, others for broader displays, each type being given a special name. Often the vases were supported by matching stands or tables, and the variety and quality of the demand had considerable influence on the production of ceramics.[83]

THE CONTEXTUALITY OF THE SYMBOLISM OF FLOWERS

We have seen how designs from China passed to the West and those from Europe to the East.[84] The border motifs of the acanthus scroll patterns of ancient Greece passed along the length of the Silk Road. In the later stages of this process, the agents were often Buddhists who gave the designs a new 'reading', incorporating what became 'the major floral emblem of spiritual attainment, the lotus'.[85] The lotus is the first flower to appear in poetry, followed by the orchid.[86] The chrysanthemum plays its part from the third century AD when it is associated with its homophones, or near homophones, longevity, wine and with the lucky number nine, its festival taking place on the ninth day of the ninth month. The colour of the favoured yellow variety was associated with the emperor and represented the centre of the earth. In the seventh and eighth centuries, Sui emperors and Tang metropolitan society developed a 'craze' for the tree peony (*mudan*, *Paeonia suffruticosa*), and it too became incorporated in the floral scrolls but as a symbol of wealth rather

---

[82] Li 1956.   [83] Li 1956:75ff.   [84] Rawson 1984.   [85] McMullen 1987:199.
[86] The word for orchid (*lan*) occurs in the *Book of Odes*, the poems in which date from the period 800–600 BC. Waley claims the word refers to a leguminous plant which he calls the 'vine-bean' (*The Book of Songs*, London, 1937, p.55, Ode 55). The hidden orchid (*you lan*) is identified with Confucius as a symbol of unrecognised worth, but only by later tradition. It occurs in the *Chu ci* (Songs of the South).

than of spirituality.[87] The tree peony is linked to the name of the Empress Wu who favoured Buddhism and whose capital at Luoyang was the centre for its cultivation. That was followed in the next century by the inclusion of the hollyhock, which became a symbol of passing time, although it never attained the status of a major floral emblem.[88]

At the same time as there were changes of meaning, in other cases there was also a loss. It has been argued that flower and animal subjects became 'no more than pleasing motifs', appreciated not for their meaning but because they were 'attractive and intriguing'.[89] The continuation of the motif combined with such a loss is frequent in the history of art; so too is the process by which the motif is endowed with new significances. The first occurred with the border motifs and ornamental scrolls. At the same time, as McMullen points out, the continuing appeal of the great floral emblems to successive generations of Chinese involved some reinterpretation.

The total repertoire was numerically small: 'To the lotus, peony, bamboo, pine and prunus should be added the peach, the chrysanthemum and the orchid.'[90] These flowers formed part of the literary tradition over many centuries, being endowed with multivocal meanings. In the case of the 'three friends of winter', the bamboo, the pine and the winter-flowering prunus, the continuity of their role over the centuries gives some support to the view that the symbolic tradition, becoming 'adapted to the aspirations of all levels of Chinese society', persisted over the long term, in substance as in form.[91] Such penetration certainly took place. Nevertheless, these traditions are strongly associated with the culture of privileged literati for whom the maintenance of symbolic value was also the maintenance of political and economic influence. Even if the transmission of that culture was often by oral and visual channels, through operas, stories, poems, paintings and displays, the tradition was embodied in written and graphic works which provided a focus for its unitary aspects. Some of the components of flower symbolism were no doubt developed in the 'pre-literate' culture but which ones we cannot be sure; others emerged from the later interactions among the common people. But the elaboration of flower culture took place largely at the hands of the literati who were also concerned with arranging for the cultivation and domestication of flowers so that it was the meanings they established that tended to be determinative. Much was elaborated in the written text. 'Popular culture', as we know it, the product of the interaction of the written and the 'oral' (that is, non-written) traditions, incorporated many elements of literati culture, such as the notion of the 'three friends of winter' or the 'four gentlemen of flowers',

---

[87] See Bartholomew 1985:23–4; it is the emblem of riches and honours, *fu-kuei hua*, a phrase used in many puns (Koehn 1952:133).   [88] I am grateful to D. McMullen for his references to flowers in Tang poetry.
[89] Rawson 1984, following Gombrich.   [90] McMullen 1987:199.
[91] On painting the pine, see Barnhart 1983:546–55.

and it employed these elements in visual motifs, in flower festivals and in rites of passage.

Some indications of the character, range and context of the symbolic significance of flowers in popular usage will emerge in discussing the contemporary situation, especially at the New Year. The lotus, associated both with the literati and with Buddhism, was opposed to the peony standing for wealth and sensuality.[92] The begonia was the feminine flower *par excellence* because it prefers cool and shady places, so that it enters into many stories of forlorn love. The iris was linked to ideas about fertility and the birth of sons. An iris broth was used in a ceremonial bath in parts of South China and one could drink an infusion in wine, which was believed to prolong life and to promote intelligence; together with artemisia, it was hung on doors for protection.[93] The red pomegranate blossom was believed to ward off bad fortune as well as signifying happiness and fertility, especially the birth of male offspring as numerous as its seeds. The day lily was the herb of forgetfulness, helpful in alleviating the pains of childbirth but also worn in pregnancy to ensure the birth of a son.[94]

As the reference to both literati and Buddhism implies, such associations were often contextual, depending upon the specific domain of discourse. Other meanings depended upon the enormous extent of punning and word play, partly tonal, partly phonic, partly allusive.[95] Used in the decorative arts, the puns become rebuses; several botanical motifs were strung together to form an auspicious phrase, as when the peony, magnolia and crab apple are combined in a design to mean 'wealth and rank in the jade hall'.[96] In most contexts flowers carried general meanings of well-being and few if any acquired the negative implications that some took on in parts of Europe, for example, the chrysanthemum and the carnation with their associations with funerals and death.[97] Flowers were uniformly positive, harbingers of good, concerned with the three basic wishes of mankind for longevity, happiness and fertility.

Flower symbolism in China was therefore multivocal, multivalent. 'Meaning was read into their habitats, their shape, and from the season of the year in which they flowered or were most conspicuous. Their ability to withstand weather, their medicinal properties, and the meaning of characters homophonous with their names were also given significance.' The transfer to Europe involved, it has been suggested, an impoverishment of meaning

---

[92] The lotus is said to bear the meaning of a wish for many sons in Guangzhou (*Introduction to Popular Traditions*, 4).   [93] Laing 1988:32; Eberhard 1952:82–5; Weidner 1988:109.

[94] For other significances of the day lily and the pomegranate, see Koehn 1952:135, 138.

[95] See Bartholomew 1985.   [96] Bartholomew 1985:24.

[97] In Seoul, Korea, in 1989, I was told that chrysanthemums were used for funerals and roses for marriage; it would be terrible to make a mistake. From Japan I have also heard the same thoughts about chrysanthemums. I view these associations as being adoptions from Western usage since I do not think they have any historical depth.

because the Western tradition was based on 'a simple one to one correlation with a single virtue or moral value'.[98] That impression is certainly given by the Language of Flowers. But those lists were a highly specialised product of a branch of the written tradition which by no means exhausted the wider 'culture of flowers' in Europe. As in China the 'higher' culture of painting, literature and religion heavily influenced symbolic usage throughout the society, often in a segmental, contextual manner. But what may appear to be a unitary scheme in the eyes of the actor reflects his participation in different segments at different times.

THE USAGE OF FLOWERS

In looking more generally at the uses of flowers in social life, I turn from historical to cultural depth, referring to the recent past where the material is more abundant. The great importance of flowers is embodied in the word *hua*, which in various combinations refers not only to a blossom but to sparks, sprays, fireworks, variegated designs, cotton prints, decorative borders, flower paintings, toilet water (*hualushui*) and nectar (*huami*). The word stands for female beauty itself in the phrase 'as beautiful as flowers and jade' (*ru hua si yu*) and it is associated symbolically not only with married love (*hua hao yueyuan*, 'blooming flowers and full moon') but with the more casual sexual congress sought by literati and merchants, by men of all classes, among the 'flower girls' (*huazi*) on the 'flower boats' of Guangzhou (Canton) of the Yangzi delta and elsewhere in the country. While the word can mean women in a general sense, more usually it refers to prostitutes and entertainers. Going to visit them was 'looking for the flowers and asking after the willows' (*xun hua wenliu*), and as a consequence venereal disease was called the 'flower willow disease'. During the Republican period, a tax, known as 'flower surcharge', *huajan*, was placed on prostitutes. Such girls were often called by the names of flowers, plum, orchid, fragrance, as was the case with 'geishas' during the Tang and, at a later period, with the actresses in the Peking Opera and indeed with household servants. They often wore flowers in their hair according to a commentator on Chinese life in nineteenth-century San Francisco, who added that the 'courtesans generally wear garments of a loud colour'.[99] However, this practice was certainly not confined to the lower orders and on festive occasions in Beijing well-dressed ladies also decorated their hair with flowers.[100]

The use of flowers in personal decoration varied in different parts of the country as well as by class. The plant-hunter, Fortune, remarked that the ladies of Suzhou (Fujian) were particularly fond of using flowers, though these were not confined to the natural; there was already a flourishing market in

---

[98] McMullen 1987:200.   [99] Gibson 1877:150.   [100] Bredon and Mitrophanow 1927:126.

artificial flowers there in the sixteenth century. 'The rustic cottage beauty employs the more large and gaudy, such as the red Hibiscus; while the refined damsels prefer the jasmine, tuberose, and others of that description: artificial flowers, however are more in use than natural ones'.[101] That was also the case in the 1930s. In his autobiographical account in *The Golden Wing*, Lin refers to artificial flowers in the bride's hair and to the sedan chair in which she travelled being decorated with cloth flowers.[102] In recent times magnolia was made up into hair ornaments and corsages, which were sold in the streets of most large cities in China, while gardenias and wintersweet are also worn in the hair.[103] Once again, bright colours seem to be associated with lower groups, more subtle shades with upper ones. On the other hand, artificial flowers seem to have no negative value in the context of self-decoration and could be used by one and all.

Jasmines, imported from South Asia and Persia during the Han Dynasty, were much used for garlands in South China. The unopened buds were gathered before sunrise and sold for perfuming tea as well as for decorating the hair.[104] A seventeenth-century account of Guangdong province recounts how women collected the buds in a wet cloth for sale to the city flower merchants, where hundreds of workers were employed to string them into headdresses, lampshades and other ornamental articles for sale.[105] The flowers were also employed to make perfume, and jasmine garlands were even used to decorate buildings during religious ceremonies. The market was well established at that time.

That was also true for the other 'flower market', that in sex. In the hierarchy of prostitution during the early part of the twentieth century the lowest facilities were the 'flower smoke rooms' (*huayan jian*) where customers could smoke opium and visit prostitutes simultaneously. More than 20,000 employees were reported in the Concession areas in Guangzhou in the late 1910s. In other places, men went mainly to drink 'flower wine' (*huajiu*), that is, wine poured by prostitutes. If a patron paid heavily for the privilege of 'deflowering' a new recruit to the profession, he would go through a 'solemn ceremony ... much like a marriage rite' and then host a banquet for his friends at the brothel, a procedure known as 'celebrating the flower' (*zuo huatou*).[106]

The concept of flowers is deeply embedded metaphorically in many other expressions. 'Too many flowers dazzle the eye' (*hua duo yan luan*) is an idiom for being faced with a wide range of options. 'Different flowers strike different eyes' is a way of indicating the range of individual tastes. 'Viewing flowers on horseback' (*zou ma kan hua*) is an expression for taking a casual glance at

[101] Fortune 1847:373, 382.
[102] Lin 1947:42. For plum blossoms in the hair in the sixth-century poem by Xiao Gang, see Bickford 1985:19.
[103] Li 1959:148, 161, 167.
[104] On jasmine 'flowers with coloured silk for use as hair ornaments' in the South in the early fourth century, see Li 1979:36. In the North the plant was grown in hothouses for the same purpose.   [105] Li 1959:127–8.
[106] Hershatter 1991:10, 24. A common expression for the same procedure is *kai bao*, to 'open the bud'.

things of beauty. *Huaxu* means 'flower bits' and refers to the odds and ends of things. Like the use of flowers in art, in literature and in life, the word is pervasive.

Flowers were and are widely employed both in public and private ceremonies in China. Writing of the period before the Second World War, Koehn notes that 'Special occasions, such as Births and Deaths, Marriages and Anniversaries, the New Year's Day and the Passing of Examinations, in fact all days of celebration, call for appropriate flowers. Each month has its flower, as does each of the Four Seasons. Definite plants are associated with particular Deities, Buddhist Saints, Taoists Immortals, as well as with certain birds and animals.'[107] Decorative designs with flowers appear on innumerable items of everyday use.

In earlier times they were not only used to give pleasure and as offerings in rituals but were themselves the receivers of offerings. Every principal kind of flower was said to have a 'fairy' in Heaven who looked after its welfare.[108] The Goddess of All Flowers herself, Hua Shen, celebrated her birthday on the twelfth day of the second month, when trees and shrubs were decorated with red papers.[109] On the day of the 'flowers' birthday', spirits of blossoms presented themselves to the Jade Emperor.[110] Under the Empress Dowager Cixi a court festival celebrated that birthday by cutting up red silk and decorating flowering trees with ribbons. In a theatrical performance that followed, female flower fairies (tree spirits were male) drank wine and sang.[111] Paintings of flowers were made especially for this occasion, just as hanging scrolls of auspicious flowers and fruit would be planted for the New Year to supplement the more usual couplets.

Nor was this the only festival devoted to flowers. The eighteenth-century novel, *The Story of the Stone*, gives an account of the festival of Grain in Ear on the twenty-sixth day of the fourth month when offerings were made to the flower spirits at the beginning of summer as the blossom is about to fall. To speed the spirits on their way girls made 'little palanquins and coaches out of willow-twigs and flowers and little banners and pennants from scraps of brocade and any other pretty material they could find, which they fastened with threads of coloured silk to the tops of flowering trees and shrubs'.[112]

It was above all the plum that formed the focus of spring viewing. A story of a famous courtesan in the twelfth century tells how the son of a minister

---

[107] Koehn 1952:121.
[108] Buddhists associate these agencies with the task of rewarding students of the text with flowers. 'One of the tasks of the Heavenly Fairy in charge of the Buddhist Kingdom of Fragrances is the scattering of Flowers, *t'ien nü san hua* . . . over students of the holy Scriptures to test their spiritual attainment. On those who have not discarded all mortal desire, the falling blossoms will cling. Not a single petal, however, ever disturbs those who have reached Perfection' (Koehn 1952:123). Is this another indication of the potential opposition between flowers (as worldly, luxurious, sensuous) and the simple virtues?
[109] Li 1956:31.   [110] Robinson 1988:85.   [111] Weidner 1988:54; Der Ling 1911:348–50.
[112] Weidner 1988:54; Cao Xueqin 1977:24.

begged her to go with him to East Village to enjoy the early plum blossom.[113] The practice was widespread. Many horticulturalists made a living planting plum trees. The magistrate's secretary, Shen Fu, writes of the area near Suzhou in the late eighteenth century where 'when the flowers bloomed all you could see for dozens of *li* appeared to be a heavy fall of snow', so the region was called the Sea of Fragrant Snow.[114] On his visit to perform the spring sacrifice at a temple in the area, he admired the blossoms and the landscape so much that he painted a set of twelve pictures of the scene to present to his host. On another occasion he travelled to see the turning leaves in the ninth month, a practice which both in China and in Japan also had a long history.

Plum trees were also used as memorials. To the east of the Zhiyong Academy of Fuzhou stood a shrine to Wang Kaitai, the founder and Governor of the province. In the courtyard were thirteen plum-blossom trees which his successor, Xie, replanted at the same time as he restored the academy's tablets and built a 'thirteen plum-blossom tree study'. These trees became an important focus of his thoughts; 'at winter's end, I open the door and gaze upon the plum trees'.[115] Like potted trees, the plum was offered as a gift to temples, for example, during the month of the winter sacrifice.[116]

While some flowers were grown for display in gardens, that was not their major function. Nor were gardens mainly for flowers, but rather the domain of water, rocks, greenery and miniature trees. As we have noted, a large number of the flowers in China appear on trees and bushes rather than on herbaceous plants. Even the latter are grown mainly as potted plants, to be placed on walls or balconies and in areas of public display. Roof gardens could be very elaborate, with terraces on the tops of buildings being extended into hanging roof gardens, with 'rocks arranged and flowers planted up there so that a visitor would never know that a building lay beneath his feet'.[117] Only on specific occasions and for particular purposes were flowers introduced into the house, although their representations abound in painting, on lacquered furniture, on porcelain, on textiles, in the form of miniatures of jade or other stone, even flowers of silk and other materials, especially in the houses of the elite. While such uses were widespread among the literati, and influenced other segments of the community, their model was largely urban, with the enclosed gardens, the floral designs etched on house windows, the decorated panels, the carved wood. According to Yuan Hongdao, 'the enjoyment of flowers is just a substitute for people living in the cities who must forsake the happiness of enjoying the natural scenery', a thesis that can also be applied to the growth of interest in nature in the West.[118] The flowers that the

[113] 'The oil vendor and the courtesan', discussed by Laing 1988:36. On the spring viewing of plum blossom, see Bickford 1985:28.   [114] Shen Fu 1983:136.   [115] Barnett 1989.   [116] Shen Fu 1983:127.
[117] Shen Fu 1983:138.   [118] Li 1956:95.

plant-hunter Robert Fortune found in the 1840s were largely in the town gardens of the 'mandarins' or literati. One at Ningbo belonged to Dr Zhang, an old man 'long retired from trade and with an independent fortune', who enjoyed gardening and was 'passionately fond of flowers'.[119] The garden was very limited in extent and arranged around artificial rock work, with little pools surrounded by dwarf trees and creepers, so that 'the resemblance to nature is perfect'.

Village houses were less marked by floral decorations, either real or 'artificial'. Nevertheless, features of the culture of flowers are today found throughout the region, certainly in South China and Taiwan. Walls display floral calendars and reproductions of paintings of a less sophisticated variety than in town apartments. These are widely available in mainland China, being constantly reproduced; a popular magazine devotes itself to the culture of flowers; desk calendars give reminders of growing seasons and the uses of flowers. Flowering shrubs are found around many habitations and dwarf trees can be purchased at high prices in rural markets.

For while the culture of flowers was elaborated by the literati, the growing and enjoyment of them was certainly not confined to that group alone. Writing of the Weihaiwei villages of the North China coast when they were under British administration at the beginning of this century, the magistrate Johnson observes that 'many of the cottages have little gardens which if chiefly devoted to vegetables are seldom quite destitute of flowers. The peony, chrysanthemum, wild lilies and roses, spiraea, hibiscus, jasmine, sunflower, campanula, iris and Michaelmas daisy are all common.'[120] Many of the flowering plants were prized for their medicinal and culinary qualities. But they were also used for other purposes, for placing on the Buddhist shrine in the house or as an offering to the ancestors on the proper occasions. Flowers were cut and used as gifts, but to divinities and to the dead rather than to the living, just as one greets gods but never mortals with palms pressed together in the Indian fashion. Indeed, both practices may have been adopted with Buddhism and reserved for the supernatural.

Flowers are particularly associated with rites to the dead. On Memorial Day in Hong Kong, families take floral and other offerings to the tombs of their ancestors, providing the dead with an array of ritual food and even with the chopsticks to consume them. They are also used at funerals for 'wreaths' and 'bouquets'. In Taiwan, and less gaudily in Hong Kong, the vans taking bodies to the place of burial are decorated with coloured blossoms, real and artificial; in smaller towns such as Xiaolan, Guangdong, the coffin is still carried through the town on a special route (along Coffin Street) bearing a large wreath of flowers (*huaquan*, flower ring) on top (Plate 12.3). Flowers are

---

[119] Fortune 1847:98.   [120] Johnson 1910:167.

12.3 Flowers on the coffin, Xiaolan, Guangdong, 1989.

also used to form a kind of placard (Plate 12.4) which is carried through the streets and can be stood upright on its legs; on either side is a black paper banner on which an appropriate couplet has been written.[121]

A similar placard, but with red banners carrying a joyous message, is used for more festive occasions, especially outside newly opened shops or offices, and even on the anniversary of their opening. These placards are made up by florists and often contain a mixture of fresh and artificial flowers, which have the obvious advantage of being longer lasting. Flowers are used to celebrate the passing of examinations, the celebration of weddings and the performance of operas. The foyer of the Lee Theatre in Hong Kong where the Cantonese Opera was playing at New Year 1989, was filled with floral and written tributes to the two stars, both women; the most prominent tributes came from their 'adopted' parents or patrons.[122] On these and other such occasions,

---

[121] Such funeral banners could also be white with black lettering, such as were placed by students before the portrait of the former leader of the Communist Party, Hu Yaobang. That commemoration led up to the events in Tiananmen Square of June 1989. Such 'wreaths' were forbidden at the earlier funeral of Zhou Enlai, in an attempt to 'bury' the ousted leader quietly. But in both cases the funeral was turned into a demonstration, a not unusual use of ritual for political ends. For an account of the offerings of wreaths, flowers and poems for Zhou Enlai in Tiananmen Square at Qingming ('Martyrs' Day') in 1976 as a form of support and protest which led to violent suppression by the authorities, see Cheng 1986:573ff.

[122] Adopted in the weakest sense of the term; 'patrons' would be a better translation, which even retains the implication of kinship. There are three degrees of 'adoption' in Guangzhou.

12.4 Placard for a funeral, Hong Kong, 1989.

flowers are also hung in baskets (*hualan*). These baskets do not form part of regular gift giving, although in Hong Kong over the New Year close friends may take elaborate ones filled with fruit when they go on visits.[123]

Nowadays weddings are often occasions when flowers are used in profusion, especially when celebrated at a hotel or restaurant. The well-attended marriages held over Christmas 1985, at the Grand Hotel in Taibei, among many others, were hardly traditional. The bride wore white, at least for her outer garment, the bridesmaids too. In the more lavish versions, the many guests, filling up to one hundred tables of twelve persons each, eat in a

---

[123] However, Li (1956) writes that 'Bouquets and baskets of flowers, which emphasize masses rather than lines, are frequently used as presents between friends.'

large room expensively decorated with set floral sprays, consisting of a green background with red and yellow flowers, the latter often chrysanthemums. Meanwhile the groom and some other guests sported a red flower, usually a rose or carnation, carefully placed in the buttonhole of the left lapel of the dark suit they were wearing. While the Western influence was strong, it did not altogether eliminate local practice.

Flowers did not play the same part in more traditional marriages. A few days later, at a wedding banquet in a provincial town in central Taiwan, there were no flowers at all on the tables and only the groom had a red rose in his buttonhole. The bride wore red rather than white, the wall of the living room was covered with pieces of cloth, donated by the mother's brother among others, on which were pinned notes (many being 1,000 NT dollar bills, that is 40 US dollars) as gifts to the couple. The total amount they received on this occasion was large since the girl's dowry included a car! But flowers were scarce.

Flowers are not only things of beauty but play a part as food and medicine. They were often served with sacrificial offerings such as pig or sheep.[124] During winter a favourite dish in Guangdong is snake and chrysanthemums. The snakes are sold in markets and often kept live in cages by restaurants, just as others keep lobsters or fish; the chrysanthemums are a small white variety, sometimes used in other dishes, that float in the soup. Another flower (*Osmanthus fragrans*) is used as an ingredient in a soup served in Shanghai restaurants. Chrysanthemums may be blended with tea, especially in Guangzhou, and sold as a beverage in special shops where it is kept hot in a huge brass container of elegant proportions. Other dried and scented flowers, which included *Olea fragrans*, *Chloranthus inconspicuus*, *Aglaia odorata*, as well as lychee and jasmine, may be added to black tea or brewed separately to be mixed with honey.[125] Yet others such as cassia can be added to wine.[126]

The culinary is not distinct from the medical. Chrysanthemum tea is seen as having a cooling effect on the body. In Hong Kong dried flowers are often included in the medicines prescribed by the local doctor and dispensed in the shop where he practises, and which often deals in Western medicines at a separate counter. Their therapeutic properties are widely valued and used in conjunction with cures from other traditions; indeed, from the actor's point of view these traditions are not 'alternative' but supplementary resources. The medicinal use especially of dried flowers stands in striking contrast to Africa where medicine is mainly the leaves, roots and bark of trees and bushes. In China during the 1950s, the use of flowers for contraceptive purposes was even advocated by official sources, in particular the honeysuckle, safflower blossoms, the buds of aubergine flowers, as well as other vegetable products.[127]

---

[124] Fortune 1847:191.   [125] Fortune 1847:219.   [126] Shen Fu 1983:125.   [127] Yuan Tien 1965:227.

The public use of flowers is not only ritual but also secular. The practice of displaying plants with hundreds of blooms goes back to the Song and is still carried on today in both China and Japan. Chrysanthemums in particular lend themselves to being trained to make elaborate patterns with large numbers of blooms emerging from a single stalk in quite astounding ways. The chrysanthemum is the special symbol of the Chongyang Festival (or Chongjiu, Double Ninth, in popular parlance) held on the ninth day of the ninth month, when it stands both for the autumnal season and for longevity. It was at this time, in the early autumn, that the court went up to a high place to view the scenery.[128] In former times, beginning with the Han Dynasty, the court celebration included floral displays and the drinking of chrysanthemum wine. These displays might consist of potted plants of the small-flowered varieties that are trained onto bamboo frames and made to cascade into a multitude of blooms by continuously plucking off the top of the growing plant so that two are produced in place of one. This process involved large amounts of specialist care which matched the more amateur attention paid by scholars.

An idea of the profound impact of flowers on the life of those literati is provided by Shen Fu's *Six Records of a Floating Life* (1809), in which he gives an account of the natural scenery he went to see and the splendid gardens he visited. In one garden at Suzhou he wanted to entertain some 'poor scholars' with wine, tea and dumplings while the rape flowers were in bloom.[129] In his trips to the mountains, he picked wild chrysanthemums which he placed behind his ear;[130] elsewhere he admired the hortensia and cassia flowers. His wife, Chen Yun, made movable screens out of live flowers, plum-flower trays for food, and placed tea leaves in lotus flowers over night to catch the perfume. Shen Fu himself always had a vase of flowers on his desk, which he himself arranged.[131] He explains how 'poor scholars' living in 'small crowded houses' could create 'an illusion amidst reality' by means of tray gardens. He himself was 'obsessed with a love of flowers' and pruned miniature trees to make them look like real ones, a lifetime's work since the 'proper training of a tree takes at least thirty or forty years'.[132] His account provides some idea of the care and expertise involved, not only in pruning but also in flower arranging; for instance, chrysanthemums should always be placed in vases in odd numbers with blooms of the same colour, no more than seven vases on one table.

The public attention paid by literati and others to the growing of flowers is demonstrated in the chrysanthemum festivals held in Xiaolan, a town of 12,000 inhabitants in the Pearl River delta in South China.[133] During the Ming period (1368–1644), military settlements were established in the region in order to reclaim the sandy banks of the numerous rivers. Migrant farmers and

---

[128] Li 1959:44.
[129] Shen Fu 1983:66.   [130] Shen Fu 1983:108.   [131] Shen Fu 1983:62.   [132] Shen Fu 1983:59.
[133] For an analysis of the ceremonies, see Siu 1990, from which this account is derived.

fishermen moved in to exploit the resources of the area, while corporate estates from the older, settled parts of the delta petitioned the imperial government for ownership rights over the largely untaxed land which they in turn farmed out to tenant farmers. The local inhabitants eventually formed lineages, built elaborate temples and ancestral halls, produced their own literati, and began to challenge the corporate estates themselves.

One of the ways of asserting and establishing the power and wealth of these newer lineages was by mounting festivals devoted to the chrysanthemum, whose cultivation had played a part in attracting settlers to the area. The town, whose name means 'Little Olive', has recently christened itself 'Chrysanthemum Town' and even exports chrysanthemum-flavoured egg-rolls manufactured by a municipally owned factory.[134] The use of flowers as centrepieces for festivals had already been a common feature of the area. The regional town of Foshan has its popular festival of 'autumn colours' and nearby Panyu its celebration of 'water colours'. But the particular form the festival at Xiaolan has taken over the last two and a half centuries seems to have its roots in the culture of the literati. In the first place the cultivation of this flower was regarded by the gentlemen-scholar as 'a luxury for the leisured'. It carried the notion of a retreat from mundane political affairs but that was a temporary retreat which 'continued to affirm attachment to the Imperial order'; distant from the vulgarities of the world, the flower could only be grown with delicate craftsmanship.[135]

The local literati displayed their culture as well as their strength by competing in displays of flowers, especially in the form of offerings to the ancestors at their lineage halls. Since the mid eighteenth century the new elites had formed poetry societies at whose dinners friends competed in composing poems, which might then be hung in the halls themselves. On the occasion of the festivals 'chrysanthemum operas' were staged, with visiting companies from the nearby town of Foshan coming to give theatrical performances on themes derived from literati culture.[136] These operas were appreciated by the peasantry too, as were the elaborate floral displays constructed by skilled gardeners; the peasants enjoyed the results as well as contributing their labour. For not only the elites were involved in these performances; the ancestral halls touched the interest of the whole of a local surname group. At this point there was a merging of popular and elite culture. Nevertheless, the literati defined much of the framework of belief and practice. While smaller festivals took place every few years, in 1814 the elites decided to hold a more elaborate ceremony every sixty years and this became a renowned feature of the region. After a period of uncertainty following the Second World War, the festivals were officially encouraged and mounted more frequently than before.

---

[134] On the uses of the Chinese olive (*Canarium sp.*), see Bartholomew 1980:48.   [135] Siu 1990:777.
[136] The themes of these operas are used to decorate the roofs and screens of especially elaborate lineage halls, like that of the Chen Academy in Guangzhou.

The campaign to promote 'native roots' aimed to attract overseas Chinese to participate in the life of the community, economically and otherwise.

Of all the uses of flowers, fruit and blossoms, both cut and potted, in South China the most striking occurs at the New Year, where they become symbols of future prosperity. The next chapter will be devoted to the production and consumption of flowers at this festival, 'actually' and 'symbolically', as we observed it in Guangdong in 1989.

THE RELIGIOUS USES OF FLOWERS: BUDDHISM AND CONFUCIANISM

In the past the use of flowers was particularly associated with Buddhism and that remains true today. On being offered a figure of Guanyin, the Buddhist goddess of mercy, by a nun to take back to her home overseas, a friend said she didn't know how to look after it. The nun replied: 'Just put a flower there from time to time' (Colour plate XII.1). The Loupao temple near Sanshui, Guangdong, consisted of three adjacent buildings, the centre one Daoist, the right Confucian and the left Buddhist. When we visited the temple in January 1989, only before the figure of Guanyin in the Buddhist section were there any significant quantities of flowers, filling a vase held by the goddess. On a stand in front of the shrine stood a larger wide-brimmed vessel, the base of which was formed by lotus petals. That association is widely accepted today. When a museum curator in Guangzhou was asked about a pattern on a piece of Han metalwork that we thought might be connected with that flower, he remarked, 'No, Buddhism had not reached us then.'[137] In fact the lotus was known before the Han but this opinion represents a widely held view of the relationship between Buddhism and the culture of flowers, in particular the lotus. Given the continuing connection, even in eclectic China, of Buddhism with vegetarianism and the avoidance of killing animals, flowers were seen as an acceptable offering to the deity.[138]

While there was not the clear-cut opposition between flowers linked to Buddhism, and foliage with Daoism or Confucianism, that one finds with Shintoism in Japan, places of non-Buddhist worship tended to be associated with offerings of meat (usually cooked, not raw in blood sacrifice) and with the use of greenery. Flowers are certainly found in temples associated with popular culture, for example in the Daoist temple of Ching Chung Koon at

[137] On the botany of the Indian lotus (*Nelumbo nucifera*), see Li 1959:64ff. Both the Indian lotus and the waterlily (*Nymphaea*) were apparently known in the China of the first millennium, the term *shui lian* being used of the latter (pp.43–4, referring to an early fourth-century source on South China).

[138] On the import of Indian exotics to China under the Tang, see Schafer 1963: Chapter 7. The strong associations of Buddhism with vegetable products continues today. Vegetarian restaurants in Hong Kong, of which there are some 200, are closely linked to Buddhism and Buddhist associations. On the first day of the lunar New Year, the inhabitants have nothing but vegetable foods (at least for the first meal); slaughter begins the following day. Nunneries such as that on Lantau Island, Hong Kong, provide only vegetarian food for the guests, while in the courtyard and in the temple itself flowers abound.

Tuen Mun, Hong Kong; nearby a new temple for commemorating the dead (a profitable business attracting private enterprise) embodied a nursery for growing plants in its planning. The groups in nineteenth-century Beijing who assisted with temple activities included ones for donating fresh flowers.[139]

In contemporary Taiwan most temples of a Daoist or popular persuasion do not appear to make a great use of flowers in worship, although the decor of the buildings themselves incorporated floral motifs.[140] In normal times there were no stalls for their purchase situated around the temples. However at festivals such as New Year matters were very different. Numerous stands with cut flowers sprang up, selling chrysanthemums, daisies, snapdragons, cat willow, birds-of-paradise, all standing for long life and prosperity. These flowers were placed within the temple; as in India, jasmine was scattered in bowls, used as offerings or fixed to wire and hung on dwarf trees and plants of different kinds. The same was true in Hong Kong where temples of popular religion, such as that to Tan Hou, the 'Empress of Heaven', were adorned with the seasonal flowers, peach, tangerine, narcissi, chrysanthemums and whatever was available in the market.

However, lineage halls, which are basically Confucian in their ideology, are not remarkable for flowers, being associated more with *penjing*, the miniaturised trees beloved by the literati. At New Year 1989, the focal lineage hall (*zumiao*) of Foshan in Guangdong had no flowers inside the temple, though the public gardens outside were glowing with yellow chrysanthemums. That of the Chen Clan in Guangzhou had a large display of dwarf trees that were being offered for sale. That there is an underlying opposition between Buddhism and Confucianism which is partly expressed in the use of flowers for worship is evident in the history of the struggle between them in China but especially in Korea where the effects of this antipathy were considerable, both on the culture of flowers and on the question of the representation of men and gods. Buddhism arrived from China in AD 372 by way of officially sanctioned missions and was welcomed by the ruling houses who used it for state ends.[141] The effect on art was far-reaching. It was strongly associated with the use of flowers in worship, in texts but above all in architecture. With Buddhism came the use of the lotus decoration on the ends

---

[139] Naquin, forthcoming.

[140] The usual offerings made in the temples were three fold in character: firstly, the incense which was presented to the 'deity' by raising the burning sticks between one's hands, inclining the head at the same time; secondly, there were the offerings of fruit, biscuits and other food placed on the flat altar in front of the 'deity' and which in most cases were removed by the givers themselves. Finally, there was the paper money burnt for prosperity at the special incinerator in the forecourt of the temple. These items could all be purchased at stalls nearby, which were sometimes incorporated in the temples themselves (especially those for paper money and incense). Sometimes boxes were provided for monetary donations in addition to the usual stalls where one could get one's fortune told by means of sticks or paper rolls inscribed with characters, although it was always possible to perform such divination oneself by using sticks or the paired crescents that lay upon the altar table.   [141] Lee 1984:59.

of roof tiles that is such a characteristic feature of the archaeological remains of temples (see Plate 12.1), together with the acanthus, arabesque and grape patterns. Sometimes these were moulded in clay, sometimes painted in bright colours such as are still used on Buddhist buildings which are adorned with real and painted flowers.[142] The same period saw the development of three-dimensional representation, for while there had been small clay figurines at an earlier date, we now have magnificent Buddhist images which formed virtually the entire repertoire of sculpture during the period of the Three Kingdoms.

From the beginning Confucianism was opposed to Buddhism, arguing against its 'otherworldly' teaching and its preference for merit rather than rank as a way to office, a logical position for those outside the high nobility.[143] It was also distinctly puritanical, opposed to the pleasure-seeking of kings and basing itself on the moral standards expounded in its well-known texts. While portraits of Confucius, of the philosophers and of the worthies were brought from China at an early date, there seems to have been no development of statuary for the purposes of worship.

In striking contrast to the gaudiness of Buddhist temples are Confucian structures. With the Li Dynasty (1392–1910) Buddhism was now suppressed and neo-Confucianism became the ideology of the ruling class. The dominant tone was very different: 'They scorned ostentation in the interior decoration of the *sarangbang* [or men's quarters], preferring simple elegance . . . Folding screens were generally avoided . . . and only an occasional calligraphic work or painting decorated the walls.'[144] While the painting and the growing of flowers were strongly linked to the neo-Confucian literati, there was more restraint in the use of bright decoration, preference being given to the blacks and whites of calligraphy in Confucian ceremonies, though weddings and funerals on the other hand brought out flowers, gay clothes and a range of colours. This situation bears a number of basic similarities to the Reformation in Europe where 'plainness' was 'opposed' to ornamentation much as the word was to the image.[145] This Confucian 'restraint' applied mainly in the context of the ancestral cult and of lineage halls, that is, the context of worship. For it was precisely these same literati who were largely responsible for the development of a culture of flowers in art and in gardens. A similar opposition seems to occur in China itself.

There too we see indications not simply of restraint but of a similar

---

[142] See *Catalogue of the National Museum of Korea 1988*. One way to recognise Silla foundations (c.600–800) in much later Korean temples is by the stone plinths carved with formal flowers, on which the main wooden structure stands.

[143] The State University (Tachak) was founded in 372 during the Three Kingdoms Period by which time Confucianism had arrived. But it received a new impetus during the Tang leading to the establishment of the National Confucian College (Kukhak) in 682 followed by a state examination for the selection of government officials in 788.   [144] *Catalogue of the National Museum of Korea 1988*:126.

[145] Summers 1968:73, quoted by Kronenfeld in her interesting discussion (1989).

preference for the verbal over the visual that we have found in various forms under the Near Eastern religions. Paintings and statues of gods appear in the folk religion, of which the lower-level literates -- school teachers, accountants, lesser monks and letter-writers – are the main carriers and, in the case of the paintings, the actual creators. The literati themselves created a secular art that focused on nature and virtually excluded deities. Indeed, they had positive objections to images of supernatural beings, possibly arising out of the general problem of representing the immaterial in material form. That problem is more likely to be made explicit by literates preoccupied with the written word than at more popular levels where the visual tends to dominate. A record of the Lius of Fengjian in the Pearl River delta refers to their early ancestral hall as a 'portrait hall' (*yingtang*), suggesting that portraits of the ancestors were originally hung there instead of tablets. 'This deviation from the official practice was corrected in the early seventeenth century after the lineage had produced descendants holding senior official degrees.'[146] The question of whether ancestral worship took place in front of portraits during the Song is a matter of much debate, but the opposition between word (script) and image (portrait) is clear. In the rich area of the delta, the shift to tablets occurred early, but in poorer areas like southern Fujian, ancestral figures were, until very recently, being carved by the same specialists who made the images for the folk religion.[147] The abstract representations of the ancestors, the concentration of much decorative art on calligraphy and banners, the aversion of literati art to representing deities, this was balanced by a secular art, practised by the same literati, that placed great emphasis on nature in all its forms, including domesticated flowers.

But the problem of the equivocal relationship of object to image extends outside the context of divinity and was expressed in an early source from the second century AD. 'By making pictures of dragons the duke of She succeeded in bringing down a real dragon.' The author Wang Chong saw the image as inferior to the word; painting failed to 'transform' and 'enlighten'.[148] That more general feeling did not prevent the development of a tradition of representation, but it did indicate the relative status assigned to the visual and the verbal in the hierarchy of communication. Then there was the matter of style, with the literati displaying a preference for painting bamboo, for black and white, of restraint generally; offerings of flowers were more characteristic of the Buddhist tradition. Such restraint touched upon a question that we have often seen related to that of iconoclasm, at least in its secular form, namely, the reaction to aspects of cultures of luxury to which I return in the following chapter. For while flowers were constantly celebrated in painting, in poetry and in social life, there was an undercurrent of doubt about both representation and usage which derived ultimately from the same concerns

---

[146] Faure 1989.   [147] H. F. Siu and D. Faure, personal communications.   [148] Cahill 1964:79, 87.

that we have traced elsewhere in Eurasia; hence the preference for orchids, plums, and bamboo over the peony.

ELITES AND POPULAR CULTURE

Two general points have been stressed in this chapter. The domestication of flowers in China was directly linked to the intensive nature of horticulture that is a virtual precondition of the emergence of an elaborate culture of flowers. The uses of flowers were greatly extended under the influence of an incoming world religion, Buddhism, and, to an even greater degree, through the activities of the literati, though each brought to the subject a different approach. Other elements of a more popular kind were present; categorisations of flowers, like the uses of blossom, referred to seasonal cycles and the promises of spring, which were connected with the activities of the rural peasantry. But it was Buddhism and the literati that imported certain varieties of flower and created others, that elaborated their symbolic and productive contexts, and that made them a focus for painting and decoration. Such cultural constructs were passed on to, and in many cases vigorously adopted by, other groups in society, mediated by locally based monks and nuns as well as by lower-level literati. Those other groups made contributions of their own; the sources of culture were not undifferentiated, neither was its practice. That differentiation applied both to flowers and to food; cultural aspirations may be similar, but their fulfilment depends on a multitude of factors. What is everyday food for the rich may be banquet food for the poor; the rich have daily access to flowers, the poor on festivals, public and private. Together their activities and beliefs make up the culture of flowers.

The cultivation of the 'love of nature' or of 'natural beauty', as we understand those phrases, is in large part a function of the written tradition. That is not to say that the appreciation of nature in a broader sense is absent in societies without writing. But it has little 'voice', even in verse and narrative. What is lacking is the consciousness that comes with the reflectivity that is encouraged, and to some extent created, by reading and writing. In the first place, such attitudes are usually associated with an elite focused on the towns to whom nature is something other than their 'natural' environment. They are the ones who most insistently attempt to bring natural things into the town and into the home, partly in the imagination as Wordsworth did with the Lake District for the audience of Londoners for whom he wrote, but also in the miniaturised form of gardens, even on the roof, the balcony, in window boxes, on pavements. Parks and formal gardens were often the creations of royalty and nobility with large estates and these played their part in elaborating the culture of flowers. However, it is frequently the enclosed gardens of the bourgeoisie, the literati and the monastery that elicit the intensive care needed for the breeding of more compact shrubs, of potted plants for restricted spaces and of house plants for the interior itself. In these contexts decorative flowers are encouraged (whereas food plants are often for others to take care of), being specifically bred for the purpose, even being the subject of grand follies from time to time – the Garlandomania of Roman Alexandria, the Peonymania of the early-ninth-century Chang'an and Luoyang,[149] the Tulipomania of seventeenth-century Holland the the chrysanthemum mania of twentieth-century Guangzhou. Both for conceptual and practical reasons miniaturisation was applied even to flowering and other trees, producing valued products of distorted but aesthetic horticulture.

Such activities had their critics who were stimulated by the very reflectivity that gave permanent 'voice' to the love of nature. We have seen the different attitudes towards flowers that were embodied in religious practices and beliefs to puritanism, restraint and the word as against ostentation, colour and the icon. These were not categorical oppositions; times changed, eclecticism prevailed. But they had a parallel in the secular sphere in attitudes to the uses of flowers. Criticism was not only directed to the occasional excesses, stimulated by the zeal of merchants for gambling or conspicuous consumption. We are dealing with aspects of a luxury culture, not a culture that was confined to one class but that was hierarchical in its origin, and to some extent in its contemporary structure and in its future creation. The mass of the population certainly participated but some aspects of that culture always remained located at some distance from them, even with the advent of mass consumption. That is especially true of the written word where the populace largely receives while the elite are the emitters and the transformers. The situation contains a number of contradictions, some explicit, some implicit. Those contradictions have to do with the nature of highly stratified cultures with luxury at one end and its absence, even poverty, at another, giving rise to an internal critique. But it also has to do with the partial rejection by some 'elite' groups of aspects of sumptuary behaviour, the deliberate restraint that rejects colours in favour of black and white, or that frames its opposition to other creeds in terms of the partial rejection of flowers in worship. These themes we want to explore in the context of the celebrations of New Year, a season that produces perhaps the most lively and far-reaching manifestations of the culture of flowers in China or anywhere else.

[149] The famous Tang literary figure, Han Yu (768–824), gave his ineducable nephew another chance when he found he was an accomplished grower of peonies and claimed to produce flowers in shades of dark blue, purple, yellow and red by feeding dyes into their roots. He was brought up in the South, so it suggests that connoisseurship also extended to the great Southern cities of Yangzhou, Hangzhou and Suzhou, see *Youyang Zazu* by Duan Chengshi (803–63), Beijing, 1981, Chapter 19, pp.185–6.

13 · 'Let a hundred flowers bloom': the New Year in South China

The role of flowers in the Chinese past, then, comes down to the present in the form of the myriad of representations in poetry and legend, in paintings, in stone carvings and in the window decoration of the houses of the literati and the local elites. Those icons persist, whatever social changes occur. Operas, texts, gardens and flowers are more vulnerable, as are the literati themselves, to the kind of revolutionary transformation we have seen following the Reformation in Europe. How has the culture of flowers been affected by the 'socialist' regime of the mainland and the 'capitalist' segment of Hong Kong, Macao and Taiwan? To look at the use of flowers under both regimes we explored the strongly marked ceremonies of the New Year that began on 6 February 1989.

THE NEW YEAR FLOWERS

The use of flowers at New Year in Guangdong has been long standing. In the 1840s the plant-collector, Robert Fortune, encountered boats 'in great numbers loaded with branches of peach and plum trees in bloom', together with the hanging bellflower, camellias, cock'scombs, magnolias, all of which were destined to decorate the houses, temples and even the boats. The two favourites of this time of year were the bellflower and the jonquil (that is, narcissus). The first was brought down from the hills in bud, then placed in water to bloom. The latter was grown in water among pebbles and used by the Chinese to 'exhibit their propensity for dwarf and monstrous growth'. As today, 'large quantities of all these flowers are exposed for sale in many of the shops and in the corners of the streets in Canton, where they seem to be eagerly bought up by the Chinese, who consider them quite indispensable at this particular season'.[1]

Today there are three main species of flower associated with the New Year in Guangdong and Hong Kong, the tangerine, the narcissus and the peach. Each of these plants has been radically transformed in a number of ways from ordinary members of the species. Of these three, the dwarf tangerine is the

---

[1] Fortune 1847:157.

most widely used. Grown in pots, the bushes are covered with diminutive fruit that hang like golden lanterns against the background of dark-green citrus leaves. Often the fruit is too heavy for the branches, which may have to be supported with bamboo canes, sometimes painted green to make them less visible; to these supports the branches and even the fruit are wired. Its particular value for the New Year celebrations is sometimes linked to the similarity of its name with the word for 'blessing' or 'fortune'.[2] Optimally you should purchase a pair but many households make do with one, especially in the restricted space in which most live whether in Hong Kong, even among the better-off, or in cities of the People's Republic of China.[3]

Several varieties of tangerine are cultivated specifically for the New Year. The most popular is that known as 'Four Seasons' (Cantonese, *sze kwai kat*), whose miniature fruit is later bottled and preserved with salt. In Guangzhou and throughout Guangdong such potted plants decorate the balconies and roofs many of which proliferate with foliage and a few flowers even in the winter months from January to March (Colour plate XIII.1). Another variety is the kumquat (Cantonese, *kam kwat*, the golden tangerine) with its small, smooth-skinned, rather bitter, oval fruit. Yet a third is the giant tangerine with its wrinkled skin that is sometimes sold on small potted trees but more usually as individual fruit.[4] Such fruits carry the significance of longevity and may be purchased to decorate the side-table and later to offer to gods and ancestors.

The second of the specialised New Year plants is the narcissus (*Narcissus tazetta*), known as the water fairy (*shuixian hua*) or luck lily, which is cultivated for its perfume and for its luxurious growth. As emblems, they suggest the bringers of Great Happiness, 'the veritable genii of the Taoist Heaven'.[5] Unlike the other New Year flowers, the narcissus is found throughout China. Yet it appears to have been introduced by Arab traders in the Song period and the cultivation of the bulbs is largely localised in a small village near Zhangzhou in Fujian, a possible port for its entry.[6] The bulbs are planted in carefully prepared and richly manured soil. Every summer for three years they are dug up, dried and stored before they are ready to be placed on the market. After they have been distributed, equal care has to go into the final stage of their growth which involves the exact timing of the blooming of the flowers by controlling temperature and sunlight. Bulbs are purchased by

---

[2] The multi-toned structure and limited range of sounds in Chinese makes punning a commonplace, but while such wordplays are common throughout China, the same pun does not work in Mandarin as in Cantonese. The characters sound like those for 'gold' and 'lucky'. See *Introduction to Popular Traditions*, 1986:5.

[3] There is more room in the rural houses on the mainland and in some of the three-storeyed, five-bedroomed houses of the *nouveaux riches* in the country areas.

[4] On the use of large fruit for decorative purposes, see Li 1956:54–5.   [5] Koehn 1952:129

[6] According to Wilson (1929:324), it was Portuguese traders, but I follow Li's suggestion about the Arab origin. For references to the Roman narcissus, see Schafer 1963:127. Koehn (1952:129) suggests it may have been developed from wild forms found in the provinces of Fukien and Chekiang.

individuals in November or December and set in bowls filled with pebbles and sometimes sand, while the roots are cut either vertically or transversely. The vertical cut produces tall, daffodil-like flowers; the transverse cut spreads the plant sideways so that can be built up into the expensive 'crab' variety, a complex cluster of linked roots. Crab-claw narcissus involves 'an incalculable amount of painstaking, skillful labour'.[7] The length of the flowers and stalks can be regulated by varying the time it is exposed to sunlight, which also controls the direction of growth.

Since the narcissus should be in full bloom on the first day of the lunar New Year, both to predict and to make certain of a happy and prosperous year, every effort is made to ensure that the blossoms come neither too early nor too late. Growth may be retarded by dipping the stems in sea water which can cause the buds to drop off if done in excess. A blotch of white tissue keeps the plant moist and ready to bloom; if too advanced, it would be left dry. Similar effects can be achieved by moving the pot into the warmer or cooler parts of the house. Both grower and purchaser are involved in this process of control, for unlike the other plants displayed at New Year, the narcissus is often raised in the house or on a balcony or roof garden, a task in which individuals take particular pride.

But of the three New Year flowers, the peach (*tao*) is the most remarkable since its blossoms are the most fragile, their growth most difficult to control, and the element of 'conspicuous waste' most apparent.[8] Firstly, like the narcissus, the blossom has to appear in full splendour on New Year's Day, and should last up to the fifteenth, the middle of that month. Secondly, the tree is grown directly in the earth in a nursery or garden rather than a pot. Just before the beginning of the New Year it is cut off some six inches above the root and then transported to the market or dispatched as an order to a customer.

The parallel with the use of Christmas trees in Western Europe and America is striking. Here too young trees are deliberately cut down to decorate the house. The outside is brought inside for temporary display but destroyed in the very act of doing so. The trees are specially cultivated for this one day of the year, in specialist nurseries by specialist households. The parallel is even closer because in some shops, restaurants and factories in both Guangdong and Hong Kong coloured lights were wound round the tree to give added glory; traditionally it was just tied with a red ribbon (Colour plate XIII.2).

There the similarity stops. In the West we are dealing with wild species (albeit often raised in plantations); that is also true of the holly, the ivy and the mistletoe which are also brought into the house at Christmas. In China they

---

[7] Li 1959:89.

[8] The word for peach can also stand for fruit and nuts in a more general sense; it is a category as well as a specific term.

use a domesticated variety, a type of fruit tree (*Prunus mume Zieb et Zuce*). Yet the trees are grown not for the fruit, which is inedible, but for the blossom, since they are employed for other purposes – decorative, ritual, propitiatory. In the case of the dwarf tangerines and kumquats, the miniature versions of the fruit are not intended for ordinary eating, being too bitter, but are dried and preserved in salt. The small berry-like fruit of the peach, however, does not even see the light of day since the tree is cut down in blossom. But while the tree itself is destroyed, the root is preserved and a shoot encouraged on which a graft can be made to produce another tree two or more years ahead. Like the tangerine, the tree is specialised for display rather than consumption, representing the accumulation of centuries of horticultural experimentation and a developed knowledge of gardening technology. The detailed attention continues, for their growth requires great care to make them bloom at the right moment and so to ensure good fortune for the coming year. If they come on too soon, steps are taken to discourage their growth and the early blooms are nipped off or salt water sprayed over them. If too slow, the leaves are plucked off earlier rather than later to encourage the flowers, and the trees wrapped in plastic to keep off the wind. When they are about to be sold, the branches are carefully tied up so that the tree can be transported without losing the blossom.

The expertise goes not only into the growing but into the consumer's choice. One hears many comments about people's ability to choose, about the price they have paid and about the quality of the tree they have chosen, whether it was symmetrical, too far advanced, full enough of blooms or would last through the festival season. For the days following New Year are ones on which relatives and friends regularly pay each other visits. First junior relatives visit senior ones on New Year's Day, the day when at least one meal is confined to vegetarian food, bringing their children along to get to know their kin; these visits are then returned and during the following days it is the turn of friends who call upon one another. Shops are closed over the holiday but some open again on the third day, and throughout this period the state of the peach blossom in home or shop, in factory or office, is a constant subject of conversation.

It is only the bigger offices and houses that have peach trees. Other families have tangerines or some cut flowers, partly on the grounds of space, partly of expense. However, in well-off merchant households, the tradition is well established, at least among the senior generation. Even so, the best specimens are reserved for the shop rather than the house, since that is clearly the basis of their present and future prosperity.

There is a phrase in Chinese meaning 'fortune from peach blossom', which is used of a man, and sometimes of a woman, who gets plenty of attention from the opposite sex. So there may be a special call for peach trees in households with unmarried daughters. When a friend in Hong Kong offered to buy either a tangerine or a peach tree for her mother-in-law, she was asked for a peach because her thirty-year-old sister-in-law was still unmarried.[9] A similar notion seems to be associated with gifts of lucky money (Cantonese, *lai sze*, Mandarin, *hongbao*) in red pockets, which are handed out until the fifteenth of the New Year.[10] Such packets are given by married seniors to juniors, but, as with Christmas 'boxes' in England, especially to those who have provided some service during the past year. They are also offered to unmarried children, one implication being that the gifts are good for prospects of marriage as well as for prosperity.

Although branches of peach trees are used in other parts of the country, the practice of bringing trees, whether peach or tangerine, into the house at New Year is now considered to be a feature of Guangdong. Visitors from Taiwan, for example, are surprised at this custom when they first come to Hong Kong. Given the colder winters in more northerly parts, such blossoms are more difficult to produce at New Year and nowadays it is often cut flowers that predominate. Nevertheless, according to the *Rixia Jiuwen Kao*, in the eighteenth century peonies, jasmine, plum and red-peach blossoms were sold in Beijing during the twelfth month, having all been raised in kilns with the help of fire.[11] The peach has long been valued for its blossom, its fruit and for its mystical qualities.[12] It is said to have originated in the Far West, the land of deities, and to confer long life. Hence its use at birthday parties in the shape of cookies and pastries (*shou tao*).[13] For the god of longevity, Xi Wangmu sovereign of the Western Air, is pictured as emerging from a peach. It was in her palace garden that a fabulous peach grew and on her birthday, which happens once every three thousand years, the fruit ripens and the immortals

---

[9] Other gifts are offered at this time of year. In Beijing formerly it was silks, ornaments and jewels for the family, and for distant friends flowers ('never cut blooms'), fine tea, rare fruits and especially food (Bredon and Mitrophanow 1927:79).

[10] For an interesting account of the interplay involved, see Mo 1978. On a limited continuation of the practice of cleaning the house, buying new clothes and giving luck money in the People's Republic in 1974, see Cheng 1987:512.

[11] The *Rixia Jiuwen Kao* was originally the *Rixia Jiuwen* written by Zhu Yizun (1629–1709) which was augmented and given its present title by Yu Minzhong (1714–80) and others. It describes how the plum was planted in a pot five Chinese feet (89 centimetres) below ground. Three feet below this a cavity was made in which horse dung was burnt to heat the earth above. The same method was used for other flowers while vegetables were grown in hothouses above the ground.

[12] Like most Chinese flowers and fruit, the peach has a range of associations. It stands for long life so that it is especially prominent at birthdays; at a banquet for a friend's grandfather on the fourth day of New Year pastry peaches were served, each standing for sixty years of life (he was already eighty-one). Peach-shaped petals were a common decorative element in Shang and Zhou times, and were later adopted as a symbol of longevity, especially among Daoists (Cheng Te-k'un 1969:296). The gods in Heaven gathered annually to eat the sacred peaches in the Imperial Peach Garden of the King of Heaven (Savidge 1977:75). Another version runs: 'In the fabulous garden of the Queen Mother of the West, peach trees bloomed once every three thousand years and ripened for another three thousand years. When the fruit was ready it became the fare at a banquet for immortals' (Laing 1988:162; Williams 1941:315–17).

[13] However, as a spring flower, the favoured season for weddings, it is also an emblem for matrimony.

assemble to take part in the Feast of Peaches. In the North all parts of the tree were thought to have a mystical power, the blossom, the gum, the wood, as well as the fruit. Its twigs played a special part on New Year's Eve, when earlier this century in Suzhou people 'still hang peach twigs over their front gates or spray water on the ground by means of peach branches to ward off evil spirits from the homes.'[14]

Peach-wood charms were 'an ancient and most potent enemy of demons' and had long been used in various parts of China.[15] As early as the Spring and Autumn period in the first millennium BC, records from the North declare that 'Every household has peach wood charms hanging on the gates.'[16] These charms were tiny plates, rectangular in shape, which were nailed to the gates and carried words intended to 'exorcise evil spirits and ask for blessings'.[17] In the second century AD peach-wood earrings were felt to have magical properties: 'The district magistrates of our time are in the habit of having peach-trees cut down and carved into human statues, which they place by the gate . . . to ward off evil influences.'[18] In the later Shu (AD 934–65), one of the ten independent kingdoms to emerge at the end of the Tang, they are said to have first carried the Spring couplets which were later transferred to paper during the following Song Dynasty.

That tradition continues in the South today. Such couplets are much used and in 1989 were being painted and sold at the stalls of calligraphers throughout Guangdong for posting up on either side of the main doorway to the house; the intention was the same, to ward off evil and to bring prosperity. On the mainland their earlier use changed either to 'describe the flourishing national construction or sing the praise of the wonderful sights of the land, or give expression to people's wishes for a still better future'.[19] But today the range of meanings expressed is much wider than this statement would imply, not only in Hong Kong but elsewhere overseas.[20] For in all Chinese communities prosperity is a constant theme and one that is often associated with flowers, especially at this time of the year. A New Year banner from San Francisco in 1988 declared: 'Flowers, Blossom, Prosperity', that is, 'When flowers bloom, prosperity comes' (Colour plate XIII.3). A couplet sold in the Pearl River delta in 1989 was less direct. It read:

The hall for welcoming the auspicious day is full with a thousand scarlets and ten thousand crimsons.

Another went:

---

[14] Li 1959:57ff. Li is a native of Suzhou.
[15] See *Introduction to Popular Traditions*, 1986 (for the South); and Bredon and Mitrophanow 1927:84 (for the North).   [16] Qi Xing 1988:6.
[17] Peach-wood images were placed over the door of the magistrate's yamen (Bredon and Mitrophanow 1927:86).   [18] Wang Ch'ung, *Lung Heng*, quoted by Cahill 1964:79.   [19] Qi Xing 1988:7.
[20] For a list of common spring couplets in current use in the South, see *Introduction to Popular Traditions*, 1986:2–3; see also the discussion in Bredon and Mitrophanow 1927:82ff. for the North.

In the song of birds abundance comes. The abundance opens the way for wealth and honour.[21]

Deeply rooted as the peach appears to be in the New Year festivities of Guangdong, that situation seems to have held only for some forty years. In earlier days in Hong Kong the hanging bellflower was a favourite at this time of year; together with budding branches like the peach or plum, they 'were exceptions to the rule that cut flowers were unwelcome in the house'.[22] Its branches fetched a high price and were widely sought by Hakka fuel collectors because of its woody stem; cutting the wood for burning did not kill the tree but stopped it coming into bloom for several seasons.[23] For both these reasons, the branches became so popular that the tree had to be legally protected.

The hanging bellflower (Cantonese, *tiu chung fa*, *Enkianthus quinqueflorus*) is a native bush of South China where it grows wild. Since its flowering period coincides with the lunar New Year, the small, waxy, pink, bell-like flowers were widely used to decorate living-rooms and business premises at this season, becoming well established in Guangzhou early in the Qing Dynasty. As with other New Year commodities, its popularity was enhanced by the fact that favourable meanings could be extracted from its various characteristics. The bells at the tips of the branches were interpreted as *Chong yuen ko chun*, meaning 'came first in the Imperial examination', while the great number of bells and seeds stood for *Dor tze dor suen*, 'having numerous descendants', as with other plants with many seeds.

The hanging bellflower was very popular at the time the plant-collector Robert Fortune visited Hong Kong in the 1840s. He noted that at New Year the inhabitants 'bring the branches down from the hills in great quantities for the decoration of their houses'. The flowers of what he regarded as the most beautiful of all plants were 'unexpanded when they are gathered, but by being placed in water, they very soon bloom in the houses', and remain for more than a fortnight as 'fresh and beautiful'.[24] Clearly the plant served much the same function as the peach tree, a harbinger of happiness that is made to bloom on the first day of New Year and lasts through to the fifteenth of the month.

The use of this flower was widespread among the residents of Hong Kong in the late nineteenth century, but the government became alarmed at the

[21] In Beijing earlier this century, a different form of tree was used at the New Year. Large pine and cypress branches were stuck in a tall vase of the kind used for peach trees, and on them were tied old coins and paper pomegranate flowers, which were called 'flowers offered to the gods'; today in the delta town of Xiaolan the same kind of red paper 'flower' is used to decorate the items making up a girl's dowry as they are carried through the streets to the house of her future husband two days before she joins him. As we have seen, the seeds of the pomegranate represent the wish for many sons. A further adaptation of custom has occurred among Chinese-American families in San Francisco where another Chinese cultigen, the quince, has replaced the peach which does not come into flower until later (Bartholomew 1985:25).

[22] *Sunday Morning Post*, 5 February, 1989.

[23] The Hakka form part of the local population of peasant farmers.   [24] Fortune 1847:22.

prospect of the extinction of the bush and an ordinance of 1913 prohibited its possession and sale.[25] However, cultivated and imported plants were exempted, so that a vigorous industry grew up in China where in a mountainous district some 100 kilometres north of Guangzhou farmers developed special techniques for its cultivation: 'In early summer, the branches selected for cutting later that year are "ring-barked" (stripped of the outer bark) at the lower end . . . This stops the flow of sap downward and the nutrients produced by the leaves are then retained at the top.'[26] In this way a wild species became increasingly domesticated when the demand rose.

With the Japanese occupation of most of Guangdong province in 1938 supplies dried up and local residents looked for alternatives. Some skilled nurserymen sought refuge in Hong Kong where they introduced the art of growing peach blossom. In the post-war years the hanging bellflower made a temporary comeback. But in 1949 the changes in landownership and in marketing in the producing areas, where the mainland authorities no longer countenanced the growing of flowers, led to its final demise for the New Year, despite some resistance from the older elements in the population.[27] External politico-economic factors encouraged a shift in the use and meanings of symbolic flowers, not merely a straightforward substitution, indicating the mutability of particular usages under pressure. Like most other flowers, the peach had symbolic significance elsewhere in China and its adoption was therefore not difficult for the younger generation who considered its reddish blossoms to be a sign of prosperity. Its use was further promoted by the development of nurseries in the New Territories where customers can choose their plants on the spot. That was not the case with the hanging bellflower whose disappearance was hastened by the fact that some hawkers added branches of other plants such as the *Michilus* species to their stock. The buds of these branches, while larger, did not produce any flowers at all but only leaves, which was a bad omen for the buyer. As a result of these various factors, the hanging bellflower fell into disfavour and peach blossom took on new meanings, becoming the New Year flower, not only here but throughout Guangdong. That extension was presumably the result of Hong Kong's dominance of the market after the Second World War. That dominance has been enhanced following the economic reforms and the re-establishment of peasant production through the contracts to 'specialist households'. Its influence extends from the economic to the cultural, beaming television into the households of the province, so that its customs have tended to spread over the border into South China.[28]

Cat willow has something of the same kind of role as these other flowering

---

[25] My information is largely derived from the article by Iu (1985).   [26] Iu 1985:208.
[27] The bloom was said to be associated with 'jilted love'.
[28] One township had built a communal aerial to get better reception from Hong Kong, whose channels are widely watched.

plants, breaking into bud at just the right time of year. Willow was used by the Buddhist goddess of mercy, Guanyin, to sprinkle sacred water on believers as a blessing.[29] As with jasmine, its budding could be advanced by the judicious peeling of the bud's protective covering at the right time. Today much of this willow is imported to Hong Kong from Japan and bought sparingly as a substitute for the more elaborate blossoms.[30]

Other flowering plants in pots are also in demand, especially chrysanthemums (Colour plate XIII.4). These were originally autumn flowers used for special festivals and displays both in China and Japan, especially in connection with ancestral graves and tablets. It is in autumn that the highly elaborate, multiflowered varieties, trained in delicate patterns from a single root, are set out in parks and other public places for the admiration of the citizens. But the growing season of chrysanthemums has been extended to the winter months when the flowers, especially the yellow varieties ('Yellow Prosperity'), are much in demand. At one nursery in the Tai Po valley in 1989, electric lightbulbs were strung across a patch of chrysanthemums to bring them into bloom at exactly the right moment; that is not uncommon as a way of forcing flowers. Since there are so many different varieties of this plant, the New Year buyer has a wide choice.[31] But other plants too are in favour, marigolds, which carry a similar meaning of 'longevity' and 'prosperity', as well as brightly coloured plants like peonies and camellias. Tree peonies, cultivated in the North since the Tang Dynasty, have a long-established association with the notion of prosperity and wealth. They too come in many different varieties and are much prized, being known as 'the flower of flowers' or 'the king of flowers'.

These festival flowers disappear by the fifteenth day of the lunar month which represents the end of the New Year festivities and is marked by the cleansing ceremony, known as the Festival of the Lanterns (*yuan xiao* or *deng jie*). Little now happens in private homes, although a competition for composing couplets, a traditional activity of the literati, is held in Kowloon Park, Hong Kong, and is associated with the courting of young men and women; indeed, it is sometimes described as the Chinese St Valentine's Day, although that occasion has caught on there as elsewhere, partly at the instigation of florists, partly as a universal celebration of sexual coupling by choice rather than by family arrangement. But in some parts a Lantern Ceremony (*kaideng*, lighting a lamp) is organised by the lineage and has a more serious aspect. For between the tenth and fifteenth days of the New

---

[29] Savidge 1977:71; for offerings of flowers to the goddess, see p.75. It was also a symbol of the sun, being used to beat the spring ox to bring on rain (Bredon and Mitrophanow 1927:133).

[30] Willows (river or weeping), as in the willow pattern, play an important part as Chinese emblems. They are one of the earliest signs of spring and act as an emblem of femininity. They are also believed to exercise power over evil spirits and are used to sweep graves as well as being fixed to the gates of houses to bring good luck (Koehn 1952:131).

[31] Tun Li-ch'en (1987) lists 117 and speaks of many more; he greatly underestimates the choice.

Year, 'Lantern' celebrations are held in rural temples and ancestral halls; any local family to whom a son has been born during the past year should bring a lantern to the hall and light it to express their aspirations for his good health.[32] On this occasion the names of males born to lineage members during the year are often placed on record. In 1989 the roof of the focal lineage hall of Long Yok Tou, near Fanling in the New Territories of Hong Kong, was being hung with lanterns on the eleventh day of the month while food was laid out for an offering to be made to the deity, Tian hou, later that day. Each of the paper lanterns stood for the son of a male lineage member born during the past year. However, while some flowers played a part in the offerings, these were no longer the special plants devoted to New Year.[33] That period was now closed.

PRODUCTION

Of the New Year favourites, the most important flowers are produced especially for the occasion and hence subject to the fluctuating profits and losses that are inevitable when supplies have to be aimed towards a specialised and time-specific market, like chrysanthemums for All Saints' in France or marigolds for Divali in India. Other flowers, which are used throughout the twelve months, carry a special meaning at this time for the prospects of family or business in the coming year. All require long and intensive care to produce, just as their emergence as domesticated species has required long and intensive care over the centuries.

Both in Hong Kong and in Guangdong some production is carried out by relatively small-scale producers when both husband and wife work in the fields and sell the product of their labour. In the flower market in the delta town of Xiaolan in 1989 most peach trees were being sold by children, which was also the case with other flowers. But family labour and local plots did not suffice for many of the growers around Hong Kong who employed wage labour to increase production. A producer we met at Tuen Mun had one nursery in the New Territories and another over the border in the New Economic Zone where labour is cheaper. The tangerines on display he planted in China with the aid of the local workforce but had already moved the plants south in August for sale in the more attractive market around Hong Kong some six months later.

Commercial nurseries of this kind have existed over a long period, especially in the delta areas of the Pearl River and the Yangzi. During the 1840s Fortune visited a number around Ningbo, near Shanghai, and was able

---

[32] *Introduction to Popular Traditions.*

[33] This Lantern Ceremony is also found in the North of China, where Bodde thinks it is post-Han (1975:394); householders bought lanterns for their houses but especially for their ancestral halls while in the South these were displayed in public gardens. Better-off parents of new-born sons would not only hang up lanterns as votive offerings but would also give dinners for the poor. Others would hang them up in the hope of getting sons in the future. The general festival atmosphere was maintained by children who took part in masquerades in the streets (*Introduction to Popular Traditions*).

to purchase plants for his collection. These nurserymen sometimes moved their places of cultivation over considerable distances for economic reasons. They also purchased plants from some distance. One man who had flower shops in the town, ordered plants from other growers far away.[34] Near Guangzhou Fortune visited the famous Fatei (Cantonese, 'Flowery Land') Gardens, from where so much had been obtained for export to Europe. 'The plants are principally kept in large pots arranged in rooms along the side of narrow paved walks, with the houses of the gardeners at the entrance through which the visitors pass to the gardens.'[35] Of these gardens there were twelve, each with stockgrounds for planting out and for starting the dwarfing process. In addition to nurseries and the florists' shops, there were stands at street corners, especially at the New Year.

During the two weeks leading up to that festival in 1989, many nurseries in Hong Kong had already sold a number of tangerine bushes which were then marked with a red tag. By direct sale a medium-size plant cost about 350 HK dollars (50 US dollars). The larger, more expensive ones had taken up to three years to grow and were planted in large jars decorated with dragons and other traditional designs, that had previously been used for preserved eggs, although nowadays such jars are specially manufactured for potting plants. While a customer may pay more by buying in advance from a nursery rather than in the open market, he or she has the advantage of dealing with a grower whose practices are known and in whom some confidence can be placed. In the open market anything can happen; a peach tree might have been placed in cold storage to delay the blossom or have been treated in some other way that would lead to its early demise. By buying from a known producer, one gains a measure of protection.[36]

Many merchants centred their production further away in the Pearl River delta where costs were much lower. In 1989 growers in the New Territories complained of the difficulty of getting enough labour, the lack of which would further increase their costs. The owner of one nursery claimed his garden was suffering from a shortage of twenty people in a nursery needing thirty skilled gardeners to maintain, because so many had shifted to more lucrative work such as driving trucks between Hong Kong and Shenzhen in the New Economic Zone over the border in China. He had only managed to keep his present workforce by raising their salaries from 200 to 350 HK dollars, plus a transport subsidy of 20 dollars.[37] As a result of the labour shortage, the owner

---

[34] Fortune 1987:133–5.   [35] Fortune 1987:152.

[36] The same principle operates even in the highly active urban markets in ways that run somewhat contrary to ideas of unrestricted competition. Shops offering similar commodities exist side by side without price competition because clients deal with the merchant they know and trust; that is the essence of established commerce in China. People are often advised to go to such shops, especially to purchase expensive items like cameras; otherwise one does not know if the lens has been changed or if the goods have been tampered with in other ways. The anonymous, open market of the bazaar did not offer sufficient guarantees against such practices.

[37] *Sunday Morning Post*, 22 January, 1989. This was the Wing Tai Yuen nursery in Sai Kung.

claimed that output had fallen by 40 per cent, although he still made a bid for fourteen stalls at two different flower markets in Hong Kong, which were being auctioned by the municipal authorities.

Despite such problems, the production of flowers was on the rise. The estimate for the total value of local production was 82.5 million HK dollars in 1988, an increase of some 15 million over the previous year.[38] Flowers and garden produce have taken over from rice in a dramatic manner. The acreage under paddy fell from 9,450 hectares in 1954 to 10 hectares in 1987. That under fruit, vegetables and flowers rose from 910 in 1954 to 2,510 in 1987, which in turn represented a fall from a peak of 4,790 in 1976, probably in vegetables rather than flowers. Much agricultural production is rapidly being driven out by the increasing price of land and labour, and by the alternative uses of land for industry and for habitation. The Yuenlong plain, whose ecology is similar to that of the Pearl River delta further to the north-west, is now becoming a peripheral zone of industrial or at least of urban activity.[39] Rice production has virtually ceased; while some vegetables and flowers are still grown, many of the plots have been leased out by their owners as parking places for containers which would incur much higher costs at the ports, or as rural dumps for old cars, building materials and other such bulk items. Much of the production of flowers and vegetables has shifted northwards over the border. Since it became politically and economically possible in the delta, the growing of mulberry leaves for silk and of some rice for the market has given way to more profitable crops intended for local consumption and for export. Guangdong does not participate directly in the world-wide market in flowers, which demands easy access to frequent air transport; instead it sends flowers to Hong Kong and Macao both for local use and for re-export. But as far as tangerine bushes, peach blossom and narcissi are concerned, the market is essentially confined to the New Year in South China.

On a small scale we find a similar cycle of displacement taking place around the urban areas in Guangdong. Xiaolan, as mentioned in the previous chapter, christened itself Chrysanthemum Town in 1958 and recast an old festival, partly with overseas Chinese in mind.[40] Under the changed socio-economic conditions of recent years the town cultivated its own blooms for its parks, its hotels, its shops and its people. In 1988 there was a large nursery with some 10,000 pots of tangerines below the Chrysanthemum Town Hotel. By the following year this had given way to a complex of swimming and paddling pools to cater for the leisure of its increasingly prosperous inhabitants, leaving a small nursery for the hotel together with a graveyard of old flower pots. With the indirect pressure from manufacture, largely small-scale and stimulated in part from Hong Kong, flower growing had moved outside the

---

[38] Hong Kong, *Annual Review*, 1988, p.353.
[39] This area was the one in which J. and R. Watson carried out their fieldwork.   [40] See Siu 1990.

town boundary. For the next festival the town intended to contract the production to a neighbouring 'brigade' or township, where flowers continued to be grown commercially.

There are still some nurseries in the vicinity of Xiaolan, on the wide banks of the polders between the fishponds that surround the town, but these ponds are rapidly being filled in to provide space for private housing and for artisanal enterprise. However, production flourishes in Shunde county between Daliang and Chencun, not far outside the city of Guangzhou. As around many major European cities in the past, and to a lesser extent in the present, the peri-urban area specialised in horticulture: vegetables and flowers were produced for the markets of the town to supply those not in a position to grow their own.

The production of flowers in the Pearl River delta has been long established, together with the symbolic and decorative use of flowers not only among the literati but also among the wider population. Popular culture was much influenced by the national written tradition that percolated down to every settlement; despite the rapid pace of recent developments, the serpentine gables of some of the old houses of the literati can still be seen overshadowing the roofs of peasant dwellings. Flowers were etched on the glass panels of their meeting rooms, decorated their furniture and cloth, and are still a major subject for drawing and painting.

Today the literati and local elites of earlier times have effectively disappeared, having been killed off, metaphorically and sometimes literally, following the events of 1949. The more demotic but more restricted culture that has emerged still prizes flowers and much the same uses at New Year are found in Guangdong and Hong Kong. However, that convergence is largely a matter of the last five to ten years, which have seen the rebirth of the cultivation of flowers and the beginning of the cycle of displacement towards the north in some of the more urban areas.

All cash crops in China had been heavily restricted by the policies of the government up to 1976. In Xinhui county the production of edible tangerines plummeted. The growing of flowers, concentrated in Shunde county, had little chance and it was only in 1984 that the market was effectively re-established. Commercial growing has sprung up again, partly to supply Hong Kong and Macao but also in response to increasing local demand. The gap of some twenty-five years under Mao's regime (and before that the long and difficult war years) meant that the horticultural expertise was not readily available among the young so that in Xiaolan and elsewhere former landlords had to be brought in to carry out the work, which is skilled, intensive and requires careful planning.

Flowers are now being produced by 'specialist households', sometimes with the help of seasonal labour from northern areas where winter agriculture is more limited. For Shunde, which like the rest of the region is semi-tropical, has long been growing flowers that cannot be cultivated in the rest of the country.[41] At present the county has a regular export of several thousand dozen flowers a day to Hong Kong where they are taken overnight by hydrofoil or by other river transport. The Guangdong region as a whole had a total export of flowers worth 11,402,00 dollars in 1987.[42] A total area of 222,000 hectares was devoted to their production, representing an increase of 13.7 per cent over the previous year; the total output has likewise increased by 16.9 per cent, which includes about 1 million dozen fresh flowers, a growth of one and a half times. These figures represent the region's massive shift in production and in marketing following the change in political direction led by economic rather than ideological considerations. They add up to the return of the culture of flowers with a vengeance.

THE MARKET AND THE MARKET PLACE

Production in South China is directed to local demands, to the requirements of Hong Kong and to an international market. On a much smaller scale the external demand for plants from China has had a long history, while China herself received species from other regions. Potted plants are still an important feature of the trade to Hong Kong, while the valued *penjing*, 'scenery in a pot', has a much wider distribution, especially in the United States. What has changed is the rise of cut flowers as a marketable item.

Cut flowers for the house were not an important part of traditional Chinese life.[43] People did not often give flowers as gifts to the living, although they were used for the dead at funerals. Even those in temples were usually provided by the priests rather than directly by the worshippers. But in Hong Kong family members took cut flowers to grave sites for special festivals. Flowers are sometimes put beside a father's tablet in the house as well as in any temple, Buddhist or Daoist, where he is commemorated. Such commemoration temples are part of commercial practice in Hong Kong, with photographs decorating the memorial plaques; one we visited in the New Territories had established its own nursery to provide flowers for decoration and remembrance.

Nowadays cut flowers are more widely used in Hong Kong, following the Western practice, being sold in florists' shops as well as on market stalls, and supplied by local, mainland and foreign producers. In that city, birthdays too attract floral gifts and the bourgeoisie use them to decorate their homes, just as hotels and restaurants do their rooms and tables. Even at New Year some people now prefer cut flowers to potted ones, while in other homes they act as a supplement. The reason is partly price, partly space, but also changing

---

[41] See Qu Dajun 1700.
[42] From the *Government Year Book* for 1988, p.271.   [43] See Bredon and Mitrophanow 1927:79.

attitudes. The same shift to cut flowers is making itself felt in the People's Republic. Customers, mainly women, buy them as gifts or more usually for themselves. Migrants formerly brought back useful gifts, whereas now, we were told, they may give flowers in the Western style. That shift is not simply an imitation of Western custom but a mark of changing economic circumstances; prosperity favours the 'non-utilitarian' as gifts, while party policy more readily accepts the association of flowers and prosperity, of economic advance and the cultivation of 'luxury' goods.

On a cold January day Guangzhou may nowadays appear to be less well endowed with flowers than Hong Kong. Nevertheless, there are a number of florists in and around the city. The roofs and balconies of houses are decorated with plants in much the same way as those of its southern neighbour, especially in the cramped accommodation of former literati and landlords. In the public domain, shops are opened with similar baskets and placards, while the public use of flowers, especially in reconstructed areas around the new international hotels, is very lavish.

There is a main flower market in all the larger towns for the daily supply to florists, hotels and to the public. In Guangzhou the long-established Flower Ground lay directly across the Pearl River from the former foreign concessions. When visited by the eighteenth-century author Shen Fu in 1792, it had many flowers and trees which, as he came from further north, he could not recognise, and some of which were not even entered in the *Handbook of Collected Fragrances*, a checklist for identification. Close to the river, the market could be readily supplied by boat from nurseries in the surrounding countryside. For the province was already well known for its flowers at this time. Coming through Foshan county, before entering the city, 'we saw that on the tops of the walls around their homes, the local people had placed potted flowers, with leaves that looked like wintergreen and blooms that resembled peonies. There were three colours of flower – red, white, and pink – and they were called camellias.'[44]

It was along the river too that another 'flower' market was held. 'Flower boats' were elaborately carved and profusely gilded. They were hired for pleasure parties and banquets by the wealthy who enjoyed the company of 'damsels highly rouged and gaily attired', 'their black hair charged with roses and orange flowers'. But as a nineteenth-century visitor explains, behaviour was very decorous and any sexual encounters took place elsewhere.[45] Shen Fu describes his visit to the boats moored in groups along the banks containing 'flower girls' from various parts of China. The madam on the first boat wore a flower behind one ear and was dressed like the actors of women's parts in a play. But Shen Fu was not to be tempted. 'People say that young men should not come to Guangdong, to keep from being led astray by the beautiful girls.

---

[44] Shen Fu 1983:118.   [45] Schlegel 1894:4.

But who could be attracted by this gaudy clothing and barbarous southern language?'[46] So he is taken off to see the boats where the girls dressed up in his native Suzhou fashion and where he meets one who looks a little like his wife, Chen Yun. With this girl he establishes a continuing friendship while he is in the town; for girls, connections of this kind may be the way to marriage, to concubinage, or at least to a position of some influence in the community because of the patronage of scholars. In Zang-Xin-hai's historical novel, *The Fabulous Concubine,* Orchid first works on a flower boat in Ningbo before becoming the partner of the man later appointed ambassador to Germany. The boats were the haunts of literati who went there to converse, compose poetry, smoke opium and enjoy the company of 'sing-song girls', whose role was not at all approved by other women. 'One can see at once she comes from a flower garden', remarks Jade Fountain in *Jinping Mei*,[47] of Cinnamon Bud, when the girl's mood changes rapidly from desolation to joy on learning that the magistrate would protect her. She even asks for a lute to sing a song, geisha-like. The flower boats have disappeared from the Pearl River; here and elsewhere in the delta the Dan fishermen too have been resettled on land where some prostitution may still linger on the river banks.[48]

The sale of flowers for the New Year begins well in advance, at least for the dwarf tangerines. By 20 January, some sixteen days beforehand, the bushes were already on display at some corner flower shops in Hong Kong as well as being available in local nurseries, which were doing a flourishing business in preparation for the Year of the Snake. Guangzhou too is transformed at the New Year with tangerine bushes arranged along a number of the main streets some ten days beforehand. These are sold to private individuals. Factories and other groups with access to transport went outside the city boundaries for better bargains.

The largest, but by no means the only, flower market in the delta is at Chencun, south-west of Guangzhou. Re-established in 1985, it now stretches for some 15 kilometres on both sides of the road running from Shunde to Guangzhou, but mainly on the traffic side, the stopping side, the right-hand side as you drive towards the city. Innumerable stalls, some with many tiers, fill the roadside, selling a variety of flowers, mainly dwarf tangerines, chrysanthemums, peonies and some dwarf trees. While this is a market aimed at the local population (export is differently handled), some of the *penjing* were being offered at 10,000 yuan, that is approximately 2,500 dollars.[49] Others are sold at twice that price. However, most flowers were of an ordinary variety and went at more reasonable rates to local customers who were shopping even as late as 9 pm. The sellers had erected rough tents at the

---

[46] Shen Fu 1983:119.   [47] *Jinping Mei* 1939:42.
[48] On the last days of the flower boats, see the short story, 'The husband', written in the 1930s by Shen Congwen (transl. in *The Border Town and Other Stories*, Beijing, 1981.).
[49] A permanent exhibition hall for *penjing* was in the process of being built.

roadside where they spent the night looking after their wares. Many nurseries were quite near to the stands, but pots of flowers were also trucked in from outlying locations.

The market at Chencun had no peach trees for sale, for it was too early to cut them from their roots. The first we saw were at the county town of Daliang (Shunde) on the morning of 1 February five days before New Year, in the street outside the Chenhui Gardens. Standing some 1–1.30 metres tall, they had been brought into the town on the back of bicycles by members of 'specialist households' which grow considerable quantities of flowers for this occasion. Some cycles even had carefully constructed wooden frames fixed to the carriers to take a tree on either side.

In contemporary Hong Kong, the main New Year fair is held at Victoria Park but this was only one of many places, a dozen or so in 1989, where the municipality sets up stalls to be auctioned to all comers. The sellers may include private as well as professional gardeners; some of the former raise flowers for the market as well as for the garden, and at New Year sell their produce in a stall in one of these areas set aside for this purpose, such as that near the old merchants' section of town. In earlier times the main market was the Wan Chai Fair stretching along the whole waterfront. Then too there were also flower fairs in Beijing, at Huguo Temple, 'where narcissus, the New Year flower *par excellence*, peonies, magnolias, early double-peach blossoms, especially cultivated in Beijing, are in flower, and "heavenly bamboos", orange trees, lemons and "Buddha's fingers" are in fruit'.[50]

Going to the flower market at this time is a tradition for many of the inhabitants of Hong Kong and on New Year's Eve itself the crowd becomes almost impenetrable. Since there is no market for these festival flowers once the New Year has begun, their price gets lower and lower towards the close. Purchasers have to judge the latest moment to buy while leaving themselves enough time to take their bargain home and erect it for the first day of the year. That takes some care. Peach trees have to be placed carefully in a tall vase which is then secured to a small table or stand by red ribbons. 'Everybody keeps a vase for New Year', commented an acquaintance, 'even if it is only for some cut flowers.' The vases used for the occasion are often highly valued as heirlooms or as acquisitions. Some specimens of ancient porcelain are said to 'preserve flowers and fruit from decay for an unusual time' and almost as much attention was paid to the container as to the contents.[51]

In earlier days it was felt that all purchases should be made before midnight, the point of transition to the New Year when firecrackers on the quays and ships' sirens in the harbour produced a deafening din. The noise was designed to frighten away evil spirits, keeping off the Skin Tiger who in a curious

---

[50] Bredon and Mitrophanow 1927:149. Large branches of peach are also on sale at New Year in the flower market at Hanoi in Vietnam, with which, as Stein (1990) points out, the Chinese possess long-standing links of a cultural kind.   [51] Fortune 1847:89.

reciprocal inversion would steal food from the poor to repay the wealthy for what they had handed out.[52] Firecrackers are now forbidden, though not on the mainland. But towards that hour, the pace of market activity increased rapidly because buyers had delayed their purchases partly in the hope of lower prices or to avoid carrying them around before leaving the market, which nowadays continues until dawn.

The sale of all flowers ended abruptly with the closing of the shops and markets over the holiday. But the florists were soon open again for personal gifts and family celebrations announcing preparations for the next great annual festival, that of St Valentine's Day, 14 February. This ritual has been adopted from the culture of the global village and, as in America, now accounts for the greatest sales for Hong Kong's five hundred or so florists, more than Christmas or Mother's Day; for it is producers rather than florists who dominate the trade at New Year when the majority of purchases are made. Prices leap up. A single long-stemmed rose, normally 8 HK dollars, jumps to 35 dollars; these flowers come mainly from Holland, New Zealand and Singapore, taking about three days from the time they are cut to get to the shop. Flower vendors proliferate in the streets and restaurants. Florists take on extra staff and begin wrapping the flowers the previous evening.[53] Even students in the Chinese University of Hong Kong had set up a booth selling red roses and white 'fillers', just like on an American campus. But the New Year market has come to an end and we now enter another phase of the ritual cycle as it affects the culture of flowers.

THE TENSIONS AND CONTRADICTIONS OF THE FLOWER CULTURE

In describing the culture of flowers in contemporary Hong Kong and Guangzhou, I have drawn attention to interdependence and convergence. That has not long been the case. In the previous chapter the differences in approach in religious traditions were interpreted as indicating a deep-seated contradiction about the way in which we address divinity and the dead, as well as about the way we conduct ourself on the earth. That discussion touched upon some internal differences in the decorative, architectural and ritual uses of flowers in Buddhism and Confucianism, differences that were partly related to the nature of offerings, partly to notions of restraint, partly to the establishment of diacritical distinctions between opposing groups. But this religious problem has a secular counterpart which earlier led to radical divergences between the 'capitalist' Hong Kong and 'socialist' Guangdong.

---

[52] In earlier times sections of bamboo culms were thrown into open fires where they exploded with a loud bang intended to frighten away the evil spirits (Koehn 1952:134). Various features of the New Year festivals were already established in the Han Dynasty – the visiting, paying off debts, the dragon dances, the ancestral sacrifices (Bodde 1975).

[53] The illustrated catalogue issued by the Flower Council of Holland and found even in small florists gives 530 varieties of cut flower that can be delivered abroad.

In the recent past the two regimes took distinctly different attitudes not only to the use of flowers but more generally to the practice of rituals and to access to (and even the existence of) luxuries. As signs of luxury, as relics of discarded customs, as distractions from the serious business of material production, flowers are obvious targets for egalitarian regimes that attempt to rectify the sins of the past. Rituals, especially those associated with supernatural beliefs, are anathema not only to atheistic elites but also to many reformist religious ones. The two elements of luxury and ritual are often associated as decorations or offerings in the temple and in the house, so that attitudes to non-utilitarian luxury combine with those towards beliefs and practices that are seen as 'the opiate of the people'. Such thoughts were overt among the more dogmatic elements represented by the Gang of Four. The New Year ceremonies were abolished under the Cultural Revolution but were reinstated under Deng Xiaoping.[54] While flowers were certainly incorporated in ceremonies organised by the party and were planted in public places, in the private domain their use was discouraged, partly by ideological means but also because the impoverishment of the elites meant that neither they nor others could indulge themselves any longer; the state had appropriated this segment of cultural activity.

During the Cultural Revolution in Shanghai the Red Guards smashed flower and curio shops, saying that only the rich had the money to spend on such frivolities. Other luxuries such as silks and cosmetics were also condemned, and people wearing them were abused[55] – and not only the objects themselves but their representations. Nien Cheng presents a harrowing account of the coming of the Red Guards to her house in Shanghai, knocking over her flower bowls and destroying china, paintings and books. Needless to say, such actions affected the production of these items which was seen as distracting the workers from 'essentials'. Nien Cheng's old gardener told her how he had lost his job because 'To plant flowers was supposed to be bad, if not counter-revolutionary.'[56] When the Red Guards came, he put his seedling boxes under the beds. Flower shops were closed and around Shanghai growing was forbidden till the mid-1970s.[57] However, even then when Nien Cheng wanted him to plant flowers in the garden, the family sharing the house objected: 'Don't you know our Great Leader Chairman Mao is against flowers?' Yet, Mao was constantly referring to flowers (as well as to the notion of the 'soul') in his many speeches, incorporating them into slogans such as 'Let a Hundred Flowers Bloom and a Hundred Schools of Thought Contend', and 'If poisonous weeds are not removed, scented flowers cannot grow.' In other words, the conditions for the reinstatement of the culture of flowers were implicit in discourse and in particular words and names. The murdered daughter of Nien Cheng was called Meiping, Flowering-Plum Vase.

[54] Cheng 1987:511.   [55] Cheng 1987:83.   [56] Cheng 1987:484.   [57] Cheng 1987:519, 605.

The attitudes lying behind the diminished role of flowers, and of personal luxuries more generally, are characteristic not only of revolutionary and reformist programmes, but constitute a subdominant theme, a submerged element in many of those societies, or in periods of their history, where these items are found. As with other elements in stratified societies, for example, food or clothing, an internal critique of 'luxury' may be generated by the very existence of difference, though its force and explicitness obviously vary with a whole set of circumstances.

One such circumstance is the existence of sumptuary laws which attempt to limit patterns of luxury consumption to distinct social groups or roles. While ordinances of this kind may serve to restrict conspicuous display, they are often the result of hierarchical competition. In any case, they do not suppress, even if they may inhibit, the existence of ambivalence and criticism. For that is an intrinsic element even in the ideology of the 'culture' of mass consumption, of egalitarian distribution. The fact is that consumerist ideologies are never complete in their practical application. The ruler or the ruling elite utilises what is forbidden or unattainable to the rest, sometimes overtly with a religious or social rationale, more often covertly as the fruits of power. Prominent cadres under one regime and successful yuppies under another have access to goods and services effectively denied to others, not in principle, not necessarily over their entire life-cycle, but as a condition of the working of the system. As a result, the commentaries persist – in the form of samizdat jokes, open envy or letters to the editor. In earlier times such criticism was the subject of comment by philosophers, creative writers or religious reformers. While these doubts are sometimes expressed as an 'individual' attitude, the sentiments are more widespread.[58] They were formulated in an early American flower manual which begins '"Flowers! The cultivation of flowers", say some; "of what use? It neither gives us meat, drink, nor clothing."'[59] Similar sentiments are to be heard in many places. As a dominant attitude, such expressions are specific to certain societies at certain times; but potentially all 'cultures of luxury' are apt to generate such comments. By this phrase I simply refer to the existence of 'luxuries', such as aesthetic, non-utilitarian gardens, which are unequally distributed. The luxuries are not necessarily confined to an elite, but expenditure on them gives rise to comments on the conspicuous consumption of others (a problem of hierarchy) as well as to ideas of distributive justice, that the poor should be fed not on the crumbs of the rich but at the expense of inessentials (an ethical problem).

Such differentiated and luxury cultures tend to give rise to actual or potential protest, on general grounds of morality as well as of access. In mass

---

[58] As one Scotsman remarked to me of his bourgeois home, which adhered to the puritanical tradition of the Kirk: 'We never had flowers in our house – you can't eat them. My mother preferred [gifts of] eggs.'

[59] Breck 1851:2.

cultures, in which the distribution of goods is widespread but nevertheless not universal, tensions appear as they do in hierarchical or minority ones; in both cases they are often aggravated by the kind of process needed to produce items that can be viewed as 'unnatural'.

In many parts of the world the evolution of crop production has involved a double measure of human control, firstly, the domestication of wild species in their native habitats, secondly, the extension of those species to different environments, as with the early efforts to grow Mediterranean cultigens such as wheat and vines in more northerly climes. But the controlled production of out-of-season crops demands shorter-term measures which are more obviously modifications of the 'natural' cycle. Forced production has long been practised in China especially for the New Year in the North where the weather is less clement than in the South. As in Europe, the emphasis is on the application of heat. The lightbulbs of the Tai Po valley are nothing new. Writing of Beijing in the earlier part of this century, Tun Li-ch'en notes that 'Flowers which have been reared by artificial heat are always called *tang* flowers by florists, and at every New Year people make presents of them to one another, especially of peonies and kumquat. The delicate beauty of the three spring months is all here within one hall, which is why they are called "hall flowers"',[60] or *tanghua*. Hothouses made of paper were necessary in the North to ensure year round production; in the last century, Fortune observed chrysanthemums at all seasons. In these hothouses the plants were bedded in loam and every bud was wrapped in paper, so that 'this skilful forcing brings the dwarf fruit-trees and the peonies into full bloom at exactly the right time'.[61]

According to the eighteenth-century *Rixia Jiuwen Kao*, peonies, blossoms and jasmine were all sold to Beijing during the twelfth month, having been reared in hothouses by means of fire. 'This method has been in existence since the Han dynasty, when in the gardens of great officials, shallot, onion, and madder used to be covered over in long sheds, and kept warm by fire day and night, so that these various vegetables, receiving the warm air, would all sprout.' The same techniques were applied to flowers which were on display at the East and West Temples all the year round. 'As to spring flowers, such as the peony, begonia, lilac, and peach, these are all made to blossom during the severe winter. [The men who cultivate these flowers] have stolen a march on the *Yueling*, and have delved deeply in their investigations into the principles of things. Alas that none have produced books on the subject!'[62] Tun Li-ch'en goes on to lament the fact that these unrecorded techniques used in growing flowers were not applied to vegetables but their expense made them practical only for luxuries. Perhaps too secretive knowledge and the absence of textbooks meant that their discoveries could not be disseminated in the way

[60] Tun Li-ch'en 1987:102.   [61] Bredon and Mitrophanow 1927:78–9.   [62] Tun Li-ch'en 1987:19.

that other agricultural techniques had been spread throughout the country. Nevertheless, such intensive methods had in fact been applied to foodstuffs as early as the Han, at least in the gardens of the rich. For the methods used to grow flowers, including out-of-season ones, are part of a system of highly intensive horticulture, probably the most intensive in the world, that uses heat, water, manure and a whole range of technical skills to develop new varieties, extend the growing season, improve the product, diversify colours, all of which procedures make use of a practical knowledge of botany and biology.

Such developments did not take place without opposition. At the most general level, philosophers criticised the luxury and the hierarchy involved in a system where the many produced for the enjoyment of the few or where the poor wasted their subsistence on 'inessentials'. Already during the Han Dynasty, New Year offerings took such conspicuous forms that they led to critical comments. An edict of AD 69 protested that the poor wasted their food on the dead and a few years later the rich are similarly criticised. At a gathering of literary figures of the court in the fourth century AD, a young peer decorated a room with the portrait of the ancient philosopher, Zuangzi. When called upon to compose an essay praising the occasion, Ji Han wrote a 'mourning paper' to be burnt at the grave of a friend which criticised the extravagance displayed.[63] The connection between philosophy and social criticism is clear.[64]

Luxury was criticised not only by philosophers and politicians on the wider moral and social grounds but more generally by religious functionaries. While literary sources such as *Jinping Mei* are to be treated with caution, the Abbess in that picaresque novel of the eighteenth century makes a significant comment upon the eating and drinking habits of nuns and monks: ' "We nuns, of course display a little self-control in that respect . . . In the Tripitaka it is written: What one wastes in luxury in this life one must make good in a subsequent existence." "Good gracious!" said sister-in-law Wu, in dismay, "then we who are spending the whole day in feasting and luxurious living will have to atone for it abundantly in our subsequent existence!" '[65] The Abbess' restraint caused the laity to rethink their lives. Penance might be exacted for indulgence in luxury just as restraint could be a source of pride and strength. That was so with Confucians as well as with Buddhists. It was also a theme of dynastic conquerors, at least in the initial stages. The Manchu rulers from the North extolled their 'august frugality' as against the wasteful and 'childish' luxury of their predecessors,[66] just as their subjects used flower paintings to make political statements against their domination.

The objections are to luxury in general. But the growing of out-of-season plants and particularly flowers raises related questions of an ecological kind. Some commentators remarked on the diversion of human effort in raising

---

[63] Li 1979:8.   [64] Bodde 1975:64.   [65] *Chin P'ing Mei* 1939:415.   [66] Bodde on Tun Li-ch'en (1975).

non-edible plants when others were short of food; that is the problem of poverty in the midst of riches. The major ecological objection is contained in Tun Li-ch'en's reference to the *Yueling*, one of the oldest of the Chinese almanacs which now forms a chapter of the *Liji*.[67] This source frequently warns against the unnatural disasters that will overtake a person who at any one season follows the rules proper to another. At the same time, the author's ambivalence about meddling with nature is revealed in his reference to the well-known sentence of the first section of *Daxue* (Great Learning), which runs: 'The extension of knowledge lies in the investigation of things', but the methods of investigation are not immune from criticism. Such attitudes, which are more explicit in written cultures, smack of having it both ways, of enjoying the benefits of experiment and of disapproving its methods. Nevertheless, similar criticisms came from many sources. As long ago as 33 BC, Shao Xinchen, the Minister of Natural Resources Revenues, declared that products such as hothouse plants were all untimely things, whether flowers or not, and would be injurious to men and inauspicious as offerings. And he went so far as to ask that they all be done away with.[68] Consumer demand, initially based on the luxury trade, presses towards an extension of the growing period, but ambivalence expresses itself in 'ecological' feelings, that tampering with nature, destroying its seasonality, is harmful for the world at large, for the balance of nature.

A remarkably similar outlook forms a major theme in that legendary, mythical, work, *Flowers in the Mirror*, a classical novel of a satirical kind written by Li Ruzhen who was born in Hebei about 1763 and died in 1830. The beginning of the book is set in one of Three Islands of the Blessed where the mountains are full of fruit, plants, grain, grass and 'flowers which are in bloom all the year round'.[69] In the Cave of Beauty on the island of Penglai lived the Fairy of a Hundred Flowers who was in charge of all the flowers on earth. On the birthday of the Queen Mother of the West in Kunlun, she flew off with a gift of hundred-flower nectar, accompanied by her friends, the Fairy of a Hundred Plants, the Fairy of a Hundred Fruits and the Fairy of a Hundred Grains, meeting on the way the wife of the Star of Literature.

When they arrived, one of the ruler's attendants, the Lady of the Moon, asked the Fairy of a Hundred Flowers to please the Queen Mother by making all the flowers bloom at once. She objected:

You see my flowers must follow a schedule . . . Before every flower blooms on earth it must first receive the approval of the Deity. The Fragrant Jade Maiden has to plan everything to the last detail in advance, such as the number of petals and the shade of

[67] *Sacred Books of the East*, XXVII, 249–310.   [68] Tun Li-ch'en 1987:102.

[69] P.17. The constant blooming of flowers in the other world is a more general sign of both immortal life and of pleasure, as it is in the European and Near Eastern notions of Paradise. Some local stories in Guangdong refer to a child coming in and going out of this world with a flower, a conception of a Wordsworthian kind. The centrality of the Queen Mother of the West, of peaches, immortality and flowers is indicated by the references made by many writers, see pp. 358, 378 and fn. 108, 391 fn. 121.

colouring. She is a genius and thinks of endless original designs. That is why there is so much variety . . . The flowers which blossom according to design are ordered to bloom on earth in private gardens and choice spots, where they are given care and nourishment and clean water, so that poets may sing their praises, and people enjoy them. (p.20)

Flowers which do not bloom in the proper way were brought before the magistrate and punished. That was her responsibility, so she asked to be excused. 'How can I suddenly ask all flowers to bloom at the same time?'

Aunt Wind, a close friend of the Lady of the Moon, protested, saying that flowers do indeed bloom out of season. 'How do you account for the fact that peony and the green-peach blossom may be induced to bloom in winter if given warmth and special nourishment?' (pp.20–1). The Fairy accepted that it is possible to force flowers to bloom through artificial means, but she refused to be held responsible. For 'as you yourself must surely know, the seasons must be respected' (p.21). So she again refused to perform the miracle asked of her, but agreed that if some earthly ruler ordered this to be done, she would have to do penance. When the remarkable Empress Wu of the Tang Dynasty, a strong supporter of Buddhism who ruled between 684 and 704, took over the throne, she did exactly this. Only the peony resisted, and for this reason was banished from the capital Chang'an (the present-day Xi'an) to Luoyang, the centre of its cultivation. The danger to seasonality comes from the unjustifiable tampering with nature by the rich and powerful.

These objections to the culture of flowers stem from notions of a kind that are embodied in the doctrines of the green movements of contemporary Europe but have long formed part of man's experience. There is also a religious aspect. If one attributes the regular rotation of the seasons to the work of divinity, as did the early Christian Father Minicius Felix, then to disturb that order is to interfere with the divinely ordered scheme of the universe.[70] But such qualms are equally appropriate in a secular worldview. In most climates seasonality has such an obvious connection with growth and rest that it is hardly necessary to elaborate on the idea that to interfere with nature is to invite disaster.[71] These notions apply with equal force to the destruction of animal or vegetable life.[72] They are reinforced when the reasons for interference have to do with the production of luxury, or non-utilitarian items, with killing animals to provide furs for women of upper groups, or cutting down trees to supply wood pulp for ephemeral magazines. While they were not unique to these societies, such ideas become especially prominent in highly differentiated cultures, in cultures of luxury.

This means that an aspect of 'class' is necessarily involved, that is, of 'class'

---

[70] Minucius Felix 1844–64:475 (cap. 17).
[71] The objections to interfering with seasonality have to do not only with divinity and the science of nature, but with aesthetics which value regular alternation, the movement between seasons of different types.
[72] Goody 1962:198.

in the widest sense of that word, of the activities of 'upper' groups and individuals in contrast to 'lower' ones. Like other aspects of the culture of luxury, a related objection to the culture of flowers is that its benefits are not equally distributed, not available to one and all; instead they constitute the very stuff of difference, of hierarchy, of deprivation. The aspirations of the lower groups may embody the wish for wider access to those items or alternatively a desire to destroy the very foundations of the system, both attitudes being found associated with revolutionary movements. But neither these attitudes nor any consequential actions are defined solely by hierarchy; the lower groups may internalise, in whole or in part, the culture of the upper, at least as a goal; even if much may remain unattainable, flowers migrate from the gardens of the rich where it is often the poor who look after them with intense care and much hard labour. Equally the critique of the culture of luxury may be generated within the upper groups themselves, especially by literati encouraged to reflect upon the contradictions of their own society. The formulators of the most important revolutionary creeds of the nineteenth century were members of the very bourgeoisie whose domination they were trying to end.

Similar tensions and ambivalences to those found in earlier China have appeared in recent times and may be regarded as one of the springs of the Revolution itself. Ideals of equality, the impoverishment of the Northern peasantry, especially in light of the comparatively easy life of the elites, such notions and facts inspired a movement that gave its first priority to the redistribution of property and the growing of grain rather than flowers. In the delta as elsewhere in the country, peasants were organised in communes and allocated high production targets for basic crops which they were expected to fulfil. The inclusion of a crop of winter wheat in addition to two of rice meant the exhaustion of land and labour, as well as the diversion of effort from the cultivation of cash crops which had been such an important part of the horticultural scene for many centuries.[73] In order to ensure that quotas were filled, cadres tried to reduce other agricultural activities, in some cases trampling down vegetable plots, cutting down fruit trees, filling in duck ponds. In any case, this demanding schedule left little time or energy for growing other crops, especially inedible ones. The Cultural Revolution further reinforced the element of utilitarianism, raising objections to the bourgeois and feudal cultures of the past; in turning temples into schools and lineage halls into factories, they not only changed their use but damaged their fabric, often unintentionally but at times deliberately destroying tablets and beheading religious figures. Religion and ritual suffered at the same time as the culture of flowers. At least in its drive against the representation of deity and the private use of flowers, the Revolution's association of iconoclasm and

[73] Siu 1989.

'puritanism' recalled the situation at the time of the rise of Christianity and later on during the Reformation. While the public use of flowers was not at issue, the state suppressed many other uses, partly for ideological reasons, partly by virtually eliminating the possibility of surplus (and hence of luxury) as well as the elites who had cultivated and enjoyed those pleasures.

The renewal of the culture of flowers, in both senses of the phrase, came after the ending of the Cultural Revolution in 1976, and especially with the preliminary opening up of the economy that began in 1979. Peasants were allowed to cultivate land themselves providing they produced a quota of grain to be sold to the state at a fixed price. With the rest they could engage in other activities, the growing of fruit, the raising of livestock, the cultivation of flowers. This they did, partly for the internal market, expanding with the relaxation of the 'puritanical' morality as well as with the greater access to wealth that depended on higher productivity, the import of capital and the export trade to Hong Kong and Macao. Nevertheless, the rapid growth of consumerism manifested in the consumption of flowers worried the party. In 1983 the government attempted to forbid their use in factories and offices, some of the main consumers at the time of the New Year; it was an aspect of the same sumptuary restrictions that had earlier been applied to funerals, festivals and banquets. The decree had a devastating effect on peasant life, at least in the short term, as growers needed to plan the production of these crops over several years. But there were corresponding effects on the consumers. One Xiaolan specialist in organising rituals pointed out that, following the earlier disappearance of many nurseries in the 1970s, the use of fresh flowers in funerals had radically diminished. Nowadays people turned largely to artificial ones. The recent proliferation of nurseries could reverse that trend, though the new attraction of ritual for the junior generation does not necessarily involve a return to earlier practice. Plastic is here to stay as its quality improves, especially as artificial flowers have long been a feature of Chinese as of European life, not only in the winter months (when they are no longer essential because of the world market and 'unseasonal' species) but also for prestigious functions such as decorating women's dress.

The renewed injunctions against flowers did not last long and their use has expanded into some new areas as well as filling older ones. Cadres reported that the government was now encouraging their use; potted plants proliferate around building developments of various kinds. They have even become an accepted indication of the prosperity of an enterprise. Many flowers mean large profits. In the words of the calligrapher who created a New Year banner for us in the market town of Shawan, Panyu county:

> The Spring Sacrifice bunch of golden branches bears abundant flowers and leaves,
> The heart of the silver tree opens, fortune and prosperity flourish.

Especially at New Year, blooming flowers spell out hopes for the future – good health and good fortune – as well as bearing witness to the nature of the present. A prosperous merchant can offer the best peach tree. As one grower in Hong Kong remarked, in expressing the hope of good sales over the New Year: 'from my experience, the consumption of flowers usually correlates to the economic atmosphere'.[74]

That was one of the problems about attempting to suppress the culture of flowers in China; for many they still carried the significance of 'prosperity', 'longevity', 'wealth', 'happiness', that is, of general well-being. Such meanings are well recognised in the 1990s. Ever since the re-establishment of the flower markets around 1984, their use has expanded rapidly both in business and at home. Even a local hotel like the Jianlibao Hotel at the county capital of Sanshui had its own nursery to provide plants for the excellent displays that decorated the entrances as well as for other needs. In the case of Sanshui, many of the town's new roads, public facilities and apartment blocks had been built with the profits from the government-owned Jianlibao beer factory. The balconies of those apartments were decorated with plants; the town nursery supplied a large variety for the city environment, including miniature trees. An experimental station worked on the genetic reproduction of species. The beer factory itself, a prosperous 'joint venture' started with West German technical help, American equipment and Hong Kong management, was bursting with flowers. A garden had been constructed in front of the main building; the statue that adorned its entrance was surrounded with blooms; in the foyer stood a magnificent peach tree, embedded in chrysanthemums, on which had been strung a chain of 'Christmas lights'. All announced the success of the factory, the high standard of living it provided for its workers and the profits that were channelled back for the improvement of the whole town. If flowers did not necessarily predict future prosperity, they were certainly indications of its presence.

I have spoken of the reappearance, in newly adapted forms, of the long-established flower culture of South China where it emerged from one of the most advanced systems of intensive horticulture in the world. The call of tradition, the economic take-off, the desires of visitors, especially 'overseas Chinese', and the attractiveness of the flowers themselves, influenced the change in policy and led to the reinstatement of flowers as symbols of prosperity. That shift was of course dependent on a change in state policy in favour of economic liberalisation, which put more money in people's pockets and less pressure on their minds. Flowers that had been largely the prerogative of the political organisation now spread to the factory, the family and even to ritual.

---

[74] *Sunday Morning Post*, 22 January, 1989.

Hong Kong itself suffered no setback of the kind that occurred in Guangdong. Yet throughout China in times past the culture of flowers, which has always been in part a culture of luxury, raised contradictions that are associated with the notion of distributive justice, the idea of equality and the aim of providing the essentials of life for all men that lay behind the Revolution of 1949. The lavish use of flowers, a mark of the differentiated cultures of Europe and Asia, calls attention to the existence of poverty in the midst of plenty. In this situation, tension and ambivalence accumulate around forms of conspicuous consumption. In China today, however, the overall level of development may lead to the crossing of a threshold so that the terms of the debate will be changed, leaving flowers in the less equivocal position they hold in contemporary Hong Kong. No longer perceived as an element of 'feudal' culture, under both regimes they have become items of mass culture, a 'luxury' accessible if not to all at least to the majority. In traditional China, flowers were used throughout the society, but that use was largely defined and managed by the old elite who have disappeared in the face of capitalist growth on the one hand and communist attack on the other. Today, under both regimes, the culture of flowers lives on and expands in new directions.

14 · *A distant reading*

BACK TO AFRICA

This enquiry began with a question about the absence of a culture of flowers in Black Africa. A recent comment on how a Glebo Christian in Liberia should behave in contrast to a 'pagan' gets to the core of the matter. 'A good Glebo Christian observed Sunday, pulled down greegrees (charms or 'fetiches'), and refused to participate in traditional sacrifices, but a good Glebo Christian also wore western clothes, built a western house, married only one wife, and *cultivated a garden of flowers*.'[1] The flowers distinguished the convert and his foreign influences. The absence of domesticated flowers in traditional Africa, except in some areas strongly influenced by Islam, was linked to the level of agriculture and to the limits hoe farming placed on the emergence of heavily stratified cultural forms and in particular of cultures of luxury, of differentiated styles of life that could develop the 'non-utilitarian', 'aesthetic' aspects of horticulture – or rather, that could develop crops not primarily oriented to food and war, but to religion, gift-giving and above all to beauty. It is the shift implied in the words of John Gerard in his *Herbal* of 1597 where he comments on plants that 'are not used either in mete or medicine but esteemed for their beauty, to deck up gardens and the bosoms of the beautiful'.

But the initial query about Africa applied not only to the domesticated but also to the wild varieties, of which only a restricted use is made. Here another order of explanation was called for. I suggested that it should be sought partly in the relative paucity of flowering species in Africa, at least those that produce blooms that last any length of time, but more importantly in the notion that a flower is a prelude to a further end, to the fruit or grain, never a thing in itself. The attitude persists in Europe as far as fruit trees are concerned: 'If you'd enjoy the fruit, pluck not the flower.' That notion implies a less autonomous, more contextualised aesthetic, a more holistic, less dichotomised view of nature. Meanwhile, a more overt interest in aspects of the wild often accompanies the growth of urban life. There is no call for zoos or botanical gardens outside societies constructed around cities.

[1] My emphasis, Moran (1990) quoting from J. Martin, The dual legacy: government authority and mission influence among the Glebo of eastern Liberia, 1834–1910. PhD dissertation, Boston University, 1968. I owe this reference to Rob Leopold.

In bold contrast to Africa stand the major societies of Europe and Asia. In China and Japan trees have long been cultivated not only for the edible fruit but specifically for the blossom. That becomes an end in itself. In South China the New Year peach is cut down before it can bear and over the centuries this particular species has been bred to produce blossom rather than fruit. This culture of flowers in Eurasia has roots that go back to the ancient Near East, and I have tried to outline its developments in Mesopotamia and Egypt, leading to the classical world and later to Western Europe. For any such account one is obviously dependent on the persistence of graphic sources, on texts, including literary ones, and on painting. These activities lead to the elaboration of symbolic meanings for flowers within a range of different contexts, religious, political, literary, even for supposedly everyday purposes as in the Language of Flowers, whose development in the urban society of post-Napoleonic France was associated with the growth of city culture, of botanical knowledge and of new practices in retailing and consumption. That paraliterary artefact was embraced in large parts of Europe and made a considerable impact on North America, then in the process of coping with the decline of the cultural effects of its Puritan tradition.[2]

FLOWERS AND RELIGION

In looking at the culture of flowers in more recent times I have turned from the text to the utterance and to observation. The chapters on Europe, India and China are based partly on my own experience. Limited as it was, that experience permitted a fuller account of the role of flowers in these cultures than is possible from written sources alone, especially of aspects of gift-giving of a religious and secular character. For such mundane activities tend either to go unnoticed or to be recorded in a highly formalised way that often bears only a limited relation to everyday life. In gift-giving the contrast with Black Africa becomes especially clear. In that part of the continent flowers simply do not enter into offerings either to men or to gods. Divinities are approached by word of mouth (as everywhere), by offerings of food, but mainly by animal sacrifice. In Greece and Rome (and in the earlier Near East) these sacrificial offerings to deities and the dead were accompanied by the wearing of flowers in the shape of garlands. Elsewhere in Asia flowers are often seen as a substitute rather than a supplement to sacrifice, being closely connected with worship in the Indic religions, Buddhism, Jainism and post-Vedic Hinduism, where the priests and at times the laity themselves forgo the flesh of animals. Flowers are given to gods as they are to humans, for which purposes they have long been specially cultivated.

---

[2] The historian D. H. Fischer writes of Harriet Beecher Stowe as living 'in the twilight of this culture', that is, in the middle of the nineteenth century (1989:113).

It is not only the living but the dead who are the recipients of flowers. In those cultures of Eurasia that practise burial, the importance of flowers stretches beyond the time of death to all other occasions when the dead are greeted or remembered, especially at the autumn festival in East Asia and at All Souls' in Catholic Europe. Cremation provides fewer opportunities for offerings or memorials of any kind after the funeral itself, for the bones are no longer with us and the dust often scattered. This giving of flowers to both the living and dead is a part of the culture of the major societies of Eurasia which sets them in such stark contrast to the traditional societies of Africa where the offerings to deities and to the dead consist mainly of blood sacrifice and the food, largely cooked, that men themselves eat.

But while most of the major societies of Europe and Asia use flowers in a multitude of ways, there have been some times, places and contexts where they have been virtually absent. Changes in the mode of communication to the divinity, at times the shift of emphasis from ritual and object to word and text, are associated with another type of historical change in human cultures which is typified by the decline of the flower culture in Europe. The contexts are religious and political. The first relates mainly to those religions having their origins in the Near East and stemming from Judaism, which paid little attention to flowers, either in reality or in representation. As representations they were prohibited by the second Commandment which forbade any 'graven images' at all. Actual flowers seem to have been associated with 'foreign' cults of which they disapproved as well as with the prominence given to the idea that communication with the immaterial God should be mediated not by material offerings but by words alone.

These ideas affected Christianity and Islam in varying ways. Islam rejected the use of flowers in worship and the representation of any of God's creation, though flowers took their place outside religion, in the splendour of their gardens, in the luxury of their carpets and in the secular paintings that appeared in the Safavid period. Christianity had a particular relationship both with flowers and with icons. It seems at first sight strange to find Europe dominated by a religion that, inheriting some of the great traditions of the classical world, allowed the use, cultivation and knowledge of flowers to fall to such a low level. That was not simply the result of neglect brought on by barbarian invasions, although the decline in economic activity and in urban populations, which began earlier, certainly cut at some of the roots of the production of 'luxury' items. An important factor here was the deliberate switch of investment from the facilities provided by towns, such as theatres, baths, markets, to the construction of church buildings, including enclosed monasteries in far-off places. In addition there was deliberate rejection. Just as the sculpture in the round of the ancient world that portrayed both men and gods virtually disappeared from Europe for a period of several centuries, effectively until the Gothic, so too did the garlands and flowers with which the pagan deities were surrounded. Nor were these much represented in two-dimensional painting which, even though concentrated on religious topics, was subject to considerable ambivalence. In principle no offerings were to be made either to God or to the departed except in words, that is, in prayer; all else should be offered to the church as alms and charity, for distribution as well as for consumption. The 'pagan' sacrifice of ancient Greece and Rome was metamorphosed into the sacrifice of Christ, recalled by consuming the bread and the wine, his body and his blood, in a ritual whose interpretation has long acted as a focus for religious controversy and for sectarian division. For extreme Protestants even that ritual was rejected. In addition, as Cressy has pointed out, Puritans disapproved of fires at Derbyshire well-dressing, and railed against the 'monstrous idolatry' of flowers at funerals.[3] When flowers did return, they did so mainly in the form of the bouquet, which one is tempted to see as a deliberate rejection of the pagan garland and crown, an elaboration of the single lily that the Archangel Gabriel brings, and appears sometimes to offer, to the Virgin Mary at the time of the Annunciation.

The situation was very different in the Eastern religions; Buddhism and Hinduism welcomed both the use and the representation of flowers. On the other hand, in the societies of East and South-east Asia, Buddhism, which had been through an early aniconic phase, did not go unchallenged, but had as its rivals Confucianism and Daoism in China and Korea, and Shintoism in Japan. One aspect of that rivalry turned around the role of flowers in worship, the role of non-domesticated nature and to some extent the role of representation, including that of flowers, as well as the idea of what constituted appropriate offerings to the gods.[4]

While Confucianism does not reject the notion of offerings either to the dead or to the deity, it has been notably 'puritanical' in other ways. There is the insistence on correct, restrained behaviour over a wide range of social action, even artistic production. It rejected the Buddhist tendency to proliferate colourful decorations over its buildings, including the use of the

---

[3] Cressy 1985:90, referring to J. Stoppford, *Pagano-Papismus: Or, an Exact Parallel Betweene Rome-Pagan, and Rome-Christian, in their Doctrines and Ceremonies*, London, 1675.

[4] In Confucian rites, it is cooked food that is offered to ancestors, although raw food is presented to the highest gods as well as at rites to founding ancestors. (My account is based on the ancestral sacrifice to founders of the Andong-Kim lineage in Korea in November 1989, and for the opportunity to be present I am most grateful to Professor Kim Kwang-ok and the International Cultural Society of Korea. I was also able to attend the offerings for the Chinese New Year through the courtesy of friends in Hong Kong.) At the ancestral commemoration of the Andong-Kim lineage there was no blood sacrifice, but drink and food, both cooked and raw, were offered to the founder and then distributed among those present for them to take home. Before the ceremony raw food was offered at the side to the Mountain God, and again taken away by some of those attending. While officiants may receive somewhat larger shares, the situation is very different from that in priestly religions where specialists not involved in the usual process of production have to be 'fed' by the congregation, through permanent bequests to the church or through the weekly money in the plate, even the filling of the monk's bowl. Such gifts are physically handed over, not simply offered to be taken back in the same material form for consumption or distribution by the participants, although transformed from the profane to the sacred. That is a 'sacrifice', a 'making holy', in a very different sense.

lotus on roof tiles. Korean lineage halls are distinctly more austere than Buddhist temples. Public ceremonies in this mode are not marked by the use of flowers as offerings, nor is there the same proliferation of holy statuary.

A parallel opposition occurs in Japan between Buddhism and Shintoism. The first was international, a fact that, together with the large-scale ownership of property, gave rise to recurrent complaints. The second was national, local, opposed to the outside. The first emphasised floral offerings and decoration, the second, foliage and greenery, things of the wild: it was the natural opposed to the cultivated. These features are not simply a question of one religion differentiating itself from another in peaceful complementarity, but part of a long-term struggle between competing creeds. While relations between the parties vary over time from active competition to passive co-existence, a significant element in the use of flowers for worship is the very active process of definition by opposition, of stressing one's own identity by rejecting the ways of the 'pagan'. There were of course other aspects to these differences than structural opposition alone, for they embodied various levels of ambivalent thoughts about practice which affected views about nature and about icons of nature. There was the problem of making any offerings at all, even flowers, to divinity, especially he who had created everything. There was the associated problem of representing an immaterial divinity in a material form, especially one so august as the Creator himself. Again there was the more general problem of the 'embarrassment of riches'. The two questions have to be looked at theologically, intellectually, as well as in terms of opposition.

In the theology of the Near Eastern religions a higher value was placed upon the word rather than the image. For the word was the word of God which had no visual counterpart other than writing itself. There seems to have been no such hierarchy in Egypt or Mesopotamia where in art the image and the word were often intertwined. It is true that after the defeat of the iconoclasts in the East, two-dimensional representation was encouraged by the church, partly for theological reasons (which were not altogether accepted in the West), partly for educational ones. It is also true that the Book, which was at first little embellished with 'illuminations', was gradually adorned in the north largely with elaborate initial letters that transformed themselves into figures, and with borders that shifted from the formal to the natural, eventually producing such masterpieces as the work of the Limbourg brothers or the master of Flémaille. But the opposition based on Old Testament sources, as well as recurrent problems about portraying divinity, continued to be felt and expressed not only by heretics but by members of the church itself. Eventually that trend burst forth in the work of the Iconoclasts of the sixteenth and seventeenth centuries.

The doctrine that forbids any attempt to imitate the unique work of God the Creator, and that consequently rejects all images, may emerge in a number of modified forms. There is the ban on images of the divinity or the major cult figures. Some variants of this prohibition excluded only sculpture in the round, and some all graven images, because of their enhanced reality. Others only prevented images from entering the sacred space itself, allowing their appearance in secular life. Yet others prohibited all images of the divinity, especially the High God. Such aniconic notions may have a wider, cultural base, troubling African societies but, as is often the case in oral cultures, in a less explicit or ideological way. For the problem of representing an immaterial deity in material form is at some point, in time or context, a problem for even the most iconic religions. In the early years of Christianity there was no image of Christ, Buddha was not sculptured for many centuries, while Islam continues to eschew these and other representations. Even in Africa, often thought of as the home of the sculpture of gods, the High God, the Creator God, rarely achieves an altar, let alone an image. After his unique act of creation, he distanced himself from mankind. To give him an image would be to draw him closer and so raise in an acute form the problem of evil in this world, whether the Creator of all would help us cope with the evil of his creation. At the same time, an image would attempt to represent what cannot be represented in that form. Other supernatural agencies in Africa, though not often the major deities, are figured in an anthropomorphic guise. But even the ancestors are often given an abstract rather than a human embodiment. Adjacent groups show a surprising diversity of response, which may be related in part to the ambivalence about giving a distinct human shape to deities and to the departed, yet having little but that one dominant model to offer of beings or forces that can effectively communicate with mankind.[5] Non-anthropomorphic images or objects solve one problem but create another. In any case the offering of flowers, incense and even prayers implies a divinity, whatever its form, who can experience human sensations and speech.

FLOWERS AND LUXURY

There is a further factor that affects the use and representation of flowers, namely, ambivalent attitudes towards the culture of luxury on which the production of 'aesthetic' horticulture ultimately depended. Because the growing and giving of flowers were often associated with conspicuous consumption, their use could give rise to objections from philosophers in China, from stoics in Rome, from clerics in Islam and from reformers in Christianity. Apart from reasons of religion, the connection of flowers with luxury was a persisting theme in the writings of the early Christian Fathers, and the force of such criticism was one element in the decline of the culture of

[5] I have presented in a very summary form an argument that is amplified in Goody 1991.

flowers, the growing as well as the use, the knowledge as well as the practice, that occurred with the gradual ending of 'paganism' in Rome; like Ibn Khaldun in the Middle Ages, some Roman moralists saw the excessive luxury of the upper groups as the harbinger of the fall of empires.[6]

High and low culture, that is, the behaviour, attitudes and material products of 'upper' and 'lower' groups, make different demands on the social system. Apart from direct conflicts in the general field of common understanding, such differences have effects, among other things, on the economy. Those Roman moralists were well aware of the problem when they criticised luxury and the amount of land given over to the growing of flowers for worship, adornment or perfume; the populace may have been less conscious, distracted by spectacle, accepting the ideology and perhaps desiring to imitate as well as to criticise the ways of their 'betters', or at least of the better-off.

The ambivalences about luxury persisted, for it is an intrinsic feature of such cultures. Schama's account of the Dutch Republic in its golden age, significantly entitled *The Embarrassment of Riches*, concludes:

So riches seemed to provoke their own discomfort, and affluence cohabited with anxiety. This syndrome, at once strange and familiar to modern sensibility, did not originate with the reformation, nor was it peculiar to the Netherlands. Both the Roman stoics' criticism of luxury and avarice (encoded in Italian sumptuary laws from the thirteenth century onwards), and the repeated attacks of Franciscans on church and lay wealth were absorbed into northern humanism.[7]

He goes on to point out that when Erasmus took up the theme of the rarity of the world's riches he rejected both the quietist retreat of the monastery and the mendicant purity of the Franciscans, demanding a direct encounter with the wealth of the material world. Such an encounter prevented neither Erasmus himself nor the merchants of Amsterdam from enjoying what they had accumulated.

The argument between the respective virtues of poverty and wealth is built into the nature of economically stratified societies of this kind and significantly it re-emerged in Europe at this period. In the Western tradition that argument is embodied in the views of the stoics and the peripatetics, the ones opting for poverty, the others for wealth, but as a means of achieving virtue rather than simply for personal enjoyment in the Epicurean manner. The Roman argument was thoroughly relevant to the Christian tradition in which Christ opted for poverty and proclaimed the difficulties in the way of the rich man receiving grace to be almost insurmountable. But the Donation of Constantine stood for the changes that success ushered in and the church

---

[6] Often it is the *nouveaux riches* who bear the brunt of these attacks, since they fail to make the more subtle dissimulations and adaptations of the long-established elites.   [7] Schama 1987:326.

now required a doctrinal defence of its accumulated riches. The Franciscans took another course, but the humanists of fifteenth-century Florence upheld the gaining of wealth as a means to achieve civic and personal virtue. It was an argument that had its consequences for art and other luxuries, even pagan ones. (Not in apostolic poverty, maintained Lapo da Castiglionchio, but in the custom of the Ancients who decorated their idols with costly gold must a model be sought.[8]) Such attitudes, prominent in the Renaissance, gave rise to individual ambivalences (which could be relieved by acts of charity), as well as to opposing doctrines that praised the simpler, non-ostentatious ways of living.

Whether played out on a societal scale between sectarian or hierarchical groups, or embodied as ambivalences within the ideological tenets of each individual, such contradictions are intrinsic to the differentiated societies that arose in the early civilisations of what has been called the Urban Revolution of the Bronze Age, and they remained a dominant feature thereafter. While specific aspects of Western societies, whether Christian or Roman, are of course unique, there is a general contradiction that lies close to the heart of all those developed cultural traditions in Eurasia. Advanced social differentiation gives birth to countervailing comment and criticism. Not at all times and by all persons but recurring frequently enough in the words of men, priests, moralists, philosophers, writers of all descriptions, to enable us to discern it as the part of their mentality, their mind set. Such expressions are especially characteristic of written cultures, partly because the critics leave indelible records of their rebellious thoughts, partly because the reflexive, inward-peering activity of writing encourages just such introspection, and partly because criticisms can build, almost physically, one on another.

Those contradictions give rise to subdominant themes and motifs that are critical of wasteful expenditure, of luxury, of the interference with nature or the ways of God, of ritual elaboration, of the taking of life, of images of the immaterial, of 'unnecessary' acts that are seen as offending both men and gods. To all these activities mankind extends a critical intelligence, while accepting, often indulging in, the very behaviour that is being criticised. He enjoys his wealth as well as being embarrassed by it. At other times, often under 'revolutionary' regimes, the subdominant takes over as the prevailing ideology, at least in the short term. For over the longer term, the ideals of revolutionaries become compromised with long-term trends, some of which are characteristic of those societies with advanced forms of agriculture and others of humanity at large. The former includes leanings towards luxury and towards conspicuous consumption, the latter the tendency to interfere with nature, to elaborate ritual and even to make images of the 'unimaginable'.

---

[8] See Baron 1938:30.

FLOWERS IN EUROPE

The culture of flowers is affected by both such trends and in early Christian Europe its rejection had multiple roots. But that reversal soon began to undergo modification. The elements that underlay the very gradual revival were several. Firstly, there was the acculturation of the invaders. That was of relatively little importance, since ideologically they were more involved in becoming Christian than in becoming Roman. Secondly, there was the weight of popular culture, though it is never easy to decide what the weight might be at any time for the influence of the church was undoubtedly radical, since it perceived pre-existing culture as 'pagan' and therefore as something to be destroyed.

Developments in the culture of flowers represented in part a reassertion of popular interests that worried elements in the church because of these 'pagan' associations, so their use was often played down or christianised over the following centuries. Just as churches were built on the sites of pagan worship, so herbs and flowers were literally christened, renamed, as Mary's wort or John's weed. Even so herbs had to be gathered while saying a prayer, just as many other acts were rendered harmless by means of the sign of a cross. For herbs, leaves and flowers continued to be important for medicinal and related purposes, whatever the church or state had to say.

At the same time, an important contributor to the rebirth of the culture of flowers was the church itself. The rejection of flowers for religious performances was but one aspect of early Christianity. The safe place for flowers was within the holy space of the monastery, together with Latin learning, so that their cultivation and later their wider use emerged again within the Catholic community. The churches too began to encourage some decoration. Paulinus of Nola (353–431) already recommended that the faithful attending the feast of St Felix should advance spring by spreading flowers on the ground. Nevertheless, only gradually did they return, especially in iconographic form, and even then with some ambivalence, to be cleared away once again by those reforming Protestants who turned back to the Biblical and religious texts in the same way that the Renaissance had returned to the secular writings, the shapes and the architecture of the classical world.

The dramatic growth of this revived European interest in flowers, and in the symbolic representations of the natural world more inclusively, goes back to the twelfth century and its socio-economic changes, with many further developments taking place during the Renaissance. In the sphere of botany, the 'return of the rose' at first consisted largely of a revival or adaptation of classical learning, which had persisted in some cloistered form throughout the Dark Ages, rediscovering the past and then building on those foundations. Eventually Europe caught up again with China. In different forms the culture of flowers was a feature of all the major Eurasian societies, at least as extensive in scale as in pre-industrial Europe. Where that continent differed was in the extent it had to make up for its earlier decline.

The representations of flowers cover a wide range with 'aesthetics' at the one end and with the techniques and technology of production at the other. And images of flowers make an important contribution to science, since with words alone it is difficult to make the critical identifications. It is not accidental that two of the great areas of botanical advance, namely medieval China and Renaissance Europe (the third was ancient Greece), were concerned with the graphic reproduction of flowers in a partially mechanised way by carving blocks of wood or other material. Quite apart from the effect on the internal development of botanical science, which as an advanced knowledge system builds up its own written tradition and acquires a degree of structural autonomy from other aspects of culture, there is the influence, through the mass reproduction of the drawings and paintings of flowers, on popular culture – what we might call with Van Gogh in mind the Sunflower effect. That became of great importance both in the West and in the East when cotton textiles from India, capable of absorbing the bright colours applied with the brush or the block, dominated the domestic life of the old world with their price, brilliance and design.

It is not surprising that one element in the revival of the European interest in flowers was the influence of the continent of Asia. Asia was also embarrassed by great riches, especially of a floral kind, and its produce was the basis of much of the luxury of the West, with its delicate silks, printed cottons (indiennes, chintz) and blue and white porcelain (china). Indeed, the impact of Indian cottons presaged the Industrial Revolution itself.[9] The quantity imported to satisfy the demand of the Western consumers brought about similar results to those Pliny complained of for Eastern silks in Roman times – they led to an unfavourable balance of trade and in the later case to complaints from local producers of cloth who called for restrictions on imports. But the positive response to the East lay not in the realm of restrictions, rather in the development of the local manufacture of cotton chintz by copying the wood blocks and later by the new mechanical processes that were central to the Industrial Revolution of the late eighteenth century, giving rise to the mass production of cottons in factory conditions.

It was from the end of the sixteenth century that flowers, and especially the representations of flowers made popular by painters of the Netherlands, began to dominate the domestic and personal space of the town, playing a greater part not only among the elite but in the icons of popular culture. It is not accidental that flowers became prominent in many forms of painting, and more particularly in designs on cloth, on canvas and in sculptural patterns.

[9] Schama 1987:326.

While flowers initially evolved to attract pollinating insects, they also proved pleasurable to much of agricultural mankind, partly as harbingers of harvests, whether of fruit or vegetables, but later as objects of distinct aesthetic pleasure to oneself, to one's friends and to one's gods. Printing followed painting, and made it easy to reproduce regular patterns, especially on paper and cotton. When these bright materials reached Europe, their success for clothing the person and for decorating the house was immediate, for neither woollen cloth nor linen could be treated in the same way. In their printed versions, flowers became a preferred decorative schema for wallpaper and for curtains, for upholstery and for women's dresses, and later on, with the printing of cloth for those flower-conscious cultures of the contemporary Pacific, for men. The mass urban use of flowers for such decorative purposes entailed emptying them, in that context, of any specific meaning. In the Middle Ages they had been given special meanings in a variety of fields, religion, heraldry, politics and literacy. But as part of the repetitive process of printing that wood, but especially metal, blocks made possible, their representations fell into the category of 'pattern' rather than 'sign', being drained of most symbolic significance.[10]

Developments in the culture of flowers were accompanied by the kinds of critical considerations that had affected not only earlier Christianity but other major societies in Asia. In his perceptive account of *Man and the Natural World*, Keith Thomas calls attention to the 'human dilemma' involved in the 'embarrassment about meat-eating', that is, the problem of reconciling 'the physical requirements of civilization with the new feelings and values which that same civilization had generated'.[11] He sees new sentiments as emerging in the recent period; by 1800 'the confident anthropocentrism of Tudor England had given way to an altogether more confused state of mind'. But Thomas also calls attention to the wider human dimension and my aim has been to suggest that mankind has had to face this dilemma at much earlier periods and in other societies. In classical times Porphyry had argued the case for vegetarianism; Buddhism has long affected large regions of the globe with its feelings not only about animals but plants. Even in the 'simpler' societies, there is an implicit ambivalence towards the killing of man and animals, and sometimes towards the destruction of vegetable matter, that compares, in feeling if not in manifestation, with the situation in 'civilised' society.[12] This wider pan-human aspect of conservation does not exclude the making of many environmental mistakes nor its genesis in self-regarding reasons rather than the higher altruism. Nor does it exclude changes over time; it is the nature, implications and causes of those changes that are at stake. Evidence for shifts in 'mentality' is difficult to demonstrate, as we know from parallel claims for childhood, sexuality and conjugal love. The documents can be

---

[10] Goody 1987:3.   [11] Thomas 1983:301.   [12] Goody 1962:115–21; 1986:13–16.

interpreted as indicating change in the manifestation rather than the nature of the 'mentalities', in the surface rather than the deeper structures. And when we are dealing with feelings and attitudes that are widespread in mankind, we have to assess shifts in balance rather than changes of a categorical kind.

Among these widespread human dilemmas, that take particular forms at particular junctures, are the questions of what to offer to the divinity and whether one can image (or even imagine) the immaterial. I have noted the role of the text, especially the printed text, in building up botanical knowledge, in developing elaborate, inventive but little-used symbolic schemes such as the 'Language of Flowers', but above all in providing a long-standing focus for attitudes towards flowers and their representations. It was also important in the formulation of these questions. Firstly, there were earlier texts to be reviewed, those of ancient Rome but above all the Biblical and patristic sources, which were constantly being explored and reinterpreted. The written text may lead to explicit discussions of what elsewhere is implicit, even to quibbling about what is a graven image and whether images exist that are not graven. The Eastern church had one answer, the Western another, Islam another and Judaism, which first put the notion in written form, yet another. Although each of these answers changed over time, the basic questions remained.

The dilemmas relating to the culture of flowers are also widely distributed but largely in those societies that developed an aesthetic horticulture and a scientific botany. For example, China and Japan had long displayed complicated feelings about the balance of nature, so that the 'new sentiments' of which Thomas speaks are new to modern England, part of the revival which we have examined, rather than to the world as a whole. There is some danger of taking developments in Western Europe as being unique in too many and too radical ways. Other urban societies that did not suffer the same heavy setbacks that afflicted Europe in the post-Roman period displayed similar interests in flowers and in nature more generally. Their development was more continuous.

As well as pursuing these themes I have tried to say something about culture and its interpretation, at least for the culture of flowers. The central question had to do with multiple contexts of knowledge, with hierarchical and vertical boundaries, as well as with the levels of competence of individuals. In this complex network, some significances are relatively new (those of chrysanthemums), some date from the distant past (those of roses); some extend from Sicily to Calais (chrysanthemums as flowers of death), others to the mid-Atlantic (the giving of odd numbers of red roses), yet others to South America (the giving of red roses themselves), while some are thoroughly local, like the practice of the village in the Tarn where the inhabitants were reported by Sébillot to cut all the flowers in a dead person's garden. That is an act that can be understood in a world-wide context as well as in a European one, but it is essentially a local custom. At the other extreme are the books on the 'Language of Flowers', a manufactured code of a formalised kind, a typical written list, in some ways a travesty, but with effects that feed back on wider cultural practice. Especially significant is it for that urban element (including the florists) who look for a simple table of equivalences, a structured formula by which to interpret the world, but don't know what it is. However, in the complex whole that constitutes the culture of flowers, meanings cannot be read off as with a diplomatic code, constructed with the intention of keeping messages hidden from outsiders, a mysterious secret to be known only by the privileged few. The patterns of meanings turn out to be much more complicated, dependent on context, capable of being manipulated by poet and peasant in generative ways. It is rather the written Language of Flowers that attempts to limit and constrain.

It is important to recall these varying boundaries of cultural practice which make it possible for humans in adjacent areas to communicate and at the same time to differentiate. With complex societies, some practices cut across groups, others are purely local. There is a temptation to designate differences in the practices and beliefs pertaining to flowers as 'cultural' and then to search for homologies within a particular unit. That may be possible in Aboriginal Australia; it is more difficult in Europe. These features like the absence of domesticated flowers affect more than one such unit and have to be looked at in relation to religious affiliation, to the ecology or to the horticulture of the region, to its past as well as its present.

Looking at the wider perspective, I have tried to map out 'culture areas' marked by an emphasis on broadly different uses of flowers, rising above the local characteristics of individual 'cultures'. There is the hand-held bouquet of cut flowers in the post-Renaissance West, the garland of South Asia, the potted plants in the gardens of the East, each making particular demands on domestic furnishings and architecture as well as on the type and shape of flowers. In the West long-stemmed ('sweetheart') roses are presented to lovers and displayed in tall vases; in South Asia garlands and bowls make use of multiheaded varieties in which the stalk is irrelevant. In East Asia the multiheaded flowers are woven into complex displays, while a few long-stalked ones are essential for flower arranging. Garlands around the shoulders, chaplets around heads, vases, bowls and pots, each has important links with domestic life over wide areas. The dominant use of forms such as the garland, the crown or the bouquet tends to be distributed over particular areas of the globe and to be linked to particular species, specific techniques and organisations of manufacture, and to distinct types of domestic furniture – the vase for bouquets – and hence with ceramic traditions.

There are regional differences among these societies marked by a culture of flowers. The external differences between those societies and Black Africa were related to systems of production and systems of communication. For the culture of flowers, in the sense of cultivation, is an adjunct of advanced horticulture. Although usually cultivated by the hoe or fork rather than the plough, it is the 'surplus' offered by a developed system of production that permits flowers to flourish. Today they do so on a world-wide scale, promoted by developments in international trade, in media and in the hegemonic spread of Western practice and ideas. Cut flowers from Colombia may arrive through the Dutch markets to Les Halles or Covent Garden, then to the local flower shop or to the seller of flowers outside the Metro, in the restaurant or at the street corner. Their sale is part of the provision of goods and services to the dominant and the better-off, frequently by women to a largely male clientele. Because they are grown by cultivators and sold by petty traders for the benefit of others, the culture of flowers has been marked by 'class' as well as by gender. Nowadays flowers have largely ceased to be part of the luxury trade in the West. Like gardens they have become items of mass consumption, although still providing ways of distinguishing the richer from the poorer. Elsewhere in the world that is not always the case; revolutionary regimes tend to discourage the consumption of 'inessentials'. Flower power is not always seen as people power. On the other hand, in the Third World the production of luxuries for richer nations, which may be profitable for reasons of climate and labour, is a way of financing the import of more-needed products. The Third World may draw benefits by producing luxuries to finance necessities, such as food imports from the richer, Northern, countries. So in the global village earlier differences of 'class' now tend to appear as differences between regions. The culture of flowers becomes more unified, more integrated commercially, on a world scale, but now marked by hierarchical differentiation between the North and the South.

References

I have resorted to various idiosyncracies in compiling this list of references. The editions of standard texts are often provided in the footnotes rather than in this list of references. Quotations from the Bible are all from the Authorised version, and all Shakespeare quotations are from Arden editions (London).

Acker, W. R. B. (transl.) 1954 *Some T'ang and Pre-T'ang Texts on Chinese Paintings*. Leiden

Adams, J. S. 1848 *Flora's Albums, Containing the Language of Flowers Poetically Expressed*. New York

Agnew, J. C. 1986 *Worlds Apart: The Market and the Theater in Anglo-American Thought, 1550–1750*. Cambridge
    1989 Coming up for air: consumer culture in historical perspective. MS

AGREX report 1974 *Le Marché des fleurs et des feuillages en Grande Bretagne*. August

Alexander, J. J. G. 1970 *The Master of Mary of Burgundy*. London
    1977 *Italian Renaissance Illuminations*. New York

Alexander, J. J. G. and Kaufmann, C. M. 1973 *English Illuminated Manuscripts 700–1500* (exhibition catalogue, Bibliothèque Royale Albert). Brussels.

Almanach 1817 *Almanachs de mode: oracles des fleurs*. Paris

Ambalai, Amit 1987 *Krishna and Shrinathji*. Ahmadabad

Amherst, A. 1896 *A History of Gardening in England* (2nd edn) London

Anon. 1816 *Les Emblèmes des fleurs: pièce de vers, suivie d'un tableau emblématique des fleurs*. Paris
    1819 *Le Langage des fleurs ou les sélams de l'Orient*. Paris
    1830 *The Language of Flowers, with Illustrative Poetry; to which is now first added the Calendar of Flowers* (revised by the editor of *Forget-Me-Not*, Frederick Shoberl, 2nd edn 1835, 3rd edn 1848). Philadelphia
    1834 *The Language of Flowers, or Alphabet of Floral Emblems* (imprint on cover N. and S. S. Jocelyn, New Haven 1827, National Union Catalogue). Edinburgh and New York
    1863 Sacred trees and flowers. *Quarterly Review* 114:210–50
    1900 *Les Fleurs à travers les âges et à la fin du XIXe siècle*. Paris
    1913 *Enquête sur le travail à domicile dans l'industrie de la fleur artificielle*. Paris
    1986 Introduction to *Popular Traditions and Customs of the Chinese New Year* (exhibition booklet). London

Appadurai, A. 1986 Commodities and the politics of value. In *The Social Life of Things: Commodities in Cultural Perspective*. Cambridge

Arber, A. 1938 *Herbals* (3rd edn; 1st edn 1912). Cambridge

Ariès, P. 1981 *The Hour of Our Death*. New York

Ash, R. 1989 *Sir Lawrence Alma-Tadema*. New York

Assi, L. A. 1987 *Fleurs d'Afrique Noire: de la Côte d'Ivoire au Gabon, Sénégal à l'Ouganda*. Colmar

Athenaeus (1927–41) *The Deipnosophists* (transl. C. H. Gulick, 7 vols). London

Atran, S. 1986 *Fondements de l'histoire naturelle: pour une anthropologie de la science*. Paris

  1990 *Cognitive Foundations of Natural History: Towards an Anthropology of Science*. Cambridge

Ault, N. (ed.) 1925 *Elizabethan Lyrics*. New York

Axton, R. and Stevens, J. 1971 *Medieval French Plays*. Oxford

Ball, J. Dyer 1900 *Things Chinese: Being Notes on Various Subjects Connected with China* (3rd edn). London

Balzac, H. de 1966 *Le Lys dans la Vallée* (ed. Moïse Le Yaouanc). Paris

Barjonet, C. 1986 Profits en fleurs. *L'Expansion* May–June, 127–132.

Barnett, S. W. 1989 Academy education and 'managing affairs': Hsieh Chang-t'ing and Fu-chou's Chih-yung Academy. Paper presented to the ACLS Conference on Education and Society in Late Imperial China, Montecito, California, 8–14 June

Barnhart, R. M. 1983 *Peach Blossom Spring: Gardens and Flowers in Chinese Paintings*. New York

Baron, D. E. 1982 *Grammar and Good Taste: Reforming the American Language*. New Haven

Baron, H. 1938 Franciscan poverty and civic wealth as factors in the rise of humanistic thought. *Speculum* 13:1–37

  1955 *The Crisis of the Early Italian Renaissance: Civic Humanism and Republican Liberty in an Age of Classicism and Tyranny* (2 vols.) Princeton

Barrett, W. A. 1873 *Flowers and Festivals: Or Directions for the Floral Decoration of Churches* (2nd edn, 1st edn 1867). London

Barrett, W. P. (transl.) 1932 *The Trial of Jeanne d'Arc*. New York

Barth, F. 1987 *Cosmologies in the Making: A Generative Approach to Cultural Variation in Inner New Guinea*. Cambridge

Bartholomew, T. T. 1980 Examples of botanical motifs in Chinese art. *Apollo* 48–54

  1985 Botanical puns in Chinese art from the collection of Asian Art, Museum of San Francisco. *Orientations* 18–24 September

Baskerville, C. R. 1920 Dramatic aspects of medieval folk festivals in England. *Studies in Philology* 17:19–87

Bateson, G. and Mead, M. 1942 *Balinese Character: A Photographic Analysis*. New York

Baus, K. 1940 *Der Krantz in Antike und Christentum*. Bonn

Baxandall, M. 1972 *Painting and Experience in Fifteenth Century Italy*. London

Beals, K. M. 1917 *Flower Lore and Legend*. New York

Bellair, G. A. and Bérat, V. 1891 *Les Chrysanthèmes, description, histoire, culture, emploi*. Compiègne

Belmont, A. 1896 *Dictionnaire historique et artistique de la rose, contenant un résumé de l'histoire de la rose chez tous les peuples anciens et modernes, ses propriétes, ses vertus, etc.* Melun

Belo, J. 1949 *Bali: Rangda and Barong.* New York
  1953 *Bali: Temple Festival.* American Ethnological Society. Locust Valley, New York
  1960 *Trance in Bali.* New York

Belo, J. (ed.) 1970 *Traditional Balinese Culture: Essays.* New York

Bergström, I. 1956 *Dutch Still-Life Painting in the Seventeenth Century* (Swedish edn 1947). London

Berkhofer, R. F. 1973 Clio and the culture concept: some impressions of a changing relationship in American historiography. In L. Schneider and C. M. Bonjean (eds.), *The Idea of Culture in the Social Sciences.* Cambridge

Berkson, C. 1986 *The Caves at Aurangabad: Early Buddhist Tantric Art in India.* Ahmadabad

Bernage, B. and de Corbie, G. 1971 *Le Nouveau savoir-vivre: convenances et bonnes manières.* Paris

Berrall, J. S. 1969 *A History of Flower Arrangement* (revised edn 1978). London

Besson, E. 1975 Les colporteurs de l'Oisans au XIXe siècle. Témoignages et documents. *Le Monde alpin et rhodanien* 3:7–55

Bickford, M. (ed.) 1985 *Bones of Jade, Soul of Ice: The Flowering Plum in Chinese Art.* New Haven

Bieler, L. (ed.) 1963 *The Irish Penitentials.* Scriptores Latini Hiberniae, v. Dublin

Binion, S. A. 1909 *Phyllanthography: A Method of Leaf and Flower Writing.* New York

Blake, J. W. 1942 *Europeans in West Africa, 1450–1560* (2 vols., *The Hakluyt Society*, 2nd series, 86–7). London

Blanchan, N. 1909 *The American Flower Garden.* New York

Blessington, Countess of 1842 *The Idler in France* (2 vols., 2nd edn). London

Blismon, Ana-Gramme (S. Blocquel) 1851 *Nouveau Manuel allégorique des plantes, des fleurs, des fruits, des couleurs, etc.*
  1857 *Nouvelle Sélamographie, langage allégorique, emblématique, ou symbolique des fleurs et des fruits, des animaux, des couleurs, etc.* Paris

Bloch. H. 1982 The new fascination with ancient Rome. In R. L. Benson and G. Constable (eds.), *Renaisssance and Reversal in the Tenth Century.* Oxford

Blondel, S. 1876 *Recherches sur les couronnes de fleurs* (2nd edn). Paris

Blunden, C. and Elvin, M. 1983 *Cultural Atlas of China.* Oxford

Blunt, W. 1950 *Tulipomania.* Harmondsworth, Middlesex
  1976 The Persian garden under Islam. *Apollo* 70:302–6

Boardman, J. 1985 Art. The history of Western architecture: ancient Greek. *Encyclopaedia Britannica* (15th edn). Chicago

Bodde, D. 1975 *Festivals in Classical China.* Princeton

Bohannan, P. J. 1960 Conscience collective and culture. In K. H. Wolf (ed.), *Emile Durkheim 1858–1917.* Columbus

Bologna, G. 1988 *Illuminated Manuscripts: The Book before Gutenberg.* New York

Book of the Dead: The Papyri of Ani, Hunefer, Annaï (1979) (ed. E. Rossiter). Geneva

Boon, J. 1973a *Dynastic Dynamics: Caste and Kinship in Bali Now*. Dissertation, University of Chicago

   1973b Further operations of 'culture' in anthropology: a synthesis of and for debate. In L. Schneider and C. M. Bonjean (eds.), *The Idea of Culture in the Social Sciences*. Cambridge

   1977 *The Anthropological Romance of Bali, 1597–1972: Dynamic Perspectives in Marriage and Caste, Politics, and Religion*. Cambridge

Bordenare, J. and Vallele, N. 1973 *La mentalité religieuse des paysans de l'albigeois médiéval*. Toulouse

Bossy J. 1985 *Christianity in the West 1400–1700*. Oxford

Bouillet, A. and Servières, L. 1900 *Sainte-Foy, vierge et martyre*. Rodez

Bourne, H. 1833 *Flores Poetici. The Florists' Manual: Designed as an Introduction to Vegetable Physiology and Systematic Botany, for Cultivators of Flowers*. Boston

Braudel, F. 1982 *The Wheels of Commerce* (English transl.) New York

Bravmann, R. A. 1974 *Islam and Tribal Art in West Africa*. Cambridge

   1981 *Islam in Africa*. Washington, DC

Bray, F. 1984 *Biology and Biological Technology*. pt 2, *Agriculture*. Vol. 6, J. Needham (ed.), *Science and Civilisation in China*. Cambridge

   1986 *The Rice Economies: Technology and Development in Asian Societies*. Oxford

Breck, J. 1833 *The Young Florist: Or Conversations on the Culture of Flowers and on Natural History*. Boston

   1851 *The Flower-Garden; or, Breck's Book of Flowers; in which are Described all the Various Hardy Herbaceous Perennials, Annuals, Shrubby Plants, and Evergreen Trees, Desirable for Ornamental Purposes, with Directions for their Cultivation*. Boston

Bredon, J. and Mitrophanow, I. 1927 *The Moon Year* (repr. 1982). Hong Kong

Brereton, G. E. and Ferrier, J. M. (eds.) 1981 *Le Menagier de Paris*. Oxford

Briggs, C. K. 1986 The language of flowers in O'Pioneers. *Willa Cather Pioneer Memorial Newsletter* 30:29–33. Red Cloud, Nebraska

Britten, J. and Holland, R. 1878–86 *A Dictionary of English Plant Names*. English Dialect Society. London

Brookes, J. 1987 *Gardens of Paradise: The History and Design of the Great Islamic Gardens*. New York

Brosses, C. de 1836 *L'Italie il y a cent ans; ou, Lettres écrites d'Italie à quelques amis, en 1739 et 1740*. Paris

Brown, J. P. 1980 The sacrificial cult and its critique in Greek and Hebrew (II). *Journal of Semitic Studies* 25:1–21

Brown, P. 1988 *The Body and Society: Men, Women and Sexual Renunciation in Early Christianity*. New York

Browne, T. 1928 Of garlands and coronary or garland-plants. *The Works of Sir Thomas Browne* (ed. G. Keynes). London

Bruce, P. A. 1927 *Social Life of Virginia in the Seventeenth Century* (2nd edn). Lynchburg, Virginia

Bruce-Mitford, R. 1972 *The Sutton-Hoo Ship-burial: A Handbook* (2nd edn). London

Brückner, A. 1961 *Quellenstudien zu Konrad von Megenberg: Thomas Cantiprata-*

nus 'De animalibus quadrupedibus' als Vorlage im 'Buch der Natur'. Dissertation, Frankfurt am Main

Brydon, G. M. 1947 *Virginia's Mother Church and the Political Conditions under which it Grew*. Virginia Historical Society. Richmond

Buck, J. L. 1937. *Land Utilization in China*. Shanghai

Bulwer-Lytton, E. 1834 *The Last Days of Pompeii*. London

Bumpus, Judith 1990 *Impressionist Gardens*. Oxford

Burke, P. 1974 *Venice and Amsterdam: A Study in Seventeenth-Century Elites*. London

   1978 *Popular Culture in Early Modern Europe*. London

Burkhill, I. H. 1965 Chapters on the history of botany in India. *Botanical Survey of India*. Calcutta and Delhi

Burne, C. S. (ed.) 1883 *Shropshire Folk-Lore*. London

Burra, Neera n.d. Ambedkar: vision and achievement: a report from the field. MS

Burrows, E. 1963 *Flower in My Ear: Art and Ethos of Ifeluk Attol*. Seattle

Cafagna, A. C. 1960 A formal analysis of definitions of 'culture'. In G. E. Dole and R. L. Carneiro (eds.), *Essays in the Science of Culture*. New York

Cahill, J. 1960. *Chinese Painting*. Geneva

   1964 Confucian elements in the theory of painting. In A. F. Wright (ed.), *Confucianism and Chinese Civilization*. New York

Calder, W. M. 1920 Studies in early Christian epigraphy. *Journal of Roman Studies* 10:42–59

Calmettes, P. 1904 *Excursions à travers les métiers*. Paris

Campenhausen, H. von 1968 *Tradition and Life in the Church: Essays and Lectures in Church History* (transl. A. V. Littledale). London

Cao Xueqin (1977) *The Story of the Stone*. Harmondsworth, Middlesex

Celnart, Mme E. F. (pseud. Bayle-Mouillard) 1829 *Manuel du fleuriste artificiel, ou l'Art d'imiter d'après nature toute espèce de fleurs: en papier, batiste, mousseline et autres étoffes de coton, en gaze, taffetas, satin, velours; de faire des fleurs en or, argent, chenille, plumes, paille, baleine, cire, coquillages suivi de l'art du plumassier*. Paris

Céüse, A. de 1908 *La fleur qui parle et la plante qui guérit: principes élémentaires de botanique, figures, étymologie, description, habitat, culture, langage, emploi en médecine, application à la partie vétérinaire et aux arts, tables analytiques* (2nd edn). Paris

Chadwick, W. O. 1973 Art. Oxford Movement. *Encyclopaedia Britannica*, vol. 17, pp.13–15. Chicago

Chambers, R. (ed.) 1869 *The Book of Days: A Miscellany of Popular Antiquities in Connection with the Calendar, Including Anecdote, Biography and History, Curiosities of Literature, and Oddities of Human Life and Character* (1st edn 1862–4). London

Chambet, C. J. 1825a *Emblème des fleurs, ou parterre de flore, contenant le symbole et le langage des fleurs, leur histoire et origine mythologique, ainsi que les plus jolis vers qu'elles ont inspirés à nos meilleurs poètes, etc., etc.* Lyons

   1825b *Les Bouquets du sentiment, ou manuel de famille pour les fêtes* (3rd edn). Paris

Chang Hsin-hai 1956 *The Fabulous Concubine* (repr. 1986). Hong Kong

Charageat, M. 1962 (1930) *L'Art des jardins*. Paris

Charles-Picard, G. 1959 *La Civilisation de l'Afrique romaine*. Paris

Chartier, R. 1984 Culture as appropriation: popular cultural uses in early modern France. In S. L. Kaplan (ed.), *Understanding Popular Culture: Europe from the Middle Ages to the Nineteenth Century*. Berlin

Chaucer, G. (1894) *Works* (ed. W. W. Skeat). Oxford

Cheever, G. B. 1831 *The American Common-Place Book of Poetry: With Occasional Notes*. Boston

Cheng, Nien 1987 *Life and Death in Shanghai*. London

Cheng, Te-k'un 1969 Jade flowers and floral patterns in Chinese decorative art. *Journal of the Institute of Chinese Studies* 2:251–343

Cheng, Ji 1988 (*c.*1631) *The Craft of Gardens* (transl. A. Hardie). New Haven

Chéruel, A. 1865 Art. Redevances féodales. In *Dictionnaire historique des institutions, moeurs et coutumes de la France* (2 vols., 2nd edn). Paris

Cheshire, J. G. 1914 William Dowsing's destructions in Cambridgeshire. *Transactions of the Cambridgeshire and Huntingdonshire Archaeological Society* 3:77–91

Chowdhury, K. A., Gosh, A. K. and Sen, S. N. 1971 Art. Botany. In D. M. Bose, S. N. Sen and B. V. Subbarayappa (eds.), *A Concise History of Science in India*. New Delhi

Chowning, A. 1977 *An Introduction to the Peoples and Cultures of Melanesia* (2nd edn; 1st edn 1973). Menlo Park, California

Chin P'ing Mei 1939 (English transl. of late-sixteenth-century novel, possibly by Hsü Wei). London

Chrysès-Haceophi 1892 *Nouveau Langage symbolique des plantes avec leurs propriétés médicinales et occultes*. Paris

Chu, C. 1988 *Views from the Jade Terrace: Chinese Women Artists 1300–1912* (exhibition catalogue, Indianapolis Museum of Art). Indianapolis

Clairoix, N. C. 1913 *L'Art du bouquet*. Paris

Clanchy, M. T. 1979 *From Memory to Written Record, England, 1066–1307*. Cambridge

Clark, K. 1949 *Landscape into Art*. London

Clarke, G. W. (trans.) 1974 *The Octavius of Marcus Minucius Felix*. New York 1984–6 *The Letters of St Cyprian of Carthage*, vol. I (1984), vol. III (1986). New York

Claudian (1958) *Claudian* (transl. M. Platnauer, 2 vols.) Cambridge, Massachusetts

Clayton-Payne, A. and Elliott, B. 1988 *Flower Gardens of Victorian England*. London

Clement (1954) *Christ the Educator (Paidagōgus)* (transl. S. P. Wood). *The Fathers of the Church*, vol. 23. Washington, DC

Clément, G. 1936 Histoire des cultures du chrysanthème. *Revue horticole* 108:283

CNIH, les dossiers du 1981 *Les fleurs et plantes en tant que cadeaux* 1. Rungis 1982 *Les fleuristes* 2. Rungis

Coats, A. M. 1969 *The Quest for Plants*. London

Coats, P. 1970 *Flowers in History*. New York

Coen, L. and Duncan, L. 1978 *The Oriental Rug*. New York

Cole, W. 1659 *The Art of Simpling: An Introduction to the Knowledge and Gathering of Plants*. London

Corbin, A. 1986 *The Foul and the Fragrant: Odor and the French Social Imagination.* Cambridge, Massachusetts

Cotes, R. A. 1898 *Dante's Garden: With the Legends of the Flowers.* London

Courbaud, E. 1899 *Le Bas-relief romain à représentations historiques; étude archéologique, historique et littéraire.* Bibliothèque des Ecoles françaises d'Athènes et de Rome, 81. Paris

Cowen, P. 1979 *Rose Windows.* London

Coxe, M. 1845 *Floral Emblems: Or, Moral Sketches from Flowers.* Cincinnati

Crane, T. F. 1920 *Italian Social Customs of the Sixteenth Century and their Influence on the Literatures of Europe.* New Haven

Cressey, G. B. 1955 *The Land of the 500 Million: A Geography of China.* New York

Cressy, D. 1985 *Bonfires and Bells: National Memory and the Protestant Calendar in Elizabethan and Stuart England.* Berkeley

Crowe, S., Haywood, S., Jellicoe, S. and Patterson, G. 1972 *The Gardens of Mughal India: A History and a Guide.* London

Cuming, H. S. 1875 On funeral garlands. *Journal of the British Archaeological Society* 31:190–5

Cunliffe, B. 1981 Roman gardens in Britain: a review of the evidence. In E. B. MacDougall and W. F. Jashemski (eds.), *Ancient Roman Gardens.* Washington, DC

Curcio, M. 1981 *Manuel du savoir-vivre d'aujourd'hui.* Paris

Curl, J. S. 1980 *A Celebration of Death.* London

Cuyler, E. 1862 *The Church's Floral Kalander.* London

D'Andrea, J. 1982 *Ancient Herbs in the J. Paul Getty Museum Gardens.* Malibu, California

Daneker, C. F. P. 1816 *Oracle de fleurs.* Paris

Daniker, J. G. 1938 *Flowers, their Significance, Social Use and Proper Arrangement: How to Plant and Grow Garden and House Flowers* (2nd edn). Columbia, South Carolina

Davey, R. 1889 *A History of Mourning.* London

Davies, N. M. and Gardiner, A. H. 1936 *Ancient Egyptian Paintings* (3 vols.) Chicago

de Hamel, C. 1896 *A History of Illuminated Manuscripts.* London

de la Rue, Abbé 1834 *Essais historiques sur les bardes, les jongleurs et les trouvères normands et anglo-normands*, vol 3. Caen

de Zoete, B. and Spies, W. 1939 *Dance and Drama in Bali.* New York

Dehejia, V. 1989 Stupas and sculptures of early Buddhism. *Asian Art* 11:7–32

Delachénaye, B. 1811 *Abécédaire de flore, ou langage des fleurs, méthode nouvelle de figurer avec les fleurs les lettres, les syllabes, et les mots, suivie de quelques observations sur les emblèmes et les devises, et de la signification emblématique d'un grand nombre des fleurs.* Paris

Delenda, O. 1987 La nature divine, sur l'emblème des fleurs. In *Symbolique et Botanique: le sens caché des fleurs dans la peinture au XVIIe siècle* (exhibition catalogue). Caen

Depping, G. B. (ed.) 1837 *Réglements sur les arts et métiers de Paris, rédigés au XIIIe siècle et connus sous le nom du livre des métiers d'Etienne Boileau.* Paris

Der Ling, Princess 1911 *Two Years in the Forbidden City.* New York

Desjardins, E. 1862 *Le Parfait Langage des fleurs, d'après les plus célèbres auteurs anciens et modernes (ouvrage entièrement neuf, mis à la hauteur des connaissances nouvelles et contenant l'indication des propriétés de chaque fleur avec les diverses manières d'en faire usage).* Paris

1866 *Le Parfait Langage des fleurs et des plantes, feuilles, fruits, etc., explication historique, emblématique, poétique et pittoresque de leurs particularités et de leurs symboles, d'après les meilleurs auteurs (anciens et modernes)* (new edn). Petite bibliothèque universelle, vol. 4. Paris

Dickie, J. 1976 The Islamic garden in Spain. In E. B. MacDougall and R. Ettinghausen (eds.), *The Islamic Garden.* Dumbarton Oaks Colloquium on the History of Landscape Architecture, 4. Washington, DC

Dix, D. L. 1829 *The Garland of Flora.* Boston

Dowsing, W. 1885 *The Journal of William Dowsing* (ed. C. H. Evelyn White). Ipswich

Dubos, E. C. 1808 *Les Fleurs, idylles morales, suivies de poésies diverses.* Paris

Dubost, F. 1984 *Côté Jardins.* Paris

Dufour, Y. 1874 *La Dance Macabre des SS. Innocents de Paris d'après l'édition de 1484, précédée d'une étude sur le cimetière, le charnier et la fresque peinte en 1425.* Paris

Dugaston, G. 1920 *Les Secrets du langage des fleurs.* Paris

Dumont, J. 1694 *Nouveau voyage au Levant* (English transl. 1696, London). The Hague

Dumonteil, F. 1890 *Les Fleurs à Paris.* Paris

Dunbabin, K. M. 1978 *Mosaics of Roman North Africa: Studies in Iconography and Patronage.* Oxford

Durliat, M. 1985 *Des Barbares à l'an mil.* Paris

Durston, C. 1985 Lords of misrule: the Puritan War on Christmas, 1642–60. *History Today* 35:7–14

Dutt, S. 1962 *Buddhist Monks and Monasteries of India.* London

Dwyer, E. J. 1982 *Pompeian Sculpture in the Domestic Context: A Study of Five Pompeian Houses and Their Contents.* Rome

Eberhard, W. 1952 *Chinese Festivals.* New York

1965 *Folktales of China* (1st edn 1937, New York). Chicago

Ebin, V. 1979 *The Body Decorated.* London

Eck, D. L. 1983 *Banaras: City of Light.* London

Egidi, P. *et al.* 1904 *Monasteri di Subiaco* (2 vols.) Rome

Eliot, B. 1984 The Victorian language of flowers. *Plant-lore Studies*, pp.61–5. Folklore Society. London

Elliot, T. S. 1948 *Notes towards the Definition of Culture.* London

Elvin, M. 1973 *The Pattern of the Chinese Past.* London

Empedocles: The Extant Fragments (1981) (ed. M. R. Wright). New Haven

Emsweller, S. L. 1947 The chrysanthemum: its story through the ages. *Journal of the New York Botanical Garden* 48:26–9

Enlart, C. 1916 *Manuel d'archéologie française depuis les temps mérovingiens jusqu' à la Renaissance.* Vol. III, *Costume.* Paris

Erec et Enide (1953, ed. M. Roques). Paris

Etlin, R. A. 1984 *The Architecture of Death: The Transformation of the Cemetery in Eighteenth-Century Paris.* Cambridge, Massachusetts

Ettinghausen, R. 1976 Introduction to R. Ettinghausen (ed.), *The Islamic Garden.* Washington, DC

Evans, J. 1931 *Pattern: A Study of Ornament in Western Europe from 1180–1900.* Oxford

Evans-Pritchard, E. E. 1956 *Nuer Religion.* Oxford

Evelyn, J. 1907 *The Diary of John Evelyn* (ed. W. Bray, 2 vols.) London

Faris, J. 1972 *Nuba Personal Art.* London

Faucon, E. 1870 *Nouveau Langage des fleurs.* Paris

Faure, D. 1989 The lineage as a cultural invention: the case of the Pearl River delta. *Modern China* 15:4–36

Fertiault, F. 1847 *Le Langage des fleurs illustré.* Paris

Finley, M. I., Mack Smith, D. and Duggan, C. J. H. 1986 *A History of Sicily.* London

Firth, R. W. 1951 *Elements of Social Organization.* London

Fischer, D. H. 1989 *Albion's Seed: Four British Folkways in America.* Oxford

Flinders Petrie, W. H. 1889a *Hawara, Biahmu and Assino.* London
  1889b Roman life in Egypt. *The Archaeological Journal* 46:1–6
  1890 *Kakun, Gurab and Hawara.* London

Fontaine, L. 1984 *Le Voyage et la mémoire: colporteurs de l'Oisans au XIXe siècle.* Lyons

Forge, A. 1978 *Balinese Traditional Paintings.* Sydney

Forsythe, I. H. 1972 *The Throne of Wisdom: Wood Sculptures of Romanesque France.* Princeton

Fortes, M. 1987 *Religion, Morality and the Person.* Cambridge

Fortes, M. and Evans-Pritchard, E. E., 1940 *African Political Systems.* London

Fortune, R. 1987 (1847) *Three Years Wandering in the Northern Provinces of China. Including a Visit to the Tea, Silk and Cotton Countries: With an Account of the Agriculture and Horticulture of the Chinese, New Plants, etc.* London

Foucart, G. 1896 *Histoire de l'ordre lotiforme: étude d'archéologie égyptienne.* Paris

Fowler, A. 1980 Robert Herrick. *Proceedings of the British Academy*, pp.243–64. London

Francal, A. 1862 *Le Dictionnaire du langage des fleurs précédé de la distribution des emblèmes des fleurs pour chaque mois de l'année; les attributs de chaque heure du jour chez les anciens; les emblèmes de saisons; les éléments de la nature et des couleurs principales; l'expression d'une bague portée par l'homme ou la femme à tel et tel doigt de la main et suivi de quelques bouquets parlants.* Paris

Frankel, H. H. 1976 *The Flowering Plum and the Palace Lady: Interpretations of Chinese Poetry.* New Haven

Frankel, S. 1986 *Huli Response to Illness.* Cambridge

Freedberg, D. 1981 The origins and rise of the Flemish Madonnas in flower garlands: decoration and devotion. *Münchener Jahrbuch der Bildings Kunst* 32:115–50
  1985 *Iconoclasts and their Motives.* Maarsen, Netherlands
  1988 (1972) *Iconoclasm and Painting in the Revolt of the Netherlands, 1566–1609.* New York

Freeman, R. 1978 *English Emblem Books.* New York

French, S. 1975 The cemetery as a cultural institution: the establishment of Mount Auburn and the 'rural cemetery' movement. In D. E. Stannard (ed.), *Death in America.* Philadelphia

Fresne, la Baronnesse de 1858a *Le Nouveau Langage des fleurs, des dames et des demoiselles, suivi de la botanique à vol d'oiseau.* Paris
    1858b *De l'Usage et de la politesse dans le monde.* Paris
Friedländer, M. J. 1963 *Landscape, Portrait, Still-life: Their Origin and Development.* New York
Furnivall, J. S. 1948 *Colonial Policy and Practice: a Comparative Study of Burma and Netherlands India.* Cambridge
Fusek, L. (transl.) 1982 *Among the Flowers: The Hua-chien chi.* New York
Gaillard, J. 1980 Preface to E. Zola, *Au Bonheur des dames*, Paris
Gamble, S. G. 1963 *North China Villages: Social, Political, and Economic Activities Before 1933.* Berkeley
Gaudouin, J. C. 1984 *Guide du protocole et des usages.* Paris
Geddes, G. E. 1976 Welcome joy: death in Puritan New England, 1630–1730. Ph.D dissertation. University of California, Riverside
Geertz, C. 1957 Ritual and social change: a Javanese example. *American Anthropologist* 59:32–54
    1960 *The Religion of Java.* Glencoe, Illinois
    1965 The impact of the concept of culture on the concept of man. In J. R. Platt (ed.) *New Views on the Nature of Man.* Chicago
    1966 *Person, Time and Conduct in Bali: An Essay in Cultural Analysis.* New Haven
    1973 *The Interpretation of Cultures: Selected Essays.* New York
    1980 *Negara: The Theater State in Nineteenth-Century Bali.* Princeton
Geertz, C. and Geertz H. 1975 *Kinship in Bali.* Chicago
Geiger, W. (transl.) 1950 *The Mahāyaṃsa or the Great Chronicle of Ceylon.* Columbo
Genlis, Madame de 1810 *La Botanique historique et littéraire.* Paris
Giamatti, A. B. 1966 *The Earthly Paradise and the Renaissance Epic.* Princeton
Gibault, J. 1896a Les couronnes de fleurs et les chapeaux de roses dans l'antiquité et au moyen age. *Revue horticole* 454–8
    1896b L'ancienne corporation des maîtres jardiniers de la ville de Paris. *Journal de la Société nationale d'horticulture de France* 18:1–22
    1898a La condition et les salaires des anciens jardiniers. *Journal de la Société nationale d'horticulture de France* 20:65–82
    1898b Les origines de la culture forcée. *Journal de la Société nationale d'horticulture de France* 20:1109–17
    1901 Les dieux des jardins dans l'antiquité. *Revue horticole* 286–9, 311–13
    1902a Les fleurs et les couronnes de fleurs naturelles aux funérailles. *Revue horticole* 509–13
    1902b Les fleurs et les tombeaux. *Jardin*, 16pp.
    1902c Les fleurs aux funérailles et la tradition chrétienne. *Revue horticole*
    1904 *Les Fleurs nationales et les fleurs politiques.* Paris
    1906a *Les anciens jardins de IVe arrondissement de Paris.* Paris
    1906b Les fleurs, les fruits et les légumes dans l'ancien Paris. *Revue horticole* 65–9
    1912 Les anciennes lois relatives au jardinage. *Journal de la Société nationale d'horticulture de France* 13:824–30
Gibault, J. and Bois, D. 1900 *L'approvisionnement des halles centrales de Paris en 1899, les fruits et les légumes.* Paris

Gibson, O. 1877 *The Chinese in America*. Cincinnati

Girouard, M. 1978 *Life in the English Country House: A Social and Architectural History*. New Haven

Gitomer, D. 1984 The theatre in Kālidāsa's art. In B. Miller (ed.), *Theater of Memory*. New York

Giumelli, C. (ed.) 1982 *I Monasteri Benedettini di Subiaco*. Milan

Gnudi, C. 1959 *Giotto* (transl. R. H. Boothroyd). London

Godman, P. 1985 *Poetry of the Carolingian Renaissance*. Norman, Oklahoma

Goethe, J. W. von 1819 *West-Oestlicher Divan* (English transl. J. Whaley). Stuttgart

Goldman, L. 1983 *Talk Never Dies: The Language of Huli Disputes*. London

Goldstein, L. J. 1957 On defining culture. *American Anthropologist* 59:1075–81

Golson, J. 1982 The Ipomoean revolution revisited: society and the sweet potato in the upper Wahgi valley. In A. Strathern (ed.), *Inequality in New Guinea Highlands Societies*. Cambridge

Gombrich, E. H. 1979 *The Sense of Order: A Study in the Psychology of Decorative Art*. Ithaca

Goodenough, W. H. 1957 Cultural anthropology and linguistics. In P. Garvin (ed.), *Report of the Seventh Annual Round Table Meeting on Linguistics and Language Study*. Washington, DC

Goody, J. 1961 Religion and ritual: the definitional problem. *British Journal of Sociology* 12:142–63

    1962 *Death, Property and the Ancestors*. Stanford

    1971 *Technology, Tradition and the State in Africa*. London

    1972 *The Myth of the Bagre*. Oxford

    1977a *The Domestication of the Savage Mind*. Cambridge

    1977b Against ritual: loosely structured thoughts on a loosely defined topic. In S. Falk-Moore and B. Meyerhof (eds.), *Secular Rituals Considered: Prolegomena Towards a Theory of Ritual, Ceremony and Formality*. Amsterdam

    1982 *Cooking, Cuisine and Class: A Study in Comparative Sociology*. Cambridge

    1983 *The Development of the Family and Marriage in Europe*. Cambridge

    1986 *The Logic of Writing and the Organization of Society*. Cambridge

    1987 *The Interface between the Written and the Oral*. Cambridge

    1989 Cooking and the polarization of social theory. *Food and Foodways* 3:203–21

    1990 *The Oriental, the Ancient and the Primitive*. Cambridge

    1991 Icones et iconoclasme en Afrique. *Annales ESC*, 1235–51

Goody, J. and Gandah, S. W. D. K. 1981 *Une Récitation du Bagre*. Paris

Goody, J. and Watt, I. P. 1962 The consequences of literacy. *Comparative Studies in Society and History* 5:304–45 (repr. 1968 in J. Goody (ed.), *Literacy in Traditional Societies*. Cambridge)

Goodyear, W. H. 1891 *The Grammar of the Lotus: A New History of Classic Ornament as a Development of Sun Worship*. London

Gorer, R. 1970 *The Development of Garden Flowers*. London

    1975 *The Flower Garden in England*. London

    1978 *The Growth of Gardens*. London

Gosset, M. n.d. *Le Savoir-vivre moderne* (Editions de Vecchia). Paris

Grabar, A. 1968 *Christian Iconography: A Study of Its Origins*. Princeton

Grand-Carteret, J. 1896 *Les Almanachs français, 1600–1895*. Paris

Gray, B. 1930 *Persian Painting*. London

Greenaway, K. (illustrator) 1884 *The Language of Flowers*. London

Grigson, G. 1955 *An Englishman's Flora*. London

Grimal, P. 1969 *Les Jardins romains* (2nd revised edn, 1st edn 1943). Paris

Grimm, J. 1844 *Deutsche Mythologie* (2nd edn). Göttingen

Gueusquin, M. F. 1981 *Le Mois des dragons*. Paris

Gurevich. A. 1988 *Medieval Popular Culture: Problems of Belief and Perception*. Cambridge

Haig, E. 1913 *The Floral Symbolism of the Great Masters*. London

Hairs, M. L. 1965 *Les Peintres flamands de fleurs au XVIIe siècle* (1st edn 1955; English edn 1985). Brussels

Hale, S. J. (Buell) 1832 *Flora's Interpreter, or the American Book of Flowers and Sentiments*. Boston

Hall, D. 1984 Introduction. In S. L. Kaplan (ed.), *Understanding Popular Culture: Europe from the Middle Ages to the Nineteenth Century*. Berlin

Halphen, J. (transl.) 1900 *Miroir des fleurs: guide pratique du jardinier amateur en Chine au XVIIe siècle*. Paris

Halsband, R. (ed.) 1965 *The Complete Letters of Lady Mary Wortley Montagu*, vol. 1. Oxford

Hammer-Purgstall (Hammer), J. 1809 Sur le langage des fleurs. *Fundgruben des Orients*. Vienna (also *Annales des Voyages* 9:346–60)

Hanan, P. 1981 *The Chinese Vernacular Story*. Cambridge, Massachusetts

Hanaway, W. L. Jr 1976 Paradise on earth: the terrestrial garden in Persian literature. In R. Ettinghausen (ed.), *The Islamic Garden*. Washington, DC

Hann, C. M. 1990 Socialism and King Stephen's right hand. *Religion in Communist Lands* 18:4–24

Hardy, J. E. 1962 *The Curious Frame: Seven Poems in Text and Context*. Notre Dame, Indiana

Haring, D. G. 1949 Is 'culture' definable? *American Sociological Review* 14:26–32

Harvey, J. H. 1976 Turkey as a source of garden plants. *Garden History* 4:21–42
     1978 Gillyflower and carnation. *Garden History* 6:46–57

Haskins, C. H. 1927 *The Renaissance of the Twelfth Century*. Cambridge, Massachusetts

Havard, H. 1887–90 Art. Papier peint. *Dictionnaire de l'ameublement* (4 vols.) Paris

Hay, D. 1977 *The Italian Renaissance in its Historical Background*. Cambridge

Hay, J. Stuart 1911 *The Amazing Emperor Heliogabalus* (repr. 1972 Rome)

Hayashi, R. 1975 *The Silk-road and the Shoso-in*. New York

Hazlewood, C. H. 1850 *Lizzie Lyle: Or the Flower Makers of Finsbury: A Tale of Trials and Temptations*. London

Heers, J. 1971 *Fêtes, jeux et joutes dans la société d'occident à la fin du Moyen Age*. Paris

Heinemann, M. 1980 *Puritanism and Theatre: Thomas Middleton and Opposition Drama under the Early Stuarts*. Cambridge

Heliodorus n.d. *An Aethiopian Romance* (transl. T. Underdowne, revised F. A. Wright). London

Hellerstedt, K. J. 1986 *Gardens of Earthly Delight: Sixteenth- and Seventeenth-Century Netherlandish Gardens*. Pittsburgh

Hendry, J. 1981 *Marriage in Changing Japan: Community and Society*. London

Henrion, C. 1800 *Encore un tableau de Paris*. Paris

Hepper, F. N. 1990 *Pharaoh's Flowers: The Botanical Treasures of Tutankhamun*. London

Herbermann, C. G. *et al.* 1907 Art. Joan of Arc. *Catholic Encyclopaedia*, vol. 8. New York

Herrick, Robert (1915) *Poetical Works* (ed. F. W. Moorman). Oxford

Hershatter, G. 1991 Prostitution and the market in women in early twentieth-century Shanghai. In P. Ebrey and R. Watson (eds.), *Marriage and Inequality in China*. Berkeley

Hervilly, E. d' 1891 *Le Langage des fleurs: ce que disent les fleurs, les plantes, les fruits*. Paris

Hild, J. A. 1896 Arts. Flora, Floralia. *Dictionnaire des antiquités grecques et romaines*, vol. 2. Paris

Hobsbawm, E. 1984 *Worlds of Labour: Further Studies in the History of Labour*. London

Hone, W. 1826 *The Everyday Book*. London

Hooper, L. (ed.) 1842 *The Lady's Book of Flowers and Poetry: To Which are Added, a Botanical Introduction, a Complete Floral Dictionary; and a Chapter on Plants in Rooms*. New York

Horstmann, C. (ed.) 1887 *The Early South–English Legendary* or *The Lives of Saints*. vol. 1. Early English Text Society. London

Hoskins, C. N. 1927 *The Renaissance of the Twelfth Century*. Cambridge, Massachusetts

Hsu, F. L. K. 1975 *Iemoto: The Heart of Japan*. Cambridge, Massachusetts

Hubert, J. and M. C. 1985 Piété chrétienne ou paganisme? Les statues-reliquaires de l'Europe carolingienne. In J. Hubert (ed.), *Nouveau recueil d'études d'archéologie et d'histoire*. Mémoires et documents de la Société de l'Ecole des Chartes, 29. Geneva

Hubert, J., Porcher, J. and Volbach, W. F. 1970 *The Carolingian Renaissance (The Arts of Mankind*, ed. A. Malraux and A. Perrot). New York

Hulton, P. and Smith, L. 1979 *Flowers in Art from East and West*. London

Hunt, T. 1989 *Plant Names of Medieval England*. Cambridge

Hunt, W. 1983 *The Puritan Movement: The Coming of Revolution in an English County*. Cambridge, Massuchusetts

Hunter, R. L. (ed.) 1983 *Eubulus: The Fragments*. Cambridge

Huntingdon, J. C. 1985. Origins of the Buddha image: early image traditions and the concept of Buddhadarsanapunya. In A. K. Narain (ed.), *Studies in the Buddhist Art of South Asia*. New Delhi

Huntingdon, S. 1985 *The Art of Ancient India*. New York

Huntingford, G. W. B. 1953 *The Nandi of Kenya: Tribal Control in a Pastoral Society*. London

Hurst, R. 1967 The Minoan roses. *The Rose Annual 1967*. Royal National Rose Society. St Albans

Hyams, E. 1970 *English Cottage Gardens*. London (also pub. 1987, Harmondsworth, Middlesex)

Hyers, C. 1989. The paradox of early Buddhist art. *Asian Art* 11:2–6

Iliffe, J. 1987 *The African Poor: A History*. Cambridge

Industria de las flores en Colombia: desarrollos recientes. *Revista de la Asociación Colombiana de Exportadores de Flores*. April

Irwin, J. and Brett, K. 1970 *The Origins of Chintz*. London

Iu, K. C. 1985 The decline of Tiu Chung as a Chinese New Year flower. *Journal of the Royal Asiatic Society* (Hong Kong Branch) 25:207–9

Jacquemart, A. 1840 *Flore des dames: botanique à l'usage des dames et des jeunes personnes*. Paris
　1841 *Flore des dames. Nouveau langage des fleurs, nouvelle édition entièrement revue et considérablement augmentée: complétée par une grammaire florale et un traité de composition du sélam, etc.* Paris

James, E. 1981 Archaeology and the Merovingian monastery. In H. B. Clarke and M. Brennan (eds.), *Columbanus and Merovingian Monasteries*. Oxford
　1988 *The Franks*. Oxford

Jashemski, W. F. 1979 *The Gardens of Pompeii: Herculaneum and the Villas Destroyed by Vesuvius*. New Rochelle, New York

Jashemski, W. F. (ed.) 1981 *Ancient Roman Gardens*. Dumbarton Oaks Colloquium on the History of Landscape Architecture, 7. Washington, DC

Jellicoe, S. 1976 The Mughal Garden. In R. Ettinghausen (ed.), *The Islamic Garden*. Washington, DC

Johnson, D. 1985 Communication, class and consciousness. In D. Johnson, A. J. Nathan and E. S. Rawski (eds.), *Popular Culture in Late Imperial China*. Berkeley

Johnson, R. F. 1910 *Lion and Dragon in Northern China*. New York

Jones, J. and Deer, B. 1989. *The National Trust Diary of Garden Lore*. London.

Jongh, E. de 1968–9 Erotica in Vogelperspectief: de dubbelzinnigheid van een reeks 17de eeuwse genrevoorstellingen. *Simiolus* 3:22–74

Joret, C. 1892 *La Rose dans l'antiquité et au moyen âge: histoire, légendes et symbolisme*. Paris
　1894 *Les Jardins dans l'ancienne Egypte*. Le Puy
　1897–1904 *Les Plantes dans l'antiquité et au moyen âge, histoire, usage et symbolisme* (2 vols.) Paris
　1901 *La Flore de l'Inde d'après les écrivains grecs*. Paris

Josephus (1930) *Jewish Antiquities*, bk 3. New York
　(1943) *Jewish Antiquities*, bk 13. Cambridge, Massachusetts

Jung, C. G. 1961 *Memories, Dreams, Reflections* (English transl.) London

Juranville, C. 1867 *La Voix des fleurs, comprenant l'origine des emblèmes donnés aux plantes, les souvenirs et les légendes qui y sont attachés, les proverbes auxquels elles ont donné lieu*. Paris

Kaeppler, A. 1989 Art and aesthetics. In A. Howard and R. Borofsky (eds.), *Developments in Polynesian Ethnography*. Honolulu
　n.d. Lament and eulogy in Tonga: verbal expressions of grief in a hierarchical society. MS

Kaplan, D. and Manners, R. A. 1972 *Culture Theory*. Englewood Cliffs, New Jersey

Kaplan, S. (ed.) 1984 *Understanding Popular Culture: Europe from the Middle Ages to the Nineteenth Century*. Berlin

Katzenstein, R. and Savage-Smith, E. 1988 *The Leiden Aratea: Ancient Constellations in a Medieval Manuscript*. Malibu, California

Kawada, J. 1985 *Textes historiques oraux des Mossi méridionaux (Burkina-Faso)*. Tokyo

Keesing, R. M. 1974 Theories of culture. *Annual Review of Anthropology* 3:73–97

Kejř, J. 1988 *The Hussite Revolution*. Prague

Keswick, M. 1978 *The Chinese Garden* (2nd revised edn 1986). London

Kibbey, A. 1986 *The Interpretation of Material Shapes in Puritanism: A Study of Rhetoric, Prejudice, and Violence*. Cambridge

Kim, Duk-whang 1988 *A History of Religions in Korea*. Seoul

King, R. 1985 *Tresco, England's Island of Flowers*. London

Kirk, M. 1981 *Man as Art: New Guinea Body Decoration* (intro. by A. Strathern). London

Kitzinger, E. 1977 *Byzantine Art in the Making* (1st edn 1954). Cambridge, Massachusetts

Kjellberg, P. 1963. La tapisserie gothique, sujet de constantes recherches; nouveaux trésors divulgués. *Connaissance des Arts*, December 161–72

Knight, P. 1986 *Flower Poetics in Nineteenth-Century France*. Oxford

Kock, P. de 1839 *La Bouquetière des Champs-Elysées, drame-vaudeville en 3 actes.* Paris

  1841 *Jenny, ou les trois marchés aux fleurs de Paris*. Paris

  1843/4 *La Grande Ville, nouveau tableau de Paris, comique, critique et philosophique* (2 vols.) Paris

  1855 *La Bouquetière du Château-d'Eau*. Paris

  1863 *Les Démoiselles de magasin*. Paris

Koehn, A. 1952 Chinese flower symbolism. *Monumenta Nipponica* 8:121–46

Krahl, R. 1987 Plant motifs of Chinese porcelain: examples from the Topkapi Seray identified through the *Bencao Gangmu*, parts I and II. *Orientations* May, 52–65; June, 24–37

Kren, T. (ed.) 1983 *Renaissance Painting in Manuscripts: Treasures from the British Museum*. London

Krishna, V. 1967 Flowers in Indian textile design. *Journal of Indian Textile History* 7:1–20

Kristeller, P. O. 1961 *Renaissance Thought: The Classic, Scholastic, and Humanist Strains*. New York

Kronenfeld, J. Z. 1981 Herbert's 'A Wreath' and devotional aesthetics: imperfect efforts redeemed by grace. *ELH* 48:290–309

  1989 Post-Saussurean semantics, reformation, religious controversy, and contemporary critical disagreement. *Assays: Critical Approaches to Medieval and Renaissance Texts*. Philadelphia

Lactantius (1964) *The Divine Institutes, I–VII* (transl. M. F. McDonald), *The Fathers of the Church*. Washington, DC

Laëre, Mme L. de 1856 *La Fleuriste des salons: Ie partie. Traité complet sur l'art de faire les fleurs artificielles*. Brussels. (The second part is F. Fertiault, *Langage des fleurs*, and the third M. and Mme F. de Mellecey, *Le Jardinier des appartements, des terrasses, des balcons et des fenêtres*.)

Laing, E. 1988 Wives, daughters and lovers: three Ming dynasty women painters. *Views from the Jade Terrace: Chinese Women Artists 1300–1912* (exhibition catalogue, Indianapolis Museum of Art). Indianapolis

Lambek, M. 1981 *Human Spirits: A Cultural Account of Trance in Mayotte.* Cambridge

Lambert, A. 1878 The ceremonial use of flowers. *The Nineteenth Century* 4:457–77
    1880 The ceremonial use of flowers: a sequel. *The Nineteenth Century* 7:808–27

La Mottraye, A. de 1723–32 *Travels through Europe, Asia, and into Parts of Africa, etc.* (3 vols. transl. from French 1722, 2 vols.) London

Lane Fox, R. 1986 *Pagans and Christians.* New York

Lansing, S. J. 1977 *The Three Worlds of Bali.* New York

Lattès, J. C. 1983 *Les Fleurs et leur langage.* Paris

Latour, Charlotte de (Mme Louise Cortambert) 1819 *Le Langage des fleurs.* Paris; German transl. 1820 *Die Blumensprache, oder Symbolik des Pflanzenreichs.* Berlin; English transl. 1834 *The Language of Flowers.* London

Laufer, B. 1919 *Sino-Iranica: Chinese Contributions to the History of Civilization in Ancient Iran with Special Reference to the History of Cultivated Plants and Products.* Field Museum of Natural History, Publication 201, Anthropological Series XV:185–597. Chicago

Laughlin, C. J. 1948 Cemeteries of New Orleans. *The Architectural Review* 103:47–52

Laurie, A. 1930 *The Flower Shop.* Chicago

Layard, A. H. 1849–53 *The Monuments of Nineveh: From Drawings Made on the Spot* (2 vols.) London

Leakey, M. 1983 *Africa's Vanishing Art: The Rock Paintings of Tanzania.* New York

Le Blant, E. 1886 *Les Sarcophages chrétiens de la Gaule.* Paris
    1856–65 *Les Inscriptions chrétiennes de la Gaule antérieures au VIIe siècle* (2 vols.) Paris

le Folcalvez, F. 1976 *Savoir-vivre aujourd'hui.* Paris

Le Goff, J. 1984 *The Birth of Purgatory* (French edn 1981). Chicago
    1985 *L'Imaginaire médiéval: essais.* Paris

Lenoir, A. 1852–6 *Architecture monastique.* Paris

Le Roux, H. 1890 *Les Fleurs à Paris.* Paris

Le Roy Alard, R. R. 1641 *La Saincteté de vie tirée de la considération des plantes.* Liège

Lee, Kwang-Kyu 1989 The practice of traditional family rituals in contemporary urban Korea. *Journal of Ritual Studies* 3:167–83

Lee, S. E. 1988 Ming and Qing painting. In *Masterworks of Ming and Qing: Paintings from the Forbidden City.* Lansdale, Pennsylvania

Legner, A. (ed.) 1989 *Reliquien: Verehrung und Verklärung: Skizzen und Noten zur Thematik, und Katalog zur Ausstellung der Kölner Sammlung Louis Peters im Schnütgen-Museum.* Cologne

Lehrman, J. 1980 *Earthly Paradise: Gardens and Courtyards in Islam.* Berkeley

Leighton, A. 1986 *American Gardens of the Eighteenth Century: 'For Use or for Delight'.* Amherst
    1987 *American Gardens of the Nineteenth Century: 'For Comfort and Affluence'.* Amherst

Leneveux, L. P. 1827 *Les Fleurs emblématiques, leur histoire, leur symbole, leur langage* (new edn). Roret's Encyclopédie. Paris

    1837 *Nouveau Manuel des fleurs emblématiques, ou leur histoire, leur symbole, leur langage* (3rd edn). Roret's Encyclopédie. Paris

    1848 *Les Fleurs parlantes.* Paris

    1852 *Les Petits Habitants des fleurs.* Paris

Leroi-Gourhan, A. 1975 The flowers found with Shandar IV, a Neanderthal burial in Iraq. *Science* 190:562–4

Lespinasse, R. de, and Bonnardot, F. 1879–97 *Les Métiers et les corporations de la ville de Paris* (Histoire générale de Paris). *Histoire de l'industrie française et des gens de métiers.* Paris

Levi d'Ancona, M. 1977 *The Garden of the Renaissance: Botanical Symbolism in Italian Paintings.* Arte et Archeologia, Studi e Documenti, 16. Florence

Lewis, G. 1975 *Knowledge of Illness in a Sepik Society: A Study of the Gnau, New Guinea.* London

    1980 *Day of Shining Red: An Essay on Understanding Ritual.* Cambridge

    1986 The look of magic. *Man* 1986:414–35

Lewis, N. 1983 *Life in Egypt under Roman Rule.* Oxford

Li, Hui-lin 1956 *Chinese Flower Arrangement.* Philadelphia

    1959 *The Garden Flowers of China.* New York

    1979 *Nan-fang ts'ao-mu chuang: a Fourth Century Flora of Southeast Asia.* Hong Kong

Li, Ju-chen 1965 (c.1815) *Flowers in the Mirror* (transl. Ching Hua Yuan). London

Li, Ki-baik 1984. *A New History of Korea.* Seoul

Lin, Yueh-hwa, 1947 *The Golden Wing: A Sociological Study of Chinese Familism.* New York

Lindon, R. n.d. *Guide de nouveau savoir-vivre.* Paris

Lindsay, J. 1965 *Leisure and Pleasure in Roman Egypt.* London

l'Isle, Mme de 1861 *Livre-manuel des fleurs en papier, en cheveux, en soie, etc.* Paris

Litten, J. 1991 *The English Way of Death.* London

Littlewood, A. R. 1987 Ancient literary evidence for the pleasure gardens of Roman country villas. In E. B. MacDougall (ed.), *Ancient Roman Villa Gardens*, Dumbarton Oaks Colloquium on the History of Landscape Architecture, 10. Washington, DC

Loudon, J. C. 1822 *An Encyclopaedia of Gardening.* London

    1843 *On the Laying Out, Planting and Managing of Cemeteries, etc.* London

Lucius of Patras (1822) *La Luciade ou l'âme de Lucius de Patras* (transl. P. L. Courier). Paris

Ludwig, A. I. 1966 *Graven Images: New England Stonecarving and its Symbols, 1650–1815.* Middletown, Connecticut

Lyons, Faith. 1965 *Les Eléments descriptifs dans le roman d'aventure au XIIIe siècle (en particulier Amadas et Ydoines, Gliglois, Galeran, L'Escoufle, Guillaume de Dole, Jehan et Blonde, Le Castelain de Couci).* Geneva

MacCormack, S. 1981 *Art and Ceremonial in Late Antiquity.* Berkeley

McCormick, M. 1986 *Eternal Victory.* Cambridge

MacDougall, E. B. (ed.) 1986 *Medieval Gardens.* Dumbarton Oaks Colloquium on the History of Landscape Architecture, 9. Washington, DC

1987 *Ancient Roman Villa Gardens*. Dumbarton Oaks Colloquium on the History of Landscape Architecture, 10. Washington, DC

1989 Flower importation and Dutch flower paintings, 1600–1750. *Still Lifes of the Golden Age* (exhibition catalogue, National Gallery of Art). Washington, DC

MacDougall, E. B. and Ettinghausen, R. (eds.) 1976 *The Islamic Garden*. Dumbarton Oaks Colloquium on the History of Landscape Architecture, 4. Washington, DC

McKendrick, N. 1960. Josiah Wedgwood: an eighteenth century entrepreneur in salesmanship and marketing techniques. *Economic History Review* 12:408–33

McKendrick, N., Brewer, J. and Plumb, J. R. 1982 *The Birth of a Consumer Society*. Bloomington, Indiana

McLean, T. 1981 *Medieval English Gardens*. London

McLeod, M. 1981 *The Asante*. London

McMullen, D. L. 1987 Review of Jessica Rawson, Chinese ornament: the lotus and the dragon. *Modern Asian Studies* 21:198–200

McNeill, J. T. and Gamer, H. M. 1938 *Medieval Handbooks of Penance: A Translation of the Principal Libri Poenitentiales and Selections from Related Documents*. New York

McPhee, C. 1946 *A House in Bali*. New York

1966 *Music in Bali: A Study in Form and Organization in Balinese Orchestral Music*. New York

Macura, V. 1983 *Znamení Zrodu: České obrození ieko kulturní typ*. Prague

Maeterlinck, M. 1907 *L'Intelligence des fleurs*. Paris

Magnat, Abbé C. 1855 *Traité du langage symbolique, emblématique et religieux des fleurs*. Paris

Maiuri, A. 1953 *Roman Painting*. Lausanne

Mallet, J. 1959 *Jardins et Paradis*. Paris

Mâle, E. 1932 *L'Art religieux après le Concile de Trente: étude sur l'iconographie de la fin du XVIe siècle, du XVIIe, du XVIIIe siècle: Italie, France, Espagne, Flandres*. Paris

Malo, C. 1816 *Guirlande de Flore* (calendrier pour l'année 1816). Paris

1819 *Parterre de Flore*. Paris

n.d. *Histoire des roses*. Paris

n.d. *Histoire des tulipes*. Paris

Mandel, G. 1983 *Oriental Erotica*. New York

Maraval, P. 1987 Epiphane, docteur des Iconoclastes. In E. Boesplug *et al.* (eds.), *Nicée II 787–1987: douze siècles d'images religieuses*. Paris

Marçais, G. 1957a Les jardins de l'Islam. *Mélanges d'histoire et d'archéologie de l'Occident musulman*. Algiers

1957b La question des images dans l'art musulman. *Mélanges d'histoire et d'archéologie de l'Occident musulman*. Algiers

Marcus, L. S. 1986 *The Politics of Mirth: Jonson, Herrick, Milton, Marvell, and the defense of old holiday pastimes*. Chicago

Marriott, M., 1966 The feast of love. In M. Singer (ed.), *Krishna: Myths, Rites and Attitudes*. Hawaii

Martin, L. Aimé 1810 *Lettres à Sophie sur la physique, la chimie et l'histoire naturelle* (2 vols.) Paris

Mason, R. H. P. and Caiger, J. G. 1972 *A History of Japan*. Melbourne

Maspero, G. 1895 *Histoire ancienne des peuples de l'Orient classique: les origines, Egypte et Chaldée*. vol. 1. Paris

Massilie, Sirius de 1891 *Le Langage des fleurs*. Paris
    1901 *L'Oracle des sexes, prédiction du sexe des enfants avant la naissance*. Paris
    1902 *L'Oracle des fleurs, véritable langage des fleurs d'après la doctrine hermétique, Botanologie, Hiérobotanie, Botomancie*. Paris
    1911 *La Sexologie, prédiction du sexe des enfants avant la naissance, L'oracle des sexes* . . . Paris

Matheson, S. B. 1982 *Dura-Europos: The Ancient City and the Yale Collection*. New Haven

Mauméné, A. 1897 *Les Fleurs dans la vie: l'art du fleuriste, guide de l'utilisation des plantes et des fleurs dans l'ornamentation des appartements, du montage des fleurs et de la composition des bouquets, des corbeilles et des couronnes*. Paris
    1900 *L'Art floral à travers les siècles*. Paris

Mead, M. 1940 *The Mountain Arapesh. II. Supernaturalism*. Anthropological Papers of the American Museum of Natural History 37:317–451

Mead, M. and Macgregor, F. C. 1951 *Growth and Culture: A Photographic Study of Balinese Childhood*. New York

Meiss, M. 1951 *Painting in Florence and Siena after the Black Death*. Princeton

A Member of the Lichfield Society for the Encouragement of Ecclesiastical Architecture 1843 *Tract upon Tombstones or Suggestions for the Consideration of Persons Intending to set up that Kind of Monument to the Memory of Deceased Friends*. Rugeley

Menocal, M. R. 1987 *The Arabic Role in Medieval Literary History*. Philadelphia

Messire, J. B. 1845 *Le Langage moral des fleurs, suivi des principales curiosités de la Touraine*. Tours

Meyvaert, P. 1986 The medieval monastic garden. In E. MacDougall (ed.), *Medieval Gardens*. Dumbarton Oaks Colloquium on the History of Landscape Architecture, 9. Washington, DC

Middleton, J. and Tait, D. 1958 *Tribes Without Rulers: Studies in African Segmentary Systems*. London

Migne, J. P. *see under* Minucius Felix

Miles, C. A. 1912 *Christmas in Ritual and Tradition, Christian and Pagan* (repr. 1990, Detroit)

Miller, B. S. (ed.) 1984 *Theater of Memory: The Plays of Kālidāsa*. New York

Miller, J. I. 1969 *The Spice Trade of the Roman Empire, 29 BC to AD 641*. Oxford

Miller, M.B. 1981 *The Bon Marché: Bourgeois Culture and the Department Store, 1869–1920*. London

Ministry of Agriculture and Fisheries 1988 *Floriculture in the Netherlands*. The Hague

Minns, G. W. 1905 Funeral garlands at Abbott's Ann. *Hants. Field Club, Papers and Proceedings* 4:235–9

Mintz, S. W., 1985 *Sweetness and Power: The Place of Sugar in Modern History*. New York

Minucius, Felix M. 1844–64 *Patrologiae cursus completus, series latina* and *series graeca*. J. P. Migne. vol. 221, pt 3. Paris

Mitford, J. 1963 *The American Way of Death*. London

Mo, T. 1978 *The Monkey King*. London

Moens, W. J. C. 1887–8 *The Walloons and their Church at Norwich*. Huguenot Society. London

Mollevaut, C. L. 1818 *Les Fleurs; poème en quatre chants*. Paris

Montagu, Lady Mary Wortley 1965 *The Complete Letters* (ed. R. Halsband), vol. 1, 1708–1720. Oxford

Monteil, A. A. 1872 *Histoire de l'industrie française et des gens de métiers*. Paris

Montias, J. M. 1982 *Artists and Artisans in Delft: A Socioeconomic Study of the Seventeenth Century*. Princeton

Moore, O. K. 1952 Nominal definitions of 'culture'. *Philosophy of Science* 19:245–56

Moran, M. H. 1990 *Civilized Women: Gender and Prestige in Southeastern Liberia*. Ithaca

Morgan, W. B. 1985 Cut flowers in Warsaw. *Geojournal* 11:339–48

Morton, T. 1883 *The New Canaan*, Boston

Moss, F. J. 1889 *Through Atolls and Islands in the South Seas*. London

Moynihan, F. B. 1979 *Paradise as a Garden in Persia and Mughal India*. New York

Mukerji, C. 1983 *From Graven Images: Patterns of Modern Materialism*. Columbia

Mullen, N. 1880 *Janet, the Flower Girl: A Drawing-room Drama, in One Act*. New York

Muller, C. R. and Allix, A. 1979 (1925) *Les Colporteurs de l'Oisans*. Grenoble

Müller, F. M. (transl.) 1881 *Dhammapāda: A Collection of Verses, Being One of the Canonical Books of the Buddhists, The Sacred Books of the East*, vol. 10. Oxford

Murray, A. 1986 A medieval Christmas. *History Today* 35:31–9

Nakao, S. 1986 *A Cultural History of Flowers and Plants* (Japanese). Iwanami-shinsho

Naquin, S. 1992. The Peking pilgrimage to Miao-feng-shan: religious organizations and sacred site. In Susan Naquin and Chün-tang Yü (eds.), *Pilgrims and Sacred Sites in China*. Berkeley.

Needham, J. (ed.) 1986 *Biology and Biological Technology*, pt 1, Botany. vol. 6, *Science and Civilisation in China*. Cambridge

Nelson, Christina H. 1985 *Directly from China: Export Goods for the American Market, 1784–1930*. Salem, Massachusetts

Neuer, R. and Libertson, H. 1988 *Ukiyo-e: 250 Years of Japanese Art*. New York

Neuville, A. de 1866 *Le Véritable Langage des fleurs; précédé de légendes mythologiques*. Paris

Newberry, P. E. 1889 On some funeral wreaths of the Graeco-Roman period, discovered in the cemetery of Hawara. *The Archaeological Journal* 46:427–32

Noël, F. Abbé 1867 *Le Véritable Langage des fleurs interprété en l'honneur de la plus grande dame de l'Univers, par l'un de ses plus dévoués admirateurs. Ouvrage formant une série de bouquets, couronnes et guirlandes symboliques, suivi de l'écrin de Marie*. Librairie Catholique de Perisse Frères

O'Hanlon, J. 1979 In the language of flowers. *A Wake Newsletter: Studies in James Joyce's Finnegan's Wake* 16:9–12

Ohrbach, Barbara M. 1990 *A Bouquet of Flowers*. New York

Olk, F. 1894–1940 Art. Gartenbau. von Pauly-Wissova, *Real-Encyclopädie der classischen Altertumwissenschaft*. Stuttgart

Orgel, S. 1975 *The Illusion of Power: Political Theatre in the English Renaissance.* Berkeley

1981 (1967) *The Jonsonian Masque.* New York

Pal, P. 1989 Art and ritual of Buddhism. *Asian Art* 11:33–55

Panofsky, E. 1946 *Abbot Suger on the Abbey Church of St-Denis and its Art Treasures.* Princeton

1958 *Early Netherlandish Painting: Its Origin and Character* (2 vols.) Cambridge, Massachusetts

1970 *Meaning in the Visual Arts.* London

1972 *Renaissance and Renascences in Western Art* (1st edn 1960, Stockholm). New York

Parkinson, J. 1975 (1629) *Paradisi in sole paradisus terrestris.* Norwood, New Jersey

Parrot, A. 1953 *Mari. Collection des idées photographiques.* Neuchâtel

1961a *Sumer: The Dawn of Art.* New York

1961b *The Arts of Assyria.* New York

Paschalius, P. 1610 *Coronae opus, quod hunc primum in lucam editor.* Paris

Pasternak, B. 1969. The role of the frontier in Chinese lineage development. *Journal of Asian Studies* 41:747–65

Pearsall, D. A. and Salter, E. 1973 *Landscapes and Seasons of the Medieval World.* London

Pelikan, J. 1990 *Imago Dei: The Byzantine Apologia for Icons.* Princeton

Pendrill, C. 1937 *Old Parish Life in London.* London

Perkins, D. H. 1969 *Agricultural Development in China, 1368–1968.* Chicago

Perrot, G. and Chipiez, C. 1883 *A History of Art in Ancient Egypt* (transl. from French, 2 vols.) London

1884 *A History of Art in Chaldaea and Assyria* (2 vols.) London

Phillips, H. 1825 *Floral Emblems.* London

1829 *Flora Historica: Or the Three Seasons of the British Parterre Historically and Botanically Treated: with Observations on Planting to Secure a Regular Succession of Flowers from the Commencement of Spring to the End of Autumn* (2 vols., 2nd revised edn; 1st edn 1824). London

Phillips, J. 1973 *The Reformation of Images: Destruction of Art in England, 1535–1660.* Berkeley

Picinelli, F. 1694 *Mundus Symbolicus.* Cologne (facsimile, New York, 1976)

Pieper, P. 1980 Das Blumenbukett. *Stilleben in Europa* (exhibition catalogue, Westfälisches Landesmuseum für Kunst und Kulturgeschichte). Munster

Piesse, G. V. Septimus 1879 *Art of Perfumery.* Quoted in art. Dress and adornment. *Encyclopaedia Britannica* (15th edn), 1974. Chicago.

Pinder-Wilson, R.H. The Persian garden: Bagh and Chahar Bagh. In MacDougall and Ettinghausen 1976

Pitt-Rivers, J. 1974 *Mana.* London

1984 De lumière et de lunes: analyse de deux vêtements andalous de connotation festive. *L'Ethnographie* 80:245–54

Planche, A. 1987 La parure du chef: les chapeaux de fleurs. *Le Corps paré: ornements et atours, Razo,* Cahiers du Centre d'Etudes Médiévales de Nice

Pleyte, W. 1885 La couronne de la justification. *Actes du Sixième Congrès International des Orientalistes,* pt 4, pp.1–30. Leiden

Plinvall, G. de 1951 Tertullien et le scandale de la Couronne. *Mélanges Joseph de Ghellinck*. Gembloux

Poisle-Desgranges, J. 1868 *Le Véritable Langage des fleurs, ou flore emblématique.* Paris

Posthumus, N. W. 1929 The tulip mania in Holland in the years 1636 and 1637. *Journal of Economic History* 1:435–65

Potter, J. 1970 Land and lineage in traditional China. In M. Freedman (ed.), *Family and Kinship in Chinese Society*. Stanford

Prest, J. 1981 *The Garden of Eden: The Botanic Garden and the Re-creation of Paradise*. New Haven

Prior, R. C. A. 1863 *On the Popular Names of British Plants, Being an Explanation of the Origin and Meaning of the Names of our Indigenous and Most Commonly Cultivated Species*. London

Prudentius (1962) *The Poems of Prudentius* (transl. M. C. Eagan). *Fathers of the Church*. Washington, DC

Proust, M. 1954 *A la recherche du temps perdu: du côté de chez Swann* (Pleiade edn). Paris

Purcell, N. 1987 Town in country and country in town. In E. B. MacDougall (ed.), *Ancient Roman Villa Gardens*. Dumbarton Oaks Colloquium on the History of Landscape Architecture, 10. Washington, DC

Pye, L. W. 1973 Culture and political science: problems in the evolution of the concept of political culture. In L. Schneider and C. M. Bonjean (eds.), *The Idea of Culture in the Social Sciences*. Cambridge

Qi Xing (ed.) 1988 *Folk Customs and Traditional Chinese Festivities*. Beijing

Qu Dajun 1985 (c.1700) *Guangdong Xinyu* (New Items Relating to Guangdong). (Repr.) Beijing

Quarré-Reybourbon, L. F. 1897 *Les Bouquets et l'assemblage artistique des fleurs au XVIIe siècle*. Lille

Radcliff-Brown, A. R. 1922 *The Andaman Islanders* (repr. 1964, Glencoe, Illinois). Cambridge

Rahim, H. 1987 Art. Incense. *The Encyclopedia of Religion*, vol. 7, pp.161–3. New York

Ramanujan, A. K. (transl.) 1985 *Poems of Love and War: From the Eight Anthologies and Ten Long Poems of Classical Tamil*. New York

Ramseyer, U. 1977 *The Art and Culture of Bali*. Oxford

Randall, L. M. C. 1966 *Images in the Margins of Gothic Manuscripts*. Berkeley

Rattray, R. S. 1927 *Religion and Art in Ashanti*. Oxford

Rawson, J. 1984 *Chinese Ornament: The Lotus and the Dragon*. London

Rawson, P. 1977 *Erotic Art of India*. London

Raymond, E. 1884 *L'Esprit des fleurs, symbolisme, science*. Paris

Razina, T. *et al.* 1990 *Folk Art in the Soviet Union*. New York

Rebérioux, P. M. (ed.) 1989 *1789: Cahiers des doléances des femmes*. Paris

Reeds, K. 1980 Albert on the natural philosophy of plant life. In J. A. Weisheipl (ed.), *Albertus Magnus and the Sciences: Commemorative Essays 1980*. Toronto

Revel, J. 1984 Forms of expertise: intellectuals and 'popular' culture in France (1650–1800). In S. L. Kaplan (ed.), *Understanding Popular Culture: Europe from the Middle Ages to the Nineteenth Century*. Berlin

Rhys Davids, T. W. (transl.) 1881 *Buddhist Suttas, translated from the Pali. The Sacred Books of the East*, vol. III. Oxford

Rice, K. A. 1980 *Geertz and Culture*. Ann Arbor, Michigan

Ridgway, B. S., 1981 Greek antecedents of garden sculpture. In E. B. MacDougall and W. F. Jashemski (eds.), *Ancient Roman Gardens*. Dumbarton Oaks Colloquium on the History of Landscape Architecture, 7. Washington, DC

Riegl, A. 1891 *Altorientalische Teppiche*. Leipzig

   1893 *Stilfragen: Grundlegungen zu einer Geschichte der Ornamentik*. Berlin

Rimmel, E. 1865 *A Lecture On the Commercial Use of Flowers and Plants, delivered on the 27th July, 1865, at the Royal Horticultural Society* (privately printed). London

Riols, E. N. de (Satine de) 1896 *Le Langage des fleurs expliqué*. Paris

Rizvi, S. A. A. 1978–83 *A History of Sufism in India* (2 vols.) New Delhi

Robinson, C. 1878 (1584) *A Handeful of Pleasant Delites* (ed. E. Arber, repr.) London

Robinson, J. 1988. *Views from Jade Terrace: Chinese Women Artists, 1300–1912* (exhibition catalogue, Indianapolis Museum of Art). Indianapolis

Roger, A., n.d. *Le Savoir-vivre d'aujourd'hui*. Paris

Rogers, H. 1988 Catalogue, *Masters of Ming and Qing Painting from the Forbidden City*. Lansdale, Pennsylvania

Roth, K. 1990 Socialist life-cycle rituals in Bulgaria. *Anthropology Today* 6(5): 8–10

Rubin, A. (ed.) 1988 *Marks of Civilisation: Artistic Transformations of the Human Body*. Los Angeles

Runciman, S. 1975 *Byzantine Style and Civilization*. Harmondsworth, Middlesex

Rutter, M. and Lacam, J. 1949 Les jardins suspendus de Babylone. *Revue horticole* 88–92, 123–7

Sackville-West, V. 1953 Persian gardens. In A. J. Arberry (ed.), *The Legacy of Persia*. Oxford

Sahas, D. J. 1986 *Icon and Logos: Sources in Eighth-Century Iconoclasm*. Toronto

Sahlins, M. D. 1976 *Culture as Practical Reason*. Chicago

St Augustine (1957–72) *The City of God against the Pagans* (7 vols.) London

Saklatvala, B. 1968 *Sappho of Lesbos: her works restored*. London

Salaman, R. N. 1989 *The History and Social Influence of the Potato* (revised edn). Cambridge

Saldivar, R. 1983 Bloom's metaphors and the language of flowers. *James Joyce Quarterly* (Tulsa, Oklahoma) 20:399–410

Sales, François de (St) 1874 *Flore mystique de Saint François de Sales, ou la vie chrétienne sous l'emblème des plantes*. Paris

Salin, E. 1959 *La Civilisation mérovingienne, d'après les sépultures, les textes et le laboratoire*, vol. 4. Paris

Sansom, G. B. 1952 (1931) *Japan: A Short Cultural History*. Stanford

Sanzo Wada 1963 Preface to Japanese edn of *Chintz anciens: les cotonnades imprimées d'Asie*, by Tamezo Osumi. Fribourg and Tokyo

Sarton, G. 1951 *The Incubation of the Western Culture in the Middle East*. Washington, DC

Savidge, J. 1977 *This is Hong Kong: Temples*. Hong Kong

Schafer, E. H. 1963 *The Golden Peaches of Samarkand: A Study of T'ang Exotics*. Berkeley

   1967 *The Vermilion Bird: T'ang Images of the South*. Berkeley

Schama, S. 1987 *The Embarrassment of Riches: An Interpretation of Dutch Culture in the Golden Age*. London

Schimmel, A. 1976 The celestial garden in Islam. In R. Ettinghausen (ed.), *The Islamic Garden*. Washington, DC

Schlegel, G. 1894 A Cantonese flower-boat. *Internationale Archiv für Ethnographie* 7:1–9

Schmitt, J. C. 1987 L'Occident, Nicée II et les images du VIIIe au XIIIe siècle. In F. Boespflug *et al.* (eds.), *Nicée II 787–1987: douze siècles d'images religieuses*. Paris

Schneider, D. M. 1976 Notes toward a theory of culture. In K. H. Basso and H. A. Selby (eds.), *Meaning in Anthropology*. Albuquerque

Schneider, N. 1980 Vom Klostergarten zur Tulpenmanie, Hinweise zur materiellen vorgeschichte des Blumenstillebens. *Stilleben in Europa* (exhibition catalogue, Westfälisches Landesmuseum für Kunst und Kulturgeschichte). Munster

Schnitzler, A. 1914 *Playing with Love*. London

Schrijnen, J. 1911 La couronne nuptiale dans l'antiquité chrétienne. *Mélanges d'archéologie et d'histoire de l'Ecole française de Rome* 31:309–19

Schürmann, U. 1979 *Oriental Carpets* (revised edn). London

Scott, F. J. 1870 *Art of Beautifying Suburban Home Grounds of Small Extent*. New York

Scott-James, A., Desmond R. and Wood, F. 1989 *The British Museum Book of Flowers*. London

Seager, H. W. 1896 *Natural History in Shakespeare's Time, Being Extracts Illustrative of the Subject as He Knew It*. London

Seaton, B. 1980a The flower language books of the nineteenth century. *Morton Arboretum Quarterly* 16:1–11

   1980b French flower books of the early nineteenth century. *Nineteenth Century French Studies* 11:60–72

   1985a A nineteenth-century metalanguage: le langage des fleurs. *Semiotica* 57:73–86

   1985b Considering the lilies: Ruskin's 'Proserpina' and other Victorian flower books. *Victorian Studies* 28:255–82

Sébillot, P. 1906 *Le Folk-lore de France; vol. 3, La Faune et la flore*. Paris

Segalen, M. and Chamarat, J. 1979 Les rosières se suivent et ne ressemblent pas ou notes pour une analyse historique et sociologique de fêtes de la rosière de Nanterre. *Bulletin du Centre d'Animation de l'Histoire de Nanterre* 8:1–8

   1983 La Rosière et la 'Miss': les reines des fêtes populaires. *L'Histoire* 53:44–55

Seneca (1959) *Epistolae morales* (transl. R. M. Gummere), 3 vols. Cambridge, Massachusetts

Shahar, S. 1989 *Childhood in the Middle Ages*. London

Shaver-Crandell, A. 1982 *The Middle Ages*. Cambridge Introduction to the History of Art

Shen Fu 1983 (c.1809) *Six Records of a Floating Life* (transl. L. Pratt and Chian Su-hui). Harmondsworth, Middlesex

Shepherd, J. R. 1988 Rethinking tenancy: explaining spatial and temporal variation in late imperial and republican China. *Comparative Studies in Society and History* 30:403–31

Sillitoe, P. 1983 *Roots of the Earth: Crops in the Highlands of Papua New Guinea.* Manchester

Singer, M. 1968 The concept of culture. *International Encyclopedia of the Social Sciences*, vol. 3, pp.527–43. New York

Sircar, N. N. 1950 An introduction to the Vṛkṣāyursveda of Parāśara. *Journal of the Royal Asiatic Society of Bengal* (Letters) 16:123–39.

Sitenský, L. n.d. *Prague of My Youth.* Prague

Siu, H. F. 1989 *Agents and Victims in South China: Accomplices in Rural Revolution.* New Haven

　1990 Recycling tradition: culture, history, and political economy in the chrysanthemum festivals of South China. *Comparative Studies in Society and History* 32:765–94

Sivaramamurti, C. 1980 *Approach to Nature in Indian Art and Thought.* New Delhi

Smith, L. (ed.) 1988 *Ukiyoe: Images of Unknown Japan.* London

Snellgrove, D. L. (ed.) 1978 *The Image of the Buddha.* Paris

Sol, E. 1929 *Le Vieux Quercy.* Cahors

Sourdon-Clélie, Mlle 1858 *Nouveau manuel simplifié du fleuriste artificiel.* Paris

Southern, R. W. 1953 *The Making of the Middle Ages.* London

Spieth, J. 1985 The language of flowers in Senghor's *Lettres d'Hivernage.* In D. W. Tapper (ed.), *French Studies in Honor of Philip A. Wordsworth.* Birmingham, Alabama

Srinivas, M. N. 1976 *The Remembered Village.* Berkeley

Stannard, D. E. (ed.) 1975 *Death in America.* Pennsylvania

　1977 *The Puritan Way of Death: A Study in Religion, Culture, and Social Change.* Oxford

Stannard, J. 1980 Albertus Magnus and medieval herbalism. In J. A. Weisheipl (ed.), *Albertus Magnus and the Sciences: Commemorative Essays 1980.* Toronto

　1986 Alimentary and medicinal use of plants. In E. MacDougall (ed.), *Medieval Gardens.* Dumbarton Oaks Colloquium on the History of Landscape Architecture, 9. Washington, DC

Stein, R. A. 1990 *The World in Miniature: Container Gardens and Dwellings in Far Eastern Religious Thought* (French edn 1987). Stanford

Sterling, C. 1985 *La Nature morte.* Paris

Stevenson, F. V. de G. 1915 *The Cruise of the 'Janet Nicol' among the South Sea Islands: A diary by Mrs Robert Louis Stevenson.* London

Stewart, D. C. n.d. *The Kitchen Garden: A Historical Guide to Traditional Crops.* London

Stock, B. 1983 *The Implications of Literacy: Written Languages and Models of Interpretation in the Eleventh and Twelfth Centuries.* Princeton

Stokstad, M. 1986 *Medieval Art.* New York

Strathern, A. (ed.) 1982 *Inequality in New Guinea Highlands Societies.* Cambridge Papers in Social Anthropology, 11

Strathern, M. and A. 1971 *Self-decoration in Mount Hagen.* London

Sullivan, M. 1974 *The Three Perfections: Chinese Painting, Poetry and Calligraphy.* London

Summers, G. 1968 *George Herbert: His Religion and His Art.* Cambridge, Massachussets

Susman, W. 1984 *Culture as History: The Transformation of American Society in the Twentieth Century.* New York

Symanski, J. D. 1821 *Selam, oder die Sprache von Blumen.* Berlin

Sze, Mai-mai 1956 *The Tao of Painting: A Study of the Ritual Disposition of Chinese Painting; With a Translation of the Chieh Tzu Yuean Chuan or Mustard Seed Garden Manual of Painting, 1679–1701.* New York

Tait, G. A. O. 1963 The Egyptian relief chalice. *Journal of Egyptian Archaeology* 49:93–139

Tambiah, S. J. 1970 *Buddhism and the Spirit Cults in North-east Thailand.* Cambridge

Tapié, A. 1987 La nature, l'allégorie. In A. Tapié and C. Joubert, *Symbolique et botanique.* Caen

Tapié, A. and Joubert, C. 1987 *Symbolique et botanique: le sens caché des fleurs dans la peinture au XVIIe siècle* (exhibition catalogue). Caen

Tennent, J. E. 1859 *Ceylon: An Account of the Island: Physical, Historical and Topographical, with Notices of its Natural History, Antiquities and Productions.* London

Tertullian (1950) *Apologetic Works* (transl. R. Arbesmann *et al.*) *The Fathers of the Church.* vol. 10. Washington, DC

  (1959) *Disciplinary, Moral and Ascetical Works* (ed. J. Deferrasi). Washington, DC

Terukazu, A. 1961 *Japanese Art.* Geneva

Thacker, C. 1979 *The History of Gardens.* Berkeley

Thiers, J. B. 1679 *Traité des superstitions selon l'Ecriture sainte, les décrets des conciles et les sentiments des Saints Pères et des théologiens.* Paris

Thomas, A. 1986 The *Fātele* of Tokelau; approaches to the study of dance in its social context. MA dissertation, Victoria University of Wellington

Thomas, K. V. 1971 *Religion and the Decline of Magic.* London

  1983 *Man and the Natural World: Changing Attitudes in England 1500–1800.* London

Thornton, P. 1978 *Seventeenth-century Interior Decoration in England, France and Holland.* New Haven

Tiérant, C. 1981 *La Bretagne: almanach de la mémoire et des coutumes.* Paris

Tolstoy, V. *et al.* 1990 *Street Art of the Revolution: Festivals and Celebrations in Russia 1918–33.* London

Toynbee, J. M. C. 1971 *Death and Burial in the Roman World.* Ithaca, New York

Trapp, J. B. 1958 The owl's ivy and the poet's bays. *Journal of the Warburg and Courtauld Institutes* 21:227–55

Tun Li-ch'en 1987 *Annual Customs and Festivals in Peking* (transl. and annotated by D. Bodde; revised edn 1936). Hong Kong

Turnbull, C. M. 1972 *The Mountain People.* New York

Tylor, E. B. 1871 *Primitive Culture.* London

Underdown, D. 1985 *Revel, Riot and Rebellion: Popular Politics and Culture in England 1603–1660.* Oxford

Van Dam, R. 1985 *Leadership and Community in Late Antique Gaul.* Berkeley

Van Gulick, R. H. 1961 *Sexual Life in Ancient China.* Leiden

Van Malderghem, J. 1894 *Les Fleurs de lis de l'ancienne monarchie française, leur origine, leur nature, leur symbolisme.* Paris

Vatsyayana (1963) *The Kama Sutra* (transl. R. Burton and F. F. Arbuthnot). London

Vickery, A. R. 1981 Traditional uses and folklore of *Hypericum* in the British Isles. *Economic Botany* 35:289–95

1983 *Lemna minor* and Jenny Greenteeth. *Folkore* 94:247–50

Villiers-Stuart, C. M. 1913 *Gardens of the Great Mughals.* London

Vilmorin, P. L. de 1892 *Les Fleurs à Paris, culture et commerce.* Paris

Virgil (n.d.) *Eclogues and Georgics* (transl. T. F. Royds). London

Vollmer, J. E., Keall, E. J. and Nagai-Berthrong 1983 *Silk Roads: China Ships.* Toronto

Vyas, S. N. 1967 *India in the Rāmāyaṇa Age: A Study of the Social and Cultural Conditions in Ancient India as Described in Valmīki's Rāmāyaṇa.* Delhi

Waddell, H. 1929 *Mediaeval Latin Lyrics.* London

Wagner, M. L. 1984 *The Lotus Boat: The Origins of Chinese Tz'u Poetry in T'ang Popular Culture.* New York

Wakeman, F. 1975 *The Fall of Imperial China.* New York

Walahfrid Strabo (1966) *Hortulus* (transl. R. Payne; commentary, W. Blunt). Hunt Botanical Library. Pittsburg

Waley, A. 1937 *The Book of Songs.* London

Walker, G. A. 1846 *Lectures on the Actual Conditions of the Metropolitan Grave-yards.* London

Walshe, M. (transl.) 1987 *Dīgha Nikāya.* London

Waterman (Esling), C. H. 1839 *Flora's Lexicon: An Interpretation of the Language and Sentiment of Flowers: With an Outline of Botany, and a Poetical Introduction.* Philadelphia

Waugh, E. 1948 *The Loved One.* London

Weidner, M. 1988 Women in the history of Chinese painting. In *Views from Jade Terrace: Chinese Women Artists 1300–1912.* Indianapolis

Weitzmann, K. 1977 *Late Antique and Early Christian Book Illumination.* New York

Weitzmann, K. *et al.* 1987 *The Icon* (Italian edn 1981). New York

Welch, C. 1890 *A Brief Account of the Worshipful Company of Gardeners of London* (privately printed). London

Welch, S. C. 1972 *A King's Book of Kings: The Shah-nameh of Shah Tahmasp.* New York

Wheaton, B. K. 1983 *Savoring the Past: The French Kitchen and Table from 1300 to 1789.* Philadelphia

Wheelock, A. K. 1989 Still life: its visual appeal and theoretical status in the seventeenth century. *Still Lifes of the Golden Age: Northern European Painting from the Heinz Collection* (exhibition catalogue, National Gallery of Art). Washington, DC

Wheelwright, C. 1989a Introduction to *Word in Flower* (exhibition catalogue, Yale University Art Gallery). New Haven

1989b Past and present, text and image. *Word in Flower* (exhibition catalogue, Yale University Art Gallery). New Haven

White, G. 1789 *The Natural History and Antiquities of Selborne, in the County of Southampton.* London

White, L. A. 1949 *The Science of Culture: A Study of Man and Civilization.* New York

Whitehouse, O. C. 1901 Art. Garden. *Encyclopaedia Biblica.* vol. 2,1640–44

Whitfield, J. H. 1943 *Petrarch and the Renaissance.* Oxford

Wickham, G. 1987 *The Medieval Theatre* (3rd edn). Cambridge

Wilber, D. N. 1979 *Persian Gardens and Garden Pavillions.* (1st edn 1962). Washington, DC

Wilkins, E. H. 1951 The coronation of Petrarch. In *The Making of the Canzoniere.* Rome

   (transl.) 1953 Petrarch's coronation oration. *PMLA* 68:1241–50

Wilkinson, J. G. 1837 *Manners and Customs of the Ancient Egyptians, Including their Private Life, Governments, Laws, Arts, Manufactures, Religion, and Early History; Derived from a Comparison of the Paintings, Sculptures, and Monuments still Existing with the Accounts of Ancient Authors.* London

Willard, 1726 *A Compleat Book of Divinity.* Boston

Willet, F. 1971 *African Art.* London

Williams, C. A. S. 1941 *Outlines of Chinese Symbolism and Art Motives* (3rd revised edn). Shanghai

Williams, D. 1974 *Icon and Image: A Study of Sacred and Secular Forms of African Classical Art.* London

Williams, G. 1971 *African Designs from Traditional Sources.* New York

Wilmott, P. 1986 Family flowers only. *New Society,* 2 May

Wilson, D. M. 1984 *Anglo-Saxon Art: From the Seventh Century to the Norman Conquest.* London

Wilson, E. H. 1929 *China, Mother of Gardens.* Boston

Wilson, S. 1984 *What is Pre-Raphaelitism?* London

Winlock, H. E. 1935 *The Private Life of the Ancient Egyptians.* London

Wirt, E. W. (Gamble) 1833 *Flora's Dictionary* (by a Lady). Baltimore

Wither, G. 1635 *A Collection of Emblemes, Ancient and Modern.* Renaissance Text Society Publications. London

Woodbridge, K. 1986 *Princely Gardens: The Origins and Development of the French Formal Style.* London

Wright, A. R. and Lones, T. E. 1938 *British Calendar Customs: England,* vol. II. *Fixed Festivals, January–May, inclusive.* Folklore Society. London

   1940 vol. III. *Fixed Festivals. June–December, inclusive.* Folklore Society. London

Wright, T. 1862 *A History of Domestic Manners and Sentiments in England during the Middle Ages.* London

xxxx, Marie 1867 *Voyage autour de mon parterre: petite botanique religieuse et morale, emblèmes des fleurs.* Paris

Young, A. 1986 (1945) *A Prospect of Flowers: A Book about Wildflowers.* Harmondsworth, Middlesex

Yriarte, C. E. 1893 *Les Fleurs et les jardins de Paris.* Paris (published in *Le Figaro* under pseud. Marquis de Villemen)

Yuan Tien, M. 1965 Sterilization, oral contraception, and population control in China. *Population Studies* 18:215–35

Zaccone, P. 1853 *Nouveau Langage des fleurs, avec la nomenclature des sentiments dont chaque fleur est le symbole et leur emploi pour l'expression des pensées.* Paris

Zoetmulder, P. J. 1974 *Kalangwan: A Survey of Old Javanese Literature.* The Hague

Zonabend, F. 1980 *The Enduring Memory.* Manchester (transl. of *La Memoire longue*, Paris)

Index